Every Decker book is accompanied by a CD-ROM...

Travelers' Vaccines is accompanied by a dual-platform CD-ROM, which features the complete text and *full-color* maps and illustrations. Also featured are *bonus appendices* including a checklist for safe vaccine handling and storage; an example of a vaccine information sheet; and sample screening questionnaires and vaccination administration records. The fully searchable PDF files facilitate the exploration of need-to-know information. The disc is also ideal for printing pertinent information necessary for traveler education.

The book and disc are sold only as a package; neither is available nor priced independently. We trust you will find the Book/CD package invaluable and invite your comments and suggestions.

Access information. Acquire knowledge. Please visit www.bcdecker.com for a complete list of titles in your discipline. Our innovative approach to meeting the informational needs of healthcare professionals ensures that Decker products belong in your library and on your computer.

Brian C. Decker
CEO and Publisher

TRAVELERS' VACCINES

Elaine C. Jong, MD
Department of Medicine
University of Washington School of Medicine
Seattle, Washington

Jane N. Zuckerman, MD, FFPM, FIBiol, FRCPath
World Health Organization Collaborating Centre for Reference,
Research and Training in Travel Medicine
Academic Centre for Travel Medicine and Vaccines
Royal Free and University College Medical School
London, United Kingdom

2004
BC Decker Inc
Hamilton • London

BC Decker Inc
P.O. Box 620, L.C.D. 1
Hamilton, Ontario L8N 3K7
Tel: 905-522-7017; 800-568-7281
Fax: 905-522-7839; 888-311-4987
E-mail: info@bcdecker.com
www.bcdecker.com

04 05 06 07/WWP/9 8 7 6 5 4 3 2 1

ISBN 1-55009-225-1

Printed in the United States

Sales and Distribution

United States
BC Decker Inc
P.O. Box 785
Lewiston, NY 14092-0785
Tel: 905-522-7017; 800-568-7281
Fax: 905-522-7839; 888-311-4987
E-mail: info@bcdecker.com
www.bcdecker.com

Canada
BC Decker Inc
20 Hughson Street South
P.O. Box 620, LCD 1
Hamilton, Ontario L8N 3K7
Tel: 905-522-7017; 800-568-7281
Fax: 905-522-7839; 888-311-4987
E-mail: info@bcdecker.com
www.bcdecker.com

Foreign Rights
John Scott & Company
International Publishers' Agency
P.O. Box 878
Kimberton, PA 19442
Tel: 610-827-1640
Fax: 610-827-1671
E-mail: jsco@voicenet.com

Japan
Igaku-Shoin Ltd.
Foreign Publications Department
3-24-17 Hongo
Bunkyo-ku, Tokyo, Japan 113-8719
Tel: 3 3817 5680
Fax: 3 3815 6776
E-mail: fd@igaku-shoin.co.jp

UK, Europe, Scandinavia, Middle East
Elsevier Science
Customer Service Department
Foots Cray High Street
Sidcup, Kent
DA14 5HP, UK
Tel: 44 (0) 208 308 5760
Fax: 44 (0) 181 308 5702
E-mail: cservice@harcourt.com

Singapore, Malaysia, Thailand, Philippines, Indonesia, Vietnam, Pacific Rim, Korea
Elsevier Science Asia
583 Orchard Road
#09/01, Forum
Singapore 238884
Tel: 65-737-3593
Fax: 65-753-2145

Australia, New Zealand
Elsevier Science Australia
Customer Service Department
STM Division
Locked Bag 16
St. Peters, New South Wales, 2044
Australia
Tel: 61 02 9517-8999
Fax: 61 02 9517-2249
E-mail: stmp@harcourt.com.au
www.harcourt.com.au

Mexico and Central America
ETM SA de CV
Calle de Tula 59
Colonia Condesa
06140 Mexico DF, Mexico
Tel: 52-5-5553-6657
Fax: 52-5-5211-8468
E-mail: editoresdetextosmex@prodigy.net.mx

Brazil
Tecmedd
Av. Maurílio Biagi, 2850
City Ribeirão Preto – SP – CEP: 14021-000
Tel: 0800 992236
Fax: (16) 3993-9000
E-mail: tecmedd@tecmedd.com.br

India, Bangladesh, Pakistan, Sri Lanka
Elsevier Health Sciences Division
Customer Service Department
17A/1, Main Ring Road
Lajpat Nagar IV
New Delhi – 110024, India
Tel: 91 11 2644 7160-64
Fax: 91 11 2644 7156
E-mail: esindia@vsnl.net

CONTENTS

SECTION IV: IMMUNIZATIONS FOR TARGETED POPULATIONS

PREFACE

The specialty of travel medicine has evolved rapidly as a result of the massive increase in international travel and tourism. The World Tourist Organization, for example, has predicted that international travel, currently in excess of 600 million people each year, will increase by 80% or more by the end of the year 2010. Correspondingly, this means that an increasing number of travelers will face the risks of exposure to many infectious diseases across the various geographical regions of the world.

An essential component of the practice of travel medicine is the provision of advice and clinical practice to protect the health of those who travel. Prevention of communicable diseases by immunization is an integral and important part of this practice, and thorough knowledge of current and new vaccines is essential. Not only is immunization against vaccine-preventable diseases an important aspect of travel medicine for the personal benefit of the individual traveler, the administration of travel vaccines also fulfills a public health role in contributing to the reduction of the risk that communicable diseases will be imported by infected travelers to the detriment of susceptible populations in receiving countries.

This textbook is, therefore, devoted to vaccines for travelers and includes comprehensive information by experts on the principles of immunization; practical information on vaccine requirements, recommendations, and administration; travel vaccines available currently; vaccines against enteric infections, dengue fever, and malaria; and immunization of targeted groups and groups at "special risk." Chapters are also included on vaccine safety, public policy and surveillance of adverse reactions, vaccine initiatives and programs, and vaccine health economics.

This textbook of *Travelers' Vaccines* is addressed to practicing physicians and nurses in primary care, to specialists in designated travel clinics or occupational health services, and to public health physicians, pharmacists, and health administrators, and is intended as a source textbook for undergraduate and postgraduate students.

Finally, we are most grateful to our coauthors, who contributed so willingly and with enthusiasm their considerable knowledge and expertise to this book and to the advancement of the discipline of travel medicine.

Elaine C. Jong
Jane N. Zuckerman

CONTRIBUTORS

Indran Balakrishnan, BSc, MRCP(UK),
MSc, MRCPath
Department of Medical Microbiology
Royal Free and University College Medical School
London, United Kingdom

Elizabeth D. Barnett, MD
Department of Pediatrics
Boston University School of Medicine
Boston, Massachusetts

Frank J. Bia MD, MPH
Department of Medicine
Yale University
New Haven, Connecticut

Lynne Bunnell, BA, RN
Department of International Health
Citigroup Health Services
New York, New York

James D. Campbell, MD
Department of Pediatrics
University of Maryland School of Medicine,
  Center for Vaccine Development
Baltimore, Maryland

Bambos M. Charalambous, BSc (Hons), PhD
Department of Medical Microbiology
Royal Free and University College Medical School
London, United Kingdom

Thomas Larry Hale, PhD
Department of Enteric Infections
Walter Reed Army Institute of Research
Silver Spring, Maryland

Scott B. Halstead, MD
Department of Preventive Medicine and Biometrics
Uniformed Services University of the Health Sciences
Bethesda, Maryland

Stephen L. Hoffman, MD, DTMH
Sanaria Inc.
Gaithersburg, Maryland

Betty Anne Johnson, MD, PhD
Division of General Medicine
Medical College of Virginia
Richmond, Virginia

Elaine C. Jong, MD
Department of Medicine
University of Washington School of Medicine
Seattle, Washington

Myron M. Levine, MD, DTPH
Departments of Medicine and Pediatrics
Centre for Vaccine Development
University of Maryland School of Medicine
Baltimore, Maryland

Sheila M. Mackell, MD
Mountain View Pediatrics
Flagstaff, Arizona

Punam Mangtani, MRCP, MSc, MD
Department of Infectious and Tropical Diseases
London School of Hygiene and Tropical Medicine
London, United Kingdom

Timothy D. McHugh, BSc (Hons), PhD
Department of Medical Microbiology
Royal Free and University College Medical School
London, United Kingdom

Thomas P. Monath, MD
Acambis Inc.
Cambridge, Massachusetts

Karl Neumann, MD
Department of Pediatrics
Weill Medical College of Cornell University
New York, New York

Clydette Powell, MD, MPH, FAAP, FABPN, FABPM
Department of Pediatrics
George Washington University School of Medicine
Washington, DC

Thomas L. Richie, MD, PhD
Malaria Program
Naval Medical Research Center
Silver Spring, Maryland

Jennifer A. Roberts, PhD, FFPHM
Department of Public Health and Policy
London School of Hygiene and Tropical Medicine
London, United Kingdom

Gail Rosselot, APRN, BC, MPH, COHN-S
Department of Medicine
Mount Sinai School of Medicine
New York, New York

Tanya Schreibman, MD
Department of Medicine
Yale University
New Haven, Connecticut

Tom Solomon, MD, PhD
Department of Neurological Science
Walton Center for Neurology and Neurosurgery
University of Liverpool
Liverpool, United Kingdom

David N. Taylor, MD, MPH
Department of International Health
Johns Hopkins University School of Public Health
Baltimore, Maryland

Stephen Toovey, MBBCh, CTM, FFTM
South African Airways—Netcare Travel Clinics
Sandton, South Africa

David R. Tribble, MD, MPH
Department of Enteric Diseases
Naval Medical Research Center
Silver Spring, Maryland

David W. Vaughn, MD, MPH
Department of Preventive Medicine and Biometrics
Uniformed Services University of the Health Sciences
Bethesda, Maryland

Henry Wilde, MD, FACP
Department of Infectious Diseases
Chulalongkorn University
Bangkok, Thailand

Jane N. Zuckerman, MD, FFPM, FIBiol, FRCPath
World Health Organization Collaborating Centre for
  Reference, Research and Training in Travel Medicine
Academic Centre for Travel Medicine and Vaccines
Royal Free and University College Medical School
London, United Kingdom

Chapter 1

IMMUNOLOGIC PRINCIPLES OF VACCINATION (THEORY)

Bambos M. Charalambous and Timothy D. McHugh

Microbial infections are the major cause of death in human populations. The foremost contributions in disease prevention over the past 100 years have been sanitation and vaccination. Vaccination is the administration of a substance or substances into the body in an attempt to modify its defenses and induce long-term protection without prior exposure to the pathogen, so that disease is prevented or the severity of disease is significantly reduced. If appropriate protection is elicited by the administration of a vaccine, the individual is said to be immunized. It is important to bear in mind that vaccination does not always lead to immunization. An example of this is the poor efficacy of vaccines in immunosuppressed individuals or in diseases that subvert or avoid our defenses, which are discussed later in this chapter.

Immunology as an area of scientific endeavor began from the success of Edward Jenner's vaccine against smallpox and led to the global eradication of smallpox in 1980. National and global vaccination programs, such as the United Nations' Expanded Program for Immunization (EPI), have significantly reduced mortality and morbidity caused by infectious diseases such as polio as well as provided specific vaccinations for protecting travelers against diseases such as yellow fever, rabies, meningococcal meningitis, and hepatitis A and B.

Before describing the principles of vaccination leading to immunization, an explanation of how our defense mechanisms operate will be given, providing the reader with a better understanding of how vaccines are thought to prime our defenses against previously unseen pathogens and thus preventing the onset of disease. Our knowledge of immunologic memory at the molecular level is incomplete, with only a few molecules that have important roles in this process identified and their biochemical functions partially elucidated. This lack of understanding prevents us from predicting whether a vaccine candidate will elicit immunologic responses that lead to protection against disease. Therefore, it remains necessary to establish efficacy in animal models and to develop correlates of protection that can be extended to human responses. Animal models, however, are fraught with practical and interpretive difficulties, particularly for pathogens that colonize and cause disease only in human hosts. Ultimately, the vaccine must be tested in humans in ethically approved and regulated field trials. The World Health Organization (WHO), in consultation with research scientists and vaccine-producing companies, is currently promoting standardized regulations for testing and introducing new vaccines. WHO is also committed to the global introduction of vaccines, in particular to developing countries, where resources are limited and the infrastructure is not yet available for mass vaccination but where such programs would have the most impact, for example, in the control of malaria and tuberculosis.

ORGANIZATION OF THE IMMUNE SYSTEM

The immune system is organized into two overlapping compartments, the lymphoid and the reticuloendothelial systems (RES), which provide the environment for the development and maintenance of an effective immune response (Figure 1-1). These compartments contain white cells (leukocytes), which are the main cells responsible for protection and are derived from pluripotent (undifferentiated or immature) stem cells in the bone marrow during postnatal life. Leukocytes include macrophages, monocytes, neutrophils, eosinophils, basophils, natural killer (NK) cells, and thymus-dependent (T) and B (derived from the bursa of Fabricius present in some nonhuman species) lymphocytes. Blood and lymphoid precursor cells are also derived from pluripotent stem cells.

There are two types of responses to invading organisms: the innate (natural) and adaptive responses. The innate response is rapid, lacks immunologic memory, and occurs to the same extent regardless of how frequently the infectious agent is encountered. The slower adaptive response, also known as active immunity, is remembered and improves on repeated exposure to a given pathogen. The innate and adaptive responses usually work in unison to eliminate pathogens. All the cells involved in these responses develop from stem cells in the fetal liver and in fetal bone marrow and then circulate throughout the extracellular fluid.

Adaptive immune responses are generated in the lymph nodes, spleen, and mucosa-associated lymphoid tissue in contrast to "primary lymphoid tissues" where lymphocytes are generated. These are referred to as the secondary lymphoid tissues. In the spleen and lymph nodes, the activation of lymphocytes by an antigen occurs in distinctive B- and T-cell compartments of lymphoid tissue. A morphologic feature of the B-cell area is the secondary follicle containing the germinal center, where B-cell responses occur within a meshwork of follicular dendritic cells. The mucosa-associated lymphoid tissues, including the tonsils, adenoids, and Peyer's patches in the gut, defend mucosal surfaces. Diffuse collections of lymphoid cells are also present throughout the lung and the lamina propria of the intestinal wall.

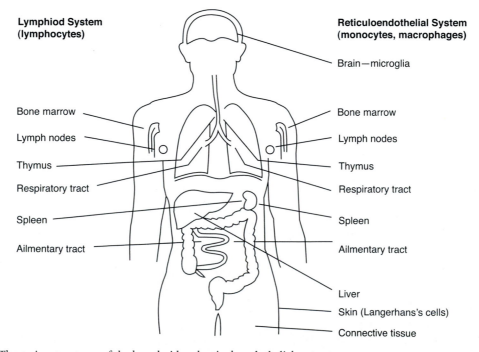

Figure 1-1. The major structures of the lymphoid and reticuloendothelial systems.

Lymphoid Cells

Lymphoid cells provide protection against foreign agents and coordinate the functions of other parts of the immune system by producing immunoregulatory chemicals called cytokines that communicate between cells. The lymphoid system consists of the thymus, bone marrow of the central lymphoid organs, and peripheral lymphoid organs (lymph nodes, spleen, and mucosal and submucosal tissues of the respiratory and alimentary tracts). The thymus instructs lymphocytes to differentiate into T lymphocytes and selects the majority to die in the thymus (negative selection) and others to exit into the circulation (positive selection). T lymphocytes enter the blood stream, where they regulate antibody and cellular immunity to defend against infections. The antibody-forming cells, the B lymphocytes and NK cells, are independent of the thymus and remain principally in peripheral lymphoid organs.

Reticuloendothelial System

Cells of the RES provide natural, or innate, immunity against microorganisms by phagocytosis and intracellular killing, the recruitment of other inflammatory cells by the secretion of cytokines, and the presentation of peptide antigens to lymphocytes for the production of antigen-specific immunity. The RES contains circulating monocytes; resident macrophages in the liver, spleen, lymph nodes, thymus, bone marrow, connective tissues and submucosal tissues of the alimentary and respiratory tracts; and macrophage-like cells, including dendritic cells in lymph nodes, Langerhans' cells in skin, and glial cells in the central nervous system.

Innate, or Natural, Defense Responses

Innate responses involve phagocytic white cells, including neutrophils, monocytes, and macrophages, which can take up and ingest foreign particles, including microbes (phagocytosis); basophils, mast cells, and eosinophils, which release inflammatory mediators, such as cytokines (eg, interleukins); and NK cells. The molecular components of innate responses include complement, acute-phase proteins, and cytokines, such as the interferons.

Pathogen Killing by the Complement Cascade

Serum contains a number of plasma proteins, called complement proteins, that interact either with antibodies or directly with molecules on the surface of the pathogen to aid in the killing and removal of extracellular pathogens. Vaccination leads to the production of antibodies that, on binding to a specific vaccine antigen (refer to section on adaptive defence mechanisms for definition), can activate complement. Activation by an antibody mediates three processes targeted toward the pathogen: opsonization (also known as phagocytosis), recruitment of macrophages, and killing by formation of a complement attack complex. Complement killing can also be activated spontaneously by the pathogen itself—the alternative pathway. Activation of the antibody-mediated classic pathway provides a component that can also initiate the alternative pathway. The alternative pathway amplifies the complement response, facilitating the rapid killing of the invading pathogen. As well as the classic and alternative pathways for activating complement killing, direct activation of complement killing can occur by the binding of a serum lectin (mannan-binding lectin) to mannose-containing carbohydrates on the pathogen surface—the mannan-binding–lectin pathway. This pathway contributes to innate primary host defenses and serum resistance. Complement activation,

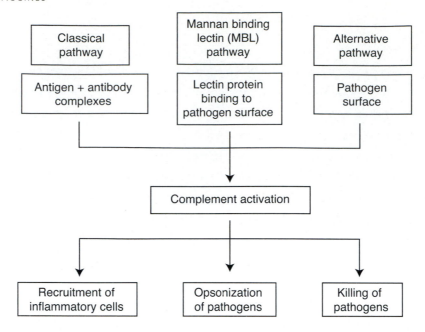

Figure 1-2. Schematic of the mechanisms for the activation of the complement cascade. There are three pathways of complement activation: the classic pathway activated by an antibody, the mannan-binding–lectin (MBL) pathway initiated by MBL protein in serum, and the alternative pathway triggered directly on pathogens. All activate a critical enzyme that activates opsonization, direct killing, and recruitment of inflammatory cells.

irrespective of the mechanism, involves a series of cleavage reactions leading to the generation of the C5b component of the pathway, which associates with the bacterial cell membrane. This triggers the terminal components to form a membrane attack complex, which causes cell death (Figure 1-2).

Acute-Phase Proteins

Cytokines secreted by macrophages and neutrophils stimulate the acute-phase response, in which some plasma protein levels decrease whereas others increase markedly. The synthesis of acute-phase proteins occurs by activation of liver cells. Acute-phase proteins, such as C-reactive protein (CRP) and mannan-binding protein (or lectin–sugar-binding protein), on binding to pathogens act as opsonins for complement killing. CRP binds to the phosphorylcholine portion of bacterial and fungal cell wall lipopolysaccharides but not to mammalian phosphorylcholine. CRP not only opsonizes the pathogen on binding but also activates the complement cascade directly by binding to the first component of the classic pathway, C1q, mimicking the action of antibodies but with far less specificity. The synthesis of mannan-binding lectin is also increased during the acute-phase response. Mannan-binding lectin is a calcium-dependent protein and a member of a structurally related family known as collectins. The sugars bound by mannan-binding lectin are present on many bacteria, and their presence activates opsonization by monocytes. The mannan-binding lectin resembles the structure of the C1q component of the complement pathway and consequently can activate complement killing. The collectins also include the pulmonary surfactant proteins, which are thought to be important in binding and opsonizing pulmonary pathogens such as *Pneumocystis carinii*. Thus, within 2 days of an infection, acute-phase proteins with the functional properties of antibodies that can bind to and initiate (with the functional properties of antibodies) the elimination of the infectious agent are induced.

The same cytokines that initiate the acute-phase response also act as endogenous pyrogens, raising body temperature. This is thought to aid in the elimination of pathogens because at elevated temperatures, bacterial and viral replication is decreased and antigen processing is increased.

Adaptive Defense Responses

Each B or T cell has multiple copies of a single type of receptor that is unique to that cell. These receptors are surface-associated antibody (immunoglobulin [Ig]) molecules specific for a single foreign molecule or antigen. Acquired responses involve the proliferation of specific B and T cells when the surface receptors of these cells bind to an antigen presented by professional antigen-presenting cells (APCs). Antigens that bind to B-cell receptors may be either intact microbial components or breakdown products of microbial components, but they are invariably protein fragments. These fragments, or peptides, are generated from partial degradation by intracellular proteolytic enzymes when the pathogen is ingested by phagocytosis. The peptides are then translocated to, and presented on, the phagocyte cell surface, where they interact with the cell surface proteins that comprise the major histocompatibility complex (MHC) and are then available to be bound by APCs that recognize the MHC-peptide complex. Two classes of MHCs (I and II) occur, and these recruit different populations of T lymphocytes, leading to different immunologic responses. Presentation of peptide antigens on MHC class I molecules recruits a subpopulation of T lymphocytes with CD8 protein on their surface. In turn, these CD8-positive (CD8+) T cells produce mediators that activate NK cells to seek out and destroy any cells with the original peptide antigen on their surface. NK cells can therefore eradicate intracellular pathogens by activating macrophages to ingest infected cells expressing pathogen-specific antigens on their surface. APCs also stimulate the proliferation of B cells, which bind to them via the peptide bound to MHC class II receptors. These activated B cells recruit T cells with CD4 on their surface (CD4+) and secrete large amounts of the unique antibody that is associated with their cell surface and is responsible for binding to the APC. The antibody consequently recognizes the peptide antigen on the surface of the infecting organism, which stimulates phagocytosis, and activates the cytotoxic complement cascade.

Adaptive immune responses to microbial antigens can be used diagnostically to determine the history of infections; for example, a latent infection of *Mycobacterium tuberculosis* (*M. tb*), which has the potential for reactivation of disease at a later date, might be identified. Tuberculin skin testing with the purified protein derivative (PPD) antigen is the screening method commonly used to determine both latent and active tuberculosis (TB) infection as well as cell-mediated immune responses to *M. tb*. To rule out generalized anergy and to validate a negative PPD skin test, positive responses to other control antigens are used. Anergy is the lack of an immune response resulting from inhibition of T-cell responses. T-cell anergy can be overcome by a co-stimulatory signal from another antigen-presenting cell. Recent evidence from Delgado and colleagues indicates that there might be a subset of patients with active TB infection who fail to respond to intradermal injection of PPD.[1] This group has also cast doubt on the value of anergy testing with control antigens as it appears to be not predictive of PPD responsiveness in the cohort they studied.

Antibody Structure and Organization

Antibodies are large, Y-shaped, glycosylated protein molecules that have two antigen-binding sites on each arm of the Y. The regions that bind to antigens are highly variable and are known as complementarity-determining regions (CDR). The structure of the tail of the Y, termed the constant region and abbreviated to Fc, is not variable. The Fc region differs according to the immunoglobulin G subclass. Antibodies are present either as freely soluble molecules in the various fluid compartments of the body, for example, serum and mucosal fluids, or as surface-associated molecules/receptors on B cells. B-cell receptors activate cellular proliferation and cytokine secretion, which mediate recruitment of T cells, leading to T cell–dependent pathways.

There are four subclasses (types) of antibodies (IgA, IgE, IgG, and IgM), and the last two are predominant in serum. IgM is a complex of five IgG molecules that have relatively high affinities for repetitive microbial antigens because of their ability to bind via 10 possible binding sites. IgM is produced early (within days of infection) in the immune response to foreign antigens, before the adaptive responses produce high-affinity antibodies specific for a particular antigen. The adaptive response takes about 2 weeks to develop after onset of the infection, and both the antibody affinity and the magnitude of antibody response are improved on re-infection by the same pathogen. The IgG subclass is produced with specific antigen targets in response to T-cell help by B cells and leads to the generation of various IgG isotypes, a process termed antibody switching. When T helper cells of the type 1 class (Th 1) are recruited, cell-mediated immunity is activated. Macrophages are stimulated, and B cells are induced to produce the IgG isotype antibodies, IgG1 and IgG3, which opsonize, activate complement killing, and sensitize for killing by NK cells. When T helper cells of the type 2 class (Th 2) are recruited, humoral immunity is activated, leading to the induction of B cells to make IgG2 and IgG4 isotypes, which can neutralize and activate complement killing. Although IgG isotypes have particular protective functions, most IgG isotypes that bind to an appropriate antigen can activate complement killing.

Other classes of immunoglobulin are produced during humoral immunity. IgA is a monomeric antibody in the serum, but when secreted into mucosal surfaces, it occurs as a dimer, known as secretory (s)IgA. Secretory IgA provides mucosal immunity to pathogens that colonize and invade via mucosal surfaces, for example *Streptococcus pneumoniae* in the nasopharynx and *Giardia lamblia* in the small intestine. IgA is produced by cells in the basement membrane of the mucosal epithelium and is translocated across the cells by an active secretion pathway that recognizes the secretory signal on the IgA molecule.

IgE is an antibody subclass produced by B cells that coats eukaryotic parasites and stimulates phagocytosis. In localized infections, host defenses are directed to the site by the initial binding of IgE antibodies. IgE is also responsible for hypersensitivity to antigens, causing allergic reactions (allergens), such as hay fever, asthma, and systemic anaphylaxis, to an infecting organism. Binding of the antibody to the allergen presents multiple copies of the Fc domain of the antibody, which bind to and activate mast cells. Mast cells are present in high concentration in vascularized connective tissue beneath epithelial surfaces of the body. This includes submucosal tissue of the gastrointestinal and respiratory tracts and the dermis beneath the epidermal layers of the skin. On activation, mast cells release the contents of cytoplasmic granules, including chemical mediators such as histamines. These initiate a rapid increase in the permeability of local blood vessels. They also secrete lipid mediators and cytokines, which mediate a concomitant influx of white cells, macrophages, and other effector lymphocytes that lasts from several minutes to a few hours. Mast cells can also trigger muscular contraction, which can facilitate expulsion of pathogens from the gut or lungs.

Partial protective immunity to some pathogens can be elicited by harmless organisms that have common antigens, so that antibodies elicited against these antigens will also cross-react with the pathogen. For example, harmless colonization of the nasopharynx by *Neisseria lactamica* elicits antigens that are cross-protective to the related organism *N. meningitidis,* which can cause meningitis and/or septicemia, with morbidity and death. Similarly, environmental contact with nonpathogenic mycobacterial species might provide partial cross-protection to *M. tuberculosis.*

Not only do our defense mechanisms recognize foreign substances, they also differentiate between self and nonself human tissues. The antibodies responsible for this surveillance are directed at antigens that are present on human cells, known as allogen antigens or alloantigens, and are unique to individuals. The alloantigen antibodies are responsible for the rejection of organs following transplant surgery. Transplantation, therefore, has been possible only since the discovery of powerful immunosuppresive drugs that limit rejection. The disadvantage of immunosuppression is the increased susceptibility to microbial infections, which, under normal circumstances, would not pose a threat; these include fungal and protozoan as well as viral and bacterial infections.

Avoiding Unwanted Antibody Responses

A major function of the immune system is to eliminate autoantibodies that recognize self-antigens by a process known as immunologic tolerance (unresponsiveness). Development of immunologic tolerance is the result of removal of autoantibodies or the autoreactive T cells that produce them. This is mediated by a number of processes, principally clonal deletion in the thymus. If this fails, then immune tolerance is broken and antibodies are produced, which can lead to destructive autoimmune disease. Tolerance can also be broken because of a genetic predisposition to immune dysregulation, altered self-antigens, exposure to microbial antigens that cross-react with self-antigens, or exposure to a self-antigen that is normally not revealed to the immune system, such as an antigen in the eye. Fortunately, there are additional mechanisms that control unwanted T-cell activation. These include immunologic ignorance, deletion, immunoregulation, and anergy. Maintenance of tolerance is also important in immune responses to some pathogens that intentionally contain antigens that mimic human cell surface antigens. For example, group B meningococcal polysaccharide contains polysialic acids that are also present on human cells, and the neurologic disorder Guillain-Barré syndrome is due to the breaking of immune tolerance by the food pathogen *Campylobacter jejuni*, which mimics neuronal structures.

IMMUNE DEFICIENCIES

Immune deficiencies, whether genetic or acquired, result in an increased susceptibility to certain infections, depending on the nature of the defect.

Genetic Defects

X-linked agammaglobulinemia is a defect in an enzyme that is essential for B-cell development, so that few B cells and low levels of antibodies are produced. This leads primarily to an increased susceptibility to highly virulent, encapsulated respiratory bacterial infections that can cause meningitis, bacteremia, and pneumonia.

Severe combined immunodeficiency is a lack of B and T cells. T-cell deficiency is the main problem, and most cases are due to an X-linked recessive gene defect in the formation of a number of cytokine receptors, although some autosomal recessive types are due to deficiencies in enzymes, such as adenosine deaminases, in the purine salvage pathway. Patients with these diseases display few T cells, decreased T-cell function, poor antibody formation, and an increased susceptibility to opportunistic infections such as *P. carinii.*

Inherited genetic defects can occur in neutrophils. For example, a decrease in leukocyte adherence leading to dysfunctional phagocytosis is due to an autosomal recessive defect of the leukocyte adherence glycoproteins, whereas in chronic granulomatous disease, a deficiency in intracellular killing is due to a deficiency in the production of cytochrome or proteins necessary for their stabilization. Thus, reactive oxygen compounds required for intracellular killing are not produced.

Acquired Immunologic Defects

Protein-energy malnutrition is the leading cause of immunologic deficiency. A second, but important, cause of acquired immunodeficiency is the human immunodeficiency virus (HIV), which attacks CD4+ T cells and macrophages. Other infections can also depress or destroy parts of the immune system.

Subversion of Human Defenses by Microbial Pathogens

Viruses

For viruses to replicate, they must enter host cells and synthesize viral proteins. These proteins are displayed on MHC class I molecules of the infected cells and trigger CD8+ T lymphocytes. Rapidly replicating viruses produce acute illnesses and are readily detected by T cells that normally control them. Some viruses can enter a latent state. For example, herpesviruses often enter latency, where replication does not occur, and therefore no disease is evident. Latent viruses can be reactivated, resulting in recurrent illness. Therefore, for herpes simplex virus, factors such as sunlight, bacterial infection, or hormonal changes can reactivate the virus. Viruses such as the herpes and pox families can also subvert immune responses, inhibiting humoral immunity by blocking effector functions of antibodies bound to infected cells, complement-mediated effector pathways, and complement activation of infected cells. They can also inhibit the inflammatory response by interfering with cytokine interactions with host cells and the adhesion of lymphocytes to infected cells. In addition, they can block antigen processing and presentation by inhibiting both expression of MHC class I molecules and translocation of processed antigen peptides to the surface of antigen-presenting cells. Last, immunosupression of the host can occur by production of a viral version of interleukin-10, which reduces Th 1 lymphocytes and inteferon-γ production.

Bacteria

The major sources of bacterial infections are organisms that we come across from our environment or are carried asymptomatically, for example, in the nasopharynx or the epidermis. In fact, in an adult, there are about tenfold greater number of bacterial cells, 10^{15}, than human cells. The bacteria that we carry invariably have a symbiotic relationship with us and obtain their nutrients for growth from sites that contain secretions such as sweat (sebum) or mucus, and only in exceptional circumstances do they cause pathology that can lead to damage or death of their host. Consequently, many of these microbes have coevolved with us and have developed highly specialized mechanisms for evading our innate and adaptive immune defenses. These range from camouflage, with surface molecules mimicking human cell-surface antigens, to the production of human cell–regulating molecules that can alter our defense responses, so that we fail to mount an appropriate inflammatory response.

Some pathogens can evade or resist the effects of host defense mechanisms. For example, *M. tuberculosis* is taken up by phagocytosis into a macrophage in the normal way, but the fusion of the lysosome to the phagosome is inhibited, preventing the bactericidal action of the lysosomal contents. This is combined with an array of protective mechanisms, such as the production of superoxide dismutase, to neutralize toxicity from highly reactive oxygen radicals. Other microorganisms, such as *Listeria monocytogenes*, escape from the phagosome into the cytoplasm of the macrophage, where they replicate. They can then spread directly to other cells by kidnapping cellular mechanisms, which leads to the formation of vacuolar projections into adjacent cells, so that the organisms never leave the protection of the cell cytoplasm and avoid attack by antibodies. However, the infected cells are still susceptible to cytotoxic T cells.

A complicating factor in the immune response is immune interference typified by mycobacterial species; for example, *M. leprae* is known to suppress the immune system, and *M. paratuberculosis* is known to cause a range of effects, from a minimal one to the rapid onset of fatal disease. A possible explanation for this diversity is a difference in the individual's genetic make-up that predisposes him or her to developing disease.

Many countries vaccinate their population against *M. tuberculosis* using the bacille Calmette-Guérin (BCG) vaccine, which is a live attenuated form of *M. bovis*, a close relative of *M. tuberculosis*. The vaccine is capable of some replication in humans and would normally be cleared by the adaptive immune response; thus, it should not be administered to immunosuppressed individuals. The protective efficacy of the BCG vaccine, measured in population-based studies, varies vastly, from very little to almost complete protection. The protective efficacy, if any, of BCG increases with increasing distance from the equator and seems to be higher in developed than in developing countries.[2,3] In populations with high infection rates, who need an effective vaccine the most, BCG offers limited protection against adult forms of bacillary (highly infectious) pulmonary tuberculosis and offers only a low level of protection in children.[4] For this reason, tuberculosis persists in many populations that have received the BCG vaccine.

Since the 1940s, it has been known that immune responses elicited to BCG vaccination do not correlate with protective immunity, and this was proven scientifically in 1967.[5] After BCG vaccination or infection with *M. tuberculosis*, both delayed-type hypersensitivity and protection against tuberculosis can be elicited, reflecting different immune responses. Protective cellular immunity produces activation of cytotoxic macrophages against mycobacteria, whereas delayed-type hypersensitivity is associated with tissue damage, including caseation (necrosis observed at the center of a granulomatous lesion caused by tuberculosis, which has a white, cheesy appearance).

Despite the worldwide use of BCG, tuberculosis is still the leading global cause of death from a single infectious disease. Studies are needed to better understand the biology and immunology of tuberculosis in humans and to find new vaccines that are effective in high-risk regions of the world. Ideally, these vaccines should stimulate development of protective immunity with no effect on tuberculin reactivity.

VACCINATION LEADING TO LONG-TERM PROTECTION AGAINST INFECTIONS

The innate system cannot be modified, whereas the acquired response can be primed to give a rapid and protective antibody response on repeat exposure to the same pathogen, that is, active immunity. The aim of vaccination is to trigger the acquired response without preexposure to a pathogen. Effective immunization leading to long-term protection (10 years or more) requires the production of memory B cells. To ensure that memory B cells generate protective antibodies, the immune system is usually primed by an initial dose of the vaccine and then boosted by additional doses of the same vaccine (Figure 1-3). This

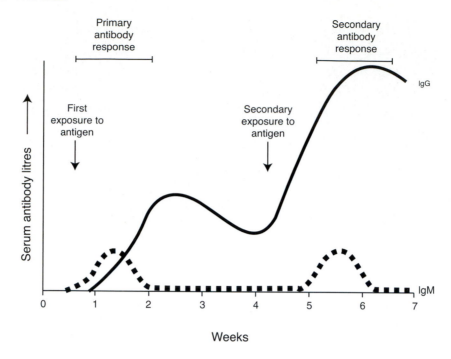

Figure 1-3. Active immunity: immunoglobulins IgG and IgM antibody levels following first and second exposure to pathogen antigen or vaccination. Ig = immunoglobulin.

regimen increases the affinity/avidity of antibodies to a specific antigen produced in the humoral immune response, termed affinity maturation. On the other hand, the vaccine candidate antigen may be poorly immunogenic, which elicits a weak immune response and generates antibodies that are nonprotective. The only definitive way of establishing the immunogenicity of vaccine components is to vaccinate and measure the immune responses associated with protective immunity and correlate these to their actual protective efficacy. (This will be discussed in Chapter 2.)

When vaccinating or developing vaccines, consideration must also be made of the age group to be immunized because at the extremes of age the immune defenses are not fully functional. In infants and children, the immune system is not fully developed, whereas in the elderly it becomes progressively weaker. This means that not only are immune responses to bacterial organisms or their components different, but responses to vaccines can also vary from poor to completely ineffective. Several bacterial pathogens, such as *S. pneumoniae*, *N. meningitidis*, and *Haemophilus influenzae*, cause morbidity and death in infants and children under age 5 years. The vaccines available consist of the outer capsular polysaccharide of the bacterium, which does not elicit an immune response in children or generate long-term memory responses in adults. Consequently, such polysaccharide vaccines are recommended only for immediate protection of adults. To overcome this problem, polysaccharides are chemically conjugated to known immunogenic proteins, such as diphtheria or tetanus toxoids, and are proving to be very efficacious in reducing diseases from these encapsulated organisms in this high-risk age group. In countries where *H. influenzae* (Hib) and *N. meningitidis* group C (MenC) conjugate vaccine programs have been introduced and where pneumococcal conjugate vaccine trials are underway, these diseases have been significantly reduced.[6–8] New vaccine strategies to enhance protection against disease in the first year of life are currently undergoing trials. New pneumococcal vaccine trials on neonates and 6-month-old infants have been initiated.

In the elderly, the efficacy of many vaccines has not been established. However, influenza vaccines have been shown to provide a 70 to 80% protective efficacy, and in the year 2000, an annual flu vaccination was recommended in the United States for all people aged 50 to 64 years. There was also a recommendation made for vaccination against pneumococcal disease in this age group. In the same year, the United Kingdom's national policy was extended to offer the influenza vaccine to all those aged 65 years and over; to all ages with chronic heart disease, chronic respiratory disease (including asthma), chronic renal disease, diabetes mellitus, and immunosuppression due to disease or treatment; and to residents in long-stay residential and nursing homes or other long-stay facilities. Healthcare workers are also being encouraged to take up vaccination. The influenza vaccine has been shown to be effective in reducing infection-associated illness and hospitalization and to reduce fatality rates in older people when the infectious and vaccine strains are closely related.[9]

What Makes an Effective Vaccine?

For a vaccine to provide protection, it needs to stimulate immunologic memory of the acquired immune response by T cell–dependent activation of B cells. Thus, vaccines need to contain molecules, usually proteins, that are able to stimulate immune responses (immunogenic). An immune response is triggered when antibody molecules associated with B cells bind to foreign molecules, either in their entirety or as peptide fragments. Some molecules can bind to an antibody but cannot elicit an adaptive immune response and are known as haptens. Some haptens can be converted to antigens that can elicit protective immune responses by conjugation to immunogenic molecules (carriers). Haptens are usually carbohydrates and have to be conjugated to proteins to become immunogenic. The region on the antigen molecule that the antibody binds to is known as the antibody epitope. The antibody-antigen interaction is very specific, analogous to a lock and key. Two identical CDRs are present, one on each arm of the Y structure of antibodies.

Some antigens, such as bacterial polysaccharides, bind to the B cell with high avidity by virtue of repeated structures and activate B cells without recruiting CD4+ T-cell help. These T cell–independent antigens do not activate germinal centers and are therefore unable to induce memory B cells or hypermutation, which generates high-affinity antibodies. The necessary switching from IgM to other antibody subclasses, such as IgG, for an effective, long-lived response is also limited in the absence of cytokines released by the helper T cells. Consequently, T cell–independent antigens elicit low-affinity IgM antibodies. As mentioned previously, most antigens are proteins and are usually T-cell dependent, activating B cells by recruitment of T-cell help. When these antigens bind to B cells, they are internalized and are broken down into short peptides, which are then brought to the surface by MHC class II molecules. CD4+ T cells that are able to bind to this complex are activated and express other stimulatory molecules on their surface, which promotes the binding of the T cell to the B cell. This binding stimulates the B cells to begin somatic hypermutation (cell division and genetic changes), which leads to affinity maturation and immunoglobulin class switching. Assistance is also provided from cytokines (interleukin-2, -4, and -5) secreted from helper T cells.

To eradicate infectious diseases, the most effective method is to introduce a comprehensive vaccine program that targets a critical portion of the population and is based on factors such as transmissibility and population density. The vaccine must target immune responses to conserved surface antigens that are accessible to antibodies. However, capsular polysaccharide conjugate vaccines can only provide protection against diseases such as meningococcal meningitis and pneumococcal pneumonia when the prevailing disease-causing capsular types are included in the vaccine formulation. The prevalent types may vary between continents, and, consequently, vaccines developed for the protection of European or American populations might not be suitable for Asia and Africa.[10,11]

The use of some microbial antigens as vaccine components may not always be suitable as they can be toxic, have poor immunogenicity, be difficult and expensive to isolate, show antigenic variability, or share epitopes with human antigens that may elicit autoantibodies. An alternative strategy for circumventing these issues is to develop oligopeptide antigenic mimics that are immunogenic and able to induce long-term protection without any of the undesirable properties.[12] Numerous studies have demonstrated that oligopeptides that mimic bacterial carbohydrates can elicit cross-reactive antibody responses to bacterial polysaccharides. Such peptides have been termed "conformational mimics" of bacterial carbohydrates. Conformational peptide mimics have been identified to a number of pathogenic bacterial capsular polysaccharides, such as *N. meningitidis* groups A, B, and C, and group B *Streptococcus* type III, as well as to lipooligosaccharides such as *Brucella melitensis* Rev1, *B. abortus* W99, and *N. meningitidis*.[13]

Adjuvants

An adjuvant is a compound or mixture that enhances the immune response to a weakly immunogenic and nonprotective antigen so that it becomes protective. Adjuvants have the capability of influencing antibody levels (titers), response duration, immunoglobulin subclass (isotype), antibody avidity, and some properties of cell-mediated immunity. Adjuvants work via three mechanisms. First, by adsorbing the antigen to form an aggregate with multiple copies on the surface, they decrease antigen solubility and therefore its rate of breakdown and clearance, which extends its release. This increases the period during which the immune system is exposed to the antigen for processing and lengthens the duration of the antibody response. Second, adjuvants can act as nonspecific mediators of immune cell function by stimulating or modulating immune cells. Third, adjuvants can act as carriers or vehicles that can stimulate macrophage phagocytosis by forming particulates with the antigen.

Intact microorganisms consist of a large variety of macromolecules, some of which are able to elicit nonspecific immune responses and act as adjuvants. For example, the bacterial cell wall component lipopolysaccharide can enhance immune responses to antigens with poor immunogenicity, whereas, sub-cellular antigen components, unlike intact live attenuated or killed vaccines, are usually weak immunogens that elicit poor protective immunity and thus are unable to prevent the onset of disease. Although the molecular bases for protective immunity have yet to be fully unraveled, some of the main methods used to determine the efficacy of vaccines and the known correlates of immunity will be described in Chapter 2.

Currently, the only adjuvants licensed for human vaccine use are aluminum hydroxide (alhydrogel) and aluminum salts, commonly termed "alum."

Mucosal Immunity

In addition to serum immunity, which protects against systemic infections and bacteremia, mucosal immunity can provide protection against the entry of pathogens via the mucosal epithelium. The mucosal epithelia line the nasopharynx, the gastrointestinal tract, and the urethral canal. The major defenses against invasion of pathogens via this route are the colonization by nonpathogenic organisms and the integrity of the epithelial structure, forming a physical barrier preventing entry into the host. The production of mucus on these surfaces reduces the organism's ability to adhere to and colonize this surface but can also provide warmth, humidity, and essential nutrients for its growth and replication. Specialized bacteria have adapted to transiently colonize these environments harmlessly for weeks or months. Colonization by these organisms is reduced by secretion of nonspecific antibodies of the IgA subclass into the mucosal lining. These bind to bacterial surface antigens to reduce adhesion to the mucosal epithelium and to promote clearance by phagocytosis. In addition, colonization can elicit adaptive immune responses that lead to the production and secretion of specific IgA, which binds with high affinity to the organism. Antigens that stimulate mucosal immunity can also be recognized by lymphomatous tissue located in the mucosa. The acquisition of immunity reduces recolonization and therefore is thought to contribute to the reduction in incidence of disease from these organisms with increasing age. An example is the reduction in incidence of pneumococcal and meningococcal disease in children over 5 years of age, as the immune system matures and cross-protective immunity is observed without development of disease.

A great deal of research is currently being undertaken to determine the most effective ways to stimulate mucosal immunity by vaccination, including other types of vaccines, such as deoxyribonucleic acid (DNA) vaccines, discussed later, and the investigation of mucosal sites for administering the vaccine.

Passive Immunity

In contrast to vaccine prophylaxis, there may be cases where an injection of antiserum that contains antibodies from another host is administered, which is known as passive immunity. The administration of antisera against bacterial toxins such as tetanus and botulinum may also be applicable when the patient has been poisoned but not vaccinated previously against these toxins. As the antisera consist of antibodies from a foreign source, they will be targets for the immune system, which will mount an appropriate response to eliminate the foreign molecule. Consequently, the effectiveness of the antiserum will wane after a few days and be almost ineffectual on repeated use, so it is critical that appropriate precautions always be taken to avoid poisoning.

Serum Sickness

Serum sickness is a form of allergic reaction caused by a delayed immune response that can occur 2 to 3 weeks after the administration of certain medications or antisera from animals or other individuals to provide passive immunization against a particular disease. However, many antisera are now prepared from humans, which greatly reduces the likelihood of serum sickness. Human serum can carry viruses, such as those that cause acquired immunodeficiency syndrome (AIDS) or hepatitis, but, fortunately, routine screening of serum for those infectious agents prevents this complication from occurring. Therefore, the use of horse serum or other animal serum in therapy is limited to cases for which no alternative is available. When only equine antitoxin is available, skin tests should be employed prior to the administration of serum, beginning with a puncture test using a 1:10 dilution. If the reaction is negative, the antiserum can be used. Many drugs, including penicillin, can also occasionally produce a condition indistinguishable from serum sickness. The mechanism involves the formation of antigen-antibody complexes that are toxic to the body.

Serum sickness presents clinically as a skin rash and intense irritation (urticaria). These are commonly accompanied by joint stiffness, swelling, and a mild fever, which last several days. Frequently, lymph nodes enlarge, particularly near the site of the injection, causing a generalized aching. In severe forms of serum sickness, the heart muscles may be involved (myocarditis), and very rarely the kidneys are affected. Kidney involvement causes a form of nephritis, with ankle swelling and high blood pressure. Occasionally, polyneuritis occurs, and recovery from this form of the disorder is seldom complete. However, most patients with serum sickness make a rapid and complete recovery within 4 weeks. Treatment depends on the severity of the symptoms, but patients usually respond well to aspirin and antihistamines. If these measures fail, corticosteroid drugs can be given to decrease the symptoms. Drug treatment is usually continued until the symptoms cease.

TYPES OF VACCINES IN USE

Immunization may be effectively achieved with a number of types of vaccine, leading to effective clearing of the causative agent by the combined innate and primed acquired defenses before serious disease ensues.

Live Attenuated or Inactivated Vaccines

The majority of antiviral vaccines are live attenuated (disabled) or inactivated (killed) viruses. Inactivated viruses are unable to replicate, whereas disabled viruses are much more effective as they can still replicate inside human cells without causing disease and therefore stimulate a greater number of responses, including cytotoxic CD8+ T cells. Attenuated viral vaccines are currently used to protect against polio, measles, mumps, rubella, varicella, and yellow fever. Because attenuated viruses are still able to replicate, albeit at a much-reduced rate, caution should be used when vaccinating antibody-deficient patients as the vaccinations can lead to disease and death. Although attenuated virus strains have many mutations, the reduced rate of clearing in antibody-compromised subjects can increase the chance of the virus's reverting to its fully virulent form and of shedding and transmitting the attenuated virus. Infants with undiagnosed inherited antibody deficiencies are at particular risk from vaccination with live attenuated polio as the virus could revert and lead to paralytic disease.

A similar approach to disabling viruses is used for developing live attenuated bacterial vaccines, the best known of which is BCG for tuberculosis. The causative bacterial agent of typhoid, *Salmonella enterica* serovar Typhi (*S.* Typhi), was manipulated by mutation to be defective in the synthetic pathway for lipopolysaccharide, a critical determinant of pathogenesis. More recent developments include attenuated *Salmonella* vaccines unable to synthesize aromatic amino acids so that they are totally dependent on an external source. The ability of these disabled organisms to grow in the gut is severely limited, but they survive long enough to elicit an effective immune response.

Toxoid Vaccines

Some vaccines, such as those for diphtheria and tetanus, are made from bacterial toxins. The toxin is inactivated to form a toxoid by treatment with aluminum, by adsorption onto aluminum salts, or by the introduction of a mutation in the gene encoding the toxin. For example, CRM_{197} is a diphtheria toxoid with a mutation in amino acid 197. Vaccines made from toxoids can induce low-level immune responses and are administered with an adjuvant. For example, diphtheria and tetanus toxoids are combined with the pertussis vaccine as a DPT immunization. In this instance, *Corynebacterium* acts as an adjuvant in this vaccine. Toxoid vaccines often require a booster every 10 years.

Tissue Culture–Derived Vaccines

Human whole, live attenuated, and inactivated viral vaccines have been produced by methods that use chicken embryos or animals. However, as vaccines produced in animals can be contaminated with residual animal components or the animals might be carrying potentially infectious agents, these vaccines pose a threat to human safety. Thus, cultured animal cells provide an ideal alternative for generating such vaccines while ensuring manufacturing quality assurance and control. At present, primary cells and human diploid cells (eg, the primary fibroblast cell line MRC-5 and WI-38 diploid fibroblasts derived from embryonic human lung primary culture) are approved for the production of licensed human viral vaccines. Continuous cell lines that are tumorigenic are not recommended, but the Vero cell, an African green monkey kidney continuous cell line, has been shown to be free of viral agents and can be maintained for many passages without inducing tumorigenicity. Vero cells have been recommended by WHO and have been used to produce human polio and rabies vaccines.[14] Vero cell propagation systems for large-scale production are used to produce poliovirus, bovine vesicular stomatitis virus, herpes simplex virus, and reovirus.

Purified Polysaccharide Vaccines

The development of bacterial vaccines to capsulated organisms such as the pneumococcus (*S. pneumoniae*) raises some important issues in vaccine development. As early as 1917, a soluble substance that was immunologically active was recovered from pneumococcal cultures and from the urine and blood of infected patients. This soluble substance was identified 6 years later by Heidelberger and Avery to be the capsular polysaccharide of the organism.[15] Following these observations, capsular polysaccharide from pneumococcal types 1, 2, and 3 was injected intradermally into human subjects. The vaccine elicited antibodies to one or more of these polysaccharide antigens. This led to large field trials on approximately 29,000 young adults in the Civilian Conservation Corps with a bivalent capsular formulation consisting of polysaccharide from types 1 and 2. Unfortunately, incomplete follow-up and bacteriologic studies resulted in inconclusive outcome data.

The mobilization of US troops during World War II led to an epidemic of pneumococcal pneumonia that provided an opportunity to evaluate the efficacy of a pneumococcal capsular vaccine. A tetravalent vaccine containing polysaccharide from types 1, 2, 5, and 7 was administered to over 8,000 recruits, and a similar number served as controls, receiving an injection of saline. No pneumonia was reported in the vaccinated individuals over the following 2 weeks, whereas 23 cases were reported in the control group. Pneumococcal pneumonia as a result of two epidemic types excluded from the vaccine formulation occurred with equal frequency in the two groups. Not only was there an impact on disease, the vaccine also influenced the carrier state. If the individual was carrying the organism, vaccination did not eliminate it. However, if the type of organism covered by the vaccine was not being carried during vaccination, the likelihood of acquiring it was reduced by about half. These findings led to the commercialization of two hexavalent vaccines of pneumococcal capsular polysaccharide for adults and children in the late 1940s. However, this coincided with the introduction of antibiotics that were effective against pneumococcus, and so the vaccines were withdrawn from the market 10 years later and their licenses revoked without prejudice. What was not predicted was that, even with optimal antibiotic treatment, pneumococcal fatality would still persist and, critically, the organism would be able to acquire antibiotic resistance relatively easily. It was not until 30 years later, in the 1970s when resistance to common antibiotics emerged, that new efficacy vaccine trials were initiated on adults, and the vaccine was relicensed in 1977. The number of serotypes covered by the vaccine was increased from 14 to 23. Vaccine studies were then initiated in children, one of the high-risk populations for pneumococcal disease. These trials were disappointing, as children up to the age of 5 years fail to respond to T-independent polysaccharide antigens, as discussed earlier; this reality has led to the development of polysaccharide conjugate vaccines (see "Polysaccharide Conjugate Vaccines," to follow).

A similar polysaccharide vaccine now exists for inducing protection in adults against meningococcal serogroups A, C, Y, and W135 disease. In preparation for the Umrah and hajj seasons each year, the Ministry of Health of the Government of Saudi Arabia has notified the Ministries of Health of all countries from which pilgrims arrive that vaccination with the quadrivalent vaccine has been added to the health requirements for arrivals.

Group B meningococcus is currently responsible for approximately 50% of endemic meningococcal infections in some developed countries in Europe, North America, and Australasia. However, the group B polysaccharide is poorly immunogenic as the molecular structure mimics neonatal neural cell surface antigens. This cross-reactivity raises safety issues as antibodies might be stimulated that break immune tolerance and lead to an adaptive immune response directed at self-antigens, which can cause autoimmune disease.

An alternative vaccine component to polysaccharide antigens is a meningococcal outer membrane vesicle (OMV) preparation. OMV-based vaccines have been developed in Norway with a protective efficacy (PE) of 57%; in Cuba the PE is 80%, and in Brazil the PE is 74% in adults. Another alternative is to avoid vaccines containing antigenically variable proteins, such as the OMV formulations. One such approach is to use peptides that mimic bacterial sugar structures as vaccine candidates.[13] Antibodies that have specificity to bacterial sugar molecules, other than those that mimic human antigens, can be used to identify peptide epitope mimics.

Polysaccharide Conjugate Vaccines

An effective acellular vaccine usually requires several components as activation of more than one type of cell is necessary for protective immunity. Polysaccharide-encapsulated bacteria are normally eliminated by antibody binding to the capsule, and so an effective, although relatively short-lived (about 3 years), vaccine strategy was developed to target antibodies to this structure in adults. However, polysaccharides are haptens in children less than 5 years old and fail to induce protective immunity as the children's immune systems are not sufficiently developed. To be converted into antigens, the polysaccharide haptens must be chemically conjugated to immunogenic proteins to form polysaccharide conjugates. The introduction of *H. influenzae* type b polysaccharide conjugated to tetanus toxoid proved to be extremely successful in eliciting protection against disease in children

In November 1999, meningococcal group C (MenC) polysaccharide conjugated to diphtheria toxoid was introduced in the United Kingdom to high-risk age groups, children under 5 years, and then to teenagers. Careful monitoring of meningococcal disease has revealed that a dramatic decline in MenC disease has occurred since the introduction of the conjugate vaccine.[6] Prior to the introduction of this vaccine, MenC was responsible for about one-third of the disease's incidence in the United Kingdom. It is still too early to predict whether replacement of the disease will occur with meningococcal group B. Currently, a combined group A and C polysaccharide and an A, C, Y, and W135 polyvalent vaccine are being developed to combat the main meningococcal groups causing disease.

Pneumococcal disease causes around five million childhood deaths annually worldwide, and a conjugate vaccine has been developed and licensed in the United States. Licensing is being sought in many other countries as well. The current formulation contains seven of the most prevalent serotypes present in the United States. A nine-valent vaccine containing two more polysaccharide serotypes that will increase the protective coverage is being developed and will be licensed within the next few years. Vaccine formulations will need to be modified for other countries if the prevalent serotypes are different.

Recombinant Vaccines

Recombinant DNA technology is already employed for the bulk production of bacterial toxoids, such as diphtheria, where the introduction of a single amino acid change makes the toxin harmless and safe as a vaccine. It is also being used to study novel conjugate carrier molecules that might have superior ability to induce long-term protective immunity when conjugated to bacterial polysaccharides. Rationally designed recombinant polyepitope proteins with the ability to interact with several antibodies might provide excellent candidates for the development and clinical testing of new conjugate vaccines.[16]

However, recombinant technology is being used to construct synthetic vaccines for the induction of protective immunity against infections such as influenza virus and *Shigella* bacteria (the cause of dysentery). Two approaches are being developed: first, synthetic peptides containing defined epitopes that lead to neutralizing antibodies and second, synthetic oligonucleotides encoding such peptides for expressing the epitopes in appropriate vectors. Using an animal model, the efficacy of a vaccine based on recombinant flagella of *Salmonella* vaccine strain, which expresses specific epitopes of the influenza virus, has been demonstrated to show protection against flu.[17] Immunization with this vaccine led to a significant reduction of lung viral load in mice challenged with the influenza virus. More recently, oligonucleotides encoding three influenza epitopes specific for human leukocyte antigen (HLA), one T helper epitope, and two cytotoxic T lymphocyte (CTL) epitopes were inserted into the *Salmonella* flagellin gene to express them as protein antigens alongside a B-cell epitope in the flagella.[18] A recombinant hemagglutinin (rHA) is being developed by Protein Sciences Corporation (Meriden, Connecticut, USA) as a potential replacement for the currently licensed influenza vaccines, which are produced in eggs. To date, rHA has completed several phase I and II human clinical trials that show safety and efficacy. The initial target market is the elderly, where the current licensed vaccine is less effective than in other populations. A strain-specific *Shigella* vaccine based on the bacterial lipopolysaccharide is also being developed.

A promising strategy is to use live attenuated viruses or bacteria, such as *M. bovis* BCG, to vaccinate against other diseases by introducing genes encoding protein antigens from other pathogenic organisms into these disabled hosts, which would elicit protective immune responses.[19,20]

DNA/RNA Vaccines

Vaccination by genes encoding protein immunogens rather than with the immunogen itself has opened up new possibilities for vaccine research and development and offers chances for new applications and indications for future vaccines. For diseases such as malaria and hepatitis, for which conventional attenuated and inactivated vaccines are not available, the prospect of producing protein vaccine components artificially from their genes in safe bacterial systems is now possible. This approach will also circumvent the safety issues related to working with such pathogens. DNA vaccines might also facilitate the identification of new immunogens as potential vaccine components. However, the efficacy of DNA vaccines in humans appears to be much lower than indicated by early studies in mice. Furthermore, important questions remain unanswered concerning the persistence and distribution of inoculated plasmid DNA in vivo, its potential to express antigens inappropriately, or the potentially harmful consequence of insertion of genes into the genome of the host cell. The possibility of inducing immunotolerance or autoimmune diseases also needs to be investigated to justify the widespread application of DNA vaccines in a healthy population.

Naked DNA vaccines are engineered from general genetic vectors, such as the replication-deficient adenoviral recombinant vector constructed to shuttle between bacterial cells for engineering and eukaryotic cells (animal or human) for expression of protein antigen. Expression of protein antigens in the host to stimulate immunity requires an appropriate DNA vector containing the gene of interest. Numerous studies in mouse models have used the replication-deficient adenovirus as a DNA vector.[21] In a mouse malaria model, the adenovirus vector was used to express a malaria antigen that successfully protected the mouse.[22] Similarly, expression of a rabies antigen from the adenovirus vector produced immune protection against this disease in mice.[23] However, naked DNA can persist much longer than had been first thought and on release or escape may lead to horizontal gene transfer to other organisms with unpredictable biologic and ecologic effects. There is also concern about harmful effects due to random insertions of vaccine constructs into cellular genomes of target or nontarget species.

Ribonucleic acid (RNA) vaccines have also been proposed but are a long way from practical use, and, although RNA is a labile molecule in the laboratory, it is surprisingly resistant to degradation under natural conditions. Recombination or shuffling between related RNA molecules is currently a major concern.

REFERENCES

1. Delgado JC, Tsai EY, Thim S, et al. Antigen-specific and persistent tuberculin anergy in a cohort of pulmonary tuberculosis patients from rural Cambodia. Proc Natl Acad Sci U S A 2002;99:7576–81.
2. Colditz GA, Brewer TF, Berkey CS, et al. Efficacy of BCG vaccine in the prevention of tuberculosis. Meta-analysis of the published literature. JAMA 1994;271:698–702.
3. Fine PEM. Variation in protection by BCG. Implications of and for heterologous immunity. Lancet 1995;346:1339–45.
4. Tuberculosis Research Centre (ICMR). Fifteen year follow up of trial of BCG vaccines in south India for tuberculosis prevention. Indian J Med Res 1999;110:56–69.
5. Hart PD, Sutherland I, Thomas J. The immunity conferred by effective BCG and vole bacillus vaccines, in relation to individual variations in tuberculin sensitivity and to technical variations in the vaccines. Tubercle 1967;48:201–10.
6. Maiden MC, Stuart MJ. Carriage of serogroup C meningococci 1 year after meningococcal C conjugate polysaccharide vaccination. Lancet 2002;359:1829–30.
7. Kyaw MH, Jones IG, Campbell H. Prevention of pneumococcal disease in children. Pneumococcal conjugate vaccines. Their use globally could have a major impact on public health. Acta Paediatr 2001;90:473–6.
8. Lee LH, Lee CJ, Frasch CE. Development and evaluation of pneumococcal conjugate vaccines. Clinical trials and control tests. Crit Rev Microbiol 2002;28:27–41.
9. Ahmed AH, Nicholson KG, Nguyen–Van-Tam JS. Reduction in mortality associated with influenza vaccine during 1989–90 epidemic. Lancet 1995;346:591–5.
10. Saha SK, Rikitomi N, Biswas D, et al. Serotypes of *Streptococcus pneumoniae* causing invasive childhood infections in Bangladesh, 1992 to 1995. J Clin Microbiol 1997;35:785–7.
11. Rusen ID, Fraser-Roberts L, Slaney L, et al. Nasopharyngeal pneumococcal colonization among Kenyan children. Antibiotic resistance, strain types and associations with human immunodeficiency virus type 1 infection. Pediatr Infect Dis J 1997;16:656–62.
12. Charalambous BM, Feavers IM. Mimotope vaccines. J Med Microbiol 2001;50:937–9.
13. Brett PJ, Tiwana H, Feavers IM, Charalambous BM. Characterisation of oligopeptides that cross-react with carbohydrate specific antibodies by real-time kinetic, in-solution competition ELISA and immunological analyses. J Biol Chem 2002;277:20468–76.

14. Montagnon BJ. Polio and rabies vaccines produced in continuous cell lines. A reality for Vero cell line. Dev Biol Stand 1989;70:27–47.

15. Heidelberger M, Avery OT. The specific soluble substance of pneumococcus. J Exp Med 1923;38:73–81.

16. Falugi F, Petracca R, Mariani M, et al. Rationally designed strings of promiscuous CD4(+) T cell epitopes provide help to *Haemophilus influenzae* type b oligosaccharide: a model for new conjugate vaccines. Eur J Immunol 2001;31:3816–24.

17. McEwen J, Levi R, Horwitz RJ, Arnon R. Synthetic recombinant vaccine expressing influenza haemagglutinin epitope in *Salmonella* flagellin leads to partial protection in mice. Vaccine 1992;10:405–11.

18. Levi R, Arnon R. Synthetic recombinant influenza vaccine induces efficient long-term immunity and cross-strain protection. Vaccine 1996;14:85–92.

19. Miyaji EN, Mazzantini RP, Dias WO, et al. Induction of neutralizing antibodies against diphtheria toxin by priming with recombinant *Mycobacterium bovis* BCG expressing CRM(197), a mutant diphtheria toxin. Infect Immun 2001;69:869–74.

20. Nascimento IP, Dias WO, Mazzantini RP, et al. Recombinant *Mycobacterium bovis* BCG expressing pertussis toxin subunit S1 induces protection against an intracerebral challenge with live *Bordetella pertussis* in mice. Infect Immun 2000;68:4877–83.

21. Armstrong AC, Dermime S, Allinson CG, et al. Immunization with a recombinant adenovirus encoding a lymphoma idiotype. Induction of tumor-protective immunity and identification of an idiotype-specific T cell epitope. J Immunol 2002;168:3983–91.

22. Gilbert SC, Schneider CM, Hannan JT, et al. Enhanced CD8 T cell immunogenicity and protective efficacy in a mouse malaria model using a recombinant adenoviral vaccine in heterologous prime-boost immunisation regimes. Vaccine 2002;20:1039–45.

23. Xiang Z, Ertl HC. Induction of mucosal immunity with a replication-defective adenoviral recombinant. Vaccine 1999;17:2003–8.

Chapter 2

MEASUREMENTS AND TESTS FOR IMMUNITY (APPLIED)

Bambos M. Charalambous and Indran Balakrishnan

Knowledge of previous infection or prior vaccination is important for a number of reasons. It can facilitate accurate clinical diagnosis or determine if there is a risk of infecting a newborn child with diseases such as hepatitis B and the human immunodeficiency virus (HIV). It is particularly important for women of childbearing age to be screened for rubella and vaccinated against this virus as infection during pregnancy carries a high risk of fetal abnormalities, including deafness, cataracts, heart defects, and mental retardation. Some infections caused by slowly dividing organisms can lead to disease after many years of latent infection. For example, *Mycobacterium tuberculosis*, the infectious agent causing tuberculosis, can be reactivated and cause disease after many years of dormancy. *M. tuberculosis* is not completely eradicated during treatment because many drugs act only on rapidly dividing organisms, and it can form granulomas that impede the entry of antibiotics. In addition, many microbial pathogens can acquire resistance to drugs, preventing effective treatment of the disease.

Some viruses, such as the herpes simplex virus, can persist in a latent form in neural cells and be reactivated many times in response to various factors ranging from other infections, immune suppression, or hormonal changes. Other viral diseases, such as HIV, have a protracted asymptomatic phase, subverting immune cells gradually over an extended period of time to produce symptomatic disease when the immune system is suppressed to the extent that opportunistic infections occur.

Vaccination has been established as an efficient and cost-effective strategy to prevent infection. Regulatory bodies quite correctly insist that before a new or improved vaccine is licensed, it must be proven to be safe and efficacious. In some countries, such as the United States, a new vaccine must be shown to be more effective than vaccines already available against the same disease before it can be licensed. As it is currently unethical to obtain safety and efficacy data on new vaccines in humans, animal models are used to obtain these data. However, in contrast to safety trials, which are relatively straightforward in animals, the assessment of protective efficacy is much more problematic, not only because many diseases are species-specific but also because we have an incomplete understanding of the molecular and cellular mechanisms that are required for protection. Interestingly, in early studies of vaccines, animal models were not used, and researchers tested their vaccine candidates directly on humans (see "Purified Polysaccharide Vaccines" in Chapter 1, "Immunologic Principles of Vaccination"). Determination of the protective efficacy of vaccines is further complicated by the nature of the pathogen; viruses are intracellular and are eliminated by different immune processes than extracellular bacterial pathogens. Our protective defenses consist of the rapid innate response and the slower adaptive response, which can proceed along a number of pathways (refer to Chapter 1 for a more detailed description of these two mechanisms).

The effectiveness of vaccination, which modulates only the adaptive response, predominantly depends on the B-cell and T-cell status of the individual. Hence, they might be much less effective in the very young, in whom B cells are poorly developed, and in immunocompromised subjects with impaired T-cell responses, in whom live attenuated vaccines are contraindicated. Many vaccine trials have shown that there can be considerable variation in protective efficacy that cannot be explained by differences in adaptive immune responses—protection is also likely to be dependent on the effectiveness of the individual's innate response to the pathogen—and an increasing amount of research is currently being undertaken in this area at the molecular level.[1–3] The innate response can vary according to the genetic background of the individual, his or her nutritional status, and the level of disease exposure.

MEASUREMENT OF HOST DEFENSE RESPONSES

On antigenic stimulation of the immune system, whether by infection or vaccination, a number of complex processes are triggered. These processes vary according to the nature of the immunogen and include phagocytosis of bacteria; antibody-mediated phagocytosis, termed opsonophagocytosis; and secretion of cytokines (cell-to-cell chemical signals) from macrophages and T cells. Circulating antibodies are produced by plasma cells located in regional lymph nodes and the spleen, and activation of the complement system can occur either directly by the invading organism or by antibodies. Central to many effector arms of the immune response are the functions of circulating antibodies, which are dictated by the constant region (Fc) of the antibody molecule (the tail of the Y-shaped immunoglobulin structure). The constant region also defines the subclass (IgA, IgE, IgG, and IgM) and isotype (IgG1, IgG2, and IgG3) of the antibody. To differentiate into the various subclasses and isotypes, the B lymphocytes (B cells), which produce antibodies, undergo genetic rearrangements, or recombinations, in the constant regions of their immunoglobulin genes. Once "switched," the genetic rearrangement is permanent, but it can be further fine-tuned by a process known as "somatic mutation" in the antigen-binding region (Fab), which is present in the arms of the Y-shaped structure. This results in higher affinity antibodies, which retain their specificity to the same antigen, and yields an improved protective function (affinity maturation).

Antibodies of the IgM subclass are located exclusively in the intravascular circulation; they bind to an invading pathogen and activate the classic complement pathway, resulting in the formation of cytotoxic complement attack complexes and opsonins, which facilitate the removal of antigen-antibody complexes by the reticuloendothelial system (refer to Chapter 1 for details). IgG subclass antibodies are the dominant immunoglobulins in extracellular fluids. They can neutralize toxins and viruses, opsonize particles for ingestion by phagocytes (opsonophagocytosis), and, when complexed to antigens, activate the classic complement pathway. The subclass IgA is present as either monomers in blood or as dimers that are secreted and protect mucosal surfaces. They can bind to and neutralize toxins or can reduce the adhesion of mucosal organisms that precedes colonization of the nasopharyngeal, genitourinary, and gastrointestinal mucosae. IgE subclass antibodies are found on the surface of mast cells and basophils; their primary role is to defend against parasites and mediate immediate hypersensitivity reactions, but they also provide a second-line defense against any pathogens that penetrate the mucosal epithelium. The functions of the different IgG isotypes will be described later in this chapter.

The magnitude of the antibody response following an infection or vaccination can be estimated by measuring the levels of serum antibodies (titer) using enzyme-linked immunosorbent assay (ELISA).

To assess their protective function, the antibody subclass and isotype can also be determined by ELISA using class- or type-specific detecting antibody. Immunoglobulin isotypes are also known to correlate with the T-helper response that is mediated; T helper 1 (Th 1) responses are associated with cell-mediated protection, which includes phagocytosis and complement-mediated killing; Th 2 responses are associated with the humoral response, eliciting immunologic memory and neutralizing antibodies.

To ascertain the type of T-helper response being stimulated, cytokine secretion assays can be performed and will be described with relevant examples. A new immunologic technique, enzyme-linked immunospot (ELISPOT), that detects cytokine secretion at a single cell level, enabling the characterization of individual CD4+ and CD8+ cells, will also be described.

As an estimate of the protective efficacy of vaccines and their ability to elicit immunologic memory, the strength of binding, or avidity, of the antibodies elicited to a specific pathogenic antigen can be measured. Avidity can be measured by performing an ELISA with serum antibodies preincubated with increasing concentrations of a denaturing chemical that disrupts antibody-antigen interactions, such as sodium isothiocyanate.

In the protection against bacterial pathogens that have a polysaccharide capsule, such as *S. pneumoniae*, evidence suggests that the rapid defensive mechanisms of complement killing and opsonophagocytosis are critical. High-avidity antibodies targeting the pathogen mediate both of these mechanisms. The in vitro methods used to measure complement killing are the serum bactericidal assay (SBA) and the opsonophagocytosis assay.

During the development of new vaccines, animal models of infectious disease can be used in two modes of protection, active or passive. Active protection involves the vaccination of animals and passive protection the injection of antisera from human vaccinees, prior to infection of the animal model with the pathogen.

The laboratory assays that are classically used to evaluate and compare immune responses are either measurements of antibody titer specific for a particular antigen or functional bioassays. Antibody-binding assays such as ELISA measure both functional and nonfunctional antibodies, which are usually of high and low avidities, respectively. Functional assays, such as passive or active immunization in animal models of infection, opsonophagocytic assay, and SBA, tend to measure only high-avidity antibodies and are better measures of the protective efficacy of vaccines. If a good correlation exists between antibody titers by ELISA and a functional assay, then the simpler ELISA assay can be used as a correlate of protection and to evaluate immune responses to vaccines.

Detection of Antibodies Elicited against Foreign Antigens

Enzyme-Linked Immunosorbent Assay

ELISA was first described in 1971 and since then has become an important technique in diagnosis and in the determination of antibody responses to vaccine components. ELISA is a solid-phase assay that involves the coating of a plastic surface with the target antigen either directly or via an antibody. When the test serum is added, antibodies that are specific for the target antigen will attach to the antigen on the solid phase. Serum antibodies can be detected by antihuman antibodies conjugated to an enzyme such as horseradish peroxidase (HRP). Adding a substrate that undergoes a color reaction in the presence of HRP will indicate the amount of antibody-HRP conjugate bound. ELISA can also be performed to detect antigens that are captured to the solid phase with antigen-specific antibody. To ensure that the detecting antibodies can bind to the captured antigen, the capture and detecting antibodies must possess nonoverlapping

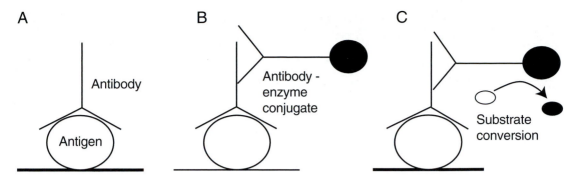

Figure 2-1. Enzyme-linked immunosorbent assay. *A*, Serum antibody binds to microbial antigen immobilized to a plastic surface. *B*, Antihuman antibody conjugated to horseradish peroxidase (HRP) binds to serum antibody. C, Substrate for HRP changes color in response to the amount of HRP present.

epitopes. ELISA kits are now commercially available for a wide range of viral and bacterial antigens and antibodies (Figure 2-1).

Antibody Subclasses and IgG Isotypes

As mentioned above, solid-phase ELISA can be used to determine immunoglobulin subclasses and isotypes. Knowing the isotype profile allows the type of T helper cell responses elicited by vaccines to be elucidated. For example, immunoglobulin isotypes IgG1 and IgG3 are produced by Th 1 responses, which elicit the cell-mediated components of the response, phagocytosis and complement-mediated killing. In contrast, isotype IgG2 is a neutralizing antibody produced by Th 2 responses associated with humoral immunity and immunologic memory. In some cases, mixed Th 1 and Th 2 responses occur, classified as Th 0.

To determine the amount of serum antibodies binding to a specific antigen, known amounts of anti-IgG antibody used in a twofold dilution series are bound to the solid phase via an IgG-specific antibody (Figure 2-2). In this way, both the unknown sample and the standards have three molecular layers. Because the standard of known antibody concentration interacts with both capture and detecting antibodies, the two antibodies must possess nonoverlapping epitopes.

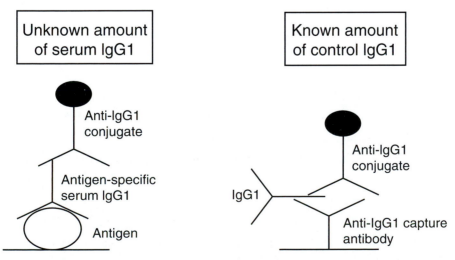

Figure 2-2. Enzyme-linked immunosorbent assay. The diagram shows the quantification of unknown antigen-specific IgG1 antibody on the left by the running in parallel of known amounts of IgG1 on the right.

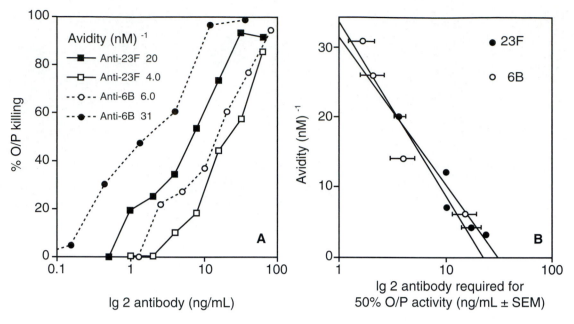

Figure 2-3. Effect of antibody avidity on opsonophagocytosis of serotype 6B and 23F pneumococci. *A,* Opsonophagocytosis (O/P killing) of serotype 6B and 23F pneumococci by two anti-PPS 6B and two anti-PPS 23F IgG2 antibodies. *B,* Correlation between avidity and the amount of antibody required for opsonophagocytosis of pneumococci. Each circle represents the amount of PPS 6B- or PPS 23F-specific IgG2 antibody required to achieve 50% opsonophagocytosis activity (O/P activity). Values shown were derived by the testing of each IgG antibody at several doses in at least three independent experiments. Reproduced with permission from Usinger WR and Lucas AH.[4]

Measurement of High-Avidity Antibodies

On a weight-for-weight basis, higher avidity antibodies are more effective than lower avidity ones. Protection against disease, consequently, depends on both antibody concentration and avidity. The measurement of high-avidity antibodies as a marker of functional antibody concentration has been developed using a modified ELISA. This involves incubation of the serum with a fixed concentration of a protein denaturant such as sodium isothiocyanate or urea prior to reacting with the antigen coating the microtiter plate.[4] Studies on serum antibodies to pneumococcal serotypes 6B and 23F indicate the importance of avidity in antibody effector functions and protection. As illustrated in Figure 2-3, the titer and avidity of antibody correlate with the percentage killing by opsonophagocytosis (left-hand panel). The correlation between avidity and opsonic activity is also shown (right-hand panel). It is important, however, to note that avidity might not serve as a universal index of antibody-mediated protection. A recent study of murine monoclonal antibodies to vesicular stomatitis virus showed a lack of correlation between antivirus avidity and protective efficacy in a mouse model of infection.[5] The majority of the antiviral antibodies had apparently exceeded a minimum avidity threshold for protection such that further increases in avidity did not lead to discernible improvements in protective function.[5,6] On the other hand, vaccine-induced human pneumococcal polysaccharide–specific antibodies differ from murine monoclonal antibodies to vesicular stomatitis virus in that they do not exceed this putative threshold; it is therefore still possible to correlate avidity with protective efficacy. Indeed, unlike antibodies to viral surface proteins, antibodies reacting with carbohydrate determinants of bacterial capsules might never achieve avidities sufficiently high to cross a threshold such that their protective function becomes independent of concentration.

Function	Human antibody (Equivalent antibody in mouse)							
	IgA	IgD	IgE	IgG1 (IgG2a)	IgG2 (IgG1)	IgG3 (IgG2b)	IgG4	IgM
Opsonization	+	−	−	+++	*	++	+	−
Neutralization	++	−	−	++	++	++	++	+
Activates complement killing	+	−	−	++	+	+++	−	+++
Sensitization of NK cells	−	−		++	−	++	−	−
Sensitization of mast cells	−	−		+	−	+	−	−

Figure 2-4. Protective functions of antibody subclasses and isotypes. The principal functions are shaded in a light grey (+++), lesser functions in a dark grey (++), minor functions (+), and no activity (−). *IgG2 is an opsonin in about 50% of Whites where Fc receptors of a particular allotype are present. As the development and testing of vaccines is usually carried out in animals, typically mice, the mouse homologues of human antibodies are also detailed.

Functional Antibody Tests

Pathogens usually invade the body by crossing the mucosal epithelial barriers of the respiratory, intestinal, and urogenital tracts, as well as through damaged skin. Infections can be localized to specific tissues. Pathogens can also be introduced directly into the blood by insects, wounds, or hypodermic needles. Therefore, mucosal surfaces, tissues, and blood all need to be protected. Consequently, antibodies are widely distributed to combat invasive pathogens and are adapted to function in different compartments. Although most antibodies are dispersed by diffusion from their site of synthesis, transport mechanisms are required to translocate them across epithelial surfaces such as the lung and intestine. The location of antibodies is determined by their subclass; this determines both their capacity for diffusion and their affinity for specific receptors that mediate translocation across various epithelia. Antibody subclasses that are directed to different compartments have distinct effector and protective functions depending on the type of immune response elicited by the infectious agent. Therefore, for vaccines to elicit protection, they must stimulate the appropriate antibody responses without exposure to the pathogen. The principal protective functions of antibodies are opsonization, neutralization, sensitization of natural killer (NK) cells, sensitization of mast cells, and activation of the complement system leading to serum bactericidal activity (Figure 2-4). Each of these will be described, with emphasis on testing for the appropriate immunologic responses required for protection following vaccination and monitoring vaccine success.

Opsonophagocytosis

Phagocytosis is thought to be an important mechanism in host defense against disease caused by capsulated organisms such as *Streptococcus pneumoniae* and *Neisserisa meningitidis*; it is the process of engulfing and digesting foreign substances or pathogens by white blood cells such as macrophages and neutrophils. As a component of the innate immune response, it occurs on interaction with pathogenic bacterial surface antigens in the absence of any previous encounter. Prior exposure to the foreign material, whether by vaccination or infection, gives rise to the adaptive immune response leading to the production of antibodies that can facilitate phagocytosis, a process known as opsonization. Opsonophagocytosis is a mechanism that protects against infection using protective antibodies, complement, and phagocytes. IgG1 and IgG3 are present in high concentrations in serum (9 mg/mL and 1 mg/mL, respectively), are transported across the placenta, and diffuse into extravascular sites. IgG2 might be able to fix complement at high epitope densities and is also the best activator of the alternate pathway at high antibody concentrations. The dimeric form of IgA, secretory (s)IgA, is translocated across the mucosal epithelium to protect mucosal surfaces, and, as a monomer, it can also diffuse into extravascular sites. All of these immunoglobulins, and to a lesser extent IgG4, play a role in opsonophago-cytosis. Antibodies bind to the target bacterium by recognition of molecules on the surface of the bacterium, such as capsular polysaccharides and surface proteins. The Fc regions of adjacent antibodies fix complement, and the deposition of complement proteins C3b or iC3b further facilitates phagocytosis. When antibodies and complement components act in this capacity they are termed "opsonins."

The opsonophagocytosis assay measures functional antibody, as opposed to ELISA, which measures total binding antibody regardless of functional capacity. This assay can be used for evaluating human responses to vaccines, both those that are currently licensed and those still in development; it is particularly useful in the assessment of capsular polysaccharide–based vaccines. Other factors, such as the type of receptors expressed on the surface of phagocytic cells, might also play a role in the efficacy of functional antibody.

An opsonophagocytosis assay has been developed to estimate the efficacy of the heptavalent polysaccharide conjugate vaccine against S. pneumoniae. A flow cytometric opsonophagocytic assay has been developed for the measurement of functional antibodies elicited after vaccination with the 23-valent pneumococcal polysaccharide vaccine.[6] Opsonophagocytic activity of serum antibodies from vaccinated subjects is determined from the number of viable cells of S. pneumoniae remaining after differentiated HL-60 human cell culture cells are activated by the addition of twofold serial dilutions of serum. The serum antibody concentration, or phagocytic titer, required to produce 50% killing provides an index of their functional activity. Although the cultured human HL-60 cells used in this assay bind antibody with low affinity, the measured opsonophagocytic activity in the presence of complement has been shown to be similar to peripheral blood lymphocytes (PBLs) from human donors. The antibody titer between vaccinated and unvaccinated individuals is compared. The early studies by Gotschlich and Goldschneider in the 1960s on capsulated organisms indicated that a minimum of a fourfold increase in the phagocytic antibody titer in response to vaccination correlated with protection.[5] Since then, this level of activation has been used as the gold standard for determining whether new vaccines targeted to capsular polysaccharide antigen can elicit protection against capsulated bacterial organisms.

Measurement of Neutralizing Antibody

One approach to the prevention of infection in adults is to screen for susceptibility by the presence of specific antibodies or by vaccination history and to administer vaccine to susceptible or antibody-negative individuals. Despite a variety of design flaws in some studies, such as selection biases and small sample sizes, most demonstrate that persons with a positive history of having received rubella vaccine are significantly more likely to be seropositive for antibodies specific for rubella than are individuals without such a history. A history of rubella infection, on the other hand, is a less reliable predictor of immunity. In rubella vaccine trials and cohort studies, most subjects with antibodies detectable by hemagglutination-inhibition (HI) are protected from clinical disease. HI testing is labor intensive and can give both false-positive and false-negative results. However, ELISA and latex agglutination, both faster and more convenient laboratory methods and with sensitivities of 92 to 100% and specificities of 71 to 100% compared with HI testing, have now replaced HI. The apparently lower specificities of these methods are due to their ability to detect low levels of rubella antibody, which are undetectable by HI methods and are therefore reported as false-positives. Although no controlled trials have been performed to determine if these low levels confer immunity against rubella, clinical and in vitro evidence suggest that they are protective. These newer tests, therefore, appear to be more accurate and convenient than HI.

Many bacteria cause disease by producing toxins that can damage or disrupt cellular function; an example is tetanus toxin, which blocks inhibitory neuron action, causing tetanic muscle contraction. Toxins frequently interact with specific receptors on the surface of target cells via a receptor-binding domain distinct from the component that mediates their toxic function. Many toxins are effective at very low concentrations; for example, one molecule of diphtheria toxin can kill a cell. Neutralizing antibodies, therefore, need to locate and bind to the toxin rapidly to minimize tissue damage. The antibody must bind to the receptor-binding domain with high affinity to prevent the toxin's displacing the antibody. The major neutralizing antibodies are IgG, predominantly IgG2, and IgA because they can attain high binding avidities and are able to diffuse rapidly to extravascular sites. Vaccines to protect against bacterial toxins usually contain modified toxin molecules, known as toxoids, that are rendered harmless by the inactivation of the region that mediates toxicity without alteration to the receptor-binding domain. Immunization thus elicits neutralizing antibodies that bind to the receptor-binding domain of the toxoid, which are able to cross-react and protect against the native toxin.[7]

In a manner analogous to toxin neutralization, protective antibodies can prevent viral disease by preventing the interaction of viral particles with their host cell. For example, the influenza virus expresses a surface protein called hemagglutinin, which binds to sialic acid residues present on the surface of epithelial cells lining the respiratory tract. Antibodies targeted toward hemagglutinin can neutralize the virus and inhibit infection. As with toxin-neutralizing antibodies, high-avidity IgA and IgG antibodies are important in virus neutralization.

Bacteria have surface-associated molecules, known as adhesins, that mediate binding to the surface of host cells. Adherence is critical to bacterial colonization and invasion regardless of whether they enter the cell (*Salmonella* sp.) or remain attached to the cell surface (*Neisseria gonorrhoeae*, the causative agent of the sexually transmitted disease gonorrhea). *N. gonorrhoeae* expresses the cell surface protein pilin, which is essential for infectivity and responsible for adhesion of the organism to epithelial cells of the urogenital tract. Antibodies against pilin can prevent adhesion and avert disease. IgA antibodies secreted onto mucosal surfaces of the respiratory, intestinal, or urogenital tracts can inhibit adhesion of bacteria, viruses, or other pathogens and prevent colonization and subsequent invasive disease.

Several strategies are employed to measure the efficacy of antibodies in neutralizing toxins or microorganisms. In vivo neutralization tests directly measure the biologic activity of antiserum by demonstrating its neutralizing properties in laboratory animals, usually mice. These sensitive tests measure primarily serum IgG. Alternatively, neutralizing antibody can be measured by an in vitro passive hemagglutination test, ELISA, or radioimmunoassay (RIA). These tests are more sensitive in detecting IgG antibodies than IgM antibodies, which are generally incapable of neutralizing toxin. Results of in vitro tests need to be interpreted carefully and verified against data obtained by the in vivo neutralization method to ensure that an accurate and reproducible correlation exists between the in vivo and in vitro tests.

Passive Hemagglutination Test

In the hemagglutination (HA) test, carrier red cells sensitized with toxoid agglutinate in the presence of antitoxin. This test has been used widely to assess the immune status of various populations in response to tetanus toxoid vaccination. In testing antibody responses to tetanus toxoid, the HA test usually correlates well with the neutralization test, although differences in titer of greater than tenfold can occur, particularly at low levels of serum antibody.

Serum Bactericidal Assays

As described in Chapter 1, complement activation occurs by three possible pathways: classic, mannan binding, and alternative. The classic pathway is activated by the formation of antigen-antibody complexes and is therefore an adaptive response that can be modified on repeated exposure to the pathogen or by vaccination.

In the measurement of the efficacy of outer membrane vesicle (OMV) vaccines against *N. meningitidis* serogroup B disease, SBA geometric mean titer (GMT) has been shown to correlate with vaccine protective efficacy and has therefore been used as a surrogate index. Evaluation of SBA was performed on data from a randomized double-blind placebo-controlled efficacy trial involving 172,000 secondary school students (aged 13 to 14 years) in Norway (1988 to 1991).[8] A vaccine efficacy of 87% was calculated for a 10-month observation period, but after 29 months, the estimated efficacy fell to 57%. A separate three-dose study on adolescents showed that after a third dose 10 months after the second, when cases of disease would usually start to appear, a strong booster response was induced. Ten months after the second dose, the GMT decreased to near preimmunization level, but after the third dose, the SBA GMT increased around 20-fold. One year after the third dose, the GMT was still higher than it was 6 weeks after the second dose. Protection observed after vaccination corresponded to the level of GMT. This analysis indicated that to attain long-term protective levels in a population, three doses of vaccine are required and that measurements of GMT will be useful for evaluating various upcoming formulations and improvements of immunization regimens for OMV vaccines.

Infant Rat Meningitis Passive Protection Assay

Several group B meningococcal vaccines based on outer membrane protein complexes have been evaluated in efficacy trials, and one is used in Latin America.[9–11] The antibody response was analyzed extensively, but uncertainty remains concerning the requirements for protective immunity. The measurement of bactericidal or opsonophagocytic activity is difficult to standardize, and their correlation to protection is not always clearly defined. Animal models for meningococcal infection have been developed but are considered for the most part unsatisfactory because of artificial set-up, the need for large inocula, or the use of adjuvants such as mucin or iron. An alternative bioassay for meningococcal meningitis was developed using infant rats aged 4 to 6 days.[12–15] The pups were injected via the intraperitoneal (IP) route with polyclonal or monoclonal antibodies. One hour later, a bacterial challenge was injected IP, and the development of bacteremia and meningitis was assessed by the culture of samples of blood and cerebrospinal fluid taken 6 hours after challenge. In this rat pup model, antibodies to capsular polysaccharides (CPS), lipooligosaccharide (LOS), and the outer membrane proteins PorB and PorA were compared; it was found that protection was regularly seen with antibodies to CPS and PorA.[6,16] Subsequently, this model has been used in the development of a PorA-based recombinant meningococcal vaccine.[16,17] Although CPS antibodies have been shown to be protective in the infant rat model, the CPS of group B meningococci is poorly immunogenic in humans because the polysaccharide is similar to human cell surface antigens and fails to elicit protection; therefore, in some instances the results need to be treated cautiously.

The rat pup passive protection model has been extended to measure the protective ability of human serum from Norwegian vaccinees who received an outer membrane complex vaccine. Serum dilutions of 1:10 and 1:30 were shown to provide reproducible results against certain strains of group B, which varied depending on whether the subjects had received the Norwegian or Cuban group B meningococcal vaccine.[18]

SBA might be favored as a useful correlate of protection in the development of a group B meningococcal vaccine as the infant rat animal model is not able to take into account meningococcal antigens that mimic human antigens, such as the group B CPS and the outer membrane LOS, which fail to elicit protection in humans and might even stimulate autoantibodies. However, these assays might not provide the complete picture of protection. A study by Gorringe and colleagues has shown protection conferred by a meningococcal vaccine based on cross-reactive antigens present on the nonpathogenic but closely related *Neisseria lactamica* despite the absence of SBA activity.[19]

Antigen-Mediated Cytokine Secretion Assays

ELISPOT Assay

The ELISPOT assay is a powerful tool for detecting secretion of a particular molecule in an individual cell in vitro.[20,21] The assay has also been developed to measure the frequencies of cells that produce and secrete a variety of effector molecules, such as cytokines.[22] The ELISPOT assay can detect cytokine-producing cells from both activated naive and memory T-cell populations, as well as other cell types, and is very sensitive, measuring cytokine-producing cells down to 1:300,000. The specificity and sensitivity of the ELISPOT assay is dependent on high-avidity capture and detection antibodies, as well as the enzyme-amplification step necessary for visualizing the binding of the detecting antibody (Figure 2-5). The ELISPOT assay enables the immunologic responses to novel pathogen antigens to be investigated in detail and is hence a useful tool in the development of new vaccine candidates.

Splenocyte Proliferation and Cytokine Secretion Assays

Antigen-stimulated proliferation of splenocytes indicates a T cell–mediated memory response to the antigen. Previous exposure of the immune system to antigens can also result in the secretion by splenocytes of cytokines such as interferon (IFN)-γ, interleukin (IL)-4, or IL-10. The secretion of cytokines can be investigated in circulating leukocytes by capturing cells that are secreting a particular cytokine. The capture antibody consists of two antibodies conjugated to each other tail to tail, an anti-CD45 antibody on one end and an anticytokine antibody at the other. The anti-CD45 interacts with all leucocytes, and during a short incubation period, the cytokine secreted by the antigen-specific T cells binds to the other antibody. The cells secreting a specific cytokine are then identified by a cytokine-specific detection antibody, which can be used to capture this population of cells for further analysis.

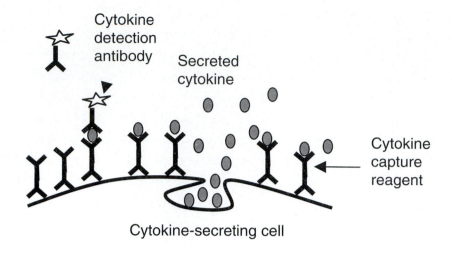

Figure 2-5. Double-ended antibodies used to label specific cytokine-secreting cells in the circulation.

CONCLUSION

In many cases, our incomplete knowledge of immunologic responses, including the interplay between the innate and adaptive mechanisms, limits our ability to predict whether a particular vaccine formulation will provide appropriate protection against a microbial pathogen. Hence, although an in vitro assay or animal model can be used to provide a correlate of protection, ultimately, the evaluation of the protective efficacy of new vaccines can be performed only in human subjects. Exceptionally, new vaccines that are based on a previously tried and tested formula, such as the group C meningococcal conjugate polysaccharide vaccine that is based on the successful *Haemophilus influenza* type b (Hib) conjugate vaccine, can be introduced without comprehensive phase III human trials.

In this chapter, we have described the tests that can be used to evaluate the immune status in response to either previous exposure to pathogen or a vaccination program. The descriptions are by no means comprehensive, but our hope is that they will inform the reader sufficiently to grasp the principles of the methods used to measure immunologic responses.

REFERENCES

1. Horng T, Barton GM, Flavell RA, Medzhitov R. The adaptor molecule TIRAP provides signalling specificity for toll-like receptors. Nature 2002;420:329–33.

2. O'Neill, LA. Signal transduction pathways activated by the IL-1 receptor/toll-like receptor superfamily. Curr Top Microbiol Immunol 2002;270:47–61.

3. Roy SK, Knox S, Segal D, et al. MBL genotype and risk of invasive pneumococcal disease. A case-control study. Lancet 2002;359:1569–73.

4. Usinger WR, Lucas AH. Avidity as a determinant of the protective efficacy of human antibodies to pneumococcal capsular polysaccharides. Infect Immun 1999;67:2366–70.

5. Gotschlich EC, Goldschneider I, Artenstein MS. Human immunity to the meningococcus. IV. Immunogenicity of group A and group C meningococcal polysaccharides. J Exp Med 1969;129:1367–84.

6. Martinez JE, Romero-Steiner S, Pilishvili T, et al. A flow cytometric opsonophagocytic assay for measurement of functional antibodies elicited after vaccination with the 23-valent pneumococcal polysaccharide vaccine. Clin Diagn Lab Immunol 1999;6:581–6.

7. Sesardic D, Corbel MJ. Testing of neutralising potential of serum antibodies to tetanus and diphtheria toxin. Lancet 1992;340:737–8.

8. Holst J, Feiring B, Fuglesang JE, et al. Serum bactericidal activity correlates with the vaccine efficacy of outer membrane vesicle vaccines against *Neisseria meningitidis* serogroup B disease. Vaccine 2003;21:734–7.

9. Bjune G, Hoiby EA, Gronnesby JK, et al. Effect of outer membrane vesicle vaccine against group B meningococcal disease in Norway. Lancet 1991;338:1093–6.

10. Sierra GV, Campa HC, Varcacel NM, et al. Vaccine against group B *Neisseria meningitides*. Protection trial and mass vaccination results in Cuba. Natl Inst Public Health Ann 1991;14:195–207.

11. Zollinger WD, Boslego J, Moran E, et al. Meningococcal serogroup B vaccine protection trial and follow-up studies in Chile. The Chilean National Committee for Meningococcal Disease. Natl Inst Public Health Ann 1991;14:211–2.

12. Frasch CE, Parkes L, McNelis RM, et al. Protection against group B meningococcal disease. I. Comparison of group-specific and type-specific protection in the chick embryo model. J Exp Med 1976;144:319–29.

13. Frasch CE, Robbins JD. Protection against group B meningococcal disease. II. Infection and resulting immunity in a guinea pig model. J Exp Med 1978;147:619–28.

14. Huet M, Suire A. An animal model for testing the activity of meningococcal polysaccharide vaccine. J Biol Stand 1981;9:67–74.

15. Saukkonen K. Experimental meningococcal meningitis in the infant rat. Microb Pathog 1988;4:203–11.

16. Idanpaan-Heikkila I, Wahlstrom E, Muttilainen S, et al. Immunization with meningococcal class 1 outer membrane protein produced in *Bacillus subtilis* and reconstituted in the presence of Zwittergent or Triton X-100. Vaccine 1996;14:886–91.

17. Nurminen M, Butcher S, Idanpaan-Heikkila I, et al. The class 1 outer membrane protein of *Neisseria meningitidis* produced in *Bacillus subtilis* can give rise to protective immunity. Mol Microbiol 1992;6:2499–506.

18. Toropainen M, Kayhty H, Saarinen L, et al. The infant rat model adapted to evaluate human sera for protective immunity to group B meningococci. Vaccine 1999;17:2677–89.

19. Gorringe AR, Oliver KJ, Reddin KM, et al. *Neisseria lactamica* protects against experimental meningococcal infection. Infect Immun 2002;70:3621–6.

20. Czerkinsky C, Andersson G, Ekre HP, et al. Reverse ELISPOT assay for clonal analysis of cytokine production. I. Enumeration of gamma-interferon-secreting cells. J Immunol Methods 1988;110:29–36.

21. Helms T, Boehm BO, Asaad RJ, et al. Direct visualization of cytokine-producing recall antigen-specific CD4 memory T cells in healthy individuals and HIV patients. J Immunol 2000;164:3723–32.

22. Fujihashi K, McGhee JR, Beagley KW, et al. Cytokine-specific ELISPOT assay. Single cell analysis of IL-2, IL-4 and IL-6 producing cells. J Immunol Methods 1993;160:181–9.

Chapter 3

TRAVEL VACCINE REQUIREMENTS AND RECOMMENDATIONS

Stephen Toovey

International travel has become available to a diverse group of travelers who, by definition, will need to seek travel health advice when spending time in foreign climes, no matter how brief. This chapter will address the issues concerning the administration of travel vaccinations, including those vaccines that are required or mandatory, and those that are recommended.

To address this question, it is convenient to classify travel-related vaccination requirements into those vaccines that are legally enforceable, for which official documentation might need to be produced when seeking entry to a country, and those that are not mandated by law. The latter can be viewed as those that constitute best clinical practice for the traveler to have but that are not demanded by the type of officialdom generally encountered by travelers at border posts and immigration controls.

The first category of vaccine, that mandated by law, is relatively easy to understand. The law is quite clear on what is required and expected of vaccinator and traveler. The second category is somewhat more problematic, as it might not always be immediately clear whether a particular vaccine does indeed constitute best clinical practice for a traveler about to embark on a particular journey. For the sake of clarity, those vaccinations that the traveler is legally compelled to have will be designated as "required" vaccines, whereas those from which the traveler might well benefit but that are not required by law will be designated "recommended" vaccines.

There is, unfortunately, a somewhat dubious category of vaccine need that hovers in a netherworld between our categories of required and recommended. These are vaccines for which no official legal requirement exists but for which immigration or port health authorities might nevertheless demand proof of vaccination. These vaccination requirements will be considered in the section under the subheading "Requirements Outside the International Health Regulations" below.

REQUIRED VACCINES

The official, and legally enforceable, vaccination requirements with which travelers wishing to cross international borders must comply are regulated by international treaty. The current International Health Regulations, which are managed by the World Health Organization (WHO) and to which individual member states accede by treaty and legislation, have been in force since 1971, when they were adopted by the World Health Assembly. They have their origin in a history that stretches back at least to the fourteenth century, when the Venetian city-state felt the need to prevent shipborne importation of disease. A maritime power and international trading port, Venice was particularly vulnerable to the unwitting importation of pathogens by docking sea vessels; accordingly, the city enacted legislation in 1377 that permitted the quarantine of ships and their crews.

The first truly global efforts directed at stemming the spread of infectious disease across frontiers date from the International Sanitary Conference of 1851 held in Paris.[1] Although this conference failed to achieve its aim of establishing an international regimen to control the spread of contagious disease, a subsequent conference held in 1892 saw the introduction of internationally agreed on measures to combat the spread of cholera, which menaced Europe at that time. From these attempts to contain the spread of contagion grew the International Sanitary Regulations, followed eventually by the current International Health Regulations.

The International Health Regulations

The intention of the current International Health Regulations is threefold:
- to detect, reduce, or eliminate sources from which infection spreads;
- to improve sanitation in and around ports and airports; and
- to prevent dissemination of vectors.[2]

It is clear that vaccination is an effective means of achieving the goal of reducing or eliminating disease, and the regulations provide the basis on which mandatory travel vaccination rests.

Previously, the International Health Regulations provided for prescribed vaccination against yellow fever, cholera, and smallpox. Although the regulations also concern themselves with the control of plague, the lack of a vaccine suitable for mass immunization has meant that mandatory vaccination against plague has never been enforced. The poor efficacy and short duration of protection offered by injected cholera vaccines and the failure of vaccination to control the spread of cholera have led to the deletion of cholera from the list of required vaccines.[3]

The global eradication of smallpox led, similarly, to the deletion of smallpox from the list of diseases mandating compulsory vaccination for travelers in 1981.[2] Accordingly, the requirement that travelers produce proof of vaccination against smallpox when traversing international frontiers has, as with cholera, been dropped from the regulations.

Currently, therefore, travelers should be required by immigration and port health authorities to produce proof of vaccination only against yellow fever. However, anomalies to these recommendations do exist and are detailed below, under "Requirements Outside the International Health Regulations."

Intention and Scope of the International Health Regulations Concerning Yellow Fever

The intention of the International Health Regulations that concern yellow fever is quite clear: to prevent the importation of yellow fever from countries where the virus might be circulating to countries free of the virus but possessing potentially competent vectors. The former are known as "endemic" countries, the latter as "receptive" countries. Travelers arriving in a receptive country within 6 days of departing an endemic country must show a valid certificate of vaccination against yellow fever to gain entry. By way of example, a traveler arriving in Los Angeles within 6 days of having departed Central Africa or tropical South America might well be incubating yellow fever. Such a viremic traveler, bitten and fed on by a competent vector mosquito in Los Angeles, might establish an ongoing cycle of virus transmission that leads to a large-scale outbreak of urban yellow fever. Such a development would be disastrous for a country currently free of yellow fever. The emergence of West Nile virus in North America serves as a suitable illustration of how exotic viruses can establish themselves in previously disease-free regions when competent vectors are present.

With this scenario in mind, the International Health Regulations, adopted by countries into their own body of legislation by statute, leave both vaccinator and traveler little leeway. The regulations clearly spell out the indications for yellow fever vaccine and the methods of administration to be employed.

Vaccination against yellow fever may be administered only by a recognized International Vaccination Center, designated by the health authority (usually the national ministry of health) in the relevant territory. Health authorities are obliged to notify WHO of the designated International Vaccination Centers in their territory, and WHO in turn maintains a register of all such centers internationally. Only vaccine sourced from a WHO-approved manufacturer may be used to immunize travelers if an International Certificate of Vaccination is to be issued. The certificate of vaccination must be in the format set out by WHO and be completed in accordance with WHO regulations in either French or English. The certificate must state, among other things, the name of the vaccine manufacturer and the batch number. Vaccination must be administered 10 days prior to arrival in a nonendemic country for an International Certificate of Vaccination to be valid.[4] This 10-day period allows time for immunity to develop and also serves to ensure that the incubation period of yellow fever has been exceeded when a traveler presents him- or herself for entry into a country.

Contraindications to the administration of yellow fever vaccine are detailed in a later chapter dedicated to yellow fever vaccine (Section III, Chapter 5, "Yellow Fever Vaccine"), but the regulations do provide for the granting of certificates of exemption or letters of waiver to travelers unable or unlikely to tolerate yellow fever vaccine. Principally, such travelers include certain categories of immunocompromised individuals, infants under 9 months of age, and pregnant women. Strict criteria apply to the granting of these letters of waiver or certificates of exemption, which must be in prescribed format. They may be issued only to travelers for whom immunization with yellow fever vaccine might pose a genuine threat to health. It is worth the vaccinator's bearing in mind that for many such individuals, the underlying condition giving rise to the contraindication might argue against travel to a destination where the risk of yellow fever exists.

Vaccinations for Departing Travelers

Travelers departing from territories infected with a disease subject to control by the International Health Regulations and preventable by vaccination might be required by the authorities within that territory to be vaccinated prior to departure. This is provided for by the International Health Regulations. The intention is to prevent the spread of a disease such as yellow fever from an endemic to an uninfected country. This requirement is rarely applied in practice, but it is quite possible that uninfected countries might increasingly demand implementation of this regulation to protect themselves against the importation of disease.

Revisions to the International Health Regulations

WHO has been conducting a review of the International Health Regulations for some while. At the time of writing, this review had not been completed, but the intention is to amend the regulations to take account of the changes that have occurred in the world since 1971.[1] The current regulations do not address issues raised by viral hemorrhagic fevers other than yellow fever, such as Ebola, Marburg, and Lassa fever. Given the difficulties of making definitive diagnoses in cases of suspected viral hemorrhagic fever, especially in developing countries, it seems likely that a syndrome-based approach to diagnosis will be adopted in the reporting of newly emerged diseases. Whatever the final form of the revised regulations, it is unlikely that significant revisions to current vaccination practice will be implemented: the current system, despite often-flawed application, has offered a measure of protection against disease importation.

Requirements Outside the International Health Regulations

There are two situations in which travelers can be expected to have been vaccinated beyond the requirements laid down by the International Health Regulations. The first is when a state requires additional vaccinations for some legitimate purpose, most usually related to public health concerns. The second occurs when immigration and port health officials make demands based on neither regulation nor law.

Legitimate Requirements for Additional Vaccinations

In certain circumstances, a state may exercise its sovereignty and decide that the interests of its citizens and arriving travelers are best served by requiring one or another additional vaccination. The best example of this is the additional vaccination requirement instituted by the authorities of the Kingdom of Saudi Arabia for Muslim pilgrims. This additional requirement affects pilgrims arriving in the kingdom with the intention of attending the annual hajj at Mecca and insists that pilgrims show proof of vaccination against meningococcal meningitis.[5] This is clearly a sensible public health measure given the history of meningitis outbreaks during previous pilgrimages to Mecca and the large numbers congregating (in excess of a million).[6] Given too that many pilgrims arrive from countries in which meningococcal meningitis is endemic, the Saudi requirement, despite its being additional to the International Health Regulations, is clearly motivated by sensible public health concerns.

In 2002, following the multicountry outbreaks of meningococcal meningitis serogroup W-135 among returned pilgrims, the Saudi authorities extended this requirement. Previously, immunization with a bivalent polysaccharide meningococcal vaccine against serogroups A and C had been deemed sufficient. The emergence of meningitis attributed to the less common W-135 serogroup led the Saudi authorities to change the requirement, so that pilgrims are now required to produce proof of immunization with a tetravalent vaccine conferring protection against serogroups A, C, Y, and the offending W-135. Pilgrims arriving in Saudi Arabia and unable to provide satisfactory proof of vaccination are immunized on the spot by Saudi authorities.

Each year, the Saudi Arabian Ministry of Health publishes its vaccination requirements for pilgrims. This forms an integral part of the process for acquiring a visa to gain admission to Saudi Arabia, and would-be pilgrims are informed clearly of the additional requirements in a transparent and consistent manner through consular channels.

Irregular Requirement for Additional Vaccinations

In contrast to the Saudi position and approach to requiring vaccination beyond the International Health Regulations, travelers sometimes encounter other, less well-intentioned demands for additional vaccination.

It is not infrequently required of travelers arriving in developing countries to show proof of additional vaccination, most usually against cholera, although inappropriate demands for yellow fever vaccination certificates are sometimes made. An example of the latter would be a traveler arriving in a yellow fever–endemic country and being asked to produce a yellow fever vaccination certificate. It is, of course, understood that such a traveler could not pose any threat of introducing yellow fever, as the virus will already be in circulation in that country, and a traveler presented with such a demand will most usually be from a nonendemic country free of yellow fever virus.

As stated, demands for proof of vaccination against cholera are not infrequently made of travelers arriving in developing countries. Such travelers, again, are most often from developed and cholera-free countries, and it would be inappropriate to ask such travelers to be immunized against cholera as they pose no threat of cholera carriage into any country; often it is officials in countries infected with cholera who make such demands.

Irregular vaccination certificate demands are made either in an attempt to extort payment from the traveler or because of ignorance of the International Health Regulations. In the first instance the traveler is often threatened with instant immunization on arrival unless he or she pays a "fine." Most travelers, who will have heard stories of unsterile medical equipment and dubious medical practices, will opt to pay the fine in lieu of immediate vaccination.

RECOMMENDED VACCINATIONS

In nearly all circumstances, travel to destinations outside the developed world will justify additional vaccination beyond the requirements of the International Health Regulations. Although the International Health Regulations offer unambiguous guidance in their prescriptions concerning yellow fever, vaccinators might seek travel health advice from other sources when considering whether an individual traveler's itinerary and medical circumstances dictate additional vaccination.

Fortunately, help is available in the form of internationally recognized guidelines and travel risk databases. These guidelines and databases will help the practitioner to decide which vaccines *might* be appropriate for the traveler. Equally important in today's litigious environment is the ability to provide a meaningful defense when faced with an accusation of negligence for not recommending a particular vaccine.

Information Systems to Assist Vaccine Selection Based on Itinerary

A number of information sources are available to assist both vaccinator and traveler with vaccine selection. However, critical appraisal of such recommendations is required. A review of some of the better known information sources follows.

Authoritative Web Sites

By it's very nature, cyberspace is a dynamic milieu, and for this reason I have confined myself to this brief review to some of the more established and authoritative sites (Table 3-1).

Centers for Disease Control Travelers' Health

The Centers for Disease Control (CDC) has one of the premier travel health information sites on the Internet and undoubtedly carries authority. A public service, it offers travelers and vaccinators information free of charge. Recommendations are made on a regional basis, with, for example, South America divided into "South America, temperate (Southern)" and "South America, tropical (Northern)." Africa is similarly divided into a number of regions: Central, North, South, West, and East. Asia, somewhat less clearly, is divided into Newly Independent States of the Former Soviet Union, Indian subcontinent, East Asia, South Asia, and Southeast Asia. The Middle East, straddling Asia and Africa, is listed separately. (**www.cdc.gov/travel/index.htm**)

Table 3-1. **Assessment Criteria for Travel Health Information Sources**

1. What is the motive of the authors?

2. Does the source carry commercial information/advertisements?

3. Is a commercial bias evident or possible in the information offered?

4. What are the institutional affiliations of the authors?

5. Have the authors' works been published elsewhere in peer-reviewed publications?

6. Is the general medical content of the information source congruent with accepted norms/consensus?

7. Is the information source consistently reliable across all destinations (check it against your own country and experience)?

8. Is the information source consistently reliable across all diseases?

9. Is the information source comprehensive?

10. When was the information source last updated?

11. Is the information source readily navigable?

12. If a log-on is required to the Web site, is the site secure?

13. What is the privacy policy of the Web site?

14. How readily can you connect to the Web site?

CDC Yellow Book (Health Information for International Travel)

Of far more practical use to vaccinators is the facility to view the CDC's "Yellow Book" on-line, with a separate entry in the publication for each country. The CDC's Yellow Book is available in hard copy and as a free download from the CDC Web Site. Vaccinators are able to view both the legal vaccine requirements for entry into a particular country and a list of the diseases likely to be of risk to the traveler for a particular itinerary. (**www.cdc.gov/travel/yb/index.htm**)

CDC The Blue Sheet (Summary of Health Information for International Travel)

The CDC's "The Blue Sheet" lists countries infected with a quarantinable disease. Quarantinable diseases, as defined by the International Health Regulations, are cholera, yellow fever, and plague. Smallpox, declared eradicated from the world, would also be a quarantinable disease should it reemerge. Such reemergence might follow its release (deliberate or accidental) from legitimate or purloined stocks. The Blue Sheet can be read in conjunction with the Yellow Book to determine the vaccinations required for a particular destination. A section is dedicated to the latest outbreaks and lists these by country. (**www.cdc.gov/travel/blusheet.htm**)

CDC National Immunization Program

This site is not specific to travel-related vaccines but instead contains the recommendations of the Advisory Committee on Immunization Practices (ACIP). Vaccinators will find it an informative source of reference on individual vaccines. (**www.cdc.gov/nip/publications/ACIP-list.htm**)

CDC Web Site Overview

The CDC sites listed above should prove useful to many vaccinators as sources of reference. This is particularly so when the question arises as to whether a particular diseases exists in a particular country. CDC Web site pages will also offer the travel medicine practitioner useful refreshers on conditions he or she might be less familiar with, at <www.cdc.gov/health/diseases.htm>. The site is not configured, and probably not intended, to provide the busy travel medicine practitioner with quick reference for a series of itineraries.

Although the lack of ready country-specific information might make the CDC sites less than ideal for travel vaccinators to consult on a regular basis, its does provide a wealth of travel health–related information on specific diseases. It is likely that many travelers will have consulted the CDC sites prior to consulting a travel medicine practitioner, and vaccinators should be familiar with the site's recommendations.

The World Health Organization

International Travel and Health *(Blue Book)*

The WHO publication *International Travel and Health* has been the definitive reference on required vaccination for many years, deriving its authority from WHO's central role in the management of the International Health Regulations. The "Blue Book" is available both electronically on the WHO Web site and in hard copy. The Blue Book provides information to vaccinators and travelers on the legal requirements for travelers presenting themselves to immigration and port health authorities. This informs merely whether proof of vaccination is required for entry into a country, not the prevalence or risk of yellow fever within a country's borders.

The WHO Blue Book lists in brief, tabular form most of the vaccines that might be administered to protect travelers but that are not legally mandated. It does not go into any detail on which of these might be appropriate for particular destinations, however, and does not purport to be a reference site of this nature. It does offer information on whether a country is malarious and whether malarial drug resistance is known to exist in that country. Along with this information, a brief recommendation on malaria chemoprophylaxis is made. This extends the utility of the WHO Blue Book but does not place it in the category of a reference that would assist the travel medicine practitioner wishing to compile a list of recommended vaccines for an individual traveler. (**www.who.int/ith/index.html**)

Other Web sites

A number of other Web sites, some authoritative, offer advice on travel-related diseases and their prevention. These include those of the Public Health Laboratory Service in England and Wales at <www.phls.co.uk> and Health Canada at <www.TravelHealth.gc.ca>.

Both sites offer advice both to the public and to professionals on specific diseases and travel hazards, whereas the Canadian site offers limited but useful country-specific vaccine advice.

The National Health Service in Scotland hosts a site at <www.fitfortravel.scot.nhs.uk> that offers immunization advice on a country-by-country basis, in a manner similar to that of the commercially available travel-risk databases. A similar service is offered by the University of Munich at <www.fit-for-travel.de>.

The ProMED site at <www.promed.org> is a respected source of information on disease outbreaks, some of which will be vaccine preventable. It offers an e-mail news service.

Table 3-2. **Web Sites Offering Useful Information on Vaccine-Preventable Travel-Related Diseases**

Web Site	Information Provided	Web Site Address
Centers for Disease Control (CDC) Travelers' Health	Recommends vaccines on a broad regional basis	www.cdc.gov/travel/index.htm
CDC Yellow Book	Vaccines required for entry to a country, diseases that might pose a threat to the traveler	www.cdc.gov/travel/yb/index.htm
CDC The Blue Sheet	Countries infected with a quarantinable disease, outbreak news	www.cdc.gov/travel/blusheet.htm
CDC National Immunization	Advisory Committee on Immunization Practices (ACIP) recommendations on individual vaccines	www.cdc.gov/nip/publications/ACIP-list.htm
CDC	Travel-related and other diseases	www.cdc.gov/health/diseases.htm
World Health Organization (WHO) Blue Book	Vaccines required for entry to a country	www.who.int/ith/index.html
Health Canada	Country-specific travel-related vaccines, advisories	www.TravelHealth.gc.ca
PHLS (UK)	Travel-related diseases, outbreaks, and guidelines	www.phls.co.uk/advice/index.htm
NHS Scotland	Country specific	www.fitfortravel.scot.nhs.uk
University of Munich	Country specific	www.fit-for-travel.de/en/reiseziele/index.html
ProMED	Outbreaks	www.promedmail.org

NHS = National Health Service; PHLS = Public Health Laboratory Service; UK = United Kingdom.

Most national governments offer their citizens some form of Internet-based travel health advice, but few of these are truly suited to addressing the needs of the busy travel medicine practitioner. Table 3-2 lists sites of recognized authority.

In general, busy travel medicine practitioners will find their needs best served by accessing preferred Internet Web sites and by consulting commercially available travel health databases. These include the Travax subscription database in the United States and the United Kingdom, the Netcare database in southern Africa, and the TMVC database in Australia. The commercial databases are updated regularly, and this feature, combined with their ready desktop availability, means that they will offer the most practical information solution for the majority of travel medicine practitioners.

The Gideon database deserves separate mention. This offers a comprehensive, country-specific review of disease prevalence data plus a diagnostic assistance program that aids in the differential diagnosis of travel-related syndromes. It is not configured to offer itinerary-specific pretravel immunization advice but can act as a definitive source of reference on disease prevalence.

Table 3-3. **Steps in the Selection of Vaccines to Recommend to Travelers**

1. Determination of traveler's current vaccine status

2. Determination of traveler's current health status and current medication use.

3. Identification of itinerary by countries to be visited

4. Elucidation of itinerary into towns and regions to be visited within each country

5. Determination of length of stay at each point along the proposed itinerary

6. Identification of "risk points" in the itinerary

7. Determination of vaccine-preventable diseases present at each risk point

8. Determination of magnitude of threat of each vaccine-preventable disease

9. Determination of the risk-benefit ratio of each vaccine contemplated

COMPILING A LIST OF RECOMMENDED VACCINES

It might be useful to break the process of developing vaccine recommendations down into a number of discrete steps. These are listed in Table 3-3.

Determination of the Traveler's Current Vaccine Status

Although this might seem self-evident, this first and essential step by way of a travel health risk assessment is identifying deficiencies in the traveler's immunity; this might even afford an opportunity to offer protection against diseases not usually considered travel hazards, such as influenza or measles. Furthermore, perusal of the traveler's vaccine record might indicate the need for vaccinations that might not have been completed at the appropriate time point. An example is the recommendation for potentially fertile female travelers to be vaccinated against rubella.

Determination of the Traveler's Current Health Status and Concurrent Medication Use

This is a critical part of the process of developing vaccine recommendations. Demographic and economic trends in developed countries mean that greater numbers of travelers of advancing age now travel. Many of these travelers will be suffering from chronic illnesses, many of which will increase the travelers' risk profiles. A review by Hill revealed that 27% of travelers consulting a Connecticut travel medicine facility had at least one chronic medical condition.[7]

The purpose of this step in the consultation and travel health risk assessment process is to understand better how a vaccine-preventable disease might affect a traveler if he or she encounters it, whether it is safe for the traveler to receive a particular vaccine, and whether the vaccine will prove to be immunogenic if administered. It might be useful at this stage to place travelers into one of the following categories:
- high-risk travelers, for example, the immunocompromised,
- members of special groups, for example, pregnant women and younger children; and
- travelers not at unusual risk.

Detailed consideration of the high-risk traveler and the needs of those in special groups are dealt with in later chapters in Section IV of this text, but the principles underlying the selection and scheduling of immunization remain the same for all potential vaccinees. Will the vaccine be immunogenic and offer protection, and will the vaccine be safe or will it harm its recipient? Reflection on these questions should reveal that the selection of vaccines has much in common with the prescription of other medical interventions, that is, consideration and weighing of the proposed intervention's safety and efficacy and the risk-benefit ratio of the vaccines. It is important, therefore, that a detailed medical history be taken from each traveler whom it is proposed to vaccinate, with attention being given to the presence of underlying medical conditions with the potential to affect vaccine efficacy and safety. This consideration relates both to the underlying disease process and to any treatment that the candidate vaccinee is receiving.

An example for consideration is a traveler suffering from rheumatoid disease. Although rheumatoid disease is not of itself usually a contraindication to vaccination, some of the agents used in its treatment might well be. It is obvious that for rheumatoid patients receiving immunosuppressant therapy, vaccination with a live viral vaccine such as yellow fever poses a risk of vaccine strain dissemination and systemic illness. What might be less obvious are other drug-vaccine interactions. Examples of this in a rheumatoid patient might include the reduced immunogenicity of rabies vaccine when given during concomitant chloroquine therapy. At least of theoretic concern is the prospect that orally administered live bacterial vaccines, such as have been developed against typhoid and cholera, might be rendered ineffective, or at the very least have their immunogenicity reduced, in the rheumatoid patient receiving oral sulfasalazine.

It is fair to say that many travelers reporting for vaccination before departure to some idyllic destination will also face a potential threat from malaria and will have malaria chemoprophylaxis prescribed for them. This places the traveler in the same situation as the rheumatoid patient considered above. Antimalaria agents will often, but not always, be prescribed at the time of consultation for travel vaccination. The travel medicine practitioner might be faced with a situation in which a traveler is already taking malaria chemoprophylaxis and in whom it will be deemed preferable not to disturb the prescribed antimalarial regimen. Vaccine selection and scheduling will in such cases have to accommodate the antimalaria regimen. Even in those cases in which the vaccinator him- or herself will be prescribing the necessary malaria chemoprophylaxis, similar considerations of drug-vaccine interaction and scheduling will apply, although the vaccinator will obviously enjoy greater latitude (Table 3-4).

Table 3-4. **Effect of Commonly Prescribed Antimalarial Drugs on Vaccine Efficacy**

Antimalarial	Oral Typhoid Vaccine[23]	Oral Cholera Vaccine[24]
Atovaquone-proguanil (Malarone)*[25]	No reduction in efficacy	No reduction in efficacy
Mefloquine	Reduced efficacy	No effect known
Doxycycline	Reduced efficacy	Reduced efficacy
Chloroquine	No effect known	Reduced efficacy
Proguanil	No reduction in efficacy	No reduction in efficacy
Dapsone-pyrimethamine (Maloprim)*	Expect reduced efficacy	Expect reduced efficacy

*Data provided by GlaxoSmithKline, which produces Malarone and Maloprim. Adapted from the Center for Disease Control and Health Canada.

Identification of Itinerary by Countries to Be Visited

Experience tells that the majority of travelers will report for vaccination with the central idea of receiving vaccine "X" for a visit to country "Y." The ready availability of such information on the Internet and the availability of information sources that present lists of vaccine recommendations against country names has perhaps perpetuated the myth that there are agreed and immutable lists of vaccine recommendations for each and every country in the world. This is clearly not so.

Automated lists serve as a useful and often expert-generated starting point for vaccine consideration, but they can be no more than one of the many inputs determining the final recommendations placed before a traveler.

Elucidation of Itinerary into Towns and Regions to Be Visited within Each Country

The country itinerary serves merely as the starting point for the drawing up of a short list of vaccines for consideration. To make truly sensible recommendations to a traveler, it is imperative for the travel medicine practitioner to have detailed knowledge of the itinerary within each country to be visited and of the activities planned at each stop along the traveler's way. The method of transport between points of sojourn should also be of relevance to the vaccinator: carriage by animal and waterborne transport will carry risks above those of reputable airlines.

The activities a traveler contemplates during his or her absence from home have great bearing on the selection of vaccines for recommendation. It is almost axiomatic in the minds of many that the more adventure oriented a traveler is, the greater will be the risk of becoming ill. Thus, business travelers confining themselves to five-star hotel accommodation will most likely imagine that they are at less risk of becoming ill than are their less affluent compatriots backpacking their way across the world's wilderness areas. This is not necessarily the case.

With respect to vaccine-preventable diseases, consider a traveler to one of Central Africa's crowded capital cities. The business traveler confining his or her stay to such a destination will unarguably be exposed to a greater risk of droplet-acquired infection than will the traveler camped out in the bush. Droplet-spread infections include, of course, meningococcal meningitis and influenza, both of which are vaccine-preventable diseases.

The same considerations might well apply to food- and waterborne disease. Urban travelers will have neither any idea of nor any control over the level of food hygiene practiced in the kitchens of the various hostelries that cater to them. Camping backpackers, by contrast, might well be preparing their own meals and attending to their own water purification.

Recreational activities will also have a bearing on the selection of vaccines for recommendation, with participants in water sports at many destinations being at obviously increased risk of a number of illnesses, some of which will be vaccine preventable.

Determination of Length of Stay at Each Point along the Proposed Itinerary

The length of time that the traveler will spend in areas of risk is obviously important, and the longer a traveler remains within a risk area, the greater will be his or her chance of contracting one or more of the diseases on offer. This often leads to the formulation of the view that the short-stay traveler need not be offered such extensive vaccination as the traveler intent on a lengthy stay away from home. Consequently, recommendations have evolved that spring or summertime travelers to the forested areas of Central and

Eastern Europe need not avail themselves of vaccination against tickborne encephalitis unless spending 3 weeks in a tick-infested area.[8] Such a recommendation should be discussed with the traveler, who might be more concerned with the issue of protection than the consideration of risk compared with duration of travel.

There is indeed evidence to support the view that risk accumulates with increasing length of stay, although a different view might prevail in the traveler's mind.[9]

Attempts have been made to aid this decision-making process by looking at the cost-effectiveness of vaccination. One such study, which set out to examine the cost-effectiveness of a number of travel-related vaccines, concluded, for British travelers at least, that immunization against typhoid and hepatitis A was not cost-effective.[10] However, this study has been criticized on a number of grounds. One of these is that the study did not segment destinations by risk profile, and another that it was not meaningful to correlate the costs borne by a nationalized and publicly funded health service with benefit accruing to individuals.[11,12] The authors of the original study acknowledge this latter difficulty in their reply to published criticism.[13] It should be understood that cost-benefit and cost-effectiveness ratios apply to populations of individuals but not necessarily to individuals. The issues raised by the results of cost-effectiveness studies are important, but it can be difficult to always relate these to the individual traveler. Each traveler should have his needs and circumstances considered on an individual basis when his travel health risk assessment is undertaken.

The risks, costs, benefits, and possible adverse effects of each vaccine contemplated, as well as the implications should the associated disease be contracted, need to be clearly and unambiguously explained to travelers and to be understood by them.

The more detailed and comprehensive databases and information sources that are likely to be at the disposal of the vaccinator will in general provide this sort of information, but such recommendations should act only as guidelines.

Identification of "Risk Points" in the Itinerary

Modern travelers come in all shapes and sizes and laden with all sorts of prejudices and misinformation about their itineraries.[14] Traveler profiles range from that of the business traveler attending meetings in capital cities to those travelers experiencing more remote regions. Between these extremes is found the affluent traveler booked on a package tour that involves an adventure element or activity. A suitable example might be travelers who, booked to see the game reserves and natural splendors of Africa, decide that white-water rafting on the Zambezi River would complete their African experience. Such travelers would be exposed to an array of risks not immediately identifiable from a list of countries to be visited.

A detailed breakdown of the itinerary into urban, rural, and wilderness sections must be undertaken, with an understanding of the activities to be pursued at each individual risk point. The length of time to be spent at each risk point identified clearly does need to be known while considering the appropriate vaccine recommendations. In addition, information on the activities to be pursued, accommodation to be occupied, and standards of hygiene prevailing in the accommodation and kitchens on which the traveler will depend will need to be considered. If in doubt, it is probably reasonable to anticipate a standard of hygiene below that prevailing in the vaccinee's home country.

The role of the travel agent in influencing vaccine uptake is well known, but less is known formally about how the health beliefs of travelers influence vaccine acceptance.[15]

Although the subject of traveler prejudices has not been investigated in any great depth, prevailing beliefs almost certainly vary across nationalities and socioeconomic classes. It is likely, for example, that European and American views will differ on this subject. Almost certainly, views within Europe, even between neighboring states, will differ.

Areas to which the vaccinator should be sensitive and that should be explored with the traveler include his or her views on the need for vaccination, and the safety and efficacy of vaccines in general. Thus, although the majority of travelers undoubtedly believe vaccines to be effective and, often, essential, many question their safety. Vaccinators faced with such travelers should endeavor to offer the necessary reassurance, but they might have to accept that logic and evidence will not always win the day. They should diligently note vaccinations declined.

In formulating vaccine recommendations, the travel medicine practitioner should, as best he or she is able, attempt to estimate just how compliant the traveler will be with nonvaccine travel hygiene practices. Considerations such as the possibility of the traveler's altering or lengthening his or her itinerary should also enter the vaccinator's mind. A traveler unlikely to comply with recommended hygiene measures and setting off on an indeterminate itinerary is arguably a candidate for multiple immunizations.

It is essential that the vaccinator discuss with the traveler accurate and up-to-date travel health information. To this end, the vaccinator is referred to the information sources listed above, under "Information Systems to Assist Vaccine Selection Based on Itinerary."

Determination of Magnitude of Threat of Each Vaccine-Preventable Disease

The best-known study of this topic is that of Steffen and colleagues.[9] These researchers looked at the incidence rate of various travel-related diseases in travelers visiting developing countries. From the type of data generated by Steffen's group, attempts are often made to deduce cost-effectiveness ratios for various vaccines. The difficulty with this approach, as discussed above, is that it adopts a macro rather than an individual perspective. The relative risk of contracting a disease does need to be explained to the traveler, alongside the risks of the particular vaccine intended to protect against it. Good practice dictates that the traveler should decide together with the travel health practitioner the risks and benefits afforded by vaccines with regard to the incidence of disease during travel. The travel medicine practitioner should advise the traveler on a destination's diseases and risks and how these might be avoided, including, where legislation demands, as with yellow fever, the necessary vaccinations.

Financial considerations might well be a significant factor in determining the final list of vaccines to be administered. This is frequently the case with younger travelers setting out to explore the world on a limited budget. Such travelers typically visit more remote areas, stay in accommodation of a lesser grade, and have less to spend on vaccination. In such cases, a prioritization of the vaccines appropriate for the itinerary needs to be made. This requires a detailed understanding not only of the itinerary but also of the activities planned, the traveler's medical history, and the availability of competent medical care while traveling. For such travelers, it might be sensible to administer the legally required vaccines, followed by those that offer protection against potentially lethal diseases; vaccines against less deadly threats would follow last.

Determination of the Risk-Benefit Ratio of Each Vaccine Contemplated

This is perhaps the most difficult and contentious part of the process of determining which vaccines a traveler should be offered, and an orderly prioritization of vaccines might not be straightforward in practice. This calculation is a different one from that of cost-effectiveness consideration, considering vaccine risk against vaccine benefit.

Part of the problem inherent in calculating even an approximate risk-benefit ratio for most vaccines is that a disease risk is rarely, if ever, known with any certainty. Correspondingly, adverse events associated with modern vaccines are usually extremely rare. There are, of course, exceptions to this, as evidenced by concerns about the Japanese encephalitis vaccine.[16] When quantified, however, serious adverse effects even from this vaccine are quite rare, with Danish investigators reporting just 101 allergic adverse events in 350,000 distributed doses.[17] The true incidence of vaccine-associated adverse events cannot in all likelihood be known, as underreporting almost certainly occurs.[18] Nevertheless, it is reasonable to believe that few serious vaccine-associated adverse events will go unreported. A large European study found that an alleged allergic reaction immediately following vaccination was reported just once for every 450,000 doses of vaccine administered.[19] This study examined the incidence of such adverse events for 15 commonly pre-scribed vaccines. It concluded that the true incidence of potentially life-threatening allergic reactions is "extremely rare": the real risk to the vaccine recipient is much less than 1:450,000. When questions of risk and benefit are raised, the vaccinator can, in most circumstances, tell the patient that the travel-related vaccines offered are extremely safe. The same applies whether single or multiple vaccines are administered.[20] This type of data will, hopefully, reassure those travelers with preconceived concerns about vaccine safety.

The caveat is that statements on vaccine safety cannot be made with such conviction for newer vaccines, for which long clinical experience is lacking, but clearly this does not apply to the established travel vaccines. Undoubtedly, newer vaccines will demand more prudent prescribing until experience elevates their safety status to that of those better known vaccines.[21] The withdrawal shortly after the commercial launch of vaccines against Lyme disease and rotavirus illustrates the need for caution with newer vaccines.[22]

Consider the case of a young traveler planning a trip through West Africa. Given a traveler possessed of limited resources and unable to afford the full panoply of protection available, should the vaccinator prioritize immunization against hepatitis A or meningococcal meningitis? The risk to the young traveler of contracting meningococcal meningitis is in the order of 5,000-fold less than his or her risk of contracting hepatitis A, according to Steffen's data.[9] The decision to be made in this rather simplistic example is whether to protect the traveler against a common illness that, although highly unpleasant and extremely inconvenient, is hardly ever fatal or, alternatively, to provide protection against the much rarer but more serious disease of meningitis. To confound the dilemma, note that it is common practice to offer travelers immunization against poliomyelitis, a disease with an incidence rate in travelers similar to that of meningococcal meningitis.[9] A subjective element will of necessity intervene in the construction of risk-benefit ratios, and the individual traveler's frame of reference will need to be subsumed into such calculations.

The utility of data such as Steffen's lies more in its persuasiveness that vaccination against diseases such as cholera might not be worthwhile for most individuals. This is a disease that, unlike meningococcal meningitis, usually lies within the power of the traveler to prevent. Even the most well-informed and counseled traveler will find it impossible to avoid airborne microdroplets of meningococcus; by contrast, the swallowing of cholera-contaminated water is easily avoided by adherence to simple food and water hygiene rules. In situations in which resource allocation is important, we can use incidence data to relegate even the newer, more efficacious cholera vaccines to the bottom of our list. It is clear that the data inform us that both cholera and meningococcal meningitis are rare diseases in travelers; what the data do not do is allow us to equate these diseases. When cost is an issue, an appropriate strategy for each disease must be offered by the vaccinator, with consideration to the nature of the disease to be prevented, the traveler's risk tolerance, and both vaccine and nonvaccine methods of prevention.

WHAT IS REQUIRED OF THE VACCINATOR

Beyond the strictures imposed by the International Health Regulations, the would-be vaccinator and the traveler need to be fully cognizant of the risks attendant on any proposed itinerary and to prioritize vaccination in accord with unavoidably subjective risk determinations. The formulation of rational vaccine recommendations demands a familiarity with the International Health Regulations and the insight that the Regulations are intended primarily to protect nations, not individuals. To consider him- or herself fully equipped, the vaccinator must have ready access to a regularly updated source of country-specific information. For the busy travel medicine practitioner, the latter will equate, in most instances, to access to a reliable and authoritative database. Finally, the vaccinator must be prepared to deal with the traveler's own preconceived notions on vaccination and travel health risk and to taper recommendations to available resources. Vaccinators should offer best clinical practice in travel medicine to their travelers by recommending the most appropriate vaccine regimens and by ensuring that these travelers are suitably protected for their journeys with the modern vaccines at our disposal.

REFERENCES

1. Revision of the international health regulations. Progress report, May 2002. Wkly Epidemiol Rec 2002;77:157–63.
2. World Health Organization. International health regulations. Available at: http://www.who.int/m/topics/international _health_regulations/en/index.html (accessed May 28, 2002).
3. World Health Organization. Cholera. Basic facts for travellers. Available at: http://www.who.int/emc/diseases/cholera/ factstravellers.html#n3 (accessed May 28, 2002).
4. World Health Organization. International travel and health. Vaccine-preventable diseases. Available at: http://www. who.int/ith/chapter06_19.html#further (accessed May 28, 2002).
5. Centers for Disease Control. Travelers' health. Saudi Arabia Hajj requirements. Available at: http://www.cdc.gov/travel/hajj.htm (accessed May 28, 2002).
6. Communicable Disease Surveillance and Response (CSR). Meningococcal disease, serogroup W135—Update 2. 22 June 2001. Available at: http://www.who.int/disease-outbreak-news/n2001/june/22june2001.html (accessed May 28, 2002).
7. Hill DR. Pre-travel health, immunization status, and demographics of travel to the developing world for individuals visiting a travel medicine service. Am J Trop Med Hyg 1991;45:263–70.
8. Travelers' Health. Encephalitis, tickborne. Available at: http://www.cdc.gov/travel/diseases/tickenceph.htm (accessed May 28, 2002).
9. Steffen R, Rickenbach M, Wilhelm U, et al. Health problems after travel to developing countries. J Infect Dis 1987;156:84–91.
10. Behrens RH, Roberts JA. Is travel prophylaxis worth while? Economic appraisal of prophylactic measures against malaria, hepatitis A, and typhoid in travellers. BMJ 1994;309:918–22.
11. Walker E. Travel prophylaxis. BMJ 1995;310:401–2.
12. Van Damme P, Van Doorslaer E, Tormans G, Beutels P. Assumptions were confusing. BMJ 1995;310:402.
13. Behrens RH, Roberts JA. Travel prophylaxis. BMJ 1995;310:533.
14. Gubler DJ. Human behavior and cultural context in disease control. Trop Med Int Health 1997;2(11)A1–2.
15. MacDougall LA, Gyorkos TW, Leffondre K, et al. Increasing referral of at-risk travelers to travel health clinics. Evaluation of a health promotion intervention targeted to travel agents. J Travel Med 2001;8:232–42.
16. Robinson P, Ruff T, Kass R. Australian case-control study of adverse reactions to Japanese encephalitis vaccine. J Travel Med 1995;2:159–64.

17. Plesner AM, Ronne T. Allergic mucocutaneous reactions to Japanese encephalitis vaccine. Vaccine 1997;15:1239–43.

18. Duclos P, Hockin J, Pless R, Lawlor B. Reporting vaccine-associated adverse events. Can Fam Physician 1997;43:1551–6, 1559–60.

19. Zent O, Arras-Reiter C, Broeker M, Hennig R. Immediate allergic reactions after vaccinations—a post-marketing surveillance review. Eur J Pediatr 2002;161:21–5.

20. Halsey NA. Combination vaccines. Defining and addressing current safety concerns. Clin Infect Dis 2001;33 Suppl 4:S312–8.

21. Ward BJ. Vaccine adverse events in the new millennium. Is there reason for concern? Bull World Health Organ 2000;78:205–15.

22. Jacobson RM, Adegbenro A, Pankratz VS, Poland GA. Adverse events and vaccination—the lack of power and predictability of infrequent events in pre-licensure study. Vaccine 2001;19(17–19):2428–33.

23. MMWR recommendations and reports. Typhoid vaccination. Dec 9 1994/Vol 43/RR-14. Available at http://ftp.cdc.gov/pub/Publications/mmwr/rr/rr4314.pdf (accessed May 30, 2002).

24. Health Canada Statement on Oral Cholera Vaccination. Available at: http://www.hcsc.gc.ca/hpb/lcdc/publicat/ccdr/98vol24/24sup/acs5.html (accessed May 30, 2002).

Chapter 4

VACCINE ADMINISTRATION: TECHNICAL ASPECTS

Gail Rosselot and Lynne Bunnell

Travel health clinics and providers should adopt recognized standards of vaccination care to ensure quality immunization services. Vaccination recommendations presented in this chapter are based on expert guidelines published in the United States. Resources for these guidelines include the Advisory Committee on Immunization Practices (ACIP), the National Immunization Program (NIP), the American Academy of Pediatrics (AAP), the American Academy of Family Physicians (AAFP), and other governmental, professional, and private groups concerned with immunization services.

Most immunization principles are universal and will apply in many international settings. However, immunization recommendations and practices do differ between countries. The World Health Organization (WHO) has published training and reference materials that are the recognized standard of immunization care in many nations.[1,2] Canada and Australia are two countries that have formulated their own national standards.[3,4] In this chapter, we have noted some international differences in vaccination practices and standards. Additional resources for this information can be found in the chapter resource list and references.

With the development of new vaccines and new vaccine administration technology, immunization standards change over time. It is important for travel health clinicians to keep current with all applicable country and institutional guidelines for immunization care.

This chapter is organized into three sections as follows[5]:

1. pre-encounter quality elements, including
   - policies and procedures,
   - maintaining the cold chain,
   - vaccine administration supplies and equipment,
   - vaccine ordering and vaccine shortages,
   - patient and staff safety,
   - staff orientation and training, and
   - vaccine administration resources;
2. the patient encounter, including
   - risk communication,
   - patient screening for contraindications and precautions,
   - administration of nonparenteral vaccines,
   - administration of parenteral vaccines, and
   - special administration issues, and

3. postencounter considerations, including
   - documentation and record keeping,
   - postadministration complications, and
   - reporting adverse vaccine events.

TRAVEL VACCINE ADMINISTRATION: PRE-ENCOUNTER QUALITY ELEMENTS

Every travel health clinic should establish written policies and procedures, maintain the vaccine cold chain, and comply with all applicable regulations for patient and staff safety. In addition, the clinic should support ongoing staff training and provide ready access to current vaccination resource materials.

Policies and Procedures

According to Campbell, "Clear policies and procedures have a profound effect on an organization. Systems operate properly. People operate properly. We all get the information we need clearly and quickly."[6] Policies and procedures (P&P) are essential for a quality immunization program because they
- define a safe and consistent way for all caregivers to provide vaccination care,
- serve as "standing orders" for nursing staff to practice with physicians,
- standardize orientation of new employees, and
- demonstrate compliance with the current standards of care in the field.

Policies
Policies are the "what" and "why" of the travel clinic, the statements that establish the organization's position on particular issues.[6] Examples of vaccine administration policies include vaccine dosage schedules and after-hours care. Policies are based on standards of care and serve as a framework for clinic quality assurance programs and staff evaluations. They evolve over time and reflect the changing scope of travel health practice and new knowledge in the field.

Procedures
Procedures tell "how to" and define specific actions to accomplish a particular task or set of tasks.[6,7] Examples of vaccine administration procedures include vaccine storage and intramuscular injection technique. Procedures are based on current published information and reflect organizational policies.

Writing Policies and Procedures
When writing P&Ps for the travel health clinic, the goal is to have readable documents that define the way care will be delivered. The practical details of the P&P should translate easily into actions. Regardless of how they are formatted (and the format is chosen by the users), the following should be included for each clinic P&P: title, date issued or revised, purpose, step-by-step procedure, and references. In addition, a list of pertinent supplies can be included in the P&P. See Appendix 1 "The Vaccine Refrigerator"; Appendix 2, "After-Hours Care"; and Appendix 3, "Administration of Intradermal Injections."

Immunization Policies and Procedures for a Travel Health Clinic

It is recommended that clinics include a number of vaccine administration policies and procedures in their manuals. For a complete listing of these P&Ps see Appendix 4.

International Perspective

The WHO Global Programme for Vaccines Expanded Programme on Immunizations (EPI) has published in print and on the Internet two companion vaccination documents: *Safe Vaccine Handling, Cold Chain and Immunizations* and *Immunizations in Practice*.[1,2] Travel health clinics will find numerous practice protocols in these two resources and other EPI training materials. Canada and Australia have developed policies and procedures useful for travel health clinics in those countries.[3,4] In the United Kingdom, practice nurses published immunization guidelines in 2001 and subsequently developed a companion CD-ROM and Web site.[8,9] Clinicians in other nations will want to keep apprised of protocol resources within their own countries and around the world.

Maintaining the Cold Chain: Vaccine Transport, Storage, and Handling

Vaccines are a valuable and fragile biologic supply that can lose effectiveness if improperly refrigerated or exposed to light. Some damaged vaccines show evidence of alteration, such as clumping, but others will never show signs of reduced potency. Once a vaccine has lost its potency, it cannot be restored.[10,11]

According to the EPI, the cold chain is the system of shipping, storing, and handling vaccines within a safe temperature range. Strict cold-chain management is critical to the safety and efficacy of travel vaccinations. Key elements of this system are clinic personnel, vaccine storage equipment, and clinic procedures.[5] Failure to protect the vaccine supply can have serious and costly consequences for a travel health clinic.[5]

General Principles of Cold-Chain Management

The following are 10 elements critical for the successful maintenance of the cold chain in a travel health clinic: (1) staff responsibility, (2) vaccine handling requirements, (3) the immunization coordinator, (4) cold-chain management equipment and supplies, (5) monitoring vaccine temperature control, (6) cold-chain policies and procedures, (7) receiving vaccine supplies, (8) vaccine storage, (9) vaccine wastage, and (10) transporting vaccines off-site.

Staff Responsibility

It is the responsibility of all personnel handling vaccines to maintain the cold chain system. Staff training should address the specific storage requirements of every vaccine in the clinic. Each facility should develop and maintain a detailed and accessible site protocol for the correct storage and handling of all stocked vaccines.[5]

Vaccine Handling Requirements

Most travel vaccines should be refrigerated at 36 to 45°F (2 to 8°C) and never frozen. Varicella must be frozen at −5°F (−15 °C). Current recommendations for handling and storing specific vaccines can be found in the manufacturer's package insert or by contacting the manufacturer directly.[12] ACIP and AAP also publish vaccine storage and handling recommendations.[10,12,13] The Centers for Disease control and Prevention (CDC) publishes a useful clinic manual *Vaccine Management: Recommendations for Handling and Storage of Selected Biologicals.*[14]

The Immunization Coordinator

Travel health clinics should appoint one person as site immunization coordinator. This professional has overall responsibility for cold-chain system monitoring and quality control, which includes system design, implementation, and evaluation. Responsibilities include selection and maintenance of cold-chain equipment and supplies, cold-chain policy and procedure development, and staff training. To prevent lapses during an absence, every clinic should appoint a back-up coordinator.

Cold-Chain Management Equipment and Supplies

Travel clinics will need a dedicated vaccine refrigerator with a separate freezer to maintain consistent storage temperatures. Additional equipment and supplies include thermometers, ice packs, and cold boxes for transporting vaccines; charts for recording daily temperature readings; plug locks to prevent disconnection of electrical plugs; and appropriate refrigerator signage.

The Vaccine Refrigerator-Freezer Unit. Vaccines have special temperature requirements. To protect the valuable vaccine supply, the clinic should invest in a quality refrigerator-freezer. The unit must meet certain criteria to ensure proper temperature control with minimal temperature variance. Do not purchase a cyclic-type domestic model.[4] To avoid heating cycles and fluctuating temperatures, the vaccine refrigerator should either be a household frost-free design or a commercial vaccine model. Contact the unit manufacturer directly, as may be necessary, to confirm a specific model's suitability for vaccine storage. Always verify adequate temperature control before ordering vaccines.[15] The refrigerator unit size should accommodate the clinic's average vaccine supply on the middle and upper shelves. Allow air to circulate; do not crowd the vaccines. Nayda and colleagues recommend that the unit be filled to at least 50% of capacity to sustain even temperatures.[16] The freezer compartment should be separate with its own door and temperature control. (This is especially critical if the clinic stocks varicella vaccine.) Consult state immunization programs for their equipment recommendations.

Refrigerator-Freezer Thermometers. It is important to monitor both the current temperature and the minimum and maximum temperatures over a 24-hour period. At least two thermometers will be needed to monitor the refrigerator and freezer compartments separately. Thermometers should be placed in central parts of the refrigerator and freezer sections, not against the walls or coils. Several thermometer types are available, including the continuous graph recording type, the digital electronic minimum-maximum type, and biosafe liquid minimum-maximum models.[5]

Monitoring Vaccine Temperature Control

The immunization coordinator should monitor and document core refrigerator and freezer temperatures twice daily, at the beginning and end of the clinic day.[5] Preprinted temperature logs from the Immunization Action Coalition (IAC) are available for this purpose from <www.immunize.org/catg.d/p3039. pdf>.[17] Any power outages or mechanical problems should be documented as to day and time of the event. According to the CDC, temperature logs should remain on file at the clinic for a minimum of 3 years (Figure 4-1).[5]

Kendal and colleagues have cited vaccine freezing as a common problem in temperate climates.[18] To stabilize the refrigerator-freezer temperature, the immunization coordinator can take these actions:
- fill space in the central storage compartments with bottles of water or ice packs,
- install signage that discourages unnecessary opening of the doors or accidental unplugging of the unit,

Protect Your Vaccines: Check Temperatures Twice a Day!   Mo./Yr: _____   Days 1–15

Instructions: Place an "X" in the box that corresponds with the temperature. The hatched zones represent unacceptable temperature ranges. If the temperature recorded is in the hatched zone: 1. **Store the vaccine** under proper conditions as quickly as possible. 2. **Call the vaccine manufacturer(s)** to determine whether the potency of the vaccine(s) has been affected. 3. **Call the immunization program at your local health department** or further assistance: (_____) _____ and 4. **Document the action** taken on the reverse side of this log.

Day of Month	1		2		3		4		5		6		7		8		9		10		11		12		13		14		15	
Exact Time																														
°F Temp	am	pm	am	pm	am	pm	am	pm	am	pm	am	pm	am	pm	am	pm	am	pm	am	pm	am	pm	am	pm	am	pm	am	pm	am	pm
≥49°																														
48°																														
47°																														
46°																														
45°																														
44°																														
43°																														
42°																														
41°																														
40°																														
39°																														
38°																														
37°																														
36°																														
35°																														
34°																														
33°																														
32°																														
31°																														
30°																														
29°																														
28°																														
8°																														
7°																														
6°																														
5°																														
4°																														
3°																														
Room temp																														
Staff Initals																														

Refrigerator temperature   Freezer temp

Immunization Action Coalition • 1573 Selby Ave., Ste. 234 • St. Paul, MN 55104 • (651) 647-9009 • **www.immunize.org** • admin@immunize.org

www. immunize.org/catg.d/p3039.pdf • Item #3039 (7/02)

Figure 4-1. A sample vaccine temperature control log. Adapted from the Immunization Action Coalition courtesy of the Michigan Department of Community Health.

- install door locks to prevent unnecessary opening or improper storage of nonvaccine items (eg, food),
- install a plug lock or safety guard to prevent the accidental disconnection of the electrical plug,
- install a temperature alarm (with connection to an automated telephone system, if possible),[19]
- in the event of a power failure, activate the clinic policy for emergency malfunction or disaster, and
- anticipate the need to empty the unit periodically for cleaning and have temporary cold storage readily available.

Note: It is critical not only to monitor temperatures but also to take immediate and corrective action if temperatures exceed acceptable ranges. The immunization coordinator must have the authority, training, and resources to take all measures necessary to preserve the vaccine cold chain.

Cold-Chain Policies and Procedures

These policies and procedures should be included in the travel health clinic operating manual: receipt of vaccine supplies, refrigerator selection and maintenance, procedure in the event of a power failure, transporting of vaccines off-site, staff training for cold-chain compliance, maintaining the refrigerator temperature log, and vaccine wastage.

Receiving Vaccine Supplies

Careful adherence to a written procedure will ensure that vaccine shipments are accepted, inventoried, and properly stored to preserve temperature and potency. On receipt, the coordinator or designee should take the following actions:

- Examine shipping containers and packing slips carefully.
- Examine shipments for breaks in the cold chain, outdated vials, shipping damage, and incorrect orders.
- Check shipping dates to confirm that the product was not delayed excessively in transit. Vaccines cannot be allowed to sit in shipping areas or mailrooms for extended periods of time without proper temperature control. Confirm delivery schedules with suppliers to ensure vaccine viability and avoid breaks in the cold chain.
- Record each shipment on arrival in the vaccine inventory log. Include the vaccine name, the number of doses received, the date of receipt, the condition of the vaccines on arrival, lot numbers, expiration dates, and manufacturers' names (Figure 4-2).
- Before accepting any questionable shipment, contact the vaccine supplier or manufacturer directly. Clearly label the shipment "Do Not Use," store it as recommended, and await the decision regarding final disposition.[5] A list of pharmaceutical company contacts is in Appendix 5.

Vaccine Storage

All travel vaccines should be refrigerated immediately on receipt in strict compliance with the manufacturer's package insert instructions. Guidelines for proper storage are the following:

- Place vaccines of the same type in rows in the central storage compartments of the refrigerator or freezer unit.
- Place new stock behind old stock and use the "first in, first out" principle to reduce wastage.
- Vials should not be placed on refrigerator doors or bottom shelves where temperature fluctuations occur.
- Vaccines at risk of freezing should not be placed near the freezer plate.
- Prompt removal of outdated vaccines will reduce the risk of inadvertent use.

Vaccine Inventory Log

Date Received	Vaccine	# of Doses*	Manufacturer	Lot #	Expiry Date	Cold-Chain Maintained in Transit (check†)	Signature of Staff Member Receiving Shipment

Figure 4-2. Sample vaccine inventory log form. If multidose vial write "M" after the number. Otherwise, all doses are unit dose. †If cold-chain was not maintained, contact site immunization coordinator and/or manufacturer **immediately.**

- Open vials of multidose vaccines should be placed on a tray and properly labeled with the date and time of opening.
- Multidose vials not requiring reconstitution (eg, tetanus/diphtheria [Td] or inactivated polio vaccine [IPV]) contain a bacteriostatic agent and can be used until the expiration date unless contaminated.[4,5,15]

A checklist for vaccine storage and handling can be viewed in Appendix A, which is located on the accompanying CD-ROM only.

Vaccine Wastage

Every effort should be made to prevent vaccine destruction or loss of potency. According to the CDC, causes of vaccine wastage include overstocking, not rotating stock, power failures, not closing the refrigerator door, predrawing syringes, opening more than one multidose vial, and allowing vaccines to go past their expiration date.[5] Although multidose vials can be less costly, use of vaccines in manufacturer-prefilled syringes might reduce wastage.[5] It should be the responsibility of the immunization coordinator to make decisions regarding vaccine wastage after consultation with the manufacturer. Following a wastage episode, the coordinator should review, and revise as needed, cold-chain policies and procedures and institute equipment modifications and staff retraining as indicated.

Transporting Vaccines Off-Site

When a clinician finds it necessary to transport a vaccine out of the clinic, careful attention must be paid to cold chain compliance. Temperature monitoring and control must be strictly maintained. The clinician should contact the vaccine manufacturer for specific transport recommendations. Monitoring thermometers should be placed in all cold storage boxes.[5]

International Perspective

Travel clinics outside the United States might stock vaccines with different storage requirements (eg, bacille Calmette-Guérin [BCG], oral polio vaccine [OPV], or cholera). Some international settings present special challenges for vaccine storage and handling, and vaccine wastage can be a significant problem. The cold chain can be difficult to control when vaccines are shipped to regions with high temperatures, transportation problems, too few refrigerators, and unreliable power supplies. The EPI has set standards for vaccine transport and storage and has supported the development of alternative technology to maintain the vaccine cold chain (eg, kerosene and solar power refrigerators, ice-lined refrigerators, time and temperature vaccine monitor cards).[20] It has issued maintenance protocols and supported national and regional education programs to train all levels of personnel in cold chain management.[21] In 1998, WHO issued its updated manual *Safe Vaccine Handling, Cold Chain and Immunizations*, which outlines WHO policy and practice to preserve vaccine potency.[1]

In 1999, WHO and UNICEF issued a joint statement in support of manufacturers supplying vaccine vial monitors (VVMs) for all vaccines. VVMs are chemically treated labels that can change color, indicating vaccine damage due to excessive heat exposure. Their use can help detect failures in the cold chain and reduce vaccine wastage.[22]

In addition to WHO efforts, some countries have issued national cold-chain management guidelines. The *Canadian Immunization Guide* and the *Australian Immunisation Handbook* are two such valuable publications.[3,4]

Vaccine Administration Supplies and Equipment

To provide quality immunization services, clinic staff will need to assemble and maintain certain clinical and nonclinical supplies and equipment. See Appendix 6 for a checklist that identifies many of the usual items needed for vaccine administration.[23]

International Perspective

Travel clinics outside US borders need to include other equipment, supplies, documents, or resources as recommended by WHO, national standards, and institutional and agency requirements. For example, in place of the VAERS (Vaccine Adverse Event Reporting System) form, many international sites will stock an AEFI (adverse effects following immunization) form approved by their national health programs.[3,4]

Vaccine Ordering and Vaccine Shortages

As a general rule, it is recommended that clinics keep vaccine stock to a minimum to avoid storage problems and wastage. New clinics and settings with fewer pretravel visits might want to order week to week or month to month. Established clinics can track and project vaccine use patterns. Formulas for calculating vaccine quantities have been developed by groups such as the Australian National Immunization Committee and WHO.[1,16] Generally, it is recommended that travel clinic staff conduct a monthly inventory to check expiration dates, rotate stock, and order new product. The immunization coordinator must take many variables into account when determining minimum and maximum stock levels and placing vaccine orders. These variables include disease outbreaks, seasonal variations, changes in client base or travel patterns, introduction of new vaccines or combination vaccines, special vaccination activities (eg, an influenza campaign), vaccine shortages, and vaccine reserve requirements (W. Atkinson, personal communication, November 2002).

Anticipating Shortages

Vaccine shortages can occur at any time and for different reasons. A consolidation of vaccine manufacturers in the United States has resulted in sporadic shortages of several travel vaccines (eg, Td). In recent years, production problems have delayed influenza shipments and interrupted oral typhoid supplies. Clinic staff can access the National Immunization Program Web site at <www.cdc.gov/nip> for the latest information about vaccine shortages in the United States.[24] Clinicians faced with vaccine shortages should keep abreast of any temporary changes in national immunization guidelines (eg, postpone fifth dose of diphtheria and tetanus toxoids and acellular pertussis vaccine, [DTaP]), prioritize patients at highest risk, and work with manufacturers to secure necessary supplies.

Urgent Vaccine Need

Any travel health clinic can face an acute vaccine shortage due to restricted supply, delayed delivery, or unexpected patient volume. Clinicians should contact manufacturers and wholesalers directly for possible express delivery. State and local health departments might also ship doses overnight. Colleagues at other clinics might offer one or more "emergency" doses.

Patient and Staff Safety

Strict compliance with all applicable standards will help ensure the health and safety of vaccine recipients and travel health clinic staff. Areas for attention include staff immunizations, infection control practices, compliance with the Occupational Safety and Health Administration (OSHA), state and local health care worker regulations, and emergency equipment and training.

Staff Immunizations

AAP recommends that all clinicians administering vaccines have evidence of immunity to measles, mumps, rubella, varicella, hepatitis B virus (HBV), influenza, tetanus, and diphtheria to reduce the risk of contracting these diseases or transmitting them to patients.[10] ACIP has also issued health care worker immunization guidelines.[25] In addition, clinicians should know and comply fully with all state, professional, and site policies.

Infection Control

Clinics must comply with state and institutional infection control training and practice requirements. These include hand washing and gloving practices; proper disposal of syringes, needles, and other patient material; and staff education. (For more information on hand washing and gloving, see the "Administration of Parenteral and Nonparenteral Vaccines" section to follow.)

Occupational Health and Safety Regulations

All clinicians providing immunization services within the United States are required to follow federal regulations designed to protect health care workers from work-related injury and illness. The regulations include the OSHA blood-borne pathogen standard and the US Public Health Service (USPHS) guidelines for the management of occupational exposures to HBV, hepatitis C virus (HCV), and human immunodeficiency virus (HIV).

OSHA Blood-Borne Pathogen Standard. To prevent the transmission of blood-borne pathogens, health professionals are required to follow standard precautions when providing first aid and health care services. In recognition of the serious risk of needlestick injuries, these regulations were updated and expanded in 2001 to include the requirements of the Needlestick Safety and Prevention Act.[26] Travel clinics should comply fully with the following safety measures:

- formation of a site committee to select safer injection devices;
- proper use and disposal of all sharps—no needles should be removed from syringes after use, recapped, or cut, and after injection, all syringes and needles should be deposited immediately into puncture-proof receptacles;
- timely reporting of all needlestick injuries to the appropriate agency personnel, and
- maintenance of a needlestick/sharps injury log in settings with 10 or more employees.

Web site resources for safety needles and needle-free devices are available.[27]

USPHS Guidelines for the Management of Occupational Exposures to HBV, HCV, and HIV and Recommendations for Postexposture Prophylaxis. All US health care settings are required to establish and maintain a postexposure management plan to provide health care workers with prompt evaluation and treatment for HIV, HBV, and HCV exposures.[28] CDC recommendations include indications for the use of HIV postexposure prophylaxis (PEP) with antiretroviral therapy.[15,28]

In addition to these federal regulations, travel health clinicians need to comply with all applicable state, professional, and institutional standards (eg, filing incident reports, fulfilling worker's compensation requirements).

Emergency Equipment and Training

All staff must be trained in emergency policies and procedures (eg, fire, anaphylaxis), and the clinic must acquire and maintain all necessary equipment and supplies. Regular staff drills should be scheduled and documented.

International Perspective

The international community recognizes the importance of injection safety for patients and staff. For many years, the EPI has had a policy in support of single-use needles and syringes. In 1999, WHO, the United Nations International Children's Emergency Fund (UNICEF), and the United Nations Population Fund (UNFPA) issued a joint statement in support of quality injection equipment and "safety boxes," puncture-proof containers for collecting syringes and needles. This group also called for all countries to use only "auto-disable" needles by the end of 2003.[29] In 2001, WHO and UNICEF published its first issue of *Vaccine and Immunization Update* to help EPI immunization managers achieve these injection safety goals. It included a tool for assessing injection safety worldwide.[30] Other international collaboration organizations, including PATH (Program for Appropriate Technology in Health, available at: <www.path.org>) and SIGN (Safe Injection Global Network, available at: <www.who.int/injection_safety/sign/en>), are working to reduce the dangers of unsafe injection practices.[31,32] National health authorities also have established practice guidelines to prevent and track injection injuries in their own countries.[3,4]

Staff Orientation and Training

Staff orientation and ongoing education are critical to the provision of quality immunization care in the travel health setting. According to NIP, all personnel engaged in immunization services should be trained to provide "knowledgeable, safe, and comprehensive care consistent with practice policies and the specialty's quality standards."[5] The site's immunization coordinator should employ standardized, competency-based materials and testing to ensure that all clinicians are fully compliant with clinic training goals. Simple reference materials such as charts, tables, manuals, and diagrams should be readily available at the clinic.[5,23] Attendance and teaching content of all staff training programs should be documented and these records retained in accordance with clinic record-keeping policies.

International Perspective

International organizations are committed to training clinicians in safe vaccine administration using the latest technology. EPI, PATH, and GAVI (Global Alliance for Vaccines and Immunization, available at: <www.vaccinealliance.org>) have published training modules and resources on the Internet.[30,31,33] Travel clinics outside the United States may contact these resources and their own national health authorities for training standards and materials.

Vaccine Administration Resources

For the purpose of staff training and to address everyday issues in clinical practice, travel health clinics should maintain a library of immunization reference books and materials. Suggested print items for a United States–based clinic include the latest editions of

- ACIP *General Recommendations on Immunization*,[34]
- ACIP *Vaccine Recommendations*,[35]

- CDC *Epidemiology and Prevention of Vaccine-Preventable Diseases* ("The Pink Book"),[36]
- AAP Red Book—*Report of the Committee on Infectious Diseases,*[37]
- Immunization Action Coalition *Directory of Immunization Resources,*[38]
- CDC *Vaccine Information Statements,*[39] and
- Thompson's *Routine and Travel Immunizations.*[15]

Many governmental, professional, nonprofit, and private organizations provide valuable, updated information about vaccine administration practices. For a listing of resources that offer the most print and Web-based materials for the US travel health clinic, see Table 4-1. In addition, see Table 4-2 for a vaccine administration URL list.

State Health Departments

Each of the 50 US states has a state immunization program. Professionals may contact their state program manager about state-specific vaccine questions, local resources for professional training, and patient education materials. The CDC lists State Health Department contact information on its Web site at <www.cdc.gov/other.htm#states>.[40]

International Perspective

Vaccination resources for the travel health clinician are expanding rapidly worldwide. WHO and other international organizations provide extensive information and materials on their Web sites. For a listing of some important international resources see Table 4-1.

TRAVEL VACCINE ADMINISTRATION: THE PATIENT ENCOUNTER

Clinicians who immunize patients must comply with federal regulations for risk communication, the use of Vaccine Information Statements (VISs), and the documentation of care. In addition, they should adhere to professional standards for patient screening and vaccine administration technique.

Risk Communication

In the United States, CDC recommends that all providers inform patients about the specific indications, contraindications, and adverse effects of any vaccine they will receive.[13] To assist in this process, federal law requires the use of VISs for a select group of vaccines.[41] (See "Vaccine Information Statements," below.)

Vaccine risk communication should be viewed as a dynamic effort. It is an active interchange between provider and patient that occurs prior to vaccine administration. It is an educational process best termed "informed decision making." Patients want to know about the immunizations they will receive. Risk communication is designed to build trust, give guidance, and help ensure better vaccination outcomes.[5] To improve risk communication practices, the clinician should

- recognize that vaccination is a patient's choice;
- provide information about the diseases that the vaccine helps to prevent;
- know and use reputable resources for vaccine information;
- provide adequate opportunity to hear patient concerns and answer all questions;

Table 4-1. Vaccine Administration Resources

The Centers for Disease Control and Prevention (CDC) at <www.cdc.gov> is the federal agency within the U.S. Department of Health and Human Services responsible for protecting the public's health and safety. It provides a number of valuable resources for professionals who immunize.

CDC Resource	Description	URL or Phone Number
National Immunization Program	Maintains website with multiple resources for the immunization professional, including: • Vaccine information updates • Safety information • Online ordering for immunization materials • Updates on vaccine shortages • Vaccine Information Statements • Immunization training programs and research initiatives • Separate travel immunization page • Provides US federal leadership for national immunization activities • Information also available in Spanish	www.cdc.gov/nip www.cdc.gov/travel/
"Immunization Works!"	A monthly e-mail newsletter published by CDC offers a number of articles pertinent to persons in the immunization community	www.cdc.gov/nip/news/newsltrs/imwrks/imwrks.htm
Immunization Information Hotline	Toll-free telephone line for health professionals to speak with an immunization specialist about vaccines, vaccine-preventable diseases, and immunization requirements	1-800-232-2522
ACIP Statements CDC's Advisory Committee on Immunization Practices	Public health recommendations on individual FDA approved vaccines	www.cdc.gov/nip/publications/ACIP-list.htm
MMWR Morbidity and Mortality Weekly Report	Weekly publication providing information and recommendations for vaccine-preventable diseases and other public health topics; source for ACIP vaccine statements and updates	www.cdc.gov/nip/subscribe.html
Epidemiology and Prevention of Vaccine-Preventable Diseases ("Pink Book")	Reference book for general principles of vaccination	www.cdc.gov/nip/publications/pink/
CDC satellite broadcasts	Periodic live broadcasts for health care providers address new ACIP vaccine information and vaccine administration issues	www.phppo.cdc.gov/phtn/default.asp

ACIP = Advisory Committee on Immunization Practices; FDA = Food and Drug Administration.

Continued on next page

Table 4-1. Vaccine Administration Resources *(Continued)*

CDC Resource	Description	URL or Phone Number
National Center for Infectious Diseases Travelers' Health Web site and hotline	For travel health information including vaccine-preventable disease information and travel immunization recommendations	Toll-free telephone 1-877-FYI-TRIP Toll-free fax service 1-888-232-3299
Health Information for International Travel ("Yellow Book")	Professional reference for travel health care updated in print every two years; includes yellow fever requirements and discussion of vaccine-preventable diseases of travelers	Online version updated as information changes: www.cdc.gov/travel/yb/
Summary of Health Information for International Travel ("Blue Sheet")	Updated reference for countries requiring an International Certificate of Vaccination	www.cdc.gov/travel/bluesheet.htm

The **Immunization Action Coalition (IAC)** at <www.immunize.org> is a nonprofit organization that promotes vaccinations for children and adults.

IAC Resource	Description	URL or Phone Number
Needle Tips and Vaccinate Adults!	Two semiannual publications mailed without charge to many health professionals; *Needle Tips* includes the "Ask the Expert" column written by CDC immunization experts	www.immunize.org/nt/ www.immunize.org/va/
Directory of National Immunization Resources	Comprehensive catalog of immunization resources including organizations, Web sites, and hotlines	www.immunize.org/resources/index.htm
IAC Catalog	Includes over 100 patient education items available for order, such as brochures, posters, slide sets, and training videos	www.immunize.org/nslt.d/n17/catalg1.htm
IAC Express	Free e-mail subscription service that provides timely Internet updates on new and important immunization information	www.immunize.org/genr.d/ntn.htm

The **American Academy of Pediatrics (AAP)** is a professional society of pediatric medical specialists in the United States, Canada, and Latin America that provides two resources for information about vaccine administration and childhood vaccine issues.

AAP Resource	Description	URL or Phone Number
Red Book Report of the Committee on Infectious Diseases	Comprehensive and definitive resource for the control of all childhood infectious diseases, including vaccine-preventable illnesses	aapredbook.aappublications.org/
AAP Web site	Includes information about vaccines, vaccine policy, and AAP immunization policies, as well as a bookstore to order immunization references, patient brochures, and charting documents	www.aap.org

Continued on next page

Table 4-1. Vaccine Administration Resources *(Continued)*

The World Health Organization (WHO) Department of Vaccines and Biologics at <www.who.int/vaccines> is committed to the global prevention of vaccine-preventable disease and includes the following resources on its Web site.

Resource	Description	URL or Phone Number
International Travel and Health ("Green Book")	Reference book redesigned in 2002 to reflect better knowledge about the risks to which travelers are exposed and the precautions needed to protect their health. With abundant new material and a revised organizational structure, this book offers guidance on the full range of health risks likely to be encountered at specific destinations and associated with different types of travel (includes vaccine section).	www.who.int/ith
Running Immunization Services	Information on cold-chain management, vaccine supply, and training resources	www.who.int/vaccines/ _(scroll down on the page)
"Other Web sites" section	Links to WHO immunization partners	www.who.int/medicines/organization/qsm/activities/ drugregul/other_websites.doc

Other International Resources

Resource	Description	URL
Australia		
Immunise Australia Programme	The Australian national resource for immunization and vaccine information where professionals can download copies of the *Australian Immunisation Handbook* and link to the national system for reporting vaccine adverse events.	www.health.gov.au/pubhlth/immunise/
Canada		
The Committee to Advise on Tropical Medicine and Travel (CATMAT)	The Health Canada resource for travelers and travel medicine professionals that includes access to the *Canadian Immunization Guide*	www.hc-sc.gc.ca/pphb-dgspsp/tmp-pmv/catmat-ccmtmv/index.html
Travel Medicine Program (TMP) Web site	Information for Travel Medicine Professionals: • Travel health advisories • Vaccine information for travel clinics • Links to national vaccine-associated adverse events reporting system • National guidelines for vaccine storage and conservation • Resources for professional conferences • References	www.hc-sc.gc.ca/pphb-dgspsp/tmp-pmv/prof_e.html

Table 4-2. Vaccine Administration URL List

Organization or Country	Resource	Web Site
American Academy of Family Physicians (AAFP)	Home page	www.aafp.org
American Academy of Pediatrics (AAP)	Home page	www.aap.org
	Red Book—*Report of the Committee on Infectious Diseases*	www.aap.org/pubserv/ redbookonline.htm
Advisory Committee on Immunization Practices (ACIP, Centers for Disease Control and Prevention)	List of publications	www.cdc.gov/nip/publications/ ACIP-list.htm
Australia	*Australian Immunisation Handbook-9*	www.health.gov.au/pubhlth/ immunise/handbook_7.pdf
Canada: The Committee to Advise on Tropical Medicine and Travel (CATMAT)	*Canadian Immunization Guide-8*	www.hc-sc.gc.ca/pphb-dgspsp/ publicat/cig-gci/index.html
Centers for Disease Control and Prevention (CDC)	Yellow Book—*Health Information for International Travel*	www.cdc.gov/travel/yb
	Blue Sheet—*Summary of Health Information for International Travel*	www.cdc.gov/travel/bluesheet.htm
	The Pink Book—*Epidemiology and Prevention of Vaccine-Preventable Diseases*	www.cdc.gov/nip/publications/pink
	Vaccine Management: Recommendations for Handling and Storage of Selected Biologicals	www.cdc.gov/nip/publications/ vac_mgt_book.pdf
	List of state health departments	www.cdc.gov/other.htm#states
	MMWR Morbidity and Mortality Weekly Review	www.cdc.gov/mmwr/ mmwrsubscribe.html
	National Childhood Vaccine Injury Act (NCVIA)	www.cdc.gov/mmwr/preview/ mmwrhtml/00000005.htm
	National Immunization Program (NIP)	www.cdc.gov/nip
	Vaccine Information Statements (VIS)	www.cdc.gov/nip/publications/ VIS/default.htm
Expanded Program on Immunizations (EPI, World Health Organization Global Program for Vaccines)	Global immunization coverage	www.who.int/vaccines-documents/ DoxNews/pdf-updt/updat33e.pdf
Global Alliance for Vaccines and Immunization (GAVI)	Home page	www.vaccinealliance.org

Continued on next page

Table 4-2. Vaccine Administration URL List *(Continued)*

Organization or Country	Resource	Web Site
Immunization Action Coalition (IAC)	Checklist for vaccine storage and handling	www.immunize.org/catg.d/ p3035chk.pdf
	Directory of immunization resources	www.immunize.org/resources/ index.htm
	Home page	www.immunize.org
	Pharmaceutical company contacts	www.immunize.org/resources/ pharmac.htm
	Temperature log	www.immunize.org/catg.d/ p3039.pdf
Occupational Safety and Health Administration (OSHA, US Department of Labor)	"Needlestick Prevention"	www.osha.gov/SLTC/needlestick
Program for Appropriate Technology in Health (PATH)	Home page	www.path.org
Shoreland, Inc.	Shoreland's *Clinic Guide*	www.shoreland.com
United Nations International Children's Emergency Fund (UNICEF)	Online information	www.unicef.org
United Nations Population Fund (UNFPA)	Online information	www.unfpa.org
US Public Health Service (USPHS)	USPHS Guidelines for the Management of Occupational Exposures to HBV, HCV, and HIV and Recommendations for Postexposure Prophylaxis	www.cdc.gov/mmwr/preview/ mmwrhtml/rr5011a1.htm
Vaccine Adverse Event Reporting System (VAERS)	Vaccine adverse event reporting form (United States)	www.vaers.org
World Health Organization (WHO)	Adverse effect following immunization (AEFI)	www.who.int/vaccines/en/avi/ haefi.ppt
	Online information	www.who.int/en
	Green Book—*International Travel and Health Manual*	www.who.int/ith
	Safe vaccine handling, cold chain, and immunizations	www.who.int/injection_safety/sign/en
	Department of Vaccines and Biologics	www.who.int/vaccines
	International Certificate of Vaccination	www.cdc.gov/travel/icv.htm, www.who.int/ith/chapter06_19.html#7

- be prepared to address concerns about safety, side effects, additives, and contraindications;
- acknowledge uncertainty; and
- communicate in a caring, culturally sensitive manner with language that is understandable and free of jargon.[3,4,5,15,23]

The provision of VIS forms alone is not an acceptable alternative to this process, although these forms may be used as part of the interchange. Providers may offer supplemental risk communication materials but not as a substitute for in-person dialogue. When the patient is a child, the clinician must discuss vaccine safety issues with the parent or legal guardian.

In addition to these CDC guidelines, individual health care settings may have their own risk communication policies. Clinicians need to stay informed and comply with all applicable practices.

Vaccine Information Statements

VIS forms are information statements that describe vaccines and are created and updated by the CDC. Federal law mandates the documented use of VISs for all vaccines covered by the National Childhood Vaccine Injury Act (NCVIA). As of January 2003, all public and private health care providers are required to give patients (adults and guardians) copies to keep of relevant VIS forms for these vaccines: DTaP, Td, measles-mumps-rubella (MMR), polio, hepatitis B, *Haemophilus influenzae* type b (Hib), varicella, and pneumococcal conjugate.[42] In addition, CDC strongly encourages clinicians to use other available VIS forms for vaccines not covered by the NCVIA: hepatitis A, influenza, pneumococcal polysaccharide, anthrax, meningococcal disease, smallpox, and yellow fever.

Additional CDC requirements concerning VIS use are as follows:

- VIS forms must be given to the patient prior to any immunization.
- Clinicians must provide the most recent edition of a VIS as these are revised periodically.
- Applicable VIS forms must be provided for each dose of a vaccine given in a series. Whenever a combination vaccine such as Twinrix (GlaxoSmithKline, Philadelphia, PA) is administered, the VIS for each component vaccine must be given (ie, Hepatitis A VIS and Hepatitis B VIS).
- Patients' signatures are not required to acknowledge receipt of VIS forms. VIS forms are *not* informed consent documents.
- To document VIS use, the clinician should note in the permanent chart record the VIS title, VIS publication date, and date given to patient, parent, or legal representative.[41]

It is important for travel health providers to know that VIS forms are not available for all travel vaccines, such as Japanese encephalitis. VIS forms have been translated into many languages, for example Spanish, Turkish, Haitian, and Vietnamese. Foreign-language versions are available at the IAC Web site at <www.immunize.org/vis/index.htm>.[43]

Camera-ready copies of VIS forms are sent to all CDC Immunization Projects for printing and distribution to public health clinics. Immunization Project coordinators are also responsible for distributing camera-ready copies to all private providers in their state or metropolitan area. In addition, VIS forms are available on the Internet. For a complete listing of current Vaccine Information Statements, and to order or download the latest edition, the clinician can contact the NIP's Web site at <www.cdc.gov/nip>.[42]

Before providing risk communication services to patients, travel health professionals should consult legal counsel to determine if additional informational requirements must be met for their state or institution.

A VIS example can be viewed in Appendix B, which is located on the accompanying CD-ROM only.

Consent Forms

In some practice settings, clinicians may elect to administer informed consent forms to document the vaccination risk communication process. Typically, consent forms require that the patient or legal guardian signs a statement that acknowledges the risks and benefits of a vaccine and gives permission for the immunization. Consents are not standardized documents; rather, they are written according to institutional or clinic policy. State law determines informed consent requirements. They are not a federal mandate.[44] Immunization consents are legal documents that should be drafted, reviewed, approved prior to use, and updated as needed by the appropriate legal counsel or risk management department of a health care setting. Consents require the dated signature of the patient or, in the case of a child, the parent or legal guardian. Originals should be filed in the permanent patient record. As noted previously, VIS forms are *not* consent forms.

Waivers or Refusal Forms

Anyone can refuse an immunization. In the event that a patient refuses a vaccination that is recommended by a clinician or required by some authority (eg, for country or school entry), the clinician may choose to document this refusal with a waiver form. A waiver confirms in writing that a patient has chosen not to receive a particular vaccine at this time. The waiver document includes the patient's dated signature and becomes part of the patient's permanent record. In the case of a child, the signature of a parent or legal guardian is required. Like consent forms, waivers are legal documents that should be drafted, reviewed, approved prior to use, and updated as needed by the appropriate legal counsel or risk management department of a health care setting. The AAP has published a sample vaccination refusal form.[45]

International Perspective

Informed consent is an important component of the vaccination procedure outside the United States. As 2 of 13 "standard vaccination procedures," Australia mandates documented risk-benefit discussions and informed consent prior to every vaccination.[4] Canada has devoted a special section in its immunization manual to risk communication and identifies four critical components of the consenting process: provider communication of existing vaccine knowledge, respect for different opinions, balanced presentation of risks and benefits, and a focus on provider-patient partnership.[3] WHO addresses the consent issue for individuals and mass vaccination campaigns in its publication *Supplementary Information on Vaccine Safety.*[46]

Patient Screening for Contraindications and Precautions

Every clinician who immunizes should screen *every* patient for vaccine contraindications and precautions. Contraindications and precautions are conditions, usually temporary, that determine when vaccines should not be administered. Contraindications and precautions may be either general (apply to every vaccine) or specific (apply to one vaccine).[47] Screening is an important measure to prevent serious adverse events while also building patient rapport.

Contraindications

Contraindications are conditions within the vaccine recipient that *greatly* increase the risk of a serious adverse event. If a patient has a vaccine contraindication, the immunization should *not* be given. Most contraindications are temporary, and the immunization can be scheduled for a later visit. CDC recognizes only two permanent contraindications to vaccination: (1) severe allergy to a previous vaccine dose or to a vaccine component and (2) encephalopathy within 7 days of a pertussis vaccination. True egg allergy is an example of a permanent contraindication to influenza vaccine. Pregnancy is an example of a temporary contraindication to a live vaccine.[48]

Precautions

Precautions are conditions within the patient that *might* increase the risk of a serious adverse event or compromise the vaccine's ability to build immunity. Two examples of vaccination precautions include (1) moderate or severe illness with or without fever as a precaution for all vaccines and (2) recent receipt of immune globulin (Ig) as a precaution to live injected vaccines. Generally, when a precaution is present, the immunization is postponed. The clinician, however, may make exceptions if the risk of travel outweighs the risk of vaccine adverse reaction.[48]

To determine the presence of a vaccine contraindication or precaution, the clinician needs to question the patient or legal guardian carefully about certain concerns prior to immunization.[49] These include:

- current illness with or without fever;
- allergies to medication, food, vaccines, or vaccine components;
- a previous severe reaction to a vaccine;
- a history of seizures;
- immunodeficiency disease, such as acquired immunodeficiency syndrome (AIDS) or leukemia;
- use of drugs or treatments that depress the immune system, such as chemotherapy, corticosteroid use, or radiation;
- receipt of blood or blood products (eg, Ig) in the past year;
- vaccinations in previous 4 weeks; or,
- for women, pregnancy or planned pregnancy.

Information gained in this screening process will help the clinician determine if the patient can be vaccinated at this visit. The Immunization Action Coalition has published a standardized screening tool that can be used for this purpose (see Appendix C, which is located on the accompanying CD-ROM only).[49]

To learn of vaccine-specific contraindications and precautions, the travel health clinician should refer to the manufacturer's product insert or the *Physicians' Desk Reference* (PDR).[12]

Note: Although it is important to defer immunization for valid contraindications and precautions, too often vaccination is postponed for invalid reasons, causing so-called "missed opportunities to immunize."[13,15] Conditions commonly misconstrued as contraindications include acute mild illness, such as an upper respiratory tract infection (URI), and exposure to an infectious illness. A list of misconceptions concerning contraindications to vaccination can be found in Appendix 7.

International Perspective

WHO and the Canadian and Australian immunization programs all recommend the careful screening of patients for vaccine contraindications and precautions.[2–4] Specific deferral guidelines vary among countries, however, and travel health clinicians should be aware of all applicable guidelines for their practice setting.

Administration of Parenteral and Nonparenteral Vaccines

Travel vaccines are administered by different routes. These include intramuscular (IM), subcutaneous (SC), and intradermal (ID) injection, as well as oral and intranasal administration. The manufacturer's recommendation for one or more routes of administration is printed in the product insert.[12] Both AAP and ACIP also publish recommendations.[10,13] Routes of administration are selected to produce maximum vaccine response and to minimize local and systemic adverse effects.[50,51]

Proper administrative technique is necessary to ensure safe and effective vaccine delivery. The travel health clinician must follow all applicable standards of care for vaccine administration, including the manufacturer's product guidelines, national and state guidelines, professional standards, and institutional and site policies. As a routine practice, the clinician should follow the vaccine administration "5R rule" and check for the right vaccine, right dose (for age), right schedule, right route of administration, and right technique plus a valid vial expiration date.[51]

Other general guidelines include (1) adherence to approved schedules, (2) preparation of the patient, and (3) hand washing and infection control.

Adherence to Approved Schedules

Travel vaccines should be administered in accordance with the manufacturers' recommendations and the latest CDC routine and accelerated schedules. Failure to follow these guidelines might affect vaccine efficacy or safety.

Preparation of the Patient

The clinician should encourage the patient, parent, or guardian to take an active role during vaccine administration. All patients should be screened for vaccine precautions and contraindications. The clinician should provide any relevant VIS forms and encourage a risk communication dialogue that allows for informed decision making (see "Risk Communication," above). The vaccine administration procedure should be explained and the patient positioned for site access, comfort, and safety.[52] Most commonly, travel vaccines are administered with the patient sitting.

Hand Washing and Infection Control

The CDC recommends that all clinicians follow standard precautions during the immunization procedure.[5] Hand washing with soap and water or cleaning with an alcohol-based antiseptic before and after injecting vaccines is a critical first step to prevent the spread of disease. The AAP and ACIP do not mandate the use of gloves by the provider unless there is a risk of exposure to blood or bodily fluids or the provider has an open hand lesion.[10,13] Some agencies and institutions, however, have site policies that do require gloving, and the clinician needs to know and comply with all applicable guidelines.

Sterile disposable needles and syringes should be used to prevent transmission of blood-borne pathogens or contamination at the injection site. After single use, needles and syringes should be discarded as one unit into labeled, puncture-proof containers. To prevent inadvertent needlestick injuries, needles should not be recapped after use. In accordance with the latest federal guidelines, safety needles should be used to reduce the risk of injury.[26]

Administration of Nonparenteral Vaccine: Oral and Intranasal Routes

Although few vaccines are currently administered via the oral or intranasal route, more are planned for the future. As the Federal Drug Administration (FDA) approves new vaccines, the travel health clinician should review the package insert for proper dispensing guidelines.

The Oral Route

As a general rule, it is important for the patient to swallow and retain any vaccine given orally. If the patient spits out the vaccine or vomits within 10 minutes, a replacement dose should be administered.[47] In addition, some manufacturers stipulate additional guidelines for oral administration. For example, oral typhoid tablets are to be taken 1 hour preceding a meal.[12]

The Nasal Route

The proper use of a nasal medication (spray, drops, or pump) usually requires some skill and practice. When intranasal vaccines (eg, FluMist; Med Immune Vaccines Inc., Wyeth Vaccines) are used in the travel health clinic, it is important for clinicians to master the recommended administration procedure, which includes patient education, patient positioning, and administrative technique.[50,51]

Administration of Parenteral Vaccines

Injecting vaccines correctly is a skill that requires training and practice. As a critical component of staff orientation, all clinicians who immunize should be competency-tested for compliance with parenteral administration procedures.

Positioning a Child for Vaccination

It is important that a child receiving vaccines does not move during the injection. The child should be restrained as may be necessary for safety but not frightened. If the parent or guardian is willing to assist, the clinician should explain the procedure fully. Parents may hold children on their laps or place the child supine on a table. Clothing should be removed to ensure that injection access sites are fully exposed. Travel health clinicians seeking more guidance on child positioning should consult the section on "Comforting Restraint" in *Epidemiology and Prevention of Vaccine-Preventable Diseases*.[48]

Pain Control

Several techniques are available to reduce vaccine injection discomfort. Local anesthetics (eg, EMLA Cream, AstraZeneca International, Waltham, MA) or topical refrigerant sprays can be used in young children in accordance with manufacturers' guidelines to reduce site pain.[53] In some patients, acetaminophen, ibuprofen or nonaspirin analgesics can be used for pain and fever. Distraction techniques (eg, "blowing away the pain," listening to music) can also be used with children and adults.[47,50]

Vaccine Inspection and Reconstitution

Vaccine vials should remain in the refrigerator until immediately before use. Multidose vials should be returned to the refrigerator promptly after a dose is removed. All vaccine containers should be examined for signs of improper storage, tampering, or contamination. Vaccines should not be used past their expiration dates. Outdated vaccines and those with particulate matter, unusual coloring, or insufficient fluid should be labeled and set aside for review and discarding, if indicated.[5]

Certain travel vaccines require reconstitution with their own sterile diluents prior to use. The clinician needs to review the manufacturer's package insert for this procedure and follow all instructions carefully. Some reconstituted vaccines should be shaken well prior to filling the syringe; others should not. When reconstituted, a vaccine should match the color described by the manufacturer. Reconstitution of multiple single-dose vials in advance is not recommended.

After reconstitution, most vaccines must be used within a certain time period to maintain efficacy (eg, varicella within 30 minutes, yellow fever within 1 hour, MMR within 8 hours).[13,15] The clinician should discard any reconstituted vaccine that exceeds the time interval listed in the manufacturer's insert.

Filling the Syringe

The use of prefilled syringes can reduce the risk of contamination during filling and the mislabeling of immunizations.[5] Prefilled syringes should be kept refrigerated until just before use. *Note:* some manufacturers instruct the clinician to shake these syringes prior to administration.

When filling a syringe for vaccination, the general procedure is as follows:

1. Maintain sterile technique.
2. Verify the vaccine ordered, check the expiration date, and confirm the dosage and route of administration: IM, SC, or ID.
3. Uncap the vaccine vial.
4. Clean the vial top with an alcohol wipe.
5. Uncap the needle.
6. Pull back the syringe plunger to draw in an amount of air equal to the amount of vaccine fluid that will be withdrawn (eg, 1 mL or 0.5 mL).
7. Inject the air into the vial, invert the vial, and remove the desired amount of vaccine, keeping the bevel within the fluid to prevent air from being drawn back into the syringe.
8. Remove the needle and expel any air by tapping the syringe.
9. Recap the needle.
10. Label the syringe, as necessary, to prevent mix-ups.[50,52,54]

According to ACIP, it is not necessary to change needles before injection.[13] Different vaccines should never be mixed in the same syringe unless permitted by the manufacturer's instructions.

The practice of drawing up vaccines in batches, well in advance of their use, is not recommended and can lead to administration errors.

Some manufacturers provide special recommendations for removing vaccine fluid and filling syringes. Travel health clinicians should read product inserts carefully and follow all applicable guidelines (eg, RabAvert; Chiron, Emeryville, CA).

Evaluation and Preparation of the Skin

Prior to giving an injection, the clinician should observe the skin at the selected anatomic site for rashes or lesions that would make it unsuitable for immunization. The skin should be carefully wiped with either 70% isopropyl alcohol or a similar disinfecting agent to reduce surface pathogens and then allowed to dry.[50,52,55]

Selection of Injection Equipment

The choice of syringe and needle size depend on the route of administration, anatomic site, and manufacturer's recommendations. For each immunization, the clinician should use a separate sterile disposable syringe and needle. Clinicians will want to stock a selection of syringes and needles to ensure availability and choice at the time of vaccine administration.

Selection of the Anatomic Injection Site

Parenteral vaccines should be injected into sites that minimize the risk of tissue, nerve, and vascular injury. The choice of anatomic site will depends on manufacturers' recommendations, the route of administration, the age of the recipient, his or her muscle size, and the amount of vaccine fluid.[9, 50,52,54]

Certain vaccine manufacturers will allow some flexibility in the selection of injectable sites. The clinician should review the package insert or contact the manufacturer directly to learn about acceptable alternatives.

For multiple immunizations, it is recommended to use more than one anatomic site. If multiple injections are administered in the same limb, the CDC and others recommend that a minimum distance of 1 inch (2.5 cm) be maintained between injections to prevent overlapping local reactions.[5,47]

Routes of Administration

There are three routes of parenteral administration for travel immunizations: IM, SC, and ID. Per ACIP, failure to comply with the manufacturer's guidelines can result in reduced vaccine potency or increased adverse reactions.[13] See Figure 4-3 for a diagram depicting injection techniques and Figures 4-4 and 4-5 for anatomic site selection.

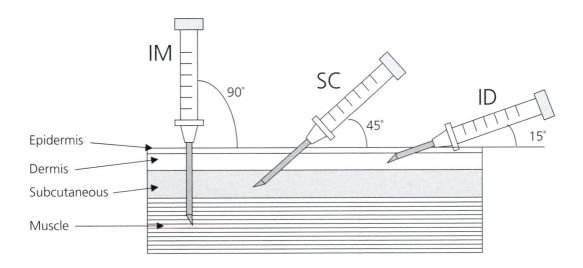

Figure 4-3. Diagram of needle placement for intramuscular (IM), subcutaneous (SC), and intradermal (ID) injections. Adapted from Timby BK[50]; Dietrich T et al[51]; Hahn K [52]; Newtown M et al[54]; Fulginiti VA[55]; Poland GA et al[56]; Zuckerman J.[57,89]

Intramuscular Injection. In general, most inactivated travel vaccines contain irritating adjuvants and should be injected deep into the muscle mass to reduce localized reactions and tissue damage (eg, inflammation or irritation).[13]

The choice of anatomic injection site and needle size for an IM immunization should be made based on the manufacturer's recommendations and individual patient factors such as age, vaccine fluid volume, and muscle size.[9,13,50,52] Poland and colleagues have suggested gender as another factor, as women might require the use of longer needles to accommodate a thicker adipose layer.[56] A different needle may be used if recommended or provided by the manufacturer or if the patient is either very thin or obese. It is important to use the correct size of needle to ensure delivery of the vaccine fluid into the muscle, not the overlying subcutaneous layer or the nerves, blood vessels, or bone below. Zuckerman supports the use of longer, larger-gauge needles to reduce local reactions in selected patients.[57]

IM Anatomic Sites and Needle Selection. See Figure 4-4 for the recommended sites by age and also the recommended needle length and gauge. In infants and children, the area selected should be adequately developed to receive the volume of injectable vaccine.

The ventrogluteal site is an alternative or additional site for IM injections for all ages, such as large volumes (1–5 mL) of immune globulin.[50,51] This triangular site spares nerves and vessels and is located in the gluteus medius muscle between the great trochanter of the femur and the iliac crest.

Not recommended: Generally, the gluteus (buttock) should not be selected because of the risk of sciatic nerve injury. Hepatitis B and rabies should *never* be administered in the buttock as studies have demonstrated reduced vaccine effectiveness with this site.[58,59]

Injection Technique. When injecting via the IM route, the syringe and needle are positioned at a 90° angle to the skin and projected into the muscle tissue with a dart-like, thrusting motion. If there is much cutaneous fat, the provider might want to stretch out the skin with the thumb and index finger of the nondominant hand to ensure better access to the muscle below.[50,52,54] The needle should enter the skin and go deep into the muscle and then the plunger should be pushed down fully. The needle should be removed quickly and the syringe disposed of properly.[9]

Note: In spring 2002, ACIP determined that it was *no longer necessary* to pull back on the plunger (aspirate) to check for possible placement in a vein or artery.[13]

Subcutaneous Injection. Yellow fever, MMR, varicella, and meningococcal vaccines are administered via the SC route. IPV and pneumococcal polysaccharide can be administered SC or IM.

SC Anatomic Site and Needle Selection. Variation to the selections shown in Figure 4-5 can occur if the manufacturer recommends or provides different equipment. It is important to use the correct size of needle to ensure delivery of the vaccine fluid into the subcutaneous layer, not the underlying muscle.

SC Injection Technique. Using the nondominant hand, the clinician should squeeze, or "bunch up," a 1-inch (2.5 cm) layer of skin over the preferred site. With the dominant hand, the needle should be placed at a 45° angle to the skin with the bevel pointing up.[51] The provider should inject rapidly, avoiding injection into the underlying muscle, release the skin fold, and depress the plunger fully. The needle then should be removed and all equipment disposed of in accordance with needlestick safety policies.[50,52,54]

Intradermal Injection. This route is used to produce a local effect (eg, tuberculin testing and allergy testing). In the international setting, this small-volume administration technique also is used for ID rabies and BCG.

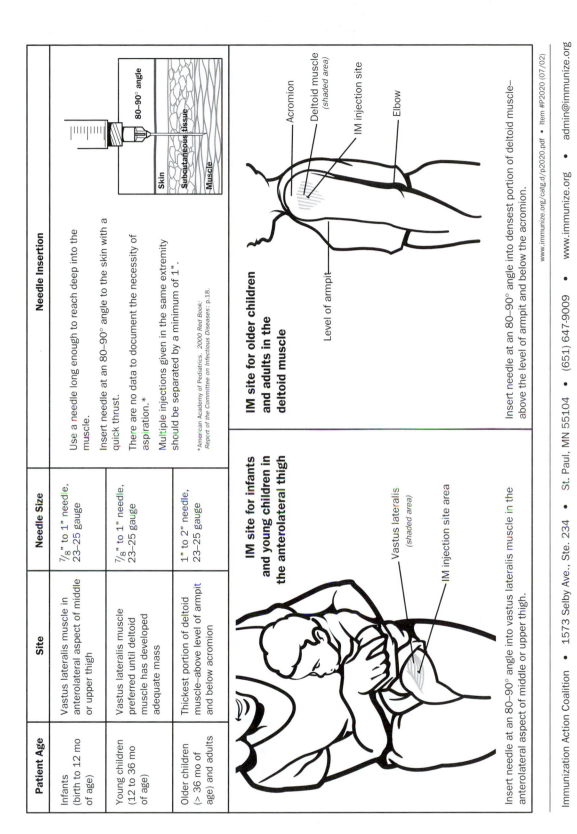

Patient Age	Site	Needle Size	Needle Insertion
Infants (birth to 12 mo of age)	Vastus lateralis muscle in anterolateral aspect of middle or upper thigh	⁷⁄₈" to 1" needle, 23–25 gauge	Use a needle long enough to reach deep into the muscle. Insert needle at an 80–90° angle to the skin with a quick thrust. There are no data to document the necessity of aspiration.* Multiple injections given in the same extremity should be separated by a minimum of 1".
Young children (12 to 36 mo of age)	Vastus lateralis muscle preferred until deltoid muscle has developed adequate mass	⁷⁄₈" to 1" needle, 23–25 gauge	
Older children (> 36 mo of age) and adults	Thickest portion of deltoid muscle–above level of armpit and below acromion	1" to 2" needle, 23–25 gauge	

*American Academy of Pediatrics. *2000 Red Book: Report of the Committee on Infectious Diseases*: p.18.

IM site for infants and young children in the anterolateral thigh

Vastus lateralis *(shaded area)*

IM injection site area

Insert needle at an 80–90° angle into vastus lateralis muscle in the anterolateral aspect of middle or upper thigh.

IM site for older children and adults in the deltoid muscle

Acromion

Deltoid muscle *(shaded area)*

IM injection site

Elbow

Level of armpit

Insert needle at an 80–90° angle into densest portion of deltoid muscle—above the level of armpit and below the acromion.

80–90° angle

Skin

Subcutaneous tissue

Muscle

www.immunize.org/catg.d/p2020.pdf • Item #P2020 (07/02)

Immunization Action Coalition • 1573 Selby Ave., Ste. 234 • St. Paul, MN 55104 • (651) 647-9009 • www.immunize.org • admin@immunize.org

Figure 4-4. How to administer intramuscular (IM) injections. Administer these vaccines via IM route: diptheria and tetanus toxoids and acellular pertussis (DTaP), DT, adult tetanus/diptheria(Td), *Haemophilus influenzae* group B (Hib), hepatitis A, hepatitis B, influenza, and PCV7. Administer polio vaccine (PV) and pneumococcal polysaccharide vaccine (PPV23) either IM or SC. Adapted by the Immunization Action Coalition. Courtesy of the Minnesota Department of Health.

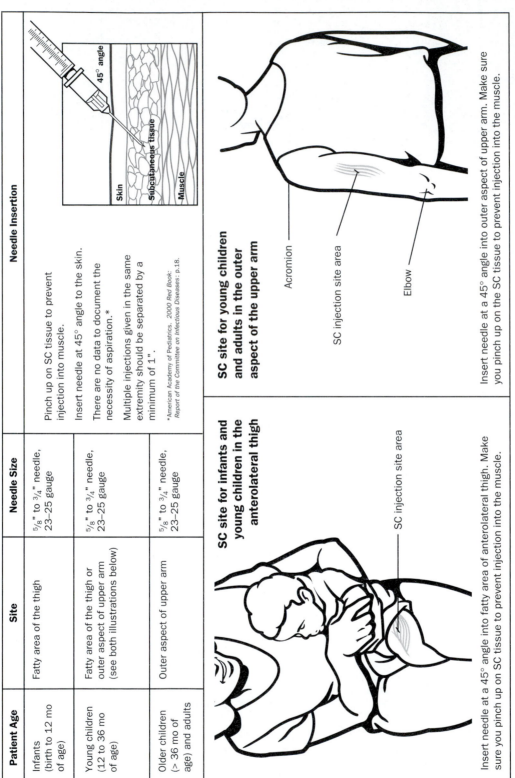

Patient Age	Site	Needle Size	Needle Insertion
Infants (birth to 12 mo of age)	Fatty area of the thigh	5/8" to 3/4" needle, 23–25 gauge	Pinch up on SC tissue to prevent injection into muscle.
Young children (12 to 36 mo of age)	Fatty area of the thigh or outer aspect of upper arm (see both illustrations below)	5/8" to 3/4" needle, 23–25 gauge	Insert needle at 45° angle to the skin. There are no data to document the necessity of aspiration.* Multiple injections given in the same extremity should be separated by a minimum of 1".
Older children (> 36 mo of age) and adults	Outer aspect of upper arm	5/8" to 3/4" needle, 23–25 gauge	

*American Academy of Pediatrics. 2000 Red Book: Report of the Committee on Infectious Diseases: p.18.

SC site for infants and young children in the anterolateral thigh

SC injection site area

Insert needle at a 45° angle into fatty area of anterolateral thigh. Make sure you pinch up on SC tissue to prevent injection into the muscle.

SC site for young children and adults in the outer aspect of the upper arm

Acromion

SC injection site area

Elbow

Insert needle at a 45° angle into outer aspect of upper arm. Make sure you pinch up on the SC tissue to prevent injection into the muscle.

45° angle

Skin

Subcutaneous tissue

Muscle

www.immunize.org/catg.d/p2020.pdf • Item #P2020 (07/02)

Immunization Action Coalition • 1573 Selby Ave., Ste. 234 • St. Paul, MN 55104 • (651) 647-9009 • www.immunize.org • admin@immunize.org

Figure 4-5. How to administer subcutaneous (SC) injections. Administer these vaccines SC route: measles, mumps, and rubella (MMR), varicella, and meningococcal. Administer inactivated polio virus (IPV) and pneumococcal polysaccharide vaccine (PPV23) either SC or IM. Adapted by the Immunization Action Coalition. Courtesy of the Minnesota Department of Health.

ID Anatomic Site and Needle Selection. In general, the preferred site for all ages is the volar (ventral) surface of the forearm; however, the clinician should consult the manufacturer's package insert for rabies ID and BCG site selection. For all ages, a 25- to 27-gauge, ⅜- to ¾-inch (1–2 cm) needle and 1 mL syringe should be used.[13,23,50–52,54]

ID Injection Technique. To administer an ID injection, the clinician should follow this protocol (see Figure 4-3).

1. Stretch the forearm skin taut with the nondominant thumb.
2. Place the syringe and needle parallel to the long axis of the skin surface with the bevel pointing up.
3. Enter the skin only until the entire bevel penetrates the dermis layer.
4. Slowly inject all the immunization fluid to produce a bleb or wheal just below the skin surface. The bleb will have a "mosquito bite" appearance. Avoid injecting subcutaneously.
5. Remove the needle and safely dispose of the equipment. Do not rub or cover the injection site.[13,23,50–52,54]

International Perspective

Recommendations for injection equipment and administration technique can vary among nations. For example, in the United Kingdom, the Royal College of Nursing refutes the need for formal skin cleansing prior to administration.[60] Travel health clinicians practicing outside the United States should be aware of, and adhere to, local standards of care.

Special Administration Issues

During patient screening or vaccine administration, issues might arise that will alter the standard immunization protocol. Travel health clinics should develop site policies and train staff to address these special circumstances.

Allergies to Vaccine Components

Prior to immunization, all patients should be questioned carefully about true allergies to vaccines; vaccine additives, such as bacteriostatic agents; and products used in vaccine manufacturer, such as gelatin. Vaccine components include many substances, such as egg protein, yeast, thimerosal, neomycin, aluminum hydroxide, beef protein, and formaldehyde. Clinicians need to keep a reference list of all current vaccine components for use during patient screening.[61]

Influenza and yellow fever vaccines both have egg protein. Prior to immunizing with these vaccines, the provider should ask patients if they can eat eggs or egg products without adverse effects.[62] If warranted, patients with a hypersensitivity to vaccine components can be referred to an allergist for further evaluation and possible desensitization.[47]

Patient with a Bleeding Disorder or Using Anticoagulant Therapy

Hematoma formation at an IM injection site is a risk for persons with bleeding disorders and persons receiving anticoagulation therapy. To avoid using the IM route, the clinician might be able to select another brand of vaccine that is not administered IM.[15] Alternatively, the clinician can contact the manufacturer directly to learn if a vaccine can be given safely by the subcutaneous or intradermal route. For a vaccine that must be administered IM, AAP and ACIP provide these guidelines:

- The clinician can provide the IM vaccination if a physician familiar with the patient's bleeding risk agrees to the safety of this route of administration.
- If the patient receives an infusion of blood products or similar therapy, the IM injection should be given shortly after the treatment.
- The use of a small-gauge needle (23 or smaller) and the application of firm, steady pressure (without rubbing) at the site for at least 2 to 10 minutes can help reduce the risk of bruising with IM injections.[10,13,63]

Inadequate Vaccination Documentation

Travel health clinicians are often faced with the problem of inadequate immunization records. Per ACIP, if a patient cannot provide written and dated proof of an immunization, the clinician should discount that vaccination.[13] To avoid unnecessary revaccination, clinicians should assist patients in collecting and maintaining their immunization records. Immunization information from pediatric visits, school entry, immigration, and military service can be useful in piecing together a patient's vaccination history. If vaccination records are not available, then the clinician should start the patient on the age-appropriate primary immunization schedule. Serologic testing for immunity may be an alternative for some vaccinations (eg, MMR, hepatitis B, or varicella).

Immunizing Patients with Moderate or Severe Illness

As previously discussed in this chapter, travelers with mild illnesses, with or without fever, can be vaccinated. However, CDC does recommend postponing vaccination when a patient has a moderate or severe illness to avoid "superimposing adverse effects from the vaccine on underlying illness or mistakenly attributing a manifestation of underlying illness to the vaccine."[62]

Inadequate Time Interval for Multiple Doses of the Same Vaccine

Some travel vaccines require more than one dose for the primary series (eg, Japanese encephalitis, hepatitis B). Clinicians are encouraged to follow the minimum age and dosing intervals of the routine or accelerated schedules published by the vaccine manufacturer or as recommended by AAP or ACIP.[10,13] Administering a dose too early can result in inadequate vaccine response. However, when circumstances require, ACIP does recommend that vaccine doses given ≤ 4 days from the minimum age or interval ("the 4-day grace period") be counted as valid. Rabies vaccine is the one exception; the rabies prevaccination protocol should be followed as published.[13]

Interruption of the Dosing Schedule

According to CDC's *Health Information for International Travel 2003–2004*, "it is unnecessary to restart an interrupted series of a vaccine or toxoid or to add extra doses."[62] For example, if the recommended intervals between multiple doses in the primary series have been exceeded for hepatitis A or B vaccines, the clinician does not need to restart the series nor administer additional doses. On the other hand, the manufacturer of Ty21a, an oral typhoid vaccine, does recommend a restart of the series for certain lapses in the dosing schedule.[12] For guidance concerning lapses in the rabies preexposure series or Japanese encephalitis series, the clinician might want to contact the vaccine manufacturer.

Interchangeability of Vaccines

Vaccine manufacturers around the world produce many different travel vaccines; the interchangeability of only some has been documented. For example, according to ACIP, all hepatitis A and B products are interchangeable.[13] When possible, clinicians are encouraged to use the same vaccine product for sequential doses. If the same product is not available, then the clinician is encouraged to complete the series with another vaccine brand used as licensed and recommended.[47]

Simultaneous Administration of Multiple Injections

It is important to offer simultaneous administration of different vaccines when preparing a traveler on short notice or when the patient might not or cannot return for subsequent visits. Unless permitted by the manufacturer, two or more vaccines should always be administered in separate syringes at separate anatomic sites. If two or more vaccines must be administered into one limb in young children, ACIP recommends the thigh as the preferred site.[13] For older children and adults, the deltoid area can be used for multiple injections. ACIP recommends that injections into the same limb be separated by at least one inch (2.5 cm) to prevent overlapping local reactions and the location of each injection documented.[13] According to ACIP and others, there is no evidence that simultaneous administration of multiple vaccines results in a greater probability of adverse effects or more severe local or systemic reactions.[13,64] However, if the clinician is administering more than one vaccine associated with local or systemic reactions, CDC recommends giving these immunizations at separate visits.[62]

Tuberculosis Testing

If a patient will be receiving a live virus vaccine (eg, yellow fever, MMR, varicella), then tuberculin (TB) testing (PPD) can be given on the same day or 4 to 6 weeks later.[13,15]

Recipient of Other Vaccines in Previous Four Weeks

According to ACIP, if two live virus vaccines (eg, MMR, varicella, or yellow fever) are not given on the same day, the doses must be separated by at least 28 days.[13] However, Ty21a oral typhoid vaccine should not be postponed because of live virus vaccination, and yellow fever vaccine and monovalent measles may be administered at any time before or after each other.[13,65] Inactivated vaccines do not alter the response of live vaccines or other inactivated vaccines and can be given at any spacing interval if they are not administered simultaneously.

Recipient of Immune Globulin Products

The receipt of Ig products can interfere with the immune response of MMR and varicella vaccines. For questions concerning the proper scheduling of MMR (or its components) and varicella vaccines in a patient who has received Ig in the past year or who will do so in the next 2 weeks, the clinician should consult the manufacturer's package insert, the *PDR*, or the ACIP recommendations for additional guidance.[12,13,62]

Latex Allergy

Per ACIP, if a patient reports an anaphylactic allergy to latex, vaccines supplied in vials or syringes with natural rubber should not be administered unless the vaccination benefit outweighs the latex risk. If the patient reports other types of allergic reactions to latex, then vaccine vials or syringes with natural or dry rubber can be administered.[13]

Needle Fear and Phobia

Clinicians should question reluctant or anxious patients about a fear of needles and injections. Such fears can interfere with a patient's acceptance of appropriate vaccines and undermine provider attempts at vaccine risk communication. Injection fear often results from anxiety or bad experiences with injections in the past, especially during childhood. The clinician should allow patients to verbalize their fears and reassure them that talking about the fear helps to dispel the feelings. He or she should explain that distractions such as talking or singing during the immunization can be effective. Those people who fear a loss of control or fainting can receive the injections lying down. After the immunization, the person should stay supine for several minutes before gradually getting up in stages to minimize any postural hypotensive effects. For people with extreme phobia, who do not respond to these methods, psychiatric consultation might be needed.

Limited Anatomic Sites

Most travel vaccines are administered into the upper arm in older children and adults. When the manufacturer's preferred anatomic site is not available for injection (because of amputation, postmastectomy restrictions, etc), the clinician should contact the vaccine manufacturer for clinical direction regarding the best alternative site.

Use of Corticosteriods

See Chapter 17, "Travel Immunizations for Special Risk Groups: Pregnant and Immune Compromised."

Altered Immunity

See Chapter 17, "Travel Immunizations for Special Risk Groups: Pregnant and Immune Compromised."

Tetanus-Diphtheria Injections

It is advisable for the clinician to follow approved Td dosing protocols. When administered too frequently, Td vaccination can produce increased rates of local reactions.[66] In the United States, it is common practice among travel health providers to administer Td into the nondominant arm in an effort to reduce postinjection discomfort.

Altering Vaccine Volume

It is recommended that clinicians not reduce or increase the recommended fluid volume when injecting a vaccine. "Splitting doses" and administering smaller volumes of vaccine can reduce protective efficacy. Administering larger-than-recommended volumes might increase adverse effects.[48,50]

Adherence to Minimum Age Requirements

Vaccines should not be given to recipients younger than the approved minimum age as this can produce a suboptimal immune response and might increase the risk of adverse effects. For example, yellow fever vaccine should never be given to infants under 6 months of age because of an increased risk of encephalitis.[62]

TRAVEL VACCINE ADMINISTRATION: POSTENCOUNTER CONSIDERATIONS

After the vaccine has been administered, the travel health clinician is obligated to document the visit carefully and respond, as needed, to any postimmunization complications.

Documentation and Record Keeping

Careful and complete documentation is an essential requirement of the vaccine administration process. The travel health clinician needs to complete and properly store a number of administrative and clinical documents to ensure adequate immunization record keeping. Previously, the authors addressed the documentation required for cold-chain management, including the vaccine inventory log, temperature log, and staff training records. In the postencounter period, the clinician will need to complete these documents:

- the patient's medical record or chart;
- WHO International Certificate of Vaccination or exemption letter;
- patient vaccination record, if applicable;
- state immunization record or registry, if applicable; and
- the immunization logbook.

Patient Medical Record or Chart

Maintaining accurate and organized patient charts is a critical element of a quality travel health program. Dr. William Atkinson at CDC in Atlanta, Georgia, has said that the "medical record is the backbone of a patient care plan."[5] During the visit, the clinician collects information about the patient, the planned trip, and the immunizations administered. The following minimum information *specific to vaccine administration* should be noted in the patient's permanent record.

Demographic Data, Medical History, Allergies, Medications, and Trip Information. Collecting these data will help the clinician document the rationale for recommended vaccinations, screen patients for vaccine contraindications or precautions, and meet the legal requirements for treating a minor.

Immunization History. The clinician should take a thorough immunization history and record it for future reference. Using a consolidated form will help with the organization of the information and the easy retrieval of data. Many patients find it difficult to provide a complete immunization history. To facilitate this important process, the patient should be asked to bring all prior immunization records plus any information about prior vaccine-preventable diseases such as measles, mumps, rubella, and varicella. The travel health provider should know the current and historic vaccine schedules and standards for their own countries. For example, in the United States, persons born in 1956 or before are considered naturally immune to MMR and varicella, even if they cannot recall having had the diseases. When in doubt, titers can be drawn or the vaccines given. The clinician should also record BCG vaccinations and TB test history.

Vaccination Documentation. The 1986 National Childhood Vaccine Injury Act mandates that health providers keep complete and accurate records for all administered immunizations. Federal law requires that the following information be documented for every vaccine given: date of administration, vaccine name, vaccine manufacturer, lot number, and immunizer's name, clinic address, and professional title.[67]

The AAP and other professional groups recommend that the notation also include dose, injection site, route of administration, and vaccine expiration date.[10,15,47]

For a sample adult vaccine administration record, see Appendix D, which can be viewed on the accompanying CD-ROM only.

Vaccine Information Statements. The clinician is required to document VIS use as discussed previously in this chapter. Chart the VIS title, VIS publication date, and date given to patient, parent, or legal representative.

Informed Consents and Waivers. The patient record should include signed and witnessed original copies of these documents, if applicable. (See the "Risk Communication" section in this chapter for a discussion of the use of consent forms and waivers.)

Adverse Events and Allergic Reactions. Any adverse event (AE) or suspected vaccine allergy should be documented in the patient record. The clinician should note patient signs and symptoms and provider interventions, including follow-up care and referrals, and affix warning labels to the chart cover for any vaccine allergy. He or she should follow federal guidelines for filing reports to the VAERS (see below) as well as to all applicable institutional or agency policies.

WHO International Certificate of Vaccination or Exemption Letter

In the United States, yellow fever vaccination must be given at a designated, official yellow fever center and documented in the WHO International Certificate of Vaccination.[62] Clinicians may choose to issue the WHO yellow immunization record to all travel vaccine recipients, as it is a document recognized throughout the world. However, some clinics reserve its use exclusively for documenting immunizations when yellow fever vaccine is administered.

Travel health clinicians need to know how to complete this certificate, as it has several different sections for recording vaccination data, medical contraindications to vaccination, and personal health history, including medications, allergies, and ophthalmic information. The special section reserved for documentation of the yellow fever vaccine must be completed accurately with all of the following:
* the patient's name, printed and signature;
* the patient's sex and date of birth;
* the date of yellow fever vaccination;
* the signature and professional status of the vaccinator and the address of the vaccination center; and
* the manufacturer and batch number of the vaccine.[62]

The Uniform Stamp (official yellow fever stamp) of the vaccinating center must be used to validate the entry. In the United States, state health departments issue this stamp to designated nonfederal yellow fever vaccination centers. Travel health clinics seeking designation as "yellow fever centers" need to contact their state and file the appropriate documents.

Note: According to the CDC, travelers without proper validation of their yellow fever immunization may be denied entry at a border or become subject to quarantine or revaccination.[62]

Other certificate requirements include the following.
* All travelers, including children, should have their own certificates. (Some countries do not require a certificate for children younger than 6 to 12 months.) A parent or guardian may sign the certificate for a young child.

- Dates recorded in the International Certificate of Vaccination should be written in the *international* format: day-month-year, for example *8 MAR 03.*
  Note: this differs from the routine US dating format of month-day-year.
- Per CDC, the International Certificate of Vaccination must be signed by a licensed physician or by a person designated by the physician. A signature stamp is not acceptable.[63]

For an example of a completed WHO International Certificate of Vaccination see Appendix E, which can be viewed on the accompanying CD-ROM only.

The certificates can be ordered from the World Health Organization by fax (+41 22 791 48 57), e-mail (bookorders@who.int), or mail. The postal address is WHO/Marketing & Dissemination, CH-1211 Geneva 27, Switzerland. In the United States, the certificates are sold by the US Government Printing Office (GPO), Superintendent of Documents, Mail Stop: SSPO, Washington, DC 20402-9328. Copies are also available at GPO branches in major US cities.

Per CDC, if there are medical grounds for a vaccination exemption, then the physician should write an exemption letter that documents these findings. This letter should be written on letterhead stationery and include the physician's signature and the date.[15,62]

Patient Vaccination Record

All vaccine recipients should retain a record of their immunizations. If the International Certificate of Vaccination is not used for this purpose, then the travel health clinician should issue a suitable substitute document, such as the one available on the IAC Web site at <www.immunize.org/adultizcards/adult izcard.pdf>.[68] ACIP recommends recording documented AEs and results of any serologic testing for immunity on this patient vaccination record.[13]

State Immunization Record or Registry

Every US state has adopted the use of official childhood immunization cards. The travel health clinician should document all vaccines given to children in these state mandated documents. In compliance with *Healthy People 2010*, travel clinics also should participate in any community computerized vaccination registries for children.[69]

The Immunization Logbook

Clinicians will find it useful to maintain a master record of all vaccines administered, noting the date of administration, the recipient's name, and the vaccine name and lot number. In the event of a manufacturer's recall of a vaccine lot, it might be necessary to contact affected patients. An immunization logbook (print or computerized format) can facilitate this contact process and prevent time-consuming manual chart review.

Postadministration Complications

Any vaccine can have a side effect or adverse reaction. ACIP recognizes three categories of vaccine adverse effects: local, systemic, and allergic reactions.[70] Local effects are the relatively frequent, usually mild, short-lived reactions, such as pain and swelling at the injection site. Systemic reactions occur less frequently and can range from fever and headache to the paralysis associated with OPV.[56] Allergic reactions (eg, anaphylaxis) are the least frequent but can be life threatening. Manufacturers are required to describe the recognized side effects of a specific vaccine in the package insert. Each ACIP vaccine statement discusses side effects and adverse events. The PDR will also list known effects.[12]

Prevention of Adverse Reactions

The prevention of serious vaccine side effects begins with careful and consistent screening of all vaccine recipients.[5] Each patient should be questioned about vaccine contraindications and precautions prior to vaccine administration. IAC and others have published standardized screening guidelines to reduce the risk of serious AEs (see previous section, "Special Administration Issues").[49]

Emergency Preparedness and the Management of Serious Adverse Events

Travel health providers should be prepared to respond to any vaccination emergency, including anaphylaxis, syncope, and bleeding. All clinicians who vaccinate should be certified in cardiopulmonary resuscitation (CPR) and trained in clinic emergency procedures. The travel health clinic should have updated protocols for the diagnosis and treatment of postadministration complications. All clinicians should be able to recognize the differences between anaphylaxis, syncope, and convulsions.[4] Every immunization site should have appropriate resuscitation equipment and medications, and these supplies should be checked prior to each vaccination session.[4]

Postvaccination Patient Instructions

Vaccine recipients or their guardians should be reminded about common AEs that can occur following immunization. If applicable, the clinician might want to refer to the VIS form where common side effects are listed. When no VIS form is available (eg, typhoid), the provider may use other educational materials. Patients should be instructed to remain 15 to 20 minutes after vaccination in a designated location for observation and told how to reach the clinician if an AE occurs after the visit.[10]

 Note: Japanese encephalitis vaccine has a known risk of delayed AEs, and the clinician will need to counsel the patient regarding follow-up.[15,71]

Anaphylaxis

Anaphylaxis is a rare, but life-threatening, IgE-mediated allergic reaction that can occur following any immunization. Generally, anaphylaxis presents rapidly within minutes. The patient may experience any of these symptoms: flushing or pallor; face, mouth, or throat swelling; itching, urticaria, wheezing, difficulty swallowing or breathing, or other symptoms of respiratory obstruction or cardiovascular collapse. Travel health clinicians should be prepared with training, equipment, and medications to respond immediately and effectively to this vaccination emergency. Epinephrine and life support equipment should be readily available. Successful management requires immediate intervention, transfer to an emergency facility, and follow-up evaluation and treatment.[72–76] A sample clinic policy for anaphylaxis can be found in Appendix 8.

Syncope or Vasovagal Reaction

A syncopal reaction can occur after immunization. In one review of syncope after vaccination, 63% of episodes occurred in less than 5 minutes, and 89% occurred within 15 minutes of vaccination.[77] If syncope occurs, the patient should be monitored carefully until the symptoms resolve fully. Travel health providers should be prepared to intervene to prevent fall injuries, including skull fracture and intracranial bleeding. As a preventive measure, some vaccine specialists recommend assessing patients for previous vasovagal episodes. Observing patients for 15 to 20 minutes after immunization is also recommended.[10]

Site Abscess

Site abscess can occur with bacterial contamination of the injection site. Strict attention to sterile technique can help prevent this complication. Patients should be advised to seek follow-up care for any persistent injection site inflammation. Clinicians should evaluate the affected area and determine the need for site drainage, antibiotic therapy, or further care measures.

Reporting Adverse Vaccine Events

In the United States, health care providers are required by the National Childhood Vaccine Injury Act (NCVIA) to report certain AEs occurring after immunization with these vaccines: DTaP, DT, Td, MMR, MR, measles, OPV, IPV, varicella, Hib, hepatitis B, pneumococcal conjugate, and yellow fever vaccines.[13,17,67] A full listing of these reportable events can be found in the federal Vaccine Injury Table.[67] In addition, the CDC recommends that all temporally associated events following any vaccination and warranting medical attention be reported (see Chapter 18, "Vaccine Safety").[62]

AEs should be reported to the VAERS, a program maintained by CDC and the FDA as part of their postmarketing vaccine surveillance network. To ask questions or obtain VAERS reporting forms, the clinician can call 1-800-822-7967 or visit the VAERS Web site at <www.vaers.org>.[78] For a sample VAERS form see Appendix F, which can be viewed on the accompanying CD-ROM only.

Travel health clinicians must comply with any additional state, agency, or site reporting requirements. The patient's chart should fully document any AE and appropriate warning labels should be placed on the cover. The clinician should educate the patient carefully about the AE, any follow-up therapeutic care, and future vaccination precautions, if indicated.

International Perspective

Some countries, in addition to the United States, have established their own national systems for reporting vaccine AEs. Australia has the Adverse Drug Reactions Advisory Committee (ADRAC), which mandates the reporting of some 31 AEs at any time following immunization.[4] Canada has its own procedure and reporting forms.[3]

In 1996, WHO published a report that recognized the contribution of program failures (eg, wrong diluent, contaminated needles) to vaccine AEs in developing countries.[79] WHO and UNICEF have programs to help countries set up AEFI tracking and response systems.[80] The EPI has published several AEFI training documents and recommends that vaccination field managers, at a minimum, report cases of severe vaccination reactions.[81]

CONCLUSION

Proper vaccine administration helps ensure vaccine effectiveness. Ultimately, it is the responsibility of every travel health clinician who immunizes to know and comply with vaccine administration standards of care.

The authors of this chapter have endeavored to review in detail best practices in vaccine administration in the travel health care setting. These practices are based on expert guidelines published in the United States with additional discussion of the international perspective on these topics. The reader has been presented with a road map for the administration of travel immunizations, with recommendations for addressing common vaccination concerns. Tables and figures presented in the appendices expand on the text and can serve as useful clinic tools.

REFERENCES

1. World Health Organization. Safe vaccine handling, cold chain and immunizations. Available at: http://www.who.int/vaccines-documents/DocsPDF/www9825.pdf (accessed July 6, 2003).

2. World Health Organization. Immunization in practice. Available at: http://www.who.int/vaccines-documents/DoxTrng/h4iip.htm (accessed July 20, 2003).

3. National Advisory Committee on Immunization. Canadian immunisation guide. 6th ed. Ottawa (Canada): Canadian Medical Association; 2002.

4. National Health and Medical Research Council (Australia). The Australian immunization handbook. 7th ed. Canberra (Australia): National Health and Research Council; 2000.

5. Centers for Disease Control and Prevention. The immunization encounter. Critical issues [Webcast, June 27, 2002]. Available at: http://www.phppo.cdc.gov/phtn/webcast/imm-encounter/webcast.asp (accessed July 3, 2003).

6. Campbell NJ. Writing effective policies and procedures. A step-by-step resource for clear communication. New York: AMACOM, a division of American Management Association; 1998.

7. Amann MC. The policy and procedure manual—keeping it current. AAOHN J 2001;49(2):69–71.

8. The Vaccine Administration Taskforce. UK guidance on best practice in vaccine administration. London: Shire Hall Communications; 2001.

9. The Vaccine Administration Taskforce. Getting to the point. Best practice in vaccine administration. Available at: http://www.vaccine-administration.org.uk (accessed July 16, 2003).

10. American Academy of Pediatrics. Active immunization. In: Pickering LK, editor. 2000 Red book. Report of the Committee on Infectious Diseases. 25th ed. Elk Grove Village (IL): American Academy of Pediatrics; 2000.

11. Immunization Action Coalition. How to protect your vaccine supply ("Ice, Champagne, and Roses") [video]. St. Paul (MN): IAC; 2002.

12. Medical Economics Staff, editor. Physician's desk reference. 56th ed. Montvale (NJ): Medical Economics Company; 2002.

13. Centers for Disease Control and Prevention. General recommendations on immunization. Recommendations of the Advisory Committee on Immunization Practices (ACIP) and the American Academy of Family Physician (AAFP). MMWR Morb Mortal Wkly Rep 2002;51(RR-02):1–32.

14. Centers for Disease Control and Prevention. Vaccine management: recommendations for handling and storage of selected biologicals. Atlanta (GA): Department of Health and Human Services; 2001.

15. Thompson R. Routine and travel immunizations. A practical guide for the medical office. Annual. Milwaukee (WI): Shoreland; 2003.

16. Nayda C, Kempe A, Miller N. Keep it cool. The vaccine cold chain guidelines for immunisation providers on maintaining the cold chain. 2nd ed. Canberra: Commonwealth of Australia; 2001. Available at: http://www.immunise.health.gov.au/cool.pdf (accessed May 22, 2002).

17. Immunization Action Coalition. Celsius (C) temperature log. Available at: http://www.immunize.org/news.d/celsius.pdf (accessed July 10, 2003).

18. Kendal AP, Snyder R, Garrison PJ. Validation of cold chain procedures suitable for distribution of vaccines by public health programs in the USA. Vaccine 1997;15:1459–65.

19. Adler and Allan, Ltd. SensorPhone. Available at: http://www.adlerandallan.co.uk (accessed July 20, 2003).

20. World Health Organization/Expanded Program on Immunizations. EPI equipment performance specifications and test procedures. Available at: http://www.who.int/vaccines_access/vacman/pis/e03.pdf (accessed July 8, 2003).

21. World Health Organization. Available at: http://www.who.int/vaccines-access/vacman/coldchain/the_cold_chain_.htm (accessed July 12, 2003).

22. World Health Organization Department of Vaccines and Biologics, UNICEF Programme Division. Quality of the cold chain. WHO/UNICEF policy statement on the use of vaccine vial monitors in immunization services. WHO/V&B/99.18. Available at: http://www.who.int/vaccines-access/vacman/vvm/vvmmainpage.htm (accessed July 1, 2003).

23. Bunnell L, Rosselot G, Berry L. The clinic guide. Milwaukee (WI): Shoreland; 1997.

24. National Immunization Program. Vaccine shortages. Available at: http://www.cdc.gov/nip/news/shortages (accessed July 20, 2003).

25. Centers for Disease Control and Prevention. Immunization of health-care workers. Recommendations of the Advisory Committee on Immunization Practices (ACIP) and the Hospital Infection Control Practices Advisory Committee (HICPAC). MMWR Morb Mortal Wkly Rep 1997;46(RR-18):1–42.

26. Occupational Safety and Health Administration. Occupational exposure to bloodborne pathogens, needlestick and other sharps injuries. Final rule (29 CFR Part 1910). Federal Register 2001;66:5318–25. Available at: http://www.osha-slc.gov/FedReg_osha_pdf/FED20010118A.pdf (accessed September 10, 2002).

27. International Health Care Worker Safety Center. List of safety-engineered sharp devices and other products designed to prevent occupational exposures to bloodborne pathogens. Charlottesville (VA): University of Virginia; 2001. Available at: http://www.med.virginia.edu/medcntr/centers/epinet/safetydevice.html (accessed July 20, 2003).

28. Centers for Disease Control and Prevention. Public Health Service guidelines for the management of health-care worker exposures to HIV and recommendations for postexposure prophylaxis. MMWR Morb Mortal Wkly Rep 1998;47(RR-7):1–28.

29. World Health Organization Department of Vaccines and Biologics, UNICEF Programme Division, UN Population Fund. Safety of injections. WHO/V&B/99.25. Available at: http://www.who.int/vaccines-documents/DocsPDF99/www9948.pdf (accessed July 20, 2003).

30. World Health Organization Department of Vaccines and Biologics, UNICEF Programme Division. Vaccination and immunization update. 1st ed. Available at: http://www.who.int/vaccines/en/final.pdf (accessed July 21, 2003).

31. Program for Appropriate Technology in Health. Available at: http://www.path.org (accessed: July 1, 2003).

32. World Health Organization. Safe injection global network. Available at: http://www.who.int/injection_safety/sign/en (accessed July 1, 2003).

33. Global Alliance for Vaccines and Immunization [home page]. Available at: http://www.vaccinealliance.org (accessed July 1, 2003).

34. Centers for Disease Control and Prevention. ACIP general recommendations on immunization. Available at: http://www.cdc.gov/nip/publications/ACIP-list. htm (accessed September 29, 2003).

35. Centers for Disease Control and Prevention. ACIP vaccine recommendations. Available at: http://www.cdc.gov/nip/publications/ACIP-list.htm (accessed September 29, 2003).

36. Centers for Disease Control and Prevention. Epidemiology and prevention of vaccine-preventable diseases. Available at: http://www.cdc.gov/nip/publications/pink (accessed September 29, 2003).

37. American Academy of Pediatrics. Red book–Report of the Committee on Infectious Diseases. Available at: http://www.aap.org/pubserv/redbookonline.htm (accessed September 29, 2003).

38. Immunization Action Coalition. Directory of immunization resources. Available at: http://www.immunize.org/resources/index.htm (accessed September 29, 2003).

39. Centers for Disease Control and Prevention. Vaccine information statements. Available at: http://www.cdc.gov/nip/publications/VIS/default.htm (accessed September 29, 2003).

40. Centers for Disease Control and Prevention. Information networks and other information sources. Available at: http://www.cdc.gov/other.htm#states (accessed July 22, 2003).

41. Centers for Disease Control and Prevention. What you need to know about vaccine information statements. Atlanta (GA): Department of Health and Human Services, 2000.

42. National Immunization Program. Vaccine information statements. Available at: http://www.cdc.gov/nip/publications/VIS/default.htm (accessed June 5, 2002).

43. Immunization Action Coalition. Vaccine information statements (VISs). Available at: http://www.immunize.org/vis/index.htm (accessed July 1, 2003).

44. Oregon Department of Human Services. Vaccine information statements. Questions and answers. Available at: http://www.ohd.hr.state.or.us/imm/vis/questions.cfm (accessed July 9, 2003).

45. American Academy of Pediatrics. Refusal to vaccinate. Available at http://www.cispimmunize.org/pro/pdf/Refusalto Vaccinate.doc (accessed July 10, 2003).

46. World Health Organization. Supplementary information on vaccine safety. Available at: http://www.who.int/vaccines-documents/DocsPDF00/www522.pdf (accessed July 22, 2003).

47. Watson JC, Peters G. General immunization practices. In: Plotkin SA, Orenstein WA, editors. Vaccines. 3rd ed. Philadelphia: WB Saunders; 1999. p. 47–73.

48. Centers for Disease Control and Prevention. Epidemiology and prevention of vaccine-preventable diseases. 7th ed. Atlanta (GA): Department of Health and Human Services, 2002.

49. Immunization Action Coalition. Screening questionnaire for adult immunization. Available at: http://www.immunize.org/catg.d/p4065scr.pdf (accessed May 20, 2003).

50. Timby BK. Fundamental skills and concepts in patient care. 7th ed. Philadelphia: Lippincott, Williams, and Wilkins; 2002.

51. Dietrich T, Runta N, Rhorer J. Drug administration. In: Springhouse Corp, editors. Nursing procedures. 3rd ed. Springhouse (PA): Springhouse; 1999. p. 214–71.

52. Hahn K. Brush up on your injection technique. Nursing 1990;20(9):54–8.

53. Reis E, Holubkov R. Vapocoolant spray is equally effective as EMLA cream in reducing immunization pain in school-aged children. Pediatrics 1997;100(6):1025, e5.

54. Newtown M, Newton D, Fudin J. Reviewing the "big three" injection routes. Nursing 1992;22(2):34–41.

55. Fulginiti VA, editor. Immunization in clinical practice. Philadelphia: JB Lippincott; 1982.

56. Poland GA, Borrud A, Jacoban RM, et al. Determination of deltoid fat pad thickness. Implications for needle length in adult immunization. JAMA 1997;277(21):1709–11.

57. Zuckerman J. Importance of needle size for effective intramuscular delivery of vaccines. [letter]. Br J Gen Pract 2000;50(9):753.

58. Shaw FE Jr, Guess HA, Roets JM, et al. Effect of anatomic injection site, age and smoking on the immune response to hepatitis B vaccination. Vaccine 1989;7(5):425–30.

59. Fishbein DB, Sawyer LA, Reid-Sanden FL, Weir EH. Administration of human diploid-cell rabies vaccine in the gluteal area [letter]. N Engl J Med 1988;318:124–5.

60. Royal College of Nursing. Position statement on injection technique. Available at: http://www.rcn.org.uk/rcn_extranet/media/injection-technique.pdf (accessed February 15, 2003).

61. Grabenstein JD. ImmunoFacts. Vaccines and immunologic drugs. St. Louis (MO): Wolters Kluwer, Facts and Comparisons; 2001. p. K1–5.

62. Centers for Disease Control and Prevention. Health information for international travel, 2003–2004. Atlanta (GA): Department of Health and Human Services; 2003.

63. Evans DIK, Shaw A. Safety of intramuscular injection of hepatitis B vaccine in haemophiliacs. BMJ 1990;300:1694–5.

64. King GE, Hadler SC. Simultaneous administration of childhood vaccines. An important public health policy that is safe and efficacious. Pediatr Infect Dis J 1994;13:394–407.

65. Centers for Disease Control and Prevention. Typhoid immunization. Recommendations of the Advisory Committee on Immunization Practices (ACIP). MMWR Morb Mortal Wkly Rep 1994;43(RR-14):1–7.

66. Levine L, Edsall G. Tetanus toxoid. What determines reaction proneness? [letter]. J Infect Dis 1981;144:376.

67. Centers for Disease Control and Prevention. Current trends. National Childhood Vaccine Injury Act. Requirements for permanent vaccination records and for reporting of selected events after vaccination. MMWR Morb Mortal Wkly Rep 1988;37(13):197–200.

68. Immunization Action Coalition. Adult immunization record cards. Available at: http://www.immunize.org/adultizcards/index.htm (accessed July 11, 2003).

69. Department of Health and Human Services. Immunization and infectious diseases [Goal 14-26]. In: Healthy People 2010. Washington (DC): US Government Printing Office; 2000.

70. Centers for Disease Control and Prevention. Update. Vaccine side effects, adverse reactions, contraindications, and precautions. Recommendations of the Advisory Committee on Immunization Practices (ACIP). MMWR Morb Mortal Wkly Rep 1996;45 (RR-12):1–35.

71. Andersen MM, Ronne T. Side effects with Japanese encephalitis vaccine. Lancet 1991;337:1044.

72. Beck S. Taking action against anaphylaxis. Contemp Pediatr 1999;16(8):87–96.

73. Bochner BS, Lichtenstein LM. Anaphylaxis. N Engl J Med 1991;324:1785–90.

74. Mackan M. Managing the patient with anaphylaxis, part 1. Mechanisms and manifestations. Emerg Med (Fremantle) 1995;27(2):68–79.

75. Mackan M. Managing the patient with anaphylaxis, part 2. Therapeutic strategies. Emerg Med (Fremantle) 1995;27(3):20–35.

76. Barbarito C. Anaphylaxis. Am J Nurs 1999;99(1):33.

77. Braun MM, Patriarca PA, Ellenberg SS. Syncope after immunization. Arch Pediatr Adolesc Med 1997;151:255–9.

78. Centers for Disease Control and Prevention and the Food and Drug Administration. Vaccine adverse event reporting system. Available at: http://www.vaers.org (accessed July 12, 2003).

79. World Health Organization. Vaccine supply and quality. Surveillance of adverse events following immunization. Wkly Epidemiol Rec 1996;71(32):237–41.

80. World Health Organization. Developing a national system for dealing with adverse events following immunization. Bull World Health Organ 2000;78(2). Available at: http://www.who.int/vaccines-surveillance/ISPP/CDRom/alldocs/allothers/bullwhodevelsystaefiseng.pdf (accessed September 2, 2002).

81. World Health Organization. Surveillance of adverse events following immunization. Field guide for managers of immunization programmes. Available at: http://www.who.int/vaccines-documents/DocsPDF/www9541.pdf (accessed September 3, 2002).

82. Immunization Action Coalition. Measles, mumps & rubella vaccines. What you need to know. Available at: http://www.immunize.org/vis/mmr03.pdf (accessed July 22, 2003).

83. Centers for Disease Control and Prevention. Standards for pediatric immunization practices. Recommended by the National Vaccine Advisory Committee. Approved by the US Public Health Service. MMWR Morb Mortal Wkly Rep 1993;42(RR-5):1–13.

84. Fisher Scientific Company. Fisherbrand* Traceable* Refrigerator/Freezer Alarm Thermometer (Product #0666411). Available at: http://www.fishersci.com (accessed July 22, 2003).

85. Centers for Disease Control and Prevention. Health objectives for the nation public health burden of vaccine-preventable diseases among adults. Standards for adult immunization practice. MMWR Morb Mortal Wkly Rep 1990;39(41):725–9.

86. Immunization Action Coalition. Pharmaceutical company websites and telephone numbers. Available at: http://www.immunize.org/resources/pharmac.htm (accessed July 22, 2003).

87. Immunization Action Coalition. Checklist for safe vaccine handling and storage. Available at: http://www.immunize.org/catg.d/p3035chk.htm (accessed July 22, 2003).

88. Centers for Disease Control and Prevention. General recommendations on immunizations. MMWR Morb Mortal Wkly Rep 1994;43(RR-1):236.

89. Zuckerman J. The importance of injecting vaccines into muscles. Different patients need different needle sizes. BMJ 2001;321:1237–8.

APPENDIX 1

Policies and Procedures

The Vaccine Refrigerator

Policy: Guidelines for choosing and maintaining the travel clinic vaccine refrigerator/freezer unit.

Purpose: To ensure proper storage of vaccines in the travel clinic vaccine refrigerator.

Procedure:

1. Be sure all clinical personnel know that the clinic vaccine supply is valuable and fragile. It is the responsibility of the site immunization coordinator to provide orientation and ongoing staff training on cold-chain management. *Every staff member is responsible for cold-chain compliance.* Staff need to understand that a proper inventory must be made for all vaccine shipments on arrival, and vaccines must be placed quickly in the refrigerator or freezer so vaccine potency is maintained in accordance with the manufacturer's temperature requirements.

2. Purchase a frost-free refrigerator with a separate freezer door for your dedicated vaccine storage. Contact the manufacturer to ensure that the unit is suitable for vaccines. The unit should be adequately sized to accommodate your vaccine supply on the middle and upper shelves only.

3. Locate the refrigerator in a place convenient for the staff. Do not locate it in a patient examination room. Position it to ensure adequate air circulation around the unit.

4. Have padlocks on the refrigerator and freezer doors, and keep them locked to prevent access by unauthorized personnel.

5. Set the refrigerator thermostat to the proper storage temperature. The US Centers for Disease Control and Prevention (CDC) recommends a refrigerator temperature of 36 to 45°F (2–8°C). If you stock varicella vaccine, the freezer will need to maintain a temperature of −5°F (−15°C).

6. Place quality thermometers in both the refrigerator and freezer units. These should monitor current temperatures and 24-hour minimum and maximum temperatures.* Document thermometer readings twice each day (start and end of day) on a temperature log affixed to the front of the units. Direct all staff to report temperature variances or other refrigerator problems promptly to the immunization coordinator for follow-up. Maintain temperature logs for at least 3 years.

7. As may be needed to help stabilize unit temperatures, store containers of water in open refrigerator space and ice or ice packs in open freezer space. Also, limit refrigerator access to travel clinic staff to prevent frequent door openings that can affect unit temperature.

8. Prohibit food storage in the travel clinic refrigerator to limit door openings and possible overheating of the vaccines. Place signage on the unit door that discourages inappropriate door opening or storage.

9. Make sure the unit remains plugged in at all times. The following actions will help prevent a power failure.
   - Place a safety lock on the refrigerator plug—one that makes it difficult to remove the plug from the socket.

Continued on next page

APPENDIX 1 *(Continued)*

- Post warning signs so that electricians, janitors, or other personnel do not unknowingly damage vaccines by unplugging the refrigerator or turning off the circuit or electricity.
- Place "Warning—Do Not Unplug" signs on the plug, wall outlet, refrigerator door, and circuit breaker box door.

10. As may be feasible, connect the unit to an alarm system or an alarm system with a telephone connection to alert staff to power failures.

11. Stock vaccines to maintain potency:
    - Do not place vaccines in a refrigerator/freezer until the proper temperatures have been maintained and documented.
    - Place new vaccine shipments in the refrigerator or freezer as soon as they arrive at the clinic. Varicella will go into the freezer compartment. If a shipment arrives warm or damaged, mark the batch "Do Not Use," place it separate in the unit, and contact the immunization coordinator and drug manufacturer for recommendations.*
    - Place vaccines on the upper and middle shelves, and do not crowd the supply. Keep vaccines in their original containers to permit checking of expiration dates.
    - Rotate vaccines on refrigerator shelves to avoid expiration. Follow the "first in, first out" rule. Place the newest vaccines toward the back of the shelf, and move older vaccines forward.
    - Do not store vaccines on the refrigerator door, on the lowest shelf, or in bottom bins, as temperatures can vary from the rest of the unit.

12. When storing and using vaccines, follow the manufacturer's guidelines carefully to maintain the cold chain. For easy reference, keep vaccine package inserts and a list of vaccine lot numbers on file near the refrigerator. If vaccines are inadvertently left out of the refrigerator, inappropriately frozen, or in any other way not maintained in a manner consistent with the manufacturer's guidelines, mark the batch, place it separate in the unit, and contact the immunization coordinator and vendor for recommendations.

13. Follow the manufacturer's guidelines for regular refrigerator maintenance. When the unit requires cleaning, store vaccines temporarily in a cold storage box with a thermometer to maintain the cold chain.

14. If vaccines will be transported off-site, contact the drug manufacturer for detailed guidelines.

15. Every travel clinic should have a separate Disaster Recovery Plan in the event that the unit sustains a power failure. Anticipate the need to relocate the vaccine supply to another refrigerator if power is out for more than 3 hours. Contact local hospitals, other clinics, or local health departments to identify the designated backup unit for the clinic.*

16. Whenever there is a breach in this policy or an episode of vaccine wastage, the immunization coordinator should use the opportunity for policy review and staff retraining, as needed.

17. Review and revise this policy and procedure every 6 months and as needed.

Adapted from Bunnell L et al[23]; also adapted from Immunization Action Coalition (IAC)[1,11,82]; National Health and Medical Research Council (Australia)[4]; Centers for Disease Control and Prevention (CDC)[5,48,83]; Thompson R[15]; Nayda C et al[16]; Adler and Allan[19]; Fisher Scientific Company.[84]

* CDC.[36]

APPENDIX 2

Policies and Procedures

After-Hours Care

Policy: The travel clinic will establish and maintain a system whereby patients can access care when the office is closed.

Purpose: To ensure that all travel clinic patients have knowledge of and access to after-hours medical care in the event they experience a vaccine adverse event (AE).

Procedure:

The travel clinic administrator/coordinator and medical director should proceed as follows:

1. Identify at least two local resources for appropriate after-hours medical care: the clinic's on-call provider, community emergency departments, or local 24-hour urgent care centers.

2. Inform local emergency providers in writing (include a copy of your policy) that travel clinic patients might contact them for after-hours care. For each resource, the administrator should ascertain the name and telephone number of the resource administrator, patient phone access number(s), driving directions to the facility, and payment policy.

3. Develop a handout for distribution to all patients receiving vaccines and medications. Include this information:
   - an explanation about the possible need for after-hours care,
   - a list of emergency providers with phone numbers and directions (tell patients they also can try to contact their primary care provider or, for a true emergency, call 911),
   - instructions to inform the travel clinic of any after-hours contact as soon as possible, and
   - payment responsibilities (insurance, Health Maintenance Organization coverage, etc.).

4. Review and update the patient's chart following any after-hours contact. Patient follow-up—by phone or visit—should be documented in the records, including a Vaccine Adverse Events reorting System (VAERS) report if necessary.

5. Review and update the emergency resource list every 6 months, or as needed.

6. Review and revise this policy and procedure yearly, or as needed.

Adapted from Bunnell L et al[23]

APPENDIX 3

Policies and Procedures

Administration of Intradermal Injections

Administration of a substance into the dermis for slow absorption through the capillaries

Policy: This is a clinical protocol for the intradermal administration (ID) of parenteral substances.

Purpose: To ensure the safe and effective administration of biologics via the intradermal route of administration.

Procedure:

1. Intradermal injections generally are performed for diagnostic purposes, such as to identify allergens or diagnose patients who have developed specific antibodies (eg, tuberculosis). Outside the United States, the ID route is also used for rabies and BCG (bacille Calmette-Guérin) administration.

2. Intradermal injections have the longest absorption time of any parenteral route and involve small amounts of solution, usually not more than 0.5 mL. The Mantoux (PPD) tuberculosis test is an example of an intradermal injection.

3. Selecting the ID syringe and needle:
   - A 1 mL tuberculin syringe with a ½- to ⅝- inch, 25- to 27-gauge needle usually is used.

4. Selecting an appropriate ID site:
   - Choose an easily observed site to facilitate the assessment of a local reaction.
   - The most common site is the inner surface of the forearm, but the upper arm, upper chest, and upper back beneath the scapulae also are suitable.

5. Clean the injection site.
   - Use an alcohol swab.
   - Use a circular motion moving outward from the site of the injection to a distance of about 2 inches in diameter.
   - Allow the site to dry to avoid injecting alcohol under the skin.

6. Administering the injection:
   - With the nondominant hand, spread the skin taut at the site.
   - Place the needle almost flat against the patient's skin with the bevel up.
   - Insert the needle at a 5 to 15° angle beneath the skin until the entire bevel of the needle penetrates the dermis. Avoid injecting subcutaneously.
   - Slowly inject the solution, observing for a small, well-defined wheal or bleb to appear. If none appears, withdraw the needle slightly. The bleb will have a "mosquito bite appearance."
   - Withdraw the needle quickly at the same angle as inserted.
   - Do not massage the area.

7. Observe the ID site at prescribed intervals. For Mantoux, check the site at 48 to 72 hours. For ease of observation, consider drawing a circle around the injection site. Carefully explain to the patient the rationale and schedule for observations.

Adapted from Bunnell L et al[23]; also adapted from Dietrich T et al[51]; Hahn K[52]; Reis E, Holubkov R[53]; Fulginiti VA[55]; Poland GA.[56]

APPENDIX 4

Immunization Policies and Procedures for a Travel Health Clinic

It is recommended that travel health clinics include the following vaccine administration policies and procedures in their clinic manual.

Immunization coordinator job description

Describes the duties and obligations of the staff member responsible for immunization quality control

Immunization standards

Master list of all applicable standards of care and copies of these materials: federal standards for child, adolescent, and adult immunization practices; latest edition of the Advisory Committee on Immunization Practices (ACIP) *General Principles of Immunization*; latest editions of all ACIP vaccine recommendations, state vaccination guidelines, agency or institutional guidelines, and professional standards of care

Vaccine standing orders

Master list of all vaccines stocked in the practice and a signed medical order for each vaccine that includes this information: the indications for vaccine use, regular and accelerated schedules, precautions and contraindications, and handling and administration guidelines

Cold-chain policies and procedures

- receipt of vaccine supplies
- refrigerator selection and maintenance
- procedure in the event of a power failure
- transporting of vaccines off-site
- staff training for cold chain compliance
- maintaining the refrigerator temperature log
- vaccine wastage

Patient and staff safety

Includes OSHA regulations for blood-borne pathogens and needlestick injuries as well as any state and site infection control guidelines and mandated log for needlestick injuries

Vaccine ordering policy and procedures

Includes vaccine inventory log and instructions for its use; supplier contact information (see Appendix 5, for pharmaceutical company Web sites and telephone numbers)

Vaccine supply quality control

Cold-chain management policies and procedures, includes emergency plan for coping with power failures, refrigerator policy, temperature monitoring policy, vaccine receipt and storage procedures, vaccine wastage protocol, and protocol for off-site vaccine transport, if applicable

Risk communication and informed decision making

Includes policies regarding patient education about vaccines, vaccine education checklist, use of consent and refusal documents with sample copies of all documents, and master list of all Vaccine Information Statements (latest edition) with instructions for use

Continued on next page

APPENDIX 4 *(Continued)*

Vaccine administration supplies, drugs, and equipment

A master list of all clinical and nonclinical vaccine administration supplies, drugs, and equipment; includes vaccine supply as single vials, multidose vials, and prepackaged syringes as well as other clinical supplies, including syringes, needles, infection control supplies, and emergency response medications, supplies, and equipment

Vaccine administration

Includes injection technique policy for subcutaneous, intramuscular, and intradermal injections; vaccination training policy and procedure; and site guidelines for special immunizations issues (eg, multiple injections, lapsed dosing) (see Figures 4-3 and 4-4 for diagrams)

Postvaccine monitoring and complications management

Includes postinjection waiting time policy, after-hours care policy, protocols for managing anaphylaxis and syncope, and guidelines for the use of the Vaccine Adverse Event Reporting System form (VAERS) in the United States or appropriate AEFI (adverse effect following immunization) forms in other countries

Documentation and record keeping

Includes master list of all clinical and clerical documents used for immunization services, such as charting forms, patient questionnaires and screening documents, consent and waiver forms, and any customized clinical documents (eg, medical exemption letter); also includes all administrative documents, such as vaccine inventory log, temperature logs, immunization logbook, and staff training logs; and provides current samples of each document with guidelines for their completion and proper filing

Immunization referrals

Includes clinic procedure, resource list, and any applicable forms for referring patients for additional immunization care

Program evaluation/quality assurance monitoring

Includes plan for ongoing evaluation and improvement of immunization services

Professional issues

Includes cardiopulmonary resuscitation (CPR) and infection control training policies, malpractice insurance information, human immunodeficiency virus/postexposure prophylaxis policy, and a policy on professional continuing education credits

Staff training materials

Includes list of all standardized education materials and resources used for staff orientation and ongoing training, skill-training checklists and competency-based testing documents, and schedule and attendance log for continuing education programs

Vaccination administration resources

Master list of all site-approved print and Web resources for professionals and patients

Policy on manual maintenance

Includes guidelines for the regular review and revision of the clinic policy and procedure manual

Adapted from Centers for Disease Control and Prevention[5,13,48,85]; Campbell NJ[6]; Amann MC[7]; Thompson R[15]; Immunization Action Coalition[17,86]; Bunnell L et al[23]; Evans DIK and Shaw A.[63]

APPENDIX 5

Pharmaceutical Company Web Sites and Telephone Numbers

Pharmaceutical companies publish health education materials in a variety of formats, including print, video, slides, and posters. These materials are available for health professionals, usually at no cost. The following phone numbers and Web sites can put you in touch with vaccine manufacturers to find out what resources they make available. You may be able to find names of local sales representatives as well.

Aventis Pasteur, Inc.: (800) 822-2463
www.us.aventispasteur.com

Bayer Pharmaceutical Group: (800) 468-0894
www.pharma.bayer.com

Berna Products Corp.: (800) 533-5899
www.bernaproducts.com

BioPort Corp.: (517) 327-1500
www.bioport.com

Chiron Vaccines: (800) 244-7668
www.chiron.com
www.rabavert.com (provides information on rabies prevention and treatment)

Evans Vaccines, Ltd.: (800) 200-4278
www.powderject.com

GlaxoSmithKline: (888) 825-5249
www.gskvaccines.com
us.gsk.com (corporate Web site)
www.worldwidevaccines.com

MedImmune, Inc.: (877) 633-4411
www.medimmune.com

Merck & Co.: (800) 672-6372
www.merckvaccines.com
www.chickenpoxinfo.com (information to the public and health care providers about varicella prevention)
www.hepbinfo.com (information for adolescents about hepatitis B and its prevention)

Nabi: (800) 458-4244
www.nabi.com

Wyeth Lederle Vaccines: (800) 358-7443
www.vaccineworld.com
www.pneumo.com (information on pneumococcal disease and its prevention in infants and young children)
www.prevnar.com (information about the Prevnar vaccine)

Immunization Action Coalition
1573 Selby Avenue St. Paul MN 55104
E-mail: **admin@immunize.org**
Web: www.immunize.org/
Tel: (651) 647-9009   Fax: (651) 647-9131

Adapted from Immunization Action Coalition. This page was updated on March 4, 2003.[87]

APPENDIX 6

Vaccine Administration Equipment and Supplies Checklist

To provide quality vaccine administration services, the travel health clinic should acquire and maintain the following recommended items:

Clinical equipment and supplies
- Frost-free or commercial grade refrigerator with separate freezer unit and 2 (or more) thermometers suitable for 24-hour temperature monitoring
- Puncture-proof container for disposal of syringes and needles
- Assorted safety syringes—1 mL, 3 mL, plus tuberculin syringes
- Assorted 22- to 25-gauge needles for syringes—⅝ inch (15 mm), ⅞ inch (21 mm), 1 inch (25 mm), 1¼ inch (31 mm) and 1½ inch (38 mm)
- Alcohol wipes
- Small adhesive bandages for injection site
- Gauze pads, small
- Gloves for use, as needed
- Spray bottle of 10% bleach solution for cleaning up blood spills
- Stethoscope
- Sphygmomanometer with cuffs for children, adults, and large adults
- Telephone
- Sink and hand sanitizer solution
- Good lighting
- Table or bench for patient to recline, if necessary, or for use with infants and young children
- Emergency response equipment, medications, and supplies (including epinephrine 1:1000 and diphenhydramine for oral administration or injection)

Documentation materials
- Vaccine logs: inventory, temperature, vaccination lot numbers
- Vaccine Information Statements (VIS) for each vaccine (latest edition, multiple languages as may be needed in clinic)
- Consents and waivers, if used in clinic
- Patient medical record/chart; chart documents, including customized questionnaires and any applicable state, school, or agency vaccination records
- World Health Organization (WHO) International Certificates of Vaccination
- Vaccine Adverse Events Reporting Systems forms (VAERS form in the United States)
- Prescription pads
- Calendar for scheduling additional doses
- Billing forms

Print resources
- Policy and procedure manual with standing orders
- Advisory Committee on Immunization Practices (ACIP) *General Principles of Immunization* (latest edition)
- Manufacturer's vaccine package inserts
- Others, as deemed valuable for clinical care

Adapted from Bunnell L et al.[23]

APPENDIX 7

Misconceptions Concerning Contraindications to Vaccination

Note: The CDC published an updated statement on the General Recommendations on Immunization on February 8, 2002.[13]

Some health care providers might inappropriately defer administering a vaccine by considering certain conditions or circumstances to be contraindications to vaccination. The following conditions *are not* routine contraindications and immunizations should not be deferred:

- Mild acute illness with low-grade fever (eg, otitis media, upper resipiratory infection [URI], and colds) or mild diarrheal illness in an otherwise well child
- Current antimicrobial therapy or the convalescent phase of illnesses
- Recent exposure to an infectious disease
- Prematurity. The appropriate age for initiating most immunizations in the prematurely born infant is the usual chronologic age. Vaccine doses should not be reduced for preterm infants. Exception: Administration of hepatitis B vaccine in premature infants born to hepatitis B surface antigen (HBsAg)-negative mothers should be deferred until discharge from the nursery and the infant achieves a weight of 2 kg
- Pregnancy of mother or other household contact (ie, pregnancy is not a contraindication for immunization of *the infant or child*)
- Breast-feeding. The only vaccine virus that has been isolated from breast milk is rubella vaccine virus. There is no good evidence that breast milk from women immunized against rubella is harmful to infants
- A history of *nonspecific* allergies or relatives with allergies
- Allergies to duck meat or duck feathers. No vaccine available in the United States is produced in substrates containing duck antigens
- Allergies to penicillin or any other antibiotic, except anaphylactic reactions to neomycin (eg, measles, mumps, rubella [MMR]-containing vaccines and/or varicella) or streptomycin (eg, inactiviated poliovirus vaccine [IPV]): None of the vaccines manufactured in the United States contain penicillin
- Nonanaphylactic allergies to eggs or egg products
- Reaction to a previous dose of diphtheria and tetanus toxoids and acellular pertussis (DTaP) vaccine that involved only soreness, redness, or swelling in the immediate vicinity of the vaccination site or temperature of less than 105°F (40.5°C)
- Family history of convulsions in persons considered for pertussis or measles vaccination
- Acetaminophen given before administering DTaP and thereafter every 4 hours for 24 hours should be considered for children with a personal or family history of convulsions in siblings or parents
- Family history of sudden infant death syndrome in children considered for DTaP vaccination
- Family history of an adverse event, unrelated to immunosuppression, following vaccination
- Malnutrition
- Need for a purified protein deriavative (PPD) test for tuberculosis at the same time as other vaccines
  Vaccine recipients and caregivers of young children being vaccinated might also have misconceptions concerning the benefit and risk of immunization.

Adpted from American Academy of Pediatrics[10]; Thompson R[15]; Centers for Disease Control and Prevention[48,88]; Immunization Action Coalition.[89]

APPENDIX 8

Policies and Procedures

Postimmunization Anaphylaxis

Policy: This is a clinical protocol to provide care for a patient with anaphylaxis following vaccine administration.

Purpose: To ensure appropriate intervention for this acute life-threatening allergic reaction.

Medical Director Review: *Required*

Confirm that this statement of policy and procedure has the dated signature of the current medical director of the travel clinic as confirmation of his or her review and agreement with this emergency protocol.

Procedure

1. All clinical staff should be trained in cardiopulmonary resuscitation (CPR) and competency-tested in the recognition and initial care of anaphylaxis, syncope, and convulsions. The immunization coordinator should orient clinicians to important clinical features of this postvaccination emergency. There should be regular scheduled drills of this policy and procedure (P&P).

2. Each clinic should be fully stocked with resuscitation equipment and emergency medications. This emergency kit/cart should be readily accessible to the immunization area and should be checked prior to each vaccination session.

3. To prevent serious adverse events of vaccination, every clinician should screen every vaccine recipient for immunization contraindications and precautions prior to administration.

If a patient is experiencing anaphylaxis following vaccination, the clinician should follow this procedure:

4. Assess ABC's and keep airway open. Quickly evaluate the patient's cardiac and respiratory status. Immediately initiate CPR if needed.

5. If the patient is hypotensive, place him or her in a recumbent position with legs elevated.

6. Give epinephrine 0.3 to 0.5 mg (0.3–0.5 mL of 1:1000 solution) IM (intramuscularly) or SC (subcutaneously). Repeat every 10 to 30 minutes, as needed, × 3 doses.

7. Do not leave the patient alone. Call site emergency telephone number_____ (eg, 911, hospital code number) and report the medical emergency.

8. Administer oxygen at moderate to high flow via nasal cannula or mask as needed for cyanosis, severe dyspnea, or wheezing.

9. Give diphenhydramine hydrochloride 25 to 50 mg IM (or other antihistamine, per site policy).

10. Monitor vital signs.

11. In some settings, be prepared to start IV (intravenous) lines, implement endotracheal intubation, and administer medications IV (including corticosteriods and vasopressors).

12. Patients experiencing anaphylaxis should be monitored closely and transported as soon as possible to an emergency unit for further evaluation and care. Inform patients that follow-up care is essential because anaphylactic symptoms sometimes recur within 24 hours (biphasic presentation).

Continued on next page

APPENDIX 8 *(Continued)*

13. Document fully all reactions, and file a VAERS (Vaccine Adverse Event Report System) report if reaction is associated with a vaccine injection. Label patient's chart clearly with an allergy alert.

14. All patients with severe allergic reactions require extensive patient counseling that is fully documented in their medical records. The travel health clinician or another provider should instruct the patient never to receive another dose of the vaccine. Provide reassurance and address any questions, anxiety, and fears. For a life-threatening reaction, or as may be indicated, consider referring the patient to an allergist for further evaluation and/or desensitization therapy.

15. Restock emergency supplies, as needed.

16. Review and revise clinic guidelines as needed for preventing and responding to severe adverse events.

_____   _____   _____

Medical Director Signature   Date   Date for Review

Training Content

Description of Anaphylaxis

Anaphylaxis following vaccination is a severe adverse event and a medical emergency. It is an immediate, often life-threatening hypersensitivity reaction that occurs without warning. Anaphylaxis is an acute clinical complex that can include any or all of these signs and symptoms: apprehension, anxiety, facial flushing, generalized erythema, pallor, pruritus, urticaria, angioedema, nausea, vomiting, abdominal cramps, diarrhea, respiratory difficulty, hypotension, bronchial constriction, laryngeal edema or laryngospasm, cardiac arrhythmia, and loss of consciousness, with or without cardiovascular collapse.

Subjective	
History (Hx)	Patient might report personal or family history (Hx) of allergies, such as hay fever, asthma, eczema, drug reactions, bee sting allergies, or anaphylaxis; check for medical alert bracelet
Onset	Determine the time interval between exposure and onset of symptoms (most acute anaphylactic reactions occur within one hour); generally, the faster the onset of symptoms, the more severe the reaction, although delayed reactions are possible
Drug Hx	Determine current drug usage: what drugs and time of last doses
Medical Hx	Confirm any cardiac or pulmonary diagnosis or pregnancy
Mental status	Patient might report anxiety, agitation, and/or decreased mental status

Objective	
Vital signs	Check for tachycardia, bradycardia, arrhythmia, hypotension, or tachypnea
HEENT (head and neck, eyes, ears, nose, and throat)	Look for angioedema, rhinorrhea, and sneezing
Neck	Listen for stridor
Lungs	Auscultate for wheezing or decreased breath sounds
Abdomen	Note tenderness, diarrhea, emesis, or hyperactive bowel sounds
Extremities	Note if extremities are cold, clammy, cyanotic, or limp; if patient fell, check for fractures, abrasions, or lacerations
Skin	Examine skin carefully for erythema, pallor, or urticaria

Continued on next page

APPENDIX 8 *(Continued)*

Assessment	
Local reaction	Skin changes only
Generalized non–life-threatening reaction	Pruritus, urticaria, nausea, vomiting, dizziness
Generalized life-threatening reaction	Wheezing or asthma, dysphagia with tongue swelling, hoarseness with laryngeal edema, hypotension, syncope, seizures, shock, coma, or cardiac arrest
Plan	**Activate postimmunization anaphylaxis P&P**
	Consult/refer with physician: all cases of anaphylaxis

Adapted from National Health and Medical Research Council (Australia)[4]; Centers for Disease Control and Prevention[5,78]; Beck[71]; Andersen MM and Ronne T[72]; Bochner BS and Lichtenstein LM[73]; Mackan[74,75]; Barbarito C[76]; Braun MM et al.[77]

Author's Note: This is a **sample protocol only** for use in a medical emergency. Prior to its implementation, the travel clinic medical director and risk manager should review this policy and revise as needed. To complete this protocol, the medical director should attach an emergency medication list with recommended dosages for adults and children.

Chapter 5

YELLOW FEVER VACCINE

Thomas P. Monath

Yellow fever (YF) is the prototype member of the Flaviviridae (L *flavus* yellow), which includes approximately 70 single-stranded ribonucleic acid (RNA) viruses, most of which are transmitted by mosquitoes or ticks. The disease caused by the YF virus is the original "viral hemorrhagic fever"—a systemic illness characterized by high viremia; hepatic, renal, and myocardial injury; hemorrhage; and high lethality. Yellow fever virus is a single species defined by serologic (neutralization) methods, and its strains belong to at least seven distinct genotypes (two in South America and five in Africa) defined by nucleotide sequencing.[1] The genomic data support the conclusion that the YF virus evolved in Africa.

Yellow fever was recognized as a major epidemic disease in the eighteenth century in colonial settlements in the Americas and West Africa, caused enormous morbidity in the nineteenth century, and was substantially controlled during the first half of the twentieth. Two events contributed to control of the disease: (1) the discovery by Walter Reed and colleagues[2] in 1900 that the etiologic agent was transmitted by *Aedes aegypti* mosquitoes, leading to vector control; and (2) the development of vaccines in the 1930s.

Yellow fever is a zoonotic disease that cannot be eradicated. Although vector control was useful as a means of combating urban (*A. aegypti*–borne) YF in the first half of the previous century, it is less useful today and has no place in the control of sylvatic or jungle YF. Vaccination is the most effective weapon for prevention and control. Because the virus circulates in nature independently of humans, a sustained program of vaccination of populations inhabiting endemic regions is required, and persons traveling to these regions must be immunized.

Vaccine development proceeded only after isolation of the etiologic agent in 1927 by independent research groups at the Pasteur Institute in Senegal and the Rockefeller Commission laboratory in Nigeria. Beginning in 1928, attempts were made to produce an inactivated vaccine but the lack of a method for production of high-titer viral antigen precluded success. The first successful live vaccine was prepared from the 1927 French strain, which was attenuated by serial passages in mouse brain. The mouse brain–adapted virus lost its ability to produced lethal viscerotropic infection (hepatitis) but had enhanced neurotropism. Small trials involving humans were conducted in 1931 to 1932, and field trials were initiated in 1934.[3,4] Workers at the Rockefeller Foundation believed the French neurotropic strain to be insufficiently attenuated. They developed a live vaccine (17D) attenuated by serial passage of the Asibi strain in cell cultures prepared from mouse tissues and, subsequently, embryonated chicken eggs. The 17D strain was also incapable of producing hepatitis but was significantly less neurovirulent than the French vaccine. In 1936, the 17D vaccine was tested in a small number of human volunteers in New York, followed by field trials in Brazil in 1937.[5,6]

During the 1940s, control of YF by wide-scale vaccination with the French strain was undertaken in francophone Africa and with the 17D vaccine in Brazil. The French neurotropic vaccine had the advantage that it was relatively thermostable and, having a high virus titer, could be delivered by scarification, the same method employed for smallpox vaccination. The 17D vaccine was less stable and required injection by syringe and needle because immunogenicity by the scarification method was poor. For a historic account of early vaccine development and testing see Monath.[7]

During the 1950s and 1960s, increasing concern about the safety of the French neurotropic vaccine followed recognition of a high incidence of postvaccinal encephalitis in children. Manufacture and use of this vaccine finally ceased in 1982. In contrast, the17D vaccine came into routine use for protection of persons traveling to and living in the endemic areas. More than 400 million persons have received YF 17D, which is widely regarded as the most effective viral vaccine ever developed as a single dose provides lifelong immunity. Nevertheless, availability of the 17D vaccine has not ensured adequate control of the disease because of low vaccination coverage in many countries and continued exposure of unvaccinated travelers. Indeed, within the past 15 years, there has been a resurgence of YF and more frequent reports of disease among unvaccinated tourists.[8–10] Reinvasion of South America by *A. aegypti* (the mosquito responsible for urban interhuman transmission of the virus), increasing human population density, movement of people in and out of endemic regions, and the rise in air travel combine to increase the risk of urban epidemics in the Americas and to introduce of YF into other susceptible regions, particularly Asia.

ETIOLOGIC AGENT, REPLICATION, AND CELL PATHOLOGY

Flaviviruses, exemplified by YF virus, are small (50 nm), positive-sense, single-stranded RNA viruses. Flaviviruses enter cells by attachment to as yet undefined receptors. The viral nucleocapsid is released from lysosomal vesicles into the cytoplasm by fusion with the endosomal membrane, resulting in uncoating of the RNA, which enters the cytoplasm. The positive-sense RNA is transcribed, producing complementary negative RNA strands that serve as templates for progeny plus-strands. The RNA encodes replicase, helicase, and other enzymes required for continued replication; protease involved in post-translational processing of viral proteins; and structural proteins for assembling new virus particles. Assembly of virus particles occurs in close association with the endoplasmic reticulum (ER). Virus infection proceeds rapidly, with intracellular virus reaching maximal levels in approximately 24 hours. The most prominent morphologic changes in the infected cell are proliferation and hypertrophy of the ER to accommodate accumulating virions. Large cytoplasmic vacuoles containing virus particles appear. As the cell disintegrates, the cytoplasm becomes rarified and, subsequently, condensed. Virus particles are released from infected cells by exocytosis from plasma membranes or by cell rupture when cytopathic effects are at a very advanced stage.

Morphologic and biochemical studies suggest that flaviviruses, including YF, induce cell death by apoptosis rather than by necrosis. Thus, flavivirus-infected cells are characterized by shrinkage and condensation of cytoplasmic and nuclear material, surface membrane blebbing, and fragmentation of cellular deoxyribonucleic acid(DNA). YF virus–induced apoptotic cell death of human hepatocyte cells has been demonstrated in cell culture.[11,12] Apoptosis represents a protective mechanism whereby the host eliminates virus-infected cells, and the propensity of YF virus to program cell death only at a late stage of the infection might explain the severe damage to liver tissue in human infection.

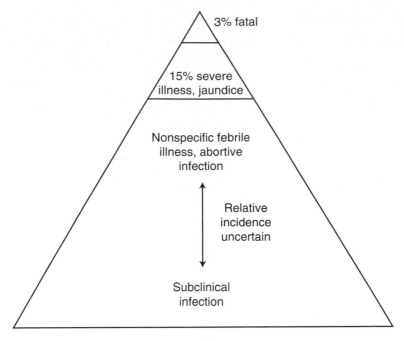

Figure 5-1. "Iceberg" phenomenon applied to yellow fever disease expression in the human host showing that pathognomonic infection with hepatitis and multiple organ failure occur in a minority of cases (~15%) and that death occurs in only about 3% of individuals infected.

THE DISEASE SYNDROME

Infection with YF virus causes a systemic disease with fever, jaundice, and renal dysfunction in approximately 15% and death in approximately 3% of persons infected (Figure 5-1). Abortive infections with nonspecific, grippe-like symptoms (headache, malaise, myalgia) are common, and many infections escape medical attention or are truly subclinical. This variability in response is associated with differences in both the pathogenicity of virus strains and genetic and acquired host resistance factors, especially cross-protective immunity to related flaviviruses.

After an incubation period of 3 to 6 days, the onset of illness is abrupt, with fever, chills, and headache. Three stages of disease have been described in humans.[13–15] The initial period of infection lasts several days, during which virus is present in blood and the patient can serve as the source of infection for blood-feeding mosquitoes. There are few data on the height of viremia, but, in one report, viremia peaked on day 2 or 3 after onset of illness at a titer of 5.6 $\log_{10}$ mouse intracerebral (IC) median lethal doses (LD_{50})/mL (approx 7 $\log_{10}$ plaque-forming units [PFU]/mL).[16]

Symptoms during the period of infection include generalized malaise, headache, photophobia, lumbosacral pain, generalized myalgia, nausea, vomiting, restlessness, irritability, and dizziness. On physical examination, the patient appears acutely ill, with hyperemia of the skin, conjunctival injection, and tenderness and enlargement of the liver. The heart rate can be slow relative to the height of the fever (Faget's sign). The average fever is 102 to 103°F and lasts 3.3 days, but the temperature can reach 105°F, portending a fatal outcome. During this phase of illness, clinical laboratory tests show leukopenia, relative neutropenia, and minimal elevations of serum aspartate transaminase (AST) and alanine transaminase (ALT).

The period of infection is sometimes followed by a period of remission, with abatement of fever and symptoms lasting a few hours or up to 2 days. In cases of abortive infection, the patient can recover rapidly at this stage.

The third stage, the period of intoxication, begins on the third to sixth day after onset. Symptoms and signs include fever, severe asthenia, nausea, vomiting, epigastric pain, jaundice, oliguria, cardiovascular instability, and hemorrhage. Virus disappears from the blood, and antibodies appear. Initially, the liver is typically enlarged and tender, and the patient becomes jaundiced. In contrast to other viral hepatitides, AST levels exceed ALT, presumably because of viral injury to myocardium and skeletal muscle. The rise in serum transaminases and bilirubin is proportional to disease severity, and very high levels carry a poor prognosis.[17,18]

Renal dysfunction is characterized by albuminuria, oliguria, and azotemia. Urinalysis shows elevated albumin, microscopic hematuria, and proteinaceous casts. Unlike many other viral hemorrhagic fevers, edema, ascites, and pleural effusion are not often clinically apparent despite the severity of renal failure, but most patients have not received intensive care, which can result in fluid overload.

The most dramatic hemorrhagic manifestation is coffee-grounds hematemesis ("black vomit"), but melena, hematuria, metrorrhagia, petechiae, ecchymoses, bleeding from the gums and nose, and prolonged bleeding at needle puncture sites are also common. Thrombocytopenia and prolonged clotting, prothrombin, and partial thromboplastin times reflect the bleeding diathesis.

Electrocardiograpic abnormalities include sinus bradycardia without conduction defects and ST-T changes, particularly elevated T waves, reflecting virus replication and damage to the myocardium.[19] Bradycardia can contribute to the physiologic decompensation associated with hypotension, reduced perfusion, and metabolic acidosis in severe cases. Acute cardiac enlargement indicative of heart failure can occur during the course of YF infection.[13]

Central nervous system (CNS) signs include delirium, agitation, convulsions, stupor, and coma. In severe cases, the cerebrospinal fluid is under increased pressure and might contain elevated protein without inflammatory cells. In patients dying of YF, CNS signs appear to result from cerebral edema or metabolic factors, based on the virtual absence of inflammatory changes in brain tissue. Pathologic changes include petechiae, perivascular hemorrhages, and edema.[20]

The critical phase of the illness occurs between the fifth and tenth day, at which point the patient either dies or rapidly recovers. The terminal illness is characterized by hypotension, shock, hemorrhage, hepatorenal failure, hypothermia, and metabolic acidosis. Case fatality rates in patients with jaundice during recent outbreaks approximated 20%, a rate consistent with historic accounts.[21,22] Severity of illness and case fatality rates are highest in infants and the elderly.[14,23] The case fatality rate in travelers who have acquired the disease is 80%. The lower case fatality in field studies might reflect the inclusion of milder cases or dilution of the denominator by illnesses with jaundice other than YF. A corollary is that milder cases in travelers are escaping medical attention.

Pathology and Pathogenesis

The virus is introduced into the epidermis or dermis in saliva from a blood-feeding mosquito and is disseminated via lymphatic channels to the draining lymph nodes. Virus is released into the bloodstream, seeding multiple organized tissues, including the reticuloendothelial system. These tissues in turn release virus, causing a secondary viremia with subsequent involvement of other target tissues such as the kidney and heart. The cells involved in early infection at the cutaneous portal of entry are unknown, but observations on dengue viruses suggest that dendritic cells play a primary role.[24] Evidence from experimental animals also suggests that lymphoid cells are important targets for YF virus replication.[25,26] It was concluded that Kupffer's cells play a critical role in innate resistance, initially protecting the hepatocyte from YF infection. In the rhesus monkey model, liver biopsies revealed only Kupffer's cell degeneration, without pathologic changes in hepatocytes or elevated liver enzymes until the last 24 hours of life, at which point coagulative degeneration began and chemical dysfunction occurred.[26]

YF virus produces two distinct patterns of infection: viscerotropism and neurotropism. Viscerotropism refers to the ability of YF virus to infect and damage extraneural organs, including the liver, spleen, heart, and kidneys, whereas neurotropism refers to the ability of the virus to infect the brain and cause encephalitis. Wild-type YF virus strains are viscerotropic in monkeys and humans but are neurotropic when inoculated intracerebrally in rodents. Wild-type YF virus inoculated directly into the brain of a monkey causes viscerotropic infection and death from hepatorenal failure and shock. As would be expected from the latter observation, true encephalitis due to viral invasion of the brain (as opposed to metabolic encephalopathy) is very rarely seen in humans following natural infection. However, as will be discussed later, 17D vaccine, which has virtually lost its ability to induce viscerotropic infection in monkeys and humans, retains its neurotropism for rodents. The 17D vaccine virus causes mild encephalitis in monkeys after intracerebral infection and occasionally invades the brain and causes encephalitis in humans.

There are five major pathologic features induced by YF virus in the liver: (1) eosinophilic degeneration (apoptosis) of hepatocytes and Kupffer's cells; (2) midzonal hepatocellular necrosis; (3) absence of inflammation; (4) microvesicular fatty changes; and (5) retention of the reticulin structure, with return to normal histology without cirrhosis in survivors. A unique feature of YF is the predominance of hepatocellular damage in the midzone (zone 2) of the liver lobule, with sparing of cells around the central vein and portal tracts (Figure 5-2). The reason for this peculiar distribution of hepatic cell injury is unknown. YF virus antigen and RNA have been observed principally in hepatocytes in the midzone, suggesting a predilection of these cells for virus replication.[27]

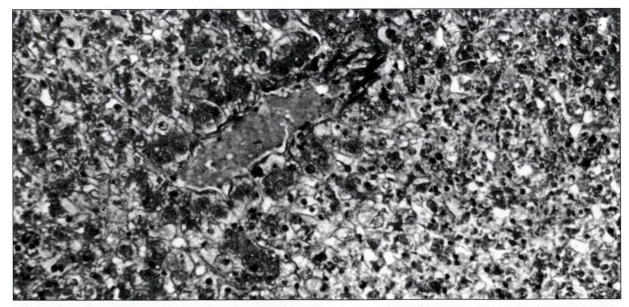

Figure 5-2. Histopathologic changes in the liver of a fatal case of yellow fever, showing midzonal necraptosis, eosinophilic degeneration of hepatocytes, microsteatosis, and virtual absence of inflammation (hematoxylin and eosin, × 500 original magnification).

The spleen and lymph nodes undergo significant changes in YF infection, with depletion of lympho-cytes in the germinal centers of spleen, lymph nodes, tonsils, and Peyer's patches and the appearance of large histiocytic cells accumulating in the splenic follicles.

Renal damage is characterized by eosinophilic degeneration and microvesicular fatty change of the renal tubular epithelium without inflammation, analogous to the injury to the liver. Antigen is demon-strable by immunocytochemistry in the renal tubular cells of fatal human cases.[28] Glomerular lesions include cloudy swelling and degeneration of cells lining Bowman's capsule, contributing to the severe albuminuria seen in YF. The pathogenesis of renal injury is poorly understood. In one study of experi-mental YF in rhesus monkeys, the disturbance in function was prerenal (characterized by normal his-tology on needle biopsy, oliguria, and diminished urine Na^+ excretion, indicative of reduced renal perfusion) until the terminal 24 hours of life.[26] During the terminal phase of infection, oliguria was accompanied by proteinuria, cylindruria, azotemia, acidosis, hyperkalemia, and shock and pathologic changes of severe tubular necrosis. The observations in this model suggested that hemodynamic factors (renal ischemia) contribute significantly to renal failure.

Myocardial cells also undergo apoptotic changes and microsteatosis without a significant inflammatory response. These effects are typically patchy in distribution. Lesions have been noted in the sinoauricular node and bundle of His, explaining the paradoxic bradycardia (Faget's sign).[28] Antigen is found by immunocytochemistry, indicating direct viral damage to myocardial fibers. As in the liver, the reticulin structure is preserved, and no fibrosis occurs after recovery.

Damage to and plasma leakage from capillaries is a characteristic of YF and many viral hemorrhagic fevers. Petechial hemorrhages occur in skin and mucosae; edema of the brain and other organs, particu-larly around blood vessels, is seen on microscopic examination; and cardiovascular shock occur during the terminal stage of illness. The pathogenesis of vascular leakage in YF is unknown. By analogy to dengue hemorrhagic fever, which is much better studied, cytokine dysregulation, particularly activation of NF-κ B and increases in expression of proinflammatory cytokines, especially interleukin-8 (IL-8), is suspected to cause plasma leakage.[29] Endothelial cells are hypothesized to play a central role in the pathogenesis.[30] Infection of endothelial cells and monocyte/macrophages leading to a cascade of events characterized by the release of cytokines and oxygen free radicals can trigger a series of events, including coagulation, fibrinolysis, plasma leakage, and hypotension. Although cytokine dysregulation and endothelial infection have not been evaluated in YF, it is likely that they play a role in pathogenesis of the infection. Changes in tissue concentrations of water and electrolytes in various compartments of the CNS have been described in experimental YF, in particular intracellular dehydration of thr medulla, cerebellum, and spinal cord.[31] These effects, plus liver failure, probably contribute to the encephalopathy. Elevated plasma ammonia levels have been noted in one human case.[32]

Experimental studies in monkeys have revealed an array of acid-base and electrolyte disturbances, principally occurring in the last 24 to 48 hours of life.[26,31] Significant findings include increased plasma and total circulatory K^+; increased extracellular water, Na^+, and K^+, reflecting modification of cell trans-port mechanisms; and increased cell membrane permeability. These effects are likely the result of both direct YF viral injury and poor perfusion resulting in hypoxia. During the preterminal period, a decrease in arterial partial pressure of carbon dioxide (P_{CO_2}) occurs (reflecting respiratory compensation for metabolic acidosis). In the last few hours of life, severe metabolic and a rise in P_{CO_2} (combined respiratory and metabolic acidosis) accompany hypotension and shock.

Few human patients have been studied with respect to coagulation defects.[33–35] Global reduction in clotting factors suggests that reduced synthesis of clotting factors by the liver is probably the preeminent explanation for abnormal bleeding, although disseminated intravascular coagulation might also play a role. Similar conclusions were reached in studies involving experimental YF infections of monkeys, which also show global coagulation abnormalities.[26,36] Evidence for consumption coagulopathy was not striking, as fibrin split products were modestly elevated and platelet counts were only mildly depressed, and heparin therapy did not change the outcome.[36] It can be concluded that the preeminent contributor to bleeding in YF is decreased synthesis of clotting factors by the diseased liver.

Immune Response to Infection

In persons undergoing primary infection with YF virus, nonspecific innate immune responses provide the first line of defense against infection. Because approximately 1 in 7 persons infected with YF virus develops clinical illness, it is clear that the innate immune system usually protects the host.[21] Natural killer (NK) cells and type 1 interferons control the early phase of virus replication before the appearance of specific cytotoxic T cells and antibodies. Rhesus monkeys treated with an interferon inducer before or shortly after infection were protected against lethal YF.[37] During the early phase of infection with YF virus, elevated levels of the interferon-dependent enzyme, 2′5′-oligoadenylate synthetase occur in T and B cells.[38] Recent studies indicate that the 2′5′-oligoadenylate synthetase system is under genetic control, at least in the mouse.[39] This or another genetically controlled host resistance mechanism could be important in determining the susceptibility of humans to YF virus.

Interferon-γ activates NK cells and CD14+ monocyte/macrophages, as well as adaptive immune responses, T helper cell 1 (Th 1)–dependent immunoglobulin synthesis, and cytotoxic T lymphocytes.[40,41] Treatment with interferon-γ resulted in partial protection of monkeys against YF, and interferon-γ knockout mice had reduced YF viral clearance compared to control mice.[42,43]

Infection with YF virus or vaccine is followed by a rapid, immunologically specific (adaptive) immune response. Neutralizing antibodies, cytolytic antibodies against viral proteins on the surface of infected cells, antibody-dependent cell-mediated cytotoxicity (ADCC), and cytotoxic T cells mediate clearance of primary infection. Neutralizing antibodies appear 7 to 8 days after YF virus infection (4 to 5 days after disease onset).[13] Virus-specific cellular immune responses probably occur earlier than antibodies. Thus, the appearance of adaptive immunity coincides with the clinical crisis and viscerotropic injury during the period of intoxication, suggesting the possibility that immune clearance (virus-antibody complexes, complement activation, cytotoxic T lymphocyte [CTL]-mediated clearance of infected cells, and release of cytokines) might contribute to pathogenesis, particularly capillary leak, hemorrhage, and shock. Although there is no evidence that immunopathologic mechanisms occur in YF, this is an area for future investigation.

Individuals with prior immunity to heterologous flaviviruses develop broadly cross-reactive antibody responses following infection with YF virus. There is ample evidence that heterologous flavivirus immunity cross-protects against YF. For example, monkeys previously infected with dengue virus were protected against YF virus challenge, whereas passive transfer of the dengue antibody had no effect, suggesting that cellular immunity was responsible.[44,45] Monkeys immunized with the African flaviviruses (Zika and Wesselsbron) were protected against YF virus challenge.[46] Epidemiologic studies also found that persons with immunity to unspecified African flaviviruses experienced a lower incidence of YF disease than those with primary YF infections.[21] These observations indicate that prior flavivirus immunity protects against rather than enhance of YF infection.

Neutralizing antibodies are directed principally against the envelope (E) glycoprotein of YF virus, which contains redundant neutralizing epitopes. In the vaccinated or naturally immune host, preformed antibodies against the E glycoprotein rapidly neutralize virus inoculated in the saliva of a blood-feeding infected mosquito. Antibodies are also generated against the nonstructural protein NS1 that is present in and is secreted from infected cells. Animals actively immunized with YF NS1 protein or passively immunized with anti-NS1 antibody were protected against YF challenge.[47–50] Anti-NS1 antibodies apparently work by complement-mediated cytolysis and clearance of infected cells. It is presently uncertain whether anti-NS1 contributes to protective immunity against re-infection in humans or whether it plays a role in virus clearance and recovery from infection, or both.

Cytotoxic T lymphocytes mediate killing of flavivirus-infected cells and contribute to viral clearance during primary infection. There are no studies on human CTL responses to wild-type YF, and only four human subjects vaccinated with YF 17D have been studied (see "Immune Responses to YF Vaccine").[51]

Antibody-dependent enhancement (ADE) of YF virus replication has been demonstrated in vitro.[52] ADE is mediated by non-neutralizing antibodies that bind virus and increase the uptake of infectious virus-antibody complexes via Fc-γ receptor–bearing monocyte/macrophages. Some evidence has been obtained for ADE in vivo by YF antibodies. Subjects previously vaccinated against YF had higher antibody responses to a live dengue vaccine, suggesting that prior immunity had increased replication of the dengue virus.[53,54] Similarly, subjects with prior YF immunity who were given a live chimeric YF/Japanese encephalitis or YF/dengue vaccine had higher viremias than naive subjects.[55] Based on these observations, it seems that YF immunity enhances disease expression by dengue viruses (dengue hemorrhagic fever). The natural experiment is underway in South America, where dengue viruses have recently invaded the region endemic for YF.

Host Factors Affecting Susceptibility

YF appears to be more severe in infants and in the elderly.[14,16,23,56] The disease affects males more frequently than females. The gender difference in South America is determined by occupational exposure to infected mosquitoes, but an epidemiologic explanation for the excess of male cases in Africa is lacking. In a large clinical trial of YF 17D vaccines, the antibody response was statistically significantly higher in males than in females.[57] Moreover, the incidence of postvaccinal encephalitis caused by the French neurotropic vaccine and 17D vaccine (see "Vaccine Safety") is higher in males than in females, suggesting that males undergo more active replication of YF viruses than females.[58]

The high prevalence of human immunodeficiency virus (HIV) in YF-endemic areas represents a potential risk factor for increased severity of disease expression and YF 17D vaccine–associated adverse events.

Diagnosis

The textbook picture of triphasic acute illness, jaundice, relative bradycardia, leukopenia, albuminuria, oliguria, and black vomit in an unvaccinated patient with a history of residence or recent travel to a YF-endemic zone poses little difficulty in clinical diagnosis. Other diseases that mimic the clinical presentation of YF include leptospirosis and louse-borne relapsing fever (*Borrelia recurrentis*), which are also characterized by jaundice, hemorrhage, disseminated intravascular coagulation, and a high case fatality rate. Other diseases that must be differentiated clinically from YF include fulminant viral hepatitis; Q fever; West Nile virus hepatitis; Rift Valley fever; typhoid; malaria; dengue hemorrhagic fever; Lassa, Marburg, and Ebola virus diseases; South American hemorrhagic fevers; and Crimean-Congo hemorrhagic fever. Mild YF can resemble many other arboviral infections and influenza, which are characterized by fever, headache, malaise, and myalgias.

Specific diagnosis is made by the detection of virus, viral RNA, or viral antigen in blood or by serology. Virus is readily isolated from blood during the first 4 days after onset. Virus isolation is accomplished by intracerebral inoculation of suckling mice, by intrathoracic inoculation of mosquitoes followed by immunofluorescence staining to detect antigen, or by inoculation of mosquito or mammalian cell cultures. The last show cytopathic effects (CPE), and the virus is identified by immunostaining or reverse transcriptase polymerase chain reaction (RT-PCR).[59] The RT-PCR method requires further field testing but will undoubtedly gain acceptance for rapid identification of virus in the serum of patients.

Examination of liver reveals the typical pathoanatomic features of YF (see "Pathology and Pathogenesis"). Liver biopsy during life should *never* be performed as fatal hemorrhage can result. Histopathologic diagnosis can be difficult in patients who die after the second week of illness. However, definitive diagnosis can be made by immunocytochemical staining for YF antigen in the liver, heart, or kidney, even in specimens stored for years at ambient temperature.[27,60–62]

Serologic methods are useful for the diagnosis of recent infection and to establish the status of immunity to YF. Older methods include the hemagglutination inhibition (HI), complement-fixation (CF), indirect immunofluorescence assay (IFA), and neutralization tests. CF antibodies are found in the second week after onset and wane rapidly, so that a positive test in a single sample provides a presumptive diagnosis.[63,64] The immunogloulin (Ig)M-capture enzyme-linked immunosorbent assay (ELISA) has largely replaced the CF test for serologic diagnosis of YF.[65] Confirmation of the diagnosis is made by a rise in antibody titer, measured by IgM-capture ELISA or other methods, between paired acute and convalescent samples or a fall in titer between early and late convalescent samples. The specificity of all test methods, including IgM ELISA, is high in primary infections. However, cross-reactions complicate the diagnosis of YF by all serologic methods, particularly in Africa where multiple flaviviruses cocirculate. The neutralization test provides the most specific diagnosis, and neutralizing antibodies are more durable than those measured by other methods. The phenomenon of "original antigenic sin" might also complicate serologic investigations. Individuals with prior heterologous flavivirus infection who develop YF might have higher responses to the original virus, and those with prior YF infection or vaccination subsequently infected with another flavivirus can have higher responses to YF.[66]

TREATMENT

There is no specific treatment for YF. Passive antibody and interferon do not have a role in treatment of the disease, and no antiviral drug has shown promise. It was widely held by nineteenth-century physicians that severely ill patients did poorly when moved to hospital. The fragility of YF patients should be considered in cases where long-range medical evacuation is contemplated. Nevertheless, intensive care might be necessary to manage hypotension, metabolic acidosis, bleeding, renal failure, and secondary bacterial infections. (See Monath for recommendations of an expert panel on the subject of supportive care for patients with YF.[15])

Orthoptic liver transplantation would appear to be a reasonable clinical intervention in fulminant hepatitis caused by YF. It is unlikely that the transplanted liver would become infected because the patient should already be mounting an immune response at the time transplantation would be required, but Ig also could be administered at the time of transplantation. Commercial lots of intravenous globulin contain titers of neutralizing antibody (See "Passive and Passive-Active Immunization"). Extracorporeal support systems (in particular the Molecular Adsorbent Recirculating System,[67] MARS) represent a possible approach to sustain life while the liver recovers. To date, neither liver transplantation nor MARS has been tested in patients with YF.[68]

EPIDEMIOLOGY

Yellow fever occurs in tropical South America and sub-Saharan Africa (Figure 5-3). Current YF activity is published in the World Health Organization (WHO) Weekly Epidemiological Record (WER) and by the Centers for Disease Control and Prevention, Division of Quarantine at <www.cdc.gov>. However, it should be noted that YF transmission in the zoonotic cycle occurs in areas that are silent with respect to official reports, in part because the indigenous human population has a high level of immunity. In addition, surveillance is poor in many areas, and human cases are often missed. Thus, the official reports do not accurately reflect the risk to unimmunized travelers. Where specific investigations have been undertaken, the ratio of cases to official notifications varies between 1 and approximately 300:1.

Figure 5-3. Yellow fever–endemic zone (shaded) in South America and Africa. Adapted from the Centers for Disease Control.[180]

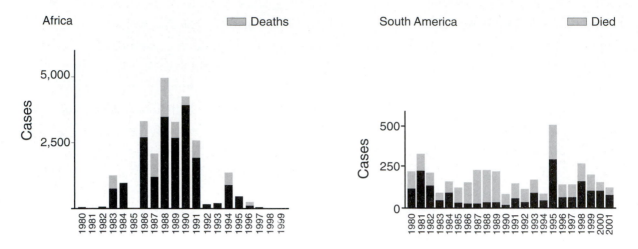

Figure 5-4. Incidence of YF cases and deaths in Africa and South America notified to the World Health Organization since 1980. The years 1986 to 1991 represented a period of major epidemic activity in Africa and 1995 to 2000 a period of intensified jungle YF virus activity in South America.

Between 1985 and 1999, 25,846 cases and 7,118 deaths were officially reported to WHO. The decade between 1986 and 1995 reflected a dramatic increase compared with previous and subsequent reporting intervals (Figure 5-4).[8] In Africa, which accounted for 89% of the cases (22,952), the annual incidence varied between 0 and 5,000 cases. Africa reported 5,357 deaths for a case fatality rate of 23%. The epidemiology in Africa reflects periodic intense epidemic activity, generally with interhuman transmission by mosquito vectors, including *A. aegypti*; high human population density and low vaccine coverage are contributing factors. Recent outbreaks have occurred in Benin (1996–97), Cameroon (1990), Ivory Coast Republic (2001), Gabon (1994–95), Ghana (1993–94, 1996), Guinea (2001), Kenya (1992), Liberia (1995, 1998, 2000–01), Nigeria (1986–91,1994–95), and Senegal (1995–96, 2002). In contrast, South America has a relatively constant and low incidence of reported disease. Between 1985 and 1999, 2,894 cases and 1,761 deaths were reported (mean, 193 cases; range 88–515 cases/year). The lower incidence of YF in South America is due to transmission by enzootic vectors (principally from monkey to human), low densities of vectors, monkey and human hosts, and relatively high vaccination coverage. The higher case fatality rate (61%) in South America probably reflects surveillance based on death reports and the postmortem examination of livers, although it remains possible that the South American genotype(s) are more virulent than those in Africa.[69,70]

The ratio of illness to infection has been estimated to be 1.7:4.[21] Because illness was defined by a case definition that included jaundice, the ratio would be lower if mild cases were included.

The burden of YF in Africa has been estimated almost entirely in terms of epidemic disease, and only limited attempts have been made to define the incidence of *endemic* YF infection. In one analysis, the incidence of YF infection with jaundice was estimated at 1.1 to 2.4 per 1,000 population and the death rate between 0.2 and 0.5 per 1,000.[71] These rates are 25- to 50-fold lower than those during epidemics and are below the threshold of detection by existing surveillance systems. It is likely that endemic YF activity varies considerably from year to year but that it causes thousands of unrecorded deaths annually in West Africa. This provides a strong rationale for preventive immunization and illustrates the risk to unvaccinated travelers.

Table 5-1. **Reported Yellow Fever Cases in Travelers, 1979 to 2002**

Year	Age/Gender	Vaccinated	Residence	Travel/Exposure	Fatal?	Reference
1979	42/M 25/M	No	France	Senegal	Yes	Bendersky et al[34]
1985	27/F	No	Netherlands	Guinea-Bissau, The Gambia, Senegal	No	WHO, 1986[238]
1988	37/F	Yes	Spain	Niger, Mali, Burkina Faso, Mauritania	No	Nolla-Salas et al[170]
1996	53/M	No	Switzerland	Brazil	Yes	Barros and Boecken[234]
1996	42/M	No	United States	Brazil	Yes	McFarland et al[236]
1999	40/M	No	Germany	Ivory Coast	Yes	WHO, 2000[239]
1999	48/M	No	United States	Venezuela	Yes	WHO, 2000[239]
2001	47/F	No	Belgium	The Gambia	Yes	Colebunders et al[32]
2002	47/M	No	United States	Brazil	Yes	Hall et al[235]

Yellow Fever in Travelers

Prior to World War II, when vaccines came into routine use, YF was a major threat to travelers and expatriates living in the tropics. Table 5-1 lists published cases in travelers between 1979 and 1992. Since 1996, there have been six recorded cases in travelers, all fatal. Two cases in 1996 occurred in unvaccinated American and Swiss tourists who had visited jungle areas near Manaus, Brazil. In August 1999, a 40-year-old unvaccinated man became ill in Germany after a visit to the Ivory Coast and died 4 days later. In September 1999, a 48-year-old male became ill in southern Venezuela, returned home to California on the fifth day of illness, and died in hospital on the eleventh day. In November 2001, an unvaccinated Belgian tourist to The Gambia returned home while ill and died in hospital, and in March 2002, an unvaccinated US citizen acquired YF while on a fishing trip on the Rio Negro (Amazonas, Brazil) and died in a Texas hospital.

The risk of acquiring YF is determined by geographic location, season, duration of travel, activities that lead to exposure to mosquito bites, and the intensity of YF virus transmission occurring at the time. Although reported cases of human disease are an important guide to YF activity, they can be absent because of a high level of immunity in the resident population or lack of detection by surveillance. Based on estimates of attack rates (see "Epidemiology"), it has been estimated that an unimmunized traveler to an epidemic area would have risks of YF illness and death of 1:267 and 1:1,333, respectively, for a 2-week trip.[72]

As noted above, the incidence of disease caused by endemic YF transmission in Africa is below the threshold of detection by surveillance. Epidemiologic silence might provide a sense of false security and lead to travel without the benefit of vaccination. The recent case in a Belgian traveler who spent a week in The Gambia is a case in point.[32] There was no evidence of YF transmission at the time and a high prevalence of vaccine immunes in the local population. In unvaccinated travelers to these areas, the risk of YF illness can be estimated at 1:1,000 per month and death at 1:5,000 (1:2,000 risk of illness and 1:10,000 risk of YF death for a typical 2-week journey), but these statistics vary considerably with the season.[72] These estimates, which are based on risk to local residents, probably overestimate the risk to travelers who take precautions against mosquito bites and have less outdoor exposure than the indigenous population has.

In South America, the incidence of disease is lower than in Africa. The risk of illness and death is probably 10 times lower than in rural West Africa, that is, 1:20,000 for illness and 1:100,000 for death per 2-week journey but varies greatly with specific location and season.[72] As in Africa, virus transmission is often silent, although sometimes deaths of howler monkeys signal an ongoing YF epizootic. The low reported incidence of YF has diminished concern among travelers. In Brazil, for example, where the majority of the population lives in coastal regions outside the endemic zone, unimmunized recreational or vocational travelers to the interior are the usual victims of YF. Four of the six cases among travelers from the United States and Europe between 1996 and 2002 were exposed in South America (see Table 5-1).

YF virus transmission depends on mosquito vectors, which, in turn, are highly dependent on rainfall because juvenile stages in the mosquito life cycle are exclusively aquatic. In South America, the incidence of YF is highest during months of high rainfall, humidity, and temperature (January to May, peak incidence February and March), corresponding to the activity of *Haemagogus* mosquitoes, which breed in tree holes. In the savanna zone of West Africa, cases appear during the middle of the rainy season (August) and peak during the early dry season (October), corresponding to the period of maximum longevity of sylvatic mosquito vectors.[73] *Aedes aegypti* breeds in receptacles used by humans for water storage and is thus less dependent on rainfall. Where this mosquito is involved in virus transmission, YF can occur in the dry season in both rural areas and heavily settled urbanizations. Thus, season is only a partially reliable guide to determine the risk of exposure and to make decisions on the need for immunization of travelers. Yellow fever vectors are diurnal biters (as opposed to malaria vectors, which bite principally at night).

The decision to vaccinate a traveler should be based principally on an assessment of the risk of exposure to mosquitoes transmitting YF virus, which, in turn, depends on knowledge of geography and epidemiology. Depending on the level of risk, the decision might be in favor of vaccination, offering vaccination with an explanation that the risk is low or uncertain, or offering advice that the risk of exposure is too low to warrant vaccination as long as the travel plan does not change but that the traveler should take sensible precautions against mosquito bites. The International Health Regulations and requirements for a valid certificate of immunization against YF must also be considered.[74] Finally, the risk of vaccine-associated severe adverse events, based on precautions described below (Contraindications and Precautions), advanced age, gender, and underlying medical conditions should be taken into consideration. As a guide, the algorithm provided in Figure 5-5, might be useful.

Transmission Cycles

The primary enzootic transmission cycle involves monkeys and tree hole–breeding mosquitoes in the rainforest ecologic zone (*Haemagogus* spp. in South America and *A. africanus* in Africa) (Figure 5-6). The density of vectors and human inhabitants is relatively low, and cases of "jungle YF" in persons entering or working in forested areas occur in a sporadic fashion at low incidence. The true reservoir of YF virus is the mosquito, and virus is maintained by vertical transmission through the mosquito ova across the dry season, when the activity of adult mosquitoes is reduced or ceases. During periods of mosquito activity, YF virus is amplified by horizontal transmission in a cycle involving nonhuman primates.

Many species of nonhuman primates are susceptible to YF infection.[74–76] The majority of African species have viremic infections sufficient to infect mosquitoes without developing clinical illness, whereas some neotropic species (eg, howler monkeys) develop lethal infections.

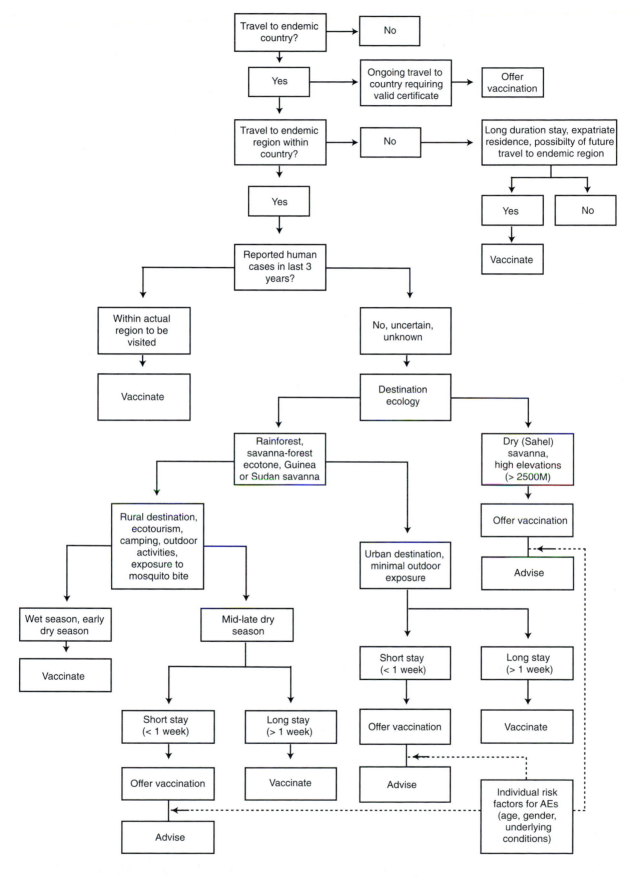

Figure 5-5. Algorithm for determining whether to vaccinate the traveler. AE = adverse effects.

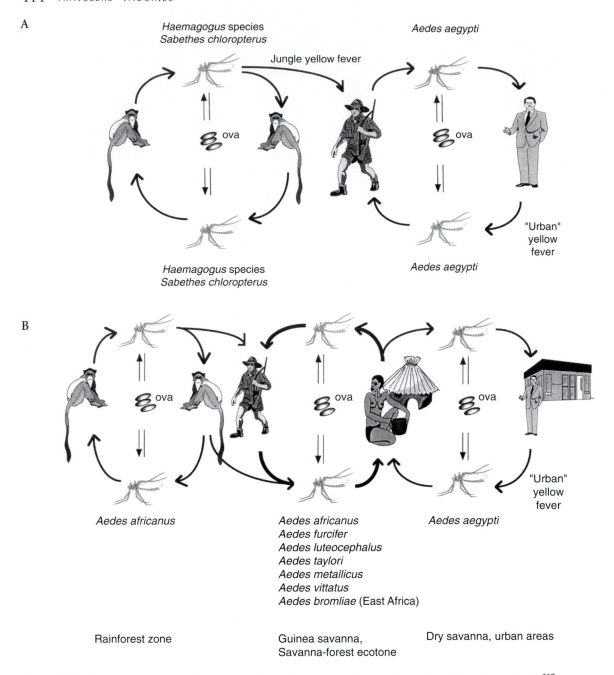

Figure 5-6. Transmission cycles of YF virus in Africa (*A*) and South America (*B*). Adapted from Monath TP.[237]

The pattern of YF activity in South America is characterized by intermittent "emergences" around the edges of the Amazon region. These outbreaks are preceded by evidence of increased virus transmission between monkeys and *Haemagogus* spp. within the Amazon basin, which moves in a circular fashion within the forest or along gallery forests of river courses. A detailed analysis of the patterns of virus activity preceding and during epidemics in Brazil is provided by Mondet.[77]

In the rainforest regions of central Africa, the ecology of YF is similar to that in South America except that *A. africanus* is the primary vector species. The ecology of YF differs dramatically in the moist (Guinea) savanna vegetational zone that extends north and south of the rainforest block (Figure 5-7).

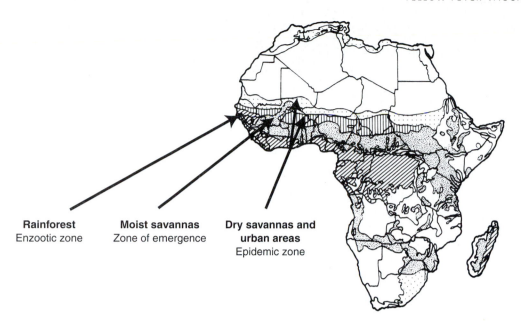

Figure 5-7. Vegetational zones of Africa corresponding to cycles of transmission of YF. Rural situations in the moist savanna zone and the transitional regions at the border of the rainforest and savanna represent the region of greatest risk to the traveler during the rainy season and early dry season (July to November in West Africa).

Here, YF transmission is effected by a wide variety of tree hole–breeding mosquito vectors, including *A. furcifer*, *A. vittatus*, and *A. luteocephalus*, as well as *A. africanus*, which reach very high densities during the rainy and early dry seasons. Vectors are active in plantation areas and in proximity to human dwellings and can enter houses. Both humans and nonhuman primates are involved as hosts in the transmission cycle, and the rate of virus transmission far exceeds that found in the rainforest zone. The savanna-forest ecotone and surrounding Guinea savanna has been described as the *zone of emergence* of YF and represents the region principally affected by epidemics.[78]

An epidemiologically distinct transmission cycle involves *A. aegypti*, which breeds in containers used to store water or in artificial containers that collect rainwater around human habitations. The vector occurs in dry areas and in heavily settled areas but is also widely dispersed in settlements in rural areas. *A. aegypti* transmits YF virus between humans, the sole viremic hosts in the cycle. Urban outbreaks have followed after the introduction of the virus by viremic persons from areas of jungle YF activity.[22,79] In the Americas, urban YF outbreaks were common prior to the successful control and eradication of the vector between the 1930s and 1960s. Since 1942, only two episodes of *A. aegypti*–transmitted YF have been recognized in the Americas (in Trinidad in 1954 and in Santa Cruz, Bolivia, in 1997).[78,79] In contrast, Africa suffers many *A. aegypti*–borne epidemics, and the vector is prevalent in urban and rural areas. *A. aegypti*–borne epidemics in the past 30 years include those in Senegal in 1965; Angola, 1971; Ghana in 1969, 1977 to 1980, and 1983; Ivory Coast, 1982; and Nigeria between 1987 and 1991.[82]

The most alarming prospect for the future involves the reemergence of urban (*A. aegypti*–borne) YF in South America and the spread of YF to heavily populated, *A. aegypti*–infested areas of the world that are currently free from the disease, including the United States, the Mediterranean region, Asia, and Australia. The re-infestation of the South American continent by *A. aegypti* in the 1970s has been followed by large outbreaks of dengue fever, illustrating the susceptibility to reemergence of urban YF.[83,84] Changes in human demography, principally the increase in urban populations and the opening up of remote rural areas to commerce within the YF endemic zone and increased air travel, have reduced barriers to the spread of YF.

ACTIVE IMMUNIZATION

The only vaccine currently used for human immunization against YF is 17D, which protects against all strains of YF virus circulating in nature.

The 17D vaccine was developed by Theiler and Smith who sequentially passed the Asibi virus in a substrate that was restrictive for growth, initially in cultures of minced mouse embryo and subsequently in cultures of minced whole chick embryo.[5] After 58 passages, the virus, now designated as passage series 17D, was propagated by subcultures in minced chick embryo cultures from which the brain and spinal cord had been removed and finally in embryonated eggs. A reduction in monkey neurovirulence and loss of viscerotropism occurred between passages 89 and 114, and reduction in mouse neurovirulence between passages 114 and 176. The initial clinical trials using virus at the 227th and 229th passage levels were conducted in 1936, first in YF immunes and then in nonimmune volunteers.[6,85] The trials showed acceptable tolerability and development of neutralizing antibodies. In early 1937, 17D vaccine was taken to Brazil where it was used in trials of increasing size, leading to the establishment of local manufacturing and initiation of a mass vaccination campaign in 1938.[86]

Between 1938 and 1941, field trials and experimental studies revealed the importance of controlling passage level and substrains derived from the original 17D by independent lines of passage. Some substrains were found to be overattenuated, and others were associated with the appearance of post-vaccinal encephalitis.[87] To prevent uncontrolled passage, a "seed-lot" system was established, in which primary seed and secondary seed lots were prepared and the latter used to prepare multiple vaccine batches. This system was formally established as a biologic standard in 1945.[88] In 1957, publication of WHO *Requirements for Yellow Fever Vaccine* further standardized the seed-lot and manufacturing procedures.[89]

Currently, there are eight active manufacturers of YF 17D vaccine (Table 5-2). Manufacturers in Brazil, France, and Senegal produce large amounts of vaccine for the Expanded Program on Immunization (EPI) and for mass vaccination campaigns during emergency operations. Four manufacturers are currently approved by WHO for use in the EPI and for purchase through the UNICEF bid market.[74] The vaccines produced elsewhere are used almost exclusively in-country for travelers and military personnel.

Two substrains (17D-204 and 17DD) are use for manufacture; these represent different passage lineages from the original 17D. Only one manufacturer (BioManguinhos, Rio de Janeiro) uses the 17DD strain. The safety and efficacy of 17D-204 and 17DD substrain vaccines are similar. Vaccines differ with respect to passage level and formulation with stabilizers.17D vaccines are not biologically cloned and are heterogeneous mixtures of multiple virion subpopulations. Not surprisingly, differences have been found in plaque size and nucleotide sequences.[90–95] There is no evidence to suggest that such variations affect safety or efficacy.

To comply with WHO requirements, vaccines must be produced according to good manufacturing practices.[96] National control authorities such as the Food and Drug Administration in the United States and the Medicines Control Agency in the United Kingdom govern approval for use, and thus biologic standards differ somewhat from country to country.

Master and working seeds are tested for bacteria, fungi, mycoplasma, and adventitious viruses (including avian leukosis virus) and are subjected to a standard safety and immunogenicity test in

Table 5-2. **Manufacturers of Yellow Fever 17D Vaccine**

Country	Manufacturer	Approved by WHO*
United States	Aventis Pasteur, Swiftwater, PA	No
Brazil	Bio Manguinhos, Rio de Janeiro	Yes
United Kingdom	Evans Vaccines, Speke, Liverpool	Yes
France	Aventis Pasteur, Marcy l'Etoile	Yes
Colombia	Instituto Nacional de Salud, Bogota	No
Russia	Institute of Poliomyelitis and Viral Encephalitides, Moscow	No
Senegal	Pasteur Institute, Dakar	Yes
Switzerland	Berna, Bern	No

WHO = World Health Organization.
*Approval by WHO allows international distribution, purchase by UNICEF, and supply to the Expanded Program of Immunization.

rhesus or cynomolgus monkeys.[96] In the standard monkey neurovirulence test, 10 animals are inoculated in the frontal lobe with 0.25 mL of virus containing 5,000 to 50,000 median lethal dose (MLD). The monkeys are scored for clinical signs of encephalitis, viremia and antibody responses are measured, and necropsy is performed on day 30, with scoring of neuropathologic lesions in the brain and spinal cord. A reference control virus seed or vaccine is inoculated into 10 other animals. The test article may not exceed the reference control with respect to clinical and neuropathologic scores, and viremia may not exceed a specified limit.

Vaccine is produced by aseptic inoculation of secondary seed into viable embryonated eggs.[97–99] Most manufacturers use eggs from special pathogen-free flocks. After incubation for 3 to 4 days, infected embryos are aseptically harvested, homogenized, and clarified by centrifugation. The bulk harvest is tested for the absence of adventitious agents. It is diluted and blended with stabilizers (eg, hydrolyzed porcine gelatin and sorbitol) to produce the drug product and is then filled into vials and lyophilized. The final vialed product is tested for identity by neutralization test, potency, thermostability, sterility, general safety in mice and guinea pigs, residual moisture, residual ovalbumin, and endotoxin. The potency titer for release must exceed the compendial minimum (1,000 MLD or equivalent in PFU). Typically, the dose in the final container exceeds the minimum specification by at least fivefold (0.7 log) to account for losses during storage. The yield of vaccine per embryonated egg is typically in the range of 100 doses and so the vaccine is relatively inexpensive to manufacture. Current pricing (in 2002) for vaccine supplied to WHO or UNICEF for use in emergencies or for the EPI is $0.35 (US) per dose (20-dose container) to $0.63 per dose (10-dose container), whereas the price for YF vaccine sold in a single-dose presentation to travelers in developed countries is as high as $55 per dose.

Molecular Determinants of Attenuation

Comparison of the genomic sequences of wild-type virus and the attenuated vaccine strains derived therefrom has provided some clues to the molecular basis of attenuation of vaccine strains. The entire genomes have been sequenced of the 17D and the French neurotropic vaccines and their wild-type parents (Asibi and the French viscerotropic virus).[92,100–105] Because a large number of mutations occurred during the 230 plus passages that separate vaccines from their parental strains, it has not been possible to define exactly which mutations are responsible for attenuation nor is it clear which determinants encode viscerotropism and neurotropism. Although some potentially important mutations have been identified, it is clear that virulence is multigenic, determined by both nonstructural and structural genes of the virus. Moreover, studies of molecular determinants of virulence have employed mouse models, which reveal only one of the two biological properties of the virus (neurotropism). Recently, hamsters were shown to be susceptible to a lethal disease with hepatic dysfunction and necrosis resembling wild-type YF after infection with virus strains adapted by serial passage in hamster liver.[106,107] This model might be useful for dissecting the molecular determinants associated with viscerotropism.

Twenty amino acid differences distinguish parental Asibi virus and attenuated 17D virus strains. In addition, there are four nucleotide differences in the 3' noncoding region (NCR) (Figure 5-8). Because of the functional importance of the E protein in attachment and entry to cells, one or more of the eight amino acid differences that separate Asibi and the vaccine strains are likely to play a role in attenuation. Four mutations in the E glycoprotein are nonconservative changes (at residues E52, E200, E305, and E380). The mutations at E299, E305, and E380 are located in a region of the E glycoprotein (domain III) that contains determinants involved in tropism and cell attachment and thus could alter neuro- or viscerotropism of the virus.

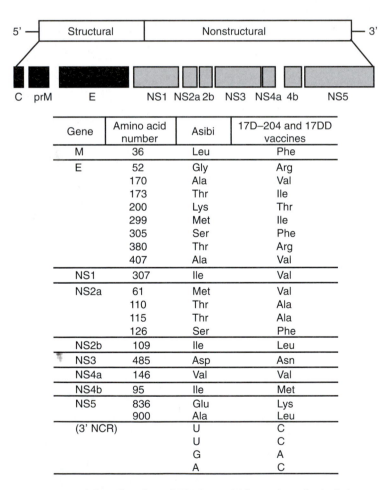

Gene	Amino acid number	Asibi	17D–204 and 17DD vaccines
M	36	Leu	Phe
E	52	Gly	Arg
	170	Ala	Val
	173	Thr	Ile
	200	Lys	Thr
	299	Met	Ile
	305	Ser	Phe
	380	Thr	Arg
	407	Ala	Val
NS1	307	Ile	Val
NS2a	61	Met	Val
	110	Thr	Ala
	115	Thr	Ala
	126	Ser	Phe
NS2b	109	Ile	Leu
NS3	485	Asp	Asn
NS4a	146	Val	Val
NS4b	95	Ile	Met
NS5	836	Glu	Lys
	900	Ala	Leu
(3' NCR)		U	C
		U	C
		G	A
		A	C

Figure 5-8. The genome organization of the yellow fever (YF) virus, which consists of a single long open reading frame (ORF) of approximately 11 kilobases and flanking short noncoding regions (NCR), is shown at the top. The ORF contains three structural genes at the 5' end (C-prM-E) and seven nonstructural genes (NS) encoding enzymes required for replication and post-translational processing of viral proteins. At the bottom are shown the location of mutations that occurred during the 230 plus passages of wild-type YF virus (Asibi strain) to generate the attenuated 17D vaccine.

The potential importance of residue E305 in the attenuation phenotype of 17D vaccine was suggested by sequence analysis of virus recovered from the brain of a 3-year-old child in the United States who died of encephalitis following 17D immunization.[108] The brain virus differed from the 17D vaccine at a locus in domain III located near the E305 residue (at E303 Glu → Lys) and was found to have increased neurovirulence for mice and monkeys.[109]

The mutation at position E407 occurs in the N-terminal portion of the stem-anchor region of the E protein. Mutations in this region of the protein can affect the structural integrity and spatial characteristics of the E protein necessary for internalization of the virus.[110,111]

Mutations in the nonstructural proteins or the 3′ NCR of the virus might also alter virulence of YF virus by restricting the rate of viral RNA and protein production.[112,113] There are 10 amino acid changes in the nonstructural proteins of 17D viruses (see Figure 5-8): one change occurs in the NS1 protein; four in NS2A; one each in NS2B, NS4A, and NS4B; and two in NS5. One change occurs in NS3 at residue 485, in a region of the protein with RNA helicase and triphosphatase activities involved in unwinding RNA during replication. Mutations in the RNA polymerase (NS5) might affect replication efficiency and could also contribute to attenuation of the 17D vaccine.

Several recent studies have illustrated the importance of the 3′ NCR of flaviviruses to replication and virulence. The 3′ NCR acts as a promoter for minus-strand synthesis during replication, and, depending on their location, mutations in the conserved stem-loop region might adversely affect replication and virulence.[114]

Less is known about the molecular basis of viscerotropism than about neurotropism. The development of a hamster model of viscerotropic YF provides a new approach to defining the molecular basis for viscerotropism.[106] The model requires adaptation of wild-type virus strains by serial passage in hamsters. Asibi virus becomes virulent between the sixth and seventh hamster passages. The genome of the hamster viscerotropic P7 virus was compared with the parental nonviscerotropic virus. Fourteen nucleotide changes and seven amino acid substitutions were found, most of which (5 of 7) were in the E protein at positions E27, E28, E155, E323, and E331. These results support an important role for the E protein in viscerotropism.[115]

Antigenic Properties of YF Vaccine

The antigenic determinants in YF wild-type virus and vaccine strains have been partially analyzed. Monoclonal antibodies define distinct epitopes in the E protein that are 17D vaccine strain–specific epitopes, YF virus specific, cross-reactive with specific heterologous flaviviruses, or broadly cross-reactive with members of the flavivirus genus. Antibodies against vaccine strain–specific, virus-specific, and flavivirus group–reactive epitopes neutralize virus, providing an explanation for the serologic cross-reactivities observed clinically. This multiplicity of neutralizing determinants also explains the protective immunity afforded by 17D vaccine against all wild YF virus strains and the partial cross-protection by heterologous flaviviruses against YF. Additional studies have defined epitopes that are substrain specific, differentiating 17D-204 vaccine from other YF viruses and 17D-204 from 17DD vaccines and even distinguishing between vaccines of the same substrain from different manufacturers.[116,117] The antigenic heterogeneity of the 17D vaccine reflects the uncloned nature and different passage histories during manufacture and laboratory manipulation.

Some neutralizing epitopes have been localized by sequencing escape mutants or wild-type antigenic variants recovered from the 17D vaccine. Neutralization determinants in the E protein have been identified at residues E71/72, E155, E305, and E325.[118–120] Antigenic determinants involved in cell-mediated immunity have been localized in the E protein and in multiple nonstructural proteins NS1, NS2B, and NS3.[51] These T-cell epitopes are highly conserved and probably contribute to the cross-protective activity of 17D vaccine against all geographic variants of wild-type YF virus.

Dose and Route of Administration

YF vaccine is given by subcutaneous injection of 0.5 mL, generally in the deltoid region. The minimum dose requirement is 1,000 MLD or the equivalent in PFU. Although differences exist across laboratories, the ratio of PFU to MLD is approximately 50 to 100:1. Because commercial vaccines contain an excess of virus to provide for losses during storage, the delivered dose is higher than the minimum standard. The actual dose contained in commercial vaccines varies but at the time of release ranges from 5 to 50 times the minimum.

Alternative routes of administration have been studied in nonhuman primates. Administration of 17D vaccine by the oral route or by the intestinal route using acid-stable capsules was not successful (contrary to an earlier report), whereas application of virus by intranasal spray resulted in seroconversion.[121,122] The residual neurotropism of the 17D virus suggests caution in extending this observation to humans because of the potential for direct neuroinvasion via olfactory neurons.

All YF vaccines are prepared in embryonated chicken eggs and formulated as lyophilized powders. Vaccines vary with respect to stabilizer additives and salt content. For example, ARILVAX (Evans Vaccines, Speke, UK) contains sodium chloride and buffer salts and is reconstituted with sterile water, whereas YF-VAX (Aventis Pasteur, Swiftwater, PA) is reconstituted with a normal saline solution. Vaccines are supplied in single- and multiple-dose containers. All require storage at point of use at 2 to 8°C and should be used within 1 hour after reconstitution. For use in the field, WHO allows vaccine supplied in multi-dose containers to be used within 4 hours of the vials being opened.

Dose-response studies indicate that a dose of 100 to 200 PFU results in seroconversion rates greater than 90% and that doses of 2,000 PFU or greater cause seroconversion in nearly 100% of subjects.[123–125]

Interestingly, an inverse relationship between vaccine dose and viremia/antibody titer has been observed in a number of studies.[123–126] This effect can be explained by the presence of interferon (produced in the infected egg), defective interfering particles, noninfectious antigen competing for cell receptors, or induction of a strong innate immune response by virus inoculated in high doses. Similar effects have been also noted with chimeric viruses using YF as a vector for the envelope genes of heterologous flaviviruses.[55] Some workers have suggested that a low dose of 17D vaccine might cause a delay in antibody response, higher viremia, and, therefore, an increased risk of encephalitis.[126,127] However, administration of small intradermal doses of 17D vaccine is practiced to evaluate hypersensitivity in persons with a history of egg allergy, and administration of low doses of YF 17D by scarification during field trials in Africa have not demonstrated a safety problem. Nevertheless, theoretic safety concerns about a low dose suggest caution against the use of lyophilized vaccine that is past its expiration date, vaccine that has been subjected to storage conditions that might degrade potency, or vaccine held for more than a few hours after reconstitution.

Vaccine Thermostability

Current WHO requirements include a stability standard and also stipulate that the minimum vaccine expiry date shall be not less than 2 years after the last satisfactory potency test.[96] The stability specification requires that the lyophilized vaccine held at 37°C for 14 days must maintain minimum potency (> 1,000 MLD or equivalent in PFU per 0.5 mL dose) and must show a mean loss of titer less than 1.0 $\log_{10}$. Major manufacturers produce stabilized vaccines that lose only 0.3 to 0.5 $\log_{10}$ per dose during this interval.

Genetic Stability In Vivo

Not surprisingly, because of the high mutation rates of RNA viruses and their quasispecies nature, 17D vaccines contain heterogeneous virus subpopulations that differ with respect to plaque size, neurovirulence for mice, and reactivity with monoclonal antibodies. Given the safety record of 17D vaccines since stabilization of the passage level, the heterogeneous composition does not pose a safety problem and, in fact, has been proposed to be a positive attribute of the vaccine.[94] Virus recovered from the sera of vaccinated subjects or from monkeys 30 days after intracerebral inoculation contained only a few mutations in a nonstructural gene (NS5), indicating a high degree of genetic stability during replication in vivo.[128] In fact, mutations tend to accumulate in the 17D virus at a rate 100- to 1,000-fold lower than expected for an RNA virus. In addition, studies employing a truly clonal YF 17D virus as a vector for foreign genes have been very successful, indicating that the quasispecies nature of 17D vaccine is not critical to safety and efficacy, and that it should be possible to develop a molecular (or biologic) clone of 17D as a vaccine.[56,129]

Nevertheless, rare mutational events in 17D vaccine have occasionally been shown to alter pathogenicity. The first of two published fatal cases of encephalitis occurred in 1965 in a 3-year-old child who received 17D vaccine manufactured in the United States. The virus from brain tissue had higher neurovirulence for mice than the commercial vaccine, caused severe encephalitis in a cynomolgus monkey, and reacted with a wild-type–specific monoclonal antibody.[109] The brain virus contained two amino acid residues in the E gene (the one at E305 suspected to be responsible for increased neurovirulence) and one in NS4B. Fortunately, such mutational events appear to be exceedingly rare. Because there are no other instances of 17D virus's having been recovered from patients with postvaccinal encephalitis (most of whom recover uneventfully), it is uncertain whether that complication is related to mutational changes in the virus or to host factors. The only other postvaccinal encephalitis death occurred in a patient who was immunosuppressed.[130]

Viremia Following 17D Vaccination

Yellow fever 17D vaccine causes a self-limited infection characterized by a transient, low-titer viremia. The cell types and tissues responsible for virus replication have not been defined, although lymphoid cells are suspected to play a prominent role. At least six independent studies have demonstrated very low levels of virus in blood for a brief period following 17D vaccination.[6,55,131–134] Viremia occurs during the latter half of the first week after vaccination, and, thus, the incubation period is similar to natural infection with YF virus. Between 30 and 60% of subjects have demonstrable viremia, depending on the sensitivity of the assay method used. The RT-PCR method was more sensitive than infectivity assays for the detection of viremia.[134] Virus is typically present between 4 and 6 days after inoculation, with the highest proportion of subjects positive on day 5. Cessation of viremia corresponds to the time of appearance of neutralizing antibodies (see "Kinetics of the Immune Response," below). Reflecting attenuation of the virus, titers in blood are much lower than those seen in natural infection and are far below the infection threshold for mosquito vectors. Titers of 17D virus in blood are generally less than 20 PFU/mL and rarely as high as 200 PFU/mL. The low viremia following 17D vaccine might also explain the apparent low risk of transmission of the virus to the fetus in women who have been immunized during pregnancy and the low incidence of postvaccinal encephalitis.

There are no data on viremia levels in infants or children. The higher rate of YF vaccine–associated neurotropic events in infants suggests that viremia levels might be higher or more prolonged, enhancing the risk of neuroinvasion or, alternatively, that immaturity of the blood-brain barrier allows access of low-titer virus from the bloodstream. Similarly, no data are available on the intensity or duration of viremia in persons who are immunosuppressed.

Immune Responses to YF Vaccine

In many studies conducted over the years since its introduction in 1936, 17D vaccine has been shown to be highly immunogenic. In the first field study in Brazil in 1937, 94% of 882 vaccinees developed neutralizing antibodies, which are considered to be the correlate of protection.[6] Subsequent trials have yielded very similar results.[135–142]

The most recent trial compared the response to YF-VAX and ARILVAX in a randomized, double-blind study in healthy adult volunteers.[57] Seroconversion rates were 99% in both treatment groups, and the geometric mean neutralizing titers ($\log_{10}$ neutralization index [LNI])[†] were 2.2 and 2.1, respectively.

The level of neutralizing antibodies required for protection against wild-type YF virus challenge has been estimated by dose-response studies in rhesus monkeys.[126,143,144] An LNI of at least 0.7 was strongly associated with protection. Antibody titers measured by serum-dilution plaque-reduction tests[†] are more variable, and no cutoff has been experimentally established as a correlate of protection. Although it is generally accepted that YF-specific neutralizing antibodies at a titer of at least 1:10 by the serum-dilution plaque-reduction method is indicative of protective immunity, this is less certain in persons with a background of heterologous flavivirus antibodies because a low titer of antibody to YF might represent a cross-reaction to another virus.

The ELISA, HI, and CF methods are less sensitive than neutralization for determining response to YF vaccine. Individuals without prior flavivirus exposure generally do not develop CF antibodies after administration of 17D vaccine.[63] The CF test has therefore been thought to distinguish recent infection with wild-type virus from vaccine-induced immunity. However, individuals with prior heterologous flavivirus immunity developed broadly cross-reactive CF antibodies to YF following 17D vaccination.[145]

The primary immune response is characterized by the appearance of neutralizing antibodies of the IgM class between days 4 and 7, several days before detection of IgG antibodies.[146] IgM antibodies measured by capture ELISA were found in 83% of volunteers within 2 weeks after primary immunization.[38,134] Titers of IgM-neutralizing antibodies were 16- to 256-fold higher than IgG antibodies during the first

---

[†] Two neutralization tests are in use, depending on the preference of the laboratory. In one method, a constant amount of serum is added to varying concentrations of the virus and the virus-serum mixtures tested by plaquing in cell cultures. The end point is the difference in $\log_{10}$ titer of the virus between the test sample and a negative control serum (or the baseline serum), expressed as a log neutralization index (LNI). In the second method, a constant amount of virus (typically containing ~100 PFU) is added to varying dilutions of test serum and the virus-serum mixtures tested by plaque assay in cell culture. The end point is the highest dilution of serum that reduces the number of plaques by a specified ratio (often 50%) compared to a negative control serum. The serum-dilution neutralization test tends to be somewhat more sensitive for detection of low levels of antibody.

4 to 6 weeks after immunization, and IgM antibodies were found to persist for at least 18 months (the longest time examined). Prolonged synthesis of IgM antibodies might indicate persistence of antigen, possibly explaining the durability of YF immunity (see "Duration of Immunity").

Kinetics of the Immune Response

Studies in rhesus monkeys established that neutralizing antibodies were detectable in serum on day 6 or 7 following inoculation of 17D virus, at which time the animals were protected against challenge with wild-type YF virus. Significant protection was present 1 to 2 days before the appearance of detectable neutralizing antibodies, suggesting that very low levels of antibody or innate immune responses induced by the vaccine (interferon, NK cells) were protective.[85,146,147]

Humans inoculated with 17D virus also rapidly develop neutralizing antibodies. Smithburn and Mahaffy found neutralizing antibodies in 10% of subjects on day 7 and in 90% on day 10 after inoculation.[148] Wisseman and colleagues found no evidence of immunity on day 6, but all subjects had seroconverted by day 14 after vaccination.[149] In a recent study, Lang and colleagues showed that 88% of adult subjects seroconverted by day 14, whereas 100% were seropositive on day 28 after vaccination.[141] Similarly, Reinhardt and associates showed that all subjects seroconverted between days 6 and 13.[134] Monath and colleagues found that 80% of subjects seroconverted by day 11 and 100% by day 31, with a marked increase in mean LNI from 1.26 to 3.98.[57] Based on conclusions from multiple studies, the International Health Regulations stipulate that the YF vaccination certificate becomes valid 10 days after administration of the 17D vaccine.[74]

Neutralizing antibody levels continue to increase during the first month after immunization, with peak titers found at 3 to 4 weeks.[146,149]

Revaccination

According to International Health Regulations, the YF immunization certificate for international travel is valid for 10 years, whereupon revaccination is required.[74] The regulation is conservative because vaccine immunity appears to last several decades, if not for life.

The immune response to revaccination is blunted compared with primary vaccination, an expected finding for a live vaccine that induces long-lasting immunity after the initial dose. In persons who are revaccinated, viremia is absent or undetectable, and the common side effects of vaccination are reduced.[55,57,138] Revaccination (or vaccination of individuals with naturally acquired immunity) might result in no increase in antibody titer (indicating sterilizing immunity) or in a booster response (indicating that sufficient virus replication had occurred or that the antigenic mass of neutralized virus in the vaccine dose was sufficient to elicit a memory response). An immune response to revaccination is more likely in individuals with a low neutralizing antibody titer prior to inoculation.[150,151]

Immunization in Individuals with Prior Flavivirus Immunity

In an immunologically naive subject, the primary neutralizing antibody response to 17D vaccine is highly specific, characterized by no or very-low-titer cross-reactive antibodies to other flaviviruses.[149] However, persons undergoing secondary responses (ie, those with preexisting heterologous flavivirus immunity) respond to 17D vaccine with a broad response characterized by the appearance of both homologous (YF) and heterologous neutralizing, HI, and complement-fixing antibodies.[145,149] Similarly, persons with prior 17D immunity respond to natural infection by heterologous flaviviruses with the development of a broad flavivirus group response. Thus, individuals with prior immunity to heterologous flaviviruses have responses that are qualitatively and quantitatively different from those of naive subjects.

Prior immunity to dengue appears to reduce the response to 17D vaccine, whereas prior infection with members of the Japanese encephalitis (JE) complex including JE and St. Louis encephalitis does not.[131,149,152] Interference by heterologous flaviviruses was particularly evident when the 17D vaccine was given by scarification, presumably due to the lower dose of 17D administered by this route.[153–155] In contrast to these observations, volunteers who had previously received a live attenuated dengue vaccine followed by the 17D vaccine had similar immune responses to YF as dengue nonimmune controls, suggesting no interference with YF vaccine replication.[53,54]

The interactions with inactivated flavivirus vaccines are fundamentally different from those with live vaccines. Prior 17D immunization might increase the response to inactivated antigens through memory responses of IgG-producing B cells and restimulation of Th and follicular dendritic cells. Thus, YF-immune subjects receiving inactivated tick-borne encephalitis (TBE) vaccine had anamnestic (earlier and in higher titer) responses that were also more cross-reactive than those of nonimmunes.[156] Similar responses to inactivated JE vaccine would be expected in YF-immune subjects.

Cytokine Responses

Yellow fever 17D induces a type 1 interferon response in serum and the interferon-induced enzyme $2'5'$-oligoadenylate synthetase in peripheral blood mononuclear cells.[38,132] These responses follow the viremic response closely, with a 24-hour delay. Increases in serum β2-microglobulin, neopterin, and tumor necrosis factor (TNF)-α have been found during the first week after 17D vaccination but not after revaccination.[134,157] The increase in β2-microglobulin reflects activation of T lymphocytes bearing major histocompatibility complex (MHC)-I, and neopterin is released by monocyte/macrophages in response to γ-interferon from activated T cells. It is likely that systemic side effects of 17D vaccine, including headache, myalgia, asthenia, and slight leukopenia, are caused by interferon-α and other cytokines (see "Vaccine Safety").

Cellular immune responses to 17D vaccine have been measured in four subjects. T cell responses were measured by lymphoproliferation, cytotoxic T cell assay, and interferon-α ELISPOT.[51]

Protection against Wild-Type Yellow Fever

Many studies in nonhuman primates have demonstrated that the 17D vaccine protects against lethal challenge with wild-type virus and that protection correlates with prechallenge neutralizing antibody responses.[144,147] The protective role of antibodies was confirmed by passive transfer of immune serum before or shortly after challenge.[158,159]

The efficacy of the 17D vaccine has not been formally tested in field trials. However, ample evidence for protection has been obtained by the demonstration of neutralizing antibodies in virtually all persons who receive the vaccine and by the control of jungle YF in Brazil in the 1930s and 1940s following immunization of the susceptible population.[160]

Because YF vaccination is the standard of care, placebo-controlled efficacy trials cannot be performed today. New vaccines against YF will be licensed based on animal data and immunologic surrogates. Further studies on the effectiveness of YF vaccines, which could be performed by case-control studies, would be useful in populations affected by HIV or malnutrition, where efficacy of the vaccine might be reduced.

Duration of Immunity

The certificate of immunization for international travel is valid for 10 years, an interval established by studies showing that neutralizing antibodies were present in 92 to 97% of persons 16 to 19 years after vaccination.[161,162] In a study of World War II veterans conducted 30 to 35 years after 17D vaccination, 80.6% had neutralizing antibodies overall, but in a subset with more reliable service records of immunization, 97% were seropositive.[163]

The basis of the long-lasting immune response to YF 17D is uncertain. Persistent infection has been documented in monocyte/macrophage cells in vitro and in brain tissue of monkeys and mice.[52,164–167] The prolonged synthesis of IgM antibodies in humans immunized with the 17D virus suggests that chronic, persistent infection or storage of antigen in vivo, possibly in follicular dendritic cells, might explain the durability of the human immune response.[146]

Primary Vaccine Failure

A very small proportion of healthy individuals (1 to 2% in clinical trials where good control of vaccine quality and injection techniques were ensured) do not respond to primary vaccination with 17D. Failure to mount a response on primary immunization might not represent an absolute refractoriness, however, because revaccination can result in the development of neutralizing antibodies.

Development of YF disease in vaccinated persons has been reported on rare occasions. Five cases (3 fatal) occurred in vaccinated military personnel in West Africa during World War II, one in a vaccinated expatriate in Uganda in 1952, and one in a vaccinated Spanish tourist traveling in West Africa in 1988.[168–170] It is uncertain whether these individuals were actually vaccinated, had received vaccine that had deteriorated, or had failed to respond to the vaccine.

Malnutrition is a recognized cause of vaccine failure. In 8 children with kwashiorkor, only 1 seroconverted after 17D vaccination, compared with 5 of 6 controls.[171] Further studies are required to assess the relevance of this finding to the use of 17D vaccine in endemic countries. Although there were no obvious adverse effects of immunization in the small series of kwashiorkor patients, the safety of YF immunization in infants with malnutrition has not been fully assessed. One study suggests that catabolic effects of the mild infection caused by 17D vaccine could result in a net loss of body nitrogen and transiently aggravate the clinical effects of protein malnutrition.[172]

Pregnancy is another potential cause of primary vaccine failure. Neutralizing antibody responses to 17D vaccine were significantly impaired in pregnant women studied in Nigeria.[173] Only 38.6% of the pregnant women developed neutralizing antibodies compared with 81.5 to 93.7% in various control groups. If YF vaccination during pregnancy is warranted because of a high risk of infection, it is important to caution patients about the possibility of vaccine failure or to test for seroconversion. Women who do not respond and remain at risk of exposure to YF should be re-immunized after parturition.

HIV infection is likely to reduce the immune response to YF 17D depending on the degree of immune suppression (and to represent a risk of adverse events; see "Vaccine Safety"). Some reports suggest that vaccination of HIV-infected subjects without severe immune suppression was followed by seroconversion.[174] In contrast, 17D vaccine was administered to 33 adult travelers with HIV infection and CD4+ cell counts > 200 per mm³, and only 70% percent had responded by 1 month after vaccination.[175] In another study, only 17% of infants with HIV infection in the Ivory Coast immunized with 17D and measles vaccines developed YF antibodies.[176]

Other Host Factors that Modulate the Response to YF 17D

Neutralizing antibody responses are higher in males than in females, in persons of the white race, and in smokers versus nonsmokers.[57] These effects have limited significance for vaccine usage. The gender and racial biases in antibody response might reflect a more active infection and higher susceptibility to adverse events.

VACCINE SAFETY

Until recently, YF 17D was widely held to be one of the safest vaccines in use. However, within the past 5 years, a new syndrome (YF vaccine–associated viscerotropic adverse events, or YEL-AVD) has been recognized to occur at a low incidence, and a higher risk of severe adverse events has been noted in the elderly, raising concerns about the safety profile of 17D vaccines.

Common Adverse Events Caused by 17D Vaccines

Because no placebo-controlled trials have been performed, the assessment of frequent adverse events must be made with caution. Nonetheless, there is little doubt that the vaccine causes local reactions at the site of injection (erythema, induration, pain) and systemic symptoms (headache, myalgia, and malaise, generally without fever) that are generally mild in severity. The reported incidence of the systemic events is dependent on the methods used for assessment. Among 2,457 persons in Brazil from whom "reasonably accurate" clinical follow-up data were obtained, 14.6% complained of headache for 1 to 2 days, 10.2% developed pains in the body (usually accompanied by headache), 1.4% missed time from work (usually only 1 day), and 0.16% spent 1 or more days in bed.[6] These reactions, which were generally considered mild, occurred on the fifth to seventh day after immunization. Reactogenicity of 17D vaccine has been monitored in 12 clinical trials conducted between 1953 and 2002. In trials where subjects have kept diaries or were prompted for adverse events, a higher incidence, in the range of 18 to 50%, has been detected.[124,137,138,141]

In a recent large clinical trial, adverse events were monitored closely in 1,440 subjects, half of whom received either YF-VAX or ARILVAX.[57] More subjects in the YF-VAX group (71.9%) experienced one or more nonserious, adverse events than in the ARILVAX group (65.3%, $p = .008$) because of a higher rate of local reactions of mild-moderate severity. The most common systemic side effects (which did not differ significantly across treatment groups) were headache (in 32 to 33% of subjects), asthenia (29 to 30%), myalgia (24 to 26%), malaise (18 to 19%), fever (14 to 15%), and chills (10 to 11%). These were generally mild or moderate but 7 to 8% of all treatment-emergent events were severe and interfered with normal activities. Injection-site reactions occurred between days 1 to 5, and the systemic adverse events also occurred with the highest incidence during this interval but then continued between days 6 and 11. Asthenia, malaise, headache, fever, injection-site inflammation, and injection-site pain occurred at a significantly lower rate in subjects who were seropositive at baseline (presumably by YF vaccination for military service that was unknown to the subject). This indicated that active replication of the vaccine virus was responsible for the adverse events and that subjects with prior immunity were protected against side effects. The systemic adverse events are presumably caused by T-lymphocyte activation and the release of cytokines, including interferons and TNF-α stimulated by virus replication.[132,157]

YF 17D vaccination is associated with minimal changes in clinical laboratory parameters. In a recent clinical trial, the mean white blood cell count decreased slightly between baseline and day 11, with a mild neutropenia.[57] Minimal, reversible elevations in serum transaminase levels were observed in 3.5 to 3.9%

(AST) and 3.9 to 4.6% (ALT) of the subjects during the 10 days after vaccination. There were no associated symptoms or other laboratory abnormalities and no relationship to concomitant medications. Future placebo-controlled trials will be required to determine whether elevations in serum enzymes are non-specific or are caused by the 17D vaccine. However, the recent discovery that 17D vaccines can rarely cause severe hepatitis (YEL-AVD) suggests the possibility that that the laboratory abnormalities observed in this trial might represent subclinical liver injury.

Rare Adverse Events Caused by 17D Vaccine

Yellow Fever Vaccine–Associated Neurotropic Disease (YEL-AND)

The YF 17D virus retains a degree of neurovirulence, as demonstrated by intracerebral inoculation of mice and monkeys and by the occurrence of rare cases of yellow fever vaccine–associated neurotropic disease (YEL-AND) (formerly designated postvaccinal encephalitis) in humans. Infant mice are susceptible to neuroinvasion and lethal encephalitis caused by YF 17D virus inoculated by the peripheral route but become refractory after about 8 days of age; after that age, mice are susceptible only to intracerebral inoculation.

Very young age is also a risk factor for humans. Of 26 published case reports of YEL-AND, 15 have occurred in infants, most of which were before recommendations were promulgated for the restriction of use of 17D vaccine to infants greater than 6 months of age.[177] The reasons for the increased risk of encephalitis in young infants is unknown. Possibilities include (1) immaturity of the blood-brain barrier, allowing access of the virus to brain parenchyma; (2) prolonged or higher viremia, increasing the risk of neuroinvasion; and (3) immaturity of the immune system, resulting in delayed clearance of the virus. There are no data on 17D viremia levels or on the kinetics of the immune response in infants or children.

Of 15 cases of YEL-AND reported in the 1950s, 13 (87%) occurred in infants ≤ 4 months of age, and all were ≤ 7 months of age. Because age limitations for the use of 17D came into practice, only 11 cases of YEL-AND have been reported in the literature. One case was a 1-month-old infant vaccinated in 1979 in France and another was a 3-year-old child vaccinated in the United States in 1965. The remaining 8 cases were in adolescents (2 cases), adults 19 to 59 years (6 cases), and elderly adults (1 case, 71 years of age).

The incidence of YEL-AND in very young infants has been estimated at 0.5 to 4 in 1,000.[178,179] In contrast, the risk of developing encephalitis in persons over 9 months of age (the current minimum age generally recommended for routine immunization) is far lower. A recent attempt by the Centers for Disease Control and Prevention (CDC) to estimate the incidence of serious adverse events associated with YF 17D involved use of the Vaccine Adverse Events Reporting System (VAERS) database. Four cases of YEL-AND in subjects 16 to 71 years of age were uncovered in 2001 to 2002 and have been recently reported.[180] During this interval, approximately 400,000 doses of YF-VAX were distributed for civilian use in the United States. Assuming all doses were used and that all cases of YEL-AND were reported to VAERS, the incidence of YEL-AND can be estimated at 1 in 50,000. Encephalitis following 17D vaccine has been more common in males (72% of the cases) than in females.

A recent report describes the occurrence of fatal meningoencephalitis in an adult male with undiagnosed HIV and low CD4+ cell counts who received YF vaccine.[130] This is the first report of a serious adverse event following YF vaccination of a patient with immunosuppression. Presumably, a delayed or dampened immune response allowed neuroinvasion and unrestrained replication of the vaccine virus in the CNS.

The interval between vaccination and onset of symptoms has ranged between 2 and 23 days, with most (70%) cases having an onset between 6 and 14 days. The disease is characterized by fever, meningismus, convulsions, obtundation, and paresis. The cerebrospinal fluid contains 100 to 500 cells (polymorphonuclear initially, lymphocytic later after infection) and an increased protein concentration. The clinical course has typically been brief, and full recovery is typical. Two patients died (a 3-year-old and the HIV/aquired immunodeficiency disease [AIDS] patient cited above), and an adult had residual mild ataxia that was still present 11 months after onset.[108,181]

YF Vaccine–Associated Viscerotropic Adverse Events

This represents a newly recognized rare complication of 17D vaccination. Cases have been associated with vaccines manufactured in Brazil (17DD substrain), France, and the United States (17D-204 substrain). At least 16 cases (9 fatal) of a syndrome closely resembling wild-type YF have been described, and 9 cases histories have been published.[180,182–185] Fourteen cases occurred in adults immunized for travel, and 2 were in children and young adults living in an endemic region. Five of the 8 cases in the United States were in elderly patients.

Detailed evaluation of three fatal cases in Brazil and Australia showed that an overwhelming infection with the 17D virus was responsible for the disease. Similarities of the syndrome to wild-type YF included rapid onset of fever and malaise within 3 to 5 days of vaccination, jaundice, oliguria, cardiovascular instability, hemorrhage, and midzonal necrosis of the liver at autopsy. Large amounts of YF viral antigen were found in liver, heart, and other affected organs. In some persons surviving long enough to assess the immune response, antibody titers to YF were significantly higher than expected ($\geq 1:10,240$), consistent with an overwhelming infection (although a secondary response in the setting of prior heterologous flavivirus exposure was not ruled out). Markedly elevated creatine kinase levels suggest that rhabdomyolysis (myopathy) has been observed (case 8). One patient with a fatal case (case 7) was taking an hydroxymethylglutaryl coenzyme A (HMG CoA) reductase inhibitor cholesterol-lowering agent (atorvastatin). HMG CoA reductase inhibitors are known to induce abnormal liver function and rhabdomyolysis in some patients, and atorvastatin has been implicated in a case of multiorgan failure.[186] The patient clearly had an overwhelming 17D infection, but it is uncertain whether atorvastatin exacerbated his illness.

The incidence of YEL-AVD in the United States was estimated at approximately 1 per 400,000, but the true incidence will remain unknown until prospective surveillance is applied to large populations undergoing primary vaccination.[182] Why has the syndrome been recognized only in the past 6 years? One possibility suggested by workers at the CDC is that immune serum globulin (ISG) usage in travelers for hepatitis A prevention has been discontinued since the introduction of hepatitis A vaccines in the mid 1990s. ISG contains relatively high titers of YF-neutralizing antibody and could have provided protection against 17D sepsis.[187]

Vaccine-associated viscerotropic adverse events are not caused by mutations arising in the virus but appear to be related to idiosyncratic susceptibility of the individuals afflicted.[188] The host factors responsible for increased susceptibility are unknown and are not currently identifiable by laboratory tests or medical history. A genetic basis is likely.[39]

The risk of acquiring YF during travel to an endemic area exceeds the risk of vaccine-associated viscerotropic adverse events (see "Epidemiology"). Nevertheless, physicians should be aware of this serious complication of 17D vaccine and that it might occur at higher frequency in primary vaccination of elderly persons. Revaccination poses no risk because the subject has preexisting immunity or immunologic memory from the original vaccination that would protect against viral sepsis.

The fact that two cases of YEL-AVD (see cases 1 and 7, Table 5-3) occurred in persons whose travel destinations were not YF-endemic areas represent tragic, preventable events. The vaccinating physician has an obligation to use YF vaccine only when justified by potential exposure to wild-type virus.

Patients who develop a febrile illness temporally associated with YF vaccination and not explicable by another cause should be investigated, and those with elevated liver enzymes or creatine kinase levels should be hospitalized for observation. To provide much-needed data on causality, serial samples for quantitative viremia and antibody studies should be undertaken and buffy coat cells or peripheral blood mononuclear cells frozen for future genetic studies. Such cases should be reported promptly to the VAERS (toll-free in USA 800-822-7967) and consultation sought with the CDC (Fort Collins, CO, 303-221-6428; or Atlanta, GA, 404-417-8000).

Allergic Reactions to Egg Proteins

YF vaccine contains multiple proteins derived from egg white and yolk, and, therefore, the vaccine is contraindicated for persons with a history of allergic reactions to eggs.[189]

Case reports in the 1940s provided the first examples of allergic reactions to 17D vaccine, including serum sickness syndrome (urticaria or erythema multiforme–like rash accompanied by malaise, fever, arthralgia, pruritus, nausea, and vomiting) and immediate-type reactions (anaphylaxis within minutes after injection).[190,91] These cases occurred in patients with known egg allergies.

The incidence of allergic reactions to YF 17D vaccine is low, principally because a prior history of intolerance or allergy to eggs or egg-based vaccines is a contraindication to the use of 17D vaccine, and few immunizations are given to such individuals. Guidelines for the use of YF 17D vaccine recommend that patients with a clear history of allergy (oral intolerance of eggs) who must be vaccinated because of risk of exposure should undergo skin testing with 1:10 diluted vaccine and a negative and positive (histamine) control. Treatment for anaphylaxis should be immediately available. If the test is negative, an intradermal test is performed with 0.02 mL of 1:100 vaccine (see package insert, YF-VAX, Aventis Pasteur).[192–194] In the case of a positive intradermal test (a wheal 5 mm or larger), the patient may undergo a desensitization procedure consisting of increasing subcutaneous doses at 15- to 20-minute intervals under the supervision of an experienced physician. It is useful to determine whether the patient has sero-converted by virtue of the intradermal test dose before proceeding to desensitization.

Forty-two members of the US military with a history of egg allergy underwent scratch and intra-dermal testing with crude egg white and a variety of egg-based vaccines, including YF 17D, and most patients also underwent oral egg challenge.[195] The study indicated that a history of egg allergy was not a strong contraindication to vaccination because only 16% of the egg-sensitive subjects experienced a mild reaction. Intradermal skin testing with vaccine had a reasonably high negative predictive value (0.80) but a low positive predictive value (0.57) for an allergic reaction.

A patient without a history of egg allergy suffered an anaphylactic reaction to YF 17D.[196] She had a history of intolerance to foods containing raw but not cooked eggs and had positive skin tests to raw egg antigen and 17D vaccine. Because few foods contain raw eggs, and these are mixed with other ingredients, persons sensitized to raw eggs might not give an allergic history when queried prior to vaccination.

There are no current precautions regarding sequential immunization with 17D vaccine and other vaccines produced in chicken embryos or chick embryo cell culture. Influenza vaccine is manufactured in eggs but contains little residual egg protein, can generally be safely given to egg allergic persons, and might not cross-sensitize to YF vaccine.[197] Excipients in YF 17D vaccine can also cause hypersensitivity reactions. In particular, hydrolyzed gelatin incorporated as a stabilizer in YF-VAX, ARILVAX, and other vaccines such as measles, varicella, and JE vaccines have been implicated in allergic reactions.[198,199]

VAERS data from 1990 to 1997 revealed 45 cases of nonfatal hypersensitivity-type reactions (urticaria, angioedema, bronchospasm, anaphylaxis) associated with YF 17D vaccine. Based on the number of vaccine doses distributed in the United States during the interval under study (5.2 million) and the assumption that all reported events are caused by 17D vaccine and that the reporting sensitivity was 50%, the incidence of allergic reactions was estimated at 1:58,000 doses.[200]

Reactions Due to Improper Handling and Use of YF Vaccine

Because YF vaccine contains no preservative, improper handling of multiple-dose vials can lead to bacterial contamination, sometimes with serious consequences. Four outbreaks of necrotizing myositis and sepsis leading to death have been associated with contamination of YF vaccine vials or inoculation equipment in Africa.[201–203] In these episodes, bacterial contamination of multidose containers, improperly sterilized jet injector equipment, or reuse of syringes and needles were implicated.

Indications for YF Vaccine

All persons inhabiting countries or areas within countries endemic for YF should be immunized, preferably at 9 months of age. Areas endemic for YF are shown in Figure 5-3.

During epidemics of YF, mass immunization should be instituted at the earliest possible stage of the outbreak. Priorities for immunizing population subsets according to geography or age group will be determined by local information on the progress of the outbreak and on the history of prior vaccination coverage.

Immigrants, travelers, and military personnel and dependents require immunization at least 10 days before arrival in endemic areas. Even a short stay in an area of virus transmission is dangerous, as was illustrated by recent cases in unvaccinated travelers to the Amazon Region (see Table 5-1). Because the indigenous population might be immune and the virus can circulate silently between monkeys and mosquitoes, the absence of recent notification of YF in an area is not an indication that it is safe to enter. On the other hand, reports of human YF cases within the past 1 to 2 years are a clear indication of a high risk of infection. The risk of infection is greatest in rural areas, and travel to large cities within endemic areas carries a low risk in the absence of a reported outbreak. Coastal areas of East Africa and most of South America are outside the area of YF transmission.

Some countries in the endemic zone require or recommend that travelers be vaccinated prior to arrival and have a valid certificate of immunization. Most countries outside the endemic zones but infested with *A. aegypti* and thus susceptible to the introduction and spread of YF require a vaccination certificate for travelers entering from endemic countries (Figure 5-9). A full listing of requirements for all countries can be found in the WHO document *International Travel and Health*, available from WHO Distribution and Sales, CH-1211 Geneva 27, Switzerland, and in CDC's *Health Information for International Travel*, available from the Superintendent of Documents, US Government Printing Office, Washington, DC 20402 (phone 202-512-1800).[74,204] Some countries require a certificate for persons who have been in transit in an endemic country even if the disembarking traveler is in transit. Controls at airports and borders are highly variable, but travelers respecting the regulations will avoid unnecessary delays. India and Bangladesh have

Table 5-3. Yellow Fever Vacine-Associated Viscerotropic Adverse Events

Case	Year	Location	Travel destination	Vaccine	Age/sex/ race	Preexisting conditions	Days to Onset	Days to Hospitalization	Syndrome Initial	Syndrome Evolving
1	1998	US	Nepal, Thailand	YF-VAX®[1]	76/M/W	Osteoarthitis, mild renal insufficiency, Crohn's (in remission)	4	7	Fever, headache, myalgia, fatigue	Transient rash, hypotension, hypoxemia, dyspnea, agitation, confusion
2	1998	US	Africa	YF-VAX®	79/F/W	Hypothyroid, polymyalgia rheumatics, hypertension	2	3	Fever, myalgia, confusion, abdominal pain, diarrhea, cough, fatigue	Dyspnea, cardiac arrythmia, hypotension, acidosis, hypoxemia, oliguria (requiring dialysis)
3	1998	US	Amazon	YF-VAX®	67/F/W	Ulcerative colitis, thymoma	5	6	Fever, myalgias, chills, nausea	Tachpnea, tachycardia, mechanical ventilation, hypotension
4	1996	US	Africa	YF-VAX®[2]	63/M/W	None	3	5	Fever, headache, myalgia, nausea, vomiting	Transient rash, fever, rhabdomyolysis, myoglobinuria, oliguria (dialysis), epistaxis, hypotension, stupor
5	1999	Brazil		BioManguinhos[3]	5/F/W	Low birthweight, repeated episodes of bronchitis and diarrhea, aseptic meningitis	3	5	Fever, diarrhea, vomiting	Respiratory distress, dehydration, hepatomegaly, jaundice, shock
6	2000	Brazil		BioManguinhos	22/F/B	None	4	8	Fever, headache, myalgia, sore throat	Epigastric pain, jaundice, oliguria, hepatomegaly, edema, hypoxemia, respiratory distress, mechanical ventilation, hemothorax, hypotension

[1] Oral typhoid vaccine administered 21 days before YF vaccine

[2] Concomitant vaccination with oral polio, meningococal vaccine; onset of non-specific syndrome occurred 3 days after 17D vaccineation, but symptoms subsided and 2 days later (5 days after 17D) hepatitis A vaccine was administered. Severe syndrome onset followed hepatatitis A by several hours

[3] Concomitant measles-mumps-rubella

Continued on next page

Table 5-3. Yellow Fever Vacine-Associated Viscerotropic Adverse Events (*Continued*)

Case	Year	Location	Travel destination	Vaccine	Age/sex/ race	Preexisting conditions	Days to		Syndrome	
							Onset	Hospitalization	Initial	Evolving
7	2001	Australia	Saudi Arabia	Stamaril®[4]	56/M/W	None	2	5	Fever, rigors, nausea, vomiting, myalgia, arthralgia	Respiratory distress, oliguria, hypotension, hypoxemia, mechanical ventilation, acidosis
8	2001	US	North Africa, Ecuador Middle East,	YF-VAX®[5]	25/M	None	1	9	Lymphadenopathy, headache, malaise, nausea, diarrhea, fever	Fulminanat hepatic and renal failure, respiratory failure, hypotension, hemorrhage and DIC, stupor, mechanical ventilation, vasopressors, dialysis
9	2002	US	Venezuala	YF-VAX®	70/M	Post thymectomy for myasthenia gravis; hypo-thyroid, hypertension	5	8	Fever, dyspnea, myalgia, malaise	Fever, thrombocytopenia, elevated liver enzymes and bilirubin and creatinine; hypotension, respiratory failure, dialysis

[4] Concominant meningococcal vaccine; treatment with atorvastatin (see text)
[5] Concomitant influenza and poliovirus vaccines

Continued on next page

Table 5-3. Yellow Fever Vacine-Associated Viscerotropic Adverse Events (*Continued*)

Outcome	Clinical lab abnormalities		Virological findings	Histopathology (liver)	Reference
	Initial	*Peak*			
Survived	AST 31 U/L; ALT 42 U/L; alk phos 41 U/L; bilirubin 49.6 mmol/L; creatinine 362 mmol/L; platelets 94,000/L	AST 122; ALT 122; alk phos 109; bilirubin 99.2; creatinine 627.7; platelets 67,000 >10,240 (day 45)	17D virus isolated from serum (days 7 and 8) and CSF (day 10). PRNT antibody titer 1:20 (day 7),		Martin et al, 2001a
Died (day 21)	AST 40 U/L; ALT 27 U/L; alk phos 77 U/L; bilirubin 8.6 mmol/L; creatinine 124 mmol/L; platelets 154,000/L	AST 301; ALT 290; alk phos 310; bilirubin 111; creatinine 265; platelets 26,000	17D virus isolated from serum (day 7) PRNT antibody titer 1:640 (day 7), 10,240 (day 11)	Not done	
Died (day 9)	AST 85 U/L; alk phos 55 U/L; bilirubin 32.5 mmol/L; creatinine 115 mmol/L; platelets 194,000/L	AST 1638;alk phos 112; bilirubin 32.5; creatinine 327; platelets 7,000	Not done	Not done	
Died (day 30)	AST 113 U/L; ALT 109 U/L; alk phos 141 U/L; bilirubin 94.1 mmol/L; creatinine 141 mmol/L; platelets 121,000/L	AST 446; ALT 190; bilirubin 133.4; creatinine 495; platelets 25,000	Liver biopsy (day 28): yellow fever antigen	Liver biopsy, minimal changes, not diagnostic	
Died (day 5)	AST 114 IU/L; ALT 160 IU/L; bilirubin 18.8 mmol/L		17D virus isolated from blood, heart, liver, spleen at autopsy; large amounts of antigen in hepatocytes and Kupffer cells	Midzonal necrosis, Councilman bodies	Vasconcelos et al, 2001
Died (day 10)	AST 430 U/L; ALT 190 U/L; creatinine 247.5 mmol/L; platelets 54,000/L; proteinuria 1+	AST 511; ALT 91; alk phos 530; bilirubin 194.9; creatinine 3447.6; platelets 38,000	Anti-YF IgM (day 10); 17D virus isolated from blood, brain, liver, kidney, spleen, lung at autopsy; YF antigen in hepatocytes, Kupffer cells	Midzonal necrosis, Councilman bodies	

Continued on next page

Table 5-3. Yellow Fever Vacine-Associated Viscerotropic Adverse Events *(Continued)*

Outcome	Clinical lab abnormalities		Virological findings	Histopathology (liver)	Reference
	Initial	*Peak*			
Died (day 10)	Normal	AST 6750 U/L; ALT 1550 U/L; creatinine 336 mmol/L	YF virus isolated and/or PCR positive serum, liver; serum, spleen, liver, muscle	Panlobular necrosis; steatosis, Councilman bodies	Chan et al, 2001
Survived	No data	AST 436 U/L; ALT 362 U/L; Bili 8.3 mg/dl; creatinine 10.4 mg/dl; creat kinase 789 U/L; platelets 64,000/mm^3	Convalescent serum ~1 yr after vaccination: YF neutralizing antibody titer 1:640	No data	CDC, 2002a
Survived	No data	AST 400 U/L; ALT 238 U/L; Bili 1.4 mg/dl; creatinine 6.2 mg/dl; platelets 50,000/mm^3	Serum on days 21, 25, 33 and pleural fluid on day 26 negative by quantitative RT-PCR; serum day 26 YF neutralizing antibody titer 1:1,280	No data	

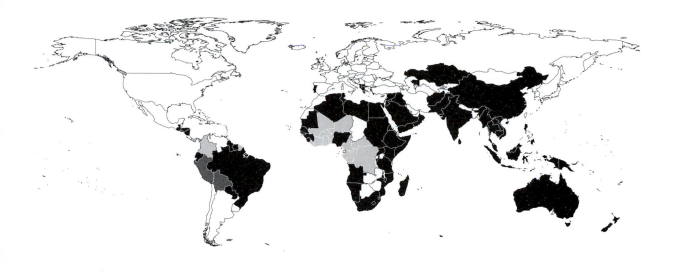

Figure 5-9. Countries requiring a valid certificate of vaccination for entry (see references for more detail).[74,203] Countries with no shading have no YF vaccination requirements. Countries shaded in black require vaccination for persons coming from endemic areas. Countries shaded in dark gray require vaccination for persons coming from endemic areas and recommend vaccination for persons coming from nonendemic areas who plan to visit endemic regions of the country. Countries shaded in medium gray recommend (but do not require) vaccination for entry (Chad) or visits to endemic regions of the country (Colombia). Countries shaded in light grey require vaccination for all visitors. Some countries (eg, Myanmar, Sudan, and Paraguay) have exit vaccination requirements. Portugal requires vaccination only for persons in or outbound from the Azores or Madeira. Consult the WHO reference for details and listings of island nations that do not appear on the map.[74]

particularly stringent regulations, requiring quarantine of unvaccinated persons coming from endemic regions. Countries vary with respect to the age at which infants require a valid certificate.[74] Persons with a contraindication to immunization (see below) should obtain a letter from their physician stating why immunization could not be performed and should be prepared to present this document to officials at ports of call.

Contraindications and Precautions

Minimum Age for Vaccination

Infants are at higher risk of YEL-AND. Published guidelines differ somewhat on the minimum age for vaccination. There is uniform agreement, however, that routine immunization can be performed at 9 months of age. The current recommendation of the Advisory Committee on Immunization Practices (ACIP) states that vaccination of infants < 6 months is contraindicated.[205] Infants between 6 and 9 months may be immunized according to the physician's judgment and an assessment as to the risk of exposure to YF virus, for example, travel to a rural area in the YF endemic zone or to an area with recent reported cases of YF.

Advanced age has been shown to be a risk factor for serious adverse events.[182,206] A retrospective analysis of VAERS data revealed a higher incidence of serious adverse events (neurologic or multisystem involvement) in elderly persons. Individuals > 65 years have a risk of severe adverse events 12 to 32 times higher than adults 25 to 44 years of age, suggesting that waning immunity with age might play a role. Travelers over 65 years of age should be cautioned about the potential for severe adverse events and a careful evaluation made of the need for vaccination.

Pregnancy and Lactation

Initially, the use of YF vaccine in pregnancy was not constrained, and hundreds of women were vaccinated without recognized problems.[6,207]

The hypothetical risk of a live viral vaccine to the developing fetus ultimately led to the recommendation that the vaccine not be administered during pregnancy unless clearly required. On theoretic grounds, should transplacental infection occur, the unborn infant might be more susceptible to neuroinvasion and encephalitis. The WHO recommends that vaccination be delayed until the last trimester, but there is no empiric evidence that this reduces the risk to the fetus.[74]

Nasidi and colleagues studied 101 women who were immunized in Nigeria in 1986.[173] Four women (4%) were immunized in the first trimester, 8 (8%) in the second trimester, and 89 (88%) in the third trimester. There were no adverse events among 40 infants who were followed up and no evidence of transplacental infection by measurement of cord-blood anti-YF IgM. As noted previously (see "Primary Vaccine Failure"), women immunized during pregnancy had a significantly lower seroconversion rate (39%) compared with controls.

During an island-wide emergency vaccination campaign in Trinidad in 1989, it was estimated that 100 to 200 women were inadvertently vaccinated during pregnancy.[208] Among 41 neonates tested, 1 (a healthy, full-term baby) had YF IgM antibody in cord blood, suggesting that congenital infection with 17D virus might have occurred without an untoward effect on the fetus.

In a separate case-control study of 17D vaccination during early pregnancy, the relative risk of spontaneous abortion was estimated to be 2.3, but the difference was not statistically significant.[209] Postmarketing safety data monitored by vaccine manufacturers contain numerous reports of inadvertent vaccination in pregnancy and a few reports of congenital abnormalities, but the relationship to the vaccine is uncertain.

Pregnant women who have inadvertently received the vaccine should be reassured that there is no risk to themselves and a very low or negligible risk to the fetus. These women should be followed to parturition, and if fetal abnormality is noted, a cord-blood sample should be obtained for IgM testing to determine whether congenital infection had occurred. Because the immune response to YF vaccination during pregnancy is impaired, revaccination is indicated at an appropriate time after delivery. If vaccination during pregnancy is required because of a high risk of exposure during travel, it is advisable to determine whether successful immunization has been achieved by a test of neutralizing antibodies 10 to 14 days or more after vaccination. If seroconversion is not evident, revaccination should be considered, preferably after parturition.

Lactation is considered a contraindication to vaccination in the United States and the United Kingdom because of the theoretic risk of transmission of 17D virus to the breast-fed infant. The concern is based on the knowledge that some tick-borne flaviviruses are secreted in milk of domesticated livestock and that West Nile virus has been transmitted via human milk. When travel cannot be postponed or where there is a high risk of exposure to YF (eg, in vaccination campaigns to combat outbreaks), lactating women may be vaccinated.

Immunosuppression

Because of the theoretic risk of neuroinvasion and encephalitis, the vaccine is contraindicated in patients with known immunosuppression due to HIV infection, leukemia, lymphoma, generalized malignancy, other conditions affecting humoral and cellular immune responses, or treatment with immunosuppressive drugs, including high-dose corticosteroids. Low-dose corticosteroid treatment ($\leq$ 20 mg prednisone or equivalent/day) or intra-articular injections of corticosteroids do not pose a contraindication to YF vaccination.[205]

Asymptomatic HIV infection is not considered a contraindication in the United States. The ACIP recommends that such patients be evaluated and that those with adequate immune function who cannot avoid exposure be offered the choice of vaccination. As noted in "Primary Vaccine Failure," preliminary studies indicate that asymptomatic HIV infection might reduce the immune response to 17D vaccine, and patients should be cautioned or serologically tested to establish a vaccine take.

The recent report of a healthy adult with low CD4+ cell counts due to HIV infection who developed fatal encephalitis following YF vaccination is the first direct evidence that immunosuppression as a risk factor.[130]

Blood, Bone Marrow, and Organ Donation

Blood donations should be delayed until 30 days after YF 17D vaccination. There are no data on whether YF 17D vaccine can induce transient false positive serologic tests for HIV or hepatitis, as has been reported for influenza vaccine.[210] No recommendations have been formulated on the suitability of persons who have received 17D vaccine at a remote point in time as organ or bone marrow donors. This issue has been raised because of the possibility that 17D virus causes a latent, persistent infection (see "Duration of Immunity") that is contained and irrelevant in the immune host but might cause systemic infection in an immuno-suppressed transplant recipient. In a single report, bone marrow from a donor twin immunized 1 month previously with YF 17D was grafted to a recipient twin without any subsequent adverse effects.[211]

Simultaneous and Combined Vaccination

Yellow fever 17D vaccine has been given simultaneously at different sites or as a mixture combined with a variety of other vaccines, including vaccinia, diphtheria-pertussis-tetanus, bacille Calmette-Guérin (BCG), measles, typhoid, cholera, hepatitis A, hepatitis B, and meningococcus A/C plus typhoid vaccines.

No increase in adverse events has been noted, nor, with few exceptions, have there been changes in immune responses compared with control groups given a single vaccine. On theoretic grounds alone, it is recommended that live vaccines (such as measles) be given either concurrently at different sites or separated by 1 month; however, where this is impractical, the schedule may be modified. Inactivated, protein, or subunit vaccines can be given concurrently with YF 17D vaccine.

Studies of YF vaccine given concurrently or at weekly intervals after live measles vaccine showed no differences in immunogenicity.[212,213] Administration of typhoid Vi vaccine appeared to enhance antibody titers to YF in one study; this effect might have been due to an adjuvant effect of lipopolysaccharide.[214] Another study looked at concomitant administration of YF 17D, inactivated hepatitis A, and typhoid Vi vaccines; no significant differences in immunogenicity were observed.[215] A possible interference with YF immune responses was noted when either vaccinia and measles vaccine or hepatitis B vaccine were combined with YF 17D, but these results have not been confirmed in other trials, and current recommendations allow concurrent vaccination with YF 17D and measles or hepatitis B.[205,216,217] An interesting observation was the mutual interference due to simultaneous or sequential administration (at intervals up to 1 month) of 17D and inactivated, parenteral whole cell cholera vaccines.[218,219] Although this cholera vaccine is no longer used, these unexpected results suggest caution in making assumptions about vaccine interactions. Trials of combined YF and live oral cholera vaccine (alone or with Ty21a live typhoid vaccine) showed no interference with anticholera immunity or YF antibody responses.[220,221]

The most problematic vaccine interactions will be with other live attenuated flavivirus vaccines. As new live vaccines against dengue, Japanese encephalitis, and other viruses are developed, careful studies will be required to evaluate interference and enhancement effects.[53,54,57]

Concomitant Treatment with Antimalarials

Chloroquine inhibits the immune response to inactivated rabies vaccine and live oral cholera vaccine, and interferes with flavivirus replication in vitro. In humans, however, no inhibitory effect on YF vaccination was demonstrated by treatment of chloroquine at doses used for malaria prophylaxis.[222]

PASSIVE AND PASSIVE-ACTIVE IMMUNIZATION

Passive immunization using convalescent human serum or hyperimmune antibodies prepared in nonhuman primates, horses, and goats was widely practiced as a means of prophylaxis prior to the development of vaccines.[223,224]

There has been some renewed interest in the use of passive immunization as a means to protect short-term travelers who have contraindications for active vaccination. Commercial lots of serum immunoglobulin contain high titers of neutralizing antibodies to YF because 5 to 10% of plasma donors have been immunized during military service in the United States.[186]

A patient with chronic lymphatic leukemia, in whom active vaccination was contraindicated, wished to visit the Amazon region. Passive immunization with commercial intravenous immune globulin (IVIG) having an log neutralization index (LNI) of 3.0 was performed, resulting in a high initial passive titer and a protective level of antibody throughout several weeks of travel (McMullen R et al, unpublished data, 2000). The level of passive antibody considered to be protective was an LNI of 0.7 based on studies in nonhuman primates.[225] Although this approach might have merit for certain individuals who cannot avoid travel to a high-risk area, it is expensive and requires monitoring of antibody levels in IVIG and the patient, and efficacy is not supported by clinical data.

Transplacental transfer of YF-neutralizing antibodies has been documented in monkeys and humans, and antibody has also been found in breast milk of immune mothers.[226–228] Because YF 17D vaccine is not administered to infants prior to 6 months of age for safety reasons, maternal immunity does not pose an obstacle to effective immunization.

"Passive-active immunization" using an excess of human or animal serum mixed with partially attenuated vaccine virus elicited active immunity without untoward effects and was standard practice in the 1930s.[3] Passive-active immunization was discontinued in 1936 with the advent of vaccines that could be administered safely without serum.

The neutralizing antibody response to YF 17D vaccine was not affected by the intramuscular administration of 5 mL of commercial pooled ISG for prevention of hepatitis A. The ISG contained high titers of F-neutralizing antibodies and was given 0 to 7 days before or at intervals after YF 17D immunization.[187] The results are not unexpected given the success of passive-active immunization and the observation that revaccination of individuals with neutralizing antibodies often results in a booster response.[151]

The original concept of passive-active immunization is being reconsidered in light of the newly recognized occurrence of severe and fatal viscerotropic adverse events and a higher incidence of neurotropic events than was previously recognized (see "Vaccine Safety").

FUTURE YELLOW FEVER VACCINES AND YELLOW FEVER–VECTORED VACCINES

The construction of a full-length complementary strand deoxyribonucleic acid (cDNA) clone of 17D virus provides a new approach to vaccine development. The cDNA can be reverse transcribed to full-length positive-strand RNA and transfected into primary chick embryo or other cells for vaccine manufacture. Unlike current YF vaccines, which are heterogeneous mixtures of virion subpopulations, a vaccine produced in this way would be genetically homogeneous. The benefits of this approach are genetic homogeneity, reduced likelihood of selection of a subpopulation during replication in vitro or in vivo, manufacture of seed virus from bacterial plasmids (reducing the risk of adventitious viruses), and production of vaccine in a cell culture system. This method would also allow the introduction of mutations or deletions that might render the 17D vaccine incapable of producing neurotropic or viscerotropic adverse events.

The use of YF 17D as a live vector is a promising approach for the development of new vaccines against other flaviviruses. Novel chimeric vaccines have been constructed in which heterologous flavivirus prM-E genes (eg, of JE virus, West Nile, or dengue) have been inserted into the YF 17D virus infectious clone.[57,129] Characterization of chimeric viruses has shown that the nonstructural genes of YF 17D confer a highly attenuated phenotype on the vaccine candidates, including the restricted ability to replicate in mosquito vectors while retaining the ability of the vaccines to efficiently immunize mice, monkeys, and humans.

Workers at BioManguinhos (Brazil) have produced a new seed stock and vaccines in primary chick embryo cell culture rather than embryonated eggs. Manufacture in cell culture would be expected to significantly increase vaccine virus yields and thereby reduce costs. Although modernization of manufacture of the 17D vaccine in cell culture has been a goal for many years, previous attempts have failed because of alterations in the virulence phenotype during passage in cell culture (a problem avoided by a genetically uniform infectious clone) or to poor yields due to in vitro interferon production. However, the tools of molecular biology were not available at those times to monitor genetic changes during cell culture propagation.

Combination vaccines are not being pursued actively by industry. Potential combinations of value might include YF and measles vaccines for the EPI and the combinations of 17D vaccine with inactivated vaccines (eg, hepatitis A, typhoid) as a means of simplifying immunization regimens for travelers. Again, it is likely that the development of chimeric YF-vectored vaccines will lead to combination vaccines against YF and dengue or against dengue and JE; the combination of these vaccines with measles vaccines would be of interest for use in the EPI.

PUBLIC HEALTH POLICY

Eradication of YF by means of human vaccination is not feasible because the virus is maintained in nature in a mosquito reservoir and is amplified in nonhuman primates.

In South America, 54 million persons (21% of the 258 million total population as of 1997) inhabit the YF-endemic zone. YF immunization has been implemented for decades in endemic areas in South America but vaccination coverage varies by country. With the leadership of the Pan American Health Organization, vaccination policy has recently changed from periodic mass campaigns to routine childhood vaccination in the EPI. Significant progress is being made toward implementation of this policy in Brazil, Bolivia, Guyana, Peru, and Ecuador. Because of the threat of reurbanization in densely populated coastal areas, some countries are also considering extending immunization beyond the endemic regions. Because the 17D vaccine induces life-long immunity, as shown by studies of populations that do not have an opportunity for boosting by natural exposure, revaccination is unnecessary.[163]

The increased incidence of epidemic YF in Africa, beginning in the mid-1980s, and the recognition that the disease predominantly affects children led to a reassessment of the vaccination policy for Africa.[8] In 1988, a joint UNICEF/WHO Technical Group on Immunization for the African Region and the EPI Global Advisory Group recommended that countries endemic for YF incorporate 17D vaccine into the routine EPI schedule, either at 6 months of age or at 9 months of age together with measles vaccine.[229,230] In 1990, this recommendation was reemphasized, with the additional suggestion that catch-up immunization of older children is needed in countries at high risk. By 1998, 17 of the 34 African countries endemic for YF had incorporated the vaccine into the EPI, although coverage is low in the majority of countries. Whereas a policy of routine immunization of infants in the EPI is an important goal, it should be emphasized that, even assuming the achievement of high coverage rates, it would take at least 15 years to create herd immunity sufficient to prevent epidemic spread without catch-up immunization of older children.[71]

Monath and Nasidi concluded that after introduction of YF vaccine into the EPI, 15 to 18 years would be required to achieve an effective immune barrier to epidemic spread, at which time routine immunization would be seven- to eightfold more efficient than emergency control in the number of cases and deaths prevented.[71] The cost of routine immunization was estimated at $763/case (US) prevented and $3,817/death prevented during epidemics, with lower costs if prevention of endemic disease was taken into account. These cost-effectiveness ratios compared favorably to those for other infections preventable by EPI vaccines in Africa.

Elimination of human YF is achievable by vaccination, but nearly 100% coverage would be necessary to prevent cases of jungle YF acquired by exposure to enzootic vectors. Prevention of epidemics involving interhuman virus transmission by *A. aegypti* or sylvatic vectors also requires a high prevalence of immunity. This was shown in the case of the severe epidemic in Senegal (1965) affecting children < 10 years, where the prevalence of immunity before the epidemic was approximately 57% and a prevalence of 90% would have been required to preclude the epidemic.[231,232] The effect of herd immunity on YF transmission under different assumptions of vector capacity was explored in a mathematic model by Monath and Nasidi.[71] The prevalence of immunity in a human population required to preclude an epidemic was estimated to be between 60 and 90%. In a more recent and separate analysis, Massad and colleagues reached a very similar conclusion, estimating that 58 to 88% YF vaccination coverage rates would be required to prevent urban YF in Sao Paulo State, Brazil.[283]

REFERENCES

1. Mutebi J-P, Wang H, Li L, et al. Phylogenetic and evolutionary relationships among yellow fever virus isolates in Africa. J Virol 2001;75:6999–7008.

2. Anon. Yellow Fever. A complication of various publications. Results of the work of Maj Walter Reed, Medical Corps, United States Army, and the Yellow Fever Commission. 61st Congress Doc No 822, Washington DC: Govt Printing Office, 1911.

3. Sawyer WA, Kitchen SF, Lloyd W. Vaccination against yellow fever with immune serum and virus fixed for mice. J Exp Med 1932;55:945–69.

4. Sellards AW, Laigret J. Vaccination de l'homme contre la fièvre jaune. C R Acad Sci Paris 1932;194:1609–11.

5. Theiler M, Smith HH. The effect of prolonged cultivation in vitro upon the pathogenicity of yellow fever virus. J Exp Med 1937;65:767–86.

6. Smith HH. Penna HA, Paoliello A. Yellow fever vaccination with cultured virus (17D) without immune serum. Am J Trop Med Hyg 1938;18:437–68.

7. Monath TP. Yellow fever vaccines. The success of empiricism, pitfalls of application, and transition to molecular vaccinology. In: Plotkin S, Fantini M, editors. Vaccinia, vaccination and vaccinology. Jenner, Pasteur and their successors. Paris: Elsevier; 1996. p. 157–82.

8. Robertson SE, Hull BP, Tomori O, et al. Yellow fever. A decade of reemergence. JAMA 1996;276:1157–62.

9. Monath TP. Epidemiology of yellow fever. Current status and speculations on future trends. In: Saluzzo J-F, Dodet B, editors. Factors in the emergence of arbovirus diseases. Paris: Elsevier; 1997. p. 143–56.

10. Tomori O. Impact of yellow fever on the developing world. Adv Virus Res 1999;53:5–34.

11. Marianneau P, Cardona A, Edelman L, et al. Dengue virus replication in human hepatoma cells activates NF-kappa B which in turn induces apoptotic cell death. J Virol 1997;71:3244–9.

12. Marianneau P, Steffan A-M, Royer C, et al. Differing infection patterns of dengue and yellow fever viruses in a human hepatoma cell line. J Infect Dis 1998;178:1270–8.

13. Berry GP, Kitchen SF. Yellow fever accidentally contracted in the laboratory. A study of seven cases. Am J Trop Med Hyg 1931;11:365–434.

14. Beeuwkes H. Clinical manifestations of yellow fever in the West African native as observed during four extensive epidemics of the disease in the Gold Coast and Nigeria. Trans R Soc Trop Med Hyg 1936;1:61–86.

15. Monath TP. Yellow fever. A medically neglected disease. Report on a seminar. Rev Infect Dis 1987;9:165–75.

16. MacNamara FN. Man as the host of the yellow fever virus [medical thesis]. Cambridge (UK): Cambridge Univ.; 1955.

17. Elton NW, Romero A, Trejos A. Clinical pathology of yellow fever. Am J Clin Pathol 1955;25:135–601.

18. Oudart J-L, Rey M. Protéinurie, protéinémie et transaminasémies dans 23 cas de fièvre jaune confirmée. Bull World Health Organ 1970;42:95–102.

19. Chagas E, De Freitas L. Electrocardiogramma na febre amarela. Mem Inst Oswaldo Cruz 1929;Suppl 7:72–85.

20. Stevenson LD. Pathological changes in the central nervous system in yellow fever. Arch Pathol 1939;27:249–66.

21. Monath TP, Craven RB, Adjukiewicz A, et al. Yellow fever in the Gambia, 1978–1979. Epidemiologic aspects with observations on the occurrence of Orungo virus infections. Am J Trop Med Hyg 1980;29:912–28.

22. Nasidi A, Monath TP, DeCock K. Urban yellow fever epidemic in western Nigeria, 1987. Trans R Soc Trop Med Hyg 1989;83:401–6.

23. Hanson H. Observations on the age and sex incidence of deaths and recoveries in the yellow fever epidemic in the department of Lambayeque, Peru, in 1921. Am J Trop Med Hyg 1929;9:233–9.

24. Marovich M, Grouard-Vogel G, Louder M, et al. Human dendritic cells as targets of dengue virus infection. J Investig Dermatol Symp Proc 2001;6:219–24.

25. Tigertt WD, Berge TO, Gochenour WS, et al. Experimental yellow fever. Trans N Y Acad Sci 1960;22:323–33.

26. Monath TP, Brinker KR, Chandler FW, et al. Pathophysiologic correlations in a rhesus monkey model of yellow fever. Am J Trop Med Hyg 1981;30:431–43.

27. Monath TP, Ballinger ME, Miller BR, et al. Detection of yellow fever viral RNA by nucleic acid hybridization and viral antigen by immunocytochemistry in fixed human liver. Am J Trop Med Hyg 1989;40:663–8.

28. Lloyd W. The myocardium in yellow fever. II. The myocardial lesions in experimental yellow fever. Am Heart J 1931;6:504–16.

29. Bosch I, Xhaja K, Estevez L, et al. Increased production of interleukin-8 in primary human monocytes and in human epithelial and endothelial cell lines after dengue virus challenge. J Virol 2002;76:5588–97.

30. Peters CJ, Zaki SR. Role of the endothelium in viral hemorrhagic fevers. Crit Care Med 2002;30 Suppl:S268–73.

31. Liu CT, Griffin MJ. Distribution of tissue water and electrolytes in normal rhesus macaques. Am J Vet Res.1978;39:1692–4.

32. Colebunders R, Mariage J-L, Coche J-C, et al. A Belgian traveller who acquired yellow fever in the Gambia. Clin Infect Dis, 2002;35:113–6.

33. Borges APA, Oliveira GSC, Almeida Netto JC. Estudo da coagulaçao sanguinea na febre amarela. Rev Patol Trop 1973;2:143–9.

34. Santos F, Pereira Lima C, Paiva P, et al. Coagulaçao intravascular disseminada aguda na febre amarela. Dosagem dos factores da coagulaçao. Brasilia Med 1973;9:9–16.

35. Bendersky N, Carlet J, Ricomme JL, et al. Deux cas mortels de fièvre jaune observés en France et contractés au Sénégal. Bull Soc Pathol Exot 1980;73:54–61.

36. Dennis LH, Reisberg BE, Crosbie J, et al. The original haemorrhagic fever: yellow fever. Br J Haematol 1969;5:455–62.

37. Stephen EL, Sammons ML, Pannier WL, et al. Effect of a nuclease-resistant derivative of polyriboinosinic-polyribocytidylic acid complex on yellow fever in rhesus monkeys (*Macaca mulatta*). J Infect Dis 1977;136:122–6.

38. Bonnevie-Nielsen V, Heron I, Monath TP, et al. Lymphocytic 2′, 5′-oligoadenylate synthetase activity increases prior to the appearance of neutralizing antibodies and immunoglobulin M and immunoglobulin G antibodies after primary and secondary immunization with yellow fever vaccine. Clin Diagn Lab Immunol 1995;2:302–6.

39. Perelygin AA, Scherbik SV, Zhulin IB, et al. Positional cloning of the murine flavivirus resistance gene. Proc Natl Acad Sci U S A 2002;99:9322–7.

40. Kurane I, Innis BL, Nisalak A, et al. Human T cell responses to dengue antigens. Proliferative responses and interferon-gamma production. J Clin Invest 1989;83:506–13.

41. Kurane I, Meager A, Ennis FA. Dengue virus-specific human T-cell clones. Serotype cross-reactive proliferation, interferon-gamma production, cytotoxic activity. J Exp Med 1989;170:763–75.

42. Arroyo, JI, Apperson SA, Cropp CB, et al. Effect of human gamma interferon on yellow fever virus infection. Am J Trop Med Hyg 1988;38:647–50.

43. Liu T, Chambers TJ. Yellow fever virus encephalitis. Properties of the brain-associated T-cell response during virus clearance in normal and gamma interferon-deficient mice and requirement for CD4+ lymphocytes. J Virol 2001;75:2107–18.

44. Snijders EP, Postmus S, Schüffner W. On the protective power of yellow fever sera and dengue sera against yellow fever virus. Am J Trop Med 1934;14:519–45.

45. Theiler M, Anderson CR. The relative resistance of dengue-immune monkeys to yellow fever virus. Am J Trop Med Hyg 1975;24:115–7.

46. Henderson BE, Cheshire PP, Kirya GB, et al. Immunologic studies with yellow fever and selected African group B arboviruses in rhesus and vervet monkeys. Am J Trop Med Hyg 1970;19:110–8.

47. Schlesinger JJ, Brandriss MW, Cropp CB, et al. Protection against yellow fever in monkeys by immunization with yellow fever virus nonstructural protein NS1. J Virol 1986;60:1153–5.

48. Schlesinger JJ, Brandriss MW, Walsh EE. Protection against 17D yellow fever encephalitis in mice by passive transfer of monoclonal antibodies to the nonstructural glycoprotein gp48 and by active immunization with gp48. J Immunol 1985;135:2805–9.

49. Gould EA, Buckley A, Barrett ADT, et al. Neutralizing (54K) and non-neutralizing (54K and 58K) monoclonal antibodies against structural and nonstructural yellow fever virus proteins confer immunity in mice. J Gen Virol 1986;67:591–5.

50. Putnak JR, Schlesinger JJ. Protection of mice against yellow fever virus encephalitis by immunization with a vaccinia virus recombinant encoding the yellow fever virus non-structural proteins, NS1, NS2a and NS2b. J Gen Virol 1990;71:1697–02.

51. Co MD, Terajima M, Cruz J, et al. Human cytotoxic T lymphocyte responses to live attenuated 17D yellow fever vaccine. Identification of HLA-B35-restricted CTL epitopes on nonstructural proteins NS1, NS2b, NS3, and the structural protein E. Virology 2002;293:151–63.

52. Schlesinger JJ, Brandriss MW. Growth of 17D yellow fever virus in a macrophage-like cell line, U937. Role of Fc and viral receptors in antibody-mediated infection. J Immunol 1981;127:659–65.

53. Bancroft WH Jr, Top FH Jr, Eckels KH, et al. Dengue-2 vaccine. Virological, immunological, and clinical responses of six yellow fever immune recipients. Infect Immun 1981;31:698–703.

54. Scott RM, Eckels KH, Bancroft WH. Dengue 2 vaccine. Dose response in volunteers in relation to yellow fever immune status. J Infect Dis 1983;148:1055–60.

55. Monath TP, McCarthy K, Bedford P, et al. Clinical proof of principle for ChimeriVax™. Recombinant live, attenuated vaccines against flavivirus infections. Vaccine 2002;20:1004–18.

56. Jones MM, Wilson DC. Clinical features of yellow fever cases at Vom Christian Hospital during the 1969 epidemic on the Jos Plateau, Nigeria. Bull World Health Organ 1972;46:653–7.

57. Monath TP, Nichols R, Archambault WT, et al. Comparative safety and immunogenicity of two yellow fever 17D vaccines (ARILVAX™ and yellow fever-VAX®) in a Phase III multicenter, double-blind clinical trial. Am J Trop Med Hyg 2002;66:533–41.

58. Rey FA, Heinz FX, Mandl C, et al. The envelope glycoprotein from the tick-borne encephalitis virus at 2Å resolution. Nature 1995;375:291–8.

59. Brown TM, Chang GJ, Cropp CB, et al. Detection of yellow fever virus by polymerase chain reaction. Clin Diagn Virol 1994;2:41–51.

60. De Brito T, Siqueira SAC, Santos RTM, et al. Human fatal yellow fever. Immunohistochemical detection of viral antigens in the liver, kidney and heart. Pathol Res Pract 1992;188:177–81.

61. De La Monte SM, Linhares AL, Travassos Da Rosa APA, et al. Immunoperoxidase detection of yellow fever virus after natural and experimental infections. Trop Geogr Med 1983;35:235–41.

62. Hall WC, Crowell TP, Watts DM, et al. Demonstration of yellow fever and dengue antigens in Formalin-fixed paraffin-embedded human liver by immunohistochemical analysis. Am J Trop Med Hyg 1991;45:408–17.

63. Lennette EH, Perlowagora A. Complement fixation test in the diagnosis of yellow fever. Use of infectious mouse brain as antigen. Am J Trop Med 1943;23:481–504.

64. Theiler M, Casals J. The serological reactions in yellow fever. Am J Trop Med Hyg 1958;7:585–95.

65. Saluzzo JF, Sarthou JL, Cornet M, et al. Intérêt du titrage par ELISA des IgM spécifiques pour le diagnostic et la surveillance de la circulation selvatique des flavivirus en Afrique. Ann Virol (Inst Pasteur) 1986;137E:155–62.

66. Filipe AR, Martins CMV, Rocha H. Laboratory infection with Zika virus after vaccination against yellow fever. Arch Virusforsch 1973;43:315–9.

67. Mitzner SR, Stange J, Klammt S, et al. Extracorporeal detoxification using the Molecular Adsorbent Recirculating System for critically ill patients with liver failure. J Am Soc Nephrol 2001;12:S75–S82.

68. Kapoor D. Molecular adsorbent recirculating system. Albumin dialysis extracorporeal liver assist device. J Gastroenterol Hepatol 2002;17 Suppl 3:S280–6.

69. Laemmert HW Jr. Susceptibility of marmosets to different strains of yellow fever. Am J Trop Med 1944;24:71–8.

70. Deubel V, Schlesinger JJ, Digoutte J-P, et al. Comparative immunochemical and biological analysis of African and South American yellow fever viruses. Arch Virol 1987;94:331–8.

71. Monath TP, Nasidi A. Should yellow fever vaccine be included in the expanded program of immunization in Africa? A cost-effectiveness analysis for Nigeria. Am J Trop Med Hyg 1993;48:274–99.

72. Monath TP, Cetron M. Preventing yellow fever in travelers to the tropics. Clin Infect Dis 2002;34:1369–78.

73. Cornet M, Chateau R, Valade M, et al. Données bioécologiques sur les vecteurs potentiels du virus amaril au Sénégal oriental. Rôles des différents espèces dans la transmission du virus. Cah ORSTOM Ser Entomol Med Parasitol 1978;16:315–41.

74. World Health Organization. International travel and health. Vaccination requirements and health advice. Geneva (Switz): WHO; 2002.

75. Monath TP. Yellow fever. In: Monath TP, editor. The arboviruses. Ecology and epidemiology. Vol 5. Boca Raton (FL): CRC Press; 1988. p. 139–231.

76. Digoutte J-P, Cornet M, Deubel V, et al. Yellow fever. In Porterfield JS, editor. Exotic virus infections. London: Chapman & Hall; 1995. p. 67–102.

77. Mondet B. Yellow fever epidemiology in Brazil. Bull Soc Pathol Exot 2001;94:260–7.

78. Germain M, Cornet M, Mouchet J, et al. La fièvre jaune en Afrique. Données récentes et conceptions actuelles. Med Trop (Mars) 1981;41:31–43.

79. Walcott AM, Cruz E, Paoliello A, et al. An epidemic of urban yellow fever which originated from a case contracted in the jungle. Am J Trop Med Hyg 1937;17:677–88.

80. Downs WG. Epidemiological notes in connection with the 1954 outbreak of yellow fever in Trinidad, BWI. In: Boshell JM, Busher J, Downs WG, et al, editors. Yellow fever. A symposium in commemoration of Carlos Juan Finlay. Philadelphia: Jefferson Medical College; 1955. p. 71–8.

81. Van der Stuyf P, Giannella A, Pirard M, et al. Urbanisation of yellow fever in Santa Cruz, Bolivia. Lancet 1999;353:1558–62.

82. Monath TP. Yellow fever. Victor, Victoria? Conqueror, conquest? Epidemics and research in the last forty years and prospects for the future. Am J Trop Med Hyg 1991;45:1–43.

83. Monath TP. Yellow fever and dengue. The interactions of virus, vector and host in the re-emergence of epidemic disease. Semin Virol 1995;5:1–13.

84. Gubler DJ. Dengue and dengue hemorrhagic fever. Its history and resurgence as a global public health problem. In: Gubler DJ, Kuno G, editors. Dengue and dengue hemorrhagic fever. Wallingford (UK): CABI; 1997. p. 1–22.

85. Theiler M, Smith HH. The use of yellow fever virus modified by in vitro cultivation for human immunization. J Exp Med 1937;65:787–800.

86. Manso, C deS. Mass vaccination against yellow fever in Brazil 1937–54. In: Smithburn KC, Durieux C, Koerber R, et al. Yellow fever vaccination. Geneva (Switz):WHO; 1956. p. 123–40.

87. Fox JP, Lennette EH, Manso C, et al. Encephalitis in man following vaccination with 17D yellow fever virus. Am J Hyg 1942;36:117–142.

88. United Nations Relief and Rehabilitation Administration (UNRRA). Standards for the manufacture and control of yellow fever vaccine. Epidemiol Inform Bull 1945;1:365–90.

89. World Health Organization. Requirements for yellow fever vaccine (Requirements for Biological Substances No. 3). Tech Rep Ser No. 136. Geneva (Switz): WHO; 1957.

90. Liprandi F. Isolation of plaque variants differing in virulence from the 17D strain of yellow fever virus. J Gen Virol 1981;56:363–70.

91. Monath TP, Kinney RM, Schlesinger JJ, et al. Ontogeny of yellow fever 17D vaccine. RNA oligonucleotide fingerprint and monoclonal antibody analyses of vaccines produced world-wide. J Gen Virol 1983;64:627–37.

92. Duarte dos Santos CN, Post PR, Carvalho R, et al. Complete nucleotide sequence of yellow fever virus vaccine strains 17DD and 17D-213. Virus Res 1995;95:35–41.

93. Dupuy A, Despres P, Cahour A, et al. Nucleotide sequence comparison of the genome of two 7D-204 yellow fever vaccines. Nucleic Acids Res 1989;17:2989.

94. Barrett ADT. Yellow fever vaccine. Biologicals 1997;25:17–25.

95. Pugachev KV, Ocran SW, Guirakhoo F, et al. Heterogeneous nature of the genome of the ARILVAX yellow fever 17D vaccine revealed by consensus sequencing. Vaccine 2002;20:996–9.

96. World Health Organization. Requirements for yellow fever vaccine (Requirements for Biological Substances No. 3). Tech Rep Series. Geneva (Switz): WHO; 1997.

97. Penna HA. Production of 17D yellow fever vaccine. In: Smithburn KC, Durieux C, Koerber R, et al, editors. Yellow fever vaccination. Geneva (Switz): WHO; 1956. p. 67–90.

98. Tannock GA, Wark MC, Hair CG. The development of an improved experimental yellow fever vaccine. J Biol Stand 1980;8:23–34.

99. Lopes O deS, de Almeida Guimarães SSD, de Carvalho R. Studies on yellow fever vaccine. I. Quality-control parameters. J Biol Stand 1987;15:323–30.

100. Rice CM, Lenches EM, Eddy SR, et al. Nucleotide sequence of yellow fever virus. Implications for flavivirus gene expression and evolution. Science 1985;229:726–33.

101. Hahn CH, Dalrymple JM, Strauss JH, et al. Comparison of the virulent Asibi strain of yellow fever virus with the 17D vaccine strain derived from it. Proc Natl Acad Sci U S A 1987;84:2019–23.

102. Post PR, Santos CND, Carvalho R, et al. Heterogeneity in envelope protein sequence and N-linked glycosylation among yellow fever virus vaccine strains. Virology 1992;188:160–7.

103. Jennings AD, Whitby JE, Minor PD, et al. Comparison of the nucleotide and deduced amino acid sequences of the structural protein genes of the yellow fever 17DD vaccine strain from Senegal with those of other yellow fever vaccine viruses. Vaccine 1993;11:679–81.

104. Wang E, Ryman KD, Jennings AD, et al. Comparison of the genomes of the wild-type French viscerotropic strain of yellow fever virus with its vaccine derivative French neurotropic vaccine. J Gen Virol 1995;76:2749–55.

105. Wang E, Weaver SC, Shope RE, et al. Genetic variation in yellow fever virus: duplication in the 3′ noncoding region of strains from Africa. Virology 1996;225:274–81.

106. Tesh RB, Guzman H, da Rosa AP, et al. Experimental yellow fever virus infection in the golden hamster (*Mesocricetus auratus*). I. Virologic, biochemical, and immunologic studies. J Infect Dis 2001;183:1431–6.

107. Xiao SY, Zhang H, Guzman H, Tesh RB. Experimental yellow fever virus infection in the golden hamster (*Mesocricetus auratus*). II. Pathology. J Infect Dis 2001;183:1437–44.

108. Anonymous. Fatal viral encephalitis following 17D yellow fever vaccine inoculation. JAMA 1966;198:671–6.

109. Jennings AD, Gibson CA Miller BR. Analysis of a yellow fever virus isolated from a fatal case of vaccine-associated human encephalitis. J Infect Dis 1994;169:512–8.

110. Allison SL, Stiasny K, Stadler K, et al. Mapping of functional elements in the stem-anchor region of tick-borne encephalitis virus envelope protein E. J Virol 1999;73:5605–12.

111. Wang S, He R, Anderson R. prM-and cell-binding activities domains of the dengue virus E protein. J Virol 1999;73:2547–51.

112. McMinn PC, Marshall ID, Dalgarno L. Neurovirulence and neuroinvasiveness of Murray Valley encephalitis virus mutants selected by passage in a monkey kidney cell line. J Gen Virol 1995;76:865–72.

113. Duarte dos Santos, Frenkiel M-P, Courageot M-P, et al. Determinants in the envelope E protein and viral RNA helicase NS3 that influence the induction of apoptosis in response to infection with dengue type 1 virus. Virology 2000;274:292–308.

114. Zeng L, Falgout B, Markoff L. Identification of specific nucleotide sequences within the conserved 3′-SL region in the dengue type 2 virus genome required for replication. J Virol 1998;72:7510–22.

115. McArthur MA, Suderman MT, Mutebi J-P, et al. Molecular characterization of a hamster viscerotropic strain of yellow fever virus. J Virol 2003;77:1462–8.

116. Buckley A, Gould EA. Neutralization of yellow fever virus studied using monoclonal and polyclonal antibodies. J Gen Virol 1985;66:2523–31.

117. Barrett ADT, Matthews JH, Miller BR, et al. Identification of monoclonal antibodies that distinguish between 17D-204 and other strains of yellow fever virus. J Gen Virol 1990;71:13–8.

118. Lobigs M, Dalgarno L, Schlesinger JJ, et al. Location of a neutralization determinant in the E protein of yellow fever virus (17D vaccine strain). Virology 1987;161:474–8.

119. Ryman KD, Ledger TN, Weir RC Jr, et al. Yellow fever virus envelope protein has two discrete type-specific neutralizing epitopes. J Gen Virol 1997;78:1353–6.

120. Ryman KD, Xie H, Ledger TN, et al. Antigenic variants of yellow fever virus with an altered neurovirulence phenotype in mice. Virology 1997;230:376–80.

121. Findlay GM, MacCallum FO. Transmission of yellow fever virus to monkeys by mouth. J Pathol Bacteriol 1939;49:53–61.

122. Niedrig M, Stolte N, Fuchs D, et al. Intra-nasal infection of macaques with yellow fever (yellow fever) vaccine strain 17D. A novel and economical approach for yellow fever vaccination in man. Vaccine 1999;17:1206–10.

123. Smith CEG, Turner LH, Armitage P. Yellow fever vaccination in Malaya by subcutaneous injection and multiple puncture. Neutralizing antibody responses in persons with and without pre-existing antibody to related viruses. Bull World Health Organ 1962;27:717–27.

124. Freestone DS, Ferris RD, Weinberg A, et al. Stabilized 17D strain yellow fever vaccine. Dose response studies, clinical reactions and effects on hepatic function. J Biol Stand 1977;5:181–6.

125. Lopes Ode S, de Almeida Guimarães SSD, de Carvalho R. Studies on yellow fever vaccine III-dose response in volunteers. J Biol Stand 1988;16:77–84.

126. Fox JP, Penna HA. Behavior of 17D yellow fever virus in rhesus monkeys. Relation to substrain, dose and neural or extra-neural inoculation. Am J Hyg 1943;38:152–72.

127. Panthier R. À propos de quelques cas de réactions nerveuses tardives observées chez des nourrissons après vaccination antimarile (17D). Bull Soc Pathol Exot 1956;49:478–94.

128. Xie H, Ryman HD, Campbell GA, et al. Mutation in NS5 protein attenuates mouse neurovirulence of yellow fever 17D vaccine virus. J Gen Virol 1998;79:1895–9.

129. Guirakhoo F, Arroyo J, Pugachev KV, et al. Construction, safety, and immunogenicity in non-human primates of a chimeric yellow fever-dengue tetravalent vaccine. J Virol 2001;75:7290–304.

130. Kengsakul K, Sathirapongsasuti K, Punyagupta S. Fatal myeloencephalitis following yellow fever vaccination in a case with HIV infection. J Med Assoc Thai 2002;85:131–4.

131. Sweet BH, Wisseman CJ Jr, Kitaoka M. Immunological studies with group B arthropod-borne viruses. II. Effect of prior infection with Japanese encephalitis virus on the viremia in human subject following administration of 17D yellow fever vaccine. Am J Trop Med Hyg 1962;11:562–9.

132. Wheelock EF, Sibley WA. Circulating virus, interferon and antibody after vaccination with the 17-D strain of yellow-fever virus. N Engl J Med 1965;273:194–8.

133. Actis DAS, Sa Fleitas MJ. Replaciones entre viremia y sero-anticuerpos secundarious a la vacunacion antiamarilica de personsas vacunadas con "Cepa" 17D-EP. Rev Sanid Mil Argent 1970;69:51–63.

134. Reinhardt B, Jaspert R, Niedrig M, et al. Development of viremia and humoral and cellular parameters of immune activation after vaccination with yellow fever virus strain 17D. A model of human flavivirus infection. J Med Virol 1998;56:159–67.

135. Tauraso NM, Coultrip RL, Legters LJ, et al. Yellow fever vaccine. IV. Reactogenicity and antibody response in volunteers inoculated with a vaccine free from contaminating avian leukosis viruses. Proc Soc Exp Biol Med 1972;139:439–46.

136. Tauraso NM, Myers MG, Nau EV, et al. Effect of interval between inoculation of live smallpox and yellow-fever vaccines on antigenicity in man. J Infect Dis 1972;126:362–71.

137. Moss-Blundell AJ, Bernstein S, Wilma M, et al. A clinical study of stabilized 17D strain live attenuated yellow fever vaccine. J Biol Stand 1981;9:445–52.

138. Pivetaud JP, Raccurt CP, M'Bailara L, et al. Clinique. Réactions post-vaccinales. A la vaccination anti-amarile. Bull Soc Pathol Exot 1986;79:772–6.

139. Roche JC, Jouan A, Brisou B, et al. Comparative clinical study of a new 17D thermostable yellow fever vaccine. Vaccine 1986;4:163–5.

140. Coursaget P, Fritzell B, Blondeau C, et al. Simultaneous injection of plasma-derived or recombinant hepatitis B vaccines with yellow fever and killed polio vaccines. Vaccine 1995;13:109–11.

141. Lang J, Zuckerman J, Clarke P, et al. Comparison of the immunogenicity and safety of two 17D yellow fever vaccines. Am J Trop Med Hyg 1999;60:1045–50.

142. Osei-Kwasi M, Dunyo SK, Koram KA, et al. Antibody response to 17D yellow fever vaccine in Ghanaian infants. Bull World Health Organ 2001;79:1056–9.

143. Mason RA, Tauraso NM, Ginn RK. Yellow fever vaccine. V. Antibody response in monkeys inoculated with graded doses of the 17D vaccine. Appl Microbiol 1972;23:908–13.

144. Mason RA, Tauraso NM, Spertzel RO, et al. Yellow fever vaccine. Direct challenge of monkeys given graded doses of 17D vaccine. Appl Microbiol 1973;25:539–44.

145. Monath TP, Craven RB, Muth DJ. Limitations of the complement-fixation test for distinguishing naturally acquired from vaccine-induced yellow fever infection in flavivirus-hyperendemic areas. Am J Trop Med Hyg 1980;29:624–34.

146. Monath TP. Neutralizing antibody responses in the major immunoglobulin classes to yellow fever 17D vaccination of humans. Am J Epidemiol 1971;93:122–9.

147. Smithburn KC. Immunology of yellow fever. In: Smithburn KC, Durleux C, Koerber R, editors. Yellow fever vaccination. Geneva (Switz.): WHO; 1956. p. 11–27.

148. Smithburn KC, Mahaffy AF. Immunization against yellow fever. Am J Trop Med 1945;45:217–23.

149. Wisseman CL Jr, Sweet B, Kitaoka M, et al. Immunological studies with group B arthropod-borne viruses. I. Broadened neutralizing antibody spectrum induced by strain 17D yellow fever vaccine in human subjects previously infected with Japanese encephalitis virus. Am J Trop Med Hyg 1962;11:550–61.

150. Boiron H. De l'influence des revaccinations antiamariles sur le taux de l'immunité humorale. C R Soc Biol (Paris) 1956;150:2219–21.

151. Wisseman CL Jr, Sweet B. Immunological studies with group B arthropod-borne viruses. III. Response of human subjects to revaccination with 17D strain yellow fever vaccine. Am J Trop Med Hyg 1962;11:570–5.

152. Pond WL, Ehrenkranz NJ, Danauskas JX, et al. Heterotypic serologic responses after yellow fever vaccination. Detection of persons with past St. Louis encephalitis or dengue. J Immunol 1967;98:673–82.

153. Meers PD. Further observations on 17D-yellow fever vaccination by scarification, with and without simultaneous smallpox vaccination. Trans R Soc Trop Med Hyg 1960;54:493–501.

154. Draper CC, Knott EG. Failure to respond to vaccination with 17D yellow fever virus by scarifiation and its significance. West Afr Med J 1964;April:78–82.

155. Fabiyi A, MacNamara FN. The effects of heterologous antibodies on the serological conversion rate after 17D yellow fever vaccination. Am J Trop Med Hyg 1962;11:817–21.

156. Kayser M, Klein H, Paasch I. Human antibody response to immunization with 17D yellow fever and inactivated TBE vaccine. J Med Virol 1985;17:35–45.

157. Hacker UT, Jelinek T, Erhardt S, et al. In vivo synthesis of tumor necrosis factor-alpha in healthy humans after live yellow fever vaccination. J Infect Dis 1998;177:774–8.

158. Bauer JH. The duration of passive immunity in yellow fever. Am J Trop Med Hyg 1931;11:451–7.

159. Davis NC. On the use of immune serum at various intervals after the inoculation of yellow fever virus into rhesus monkeys. J Immunol 1934;26:361–90.

160. Soper FL. Yellow fever. Present situation (October 1938) with special reference to South America. Trans R Soc Trop Med Hyg 1938;32:297–332.

161. Groot H, Ribeiro RB. Neutralizing and haemagglutination-inhibiting antibodies to yellow fever 17 years after vaccination with 17D vaccine. Bull World Health Organ 1962;27:699–707.

162. Rosenzweig EC, Babione RW, Wisseman CL Jr. Immunological studies with group B arthropod-borne viruses. Am J Trop Med Hyg 1963;12:230–5.

163. Poland JD, Calisher CH, Monath TP, et al. Persistence of neutralizing antibody 30–35 years after immunization with 17D yellow fever vaccine. Bull World Health Organ 1981;59:895–900.

164. Doherty RL. Effects of yellow fever (17D) and West Nile viruses on the reactions of human appendix and conjunctiva cells to several other viruses. Virology 1958;6:575–81.

165. Penna HA, Bittencourt A. Persistence of yellow fever virus in brains of monkeys immunized by cerebral inoculation. Science 1943;97:448–9.

166. Xie H. Mutations in the genome of yellow fever 17D-204 vaccine virus accumulate in the non-structural protein genes [doctoral dissertation]. Galveston: University of Texas Medical Branch; 1997.

167. Gould EA, Buckley A, Cane PA, et al . Use of a monoclonal antibody specific for wild-type yellow fever virus to identify a wild-type antigenic variant in 17D vaccine pools. J Gen Virol 1989;70:1889–94.

168. Elliot M. Yellow fever in the recently inoculated. Trans R Soc Trop Med Hyg 1944;38:231–4.

169. Ross RW, Haddow AJ, Raper AB, et al. A fatal case of yellow fever in a European in Uganda. East Afr Med J 1953;30:1–3.

170. Nolla-Salas J, Sadalls-Radresa J. Imported yellow fever in vaccinated tourists. Lancet 1989:1275.

171. Brown RE, Katz M. Failure of antibody production to yellow fever vaccine in children with kwashiorkor. Trop Geogr Med 1966;18:125–8.

172. Gandra YR, Scrimshaw NS. Infection and nutritional status. Am J Clin Nutr 1961;9:159–63.

173. Nasidi A, Monath TP, Vandenberg J, et al. Yellow fever vaccination and pregnancy. A four-year prospective study. Trans R Soc Trop Med Hyg 1993;87:337–9.

174. Receveur MC, Thiebaut R, Vedy S, et al. Yellow fever vaccination of human immunodeficiency virus-infected patients. Report of 2 cases. Clin Infect Dis 2000;31:E7–8.

175. Goujon C, Tohr M, Feuillie V, et al. Good tolerance and efficacy of yellow fever vaccine among subjects carriers of human immunodeficiency virus. Fourth international Conference on Travel Medicine; 1995 April 23–27; Acapulco, Mexico.

176. Sibailly TS, Wiktor SZ, Tsai TF, et al. Poor antibody response to yellow fever vaccination in children infected with human immunodeficiency virus type 1. Pediatr Infect Dis J 1997;16:1177–9.

177. Centers for Disease Control. Recommendations of the Immunization Practices Advisory Committee. Yellow fever vaccine. MMWR Morb Mortal Wkly Rep 1969;18:189–90.

178. Louis JJ, Chopard P, Larbre F. Un cas d'encephalite après vaccination anti-amarile par la souche 17 D. Pediatrie 1981;36:547–50.

179. Stuart G. Reactions following vaccination against yellow fever. In: Smithburn KC, Durieux C, Koerber R, et al, editors. Yellow fever vaccination. Geneva (Switz): WHO; 1956. p. 143–92.

180. Centers for Disease Control. Adverse events associated with 17D-derived yellow fever vaccination—United States, 2001–2002. MMWR Morb Mortal Wkly Rep 2002;51:989–93.

181. Merlo C, Steffen R, Landis T, et al. Possible association of encephalitis and 17D yellow fever vaccination in a 29-year-old traveller. Vaccine 1993;11:691.

182. Martin M, Tsai TF, Cropp CB, et al. Fever and multisystem organ failure temporarily associated with yellow fever vaccination: a report of four cases. Lancet 2001;358:98–104.

183. Vasconcelos PFC, Luna EJ, Galler R, et al. Serious adverse events associated with yellow fever 17DD vaccine in Brazil. Report of two cases. Lancet 2001;358:91–7.

184. Chan RC, Penney DJ, Litele D, et al. Hepatitis and death following vaccination with 17D-204 yellow fever vaccine. Lancet 2001;358:121–2.

185. Centers for Disease Control. Fever, jaundice, and multiple organ system failure associated with 17D-derived yellow fever vaccination, 1996–2001. MMWR Morb Mortal Wkly Rep 2001;50;643–6.

186. Sreenarasimhaiah J, Shiels P, Lisker-Melman M. Multiorgan failure induced by atorvastatin. Am J Med 2002;113:348–9.

187. Kaplan JE, Nelson, DB, Schonberger LB, et al. The effect of immune globulin on the response to trivalent oral poliovirus and yellow fever vaccinations. Bull World Health Organ 1984;62:585–90.

188. Galler R, Pugachev KV, Santos CLS, et al. Phenotypic and molecular analyses of yellow fever 17DD vaccine virus associated with serious adverse events in Brazil. Virology 2001;290:309–19.

189. Cohen SG, Mines SC. Variations in egg white and egg yolk components of virus and rickettsial vaccines. J Allergy 1958;29:479–82.

190. Swartz H. Systemic allergic reaction induced by yellow fever vaccine. J Lab Clin Med 1943;43:1663–7.

191. Sprague H, Barnard J. Egg allergy, significance in typhus and yellow fever immunization. US Naval Med Bull 1945;45:71–4.

192. American Academy of Pediatrics. Report of the Committee on Immunization Practices. 23rd ed. Elk Grove Village (IL): American Academy of Pediatrics 1994.

193. Patterson R, DeSwarte RD, Greenberger PA, et al. Drug allergy and protocols for management of drug allergies. N Engl Reg Allergy Proc 1986;7:325–42.

194. Mosimann B, Stoll B, Francillon C, et al. Yellow fever vaccine and egg allergy. J Allergy Clin Immunol 1995;95:1064.

195. Miller JR, Orgel HA, Meltzer EO. The safety of egg-containing vaccines for egg-allergic patients. J Allergy Clin Immunol 1983;71:568–73.

196. Kelso J. Raw egg allergy. A potential issue in vaccine allergy. J Allergy Clin Immunol 2000;106:990.

197. James JM, Zeiger RS, Lester MR, et al. Safe administration of influenza vaccine to patients with egg allergy. J Pediatr 1998;133:624–8.

198. Sakaguchi M, Nakayama T, Inoue S. Food allergy to gelatin in children with systemic immediate-type reactions, including anaphylaxis, to vaccines. J Allergy Clin Immunol 1996;98:1058–61.

199. Sakaguchi M, Yoshida M, Kuroda W. Systemic immediate-type reactions to gelatin in Japanese encephalitis vaccines. Vaccine 1997;15:121–2.

200. Kelso JM, Mootrey GT, Tsai TF. Anaphylaxis from yellow fever vaccine. J Allergy Clin Immunol 1999;103:698–701.

201. World Health Organization. Prevention and control of yellow fever in Africa. Geneva: WHO; 1986 p. 93.

202. World Health Organization. Yellow fever in 1985. Wkly Epidemiol Rec 1986;61:377.

203. Oyelami SA, Oyaleye OD, Oyejide CO, et al. Severe post-vaccination reaction to 17D yellow fever vaccine in Nigeria. Rev Roum Virol 1994;45:25–30.

204. Centers for Disease Control and Prevention. Health information for international travel 2001–2002. Atlanta (GA): Department of Health and Human Services; 2002.

205. Centers for Disease Control. Yellow fever vaccine. Recommendations of the Immunization Practices Advisory Committee (ACIP). MMWR Morb Mortal Wkly Rep 2002;51(RR-17):1–10.

206. Martin M, Weld LH, Tsai TF, et al. Advanced age is a risk factor for adverse events temporally associated with yellow fever vaccination. Emerg Infect Dis 2001;7:945–51.

207. Stefanopoulo GJ, Duvolon S. Réactions observées au cours de la vaccination contre la fièvre jaune par virus atténué de culture (souche 17 D). A propos de 20.000 vaccinations pratiquées par ce procédé à l'Institut Pasteur de Paris (1936–1946). Bull Mem Soc Med Hop Paris 1947;63:990–1000.

208. Tsai TF, Paul R, Lynberg MC, et al. Congenital yellow fever virus infection after immunization in pregnancy. J Infect Dis 1993;168:1520–3.

209. Nishioka S de A, Nunes-Araujo FR, Pires WP, et al. Yellow fever vaccination during pregnancy and spontaneous abortion. A case-control study. Trop Med Int Health 1998;3:29–33.

210. Simonsen L, Buffington J, Shapiro CN, et al. Multiple false reactions in viral antibody screening assays after influenza vaccination. Am J Epidemiol 1995;141:1089–96.

211. Starling KA, Falletta JM, Fernbach DJ. Immunologic chimerism as evidence of bone marrow graft acceptance in an identical twin with acute lymphocytic leukemia. Exp Hematol 1975;3:244–8.

212. Mouchon D, Pignon D, Vicens R, et al. Étude de la vaccination combinée rougeole-fièvre jaune chez l'enfant Africain agé de 6 à 10 mois. Bull Soc Pathol Exot 1990;83:537–51.

213. Stefano I, Sato HK, Pannuti CS, et al. Recent immunization against measles does not interfere with the sero-response to yellow fever vaccine. Vaccine 1999;17:1042–6.

214. Ambrosch F, Fritzell B, Gregor J, et al. Combined vaccination against yellow fever and typhoid fever. A comparative trial. Vaccine 1994;12:625–8.

215. Jong EC, Kaplan KM, Eves KA, et al. An open randomized study of inactivated hepatitis A vaccine administered concomitantly with typhoid fever and yellow fever vaccines. J Travel Med 2002;9:66–70.

216. Meyer HM Jr, Hostetler DD Jr, Bernheim BC, et al. Response of Volta children to jet inoculation of combined live measles, smallpox and yellow fever vaccines. Bull World Health Organ 1964;30:783–94.

217. Yvonnet B, Coursaget P, Deubel V, et al. Simultaneous administration of hepatitis B and yellow fever vaccines. J Med Virol 1986;19:307–11.

218. Felsenfeld O, Wolf RH, Gyr K, et al. Simultaneous vaccination against cholera and yellow fever. Lancet 1973;1:457–60.

219. Gateff C, Le Gonidec G, Boche R, et al. Influence de la vaccination anticholérique sur l'immunisation antiamarile associée. Bull Soc Pathol Exot 1973;258–66.

220. Kollaritsch H, Que JU, Kunz C, et al. Safety and immunogenicity of live oral cholera and typhoid vaccines administered alone or in combination with antimalarial drugs, oral polio vaccine, or yellow fever vaccine. J Infect Dis 1997;175:871–75.

221. Foster RH, Noble S. Bivalent cholera and typhoid vaccine. Drugs 1999;58:91.

222. Tsai TF, Bolin RA, Lazuick JS, et al. Chloroquine does not adversely affect the antibody response to yellow fever vaccine. J Infect Dis 1986;154:726–7.

223. Pettit A, Stefanopoulo GJ. Utilisation du sérum antiamaril d'origine animale pour la vaccination de l'homme. Bull Acad Natl Med 1933;110:67–76.

224. Theiler M, Smith HH. Use of hyperimmune monkey serum in human vaccination against yellow fever. Bull Off Intl Hyg Pub 1936;28:2354–7.

225. Mason RA, Tauraso NM, Spetzel RQ, et al. Yellow fever vaccine: direct challenge of monkeys given graded doses of 17D vaccine. Appl Microbiol 1973;25:538–44.

226. Hoskins M. Protective properties against yellow fever virus in the sera of the offspring of immune rhesus monkeys. J Immunol 1934;26:391–4.

227. Soper FL, Beeuwkes H, Davis NC, et al. Transitory immunity to yellow fever in offspring of immune human and monkey mothers. Am J Hyg 1938;27:351–63.

228. Stefanopoulo GJ, Laurent P, Wassermann R. Présence d'anticorps antiamarils dans le lait de femme immunisé contre la fièvre jaune. C R Soc Biol (Paris) 1936;122:915–7.

229. Meegan JM. Yellow fever vaccine. Unofficial report WHO/EPI/GEN/91.6. Geneva (Switz.): WHO; 1991.

230. Robertson SE. The immunological basis for immunization. 8. Yellow fever. Document WHO/EPI/GEN/93.18. Geneva (Switz): WHO; 1993.

231. Brès P, Cornet M, Ly C, et al. Une epidemie de fièvre jaune au Senegal en 1965. I. Charactéristiques de l'épidémie. Bull World Health Organ 1967;36:113–8.

232. Brès, P. Benefit versus risk factors in immunization against yellow fever. Int'l Symp Immuniz: benefit versus risk factors, Brussels, 1978. Dev Biol Stand 1979;43:297–304.

233. Massad E, Coutinho FAB, Burattini MN, et al. The risk of yellow fever in a dengue-infested area. Trans R Soc Trop Med Hyg 2001;95:370–4.

234. Barros ML, Boecken G. Jungle yellow fever in the central Amazon. Lancet 1996;348:969–70.

235. Hall P, Fojtasek M, Pettigrove J, et al. Fatal yellow fever in a traveler returning from Amazonas, Brazil, 2002. MMWR Morb Mortal Wkly Rep 2002;51:324–5.

236. McFarland JM, Baddour LM, Nelson JE, et al. Imported yellow fever in a United States citizen. Clin Infect Dis 1997;25:1143–7.

237. Monath TP. Yellow fever. In: Service MW, editor. Encyclopedia of arthropod-transmitted infections of man and domesticated animals. New York: CABI Publishing; 2001. p. 571–7.

238. World Health Organization. Yellow fever in 1985. Wkly Epidemiol Rec 1986;61:377–80.

239. World Health Organization. Yellow fever, 1998–1999. Wkly Epidemiol Rec 2000;75:322–7.

Chapter 6

Hepatitis A and Hepatitis B Vaccines

Jane N. Zuckerman

The past three decades have witnessed an explosion in knowledge of viral hepatitis, a major public health problem throughout the world affecting several hundreds of millions of people. On a worldwide basis, approximately 1.4 million cases of hepatitis A are reported every year, although the true incidence of disease might be 3 to 10 times greater.[1] More than one-third of the world's population has been infected with the hepatitis B virus.[2] It is estimated, conservatively, that there are 350 million chronic carriers of hepatitis B worldwide and 1 to 2 million deaths per year.[3]

Since 1980, with the development of the first vaccine against hepatitis B, significant advances have been made in the protection against both hepatitis A and hepatitis B, with a vaccine against hepatitis A being licensed in 1992.[4,5] Active immunization has become the preferred method of protection for hepatitis A, including in disease outbreak situations, replacing the use of human normal immunoglobulin (Ig).[6,7] In recent years, the monovalent vaccines have been complemented by the availability of multivalent vaccines, including that of a combined vaccine of hepatitis A and B (Twinrix) and hepatitis A and typhoid (Hepatyrix).[8–11]

As with all forms of immunization, patient compliance with the schedules and subsequent completion of a course of immunization is often a continuing challenge for health care professionals. Recently, the standard courses of both the monovalent and the combined vaccine have been accompanied by the availability of accelerated schedules that also confer high levels of protection against disease.

Viral hepatitis is an important cause of morbidity and mortality, both from acute infection and from the chronic sequelae. These include, with hepatitis B, C, and D infection, chronic active hepatitis and cirrhosis and with hepatitis B and C, primary liver cancer as well. The hepatitis viruses include a range of unrelated human pathogens. This chapter will be confined to the description of those vaccines that provide protection against hepatitis A and hepatitis B. Currently, there are no licensed vaccines that confer protection against hepatitis C or E.

HEPATITIS A

Epidemics of jaundice have been reported for many centuries, and the term infectious hepatitis was coined in 1912 to describe these outbreaks. The term hepatitis type A was adopted by the World Health Organization (WHO) in 1973 to describe this form of hepatitis, and the virus was visualized by electron microscopy in human fecal extracts in the same year.

Hepatitis A virus (HAV) is spread by the fecal-oral route. It remains endemic throughout the world and is hyperendemic in areas with poor standards of sanitation and hygiene. Since the end of World War II in 1945, the seroprevalence of antibodies to HAV has declined in many countries. Infection results most commonly from person-to-person contact, but large epidemics do occur.

The Nature of the Virus

In 1983, HAV was classified in the genus *Enterovirus* of the family Picornaviridae based on its biophysical and biochemical characteristics, including stability at low pH. This preempted the isolation and analysis of complementary deoxyribonucleic acid (DNA) clones that led to the determination of the entire nucleotide sequence of the viral genome. There is limited sequence homology with the enteroviruses and rhinoviruses, although the structure and genome organization are typical of the picornaviruses. The virus is classified as a hepatovirus within the *Heparnavirus* genus. There is only one human serotype of HAV and seven genotypes, but all human HAVs have a single immunodominant epitope that is responsible for generating neutralizing antibodies.

Epidemiology and Geographic Distribution

Hepatitis A occurs endemically in all parts of the world, with frequent reports of minor and major outbreaks. The exact incidence is difficult to estimate because of differences in surveillance, differing patterns of disease, and the high proportion of subclinical infections and infections without jaundice. The degree of underreporting is very high.

The mode of transmission of HAV is by the fecal-oral route, most commonly by person-to-person contact in developed countries, and infection occurs readily under conditions of poor sanitation and hygiene and overcrowding. Common source outbreaks are most frequently initiated by fecal contamination of water and food, but water-borne transmission is not a major factor in maintaining this infection in industrialized communities. On the other hand, many food-borne outbreaks have been reported. This can be attributed to the shedding of large quantities of virus in the feces during the incubation period of the illness in infected food handlers; the source of the outbreak often can be traced to uncooked food or food that has been handled after cooking. Oysters, clams, and other shellfish from contaminated water pose a high risk of infection unless heated or steamed thoroughly. There is a similar risk with uncooked vegetables and crops in countries where raw sewage is used as a fertilizer. Although hepatitis A remains endemic and common in the developed and developing countries, the infection occurs mainly in small clusters, often with only few identified cases.

Hepatitis A is recognized as an important travel-related infection in travelers from low prevalence areas to endemic countries. As a generalization, low prevalence areas include Western Europe, the United States and Canada, Australia, New Zealand, and Japan. The infection is much more prevalent in other areas of the world, and people traveling to developing countries, including many holiday destinations, are at risk of infection and are at particularly high risk of infection in rural areas.

Passive Immunization with Immunoglobulin

Human immunoglobulin is prepared from pooled human plasma specimens under rigorous conditions of donor screening and product purification. Preparations typically contain high titers of antibodies against hepatitis A virus (at least 100 IU/mL). Passive immunization with IG constituted the most common means of providing protection against hepatitis A virus infection prior to the availability of the safe, efficacious, inactivated hepatitis A vaccine products in the 1990s. Since that time, there has been a marked shift to active immunization with hepatitis A vaccine for the protection of international travelers going to areas with high endemicity for hepatitis A and for residents in such areas. Immunoglobulin is currently used for passive immunization of pediatric travelers < 2 years of age and for postexposure prophylaxis during outbreaks. A dose of 0.6 mL/kg body weight administered by intramuscular injection can provide up to 5 months protection against hepatitis A.[12] Concurrent administration of the first dose of hepatitis A vaccine and IG to international travelers when there is < 2 weeks before trip departure is no longer recommended (see "Active Immunization with Hepatitis A Vaccine").

Active Immunization with Hepatitis A Vaccine

Killed hepatitis A vaccines are prepared from virus grown in tissue culture and inactivated with formalin. The first such vaccine was licensed in 1992, and several preparations are available, including a combined hepatitis A and B vaccine. These vaccines are highly immunogenic and provide long-term protection against infection.[13] In areas of high prevalence, most children have antibodies to hepatitis A virus by the age of 10 years, and such infections are generally asymptomatic. Infections acquired later in life are of increasing clinical severity. It is important, therefore, to protect those at risk because of personal contact or because of travel to highly endemic areas.

Vaccination against hepatitis A is recommended for all travelers visiting areas outside of northwestern Europe, North America, Australia, and New Zealand where the risks of infection from contaminated food and water and close contact with the local population might be high.[14,15] Those at risk include a wide group of travelers, for example, short- and long-term travelers, expatriates, aid/health care workers, missionaries, and military personnel. Also, in travelers with underlying medical conditions, such as chronic liver disease, infection with another hepatic virus might result in a subsequent increased burden on the liver, leading to morbidity and death. The risks of infection with hepatitis A have been estimated as 3 cases in 1,000 travelers per month of travel in a tourist resort, which rises to 20 cases per 1,000 travelers per month of travel outside of tourist resorts.[16] As the incidence of infection with hepatitis A has been estimated as 1.4 million cases per annum worldwide, this supports the assertion that hepatitis A is the most frequent vaccine-preventable disease in travelers.

Other groups at risk of hepatitis A infection include staff and residents of institutions for the mentally handicapped, day care centers for children, sexually active male homosexuals, intravenous narcotic drug abusers, food handlers, sewage workers, and certain low socioeconomic groups in defined community settings. Patients with blood coagulation defects and patients with chronic liver disease should be immunized against hepatitis A.[17]

As a result of the paradoxic shift in seroprevalence, adults over the age of 40 years, including those who have a history of jaundice or have lived in an endemic area for several years, might be naturally immune to hepatitis A. In such circumstances, vaccination might not be necessary. Natural immunity can be determined by serologic testing of the presence of hepatitis A antibodies (IgG). Screening for the presence of hepatitis A antibodies in such circumstances is a cost-benefit procedure and prevents the inappropriate administration of hepatitis A vaccine.[18,19]

Table 6-1. **Selected Vaccines Against Hepatitis A and Hepatitis B**

Proprietary Name (manufacturer)	Characteristics	Route of Administration	Availability
Havrix (GlaxoSmithKline, Rixensart, Belgium)	Inactivated hepatitis A virus, aluminum absorbed	Intramuscular injection	Many countries*
VAQTA (Merck Vaccine Division, Rahway, NJ)	Inactivated hepatitis A virus, aluminum absorbed	Intramuscular injection	Many countries*
Avaxim (Aventis Pasteur, MSD, Paris, France)	Inactivated hepatitis A virus, aluminum absorbed	Intramuscular injection	Europe*
Epaxal (Berna Biotech AG, Berne, Switzerland)	Inactivated hepatitis A virus, virosome-formulated	Intramuscular injection	Many countries*
Recombivax (Merck Vaccine Division, Rahway, NJ)	Recombinant hepatitis B surface antigen	Intramuscular injection	Many countries*
Energix B (GlaxoSmithKline, Rixensart , Belgium)	Recombinant hepatitis B surface antigen	Intramuscular injection	Many countries*
Bio-Hep-B (Bio Technology General Ltd, Rehovot, Israel)	Recombinant hepatitis B surface antigen plus pre-S1 and pre-S2 epitopes	Intramuscular injection	Israel*
GenHevac B (Pasteur-Merieux, Paris, France)	Recombinant hepatitis B surface antigen plus pre-S2 epitopes	Intramuscular injection	France*
Twinrix (GlaxoSmithKline, Rixensart , Belgium)	Inactivated hepatitis A virus, aluminum absorbed, plus recombinant hepatitis B surface antigen	Intramuscular injection	Many countries*

*Consult manufacturer for current list of countries where the vaccine is licensed and distributed.

Both adult (1.0 mL) and pediatric (0.5 mL licensed for those over the age of 1 year) vaccine formulations are now available (Table 6-1). Minor side effects such as swelling and pain at the site of injection might be experienced, with systemic effects such as nausea or fever occurring infrequently. The availability of this immunogenic vaccine should obviate the use of the hepatitis A immunoglobulin preparation, whose immunologic properties are much inferior to those of the active vaccine.

Hepatitis A vaccine induces an adequate level of seroprotection within 7 to 10 days following vaccination and will provide some degree of protection to an individual traveling at short notice depending on his or her risk of exposure. However, a recent study has demonstrated that significant levels of seroprotection against hepatitis A can be achieved within 13 days of administration of the primary dose of hepatitis A vaccine, which is much shorter than the incubation period of hepatitis A virus.[20–22] This suggests that protection will be afforded to those at imminent risk of infection. Recent studies have demonstrated that administering a single dose of hepatitis A vaccine is able to prevent outbreaks of disease when used without the immunoglobulin preparation by providing either protection against or attenuation of infection with hepatitis A, which is afforded by use of the vaccine following exposure. This might therefore have implications for the use of hepatitis A vaccine for those traveling on short notice.

The available vaccines are both highly immunogenic and protective when administered intramuscularly at day 0 with a booster at 6 to 12 months, which confer long-term protection for 25 years. Immunization with a single dose of hepatitis vaccine confers protection for only up to 1 year. It is well known that compliance with the first booster at 6 to 12 months is often poor, and, so in terms of practicalities, this first booster dose can be administered safely and effectively at any time after the first dose, which represents the primary course for this vaccine. Recent studies have demonstrated that the booster dose can be administered up to 4 to 6 years later.[23,24] Previously, further booster doses were recommended at 10-yearly intervals. However, as this is a highly immunogenic vaccine, recent research has demonstrated the presence of protective antibody levels for up to 25 years by using a model of statistical extrapolation determining the kinetics of antibody decay.[25,26]

In recent years, the Public Health Laboratory Service in the United Kingdom has recommended that because of the lack of availability of human normal Ig, active vaccination using licensed hepatitis A vaccines is the preferred option for the protection of travelers. Human normal Ig will be made available only for the protection of household contacts of confirmed cases of hepatitis A and to control outbreaks.[27–29]

In some developing countries, the incidence of clinical hepatitis A is increasing as improvements in socioeconomic conditions result in infection later in life, and protection by immunization would be prudent, but strategies are yet to be agreed on. Global control of hepatitis A will require universal immunization of infants and will become possible when HAV vaccine is combined in a polyvalent form with other childhood vaccines such as diphtheria, pertussis, tetanus, measles, rubella, mumps, and hepatitis B. In recent years, several countries, including Spain, Italy, Israel, and certain states in the United States, have implemented universal immunization programs against hepatitis A.[30,31]

Combined Hepatitis A and B Vaccine

Recent advances in combination vaccines have resulted in the availability of two multivalent vaccines, one containing hepatitis A and hepatitis B antigen and the other being hepatitis A and typhoid antigen. These vaccines might be suitable for those travelers at dual risk of exposure to these diseases. The combined hepatitis A and B vaccine is licensed for both pediatric (0.5 mL; 1–15 years) and adult (1.0 mL; > 16 years) use by the intramuscular route, with the primary course being administered at day 0, day 1, and 6 months. The corresponding levels of antibody protection achieved at each of these time points are 94%, 99%, and 100%, respectively, for hepatitis A and 34%, 97%, and 99%, respectively, for hepatitis B.[32] At present, no booster with the monovalent hepatitis B vaccine is recommended after a full primary immunization series in non-medical persons.

Recently, this vaccine has been licensed to be administered as a rapid schedule at days 0, 7, and 21, with a booster at 12 months. This regimen provides effective levels of protection at 1 month of 99%, 96% at 12 months, and 100% at 13 months for hepatitis A and 82%, 94%, and 100%, respectively, for hepatitis

B.[33,34] This schedule is licensed only for adults aged 16 years and over and is of particular benefit to those traveling at short notice and to those risk groups that are at imminent risk of dual exposure.

Combined Hepatitis A and typhoid Vaccine

Hepatitis A and typhoid are travel-related diseases of similar epidemiologic profile and disease transmission as food- and water-borne diseases. Consequently, a combination vaccine has recently been licensed in the United Kingdom: hepatitis A and typhoid.[10,11] Licensed currently for those aged 15 years and over, 1.0 mL of vaccine administered intramuscularly will confer protection against hepatitis A and typhoid within 14 days. Booster doses of the monovalent typhoid vaccine must be administered at 3-year intervals, whereas the monovalent hepatitis A vaccine must be given at 6 to12 months initially, followed by 10-year intervals. Again, no serious side effects have been reported with the use of this vaccine. The availability of a combined hepatitis A and typhoid vaccine is a valuable addition to the travel vaccine portfolio. It has become a very acceptable form of immunization for the majority of travelers who are at dual risk of infection, circumventing the need for two separate injections and so encouraging compliance with immunization.

The three most frequent vaccine-preventable diseases in travelers include hepatitis A, hepatitis B, and typhoid, and clinical trials evaluating the safety and immunogenicity of new multivalent vaccines have been reported recently. These include combination vaccines against hepatitis A, hepatitis B, and typhoid. Concurrent immunization with hepatitis A, typhoid, and yellow fever vaccines have been studied also and shown to provide protective immunity.[35–37]

HEPATITIS B

Hepatitis B virus (HBV) is a large double-shelled virus of the hepadnavirus group of double-stranded DNA viruses that replicate by reverse transcription. Hepatitis B was referred to originally as serum hepatitis, the most common form of parenterally transmitted viral hepatitis and an important cause of acute and chronic infection of the liver in many countries. It is transmitted by blood-to-blood contact and by the sexual route. More than one-third of the world's population has been infected with hepatitis B virus and WHO estimates that hepatitis B virus results in 1 to 2 million deaths every year.

The clinical features of acute infection resemble those of the other viral hepatitides. The virus persists in approximately 5 to 10% of immunocompetent adults and in as many as 90% of infants infected perinatally. Persistent carriage of hepatitis B, defined by the presence of hepatitis B surface antigen (HBsAg) in the serum for more than 6 months, has been estimated to affect about 350 million people worldwide, although not all carriers are infectious. Long-term continuing virus replication can lead to chronic liver disease, cirrhosis, and hepatocellular carcinoma. Primary liver cancer is one of the 10 most common cancers worldwide, and 80% of such cancers are ascribed to persistent infection with hepatitis B virus.[38]

Epidemiology and Geographic Distribution

Although various body fluids (blood, saliva, menstrual and vaginal discharges, serous exudates, seminal fluid, and breast milk) have been implicated in the spread of infection, infectivity appears to be especially related to blood and to body fluids contaminated with blood. The epidemiologic propensities of this infection are therefore wide; they include infection by inadequately sterilized syringes and instruments and transmission by unscreened blood transfusion and blood products, by close contact, and by both heterosexual and homosexual contact. Antenatal (rarely) and perinatal (frequently) transmission of hepatitis B infection from mother to child can take place; in some parts of the world (Southeast Asia), perinatal transmission is very common.

It should be noted that transmission of the infection can result from accidental inoculation of minute amounts of blood or fluid contaminated with blood during medical, surgical, and dental procedures; immunization with inadequately sterilized syringes and needles; intravenous and percutaneous drug abuse; tattooing; ear and nose piercing; acupuncture; laboratory accidents; and accidental inoculation with razors and similar objects that have been contaminated with blood. Additional factors can be important for the transmission of hepatitis B infection in the tropics; these include traditional tattooing and scarification, bloodletting, ritual circumcision, and repeated biting by blood-sucking arthropod vectors. Investigation of the role that biting insects play in the spread of hepatitis B has yielded conflicting results. Hepatitis B surface antigen has been detected in several species of mosquitoes and in bedbugs that were either trapped in the wild or fed experimentally on infected blood, but no convincing evidence of replication of the virus in insects has been obtained. Mechanical transmission of the infection, however, is a possibility but does not appear to be an important route of transmission of hepatitis B virus.

Infection with hepatitis B virus varies between geographic regions. Survival of hepatitis B virus is ensured by the huge reservoir of carriers, estimated conservatively to number in excess of 350 million worldwide, of whom more than 75% are from Southeast Asia and the western Pacific Region.

Other hyperendemic regions include many countries in sub-Saharan Africa. Based on the prevalence of HBsAg among blood donors, a highly selected group, prevalence rates in 1970 to 1980 extrapolated to the general population were as follows: 0.1% or less in northern Europe, North America, and Australasia; up to 5% in southern Europe, the countries bordering the Mediterranean, and parts of Central and South America; and 10 to 20% or more in some parts of Africa, Southeast Asia, and the western Pacific.

Prevention of Hepatitis B

General measures are based on knowledge of the mode of transmission of hepatitis B and include measures to prevent blood-to-blood contact; the use of sterile syringes, needles, and other implements contained within a first aid or medical kit; screening of blood and blood products; protected casual sexual intercourse; and other precautions dictated by the propensity for spread of this infection and the huge number of asymptomatic carriers of hepatitis B virus in the population. The single most effective measure for prevention is active immunization.

Passive Immunization with Hepatitis B Immunoglobulin

Hepatitis B immunoglobulin (HBIG) is prepared specifically from pooled plasma with a high titer of hepatitis B surface antibody and can confer temporary passive immunity under certain defined conditions. The major indication for the administration of HBIG is a single acute exposure to hepatitis B virus, such as occurs when blood containing surface antigen (HBs) is inoculated, ingested, or splashed onto mucous membranes and the conjunctiva. It should be administered as early as possible after exposure and preferably within 48 hours, usually 3 mL (containing 200 IU of anti-HBs/mL) in adults. It should not be administered later than 7 days following exposure. It is generally recommended that two doses of hepatitis B immunoglobulin be given 30 days apart.

Results with the use of HBIG for prophylaxis in neonates born to HBV-positive mothers at risk of infection with hepatitis B virus are good if the Ig is given as soon as possible after or within 12 hours of birth. Combined passive and active immunization provides a protective efficacy approaching 90%.

Active Immunization

The major humoral antibody response of recipients of hepatitis B vaccine is to the common a epitope, with consequent protection against all subtypes of the virus. First-generation vaccines were prepared from 22 nM HBsAg particles purified from plasma donations from chronic carriers. These preparations are safe and immunogenic but have been superseded in most countries by recombinant vaccines produced by the expression of HBsAg in yeast cells. The expression plasmid contains only the 3' portion of the HBV surface open reading frame (ORF), and only the major surface protein, without pre-S epitopes, is produced. Vaccines containing pre-S1 and pre-S2, as well as those containing the major surface proteins expressed by recombinant DNA technology have undergone extensive clinical trials but as yet remain unlicensed except for Bio Hep B licensed in Israel (see Table 6-1).[39–42]

In many areas of the world with a high prevalence of HBsAg carriage, such as China and Southeast Asia, the predominant route of transmission is perinatal. Although HBV does not usually cross the placenta, the infants of viremic mothers have a very high risk of infection at the time of birth, and immunization protects the infant against perinatal infection.

Immunization against hepatitis B is now recognized as a high priority in preventive medicine in all countries, and strategies for immunization are being revised. Universal vaccination of infants and adolescents is under examination as the strategy to control the transmission of this infection. More than 130 countries, including the United States, Canada, Italy, France, and most western European countries, now offer hepatitis B vaccine to all children.[43–45]

However, immunization against hepatitis B is at present recommended in a number of countries with a low prevalence of hepatitis B only to groups that are at an increased risk of acquiring this infection. These groups include individuals requiring repeated transfusions of blood or blood products, prolonged inpatient treatment, patients who require frequent tissue penetration or need repeated circulatory access, patients with natural or acquired immune deficiency, and patients with malignant diseases. Viral hepatitis is an occupational hazard among health care personnel, including those working in institutions for the mentally handicapped and in some semiclosed institutions. High rates of infection with hepatitis B occur in narcotic drug addicts and intravenous drug abusers, sexually active male homosexuals, and prostitutes.[17] Individuals working in areas of high endemicity are also at an increased risk of infection. Women in areas of the world where the carrier state is high are another segment of the population requiring immunization in view of the increased risk of transmission of the infection to their offspring. Young infants, children, and susceptible persons living in certain tropical and subtropical areas where present socioeconomic conditions are poor and the prevalence of hepatitis B is high should also be immunized.

Hepatitis B and the Traveler

Protection against hepatitis B has gained greater importance for all types of travelers who may be exposed to hepatitis B by virtue of many risk activities as well as destination. It has been estimated that there are 2 billion people infected with hepatitis B and more than 350 million carriers of disease throughout the world. The risk of infection to travelers has been estimated to be 80 to 240 cases per 100,000 travelers per month of stay for long-term travelers and 2 to 10 times lower among short-term travelers.[46] Therefore, hepatitis B is the second most common vaccine-preventable disease in travelers. The risk of hepatitis B to the traveler should not be underestimated. Travelers must take commonsense precautions to reduce the risk of hepatitis B, as outlined previously. Great caution is required in any casual intimate or sexual contact, particularly with prostitutes and male homosexuals.

All procedures involving penetration of the skin or mucous surfaces, including injections, tattooing, ear and other body piercing, blood transfusion, and medical and dental procedures (which might follow an accident or an adventure sports activity) carried out under questionable hygienic conditions, must be avoided if possible. Other risk factors that can lead to subsequent infection with hepatitis B include acupuncture, haircuts, and sharing razors and toothbrushes, all of which can result in transmission of blood-borne viruses.[47]

Health care professionals should consider vaccination against hepatitis B for those traveling outside of northwestern Europe, North America, Australia, and New Zealand, including long- and short-term travelers and including expatriates; those at occupational risk, such as aid/health care workers, missionaries, and military personnel; those with preexisting medical conditions who might require medical attention while abroad; and young children who might be in contact with other young children in an endemic area.

Hepatitis B vaccine is licensed for administration by the intramuscular route by several schedules and is also available following the use of the combination hepatitis A and B vaccine. Monovalent hepatitis B vaccine can be administered by the following schedules:

1. Day 0, then 1 and 6 months
2. Day 0, then 1 and 2 months, with a booster at 12 months
3. Day 0, then 12 and 24 months (licensed schedule in the United States)
4. Days 0, 7, and 21, with a booster at 12 months. The accelerated course of hepatitis B vaccine administration provides seroprotection in 65% of individuals within one month of receiving the primary course, which increases to 95% one month following administration of the booster doose.[48] This schedule of immunization is ideal for those traveling at short notice. It is currently only licensed for use in Europe.
5. A two-dose schedule administered 4 to 6 months apart for those aged 11 to15 years and who might have poor compliance with the other hepatitis B vaccine schedules. Several recent studies have demonstrated the safety and immunogenicity, including cost-effectiveness, of using a two-dose schedule for hepatitis B vaccination in adolescents with rates of seroprotection achieved at months 1, 6, and 7 of 44.3%, 27.9% and 93.45%, respectively, following administration of adult doses of hepatitis B vaccine at day 0 and 4 to 6 months. This schedule of hepatitis B vaccine administration will assist in improving compliance with completion of a course of hepatitis B.[49,50]

Nonresponse (serum antibody titer to HBsAg less than 10 m IU/mL) to hepatitis B vaccine, defined as an antibody titre of < 10 IU/mL following the administration of five doses of hepatitis B vaccine, can occur in up to 15% of adult vaccinees and is associated with several factors, including incorrect administration, male gender, increasing age (> 40 years), body mass index, and haplotype.[51,52] Hepatitis B vaccine must be administered intramuscularly in the deltoid muscle or anterolateral aspect of the thigh (see route of administration). Consequently, it is advisable to check the hepatitis B antibody response following vaccination with the primary course as well as boosters in the older traveler to ensure that adequate levels of protection have been achieved. The use of booster doses remains controversial, but for those at continued high risk, such as aid/health care professionals and expatriates deployed to areas of high endemicity, the administration of booster doses of hepatitis B vaccine is recommended at 5-year intervals.[53] Travelers who have been exposed to and are at risk of infection with hepatitis B and are non- or poor responders to hepatitis B vaccine should receive hepatitis B–specific hyperimmuneglobulin as well as a booster dose of hepatitis B vaccine under specific medical guidance.

The introduction of universal immunization programs will ensure protection against infection for all high-risk groups, including travelers, both present and future. Dual and concurrent protection against both hepatitis A and B by use of the combination vaccine might also be recognized in future universal immunization programs.

CONCLUSION

Viral hepatitis remains a significant public health problem, and, consequently, immunization programs have been implemented to eradicate disease. The risk of hepatitis A and hepatitis B to the traveler should not be underestimated.

Vaccination against hepatitis A and B through the use of both monovalent and combination vaccines is a significant advance in conferring protection against disease. This is complemented by the development and licensing of accelerated schedules, which will enhance compliance with immunization. This is also likely to be facilitated by the use of two-dose regimens in the future. Such schedules currently being evaluated in terms of safety and efficacy include administration of two doses of the combined hepatitis A and B vaccine, which, when licensed, will offer a more effective method of providing protection against hepatitis A and B through both universal immunization and immunization for those at high risk of exposure.[54,55] Many people, including the diverse group at risk of infection with both hepatitis A and B through occupation, behavioral factors, and travel, will benefit from the availability of receiving rapid protection by way of accelerated administration of hepatitis A and B vaccines.

The future development of routine universal immunization programs against hepatitis A, such as those being introduced in the United States and several southern Mediterranean countries, will be of benefit to future generations of travelers who will be protected well in advance of their travels. It could also be surmised that future universal immunization programs will include use of the combination hepatitis A and B vaccine, thereby providing concurrent dual long-term protection against both of these specific types of viral hepatitis. Developments in combination vaccines are continually being formulated and are going to be of value to the clinical practice of travel medicine in the prevention of infectious disease.[56]

Immunization against hepatitis A and hepatitis B is strongly recommended for all travelers to hyperendemic areas, and immunization against hepatitis B is a sensible precaution in case of accidents that might require treatment and subsequent potential exposure to blood-borne viruses. Combined hepatitis A and B vaccines are available, are highly effective, and are strongly recommended for those travelers at risk of dual infection.

REFERENCES

1. Koff RS. Hepatitis A. Lancet 1998;351:1643–8.

2. World Health Organization. The WHO Report. Fighting disease, fostering development. Geneva: WHO; 1996.

3. Kane M. Global programme for control of hepatitis B infection. Vaccine 1995;13:51:S47–9.

4. Andre FE, Safray A. Over a decade of experience with a yeast recombinant hepatitis B vaccine. Vaccine 1999;18:57–67.

5. Andre FE, D'Hondt E, Delem A, Safray A. Clinical assessment of the safety and efficacy of an inactivated hepatitis A vaccine. Rationale and summary of findings. Vaccine 1992;10:S160–8.

6. Sagliocca L, Amoroso P, Stroffolini T, et al. Efficacy of hepatitis A vaccine in the prevention of secondary hepatitis A infection. A randomised trial. Lancet 1999;353:1136–9.

7. Crowcroft NS, Davison KL, Gungabisson U. Guidelines for the control of hepatitis A virus infection. Commun Dis Public Health 2001;4:3:213–27.

8. Thoelen S, Van Damme P, Leentvaar-Kuypers A, et al. The first combined vaccine against hepatitis A and B. An overview. Vaccine 1998;17:1657–62.

9. Joines RW, Blatter M, Abraham B, et al. A prospective, randomized, comparative US trial of a combination hepatitis A and B vaccine (Twinrix) with corresponding monovalent vaccines (Havrix and Engerix-B) in adults. Vaccine 2001;19:4701–19.

10. Van Hoecke C, Lebacq E, Beran J, et al. Concomitant vaccination against hepatitis A and typhoid fever. J Travel Med 1998;5:116–20.

11. Beran J, Beutels M, Levie K, et al. A single dose combined vaccine against typhoid fever and hepatitis A. Consistency, immunogenicity and reactogenicity. J Travel Med 2000;7:246–52.

12. Centers for Disease control and Prevention. Health information for international travel, 2003–2004. Atlanta: US Department of Health and Human Sciences; 2003.

13. Lemon SM, Thomas DL. Vaccines to prevent viral hepatitis. New Engl J Med 1997;336:196–204.

14. World Health Organization. International travel and health. Geneva: World Health Organization; 2000.

15. Department of Health, Welsh Office, Scottish Office Department of Health, DHSS (Northern Ireland), PHLS CDSC. Health information for overseas travel 2000.

16. Steffen R, Kane MA, Shapiro CN, et al. Epidemiology and prevention of hepatitis A in travelers. JAMA 1994;272:885–9.

17. Salisbury DM, Begg NT, editors. Immunisation against infectious disease. Department of Health, Welsh Office, Scottish Office Department of Health, DHSS (Northern Ireland) HMSO; 1996.

18. Zuckerman JN, Powell L. Hepatitis A antibodies in attenders of London travel clinics. Cost-benefit of screening prior to hepatitis A immunisation. J Med Virol 1994;44:393–4.

19. Van Doorslaer E, Tormans, G, van Damme P. Cost-effectiveness analysis of vaccination against hepatitis A in travellers. J Med Virol 1994;44:463–9.

20. Irwin DJ, Millership S. Antibody responses to hepatitis A vaccine in healthy adults. Commun Dis Public Health 2001;4:2:136–40.

21. Van Damme P, Lievens M, Stoffel M, Ngyuyen C. Rapid seroconversion rates after the first dose of an inactivated hepatitis A vaccine (Havrix 1440™). Results of a retrospective analysis. Poster presented at 3rd European Conference on Travel Medicine; May 2002; Florence, Italy.

22. Ambrosch F, Wiedermann G, Jonas S, et al. Immunogenicity and protectivity of a new liposomal hepatitis A vaccine. Vaccine 1997;15:1209–13.

23. Iwarson S, Lindh M, Widestrom L. Excellent booster response 4-6 y after a single primary dose of an inactivated hepatitis A vaccine. Scand J Infect Dis 2002:34:110–1.

24. Iwarson S. Are we giving too many doses of hepatitis A and B vaccines? Vaccine 2002;20:16:2017–8.

25. van Herck K, van Damme P. Inactivated hepatitis A vaccine-induced antibodies. Follow-up and estimates of long-term persistence. J Med Virol 2001;63:1–7.

26. Bovier PA, Bock J, Loutan L, et al. Long-term immunogenicity of an inactivated virosome hepatitis vaccine. J Med Virol 2002;68:489–93.

27. Scottish Centre for Infection and Environmental Health. Recommendations on hepatitis A immunisation for travellers. SCIEH Wkly Rep 1999;33:173.

28. Hepatitis A vaccines. Wkly Epidemiol Rec 2000;5:38–44.

29. Human normal immunoglobulin. Lack of availability for travellers. Commun Dis Rep Wkly 2000;10;34:301.

30. Salleras L, Brugera M, Buti M, Domingez A. Prospects for vaccination against hepatitis A and B in Catalonia (Spain). Vaccine 2000;1:580–2.

31. Prevention of hepatitis A through active or passive immunization. Recommendations of the Advisory Committee on Immunisation Practices (ACIP). MMWR Morb Mortal Wkly Rep 1999;48(RR12);1–37.

32. Reutter J, Bart PA, Francioli P, et al. Production of antibody to hepatitis A virus and hepatitis B surface antigen measured after combined hepatitis A/hepatitis B vaccine in 242 adults. J Viral Hepat 1998;5:205–11.

33. Zuckerman JN, Dietrich M, Nothdurft HD, et al. Rapid protection against hepatitis A and hepatitis B following an accelerated schedule of a combined hepatitis A/B vaccine. Antivir Ther 2000;5 Suppl 1:8.

34. Northdurft HD, Dietrich M, Zuckerman JN, et al. A new accelerated vaccination schedule for rapid protection against hepatitis A and B. Vaccine 2002;20:1557–62.

35. Dumas R, Forrat R, Lang J, et al. Safety and immunogenicity of a new inactivated hepatitis A vaccine in concurrent administration with a typhoid fever vaccine or a typhoid fever + yellow fever vaccine. Adv Ther 1997;14:160–7.

36. Jong EC, Kaplan KM, Eves KA, et al. An open randomized study of inactivated hepatitis A vaccine administered concomitantly with typhoid fever and yellow fever vaccines. J Travel Med 2002;9:66–70.

37. Proell S, Maiwald H, Nothdurft HD, et al. Combined vaccination against hepatitis A, hepatitis B, and typhoid fever. Safety, reactogenicity, and immunogenicity. J Travel Med 2002;9:122–6.

38. Harrison TJ, Dusheiko GM, Zuckerman AJ. Hepatitis viruses. In: Zuckerman AJ, Banatvala J, Pattison JR, editors. Principles and practice of clinical virology. 4th ed. Chichester (UK): Wiley; 200. p. 187–223.

39. Zuckerman JN, Zuckerman AJ. Recombinant hepatitis B triple antigen vaccine. Hepacare®. Expert Rev Vaccines 2002;1:141–4.

40. Raz R, Dagan R, Gallil A, et al. Safety and immunogenicity of a novel mammalian cell-dreived recombinant hepatitis B vaccine containing Pre-S1 and Pre-S2 antigens in children. Vaccine 1996;14:207–11.

41. Shapira MY, Zeira E, Adler R, et al. Rapid seroprotection against hepatitis B following the first dose of Pre-S1/Pre-S2 vaccine. J Hepatol 2001;34:123–7.

42. Soussan P, Stanislas P, Garreau F, et al. Vaccination of chronic hepatitis B virus carriers with preS2/S envelope protien is not associated with the emergence of envelope escape mutants. J Gen Virology 2001;82:367–71.

43. Goldstrin ST, Fiore AE. Toward the global elimination of hepatitis B virus transmission. J Pediatr 2001;139:343–5.

44. Kao JH, Chen DS. Global control of hepatitis B virus infection. Lancet Infect Dis 2002;2:395–403.

45. Van Damme P, Kane M, Mehens A. Integration of hepatitis B vaccination into national immunisation programmes. BMJ 1997;314:1033–6.

46. Steffen R. Hepatitis A and hepatitis B. Risks compared with other vaccine-preventable diseases and immunisation recommendations. Vaccine 1993;11:518–20.

47. Zuckerman JN, Steffen R. Risks of hepatitis B in travellers as compared to imunisation status. J Travel Med 2000;7:170–4.

48. Bock HL, Loscher T, Scheierman N, et al. Accelerated schedule for hepatitis B immunisation. J Trav Med 1995;2:213–7.

49. Schiff GM, Sherwood JR, Zeldis JB, Krause DS. Comparative study of the immunogenicity and safety of two doses of recombinant hepatitis B vaccine in healthy adolescents. J Adolesc Health 1995;16:12–7.

50. Marsano LS, West DJ, Chan I, et al. A two dose hepatitis B vaccine regime. Proof of priming and memory response in young adults. Vaccine 1998;16:6:624–9.

51. Zuckerman JN. Non-response to hepatitis B vaccines and the kinetics of anti-HBs production. J Med Virol 1996;50:283–328.

52. McDermott AB, Cohen SBA, Zuckerman JN, Madrigal JA. Hepatitis B third generation vaccines. Improved response and conventional vaccine non-response—evidence for genetic basis in man. J Viral Hepat 1998;5:9–11.

53. Kane M, Banatvala J, Da Villa G, et al. Lifelong protection against hepatitis B and the need for boosters. European Consensus Group on Hepatitis B Immunity. Lancet 2000;355:561–5.

54. Burgess MA, Rodger AJ, Waite SA, Collard F. Comparative immunogenicity and safety of two dosing schedules of a combined hepatitis A and B vaccine in healthy adolescent volunteers. An open randomised study. Vaccine 2001;19:4835–41.

55. Guptan RC, Thakur V, Safray A, Sarin SK. Immunogenicity and reactogenicity of a combined high dose hepatitis A and hepatitis B vaccine compared to that of Twinrix and unknown in healthy Indian children. Vaccine 2002;20:16:2101–6.

56. Le C. Combination vaccines. Choices or chaos? A practitioner's perspective. Clin Infect Dis 2001;33:S367–75.

Chapter 7

Typhoid and Cholera Vaccines

James D. Campbell and Myron M. Levine

International travel, including travel to developing nations of the world, has become increasingly common. More than 500 million people, of whom approximately 27 million are Americans, travel internationally each year.[1,2] Enteric illnesses are among the leading causes of disease in travelers. Away from home, one can avoid many of the exposures that increase one's risk of infectious disease but one cannot completely avoid exposure to foods and drinks, the vehicles that carry the organisms causing typhoid fever and cholera. A physician or other health professional counseling an international traveler should provide both verbal and written instructions on the appropriate methods of preventing the consumption of foods and beverages that may contain enteric pathogens. However, in addition, for certain organisms, such as *Salmonella enterica* serovar Typhi (hereafter referred to as *S.* Typhi) and *Vibrio cholerae*, there are vaccines that may be appropriate for certain travelers. These vaccines never replace proper counseling regarding safe food and water intake but, rather, augment it.

Decisions concerning the vaccination of a traveler against enteric diseases should occur after the traveler is fully informed of the risks of the disease and the risks and benefits of the vaccine. The risks of falling ill with these diseases relate to exposure and immunity. Exposure to enteric pathogens depends on the country and region to which one is traveling, the food and water sources one expects to use while there, and the ability to purify, cook, or otherwise decontaminate foods and beverages. Immunity to these organisms depends on previous enteric disease experience, vaccination, immunologic evidence of protection, and the presence of immunosuppressive diseases or the use of immunosuppressive medications. The vaccine risks to be considered include both common and uncommon side effects, interactions with other vaccines or medications, and the potential for those vaccinated to become complacent in their judicious choices of food and water while traveling. The benefits of the vaccine, of course, are its efficacy and the potential peace of mind afforded the vaccinee. One must also keep in mind the cost, the time from vaccination until protection is effected, and the length of protection provided.

This chapter will describe vaccines designed to protect against two enteric bacterial pathogens: *S.* Typhi and *V. cholerae*.

TYPHOID VACCINES

Causative Organism and Clinical Disease

Typhoid fever is a systemic illness characterized by fever, headache, malaise, and abdominal discomfort. Individuals with typhoid fever may also have splenomegaly, relative bradycardia, relative leukopenia, and a rash described as "rose spots." The illness may present acutely or insidiously, is typically more severe than other salmonelloses, and can be life threatening.[3]

Typhoid fever is caused by *Salmonella* Typhi, a gram-negative, non–lactose-fermenting, non–gas-forming bacillus that is host restricted to humans. *S.* Typhi is characterized by its lipopolysaccharide (LPS) antigens (O antigens 9 and 12), its flagellar antigen (H type d), and its capsular polysaccharide (Vi, for virulence).

The organism is shed in human stool during the acute illness or during prolonged periods of carriage. Carriers can excrete 10^6 to 10^9 organisms per gram of stool, with excretion tending to be higher in carriers with frequent or loose bowel movements. (Normal flora in the large intestine are inhibitory for *S.* Typhi.) Individuals who are exposed in various ways to human waste consume the organism along with food and beverage. It is taken up by M cells in the small intestine and subsequently ingested by underlying macrophages. It may also be taken up by enterocytes via pinocytosis. Most of the penetration occurs in the distal small bowel, where the highest density of Peyer's patches is found. The organism is transported to the mesenteric lymph nodes via lymphatics. It may then enter the systemic blood stream through the thoracic duct, eventually reaching and replicating in the reticuloendothelial organs (liver, spleen, and bone marrow). Following an incubation period that is typically 8 to 14 days (shorter with the ingestion of larger inocula), a sustained low-level bacteremia ensues. The diagnosis is made by recovering *S.* Typhi from blood or another body site.[3]

Although typhoid can be treated with antibiotics, *S.* Typhi strains resistant to clinically important antibiotics have emerged over the last decade.[4,5] Among 293 isolates of *S.* Typhi found in cases reported to the US Centers for Disease Control and Prevention (CDC) between June 1996 and May 1997, 25% were resistant to one or more antibiotics, and 17% were resistant to five or more. Resistant strains were especially common among US travelers to the Indian subcontinent.[6]

Protective Immunity

Immune responses against *S.* Typhi include serum anticapsular (Vi), antilipopolysaccharide (O), and antiflagellar (H) antibodies directed against the organism while it is extracellular; and cell-mediated mechanisms, including interferon-γ and cytotoxic lymphocytes, while intracellular.[7–9] The immunologic responses that are thought to play a role in protection include serum and intestinal secretory anti-O antibodies, antibody-secreting cells directed against the O antigen, anti-Vi antibodies, and cell-mediated immune responses.

Burden in Travelers and Known Risks

Although the world burden of typhoid fever still surpasses 15 million annual cases, the incidence of typhoid fever in the United States declined steadily in the first half of the last century and has remained fairly constant in recent decades.[6] However, the proportion of cases occurring in travelers has continued to increase. In 1920, there were approximately 36,000 cases of typhoid fever in the United States. In 2001, the last year for which there are published data from the CDC, there were 68 cases.[10] The true number of cases in travelers might be underestimated because of antibiotic treatment prior to diagnosis and treatment prior to return from travel.[11] From 1967 to 1972, only 33% of US typhoid cases were imported, whereas from 1975 to 1984, 62% were imported, and in 1999, 81% of cases report travel abroad in the preceding 6 weeks.[6,12,13] Americans ill with typhoid fever in 1996 and 1997 most commonly reported travel to India,

Pakistan, Bangladesh, Haiti, the Philippines, and Mexico, in that order. Many typhoid patients were foreign-born US residents returning to visit their country of origin. The median travel time for US typhoid patients was 1 month.[6] Typhoid fever is seen more commonly in the young and the old and in people who take antacids or who have other reasons for a high gastric pH. Pediatric travelers are at high risk for typhoid fever, accounting for 42% of the cases in US travelers from June 1996 to May 1997. Approximately two-thirds of American children returning with typhoid are under the age of 10 years (Figure 7-1).[6]

Vaccination is recommended for travelers to typhoid-endemic countries, including most areas of Central and South America, Africa, the Near East, the Middle East, Southeast Asia, and the Indian subcontinent.

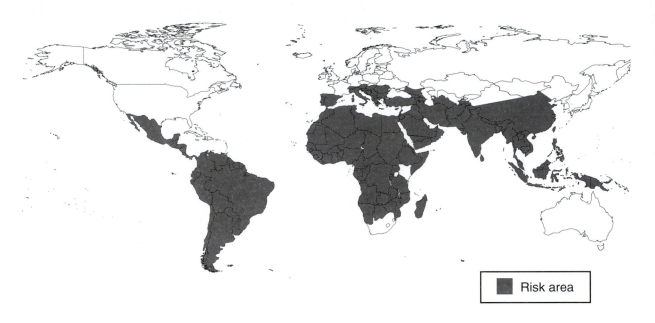

Risk area

Figure 7-1. Map of global distribution of typhoid fever.

Previously Available Typhoid Vaccines

Parenteral Whole Cell Vaccine

The parenteral whole cell vaccines against typhoid were used for many decades. They consist of *S.* Typhi bacteria inactivated by phenol, heat, or acetone. In field trials in Yugoslavia, Poland, Russia, and Guyana, the vaccines were found to range in efficacy from 51 to 88% with follow-up from 2.5 to 7 years.[3,14–19] Unfortunately, these vaccines are very reactogenic, with 16% of recipients having fever, 20% arm swelling, and 10% missing work or school owing to the vaccination.[20] As a result, the whole cell vaccines are no longer used for US travelers and have been replaced by a live attenuated oral vaccine and a parenteral subunit (purified capsular polysaccharide) vaccine.

Currently Available Vaccines

Two vaccines are available in the United States for health care workers to prescribe to travelers. The most recent CDC Advisory Committee on Immunization Practices (ACIP) recommendations for their use in the United States were published in 1994 (Table 7-1).[21]

Table 7-1. **Available Vaccines against Typhoid Fever**

	Ty21a	*Vi Capsular Polysaccharide*
Proprietary name (manufacturer)	Vivotif Berna (Berna Biotech)	Typhim Vi (Aventis Pasteur)
Characteristics	Oral live attenuated	Intramuscular subunit
Dose	1 capsule every other day to complete 4 doses	Single injection
Boosting interval	Every 5 years	Every 2 years
Time until immune	Unknown; complete series > 1 week before travel	Unknown; vaccinate > 2 weeks before travel
Estimated efficacy	~ 67–75%	~ 67–75%
Main adverse events	Abdominal complaints (< 5%)	Injection site pain, redness, induration; fever is uncommon (1%)
Contraindications	Pregnancy, immune compromise, hypersensitivity to vaccine component	Pregnancy, hypersensitivity to vaccine component; precaution in coagulopathic patients
Concomitant antimicrobials	Not to be taken within 24 hours of mefloquine or antibiotics	No restrictions
Concomitant vaccines	No restrictions	No restrictions
Children	Age 6 years and over	Age 2 years and over
Elderly	Not tested	Not tested
Where available	Many countries	Many countries

Both of the vaccines discussed here are available in the United States. Hepatyrix (GlaxoSmithKline) and ViATIM (Aventis Pasteur, Lyon, France) are combined inactivated hepatitis A and purified Vi polysaccharide typhoid vaccines. They are approved for use in some countries for travelers and others at risk. They are given as a single IM injection.

Ty21a

Background and Characteristics. In 1975, a chemically mutagenized strain of *S.* Typhi was described in which an epimerase gene was deleted and other cellular functions were altered.[22] This strain, Ty21a, was found to be tolerated well at very high doses of bacteria and to be immunogenic in humans. Field trials have been performed in Egypt, Chile, and Indonesia supporting the safety and efficacy of this strain in various formulations and dosages (Figure 7-2).[23–27]

In 1978, Egyptian schoolchildren were randomly assigned to receive 3 doses every other day of either liquid suspension (ie, reconstituted lyophilate) of Ty21a or placebo. Following 3 years of surveillance for typhoid, the vaccine was found to have 96% efficacy.[26] Subsequent formulations of the vaccine consisted of lyophilized bacteria in either gelatin capsules (accompanied by other gelatin capsules containing sodium bicarbonate) or lyophilized bacteria in enteric-coated capsules. The field trials in Chile over the following decade investigated the use of Ty21a in various doses and formulations.[23,24] In 1983, Chilean schoolchildren were randomized to receive one of four permutations of vaccine formulation/schedule or placebo. After 3 years of follow-up for culture-confirmed typhoid fever, the gelatin capsule had poor efficacy regardless of dosing interval (range 19 to 31%), but the enteric-coated vaccine had 49% efficacy with three doses at 21-day intervals and 67% efficacy with three doses at 2-day intervals. The efficacy of the

Figure 7-2. Hypothetical mechanism of action for oral typhoid vaccine Ty21a. Courtesy of Bena Biotech Ltd.

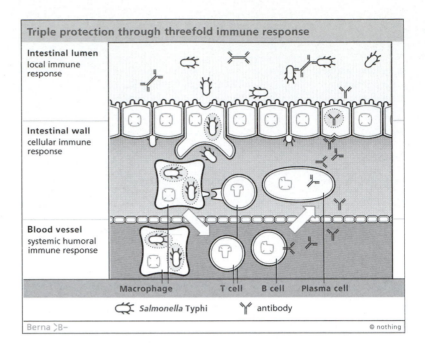

latter regimen was sustained (62%) out to the seventh year in follow-up surveillance performed after the completion of the original study.[28]

Another study of Chilean schoolchildren performed in the 1980s evaluated one versus two doses of the enteric-coated formulation compared with a placebo. A single dose had poor efficacy, and although two doses led to short-term efficacy similar to the three-dose regimen, the efficacy waned after just 2 years.[27] In a study evaluating two, three, or four doses of enteric-coated Ty21a given every other day to Chilean schoolchildren, the incidence of typhoid was significantly decreased with the addition of the fourth dose, from 161 to 96 per 100,000.[29] This large-scale effectiveness trial did not include a placebo arm.

Comparison of the enteric-coated capsule with a liquid (reconstituted lyophilate) formulation in Chilean schoolchildren found the liquid formulation more efficacious (77% vs 33%).[24] In Indonesia, where the incidence of typhoid was the highest among all the field sites at which Ty21a was evaluated, again the liquid formulation had improved efficacy (53%) over the enteric-coated capsule (42%). In this trial, the interval between doses was extended to 1 week.[25]

On the basis of these trials, Ty21a has been approved in the United States and elsewhere for use in travelers to endemic countries, in contacts of an individual chronically shedding *S.* Typhi in the stool, and in laboratory workers exposed to the organism.

Dose/Boost. The Ty21a vaccine (Vivotif Berna vaccine, Berna Biotech, Berne, Switzerland) currently used in the United States is formulated as enteric-coated capsules. Each capsule contains 2 to 6×10^9 viable (and 5 to 50 billion nonviable) lyophilized Ty21a organisms. In the United States and Canada, it is recommended that travelers ingest one capsule every other day for 7 days (ie, a total of four capsules). Most other countries recommend just 3 doses given every other day over 5 days. The capsules should be kept refrigerated (2–8°C) prior to ingestion and swallowed with cool liquid (less than body temperature) 1 hour before a meal. The capsules should not be chewed. They should remain refrigerated between doses. The Ty21a "liquid" formulation, paired sachets of lyophilized vaccine and buffer that are reconstituted with water, is available in an increasing number of countries, including Canada.

Booster doses of Ty21a are recommended for individuals who expect to remain at risk of typhoid fever. Regimens identical to the first dosing scheme are recommended for booster immunization. The manufacturer recommends a booster series every 5 years.

Efficacy and Time to Protection. The efficacy of this vaccine is not known for travelers, but estimates can be made based on studies performed in endemic countries and on the challenge model. Extrapolating from the field trials performed in endemic areas, in which three doses of enteric-coated vaccine were found to have 67% efficacy and four doses of enteric-coated vaccine were shown to effect a significantly decreased incidence compared with three doses, the vaccine as currently recommended is expected to have an efficacy in excess of 67%.[23,29] In the early clinical development phase of Ty21a, immunization with freshly harvested vaccine organisms (containing 10^{10} organisms, one log more than found in current commercial formulations) provided North American volunteers with 87% protection against experimental challenge with S. Typhi.[30]

The time from immunization until protection is also unknown, but efficacy estimates in the field trials were based on surveillance beginning 2 weeks after immunization; immune responses are evident after 2 weeks. The manufacturer recommends completing the four-dose series at least 1 week before travel to a typhoid-endemic area.

Side Effects. The Ty21a vaccine has an excellent safety profile. Pooled estimates for adverse events, compiled in a meta-analysis of all trials reported, reveal fever in 2%, vomiting in 2%, and diarrhea in 5% of vaccinees.[20] More than 150 million doses have been administered to individuals, primarily school-aged children, during trials and following licensure.[31] Adverse events occurred at the same rate in placebo recipients as in Ty21a recipients. Abdominal discomfort, nausea, headache, rash, and urticaria are additional events that have rarely been reported after Ty21a ingestion.[21]

In early clinical trials, the vaccine strain was shed transiently in the stools of volunteers who had received a 10^{10} colony-forming units (CFU) dosage (one log higher than commercial formulations).[30] The vaccine strain, as currently dosed and formulated, is not recovered in coproculture. Person-to-person transmission has not been noted. Unlike wild-type S. Typhi, the vaccine strain was not detected in the bloodstream of vaccinees.

Contraindications. The contraindications for use of this vaccine are pregnancy and an immunocompromised state, including infection with HIV, although the vaccine has not been studied in these populations. An individual with hypersensitivity to a component of the vaccine or the capsule should not be immunized. The manufacturer discourages administering the vaccine to a traveler with an acute febrile illness. The vaccine has not been studied in nursing mothers.

Interactions. Some researchers have raised the possibility that Ty21a loses immunogenicity if taken together with or in proximity to blood products containing immune globulin, antiparasitic medications, antibacterial medications, or other vaccines. Although the vaccine has not been tested for efficacy or immunogenicity in individuals who have recently received blood products that might contain antibodies against components of S. Typhi, it has been found to be immunogenic in populations with preexisting antibody due to natural infection. Therefore, it may be given, when indicated, to individuals who have received or who will receive immunoglobulin or other blood products.[21]

The ACIP recommends against giving mefloquine or antibiotics concurrently with Ty21a vaccine as either one may kill the live bacteria. It recommends waiting for 24 hours or more after a dose of mefloquine or antibiotics before beginning the Ty21a series.[21] The manufacturer's package insert discourages the use of proguanil, another antimalarial agent, but allows for either mefloquine or chloroquine.[31] These recommendations stem from a study in which individuals receiving mefloquine or chloroquine with Ty21a did not produce lower antibody responses than those receiving Ty21a alone.[32] Efficacy has not been evaluated in this situation. Because chloroquine requires very high concentrations to kill Ty21a, there are no restrictions for travelers taking chloroquine.[33,34] Proguanil should not be taken until 10 days have elapsed after the last Ty21a dose.

The vaccine has been studied when administered with other vaccines, for example, the cholera vaccine CVD 103-HgR.[32] When given together, these vaccines are clinically well tolerated, and immune responses are as strong as when Ty21a or CVD 103-HgR is taken alone. The ACIP currently places no specific precautions on simultaneous administration of Ty21a with other vaccines.

Special Populations. The manufacturer recommends use of Ty21a in individuals at risk who are 6 years of age or older. The vaccine has been shown to be tolerated well and immunogenic in preschool children.[35] The large-scale field trial in Indonesia included children as young as 3 years of age.[25,36] The parenteral Vi vaccine, approved in the United States for children aged 2 years and older, may be used in lieu of Ty21a when a preschool child is traveling to an endemic area. Ty21a has not been tested in other special populations, such as the elderly and those with inflammatory diseases of the intestines; however, the manufacturer recommends against prescribing the vaccine for a patient with an acute gastrointestinal illness.[31]

Vi Capsular Polysaccharide Vaccine

Background and Characteristics. The Vi capsular polysaccharide of *S.* Typhi is available as a parenteral vaccine. This capsule, which covers virulent typhoid organisms, is made of repeating chains of *N*-acetylgalacturonic acid. Early attempts to use this capsule as an immunogen encountered difficulties due to purification processes that denatured the sugar.[37] Subsequently, investigators succeeded in extracting the Vi without denaturing it.[38]

Early studies on safety and immunogenicity showed that purified Vi led to high anti-Vi antibody titers in American and French adult volunteers and that these responses persisted for 3 years.[39,40] Field trials were undertaken in South Africa and Nepal in the 1980s.[41,42] In the South African trial, school-aged participants were randomized to receive either Vi or meningococcal polysaccharide vaccine, serogroups A + C. Vi vaccine afforded 64% efficacy during the first 21 months following vaccination and a cumulative 3-year efficacy of 55%.[43] In Nepal, where both children and adults, ages 5 to 44 years, were randomized to receive either Vi or the 23-valent pneumococcal vaccine, Vi vaccine provided 75% efficacy over 20 months of surveillance. In a postlicensure report by the manufacturer, following the distribution of more than 22 million doses of Vi vaccine, only two confirmed cases of vaccine failure were reported to have occurred in the 2 years between recommended booster doses.[44]

Studies of efficacy in nonendemic areas are difficult to obtain given the large sample sizes that would be required to have the statistical power necessary to prove efficacy against such a low-incidence event. Studies of safety and immunogenicity have been performed in the United States and have found the vaccine to be well tolerated and able to induce fourfold increases in anti-Vi antibody levels in 88 and 96% of participants, respectively.[45,46] In Indonesian children aged 2 to 5 years, 96% had a fourfold rise in antibody titers 1 month following vaccination, and the children achieved higher geometric mean antibody concentrations than reported for adults.[45]

Vi vaccines are available to travelers from many industrialized countries, including the United States.[47] There are three commercially available products. Typhim Vi (Aventis Pasteur, Inc., Swiftwater, PA) contains only the Vi antigen and is the only one available in the United States. Hepatyrix (GlaxoSmithKline, Middlesex, UK) and ViATIM (Aventis Pasteur MSD Ltd., Berks, UK) are products with combined inactivated hepatitis A vaccine and Vi polysaccharide vaccine.

It is interesting to note that purified, injectable Vi, which includes no other antigens of *S.* Typhi, and oral Ty21a, which does not have a Vi capsule, both induce effective immune responses, presumably by different mechanisms. In addition, whereas 80% of individuals acutely infected with *S.* Typhi do not mount anti-Vi antibody responses, more than 90% of chronic carriers have very high levels of immunoglobulin (Ig)G Vi antibodies.

Dose/Boost. Vi capsular polysaccharide vaccine is given as a single 0.5 mL intramuscular injection. It contains a sterile solution of 25 µg of Vi polysaccharide precipitated from a culture supernatant. It also contains phenol as a preservative. The vaccine is recommended to be stored in refrigeration (2–8°C).

Reimmunization is recommended every 2 years. In studies to evaluate the effect of reimmunization on antibody level, American adults were reimmunized at 27 or 34 months after the first immunization. Antibody levels decayed from approximately 3 to 4 µg/mL 1 month after the first vaccination to 1 µg/mL 2 ½ years later. Repeat vaccination with Vi returns the levels to approximately 3 µg/mL. These data support the fact that the Vi polysaccharide vaccine is T-cell independent and that reimmunization does not lead to a true boost effect.[45,46]

Efficacy and Time to Protection. The efficacy of this vaccine in travelers is not known. Using the data from trials in endemic countries, immunogenicity studies in healthy adults in nonendemic countries, and vaccine failure reports, one can surmise that the vaccine most likely has efficacy in the same range as Ty21a (protecting two-thirds to three-quarters of travelers).

The manufacturer recommends an interval of no less than 2 weeks from immunization until time of expected exposure.[47] Two weeks after vaccination, approximately 80% of vaccinees will have mounted a fourfold rise in antibody titer, and the geometric mean concentration of anti-Vi antibody will be 2.5 µg/mL.[44]

Side Effects. Vi capsular polysaccharide vaccine is well tolerated and safe. In a meta-analysis in which five studies of the vaccine met the inclusion criteria for toxicity analysis, the pooled estimates of side effects were as follows: fever 1%; swelling at the injection site 4%; missed work or school 0%.[20] The manufacturer, using data from all trials and subsequent surveillance, reports the most common side effects are pain, redness, and induration at the injection site. They are usually described as mild to moderate in intensity, and they resolve spontaneously. Pain and swelling are more common in children than in adults.[44] The vaccine is well tolerated alone or when given at the same time as other vaccines.[48–51] Rare reports of other side effects that may be associated with the vaccine, including allergic reactions and rashes, have been reported by the manufacturer.[44]

Contraindications. The vaccine is not recommended for pregnant women. As of 1996, after more than 22 million doses of vaccine had been distributed, the manufacturer had collected 90 reports of vaccination occurring inadvertently during or recently before pregnancy.[44] Of these, there were 9 miscarriages or spontaneous abortions, 4 terminations, and 1 congenital anomaly (a tracheoesophageal fistula). The causal relationship between the abnormal outcomes and the vaccine is not known.

The vaccine is also contraindicated for patients with hypersensitivity to a vaccine component. Although not considered dangerous in immunosuppressed patients, the vaccine has not been tested in this population, and suboptimal immune responses may occur. Providers should follow the precautions described by the ACIP and consult the patient's hematologist when giving any intramuscular injection, including Vi, to patients with coagulation disorders.[52]

Interactions. There are no known interactions with drugs or biologics but there have been no evaluations of response to Vi in the face of concomitant antibiotics, antiparasitics, or blood products.

Special Populations. The manufacturer recommends the use of Vi capsular polysaccharide vaccine in individuals at risk who are 2 years of age or older. The vaccine is not approved for use in the United States for children below the age of 2 years. The at-risk groups are travelers to endemic countries who are likely to be exposed to contaminated food or water, microbiology laboratory workers who handle S. Typhi, and intimate contacts of a typhoid carrier. Excretion of Vi vaccine in breast milk has not been studied. Studies in the elderly have also not been done.

Future Vaccines

Ideally, new safe and effective vaccines could be developed both for travelers and for use in public health programs designed to ease the burden of typhoid fever in endemic countries. The two primary lines of research focus on rational improvements of the live attenuated oral vaccine and the capsular polysaccharide vaccine.

New Generation Live Oral Vaccines

Six attenuated strains of S. Typhi, all derived from wild-type strain Ty2 (the parent of Ty21a), have been evaluated in clinical trials.

CVD 908, CVD 908-htrA, and CVD 909

CVD 908 harbors deletion mutations in genes encoding enzymes in the aromatic amino acid biosynthesis pathway, rendering the strain nutritionally dependent on substrates that are not available in sufficient quantity in human tissues.[53] Although clinically well tolerated and immunogenic, blood cultures drawn on days 4 through 8 after vaccination detected silent, self-limited vaccinemias, as previously observed with polio and rubella vaccines, in 50% of subjects who ingested the highest doses ($5 \times 10^{7-8}$ CFU).[8,9,54–57] This phenomenon encouraged the development of strains that were more attenuated.

A gene encoding a serine protease, *htrA*, was deleted from CVD 908.[58–60] This strain, CVD 908-*htrA*, has since been administered to more than 120 young adults in phase I and II trials.[60,61] It is tolerated as well as CVD 908, is likewise excreted for only 3 days, and is similarly immunogenic. However, in contrast to CVD 908, CVD 908-*htrA* does not cause silent vaccinemias. Phase II trials in pediatric subjects in typhoid endemic areas and phase III efficacy trials are forthcoming.

CVD 908, CVD 908-*htrA*, Ty800, and X4073 (detailed below) do not stimulate serum Vi antibodies when administered as oral vaccines, as is also true in 80% of patients acutely infected with natural typhoid.[62–64] Expression of Vi is highly regulated in relation to certain environmental signals, such as osmolarity, and Vi may not always be expressed.[65–68] CVD 909 is a derivative of CVD 908-*htrA* that constitutively expresses Vi and thus may take advantage of the immune mechanisms at work in protection afforded by both Ty21a and the Vi capsular polysaccharide vaccines.[68–70] It elicits significantly higher titers of serum Vi IgG antibody in mice and is more protective against challenge with wild-type S. Typhi in a model that selectively favors the effect of Vi antibody. It has recently entered clinical trials in humans.

Ty800, X4073, and ZH9

S. Typhi strain Ty800, which harbors a deletion mutation in a regulatory system that allows for survival in the phagosome (*phoP-phoQ*), was tolerated and immunogenic in a dose/response phase I trial in young adults.[71–73] The X4073 strain harbors mutations in another regulatory system (*cya, crp*) and in a gene (*cdt*) that is involved with dissemination of *Salmonella* from gut-associated lymphoid tissue to deep organs.[74] X4073 was well tolerated in a phase I clinical trial but was less immunogenic than CVD 908-*htrA* and Ty800.[75] ZH9, from which *aroC* (a gene involved in aromatic amino acid synthesis) and *ssaV* (a gene involved in the type III secretion system) have been deleted, was also well tolerated and immunogenic in healthy volunteers given a single dose of 10^7, 10^8, or 10^9 CFU.[76] Future development of one of these new strains may provide a new oral vaccine requiring fewer doses than Ty21a while still providing protective efficacy.

New Parenteral Vaccines

Covalent binding of the Vi polysaccharide to a carrier protein (*Pseudomonas aeruginosa* exotoxin A) converts Vi to a T cell–dependent antigen, giving rise to higher antibody levels and immunologic memory.[77–80] This Vi conjugate vaccine is well tolerated and highly immunogenic in 2- to 4-year-olds, as well as in adults and school-aged children. Ninety-two percent efficacy was conferred by a two-dose immunization schedule of this vaccine tested in a large-scale, randomized controlled field trial in 2- to 5-year-old Vietnamese children.[81]

CHOLERA VACCINES

Causative Organism and Clinical Disease

Cholera, the acute diarrheal disease caused by *Vibrio cholerae* serogroups O1 and, in some parts of Asia, O139, continues to cause endemic disease and epidemic outbreaks in many parts of the world. The clinical illness of cholera encompasses a spectrum of disease states ranging from asymptomatic shedding of bacteria in the stool to life-threatening diarrhea, or cholera gravis. Up to three-quarters of cholera infections are inapparent, and among symptomatic patients only a minority will have severe purging.[82] Some patients very quickly become seriously ill from dehydration; others slowly worsen. Patients with cholera gravis may purge enough fluid (eg, one liter per hour) to cause death from dehydration within hours of the onset of illness. Patients with cholera gravis exhibit the classic signs and symptoms of severe dehydration: weak or absent peripheral pulses, hypotension, sunken eyes, poor skin turgor, and decreased urine output. Patients may also have a flat affect and muscle cramps. Stools may have a peculiar fishy odor and are referred to as "rice-water" stools: clear fluid mixed with mucus. Diagnosis can be made by stool culture.

Cholera is caused by *V. cholerae*, a gram-negative bacterium subgrouped into biotype, serogroup, and serotype and by the ability to make cholera toxin (CT).[82] The most important distinction is serogroup (also called serovar), which is based on the lipopolysaccharide O antigen. There are nearly 200 serogroups, but only two, O1 and O139, routinely express cholera toxin and cause epidemic cholera. Within strains of the O1 serogroup, there are two distinct serotypes, Inaba and Ogawa. Serogroup O1 strains are also classified into one of two biotypes, classic or El Tor. All recent outbreaks, with the exception of some O139 outbreaks in Bangladesh and in eastern India in the 1990s, have been caused by O1 El Tor strains.

Cholera is acquired from contaminated water or food. The organism is killed by heat and by acid.[83] Patients ill with cholera shed large amounts of bacteria in the stool, and large oral inocula are required to infect.[84] The bacterium is ingested orally and, after an incubation of a few hours to several days, colonizes the small intestine without invading cells or tissues producing a potent secretogenic toxin, CT. Factors important in cholera pathogenesis include those affecting colonization and those leading to toxinproduction. Toxin-coregulated pili (TCP) are required for colonization, and expression of these filamentous surface structures is correlated with expression of CT.[85] CT has a pentamer of B (binding) subunits responsible for attachment to the surface of intestinal cells and an A (active) subunit that possesses specific enzymatic activity. Through the elevation of intracellular cyclic adenosine monophosphate (cAMP) in intestinal epithelial cells, CT causes a secretory diarrhea and electrolyte perturbations. The toxin alone is sufficient to cause voluminous watery diarrhea, but removal of *ctx* genes encoding CT from the organism does not completely prevent diarrhea.[86,87]

Cholera is treated with rapid, large-volume fluid replacement and antibiotics. Fluids may be given enterally using oral rehydration solutions for mild and moderate cases; intravenous rehydration should be used in severe cases. Antibiotics are an adjunct to fluid therapy and have been shown to decrease the duration of both diarrhea and shedding of the organism.[88,89] Antibiotics should be chosen based on the susceptibility pattern of *V. cholerae* in the particular setting. Tetracyclines and fluoroquinolones have proven efficacy.

Protective Immunity

Natural cholera infection will protect most individuals from future cholera illness.[90,91] In addition, most volunteers challenged with wild-type cholera in an experimental setting are protected from cholera on future challenge.[84,92] The immune response to infection with *V. cholerae* can be separated into responses against bacterial surface structures and responses against the toxin. Although strong responses are found against both, the antibacterial response has proven the more crucial for protection.[86,87,93] Immune responses are made against LPS and other surface proteins as well as against the B subunit of CT. There is no appreciable protective cross-immunity between O1 and O139 strains, but there is substantial cross-protection between biotypes and serotypes within strains of the O1 serogroup.[82]

The best assay for determining protection following exposure to *V. cholerae* or a cholera vaccine is serum vibriocidal antibody response. Most vibriocidal activity is caused by antibodies directed against LPS, but a smaller portion of the vibriocidal response consists of antibodies directed against a protein component that has not been definitively identified.[82] Unfortunately, antibodies against any single surface molecule have not been shown to be adequate surrogates for the vibriocidal assay in determining protection. Antibodies against CT are made following infection. These antibodies are directed against the B subunit and can be measured by enzyme-linked immunosorbent assay.

Burden in Travelers and Known Risks

Cholera is found primarily in developing countries with inadequate waste disposal and contaminated water supplies. Over nearly two centuries, it has caused seven pandemics, the last of which began in 1961 and continues today. The impact that cholera has on the health of the world's population, even in the last decade, remains substantial. In 1991, cholera returned to Latin America, causing hundreds of thousands of cases, and in 1994, it killed over 12,000 Rwandan refugees.[94,95] In the year 2000, cholera was reported in 56 countries and in every region of the world.[96] In the years 2000 and 2001, large numbers of cholera cases were reported in many countries, including Niger, Guinea, Burkina Faso, Ivory Coast, Mali, Chad, and Afghanistan. India suffered tens of thousands of cases after severe flooding, and more than 86,000 cases were reported in Kwazulu-Natal in South Africa. Cholera has also found its way to the islands of Micronesia, the Marshalls, and Madagascar.[96] The worldwide case fatality rate, as reported by the World Health Organization (WHO), was 3.6% in the year 2000. Although much progress has been made, it is clear that current efforts to curb the devastation of cholera remain inadequate.

Cholera is estimated to occur at a rate of 0.2 per 100,000 returning North American and European travelers and 5 per 100,000 returning Japanese travelers.[97] Rates in US travelers have not changed substantially in recent decades.[98,99] Fifty-three cases of cholera were reported to the CDC from 1995 to 1999; one-half of the patients required hospitalization, and one person died. Two-thirds of the cases occurred following travel.[10] From 1961 to 1982, none of the reported cases in travelers occurred in children, but in 1986, two of the five reported US cases were in children (Figure 7-3).[100]

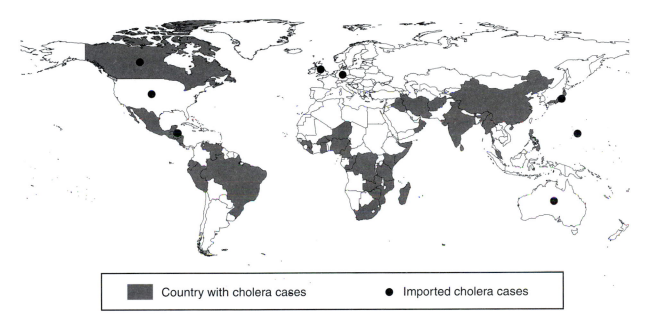

Figure 7-3. Map of global distribution of cholera.

Previously Available Vaccines

Cholera vaccine has not been required for international travel for more than a decade. Currently, the single cholera vaccine licensed for use in the United States, Wyeth-Ayerst's (Pearl River, NY) parenteral killed whole cell vaccine, is not being manufactured or sold.

Parenteral Whole Cell Vaccine

Shortly after Koch's discovery in 1884 of the bacterium responsible for cholera, a parenteral cholera vaccine was tested. Since those early efforts, numerous injectable cholera vaccines have been used.[101] The vaccine currently licensed in the United States, a whole cell inactivated *V. cholerae*, has poor efficacy, short-term protection, and a discouraging side effect profile. It contains 10^9 phenol-killed *V. cholerae* O1 organisms of both biotypes and serotypes. It protects against *V. cholerae* O1 for 3 to 6 months in approximately 50% of patients but causes injection-site pain, erythema, and induration as well as fever and other constitutional symptoms.[102] It has been given as two intradermal, subcutaneous, or intramuscular injections at a 1- to 4-week interval. It provides no protection against serogroup O139 and is not currently available to US travelers.

Currently Available Vaccines

CVD 103-HgR

Characteristics. Recombinant live oral cholera vaccine, CVD 103-HgR, was engineered by deleting from a wild-type *V. cholerae* O1 classic Inaba strain 94% of the gene encoding the A_1 subunit of cholera toxin and by inserting into the hemolysin A (*hlyA*) locus a gene encoding resistance to mercury.[103] CVD 103-HgR is a vaccine licensed in five Latin American countries (Argentina, Colombia, Guatemala, Peru, and Venezuela), Europe (Finland and Switzerland), Canada, Australia, the Philippines, and Sri Lanka, and is available under the trade names Orochol and Mutacol. It should soon be considered by the Food and Drug Administration for licensure in the United States (Table 7-2).

Table 7-2. Available Vaccines against Cholera

	CVD103-HgR	rBS-WC
Proprietary name (manufacturer)	Orochol or Mutacol (Berna Biotech)	Dukoral or Colorvac (SBL Vaccin AB and PowderJect)
Characteristics	Live attenuated oral strain	Killed oral strains plus B subunit of cholera toxin
Dose	1 dose in 100 mL clean water	2 doses in 150 mL clean water (75 mL doses in 2- to 6-year-olds) 10–14 days apart (may use 3 doses in 2 to 6 year olds and as frequent as 7-day interval as per manufacturer)
Boosting interval	Every 6 months	Every 2 years (every 6 months for 2 to 6 year olds)
Time until immune	8 days	1 week after series completion
Estimated efficacy	90% for moderate/severe cholera after challenge	85% protection over 6 months
Main adverse events	Nausea, abdominal cramps, loose stools (all at rates equivalent to placebo)	Abdominal discomfort (most likely due to buffer)
Contraindications	Immunocompromised, pregnancy, hypersensitivity to vaccine component	Hypersensitivity to vaccine component
Concomitant antimicrobials	Not to be administered to patient on antibiotics; chloroquine should be delayed by 1 week	No restrictions
Concomitant vaccines	8-hour interval before administration of Ty21a	No restrictions
Children	Age 2 years and over	Age 2 years and over
Elderly	Not tested	Not tested
Where available	Latin America, Europe, Canada, Australia, the Philippines, and Sri Lanka	Latin America, Europe, Africa, the Philippines, and New Zealand

Neither vaccine is currently available in the United States.

The safety and immunogenicity of a single oral dose of this vaccine in individuals 3 months to 65 years of age, including those infected with the human immunodeficiency virus (HIV), have been established in a number of randomized, placebo-controlled, double-blind clinical trials with active surveillance (involving more than 7,000 participants) in countries in Asia, Latin America, Africa, Europe, and North America.[104–112] A single dose of CVD 103-HgR confers on adult volunteers significant protection, from 8 days to 6 months after vaccination, against experimental challenge with pathogenic *V. cholerae* O1 of either biotype or serotype.[113–115]

In a randomized, placebo-controlled, double-blind field trial in Indonesia, 67,508 children and adults received a single dose of CVD 103-HgR vaccine or placebo.[116] The vaccine did not confer significant protection over the 4-year follow-up (13.5% efficacy) but did have a modest efficacy in blood group O recipients (45%). Unfortunately, too few cases (7 total: 5 in controls, 2 in vaccinees, giving a point estimate of efficacy of 60%) occurred in the first 4 months of follow-up after vaccination to allow a valid comparison with the previous studies using adult volunteers. The most likely reasons for decreased efficacy in the Indonesian field trial are the lower postvaccination vibriocidal titers when compared with volunteers in challenge studies and the long delay following vaccination until cholera appeared at the field trial site.[108,110,117–119] The diminished immunogenicity may result from small intestinal bacterial overgrowth, intestinal parasites, or other factors.[120–126]

The vaccine has been given as a supplement to routine public health interventions in the control of cholera epidemics in Micronesia, but efficacy estimates have not yet been published.[127]

Dose/Boost. The vaccine is manufactured by Berna Biotech and marketed as Orochol in Europe and Mutacol in North America. It is available as a travel vaccine in Canada, Europe, Latin America, Australia, and elsewhere. The vaccine is stored in refrigeration (2–8°C) and is packaged in two small sachets, one containing lyophilized CVD 103-HgR with aspartame sweetener and the other containing buffer. The contents of the two sachets are simultaneously poured into 100 mL of clean, lukewarm-to-cool water (no other beverage), mixed for 5 to 10 seconds, and swallowed immediately. Recipients should avoid food for the hour following immunization. A booster dose is recommended every 6 months.

Efficacy and Time to Protection. The efficacy of the vaccine against moderate and severe cholera, when tested in healthy adults from nonendemic countries who are challenged with wild-type cholera, exceeds 90%. The onset of protection begins 8 days following vaccination and continues out to at least 6 months after vaccination, the longest time tested to date. Efficacy was much lower when tested at a field site located in an endemic country.

Side Effects. The vaccine rarely causes adverse reactions. Recipients have complained of nausea, abdominal cramps, and loose stools but at a rate equivalent to placebo recipients.

Contraindications. The vaccine is not to be taken routinely by immunocompromised individuals. In a study in which the vaccine was given to Malians with HIV infection but without the diagnosis of acquired immunodeficiency syndrome (AIDS), it was safe and well tolerated but less immunogenic than in uninfected vaccinees.[104] Participants in the trial included individuals with CD4 T-cell counts below 400/mm^3.

The vaccine has not been studied in pregnant women and should not be used routinely in this group. It is contraindicated in individuals with hypersensitivity to a vaccine component.

Interactions. Vaccinees should not be taking antibiotics at the time of immunization or in the days following, given that the attenuated live cholera organisms could be rendered nonviable. It is recommended that chloroquine not be taken in the week following the ingestion of CVD 103-HgR, although mefloquine or proguanil use is acceptable. Despite convincing evidence that CVD 103-HgR and Ty21a immunizations can be taken together in experimental settings, it is currently recommended that the two vaccines be separated by an interval of 8 hours. Concomitant administration of oral polio vaccine or yellow fever vaccine does not cause a decrement in immunogenicity of CVD 103-HgR.[128] Other vaccines and biologics may also be taken concomitantly.

Special Populations. CVD 103-HgR has been studied in children as young as 3 months of age. In safety/immunogenicity studies in Chilean infants and toddlers and in preschoolers in Indonesia, Chile, and Peru, the formulation of CVD 103-HgR used was a suspension.[108,111,129] In very young infants, ingestion of the full recommended volume of vaccine cocktail was problematic, but the vaccine was otherwise tolerated well, and vibriocidal antibody seroconversion was similar (66% vs 63%) in children receiving the full volume of vaccine and those who drank a smaller fraction.[111] Where licensed, it is currently recommended for children over the age of 2 years only.

The manufacturer warns against use in individuals with acute gastrointestinal illness or acute febrile illness.[128] One should also be aware that aspartame is used as a sweetener in the vaccine; it therefore delivers 17 mg of phenylalanine and may be dangerous for individuals with phenylketonuria.

Oral Killed Whole Cell–B Subunit Vaccine

Characteristics. This nonliving oral vaccine contains three different strains of heat-inactivated and formalin-inactivated *V. cholerae* O1 bacteria, representing a mixture of classic and El Tor biotypes and Inaba and Ogawa serotypes. A single dose consists of 10^{11} bacteria and 1 mg of the B subunit (BS) of CT suspended in a buffer of raspberry-flavored effervescent granules. Three doses of an early formulation of the vaccine given at 6-week intervals conferred 85% protection over 6 months and 50% protection over 3 years in a field trial in Bangladesh.[130] The 3-year efficacy was lower among the subset of vaccinees aged 2 to 5 years (26%) and against the El Tor biotype (39%). A benefit of this vaccine for travelers is its provision of approximately 60% protection for 3 months against enterotoxigenic *Escherichia coli* (ETEC), a common cause of traveler's diarrhea.[131,132]

The current commercial formulation, rBS-WC, which uses a recombinant B subunit, is well tolerated by adults and children.[133] When studied during a cholera epidemic, two doses of the rBS-WC vaccine given 2 weeks apart conferred 86% protective efficacy on a group of Peruvian soldiers in the 18 to 21 weeks following vaccination.[134] In contrast, in a subsequent large placebo-controlled field trial of efficacy in Lima, Peru, which included adults and children, the same regimen had 0% efficacy during a 12-month period of follow-up.[135] However, following the administration of a third dose of vaccine 1 year later, significant (61%) protection was conferred over the next year of observation, with the highest degree of protection provided against cholera that led to hospitalization.[135] When studied in Arequipa, Peru, the rate of cholera in the first 2 years following vaccination was too low to evaluate short-term efficacy. In the third year of the trial, when cholera reemerged, efficacy in vaccine recipients was not evident.[136]

Dose/Boost. The rBS-WC vaccine, manufactured by SBL Vaccin AB (Stockholm, Sweden; now a subsidiary of PowderJect) and marketed under the names Dukoral or Colorvac, is licensed in several Latin American countries (Argentina, Honduras, Nicaragua, and Mexico), Europe (Estonia, Norway, and Sweden), Africa (Kenya, Mauritius, and Madagascar), the Philippines, and New Zealand. The vaccine is given in a glass of water together with an alkaline buffer; it is recommended that the vaccinee avoid food and beverage for 2 hours prior and 1 hour following the ingestion of the vaccine. The volume of diluent should be 150 mL for persons over 6 years old and 75 mL in those 2 to 6 years old.[137] To make 75 mL of buffer for children, the manufacturer recommends making the full 150 mL with the full amount of supplied buffer but using only 75 mL of this solution to mix with the full vaccine dose.[138] WHO recommends 2 doses 10 to 14 days apart for all ages, whereas the manufacturer recommends 3 doses for children 2 to 6 years old and intervals for all ages of at least 1 week.[138,139]

A booster dose is recommended after 2 years in those over the age of 6 years and after 6 months in those aged 2 to 6 years.[137]

Efficacy and Time to Protection. The efficacy of the vaccine against cholera in travelers is unknown but may mimic the protection afforded persons living in endemic countries. The vaccine has approximately 60% protection against traveler's diarrhea caused by heat-labile enterotoxin (LT)–producing ETEC and approximately 20% protection against all traveler's diarrhea in the 3 months following vaccination. Travelers can expect protection as early as 1 week after completing a regimen of oral vaccination.

Side Effects. The vaccine is well tolerated except for mild abdominal discomfort, which is thought to stem primarily from the buffer, sodium hydrogen carbonate.

Contraindications. The only contraindication is hypersensitivity to a vaccine component. Administration of the vaccine should be delayed in acutely ill individuals.

Interactions. There are no published data on the simultaneous administration of rBS-WC vaccine and other vaccines.

Special Populations. The vaccine is recommended for people over the age of 2 years and is considered safe in pregnancy and for nursing mothers.[139] It is known to be tolerated well by individuals infected with HIV.[139]

Future Vaccines

New parenteral vaccines, still in early stages of development, consist of the LPS of *V. cholerae* O1 and O139 conjugated to one of three protein carriers: CT, tetanus toxoid, or bovine serum albumin.[140–142] The vaccine conjugated to CT is much less reactogenic than killed whole cell vaccine. It elicits anti-CT IgG, anti-LPS antibody, and vibriocidal titers.[140]

An oral killed bivalent cholera vaccine, prepared by adding formalin-inactivated *V. cholerae* O139 to the oral recombinant O1 rBS-WC vaccine, was tolerated well and immunogenic in a phase I trial in Swedish adults.[143]

Three other oral live attenuated *V. cholerae* O1 vaccine strains are well tolerated, immunogenic, and shown to be protective in small clinical trials in volunteers: Peru 15, CVD 111, and strain 638.[144–146] Peru 15 is a genetically attenuated *V. cholerae* O1 El Tor. Three of five volunteers challenged following vaccination had no diarrhea, and the volumes of diarrhea in the two volunteers not completely protected were low (under 1 liter).[144] CVD 111 is another genetically attenuated *V. cholerae* O1 El Tor strain. Twenty-three of 25 recipients developed high-titer vibriocidal antibodies, and efficacy was 81% following challenge with the parent strain.[147]

A combined CVD 111/CVD 103-HgR bivalent vaccine has been evaluated in phase II trials in adult community volunteers in the United States, in Peruvian military personnel, and in several hundred US military personnel in Panama.[145,148] The vaccine is safe and immunogenic. The addition of CVD 111 led to an increase in the vibriocidal seroconversion rate and in Ogawa vibriocidal titers when compared with CVD 103-HgR alone.

A genetically attenuated O1 El Tor Ogawa strain, 638, developed by investigators in Cuba, has also been shown to be immunogenic.[146,149]

Two attenuated O139 strains, Bengal 15 and CVD 112, have also been shown to be reasonably well tolerated, immunogenic, and protective in experimental challenge studies.[150,151] An alternative tactic for O139 vaccine development has been the use of an O1 wild-type strain as a carrier for immunogenic O139 antigens. A strain called CH25 is a derivative of CVD 103-HgR that expresses a portion of the O polysaccharide and the capsular polysaccharide of *V. cholerae* O139.[152] Parenteral administration in rabbits led to antibody responses, but no human trials have been reported to date.

COMBINED CHOLERA AND TYPHOID VACCINE

Coadministration of CVD 103-HgR with the first dose of the live attenuated oral typhoid vaccine Ty21a is as safe and immunogenic as separate administration.[153,154]

SUMMARY

Typhoid fever and cholera are serious enteric illnesses rarely diagnosed in the more prosperous countries of the world except among travelers to more impoverished nations. Even among international travelers, these diseases are uncommon. Avoidance of exposure to enteric pathogens by careful choice of appropriate food and water sources while traveling is the best means of protection, but these precautions may be supplemented, in some cases, with a vaccine. Recommendations for vaccine use for particular travel plans are best made by consulting the appropriate national authorities that provide updates on availability of the vaccines and on typhoid and cholera epidemiology around the world. Although typhoid and cholera vaccines are available in some countries, improvements in formulation, tolerability, efficacy, or protective duration of these vaccines would be welcomed. Persons living in endemic areas, travelers to these areas, and scientists studying these diseases have high hopes for the introduction of safe, tolerable, inexpensive, and durably effective typhoid and cholera vaccines in the near future.

REFERENCES

1. Blair DC. A week in the life of a travel clinic. Clin Microbiol Rev 1997;10:650–73.
2. International Trade Administration. ITA office of travel and tourism industries home page. Available at: http://www.tinet.ita.doc.gov (accessed June 12, 2002).
3. Ivanoff B, Levine MM, Lambert PH. Vaccination against typhoid fever. Present status. Bull World Health Organ 1994;72:957–71.
4. Bhutta ZA, Naqvi SH, Razzaq RA, Farooqui BJ. Multidrug-resistant typhoid in children. Presentation and clinical features. Rev Infect Dis 1991;13:832–6.
5. Rowe B, Ward LR, Threlfall EJ. Multidrug-resistant *Salmonella typhi*. A worldwide epidemic. Clin Infect Dis 1997;24 Suppl 1:S106–9.
6. Ackers ML, Puhr ND, Tauxe RV, Mintz ED. Laboratory-based surveillance of *Salmonella* serotype Typhi infections in the United States. Antimicrobial resistance on the rise. JAMA 2000;283:2668–73.
7. Levine MM. Typhoid fever vaccines. In: Plotkin SA, Orenstein WA, editors. Vaccines. Philadelphia: WB Saunders; 1999. p. 781–814.
8. Sztein MB, Wasserman SS, Tacket CO, et al. Cytokine production patterns and lymphoproliferative responses in volunteers orally immunized with attenuated vaccine strains of *Salmonella typhi*. J Infect Dis 1994;170:1508–17.
9. Sztein MB, Tanner MK, Polotsky Y, et al. Cytotoxic T lymphocytes after oral immunization with attenuated vaccine strains of *Salmonella typhi* in humans. J Immunol 1995;155:3987–93.

10. Summary of notifiable diseases, United States, 2001. MMWR Morb Mortal Wkly Rep 2003;50:1–108.

11. Woodruff BA, Pavia AT, Blake PA. A new look at typhoid vaccination. Information for the practicing physician. JAMA 1991;265:756–9.

12. Rice PA, Baine WB, Gangarosa EJ. *Salmonella typhi* infections in the United States, 1967–1972. Increasing importance of international travelers. Am J Epidemiol 1977;106:160–6.

13. Ryan CA, Hargrett-Bean NT, Blake PA. *Salmonella typhi* infections in the United States, 1975–1984. Increasing role of foreign travel. Rev Infect Dis 1989;11:1–8.

14. Yugoslav Typhoid Commission. A controlled field trial of the effectiveness of acetone-dried and inactivated and heat-phenol–inactivated typhoid vaccines in Yugoslavia. Bull World Health Organ 1964;30:623–30.

15. Controlled field trials and laboratory studies on the effectiveness of typhoid vaccines in Poland, 1961–64. Bull World Health Organ 1966;34:211–22.

16. Hejfec LB, Salmin LV, Lejtman MZ et al. A controlled field trial and laboratory study of five typhoid vaccines in the USSR. Bull World Health Organ 1966;34:321–39.

17. Hejfec LB, Levina LA, Kuz'minova ML, et al. Controlled field trials of paratyphoid B vaccine and evaluation of the effectiveness of a single administration of typhoid vaccine. Bull World Health Organ 1968;38:907–15.

18. Hejfec LB, Levina LA, Kuz'minova ML, et al. A controlled field trial to evaluate the protective capacity of a single dose of acetone-killed agar-grown and heat-killed broth-grown typhoid vaccines. Bull World Health Organ 1969;40:903–7.

19. Ashcroft MT, Singh B, Nicholson CC, et al. A seven-year field trial of two typhoid vaccines in Guyana. Lancet 1967;2:1056–9.

20. Engels EA, Falagas ME, Lau J, Bennish ML. Typhoid fever vaccines. A meta-analysis of studies on efficacy and toxicity. BMJ 1998;316:110–6.

21. Advisory Committee on Immunization Practices (ACIP). Typhoid immunization. Recommendations of the Advisory Committee on Immunization Practices (ACIP). MMWR Morb Mortal Wkly Rep 1994;43:1–7.

22. Germanier R, Fuer E. Isolation and characterization of Gal E mutant Ty 21a of *Salmonella typhi*. A candidate strain for a live, oral typhoid vaccine. J Infect Dis 1975;131:553–8.

23. Levine MM, Ferreccio C, Black RE, Germanier R. Large-scale field trial of Ty21a live oral typhoid vaccine in enteric-coated capsule formulation. Lancet 1987;1:1049–52.

24. Levine MM, Ferreccio C, Cryz S, Ortiz E. Comparison of enteric-coated capsules and liquid formulation of Ty21a typhoid vaccine in randomised controlled field trial. Lancet 1990;336:891–4.

25. Simanjuntak CH, Paleologo FP, Punjabi NH, et al. Oral immunisation against typhoid fever in Indonesia with Ty21a vaccine. Lancet 1991;338:1055–9.

26. Wahdan MH, Serie C, Cerisier Y, et al. A controlled field trial of live *Salmonella typhi* strain Ty 21a oral vaccine against typhoid. Three-year results. J Infect Dis 1982;145:292–5.

27. Black RE, Levine MM, Ferreccio C, et al. Efficacy of one or two doses of Ty21a *Salmonella typhi* vaccine in enteric-coated capsules in a controlled field trial. Chilean Typhoid Committee. Vaccine 1990;8:81–4.

28. Levine MM, Ferreccio C, Abrego P, et al. Duration of efficacy of Ty21a, attenuated *Salmonella typhi* live oral vaccine. Vaccine 1999;17 Suppl 2:S22–7.

29. Ferreccio C, Levine MM, Rodriguez H, Contreras R. Comparative efficacy of two, three, or four doses of TY21a live oral typhoid vaccine in enteric-coated capsules. A field trial in an endemic area. J Infect Dis 1989;159:766–9.

30. Gilman RH, Hornick RB, Woodard WE, et al. Evaluation of a UDP-glucose-4-epimeraseless mutant of *Salmonella typhi* as a live oral vaccine. J Infect Dis 1977;136:717–23.

31. Swiss Serum Vaccine Institute. Vivotif Berna® vaccine, typhoid vaccine live oral Ty21a [package insert]. Berne, Switzerland: Swiss Serum Vaccine Institute; 2000.

32. Kollaritsch H, Que JU, Kunz C, et al. Safety and immunogenicity of live oral cholera and typhoid vaccines administered alone or in combination with antimalarial drugs, oral polio vaccine, or yellow fever vaccine. J Infect Dis 1997;175:871–5.

33. Brachman PS Jr, Metchock B, Kozarsky PE. Effects of antimalarial chemoprophylactic agents on the viability of the Ty21a typhoid vaccine strain. Clin Infect Dis 1992;15:1057–8.

34. Wolfe MS. Precautions with oral live typhoid (Ty 21a) vaccine. Lancet 1990;336:631–2.

35. Murphy JR, Grez L, Schlesinger L, et al. Immunogenicity of *Salmonella typhi* Ty21a vaccine for young children. Infect Immun 1991;59:4291–3.

36. Cryz SJ Jr, Vanprapar N, Thisyakorn U, et al. Safety and immunogenicity of *Salmonella typhi* Ty21a vaccine in young Thai children. Infect Immunol 1993;61:1149–51.

37. Landy M. Studies on Vi antigen. Immunization of human beings with purified Vi antigen. Am J Hyg 1954;60:52–62.

38. Wong KH, Feeley JC, Pittman M. Effect of a Vi-degrading enzyme on potency of typhoid vaccines in mice. J Infect Dis 1972;125:360–6.

39. Tacket CO, Ferreccio C, Robbins JB, et al. Safety and immunogenicity of two *Salmonella typhi* Vi capsular polysaccharide vaccines. J Infect Dis 1986;154:342–5.

40. Tacket CO, Levine MM, Robbins JB. Persistence of antibody titres three years after vaccination with Vi polysaccharide vaccine against typhoid fever. Vaccine 1988;6:307–8.

41. Klugman KP, Gilbertson IT, Koornhof HJ, et al. Protective activity of Vi capsular polysaccharide vaccine against typhoid fever. Lancet 1987;2:1165–9.

42. Acharya IL, Lowe CU, Thapa R, et al. Prevention of typhoid fever in Nepal with the Vi capsular polysaccharide of *Salmonella typhi*. A preliminary report. N Engl J Med 1987;317:1101–4.

43. Klugman KP, Koornhof HJ, Robbins JB, Le Cam NN. Immunogenicity, efficacy and serological correlate of protection of *Salmonella typhi* Vi capsular polysaccharide vaccine three years after immunization. Vaccine 1996;14:435–8.

44. Hessel L, Debois H, Fletcher M, Dumas R. Experience with *Salmonella typhi* Vi capsular polysaccharide vaccine. Eur J Clin Microbiol Infect Dis 1999;18:609–20.

45. Pasteur Merieux Connaught. Typhoid Vi polysaccharide vaccine Typhim Vi [package insert]. Lyon, France: Pasteur Merieux Connaught; 1995.

46. Keitel WA, Bond NL, Zahradnik JM, et al. Clinical and serological responses following primary and booster immunization with *Salmonella typhi* Vi capsular polysaccharide vaccines. Vaccine 1994;12:195–9.

47. Aventis Pasteur home page. Available at: www.aventispasteur.com/us/vaccines/geneinfo4.html (accessed June 12, 2002).

48. Fritzell C, Rollin PE, Touir M, et al. Safety and immunogenicity of combined rabies and typhoid fever immunization. Vaccine 1992;10:299–300.

49. Ambrosch F, Fritzell B, Gregor J, et al. Combined vaccination against yellow fever and typhoid fever. A comparative trial. Vaccine 1994;12:625–8.

50. Dumas R, Forrat R, Lang J, et al. Safety and immunogenicity of a new inactivated hepatitis A vaccine in concurrent administration with a typhoid fever vaccine or a typhoid fever + yellow fever vaccine. Adv Ther 1997;14:160–7.

51. Khoo SH, St Clair RJ, Mandal BK. Safety and efficacy of combined meningococcal and typhoid vaccine. BMJ 1995;310:908–9.

52. Advisory Committee on Immunization Practices (ACIP) and the American Academy of Family Physicians (AAFP). General recommendations on immunization. MMWR Morb Mortal Wkly Rep 2002;51:1–36.

53. Hone DM, Harris AM, Chatfield S, et al. Construction of genetically defined double aro mutants of *Salmonella typhi*. Vaccine 1991;9:810–6.

54. Tacket CO, Hone DM, Curtiss R III, et al. Comparison of the safety and immunogenicity of delta aroC delta aroD and delta cya delta crp *Salmonella typhi* strains in adult volunteers. Infect Immun 1992;60:536–41.

55. Tacket CO, Hone DM, Losonsky GA, et al. Clinical acceptability and immunogenicity of CVD 908 *Salmonella typhi* vaccine strain. Vaccine 1992;10:443–6.

56. Balfour HH Jr, Groth KE, Edelman CK, et al. Rubella viraemia and antibody responses after rubella vaccination and reimmunization. Lancet 1981;1:1078–80.

57. Horstmann DM, Opton EM, Klemperer R, et al. Viremia in infants vaccinated with oral poliovirus vaccine. Am J Hyg 1964;79:47–63.

58. Chatfield SN, Strahan K, Pickard D, et al. Evaluation of *Salmonella typhimurium* strains harbouring defined mutations in htrA and aroA in the murine salmonellosis model. Microb Pathog 1992;12:145–51.

59. Levine MM, Galen J, Barry E, et al. Attenuated *Salmonella typhi* and *Shigella* as live oral vaccines and as live vectors. Behring Inst Mitt 1997;(98):120–3.

60. Tacket CO, Sztein MB, Losonsky GA, et al. Safety of live oral *Salmonella typhi* vaccine strains with deletions in htrA and aroC aroD and immune response in humans. Infect Immun 1997;65:452–6.

61. Tacket CO, Sztein MB, Wasserman SS, et al. Phase 2 clinical trial of attenuated *Salmonella enterica serovar typhi* oral live vector vaccine CVD 908-htrA in U.S. volunteers. Infect Immun 2000;68:1196–201.

62. Levine MM, Black RE, Lanata C. Precise estimation of the numbers of chronic carriers of *Salmonella typhi* in Santiago, Chile, an endemic area. J Infect Dis 1982;146:724–6.

63. Lanata CF, Levine MM, Ristori C, et al. Vi serology in detection of chronic *Salmonella typhi* carriers in an endemic area. Lancet 1983;2:441–3.

64. Losonsky GA, Ferreccio C, Kotloff KL, et al. Development and evaluation of an enzyme-linked immunosorbent assay for serum Vi antibodies for detection of chronic *Salmonella typhi* carriers. J Clin Microbiol 1987;25:2266–9.

65. Pickard D, Li J, Roberts M, et al. Characterization of defined ompR mutants of *Salmonella typhi*. OmpR is involved in the regulation of Vi polysaccharide expression. Infect Immun 1994;62:3984–93.

66. Arricau N, Hermant D, Waxin H, et al. The RcsB-RcsC regulatory system of *Salmonella typhi* differentially modulates the expression of invasion proteins, flagellin and Vi antigen in response to osmolarity. Mol Microbiol 1998;29:835–50.

67. Robbins JD, Robbins JB. Reexamination of the protective role of the capsular polysaccharide (Vi antigen) of *Salmonella typhi*. J Infect Dis 1984;150:436–49.

68. Virlogeux I, Waxin H, Ecobichon C, Popoff MY. Role of the viaB locus in synthesis, transport and expression of *Salmonella typhi* Vi antigen. Microbiology 1995;141 Pt 12:3039–47.

69. Virlogeux I, Waxin H, Ecobichon C, et al. Characterization of the rcsA and rcsB genes from *Salmonella typhi*. RcsB through tviA is involved in regulation of Vi antigen synthesis. J Bacteriol 1996;178:1691–8.

70. Wang JY, Noriega FR, Galen JE, et al. Constitutive expression of the Vi polysaccharide capsular antigen in attenuated *Salmonella enterica* serovar typhi oral vaccine strain CVD 909. Infect Immunol 2000;68:4647–52.

71. Miller SI, Kukral AM, Mekalanos JJ. A two-component regulatory system (phoP phoQ) controls *Salmonella typhimurium* virulence. Proc Natl Acad Sci U S A 1989;86:5054–8.

72. Miller SI, Pulkkinen WS, Selsted ME, Mekalanos JJ. Characterization of defensin resistance phenotypes associated with mutations in the phoP virulence regulon of *Salmonella typhimurium*. Infect Immunol 1990;58:3706–10.

73. Hohmann EL, Oletta CA, Killeen KP, Miller SI. phoP/phoQ-deleted *Salmonella typhimurium* (Ty800) is a safe and immunogenic single-dose typhoid fever vaccine in volunteers. J Infect Dis 1996;173:1408–14.

74. Curtiss R III, Kelly SM, Tinge SA, et al. Recombinant *Salmonella* vectors in vaccine development. Dev Biol Stand 1994;82:23–33.

75. Tacket CO, Kelly SM, Schodel F, et al. Safety and immunogenicity in humans of an attenuated *Salmonella typhi* vaccine vector strain expressing plasmid-encoded hepatitis B antigens stabilized by the Asd-balanced lethal vector system. Infect Immunol 1997;65:3381–5.

76. Hindle Z, Chatfield SN, Phillimore J, et al. Characterization of *Salmonella enterica* derivatives harboring defined aroC and *Salmonella* pathogenicity island 2 type III secretion system (ssaV) mutations by immunization of healthy volunteers. Infect Immunol 2002;70:3457–67.

77. Szu SC, Stone AL, Robbins JD, et al. Vi capsular polysaccharide-protein conjugates for prevention of typhoid fever. Preparation, characterization, and immunogenicity in laboratory animals. J Exp Med 1987;166:1510–24.

78. Szu SC, Li XR, Stone AL, Robbins JB. Relation between structure and immunologic properties of the Vi capsular polysaccharide. Infect Immunol 1991;59:4555–61.

79. Szu SC, Taylor DN, Trofa AC, et al. Laboratory and preliminary clinical characterization of Vi capsular polysaccharide-protein conjugate vaccines. Infect Immunol 1994;62:4440–4.

80. Kossaczka Z, Lin FY, Ho VA, et al. Safety and immunogenicity of Vi conjugate vaccines for typhoid fever in adults, teenagers, and 2- to 4-year-old children in Vietnam. Infect Immunol 1999;67:5806–10.

81. Lin FY, Ho VA, Khiem HB, et al. The efficacy of a *Salmonella typhi* Vi conjugate vaccine in two-to-five-year-old children. N Engl J Med 2001;344:1263–9.

82. Kaper JB, Morris JG Jr, Levine MM. Cholera. Clin Microbiol Rev 1995;8:48–86.

83. Rodrigues A, Sandstrom A, Ca T, et al. Protection from cholera by adding lime juice to food—results from community and laboratory studies in Guinea-Bissau, West Africa. Trop Med Int Health 2000;5:418–22.

84. Cash RA, Music SI, Libonati JP, et al. Response of man to infection with *Vibrio cholerae*. I. Clinical, serologic, and bacteriologic responses to a known inoculum. J Infect Dis 1974;129:45–52.

85. Taylor RK, Miller VL, Furlong DB, Mekalanos JJ. Use of phoA gene fusions to identify a pilus colonization factor coordinately regulated with cholera toxin. Proc Natl Acad Sci U S A 1987;84:2833–7.

86. Levine MM, Kaper JB, Black RE, Clements ML. New knowledge on pathogenesis of bacterial enteric infections as applied to vaccine development. Microbiol Rev 1983;47:510–50.

87. Levine MM, Kaper JB, Herrington D, et al. Volunteer studies of deletion mutants of *Vibrio cholerae* O1 prepared by recombinant techniques. Infect Immunol 1988;56:161–7.

88. Lindenbaum J, Greenough WB, Islam MR. Antibiotic therapy of cholera. Bull World Health Organ 1967;36:871–83.

89. Wallace CK, Anderson PN, Brown TC, et al. Optimal antibiotic therapy in cholera. Bull World Health Organ 1968;39:239–45.

90. Glass RI, Svennerholm AM, Khan MR, et al. Seroepidemiological studies of El Tor cholera in Bangladesh. Association of serum antibody levels with protection. J Infect Dis 1985;151:236–42.

91. Clemens JD, van Loon F, Sack DA, et al. Biotype as determinant of natural immunising effect of cholera. Lancet 1991;337:883–4.

92. Levine MM, Nalin DR, Craig JP, et al. Immunity of cholera in man. Relative role of antibacterial versus antitoxic immunity. Trans R Soc Trop Med Hyg 1979;73:3–9.

93. Peterson JW. Synergistic protection against experimental cholera by immunization with cholera toxoid and vaccine. Infect Immunol 1979;26:528–33.

94. Ries AA, Vugia DJ, Beingolea L, et al. Cholera in Piura, Peru. A modern urban epidemic. J Infect Dis 1992;166:1429–33.

95. Public health impact of Rwandan refugee crisis. What happened in Goma, Zaire, in July, 1994? Goma Epidemiology Group. Lancet 1995;345:339–44.

96. World Health Organization. WHO report on global surveillance of epidemic-prone infectious diseases. Available at: www.who.int/emc-documents/surveillance/docs/whocdscsrisr2001.html/cholera/cholera.htm (accessed June 12, 2002).

97. Wittlinger F, Steffen R, Watanabe H, Handszuh H. Risk of cholera among Western and Japanese travelers. J Travel Med 1995;2:154–8.

98. Synder JD, Blake PA. Is cholera a problem for US travelers? JAMA 1982;247:2268–9.

99. Weber JT, Levine WC, Hopkins DP, Tauxe RV. Cholera in the United States, 1965–1991. Risks at home and abroad. Arch Intern Med 1994;154:551–6.

100. Preblud SR, Tsai TF, Brink EW, et al. International travel and the child younger than two years. I. Recommendations for immunization. Pediatr Infect Dis J 1989;8:416–25.

101. Koch R. An address on cholera and its bacillus. BMJ 1884;2:403–7.

102. Graves P, Deeks J, Demicheli V, et al. Vaccines for preventing cholera. Cochrane Database Syst Rev 2000;CD000974.

103. Ketley JM, Michalski J, Galen J, et al. Construction of genetically marked *Vibrio cholerae* O1 vaccine strains. FEMS Microbiol Lett 1993;111:15–21.

104. Kotloff KL, Wasserman SS, O'Donnell S, et al. Safety and immunogenicity in North Americans of a single dose of live oral cholera vaccine CVD 103-HgR. Results of a randomized, placebo-controlled, double-blind crossover trial. Infect Immunol 1992;60:4430–2.

105. Perry RT, Plowe CV, Koumare B, et al. A single dose of live oral cholera vaccine CVD 103-HgR is safe and immunogenic in HIV-infected and HIV-noninfected adults in Mali. Bull World Health Organ 1998;76:63–71.

106. Cryz SJ Jr, Levine MM, Kaper JB, et al. Randomized double-blind placebo controlled trial to evaluate the safety and immunogenicity of the live oral cholera vaccine strain CVD 103-HgR in Swiss adults. Vaccine 1990;8:577–80.

107. Suharyono, Simanjuntak C, Witham N, et al. Safety and immunogenicity of single-dose live oral cholera vaccine CVD 103-HgR in 5-9-year-old Indonesian children. Lancet 1992;340:689–94.

108. Simanjuntak CH, O'Hanley P, Punjabi NH, et al. Safety, immunogenicity, and transmissibility of single-dose live oral cholera vaccine strain CVD 103-HgR in 24- to 59-month-old Indonesian children. J Infect Dis 1993;168:1169–76.

109. Migasena S, Pitisuttitham P, Prayurahong B, et al. Preliminary assessment of the safety and immunogenicity of live oral cholera vaccine strain CVD 103-HgR in healthy Thai adults. Infect Immun 1989;57:3261–4.

110. Lagos R, Avendano A, Prado V, et al. Attenuated live cholera vaccine strain CVD 103-HgR elicits significantly higher serum vibriocidal antibody titers in persons of blood group O. Infect Immun 1995;63:707–9.

111. Lagos R, San Martin O, Wasserman SS, et al. Palatability, reactogenicity and immunogenicity of engineered live oral cholera vaccine CVD 103-HgR in Chilean infants and toddlers. Pediatr Infect Dis J 1999;18:624–30.

112. Gotuzzo E, Butron B, Seas C, et al. Safety, immunogenicity, and excretion pattern of single-dose live oral cholera vaccine CVD 103-HgR in Peruvian adults of high and low socioeconomic levels. Infect Immunol 1993;61:3994–7.

113. Levine MM, Kaper JB, Herrington D, et al. Safety, immunogenicity, and efficacy of recombinant live oral cholera vaccines, CVD 103 and CVD 103-HgR. Lancet 1988;2:467–70.

114. Tacket CO, Losonsky G, Nataro JP, et al. Onset and duration of protective immunity in challenged volunteers after vaccination with live oral cholera vaccine CVD 103-HgR. J Infect Dis 1992;166:837–41.

115. Tacket CO, Cohen MB, Wasserman SS, et al. Randomized, double-blind, placebo-controlled, multicentered trial of the efficacy of a single dose of live oral cholera vaccine CVD 103-HgR in preventing cholera following challenge with *Vibrio cholerae* O1 El Tor Inaba three months after vaccination. Infect Immun 1999;67:6341–5.

116. Richie EE, Punjabi NH, Sidharta YY, et al. Efficacy trial of single-dose live oral cholera vaccine CVD 103-HgR in North Jakarta, Indonesia, a cholera-endemic area. Vaccine 2000;18:2399–410.

117. Su-Arehawaratana P, Singharaj P, Taylor DN, et al. Safety and immunogenicity of different immunization regimens of CVD 103-HgR live oral cholera vaccine in soldiers and civilians in Thailand. J Infect Dis 1992;165:1042–8.

118. Glass RI, Holmgren J, Haley CE, et al. Predisposition for cholera of individuals with O blood group. Possible evolutionary significance. Am J Epidemiol 1985;121:791–6.

119. Tacket CO, Losonsky G, Nataro JP, et al. Extension of the volunteer challenge model to study South American cholera in a population of volunteers predominantly with blood group antigen O. Trans R Soc Trop Med Hyg 1995;89:75–7.

120. Fagundes-Neto U, Viaro T, Wehba J, et al. Tropical enteropathy (environmental enteropathy) in early childhood. A syndrome caused by contaminated environment. J Trop Pediatr 1984;30:204–9.

121. Fagundes NU, Martins MC, Lima FL, et al. Asymptomatic environmental enteropathy among slum-dwelling infants. J Am Coll Nutr 1994;13:51–6.

122. Khin MU, Bolin TD, Duncombe VM, et al. Epidemiology of small bowel bacterial overgrowth and rice carbohydrate malabsorption in Burmese (Myanmar) village children. Am J Trop Med Hyg 1992;47:298–304.

123. Lagos R, Fasano A, Wasserman SS, et al. Effect of small bowel bacterial overgrowth on the immunogenicity of single-dose live oral cholera vaccine CVD 103-HgR. J Infect Dis 1999;180:1709–12.

124. Shedlofsky S, Freter R. Synergism between ecologic and immunologic control mechanisms of intestinal flora. J Infect Dis 1974;129:296–303.

125. Cooper PJ, Chico ME, Losonsky G, et al. Albendazole treatment of children with ascariasis enhances the vibriocidal antibody response to the live attenuated oral cholera vaccine CVD 103-HgR. J Infect Dis 2000;182:1199–206.

126. Glass RI, Svennerholm AM, Stoll BJ, et al. Effects of undernutrition on infection with *Vibrio cholerae* O1 and on response to oral cholera vaccine. Pediatr Infect Dis J 1989;8:105–9.

127. Cholera, 2000. Wkly Epidemiol Rec 2001;76:233–40.

128. Swiss Serum and Vaccine Institute Berne. Mutacol Berna, Cholera vaccine live oral CVD 103-HgR [package insert]. Berne (Switzerland): Swiss Serum and Vaccine Institute Berne; 1997.

129. Lagos R, Losonsky G, Abrego P, et al. Tolerancia, immunogenicidad, excresion y transmision de la vacuna anticolera oral viva-attenuada, CVD 103 HgR, estudio pareado de doble ciego en ninos Chilenos de 24 a 59 mesas. Bol Hosp Infant Mex 1996;53:214–20.

130. Clemens JD, Sack DA, Harris JR, et al. Field trial of oral cholera vaccines in Bangladesh. Results from three-year follow-up. Lancet 1990;335:270–3.

131. Clemens JD, Sack DA, Harris JR, et al. Cross-protection by B subunit–whole cell cholera vaccine against diarrhea associated with heat-labile toxin-producing enterotoxigenic *Escherichia coli*. Results of a large-scale field trial. J Infect Dis 1988;158:372–7.

132. Peltola H, Siitonen A, Kyronseppa H, et al. Prevention of travellers' diarrhoea by oral B-subunit/whole-cell cholera vaccine. Lancet 1991;338:1285–9.

133. Sanchez J, Holmgren J. Recombinant system for overexpression of cholera toxin B subunit in *Vibrio cholerae* as a basis for vaccine development. Proc Natl Acad Sci U S A 1989;86:481–5.

134. Sanchez JL, Vasquez B, Begue RE, et al. Protective efficacy of oral whole-cell/recombinant-B-subunit cholera vaccine in Peruvian military recruits. Lancet 1994;344:1273–6.

135. Taylor DN, Cardenas V, Sanchez JL, et al. Two-year study of the protective efficacy of the oral whole cell plus recombinant B subunit cholera vaccine in Peru. J Infect Dis 2000;181:1667–73.

136. Levine MM. Immunization against bacterial diseases of the intestine. J Pediatr Gastroenterol Nutr 2000;31:336–55.

137. Ryan ET, Calderwood SB. Cholera vaccines. J Travel Med 2001;8:82–91.

138. SBL Vaccin AB. Dukoral [package insert]. Stockholm (Sweden): SBL Vaccin AB—Part of PowderJect Pharmaceuticals Plc; 2001.

139. Cholera vaccines. Wkly Epidemiol Rec 2001;76:117–24.

140. Gupta RK, Taylor DN, Bryla DA, et al. Phase 1 evaluation of *Vibrio cholerae* O1, serotype Inaba, polysaccharide-cholera toxin conjugates in adult volunteers. Infect Immun 1998;66:3095–9.

141. Boutonnier A, Villeneuve S, Nato F, et al. Preparation, immunogenicity, and protective efficacy, in a murine model, of a conjugate vaccine composed of the polysaccharide moiety of the lipopolysaccharide of *Vibrio cholerae* O139 bound to tetanus toxoid. Infect Immun 2001;69:3488–93.

142. Chernyak A, Kondo S, Wade TK, et al. Induction of protective immunity by synthetic *Vibrio cholerae* hexasaccharide derived from *V. cholerae* O1 Ogawa lipopolysaccharide bound to a protein carrier. J Infect Dis 2002;185:950–62.

143. Jertborn M, Svennerholm AM, Holmgren J. Intestinal and systemic immune responses in humans after oral immunization with a bivalent B subunit-O1/O139 whole cell cholera vaccine. Vaccine 1996;14:1459–65.

144. Kenner JR, Coster TS, Taylor DN, et al. Peru-15, an improved live attenuated oral vaccine candidate for *Vibrio cholerae* O1. J Infect Dis 1995;172:1126–9.

145. Taylor DN, Tacket CO, Losonsky, G et al. Evaluation of a bivalent (CVD 103-HgR/CVD 111) live oral cholera vaccine in adult volunteers from the United States and Peru. Infect Immun 1997;65:3852–6.

146. Benitez JA, Garcia L, Silva A, et al. Preliminary assessment of the safety and immunogenicity of a new CTXPhi-negative, hemagglutinin/protease-defective El Tor strain as a cholera vaccine candidate. Infect Immun 1999;67:539–45.

147. Tacket CO, Kotloff KL, Losonsky G, et al. Volunteer studies investigating the safety and efficacy of live oral El Tor *Vibrio cholerae* O1 vaccine strain CVD 111. Am J Trop Med Hyg 1997;56:533–7.

148. Taylor DN, Sanchez JL, Castro JM, et al. Expanded safety and immunogenicity of a bivalent, oral, attenuated cholera vaccine, CVD 103-HgR plus CVD 111, in United States military personnel stationed in Panama. Infect Immun 1999;67:2030–4.

149. Perez JL, Garcia L, Talavera A, et al. Passive protection of serum from volunteers inoculated with attenuated strain 638 of *Vibrio cholerae* O1 in animal models. Vaccine 2000;19:376–84.

150. Coster TS, Killeen KP, Waldor MK, et al. Safety, immunogenicity, and efficacy of live attenuated *Vibrio cholerae* O139 vaccine prototype. Lancet 1995;345:949–52.

151. Tacket CO, Losonsky G, Nataro JP, et al. Initial clinical studies of CVD 112 *Vibrio cholerae* O139 live oral vaccine. Safety and efficacy against experimental challenge. J Infect Dis 1995;172:883–6.

152. Favre D, Cryz SJ Jr, Viret JF. Construction and characterization of a potential live oral carrier-based vaccine against *Vibrio cholerae* O139. Infect Immun 1996;64:3565–70.

153. Cryz SJ Jr, Que JU, Levine MM, et al. Safety and immunogenicity of a live oral bivalent typhoid fever (*Salmonella typhi* Ty21a)-cholera (*Vibrio cholerae* CVD 103-HgR) vaccine in healthy adults. Infect Immun 1995;63:1336–9.

154. Kollaritsch H, Furer E, Herzog C, et al. Randomized, double-blind placebo-controlled trial to evaluate the safety and immunogenicity of combined *Salmonella typhi* Ty21a and *Vibrio cholerae* CVD 103-HgR live oral vaccines. Infect Immun 1996;64:1454–7.

Chapter 8

MENINGOCOCCAL VACCINE

Elaine C. Jong

Infections caused by *Neisseria meningitidis* bacteria result in approximately 500,000 cases per year of bacterial meningitis and sepsis and 50,000 deaths worldwide.[1] The bacteria are transmitted via infected respiratory droplets under conditions favoring close person-to-person contact. Humans serve as the natural host and reservoir for *N. meningitidis* infections, and following infection, the bacteria either colonize the human nasopharynx, mimicking harmless commensals, or become invasive pathogens causing life-threatening bacterial meningitis and sepsis. Whether a given meningococcal infection will result in an asymptomatic carrier state or in a devastating systemic disease is a delicate balance between host immunity and bacterial virulence.

The changing global epidemiology of meningococcal disease in both industrialized and developing countries, the potential for prolonged asymptomatic carriage with virulent strains, the genetic variability of virulence factors and the emergence of drug-resistant strains means that the risk of exposure associated with international travel is often unpredictable, yet exposure could be fatal. Prevention of meningococcal disease is based primarily on vaccination of susceptible individuals or populations and chemoprophylaxis in case contacts. Five meningococcal serogroups account for most human disease: A, B, C, Y, and W-135. Their geographic distribution is highly variable, and regional changes over time are possibly accelerating because of increasing international travel. Licensed vaccines exist against groups A, C, Y, and W-135, and, depending on vaccine type, are characterized by varying efficacy and duration of protection. Vaccines against group B meningococci have proven difficult to develop because of intrinsic biochemical characteristics of the group B polysaccharide capsule. However, several group B candidate vaccines are now in various stages of production, testing, and licensing.

GLOBAL EPIDEMIOLOGY

Infections with *N. meningitidis* bacteria occur globally, although large-scale epidemics due to group A and, to a lesser extent, group C have been reported, mainly from sub-Saharan Africa, since the beginning of the 1900s. The "meningitis belt," first described by Lapeyssonnie in 1963,[2] was composed of parts of Burkina Faso, Niger, Nigeria, Chad, and Sudan, and was characterized by recurrent meningococcal epidemics occurring in irregular cycles every 5 to 12 years and lasting for two to three dry seasons interrupted by intervening rainy seasons. During these epidemics, attack rates as high as 400 to 800 per 100,000 of the population were reported.[2,3]

Figure 8-1. Map of meningococcal epidemic risk areas in Africa.

The meningitis belt in Africa was expanded by the World Health Organization in 1998 to include the countries of Benin, Cameroon, Ethiopia, The Gambia, Ghana, Mali, and Senegal (Figure 8-1). Recent analyses of meningococcal disease transmission in Africa since the late 1980s have suggested a spread of high incidence rates and recurrent epidemics outside the usual boundaries of the meningitis belt, stretching from Ethiopia in the east to Senegal in the west as previously defined and, to regions in east and southern Africa composed of a band of countries around the Rift Valley and Great Lakes regions extending as far south as Mozambique and then west to Angola and Namibia (Figure 8-2).[4]

The risk of meningococcal disease transmission has been recognized for decades among pilgrims on the hajj pilgrimage in Saudi Arabia.[2] The most recent global pandemic due to intercontinental spread of *N. meningitidis* group A subgroup III has been attributed to the mass gathering at Mecca, mingling, and then dispersion of hajj pilgrims to and from home countries in Asia and Africa. Large epidemics of group A meningococcal disease occurred in China and Mongolia in the mid-1960s to 1970s and occurred again in China in the 1980s. Meningococcal group A subgroup III-1, first identified in the 1980s' China epidemic, appeared to spread westward, subsequently being reported in Nepal and India and then Saudi Arabia in 1987 following the annual hajj pilgrimage. In 1987, the incidence of disease was reported to be as high as 640 in 100,000 among pilgrims from the United States to Mecca. Group A subgroup III was subsequently identified as the causative agent in major meningitis outbreaks occurring in the 1990s throughout the meningitis belt countries in sub-Saharan Africa. In 1996, most of the 150,000 cases of meningococcal disease reported from Africa were caused by group A subgroup III.[5–7]

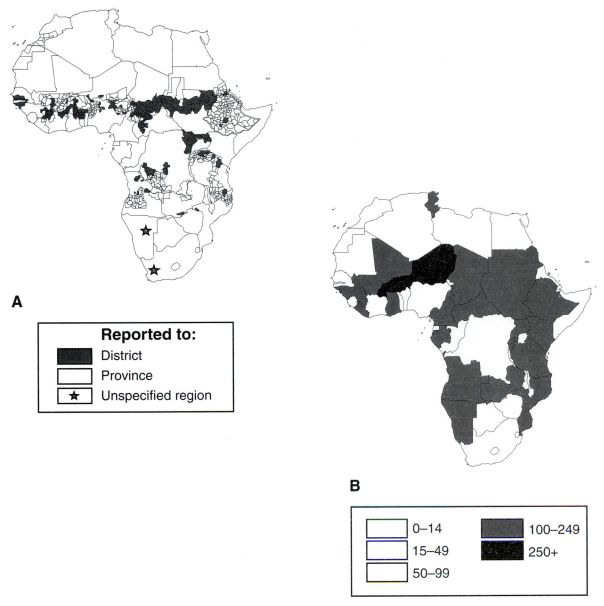

Figure 8-2. Map of expanded meningococcal epidemic risk areas in Africa. *A*, Epidemics documented in publications and internal institutional reports. *B*, Maximum rates (cases per 100,000 population) reported in routine World Health Organization (WHO) surveillance data. Adapted from Molesworth AM, et al.[4]

Following the 1987 outbreak, Saudi Arabia made meningococcal vaccine against groups A and C mandatory for all hajj pilgrims. In China, incidence rates declined in the decades following the introduction of meningococcal polysaccharide vaccines in the 1980s, and incidence rates dropped in Nepal and India for unknown reasons without implementation of widespread vaccine programs.[7]

In 2000, a large outbreak of meningococcal disease consisting of serogroup A and serogroup W-135 infections occurred among pilgrims on the hajj in Saudi Arabia, and this was the first large serogroup W-135 meningococcal disease outbreak identified worldwide. Only 53% of the epidemic cases were caused by group W-135, but transmission of group A was probably limited by widespread use of the meningococcal polysaccharide A/C vaccine among hajj pilgrims prior to travel. Following the hajj, secondary cases were reported from countries in the African meningitis belt, Europe, and the United States.[8–10] The attack rate of

W-135 disease was estimated at 25 per 100,000 pilgrims on the hajj in the year 2000, with an attack rate of 18 cases per 100,000 contacts among household contacts of returning pilgrims. Quadrivalent A, C, Y, W-135 meningococcal vaccine was administered to pilgrims on the hajj in 2001, and although there were no cases of W-135 disease reported among pilgrims, the secondary attack rate among susceptible (unvaccinated) household contacts of returning pilgrims was 28 cases per 100,000 contacts.[11,12] Group W-135 emerged as an epidemic strain during 2001 epidemics in Niger and in Burkina Faso.[13] In 2002, Saudi Arabia made documentation of receipt of quadrivalent A, C, Y, W-135 meningococcal polysaccharide vaccine a visa requirement for hajj pilgrims.

Although meningococcal group B disease is rare in Africa and other areas of the developing world, a prolonged group B epidemic (20 cases per 100,000 population) has been reported in New Zealand from 1991 through 2002. Group B epidemics also have been reported in Iceland, Belgium, Spain, Cuba, Colombia, Brazil, and Chile.[14–16]

In many industrialized countries, meningococcal disease occurs sporadically, with annual attack rates of 1 to 3 per 100,000 of the population. Sporadic nonepidemic group B meningococcal infections are responsible for a large proportion of the reported cases in Europe, notably Norway, the Netherlands, Germany, and Denmark, and they cause more than half of the meningococcal disease cases reported in the United States in the population aged less than 2 years.[15–17]

Group C strains cause a high proportion of reported cases in the Czech Republic, Slovakia, Greece, Republic of Ireland, Spain, and the United Kingdom. Local outbreaks due to group C were reported in Canada and the United States (1992 to 1993) and in Spain (1995 to 1997).[15–17] Group Y disease has been reported mainly from the United States, where it has been associated with infections in elderly people and has been reported to cause pneumonia more frequently than strains of other groups. The incidence of group Y disease in the United States increased during the early 1990s, and it accounted for 33% of cases reported in 1996.[18]

Meningococcal infections cause significant morbidity among pediatric populations, with the highest incidence in children under the age of 5 years, but there is a second peak in disease incidence among teenagers and young adults. This increase might be due to a confluence of some of the social and behavioral risk factors in this age group. Increased risks of meningococcal infection are associated historically with close exposures to large populations of persons from diverse geographic areas, and meningococcal outbreaks have been reported among military recruits, camps, and groups attending mass gatherings such as jamborees and rave concerts. In addition, cigarette smoking, viral upper respiratory infections, and alcohol consumption appear to be associated with an increased risk of disease.[19–21] In the 1990s, living on university campuses in dormitories and in catered hall accommodations and bar patronage were recognized as factors increasing the risk of meningococcal disease among college-aged students.[22–25]

The outbreaks reported among young adults in the United Kingdom and in the United States in the 1990s have been predominantly serogroup C meningococcal disease, although a rise in the proportion of W-135 disease in the United States had been noted during the 1990s.[26] In the United Kingdom, widespread immunization programs among pediatric and adolescent populations with the meningococcal serogroup C conjugate (MCC) vaccine were implemented in 1999.[27,28] In the United States, the Advisory Committee on Immunization Practices recommended that meningococcal vaccine (A, C, Y, W-135) be considered for entering freshman students planning to live in campus housing at US colleges and universities in the year 2000.[26] Some institutions have made meningococcal vaccine a requirement.

ETIOLOGY

N. meningitidis is a gram-negative diplococcus with the microscopic appearance of two kidney beans aligned side by side along their long axis (Figure 8-3). The bacteria are encapsulated by a polysaccharide coat, and this is an important determinant of potential virulence. Five antigenically distinct capsular polysaccharide serogroups, designated groups A, B, C, Y, and W-135, account for almost all human disease, although 13 groups have been identified based on antigenic characteristics (A, B, C, D, H, I, K, L, X, Y, Z, W-135, and 29E). Other important antigenic components of the meningococcus bacterial structure are the outer membrane proteins (OMP): porins (PorA, PorB) and opacity-associated proteins (OpaB, OpaD), as well as lipopolysaccharides (LPS) (Figure 8-4).

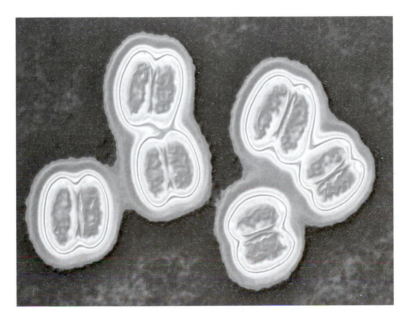

Figure 8-3. Meningococcal bacterial morphology. Reproduced with permission from Custom Medical Stock Photo.

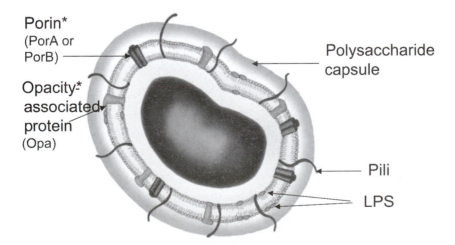

Figure 8-4. Schematic diagram of components of meningococcal bacterial structure. Reproduced with permission from Poolman JT.[31] LPS = lipopolysaccharides. *Outer membrane proteins.

Based on genetic variations in OMP and LPS, meningococcal strains can be further classified into serotypes, subtypes, and LPS types. A variety of techniques (monoclonal antibodies, multilocus enzyme electrophoresis, multilocus sequence typing) is used for studying the epidemiology of *N. meningitidis* epidemics, clusters, and sporadic cases.[6,29–33]

Infection does not invariably lead to disease, and asymptomatic meningococcal carriage is common. Up to 10% of the population in epidemic areas can serve as carriers, and carriers can remain potentially infectious to themselves and others for periods of months. Individual carriers might carry the same or entirely different organisms at different times, and carriage of a particular meningococcal strain does not necessarily protect against colonization or invasion by a homologous or heterologous strain. Carriers can develop invasive disease from the same meningococcal organisms that they carry.[28,34,35] One study conducted among university students in the United Kingdom showed that more than one-half of students identified as meningococcal carriers at the beginning of the academic year remained persistent carriers when tested 6 months later.[34]

The factors that determine bacterial virulence are incompletely understood, but properties of adhesion and invasion are thought to play a major role. The emergence of hypervirulent clones of meningococci have been reported, such as the group C electrophoretic type 37 (ET-37) clonal complex, which can cause a high proportion of cases of severe meningococcal disease despite a low carriage rate (0.3–0.4%) in the population.[27,28] A strain of the group C ET-37 complex termed ET-15, first identified in Canada, was associated with a higher than average case fatality rate of 17.8% compared with 8.1% for all other invasive meningococcal disease cases reported in the period 1985 to 1992.[35] The large outbreak of serogroup W-135 disease that occurred in 2000 among hajj pilgrims characterized by a high secondary attack rate among contacts was not caused by emergence of a new W-135 strain but rather by expansion of a single clone of the hypervirulent ET-37 complex in circulation in Africa at least since 1970; closely related strains of W-135 ET-37 had been isolated in Algeria, Mali, and The Gambia in the 1990s.[36]

Humans are the only natural reservoir for *N. meningitidis*. Following an incubation period of 2 to 10 days, the onset of acute meningococcal disease can be insidious, although the disease can rapidly progress and become fatal within a few hours. Signs and symptoms are usually associated with the onset of meningococcemia; however, the clinical presentation in the early stages—myalgia, chills, and fever—is easily confused by both patients and health care providers with other less serious diagnoses. Presentation with the more typical signs and symptoms of fever, headache, photophobia, irritability, vomiting, loss of consciousness, neck stiffness, and skin lesions will more readily suggest the diagnosis but signals more advanced disease. Despite appropriate antibiotic therapy and supportive care, the case fatality rate is typically 5% in pediatric cases and 10 to 20% in adults, although higher rates, to 80%, have been reported. The differences in reported mortality rates can be accounted for by diversity in the natural course of the disease, stage of disease at diagnosis, access to medical care, and quality of medical care and treatments. About half of the patients who die do so within 24 hours after the first symptoms appear. Survivors can have significant neurologic sequelae (including sensorineural deafness, mental retardation, spasticity, and/or seizures), and necrosis of skin and limbs requiring amputations or plastic surgery is seen in 10 to 20% of survivors.[37,38]

MENINGOCOCCAL VACCINES

Polysaccharide Vaccines

Purified capsular polysaccharide antigens of meningococcal groups A, C, Y, and W-135 stimulate bactericidal serum antibodies through T cell–independent pathways in older children and adults. Polysaccharide antigens are poorly immunogenic in children less than 2 years of age, and although partial immunity to group A and B can be elicited in children less than 2 years of age, the resulting immunity after one dose is short lived and does not appear to be boosted by additional vaccine doses.

Serum antibody against the capsular polysaccharide provides protection against disease by activation of complement-mediated bacterial lysis and also by opsonization, which is the enhancement of bacterial phagocytosis by phagocytic cells of the reticuloendothelial system and polymorphonuclear leukocytes in the peripheral blood.[39–42] Two purified polysaccharide vaccines are available for the prevention of meningococcal infections: Vaccine meningococcique polyosid A+C (Institut Pasteur, Paris) against serogroups A and C, and MENOMUNE (Aventis Pasteur, Swiftwater, PA; Aventis Pasteur MSD, Paris, France) against serogroups A, C, Y, and W-135. A single dose of A/C or A, C, Y, W-135 polysaccharide vaccine administered by subcutaneous injection elicits up to 2 years' protection against the vaccine strains in persons 2 years of age or older. Onset of immunity is 10 days or more after receipt of the vaccine. The meningococcal polysaccharide vaccines are considered very safe. Administration of the vaccine is associated with local pain and swelling at the injection site, but serious systemic side effects have not been reported. Table 8-1 lists the incidence of reported adverse effects following immunization with MENOMUNE. The vaccine is considered pregnancy category C because there is a lack of data concerning its use during pregnancy.[43]

Table 8-1. **Percentage of Patients Who Experience Adverse Events Following Immunization with Menomune**

Reaction	Mild	Moderate
*Local**		
Pain	2.6	2.0
Tenderness	36.0	9.0
Erythema	3.8	1.2
Induration	4.4	1.2
Systemic†		
Headaches	5.2	1.8
Malaise	2.5	0
Chills	2.0	0
Oral temperature	2.6	0.6

Adapted from MENOMUNE package insert.[43]
*A mild local reaction is defined as one < 2 inches; a moderate one is ≥ 2 inches.
†Mild temperature is defined as 100–101°F; moderate temperature is > 101°F.

The guidelines for meningococcal polysaccharide vaccine booster doses are not well defined. A 10-year retrospective study of US Air Force personnel immunized with the quadrivalent A, C, Y, W-135 meningococcal vaccine showed long-term anticapsular antibody response, with persistence of protective levels of antibody to serogroup C shown to last 10 years or more in the vaccinated recruits.[44] However, the phenomenon of immune hyporesponsiveness has been reported after repeated vaccination with group C polysaccharide vaccine.[45] Saudi Arabia requires meningococcal immunization within 2 years for hajj pilgrims and others entering the country during the season of the hajj .[46,47]

Immunization with meningococcal polysaccharide vaccines does not eradicate the meningococcal carrier state and transmission of the bacteria to other persons. Thus, in an outbreak situation, widespread use of meningococcal vaccine must be augmented by antimicrobial chemoprophylaxis of close contacts of diagnosed cases. A fluoroquinolone antibiotic (eg, ciprofloxacin) or rifampin is usually recommended to eradicate meningococcal nasopharyngeal carriage (Table 8-2). However, fluoroquinolones are not recommended for use in children or pregnant women because of potential adverse effects.

Polysaccharide meningococcal vaccines appear to elicit protective antibody responses in complement-deficient individuals.[39–42] Antibody responses to meningococcal polysaccharide vaccines in asplenic or hyposplenic adults depend on the underlying diagnosis and timing of any treatments. Subjects who underwent splenectomy for trauma and control subjects with a spleen showed comparable antibody responses to both antigens following immunization with bivalent A/C polysaccharide vaccine. Subjects who underwent splenectomy for nonlymphoid tumors also had normal or minimally impaired antibody responses to both antigens compared with healthy adults.[48] However, subjects with nonlymphoid tumors who had received prior chemotherapy and radiotherapy, and Hodgkin's patients who began chemotherapy less than 10 days after immunization showed greatly impaired responses to A/C and C polysaccharide vaccines, respectively.[48,49] Declines in postimmunization antibody titers were significantly greater in patients with Hodgkin's disease compared with healthy adults and did not rebound spontaneously or in response to a booster dose during the 12 months following chemotherapy.[49]

Table 8-2. **Postexposure Antimicrobial Prophylaxis against Meningococci to Eradicate Nasopharyngeal Carriage**

Drug	Dose and Schedule
Ciprofloxacin	500 mg as a single oral dose × 1 day (persons ≥ 18 years of age)
Rifampin	600 mg bid × 2 days (adults)
	10 mg/kg q12h × 2 days (children > 1 month old)
	5 mg/kg q12h × 2 days (children < 1 month old)

In another study, quadrivalent meningococcal polysaccharide vaccine was shown to be immunogenic in adult allogeneic bone marrow transplantation (BMT) recipients beginning 8 months after BMT, causing significant rises in antibody levels to group A and group C following vaccination. The presence of chronic graft-versus-host disease appeared to have no influence on the antibody response among subjects in this study.[50]

Vaccine development against group B meningococci based on capsular polysaccharides has been a challenge because of poor immunogenicity elicited by such vaccines. The glycoproteins that compose the group B capsular material contain N-acetylneuraminic acid (polysialic acid) and exhibit immune cross-reactivity with similar polysialated glycoproteins expressed in most human tissues, especially the fetal brain. This cross-reactivity can result in the phenomenon of immune tolerance and observed poor immunogenicity.[7,31,51] The pathogenic consequences of antibodies cross-reacting with tissue-polysialated glycoproteins are not known, but on a theoretical basis, such autoimmune reactions elicit concerns about long-term adverse effects in vaccine recipients, especially women of childbearing potential. Current research continues on identification of group B polysaccharide epitopes that do not cross-react with human polysialic acid.[52,53]

Conjugate Polysaccharide Vaccines

Research efforts directed toward development of vaccines against two other serious childhood illnesses, *Haemophilus influenzae B* meningitis and pneumococcal disease, showed that chemical conjugation of polysaccharide antigens to a protein carrier could elicit a T cell–dependent immune response to polysaccharide antigens. In 2002, two meningococcal group C conjugate vaccines became commercially available: Meningitec, adsorbed to aluminum phosphate and marketed by Wyeth-Lederle, Paris, France and the other adsorbed to aluminum hydroxide and marketed under two names: MENINVACT (Aventis Pasteur MSD,) and Menjugate (Chiron, Emeryville, CA).

Prior to the commercial release of the two vaccines cited above, MCC vaccine (Meningitec and Menjugate) were introduced into the routine immunization series for infants in the United Kingdom in 1999, with three doses given on a schedule of 2, 3, and 4 months of age along with the routine primary immunizations. There was no recommendation for a booster dose at the time the program was implemented. The introduction of the infant immunization program was followed by a catch-up program that targeted all children 5 to 11 months of age (2 vaccine doses) and 1 to 18 years of age (1 vaccine dose). Surveillance data obtained in the year following completion of the catch-up program showed that rates of group C invasive disease fell overall by about 80%, with approximately 70% coverage of the targeted population. There was no major increase in the number of infections due to the other serogroups. An additional finding was that among students aged 15 to 17 years, the MCC vaccination program reduced carriage of serogroup C meningococci in a similar cohort by 66% one year after MCC vaccination. Decreased carriage was thought to result from the MCC vaccine induction of sufficient levels of mucosal immunity to inhibit carriage of group C meningococci.[27,28]

The UK Meningococcal Carriage Group will continue to monitor the population centers involved in the immunization program for the selectve pressure for group C strains that are not contained in the vaccine, and capsular switching between B and C strains among meningococcal populations present in the environment; however, ongoing antigenic and genetic surveillance of meningococcal isolates in the United Kingdom since the inception of the group C conjugate vaccine program have not yet shown that either problem has occurred.[28]

Polysaccharide-protein conjugate meningococcal vaccines have made it possible to extend vaccine protection against epidemic meningococcal disease among populations of highly susceptible young infants from 2 months of age and up, and they appear to reduce nasopharyngeal carriage of the meningococci, thus reducing transmission of disease. Bivalent A plus C polysaccharide conjugate vaccines have been developed and studied in Europe and Africa in the 1990s and were shown to be safe and immunogenic in young infants less than 2 years of age as well as in children and adults and to induce long-term protection.[54–57] A quadrivalent conjugate vaccine against groups A, C, Y, W-135 is presently undergoing clinical trials in Africa, Asia, and the United States.

Outer Membrane Protein Vaccine

Outer membrane protein vesicle–based (OMV) vaccines against group B prepared by detergent extraction of meningococcal bacterial cells have been developed by the Finlay Institute in Cuba and the National Institute of Public Health in Norway.[58,59] The OMV vaccine elicits bactericidal antibodies to the PorA outer membrane proteins, but there is great antigenic diversity among group B meningococcal strains because of hypervariable regions of PorA proteins.[60,61]

In efficacy studies conducted in Cuba, Brazil, Chile, and Norway, two doses of the OMV vaccines showed an overall efficacy rate of 50 to 80% in persons 4 years of age or older and elicited strain-specific bactericidal antibodies directed at PorA but appeared to be less efficacious among infants.[62–66] In a clinical study involving a highly susceptible age group, three doses of the Cuban vaccine were given to infants at 3½, 5½, and 7½ months of age; only 27% of recipients developed serum bactericidal activity against group B. Levels of immune protection markedly declined by age 16 to 18 months.[67]

The Cuban OMV vaccine has been registered in more than a dozen countries, mainly in Latin America, and the Norwegian vaccine in others. Current researchers seek to tailor these prototypic vaccines to cover group B meningococcal PorA strain variants, which predominate in other geographic regions. For example, 20 strains would have to be considered for an OMV vaccine to cover 80% of group B disease strains in the United States.[68] GlaxoSmithKline and the Finlay Institute have reached an agreement to work together to develop new OMV vaccines. In 1998, Chiron Vaccines (Emeryville, CA) and Norway's National Institute of Public Health began collaborative efforts with the New Zealand Ministry of Health to develop a group B OMV strain–specific vaccine for the epidemic group B disease in New Zealand.[7]

A group B hexavalent recombinant PorA OMV vaccine that elicits bactericidal antibody against six PorA OMP strain variants has been developed in the Netherlands and has been assessed in clinical trials to establish efficacy and safety.[69–71] OMV vaccines have been administered by intranasal and intramuscular routes to compare the functional immune response.[72] A native outer membrane vesicle (NOMV) vaccine has been developed to retain the outer membrane proteins in a natural lipid environment, thus conserving epitopes. This vaccine is administered by the nasal route to mimic nasopharyngeal colonization by wild-type meningococcal strains. This prototype vaccine has been tested in a limited number of subjects, who showed increased IgA and IgG levels.[73,74]

Transferrin-Binding Protein B Vaccine

A serogroup B vaccine is under development by Aventis Pasteur, based on the transferrin-binding protein B (Tbp B) subunit of transferring binding protein. It is a recombinant vaccine produced in *Escherichia coli* and has completed phase I clinical trials in adult subjects. Although antigen–specific antibodies to the top TbpB antigen were elicited, serum bacterial activity was suboptimal.[7]

VACCINE RECOMMENDATIONS

Immunization against meningococcal disease is recommended for international travelers going to hyperendemic areas such as sub-Saharan Africa or to areas known to be affected by current outbreaks or epidemics. Although the disease incidence is thought to be less among most tourists than that experienced by the local population, travelers at particular risk are those whose activities might involve living and working among residents of those areas. A group at higher risk includes travelers participating in the annual hajj pilgrimage, where local travel conditions have favored large meningococcal epidemics among pilgrims in the past.

The recommendation for meningococcal vaccine will depend on vaccine product availability in the home country and the meningococcal serogroup(s) in circulation at destination. Immunization against meningococcal disease is recommended for persons at special risk of disease, including new military recruits, students living in university dormitories and residence halls, and individuals with occupational risk. International students planning to attend universities in the US should be aware of the Advisory Committee on Immunization Practices (ACIP) recommendation regarding A/C/Y/W-135 meningococcal vaccine.[26] Chapter 16 in this book covers US college health policies on meningococcal vaccine and other vaccine requirements in great detail.

Meningococcal vaccine is also indicated for persons with special risk factors for increased susceptibility to meningococcal disease whether traveling or not. This group includes individuals who have late-component complement (C3, C5−C9) deficiencies, asplenism or hyposplenism, and/ or other immune deficits.[41,50,75,76]

Recommendation of meningococcal vaccine in routine pediatric immunization schedules and in environments of occupational risk will depend on the local epidemiology of meningococcal infections and the availability of an efficacious and safe meningococcal vaccine for the meningococcal serogroup(s) implicated.

CONCLUSION

Protective capsular polysaccharide vaccines against meningococcal groups A and C were developed more than 30 years ago in the late 1960s. A group C polysaccharide vaccine was studied extensively among new recruits in the US Army in the 1970s and resulted in a significant decrease in the incidence of meningococcal disease, a trend that has been sustained until the present time following adoption of the quadrivalent A,C,Y,W-135 vaccine in 1982 for all new inductees.[77] Group A-C polysaccharide vaccine has been available in Europe for decades and was used successfully for epidemic control in sub-Saharan Africa. However, the emergence of W-135 transmission in sub-Saharan African countries may require increasing use of the quadrivalent A,C,Y,W-135 vaccine in preventive mass immunization campaigns against meningococcal meningitis.[78]

Polysaccharide-protein conjugate vaccines against group C have been licensed in Europe, and successful control of meningococcal transmission and carriage has been demonstrated in a widespread immunization program in the United Kingdom where group C disease is prevalent. The worldwide release of a quadrivalent A, C, Y, W-135 conjugate polysaccharide vaccine (Aventis Pasteur) currently in clinical trials is eagerly anticipated. Immunogenicity in infants upwards from the age of 2 months, a longer duration of immune protection, and the ability to induce eradication of nasal carriage are characteristics of the vaccine that, if borne out by present clinical trials, would lead to consideration of incorporating the new vaccine into the routine pediatric immunization schedule in areas of high endemicity for the meningococcal serogroups covered by the vaccine.[79]

Development of a safe and efficacious vaccine against meningococcal serogroup B disease is a top priority for current and future research in meningococcal vaccine development. Future vaccines may be developed from genome-derived antigens (GNAs) such as those identified by investigators at Chiron Vaccines, Italy, during the meningococcal group B genome sequence project: novel surface-exposed proteins that can elicit group B meningococcal bactericidal antibodies.[80,81]

REFERENCES

1. World Health Organization. Epidemic meningococcal disease. Fact sheet no. 105. Rev. December 1998. Available at: www.who.int/inf-fs/en/fact105.html (accessed July 29, 2002).

2. Greenwood BM. Manson lecture. Meningococcal meningitis in Africa. Trans R Soc Trop Med Hyg 1999;93:341–53.

3. World Health Organization. Emerging and re-emerging infectious diseases. Fact sheet no. 97. Rev. August 1998. Available at: www.who.int/inf-fs/en/fact097.htm 1998 (accessed July 29, 2002).

4. Molesworth AM, Thomson MC, Conner SJ, et al. Where is the meningitis belt? Defining an area at risk of epidemic meningitis in Africa. Trans R Soc Trop Med Hyg 2002;96:242–9.

5. Guibourdenche M, Hoiby EA, Riou JY, et al. Epidemics of serogroup A *Neisseria meningitidis* of subgroup III in Africa, 1989-94. Epidemiol Infect 1996;116:115–20.

6. Zhu P, van der Ende A, Falush D, et al. Fit genotypes and escape variants of subgroup III *Neisseria meningitidis* during three pandemics of epidemic meningitis. Proc Natl Acad Sci U S A 2001;98:5234–9.

7. Jodar L, Feavers IM, Salisbury D, et al. Development of vaccines against meningococcal disease. Lancet 2002;359:1499–508.

8. Yousef M, Nadeem A. Meningococcal infection among pilgrims visiting Madinah Al-Munawarah despite prior A-C vaccination. J Pak Med Assoc 2000;50:184–6.

9. Taha MK, Achtman M, Alonso JM, et al. Serogroup W135 meningococcal disease in Hajj pilgrims. Lancet 2000;356:2159.

10. Lingappa JR, Al-Rabeah AM, Hajjeh R, et al. Serogroup W-135 meningococcal disease during the Hajj, 2000. Emerg Infect Dis 2003;9:665–71.

11. Wilder-Smith A, Goh KT, Barkham T, et al. Hajj-associated strain of *Neisseria meningitidis* serogroup W135. Estimates of the attack rate in a defined population and the risk of invasive disease developing in carriers. Clin Infect Dis 2003;36:679–83.

12. Wilder-Smith A, Paton NI, S TM, et al. Meningococcal carriage in umra pilgrims returning from Saudi Arabia. J Travel Med 2003;10:147–8.

13. du Chatelet IP, Alonso JM, Taha MK. Clonal expansion of *Neisseria meningitidis* W135. Epidemiological implications for the African meningitis belt. Bull Soc Pathol Exot 2002;95:323–4.

14. Baker M, Martin D, Kieft C, et al. The evolving meningococcal disease epidemic in New Zealand. N Z Public Health Rep 1999;6:57–61.

15. Achtman M. Global epidemiology of meningococcal disease. In: Cartwright KA, editor. Meningococcal disease. Chichester (UK): John Wiley; 1995. p. 159–75.

16. Cartwright KA, Noah N, Peltola H. Meningococcal disease in Europe. Epidemiology, mortality, and prevention with conjugate vaccines. Report of a European advisory board meeting Vienna, Austria, 6–8 October, 2000. Vaccine 2001;19:4347–56.

17. Rosenstein NE, Perkins BA, Stephens DS, et al. The changing epidemiology of meningococcal disease in the United States, 1992–96. J Infect Dis 1999;180:1894–901.

18. Centers for Disease Control and Prevention. Group Y meningococcal disease—Illinois, Connecticut and selected areas, United States, 1989–1996. MMWR Morb Mortal Wkly Rep 1996;45:1010–5.

19. Stanwell-Smith RE, Stuart JM, Hughes AO, et al. Smoking, the environment and meningococcal disease. A case control study. Epidemiol Infect 1994;112:315–28.

20. Filice GA, Englender SJ, Jacobson JA, et al. Group A meningococcal disease in skid rows. Epidemiology and implications for control. Am J Public Health 1984;74:25–54.

21. Cartwright KA, Jones DM, Smith AJ, et al. Influenza A and meningococcal disease. Lancet 1991;338:554–7.

22. Froeschle JE. Meningococcal disease in college students. Clin Infect Dis 1999;29:215–6.

23. Harrison LH, Dwyer DM, Maples CT, et al. Risk of meningococcal infection in college students. JAMA 1999;281:1906–2110.

24. Imrey PB, Jackson LA, Ludwinski PH, et al. Outbreak of serogroup C meningococcal disease associated with campus bar patronage. Am J Epidemiol 1996;143:624–30.

25. Neal KR, Nguyen-Van-Tam J, Monk P, et al. Invasive meningococcal disease among university undergraduates. Association with universities providing relatively large amounts of catered hall accommodation. Epidemiol Infect 1999;122:351–7.

26. Centers for Disease Control and Prevention. Prevention and control of meningococcal disease. Recommendations of the Advisory Committee on Immunization Practices (ACIP). MMWR Morb Mortal Wkly Rep 2000;49:1–10.

27. Maiden MCJ, Spratt BG. Meningocococcal conjugate vaccines. New opportunities and new challenges. Lancet 1999;354:615–6.

28. Maiden MCJ, Stuart JM, for The UK Meningococcal Carriage Group. Carriage of serogroup C meningococci 1 year after meningococcal C conjugate polysaccharide vaccination. Lancet 2002;359:1829–30.

29. Caugant DA, Froholm LO, Bovre K, et al. Intercontinental spread of a genetically distinctive complex of clones of *Neisseria meningitidis* causing epidemic disease. Proc Natl Acad Sci U S A 1986;83:4927–31.

30. Wang J-F, Caugant DA, Morelli G, et al. Antigenic and epidemiological properties of the ET-37 complex of *Neisseria meningitidis*. J Infect Dis 1993;167:1320–9.

31. Poolman JT. Development of a meningococcal vaccine. Infect Agents Dis 1995;4:213–28.

32. Poolman JT, Kriz-Kuzemenska P, Ashton F, et al. Serotypes and subtypes of *Neisseria meningitidis*. Results of an international study comparing sensitivities and specificities of monoclonal antibodies. Clin Diagn Lab Immunol 1995;2:69–72.

33. Maiden MCJ, Bygraves JA, Feil E, et al. Multilocus sequence typing. A portable approach to the identification of clones within populations of pathogenic microorganisms. Proc Natl Acad Sci U S A 1998;95:3140–5.

34. Ala'Aldeen DA, Neal KR, Ait-Tahar K, et al. Dynamics of meningococcal long-term carriage among university students and their implications for mass vaccination. J Clin Microbiol 2000;38:2311–6.

35. Whalen CM, Hockin JC, Ryan A, et al. The changing epidemiology of invasive meningococcal disease in Canada, 1985–1992. Emergence of a virulent clone of *Neisseria meningitidis*. JAMA 1995;273:390–4.

36. Mayer LW, Reeves MW, Al-Hamdan N, et al. Outbreak of W-135 meningococcal disease in 2000: not emergence of new W-135 strain but clonal expansion with the electrophoretic type-37 complex. J Infect Dis 2002;185:1596–605.

37. van Deuren M, Brandtzaeg P, van Der Meer JW. Update on meningococcal disease with emphasis on pathogenesis and clinical management. Clin Microbiol Rev 2000;13:144–66.

38. Kirsch EA, Barton RP, Kitchen L, et al. Pathophysiology, treatment and outcome of meningococcemia. A review and recent experience. Pediatr Infect Dis J 1996;15:967–78.

39. Fijen CA, Kuijper EJ, Drogari-Apiranthitou M, et al. Protection against meningococcal serogroup ACYW disease in complement-deficient individuals vaccinated with the tetravalent meningococcal capsular polysaccharide vaccine. Clin Exp Immunol 1998;114:362–9.

40. Schlesinger M, Kayhty H, Levy R, et al. Phagocytic killing and antibody response during the first year after tetravalent meningococcal vaccine in complement-deficient and in normal individuals. J Clin Immunol 2000;20:46–53.

41. Drogari-Apiranthitou M, Fijen CA, Van De Beek D, et al. Development of antibodies against tetravalent meningococcal polysaccharides in revaccinated complement-deficient patients. Clin Exp Immunol 2000;199:311–6.

42. Gomez-Lus ML, Gimenez MJ, Vazquez JA, et al. Opsonophagocytosis versus complement bactericidal killing as effectors following *Neisseria meningitidis* group C vaccination. Infection 2003:31:51–4.

43. MENOMUNE®—A/C/Y/W-135 [package insert]. Swiftwater (PA): Aventis Pasteur; February 2001.

44. Zangwill KM, Stout RW, Carlone GM, et al. Duration of antibody response after meningococcal polysaccharide vaccination in US Air Force personnel. J Infect Dis 1994;169:847–52.

45. Granoff DM, Gupta RK, Belshe RB, et al. Induction of immunologic refractoriness in adults by meningococcal C polysaccharide vaccination. J Infect Dis 1998;178:870–4.

46. World Health Organization (WHO). International Travel and Health 2003. Available at: http://www.who.int/ith (accessed November 12, 2003).

47. Centers for Disease Control and Prevention. Health information for international travel. US 2003–2004. Available at: http://www.cdc.gov/travel/ub (accessed November 12, 2003).

48. Ruben FL, Hankins WA, Zeigler Z, et al. Antibody responses to meningococcal polysaccharide vaccine in adults without a spleen. Am J Med 1994;76:115–21.

49. Siber GR, Gorham C, Martin P, et al. Antibody response to pretreatment immunization and post-treatment boosting with bacterial polysaccharide vaccines in patients with Hodgkin's disease. Ann Intern Med 1986;104:467–75.

50. Parkkali T, Kayhty H, Lehtonen H, et al. Tetravalent meningococcal polysaccharide vaccine is immunogenic in adult allogeneic BMT recipients. Bone Marrow Transplant 2001;27:79–84.

51. Finne J, Leinonen H, Makela PH. Antigenic similarities between brain components and bacteria causing meningitis. Implications for vaccine development and pathogenesis. Lancet 1983;2:355–7.

52. Granoff DM, Bartoloni A, Ricci S, et al. Bactericidal monoclonal antibodies that define unique meningococcal B polysaccharide epitopes that do not cross-react with human polysialic acid. J Immunol 1998;160:5028–36.

53. Granoff DM, Moe DR, Giuliani MM, et al. A novel mimetic antigen eliciting protective antibody to *Neisseria meningitidis*. J Immunol 2001;167:6487–96.

54. Anderson EL, Bowers T, Mink CM, et al. Safety and immunogenicity of meningococcal A and C polysaccharide conjugate vaccine in adults. Infect Immun 1994;62:3391–5.

55. Lieberman JM, Chiu SS, Wong VK, et al. Safety and immunogenicity of a serogroup A/C *Neisseria meningitidis* oligosaccharide–protein conjugate vaccine in young children. JAMA 1996;275:1499–503.

56. Fairley CK, Begg N, Borrow R, et al. Conjugate meningococcal serogroup A and C vaccine. Reactogenicity and immunogenicity in United Kingdom infants. J Infect Dis 1996;174:1360–3.

57. Campagne G, Garba A, Fabre P, et al. Safely and immunogenicity of three doses of a *Neisseria meningitidis* A+C diphtheria conjugate vaccine in infants from Niger. Pediatr Infect Dis J 2000;19:144–50.

58. Sierra GV, Campa HC, Varcacel NM, et al. Vaccine against group B *Neisseria meningitidis*. Protection trial and mass vaccination results in Cuba. NIPH Ann 1991;14:195–207.

59. Bjune G, Hoiby EA, Gronnesby JK, et al. Effect of outer membrane vesicle vaccine against group B meningococcal disease in Norway. Lancet 1991;338:1093–6.

60. Zollinger WD, Boslego J, Moran E, et al. Meningococcal serogroup B vaccine protection trial and follow-up studies in Chile. The Chilean National Committee for Meningococcal Disease. NIPH Ann 1991;14:211–2.

61. de Moares JC, Perkins BA, Camargo MC, et al. Protective efficacy of a serogroup B meningococcal vaccine in Sao Paulo, Brazil. Lancet 1992;340:1074–8.

62. Noronha CP, Struchiner CJ, Hallaroan ME. Assessment of the direct effectiveness of BC meningococcal vacine in Rio de Janeiro, Brazil: a case control stuy. Int J Epidemiol 1995;24:1050–7.

63. Rosenqvist E, Hoiby EA, Wedege E, et al. Human antibody responses to meningococcal outer membrane antigens after three doses of the Norwegian group B meningococcal vaccine. Infect Immun 1995;63:4642–52.

64. Tappero JW, Lagos R, Ballesteros AM, et al. Immunogenicity of 2 serogroup B outer-membrane protein meningococcal vaccines: a randomized controlled trial in Chile. JAMA 1999;281:520–7

65. Fischer M, Carlone GM, Holst J, et al. *Neisseria meningitidis* serogroup B outer membrane vesicle vaccine in adults with occupational risk for meningococcal disease. Vaccine 1999;17:2377–83.

66. Morley SL, Cole MJ, Ison CA, et al. Immunogenicity of a serogroup B meningococcal vaccine against multiple *Neisseria meningitidis* strains in infants. Pediatr Infect Dis J 2001;20:1054–61.

67. Feavers IM, Fox AJ, Gray S, et al. Antigenic diversity of meningococcal outer membrane protein PorA has implications for epidemiological analysis and vaccine design. Clin Diagn Lab Immunol 1996;3:444–50.

68. Vermont CL, van Dijken HH, Duipers AJ, et al. Cross-reactivity of antibodies against PorA after vaccination with a meningococcal B outer membrane vesicle vaccine. Infect Immun 2003;71:1650–5.

69. Tondella ML, Popovic T, Rosenstein NE, et al. Distribution of *Neisseria meningitidis* serogroup B serosubtypes and serotypes circulating in the United States. The Active Bacterial Core Surveillance Team. J Clin Microbiol 2000;38:3323–38.

70. Peeters CC, Rumke HC, Sundermann LC, et al. Phase 1 clinical trial with a hexavalent PorA containing meningococcal outer membrane vesicle vaccine. Vaccine 1996;14:1009–15.

71. Cartwright K, Morris R, Rumke H, et al. Immuogenicity and retogenicity in UK infants of a novel meningococcal vesicle vaccine containing multiple class I (PorA) outer membrane protiens. Vaccine 1999;17:2612–9.

72. de Klein ED, de Groot R, Labadie J, et al. Immuogenicity and safety of a hexavalant meningococcal outer-membrane-vesicle vaccine in children of 2–3 and 7–8 years of age. Vaccine 2000;18:1456–66.

73. Aase A, Naess LM, Sandin RH, et al. Comparison of functional immune responses in humans after intranasal and intramuscular immunizations with outer membrane vesicle vaccines against group B meningococcal disease. Vaccine 2003;21:2042–51.

74. Katial RK, Brandt BL, Moran EE, et al. Immunogenicity and safety testing of a group B intranasal meningococcal native outer membrane vesicle vaccine. Infect Immun 2002;70:702–7.

75. Bisharat N, Omari H, Lavi I, et al. Risk of infection and death among postsplenectomy patients. J Infect 2001;43:182–6.

76. Davies JM, Barnes R, Milligan D, British Committee for Standards in Haematology. Working Party of the Haematology/Oncology Task Force. Update of guidelines for the prevention and treatment of infections in patients with an absent or dysfunctional spleen. Clin Med 2002;2:440–3.

77. Brundage JF, Ryan MA, Feighner BH, Erdtmann FJ. Meningococcal disease among United States military service members in relation to routine uses of vaccines with different serogroup-specific components, 1964–1998. Clin Infect Dis 2002;35:1376–81.

78. Chippaux JP, Debois H, Saliou P. A critical review of control strategies against meningococcal meningitis epidemics in sub-Saharan African countries. Infection 2002;30:216–24.

79. Rosenstein NE, Fischer M, Tappero JW. Meningococcal vaccines. Infect Dis Clin North Am 2001;15:155–69.

80. Pizza M, Scarlato V, Masignani V, et al. Identification of vaccine candidates against serogroup B meninogoccus by whole-genome sequencing. Science 2000;287:1816–20.

81. Suker J, Feavers IM. Prospects offered by genome studies for combating meningococcal disease by vaccination. Pharmacogenomics 2001;2:273–83.

Chapter 9

RABIES VACCINE

Henry Wilde

HISTORY OF RABIES VACCINATION

Pasteur and Semple Vaccines

Louis Pasteur, in the 1880s, inoculated street rabies virus into rabbits, passaging it through successive animals until the incubation period shortened and the virus had become "fixed." He then removed the spinal cords, dried them, and prepared his first attenuated vaccine. In 1886, the first successful treatments were reported in some 350 humans bitten by rabid dogs. Only one of these patients died of rabies. Thus began "postexposure rabies prophylaxis."[1] Production of these early rabies vaccines underwent many modifications over the following decades. Fermi in 1908 was responsible for the first killed nerve tissue–derived vaccine when he used phenol to inactivate the virus.[2] Semple improved inactivation and brought this new method into use in 1911.[3]

The level of efficacy in humans of these attenuated and inactivated nerve tissue–derived vaccines remains unknown. Humans are less susceptible to rabies than are the experimental animals used by Pasteur, Fermi, and Semple. Early "successful" vaccination rates were reported without data from untreated control groups. They often did not substantiate the optimistic conclusions that were reported to the scientific community and to the public. Studies by Denison and Dowling and later by McKendrick leave modern readers in doubt about the true efficacy of the then available vaccines.[4,5] Treatment failures were probably underreported.

It soon became apparent that Semple vaccines (SV) resulted in injection-site and neurologic adverse side effects consisting of pain at injection sites, encephalomyelitis and polyneuritis-like syndromes, which carried a significant mortality rate.[6] When patients who received these products as multiple (14 to 17) daily subcutaneous injections were carefully followed, it was found that up to 1 in 400 had developed serious systematic adverse reactions.[7] This ratio was exceeded in some localities, such as Indonesia, where monkey brain–derived Semple-type vaccines had been introduced by the Dutch colonialists and were used well into the early 1960s. More recently, Bhari found in Tunisia that 1 in 200 subjects came down with encephalomyelitis after the use of a locally produced SV.[8] At least one batch of phenolized sheep brain vaccine manufactured in Thailand resulted in a 1 in 120 adverse reaction rate.[9] One courageous Pakistani investigator reported that Semple vaccine, manufactured by the National Institutes of Health at Islamabad in the early 1990s, had no antigen content at all. This attested to the low production standards and absence of quality control among many of the indigenous nerve tissue–derived rabies vaccines.[10] Semple vaccines are, nevertheless, still used worldwide for postexposure rabies treatment of humans.[11]

Suckling Mouse Brain Vaccine

It soon became apparent that myelin basic protein was responsible for most of the adverse reactions to Semple-type vaccines. This led to efforts to extract this protein with ether or to use very young animals, which do not yet possess myelin. Thus came about the suckling mouse brain (SMB) rabies vaccine of Fuenzalida and colleagues and similar products from the former USSR that used young rats.[12] Some of these inactivated virus vaccines are still in common use in South America and Vietnam.[11] An SMB vaccine was manufactured in Thailand up to 1992, when all brain tissue–derived products (SV and SMB) were removed from the approved list of biologicals by local government authorities. SMB, like SV, is usually given as 14 daily subcutaneous injections (into the abdominal wall) with two later boosters. SMB is also notorious for local injection site discomfort. Several studies from South America and Asia have shown it to be inferior in immunogenicity to modern tissue culture products, even when 14 to 17 daily injections are administered.[13,14] The hope that "myelin-free" neural tissue rabies vaccines will be free of serious adverse reactions has also not materialized. Postvaccine encephalomyelitis with SMB is less frequent than with SV, but it does occur and is often fatal.[15]

The World Health Organization (WHO) has been adamant in urging that all nerve tissue–derived rabies vaccines (SV and SMB) be abolished as soon as possible. However, this recommendation has not been implemented due to several factors: lack of implementation by governments in canine rabies–endemic developing countries, resistance by current SV and SMB vaccine manufacturers to close plants, and economic considerations, which, unfortunately, might not even be based on sound fiscal analysis of actual production and administration costs.

Injectable Live Attenuated Virus Vaccines

Starting in the late 1930s, efforts were made to create a live attenuated rabies vaccine for use in animals and perhaps even humans that would confer long-lasting immunity. Thus came into being several mouse- and egg-passaged virus strains, some of which were later used as animal vaccines (Flury, Street Alabama Dufferin [SAD], Kelev, and Kissling strains).[16] However, none of these products remained on the international market for very long, primarily because of fear of reversion to pathogenicity.

MODERN RABIES VACCINES

Human Diploid Cell Vaccines

Wiktor and colleagues, working in Hilary Koprowski's laboratory at the Wistar Institute in Philadelphia, adapted the CVS, Pitman-Moore, and Flury strains of rabies virus to grow in human diploid cells (WI-38). This opened the door to the production of inactivated tissue culture rabies vaccines that proved safe and highly immunogenic in human use.[17,18] Human diploid cell vaccine (HDCV) was eventually manufactured in Canada, France and Germany and soon became the "gold standard" for all later rabies vaccine developments.

The virus is grown in flasks, inactivated with betapropiolactone, and lyophilized. However, human diploid cells have a relatively poor yield of rabies virus, and production is expensive. Serum albumin is present as a stabilizer and, combined with the betapropiolactone, can act as a hapten and cause mild serum sickness–like reactions in recipients of booster injections.[19] Later, efforts were made to eliminate the albumin from HDCV.

This was achieved, but the resulting vaccine never reached the international marketplace because of high production costs and the increasing competition of safe and immunogenic "second-generation" tissue culture vaccines using more efficient Vero cell and chick embryo cell tissue culture systems.[20,21]

Primary Hamster Kidney Cell Vaccines

As early as 1968, Fenje managed to produce a hamster kidney cell rabies vaccine using the CL-60 strain of virus. The vaccine was licensed in Canada but is no longer available.[22] Selimov in Moscow adapted the SAD "Vnukovo-32" virus strain to Syrian hamster kidney cells, and this led to a tissue culture vaccine still widely used in Russia and other former Soviet republics.[23] It was later introduced into China by Linn.[24] These primary hamster kidney cell (PHKC) rabies vaccines are still available from several firms in the former Soviet republics and China. Their potencies vary, and some batches are said to be barely above the WHO minimal acceptable level of 2.5 IU per dose. None of these vaccines should be used with the intradermal regimens because of potency problems and the fact that some of them contain adjuvants that make them unsuitable for intradermal use.

Fetal Bovine Kidney Cell Rabies Vaccine

The Institut Pasteur of Paris manufactured this highly purified and immunogenic product for a short time in the 1970s. This vaccine, based on work by Atanasiu, did not remain on the market long, as the human diploid cell vaccine had become dominant by this time.[25,26]

Adsorbed Rhesus Diploid Cell Rabies Vaccine

Scientists at the Michigan State Department of Health adapted the CVS-Kissling strain rabies virus to fetal rhesus monkey diploid lung cells, inactivated it with betapropiolactone, and adsorbed the killed virus to aluminum phosphate. Adsorbed rhesus diploid cell rabies vaccine (rabies vaccine adsorbed [RVA]), a safe and immunogenic product, is still marketed in the United States.[27] It cannot be used with any of the intradermal regimens, however, because of the adjuvant content.

Duck Embryo Vaccine

A crude fertilized duck-grown Pitman-Moore strain of rabies vaccine was used widely in Europe and the Americas in the 1960s and early 1970s. It required 14 daily intramuscular injections followed by two or three boosters, as it was of low immunogenicity. It caused an unacceptable rate of systemic and gastrointestinal allergic reactions such as abdominal pain, nausea, vomiting, and diarrhea, and its use was abandoned.[28]

Purified Duck Embryo Vaccine

The Swiss Serum and Vaccine Institute (Berna Co.) took the Pitman-Moore strain virus grown in duck embryos and concentrated and purified the betapropriolactone-inactivated product using differential centrifugation and precipitation techniques. This purification process resulted in a potent and safe lyophilized vaccine suspension. It also allowed reducing the number of vaccine injections to the new norm of the 5-shot "Essen" postexposure regimen, which had been established with the advent of HDCV. Purified duck embryo vaccine (PDEV) is a safe and highly immunogenic vaccine but, like HDCV, is rather expensive to produce. It was marketed worldwide (but not in North America) between the years 1985 and 2000 when production was discontinued in Switzerland. The technology is now being transferred to an Indian firm.[29]

Purified Vero Cell Rabies Vaccine

Vero cells are a continuous heteroploid cell line derived from kidneys of the African green monkey (*Cercopithecus aethiops*). Van Wezel developed a microcarrier culture system suitable for industrial use that was first applied to large-scale polio vaccine production in France.[30] The Van Wezel system was later successfully adapted to the cultivation of the Pitman-Moore strain rabies virus on Vero cells.[31] Purified Vero cell rabies vaccine (PVRV) was first introduced for general postexposure treatment by the Thai Red Cross Society in 1984.[32,33] It is now licensed in most countries but is not yet available in the United States.

Previous worries concerning the use of a continuous cell line containing possible oncogenes have been dispelled by the uneventful use in humans of Vero cell–based systems in millions of doses of polio vaccine. Several smaller laboratories in India and possibly other countries have experimented with Vero cell rabies vaccines, but only two, to the best of our knowledge, had succeeded by the year 2002 in manufacturing and marketing quality products. The Rockefeller Foundation, using microcarrier technology from the Institut Armand Frappier of Montreal, managed to transfer Vero cell technology for rabies vaccine production to VECOL in Bogota, Colombia. The second successful independent producer of Vero cell–derived rabies vaccine is the Indian Immunological Institute at Hyderabad, India. Similar projects may well be under way in China and South America. Even though the existing Vero cell rabies vaccines have enjoyed a reputation of very low adverse reactions and high immunogenicity, a new chromatography-purified Vero cell rabies vaccine made in France is now undergoing final clinical trials.[34,35]

Purified Chick Embryo Cell Vaccines

The low viral yield from human diploid cell–based growth systems and the resulting high production cost led many other groups to search for a safe, immunogenic, and high-yield method for the production of a tissue culture rabies vaccine. Barth and colleagues at the Behring Institute, Marburg, Germany, developed a chick embryo cell rabies vaccine using the Flury C25 virus strain.[36] Extensive field studies in many parts of the world soon led to widespread use of purified chick embryo cell vaccines (PCEC), a potent, safe, and immunogenic vaccine using both conventional intramuscular and the newly developed and economical reduced-dose intradermal schedules.[37–39]

PCEC is now Food and Drug Administration (FDA) approved and available in the United States. A PCEC vaccine made from high-passage rabies virus is also manufactured in Japan by Kaketsuken at Kumamoto. It is not generally available outside Japan and appears to be of lower immunogenicity.[40]

Rabies Vaccines in Current Use

Semple-Type and Suckling Mouse Brain Vaccines

Neither of these two rabies vaccines should be used today, and their continuing production and usage has been condemned by the WHO Expert Committee on Rabies.[11] It is to be hoped that these vaccines will be soon phased out by the few countries that still rely on them.

SVs are still being manufactured in India, Pakistan, Bangladesh, Nepal, Myanmar, and several African countries. They are used almost exclusively for the underprivileged public sector. The small affluent local population usually has access to imported tissue culture products. SVs are of poor, and occasionally even zero, immunogenicity and must be given as 14 to 17 injections subcutaneously into the abdominal wall.[10] Pain and local as well as generalized allergic reactions are common, and severe neurologic adverse effects, some leading to deaths, have been described among 200 to 400 recipients.[6–9] Neurologic reactions are due to the presence of myelin basic protein in the vaccine. Travelers should avoid receiving Semple vaccine even at the cost of immediate evacuation to the nearest place with a higher level of care.

SMB is still widely used in South America and Vietnam. Adverse neurologic reactions occur, though much less frequently than with SV.[15] SMB is also of variable immunogenicity, and postexposure treatment schedules recommended by the manufacturers vary between 6 and 17 injections. Travelers should avoid receiving SMB, even at the cost of immediate evacuation to the nearest place where tissue culture vaccines are available. SMB should never be used for preexposure vaccination even though this has been a routine practice for vaccine plant workers in Vietnam and parts of South America.

Currently available tissue culture and avian culture vaccines and their major manufacturers are shown in Table 9-1.

Table 9-1. Currently Available Tissue Culture and Avian Culture Vaccines

Vaccine	Country	Manufacturer	Formulation	Diluent (mL)	Regimen
HDCV	France[*]	Aventis Pasteur	Lyophilized	1.0	WHO
HDCV	Canada*	Connaught	Lyophilized	1.0	WHO
HDCV	Germany*	Chiron	Lyophilized	1.0	WHO
PCEC	Germany*	Chiron	Lyophilized	1.0	WHO
RVA	USA*	GlaxoSmithKline	Lyophilized adjuvant	1.0	WHO
PCEC	India	Chiron–India	Lyophilized	1.0	WHO
PCEC	Japan	Kaketsuken	Lyophilized	1.0	WHO
PDEV	India[†]	Zydus–Cadila	Lyophilized suspension	1.0	WHO
PVRV	France	Aventis Pasteur	Lyophilized	0.5	WHO
PVRV	Colombia	VECOL	Lyophilized	0.5	WHO
PVRV	India	Indian Immunologicals	Lyophilized	0.5	WHO
PVRV	India[†]	Pasteur, Coonoor	Lyophilized	0.5	WHO
PVRV	India[†]	Bharat Biotech	Lyophilized adjuvant	0.5	WHO
PVRV	China	IBP, Wuhan	Lyophilized	1.0	WHO
PVRV	China	IBP, Hainan	Lyophilized	1.0	WHO
PHKC	China	IBP, Wuhan	Lyophilized adjuvant	1.0	WHO
PHKC	China	IBP, Lanzhou	Adjuvant	1.0	WHO
PHKC	China	IBP, Changchun	Adjuvant	1.0	WHO
PHKC	China	IBP, Shanghai	Adjuvant	1.0	WHO
PHKC	Russia	Inst. Poliom., Moscow	Lyophilized	1.0	WHO
PHKC	Russia	Inst. Poliom., Moscow	Lyophilized	3.0	7–21
PHKC	Russia	Immunopreparation, Ufa	Lyophilized	1.0	WHO
PHKC	Russia	Immunopreparation, Ufa	Lyophilized	3.0	7–21

HDCV = human diploid cell vaccine; PCEC = purified chick embryo cell vaccine; PDEV = purified duck embryo vaccine; PHKC = primary hamster kidney cell vaccine; PVRV = purified Vero cell rabies vaccine; RVA = rabies vaccine adsorbed; WHO = World Health Organization.
*United States Food and Drug Administration approved.
†Still in the developmental stage (2002). Formulation, dilution volumes, and regimens for these new products have not been confirmed at time of printing.

PASSIVE IMMUNIZATION: IMMUNOGLOBULINS

It takes approximately 10 days after the start of a rabies postexposure vaccine series before adequate endogenous serum levels of neutralizing antibodies appear. Virus that has been inoculated into or near peripheral nerves may thus enter the immune-protected neural environment and no longer be accessible to the late-appearing, circulating, vaccine-induced antibodies. This is the basis for the recommendation that rabies immunoglobulin (RIG) be used for injection into and around the bite wounds on the first day of postexposure treatment.[41–45]

The search for an antirabies serum commenced with the work of Babes and others in the 1880s. However, human application and acceptance of the use of antisera, together with vaccine, did not enter clinical practice until the 1950s. An opportunity to study the protective effect of antiserum occurred in Iran, where a rabid wolf entered a village and severely mauled some 29 persons, mostly on the head and neck. Iranian scientists, together with Hilary Koprowski, observed that most patients treated with both equine antiserum and vaccine survived. Virtually all patients treated with vaccine alone died.[41] Similar results in humans were later well documented in the USSR by Selimov and colleagues, in India by Veeraraghavan and Subrahmayan, and in China by Linn and colleagues.[42–44] Careful laboratory studies and clinical experience in rabies-endemic countries also confirmed the added protection provided by the injection of bite wounds with immunoglobulins.[45,46]

The dose of equine rabies antiserum was set at 40 IU/kg body weight. Early crude commercial products of equine antiserum carried a high rate of serum sickness reactions, characteristically appearing 1 week after treatment and consisting of erythema at injection sites, hives, myalgia, fever, and arthralgia. Anaphylaxis was also reported.[47] These problems led to the development of human rabies immunoglobulin (HRIG), a product derived from the serum of hyperimmunized donors.[48] Cutter Laboratories in the United States, the Institut Merieux in France, the Swiss Serum and Vaccine Institute, and Germany's Behringwerke were the first commercial manufacturers. The dose of HRIG was set at 20 IU/kg body weight, as it was found that a higher level of passive antibodies causes interference with the production of vaccine-induced antibodies. Not surprisingly, HRIG has a longer half-life than purified and pepsin-digested equine rabies immunoglobulin (ERIG), which consists of much smaller molecules (see below).

Several other blood banks, including that of the Thai Red Cross Society in Bangkok, manufacture HRIG but in insufficient quantity and at a high production cost. This encouraged several international manufacturers to produce purified and pepsin-digested ERIGs, which have been shown to carry a very low rate of anaphylaxis (approximately the same as injected penicillins) and an acceptable delayed serum sickness rate of around 1%.[49,50] They became available in many developing countries in the late 1970s at approximately 10% of the cost of imported HRIG.[51] However, they were not used often enough, even though sold at prices close to manufacturing costs, to justify continuing production by the large international companies. The three major producers of purified ERIG discontinued production in 2001, even though ERIG is on the WHO essential drug and biologicals list.[52,53]

Several small, often government-sponsored ERIG manufacturers in Asia, South America, and Africa produce ERIG locally but in insufficient quantities and without much effort to market and export outside their home regions. Some of these would not pass modern production and safety standards. Aventis Pasteur in France has developed a chromatography-purified and heat-treated ERIG that is undergoing

Table 9-2. **Manufacturers Of Immunoglobulins**

Human Origin (HRIG) (Dose is 20 IU/kg)	Equine Origin (ERIG)* (Dose is 40 IU/kg)
Aventis Pasteur Corporation, Lyon, France	Butantan, Sao Paulo, Brazil
Chiron Corporation (Formerly Behringwerke), Marburg, Germany	Laboratorios Biologicas de Mexico (Birmax), Mexico, DF
Bayer Corporation, USA	Institut Pasteur de Tunis, Tunisia
Connaught Laboratories, Canada	Biofarma, Bandung, Indonesia
Razi Vaccine and Serum Institute, Teheran, Iran	Central Research Institute, Kasauli, India
Swiss Serum and Vaccine Institute, Bern, Switzerland	Queen Saovabha Memorial Institute, Thai Red Cross, Bangkok
National Blood Center, Thai Red Cross Society, Bangkok, Thailand	Aventis Pasteur (new chromatography-purified product)

This listing is based on information available at the time of printing and may be incomplete.

HRIG = human rabies immunoglobulin.

*Several commercial firms discontinued production of equine rabies immunoglobulin (ERIG) in 2001. It may be that some of these international firms are reconsidering their positions regarding ERIG production under WHO pressure. The ERIG producers listed here make limited quantities, mostly for local use.

further clinical trials.[54] Although these additional purification steps may be important, concerns have been raised about their impact on efficacy and cost.[51,52,55] Local production of quality ERIG in rabies-endemic countries at an affordable price must be encouraged. Table 9-2 lists current sources of ERIG.

EPIDEMIOLOGY OF RABIES

The WHO lists rabies-free countries, medium-risk rabies-endemic countries, and high-risk rabies-endemic-countries (Table 9-3). The list of rabies-free countries in Table 9-3 should be considered fluid, and reporting might not be entirely reliable in all of the listed countries. Bat rabies is known or possibly exists in many of these regions that have been declared rabies free by WHO or local authorities. For example, Australia, previously considered rabies free, was recently found to harbor a rabies virus among both fruit- and insect-eating bats. It is still considered terrestrially rabies free, and the virus strain has received the special name of Australian variant bat Lyssavirus even though it is closely related to the Asian and European street strain of rabies (Figure 9-1).

In areas of the world where terrestrial rabies is present, the virus is transmitted by canines, felines, or wild mammals. Birds, amphibians, and reptiles do not transmit rabies. Many of the terrestrial rabies–endemic countries also harbor fruit- and/or insect-eating bat rabies, and most of the human rabies cases in North America are now due to bat virus strains. Many bats are migratory animals that can travel over long distances and possibly be transported by freighters across wide bodies of water. Rare rabid bats have been identified in England and Hawaii, countries considered both terrestrial and bat rabies free.

Medium-risk rabies-endemic countries are those that by 1998 reported no locally acquired human cases but where there is still an animal reservoir. Travelers planning extensive visits to one of the highly rabies-endemic countries are urged to have rabies preexposure vaccination. They must assume that optimal postexposure treatment (PET), which includes injecting RIG for persons who have not been immunized prior to rabies exposure, may no longer be locally available in many such regions.

Table 9-3. **Epidemiology of Rabies (World Health Organization)**

Rabies-free countries
Some of these countries or regions may be free only of terrestrial rabies but harbor known or unknown bat rabies.

Africa: Cape Verde, Libya, Mauritius, Seychelles

Americas: Antigua, Aruba, Bahamas, Barbados, Bermuda, Cayman, Guadeloupe, Jamaica, Martinique, Netherlands Antilles, Miquelon, Nevis, St. Christopher, St. Martin, St. Pierre, St. Vincent, Grenadines, Uruguay, Virgin Islands

Asia: Bahrain, Brunei, Hawaii, Hong Kong, Japan, Kuwait, Malaysia (peninsular), Maldives, Qatar, Singapore, Taiwan

Europe: Albania, Cyprus, Denmark, Faroe Islands, Finland, Gibraltar, Iceland, Ireland, Isle of Man, Italy, Jersey, Macedonia, Malta, Monaco, Norway, Portugal, Spain, Sweden, United Kingdom

Oceania: Samoa, Cook Islands, Fiji, French Polynesia, Guam, Indonesia (except Java, Kalimantan, Sumatra, Sulawesi, Flores and Kiribati), New Caledonia, New Zealand, Niue, Papua New Guinea, Solomon Islands, Tonga, Vanuatu

Medium-risk rabies-endemic countries
Countries where a significant number of animal rabies is being diagnosed but where no locally acquired human cases have been reported. Reporting in some of these countries may be unreliable.

Americas: Argentina, Bolivia, Brazil, Canada, Colombia, Costa Rica, Cuba, French Guyana, Dominican Republic, Guatemala, Guyana, Haiti, Honduras, Nicaragua, Panama, Trinidad and Tobago, United States, Venezuela

Asia: Iran, Iraq, Israel, Jordan, Korea, Lebanon, Syria, Oman

Europe: Albania, Austria, Belarus, Bulgaria, Czech Republic, Denmark, Estonia, Germany, Greece, Hungary, Kosovo, Latvia, Lithuania, Poland, Macedonia, Moldova, Romania, Slovakia, Slovenia, Yugoslavia

High-risk rabies-endemic countries

Africa: Virtually the entire continent

Americas: Bolivia, Brazil, Ecuador, El Salvador, Guatemala, Honduras, Mexico, Nicaragua, Paraguay, Peru

Asia: Afghanistan, Bangladesh, Bhutan, Cambodia, China, India, Indonesia (not all), Laos, Malaysia (not peninsular part), Mongolia, Myanmar (Burma), Nepal, Oman, Pakistan, Philippines, Russia and former Asian USSR republics, Sri Lanka, Syria, Tibet, Thailand, Vietnam

Europe: Turkey, Russian Federation

MODERN TREATMENT

Preexposure Rabies Vaccination

Any of the modern tissue culture vaccines can be used effectively for preexposure vaccination. The WHO-approved schedules consist of one intramuscular dose (1.0 mL for HDCV, PCEC, or PDEV and 0.5 mL for PVRV) administered on days 0, 7, and 28. When there is insufficient time to apply the above schedule, the schedule can be abbreviated to three injections 1 week apart. The PHKC dosage depends on the manufacturer and may range from 1.0 to 3.0 mL per injection.

Intradermal preexposure vaccination results in slightly lower and shorter-lasting antibody responses.[39,56] The intradermal schedule is 0.1 mL of HDCV, PCEC, or PVRV administered on the same schedule as the intramuscular regimen, on days 0, 7, and 28. PHKC should not be used for intradermal application. There is evidence that chloroquine will impair the immune response to rabies preexposure vaccination. It is therefore recommended that a pre- exposure series be completed before a traveler commences antimalaria prophylaxis.[57]

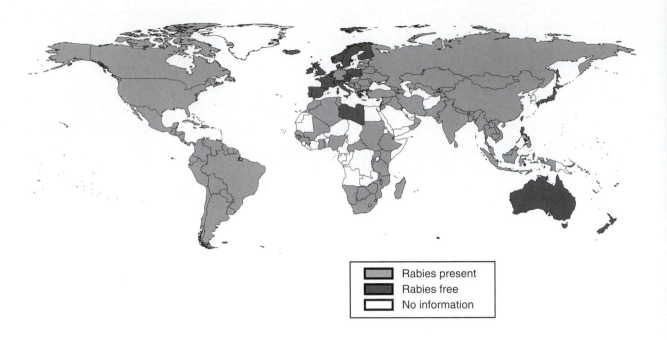

Figure 9-1. Global rabies risk.

Several studies have shown that immunity to properly applied pre- or postexposure rabies vaccination is long lasting. Our group has now followed a number of vaccine recipients for as long as 15 years, and they all still had an anamnestic response to vaccine booster doses (Khawplod P, Wilde H; unpublished data). Boosters every 5 years for individuals who are at continued risk of rabies exposures, particularly children and those that travel extensively or live in regions where optimal rabies postexposure treatment is not available, are no longer recommended. Persons who are at high risk of occupational exposure to rabies infection might require boosters or, preferably, periodic determination of their neutralizing serum antibody titers.[57]

Those who have had pre- or postexposure vaccination and are subsequently exposed to rabies must still have an intramuscular or intradermal booster injection on days 0 and 3. No immunoglobulins are given. Alternatively, it has been shown that intradermal injections of 0.1 mL on day 0 at four different lymphatic drainage sites (deltoids and anterolateral thigh) will result in higher antibody responses than the conventional two-visit intramuscular or intradermal boosters for PET of previously immunized persons.[58]

The immune response to HDCV, PVRV, and PCEC of patients with symptomatic human immunodeficiency virus (HIV) infection is impaired. Some may not develop any detectable antibody even when double-dose schedules are used. The elderly and those with chronic liver disease may also have lower neutralizing antibody levels after rabies vaccination. Whether this is clinically significant is, however, not known (experience at the Thai Red Cross).

Children constitute 30 to 50% of patients presenting to animal bite clinics in canine rabies–endemic countries, and the same is true for human rabies deaths. This makes rabies a significant pediatric problem.[59] Economic, cultural, and religious factors are a major cause for the continuing existence of rabies as a public health menace. This is particularly true in Hindu and Buddhist countries. Added to this is the

Table 9-4. Guide for Postexposure Rabies Prophylaxis

Category	Contact	Treatment
I	Touching, feeding animal, licking over intact skin	None if history reliable*
II	Licks over broken skin, minor bites or scratches with no bleeding	Start vaccine series; stop treatment if animal is FAT negative or alive after 10 days
III	Single or multiple transdermal bites at any site or licks over mucous membranes	Inject rabies immunoglobulin into and around bite sites; give the rest (if any) intramuscularly at a different site from the vaccine; start the vaccine series; discontinue treatment if animal is FAT negative or alive 10 days later

(1) Rabies vaccination of the responsible animal in a canine rabies–endemic region does not exclude rabies. This is particularly true if only one vaccination had been given. Canine and feline vaccine failures and short duration of immunity are common in endemic countries.[82]

(2) Whether an attack is provoked is often difficult to evaluate. Unprovoked attacks are more likely to come from a rabid dog or cat. However, rabid animals, which are often very irritable, bite the owner or others more readily when disturbed. The event may, therefore, be considered provoked.[83]

(3) In a low-risk or rabies-free region, observing a biting dog for 10 days before starting rabies prophylaxis may be considered. However, doing this in a canine rabies–endemic country could place patients at grave risk.

*Children may present an unreliable history. This is a good time to start preexposure vaccination in rabies-endemic countries.

worldwide shortage of immunoglobulins. This has led to increased interest in adding rabies preexposure vaccination of children to the Expanded Program on Immunization (EPI) in certain developing countries with a large, uncontrolled canine rabies problem.[60]

Present tissue culture rabies vaccines, however, are still far too expensive for such projects. The appearance of multidose, inexpensive liquid tissue culture vaccines for the public sector could change this. At least one study evaluating large-scale preexposure vaccination of children was completed in Vietnam, and another one is under way in Thailand.[61] Better means of controlling dog populations and vaccination of the huge stray canine population in these regions would, however, appear to be a more logical approach.

Suckling mouse brain vaccines have been used for preexposure vaccination of rabies laboratory staff and vaccine production workers in South America and Vietnam. This practice is disappearing as the much safer and more immunogenic tissue culture vaccines have become available.

Postexposure Rabies Vaccination Schedules

Postexposure rabies treatment is based on careful, case-by-case risk assessment. The risk depends on the geographic location of the exposure, the animal involved, and the severity and anatomic location of the animal bite or exposure (Table 9-4). Postexposure prophylaxis regimens approved by WHO using rabies vaccine and rabies immunoglobulin administration are given in Table 9-5. Intradermal schedules must be used only with high potency HDCV, PVRV, PDEV, and PCEC vaccines; those containing adjuvants cannot be used intradermally. Vaccines prepared as suspensions (PDEV) must be shaken vigorously before use with an intradermal syringe and, if there is doubt, the dose per site should be doubled from 0.1 to 0.2 mL to ensure that there is an adequate amount of antigen.

Table 9-5. Postexposure Rabies Vaccine Schedules

Essen, or five-dose, intramuscular schedule

One full dose of vaccine is given by deep intramuscular injection into the deltoid or anterolateral thigh on days 0, 3, 7, 14, and 28. This regimen confers long-lasting immunity using HDCV, PCEC, PDEV, or PVRV. The previously recommended sixth dose on day 90 can be safely omitted. The Essen schedule is considered the "gold standard" against which all other regimens are measured. It is the only regimen that is FDA approved. PHKC vaccines may vary in potency, and the schedules recommended by the manufacturer should be followed.

Zagreb, or 2-1-1, intramuscular schedule

Two full ampules are injected at two sites (deltoid or anterolateral thigh muscles) on day 0, followed by one ampule on days 7 and 14. This regimen, compared to the Essen regimen, saves two clinic visits and one ampule of vaccine. It has been shown to be safe and effective.[50,57] It is WHO approved and used in most of Europe and many developing countries. If administered concurrently with immunoglobulin, there is moderate suppression of the immune response. Whether this is clinically significant is controversial.

Thai Red Cross intradermal regimen

The intradermal reduced-dose schedules were developed in an effort to decrease vaccine costs and make quality tissue culture products affordable in the less affluent world.[58,60,61] The Thai Red Cross regimen (TRC-ID) received WHO approval in 1992.[39] It results in neutralizing antibody titers equal to those with the Essen intramuscular schedule, with reduction in the cost of the vaccine by as much as 70%. It has now been extensively used in Thailand, Sri Lanka, and the Philippines and is being introduced into India and Vietnam.[57]

The TRC-ID rabies vaccine regimen consists of the administration of 0.1 mL of HDCV, PVRV, or PCEC intradermally at 2 sites on days 0, 3, and 7 and at one site on days 28 and 90. The lyophilized vaccine in PVRV is diluted in 0.5 mL rather than 1.0 mL in the case of HDCV and PCEC. Some authorities have therefore suggested that PCEC be injected as 0.2 mL per intradermal dose using the TRC-ID method. A new modification of TRC-ID consists of two-site injections at 0, 3, 7, and 28 days (doubling the 28-day and omitting the 90-day booster dose). It has now been extensively used by the public sector in Thailand.

PDEV, a suspension rather than a solution, can also be given intradermally but requires vigorous shaking of the ampule or doubling the dose from 0.1 mL to 0.2 mL per injection site.[29] Intradermal injections are best given using tuberculin or insulin syringes. A skin "bubble" must appear intradermally after the injection to indicate that it went into the dermis—not unlike what is done with a tuberculin test or BCG vaccination (Wilde H, unpublished data).

Oxford, or eight-site, intradermal regimen

This schedule was approved by WHO in 1996 and is being used in parts of Africa and some southeast Asian countries (Wilde H, unpublished data). It produces higher but not significantly earlier antibody levels than the Essen and Zagreb intramuscular regimens and Thai Red Cross intradermal regimens.[72] It has the disadvantage that the patient is not routinely seen on day 3, the time when serious wound infections become apparent in the tropics. In addition, the fact that patients have to be undressed for the eight injections on day 0 can be a potential problem in a busy animal bite center in a developing country. The regimen consists of 8 intradermal injections of 0.1 mL at eight sites (arms, legs, chest or abdomen, and intrascapular region) on day 0, at 4 sites on day 7, and at one site on days 28 and 90.[61]

To achieve full cost savings from the two approved intradermal regimens, they must be applied in clinics that see multiple rabies-exposed patients daily. WHO and vaccine manufacturers recommend that all reconstituted vaccine be used within one working day or be discarded.[57] A recent experimental study, followed by large-scale field application in a rural Thai province, demonstrated that using normal sterile precautions, one can store reconstituted PVRV and PCEC safely and without significant loss of immunogenicity in a clinic refrigerator for reuse for at least 7 days.[84,85] This allows application of TRC-ID in small clinics at considerable savings.[52,86]

FDA = Food and Drug Administration; HDCV = human diploid cell vaccine; PCEC = purified chick embryo cell vaccine; PDEV = purified duck embryo vaccine; PHKC = primary hamster kidney cell vaccine; PVRV = purified Vero cell rabies vaccine; WHO = World Health Orginization.

Adverse Effects of Rabies Vaccines

The adverse effects of nerve tissue–derived rabies vaccines, such as Semple-type and SMB products, are well known. These dangerous and poorly immunogenic products should no longer be used. However, they still represent the most commonly used rabies vaccines in many resource-poor countries where canine rabies is endemic.

Modern tissue or avian culture–derived rabies vaccines (HDCV, PCEC, PVRV, PDEV, RVA, and PHKC) are generally very safe products that uncommonly produce systemic symptoms and are usually associated with only very minor local side effects. These vaccines are comparable to most vaccines used in the EPI. For example, in the animal bite clinic at our facility in Bangkok, nurses who treat between 20 and 40 new patients daily consider tetanus toxoid and typhoid vaccines much more reactogenic than PVRV, HDCV, PDEV, or PCEC rabies vaccines. Intradermal injections generate more local reactions (itching, swelling, mild regional lymphadenopathy), and intramuscular ones cause more systemic reactions (mild fever, myalgia, headache).[62–64]

Booster injections, particularly when HDCV is used, can result in early or delayed mild serum sickness–like reactions in approximately 6% of recipients. These are due to immune complexes formed by the betapropiolactone inactivating agent and serum albumin. We have seen similar, but less frequent, reactions when booster injections were given using PVRV, PDEV, or PCEC (Wilde H, unpublished data).

Contraindications to Rabies Postexposure Vaccination

There are no contraindications to the use of any of the modern tissue culture rabies vaccines and immunoglobulins. They have been shown to be safe in pregnancy.[65]

Adverse Reactions to Rabies Antisera and Immunoglobulins

Early equine rabies antisera had a bad reputation. Up to 40% serum sickness reactions were reported, depending on the manufacturer and batch.[47] Some unpurified antisera are still being manufactured in small laboratories and are used locally; these should be avoided whenever possible. Purified and pepsin-digested ERIG is, however, safe, as previously manufactured by Aventis Pasteur, the Swiss Serum and Vaccine Institute, and SCLAVO of Italy between 1970 and 2001, when most of the commercial firms discontinued production. These purified products carried a serum sickness reaction rate of 1 to 3 %, the signs of which occur after 1 week and are easily managed with antihistamines and analgesics. Corticosteroids should never be used in this setting unless it is known that the biting animal is not rabid and then only in a rare severe case.

A routine skin test prior to application of ERIG has been a ritually performed procedure in most centers, even though it is of dubious value in predicting very rare cases of anaphylaxis. At our institution in Bangkok, only one case of anaphylaxis occurred among more than 100,000 administrations of purified ERIG. The one patient with anaphylaxis had a negative skin test prior to ERIG injection and responded well to adrenalin and antihistamines. (No steroids were used.)

The skin test is considered of no value in predicting delayed serum sickness.[66] Nurses in our animal bite clinic, nevertheless, perform skin tests using an ERIG dilution of 1:100 and an intradermal volume of 0.2 mL and consider any wheal or erythema greater than 20 mm as a positive reaction. The fact that a simultaneously performed saline test might also be positive confuses the issue further. ERIG should be used in the presence of a positive skin test if it is indicated and HRIG is not available. None of these products (including skin testing) should be administered unless clinic staff are trained and able to manage a rare case of anaphylaxis. Equipment for resuscitation must be readily available.[68]

Human rabies immunoglobulins are safe products. Hepatitis C and B, as well as retroviruses, are inactivated by the purification methods. Very rare cases of early or delayed serum sickness–like reactions do occur, but they usually can be managed with analgesics and antihistamines alone. Equine and human immunoglobulins have been used with safety during pregnancy.[57,65]

Postexposure Rabies Treatment Failures

Human rabies deaths following postexposure treatment with tissue culture vaccines have been reported.[67] They are rare and are associated primarily with deviations from the recommendations of the WHO Expert Committee on Rabies.[64] Delay in starting treatment, failure to use immunoglobulin, and failure to inject all bite wounds diligently with immunoglobulin were the most common identifiable causes of these deaths. There have, however, been rare cases where timely optimal treatment appeared to have been rendered yet the patient succumbed to rabies.[68] Presumably, these were cases where virus was inoculated directly into peripheral nerves, and local infiltration, though attempted, did not neutralize it all.

To the best of my knowledge, only one patient has died of rabies in spite of having received preexposure vaccination. This US Peace Corps volunteer was also taking chloroquine malaria prophylaxis and did not receive any postexposure booster vaccination after a dog bite in Africa. Another patient who had received preexposure vaccine survived a neurologic illness, identified as rabies by increasing cerebrospinal fluid (CSF)-neutralizing antibody titers, after an accidental laboratory inhalation exposure (James R. Tillotson, personal communication, 1983). A review of the literature emphasizes that one must follow WHO, Thai Red Cross, or United States Centers for Disease Control (CDC) recommendations for implementing postexposure rabies prophylaxis diligently or else place patients at risk. This also leads to a great deal of overtreatment of animal bite victims worldwide, which is, however, unavoidable at the present time.

Management of Human Rabies Patients

Most readers of this chapter are unlikely to encounter a human rabies case. It is a devastating experience for the family, health care staff, and community. In developing countries, such patients are either sent home to die or placed in the "rabies room" of a public hospital, restrained, and sedated with chlorpromazine, which, in an encephalitic case, may require hundreds of milligrams to be effective.[69] Patients with paralytic rabies (20 to 30% of cases) are often misdiagnosed as having Guillain-Barré syndrome unless they present a recent history of an animal bite and are seen by staff experienced in rabies diagnosis. Patients are intermittently fully conscious and know what they have and that they are facing a terrifying and miserable death.[69] In developed countries, such patients end up in intensive care units (ICUs) and are intubated and maintained for long periods of time but all to no avail. The media become involved in virtually every case, and expensive postexposure treatment is usually applied to contacts and hospital staff, most of whom have had no real exposure.

Virtually every currently available antiviral agent has been tried to treat rabies patients. This included high-dose immune globulin given intrathecally. My colleagues and I recently treated one young Thai woman with 900 mL of intravenous HRIG to no avail. She survived for 15 days with ICU care. Central nervous system (CNS) fluid collections yielded undetectable antibody levels in the presence of high serum titers (Hemachuda T, Wilde H; unpublished data). The Canadian government and CDC recently sponsored a conference to identify appropriate management of human rabies cases. It focused on the hopelessness of all life-sustaining efforts and emphasized provision of comfort and dignity for the patient. The convened experts unanimously agreed that once the diagnosis of rabies has been confirmed, comfort care must be the priority. Titrated intravenous morphine was considered the most appropriate therapy for aerophobia, hydrophobia, muscle spasms, and the tremendous anxiety that such patients experience.[70]

Management of Special Situations

The following postexposure treatment problems are occasionally encountered in busy animal bite management centers of canine rabies–endemic countries. We present some of them with our own management approach, which may or may not represent the official views of WHO and the CDC.

Delay in Presentation for Treatment

When patients present after prolonged delay (days, weeks, even months) after an animal bite in a rabies-endemic setting, we treat as if the attack occurred the same day. The patient may not have been infected at all or the ascent of the virus into the CNS may already be in progress and any treatment may be too late. Nevertheless, a practitioner who sees and decides not to treat a patient, who develops rabies 1 week later, will not want to have to explain to the individual's family or to a judge why he or she did not instigate PET.

Multiple Wounds, Calculated Dose of RIG for Patient's Weight Insufficient

We dilute the immunoglobulin in normal saline to a volume that is sufficient to infiltrate all the wounds. This situation most commonly occurs in children, and our procedure has been approved by WHO, the Thai Red Cross, and the CDC.[57,71]

The Patient Has Gaping Wounds Requiring Suture

Whenever possible, the clinician should plan to perform secondary suture after thorough cleansing of wounds. This is a safe and usually cosmetically satisfactory procedure. Suturing rabies virus–infected wounds may hasten spread of the virus.[67] If early suture is unavoidable, the procedure is as follows: first infiltrate the wounds with RIG, wait for 1 or 2 hours, and then perform only the most necessary sutures.

There Is No Immunoglobulin Available for a Severely Exposed Patient

As an act of desperation, we would use one of the accelerated intradermal regimens (the Oxford eight-site or double-dose Thai Red Cross schedule [four-site intradermal injections on days 0, 3, and 7, with one-site boosters on days 28 and 90]). These have been shown to produce a higher but not significantly earlier antibody response. There is no convincing scientific evidence that higher but not earlier antibody levels will save lives in the absence of immunoglobulin. Hence, this is never an optimal treatment, but it is the best one can offer in this setting.[72] Furthermore, we recently experienced a rabies death in a Thai child who had received optimal and early wound care and the 8-site postexposure regimen without RIG. She died within one month of encephalitic rabies.[73]

Previous Semple or Suckling Mouse Brain Vaccine History, New Exposure

We treat as if no previous vaccine had been given. Most patients will have an anamnestic response to booster vaccination, but this is not predictable. There is no way of knowing what quality of vaccine the patient received.[10] Obtaining rabies antibody determinations is usually a slow process that is not readily available in most places and thus of no help in the emergency decision-making process.[74]

Previous Tissue Culture Vaccine (Pre- or Postexposure), New Exposure 5 Years Later

After optimal wound care, we would give the usual two boosters on days 0 and 3 or the four-site intradermal boosters on day 0 without immunoglobulin.[58]

Patient Received Vaccine But No RIG

A patient appears for his day-14 injection after having received vaccine without RIG for a severe dog bite in a canine rabies–endemic country. The patient is very anxious as he or she has learned that immunoglobulin should also have been administered on day 0.

In this situation, some of our staff would inject the bite wounds with immunoglobulin and start a new vaccine series. Others would obtain a neutralizing antibody titer and reassure the patient if it is more than 0.5 IU/mL. There is no easy solution for managing such a patient in an evidence-based manner and also providing complete reassurance.[75]

THE FUTURE OF RABIES CONTROL

Much successful work has been done worldwide in improving postexposure treatment. It is virtually 100% successful if current WHO, CDC, or Thai Red Cross recommendations are followed diligently. We have modern human and canine rabies vaccines and know how to make immunoglobulins, even though they are currently in very short supply. In other words, we have all the tools to rid the world of canine and wildlife rabies.

More than 90% of rabies exposures and human deaths, nevertheless, continue to be the result of canine attacks followed by no or inadequate postexposure treatment. The disease thus remains primarily one of poor dog population control and inadequate canine vaccination. Cultural, religious, and economic barriers are mainly responsible for this. Thailand alone has approximately 10 million dogs, mostly strays or community owned. To vaccinate them all would cost approximately $5 to 10 million (US). The country provides at least 300,000 postexposure human treatments every year at a cost of about $16 million (US). It is obvious that mass vaccination of dogs and cats would save funds and lives. However, mass dog (and even wildlife) vaccination with injectable or oral vaccines, as an ongoing and sustainable effort, is not easy to carry out in a relatively poor country. This is particularly true when dealing with mobile stray canine and feline populations that have a short life cycle. Reduction of this population by humane methods would have to be carried out. However, culling the stray dog population is not acceptable in most of Southeast Asia and the Indian subcontinent. Research for inexpensive and practical methods of canine birth control is thus urgently needed but of low priority to funding agencies.

Preexposure vaccination of children in canine rabies–endemic regions has been proposed. Whether this can be carried out in poor countries, which have many other health care priorities, is doubtful at the current high cost of rabies vaccines. It might, however, become quite feasible if the cost of tissue culture vaccines could be reduced to a level similar to that of other EPI vaccines.[62] Modelska and colleagues, from Koprowski's team in Philadelphia, were able to produce an oral rabies vaccine from spinach leaves using recombinant technology. This product was able to protect mice against a lethal rabies virus challenge.[76] DNA vaccines can also be produced for rabies.[77] Some interesting research has been published that showed that it is possible to replace ERIG and HRIG with humanized monoclonal antibodies.[78]

Research in these directions must be supported, but control of the disease in dogs is our first priority. Attenuated and recombinant oral rabies vaccines have helped to control fox rabies in Europe and North America and are now being tested in dogs and raccoons.[79,80] Rabies virus is a potential biologic warfare agent, a fact that has not been fully recognized. The street virus is readily obtainable in rabies-endemic countries and will grow in many cell culture systems. It could be weaponized by aerosolization and thus transmitted to humans in a manner similar to that of anthrax, tularemia, or smallpox.[81] Recognition of this threat in our present unstable world might, perhaps, generate more interest in this neglected disease.

ACKNOWLEDGMENTS

Professor Stanley Plotkin and Dr. Francois X. Meslin kindly reviewed this chapter and provided helpful comments. I also owe much to the nursing staff at Queen Saovabha Memorial Institute (led by Mrs. Nipa Naraporn), Mrs. Pakamatz Khawplod, head of our immunology laboratory, Dr. Veera Tepsumethanon and his veterinary researchers, my neurology colleague Professor Thiravat Hemachudha, and the present and former directors of this institute: Professors Visith Sitprija and Supawat Chutivongse. This chapter is dedicated to the memory of my friend Dr. Arthur King, a lifelong student of rabies research, who died in June of 2002 in England.

REFERENCES

1. Steel JH, Fernandez PJ. History of rabies and global aspects. In: Baer GM, editor. The natural history of rabies. 2nd ed. Boca Raton (FL): CRC Press; 1991. p. 1–24.

2. Fermi C. Immunizierung der Muriden mit tollwut und normaler Nervensubstanz gegen die nachfolgende subkutane infection von Strassenvirus. Z Hyg Infektionskr 1908;58:221.

3. Semple D. The preparation of a safe and efficient rabies vaccine. Calcutta: Government Printing Office of India; 1911.

4. Denison GA, Dowling GD. Rabies in Birmingham, Alabama. Human mortality as affected by antirabies treatment. JAMA 1939;390:390–5.

5. McKendrick AG. Ninth analytical review of reports from Pasteur Institutes on results of antirabies treatments. Bull League Nations Health Organ 1940;9:31–78.

6. Bareggi C. Su cinque casi di rabbia paralitica (de laboratorio) nell uomo. Gass Med Lombarda 1889;48:217–9.

7. Hemachudha T, Laothamatas J, Rupprecht CE. Human rabies. A disease of complex neuropathogenic mechanisms and diagnostic challenges. Lancet Neurol 2002;2:101–9.

8. Bhari F, Letaief A, Ernez M, et al. Les complications neurologiques observes chez l'adulte, secondaires au vaccin antirabique prepare sur cerveaux d'animaux. Presse Med 1996;25:491–3.

9. Swaddiwuthipong W, Wenninger BG, Wattanasri S, et al. A high rate of neurological complications following Semple anti-rabies vaccine. Trans R Soc Trop Med Hyg 1988;82:472–5.

10. Parviz S, Luby S, Wilde H, et al. Postexposure treatment of rabies in Pakistan. Clin Infect Dis 1998;27:751–6.

11. World Health Organization. World survey of rabies no 34. Geneva: WHO; 1998.

12. Fuenzalida E, Palacios R, Borgono M. The use of suckling mouse brain vaccine in man. Symp Ser Immunobiol Stand 1965;1:339–48

13. Zanetti CR, Consales CA, Rodrigues–da-Silva AS, et al. Short duration of neutralizing antibody titers after pre-exposure rabies vaccination with suckling mouse brain vaccine. Braz J Med Biol Res 1998;31:1275–80.

14. Chantavanich P, Suntharasmai P, Warrell MJ. Antibody response to suckling mouse brain rabies vaccine for post exposure treatment. Trans R Soc Trop Med Hyg 1987;81:260–3.

15. Toro G, Vergara I, Roman G. Neuroparalytic accidents of antirabies vaccination with suckling mouse brain vaccine. Arch Neurol 1977;34:694–700.

16. Bunn TO. Canine and feline vaccines, past and present. In: Baer GM, editor. The natural history of rabies. Boca Raton (FL): CRS Press; 1991. p. 415–24.

17. Wiktor TJ, Fernandes MV, Koprowski H. Cultivation of rabies virus in human diploid cell strain WI-38. J Immunol 1964;93:353–66.

18. Bahmanyar M, Fayaz A, Nour-Salehi S, et al. Postexposure treatment with the new human diploid cell rabies vaccine and antirabies serum. JAMA 1976;236:2751–4.

19. Fishbein DB, Yenne KM, Dreesen DW, et al. Risk factors for systemic hypersensitivity reactions after booster vaccinations with human diploid cell rabies vaccines. A nationwide prospective study. Vaccine 1993;11:1390–4.

20. Briggs DJ, Dreesen DW, Morgan P, et al. Safety and immunogenicity of Lyssavac Berna human diploid cell rabies vaccine in healthy adults. Vaccine 1996;14:1361–5.

21. Wilde H, Glueck R, Khawplod P, et al. Efficacy study of a new albumin-free human diploid cell rabies vaccine (Lyssavac-HDC, Berna) in 100 severely rabies-exposed Thai patients. Vaccine 1995;13:593–6.

22. Fenje P. Rabies vaccine for human use. Immunobiol Stand (Symposium series) 1974;21:148–56.

23. Selimov M. Evaluation of the inactivated tissue culture rabies vaccine from the Vnukovo-32 strain. Results of its industrial production and field use for post-exposure immunization in man. Dev Biol Stand 1978;40:57–62.

24. Linn FT. The protective effect of the large-scale use of PHKC rabies vaccine in humans in China. Bull World Health Organ 1990;68:449–54.

25. Atanasiu P, Tsiang H, Reculard P, et al. Zonal centrifuge purification of human rabies vaccine obtained on bovine fetal kidney cells. Dev Biol Stand 1978;40:69–75.

26. Fremont J, Gaudiot C, Malo JP, et al. Post-exposure rabies treatment with fetal bovine kidney cell vaccine in people bitten by animals with confirmed rabies. Lancet 1984;1:1469–70.

27. Berlin BS, Mitchell JR, Burgoyne GH, et al. Rhesus diploid rabies vaccine (adsorbed). A new rabies vaccine. II. Results of clinical studies simulating prophylactic therapy for rabies exposure. JAMA 1983;249:2663–5.

28. Rubin RH, Hattwick MA, Gregg JS, et al. Adverse reactions to duck embryo rabies vaccine. Range and incidence. Ann Intern Med 1973;78:643–9.

29. Khawplod P, Glueck R, Wilde H, et al. Immunogenicity of purified duck embryo rabies vaccine (Lyssavac N) with use of the WHO-approved intradermal postexposure regimen. Clin Infect Dis 1984;20:646–51.

30. Montagnon BJ, Fanget B, Nicolas AJ. The large scale cultivation of vero cells on microcarrier culture for virus vaccine production. Preliminary results for killed poliovirus vaccine production. Biol Stand 1981;47:55–64.

31. Montagnon BJ, Vincent-Falquet JC, Saluzzo JF. Experience with Vero cells at Pasteur-Merieux Connaught. Dev Biol Stand 1999;98:137–40.

32. Suntharasamai P, Warrell DA, Looareesuwan S, et al. New purified vero-cell vaccine prevents rabies in patients bitten by rabid animals. Lancet 1986;1:129–31.

33. Chutivongse S, Supich C, Wilde H. Acceptability and efficacy of purified vero-cell rabies vaccine in Thai children. Asia Pac J Public Health 1988;2:179–85.

34. Lang J, Cetre JC, Picot N, et al. Immunogenicity and safety in adults of a new chromatographically purified vero-cell rabies vaccine (CPRV). A randomized double-blind trial with purified vero-cell rabies vaccine (PVRV). Biologicals 1998;26:299–308.

35. Quiambao BP, Lang J, Vital S, et al. Immunogenicity and efficacy of post-exposure rabies prophylaxis with a new chromatographically purified vero-cell rabies vaccine (CPRV), a two staged randomized clinical trial in the Philippines. Acta Trop 2000;75:39–52.

36. Barth R, Bijok U, Gruschkau H, et al. Purified chicken embryo cell rabies vaccine for human use. Lancet 1983;1:700.

37. Nicholson KG, Farrow PR, Bijok U, et al. Pre-exposure studies with purified chick embryo cell culture vaccine. Serological and clinical responses in man. Vaccine 1987;5:208–10.

38. Briggs DJ, Banzhoff A, Nicolay U, et al. Antibody response of patients after postexposure rabies vaccination with small intradermal doses of purified chick embryo cell vaccine or purified Vero cell rabies vaccine. Bull World Health Organ 2000;78:693–8.

39. WHO Expert Committee on Rabies. Eighth Report. Tech Series 824. Geneva (Switz): World Health Organization; 1992.

40. Benjavongkulchai M, Kositprapa C, Limsuwan K, et al. An immunogenicity and efficacy study of purified chick embryo cell culture rabies vaccine manufactured in Japan. Vaccine 1997;15:1816–9.

41. Baltazard M, Bahmanyar M, Fayaz A, et al. Successful protection of humans exposed to rabies infection. Postexposure treatment with the new human diploid cell rabies vaccine and antirabies serum. JAMA 1976;236:2751, 1955;13:747–777

42. Selimov M, Boltucij L, Selimova E, et al. Anwendung des antirabies-Gammaglobulins bei Menshcen die von tolwutingen Wolfen und anderen Tieren schew gebissen wurden. J Hyg Epidemiol Microbiol Immunol 1959;3:168—80.

43. Veeraraghavan N, Subrahmayan TP. Value of antirabies vaccine with and without serum against severe challenges. Bull World Health Organ 1960;22:381–91.

44. Lin TF, Wang YZ, et al. Use of serum and vaccine in combination for prophylaxis following exposure to rabies. Rev Infect Dis 1988;10 Suppl 4:S766–70.

45. Dean DJ, Baer GM, Thompson WR. Studies on the local treatment of rabies infected wounds. Bull World Health Organ 1963;28:477–93.

46. Cabasso VJ, Loofbourow JC, Roby RE, et al. Rabies immune globulin of human origin. Preparation and dosage determination of non-exposed volunteer subjects. Bull World Health Organ 1971;45:303–15.

47. Karliner JS, Belaval GS. Incidence of reactions following administration of antirabies serum. JAMA 1965;193:359–62.

48. Hattwick MA, Rubin RH, Music S, et al. Postexposure rabies prophylaxis with human rabies immune globulin. JAMA 1974;227:407–10.

49. Wilde H, Chutivongse S. Equine rabies immune globulin. A product with an underserved poor reputation. Am J Trop Med Hyg 1990;42:175–8.

50. Chutivongse S, Wilde H, Supich C, et al. Postexposure prophylaxis for rabies with antiserum and intradermal vaccination. Lancet 1985;1:1059–62.

51. Wilde H, Thipkong P, Khawplod P. Economic issues in rabies treatment. J Travel Med 1999;6:238–42.

52. Wilde H, Thipkong P, Sitprija V, Chaiyabutr N. Heterologous antisera and antivenins are essential biologicals. Perspectives on a worldwide crisis [review]. Ann Intern Med 1996;125(3):233–6.

53. Wilde H. What are today's orphaned vaccines? Clin Infect Dis 2001;33:648–50.

54. Lang J, Attanath P, Quiambao B, et al. Evaluation of the safety, immunogenicity and pharmacokinetic profile of a new, highly purified, heat-treated equine rabies immunoglobulin, administered either alone or in association with a purified, Vero-cell rabies vaccine. Acta Trop 1998;70:317–33.

55. Hanlon CA, Niezgoda M, Morrill PA, et al. The incurable wound revisited. Progress in human rabies prevention. Vaccine 2001;19:2273–9.

56. Kositprapa C, Limsuwun K, Wilde H, et al. Immune response to simulated postexposure rabies booster vaccinations in volunteers who received preexposure vaccinations. Clin Infect Dis 1997;25:614–6.

57. World Health Organization. Rabines vaccines. Wkly Epidemiol Rec 2002;14:109–19.

58. Khawplod P, Benjavongkulchai M, Limusanno S, et al. Four-site intradermal boosters in previously rabies vaccinated subjects. J Travel Med 2002;9:153–5.

59. Sriaroon C, Fangmongkol P, Sitprija V, et al. A retrospective study of 2,471 animal bites and potential rabies exposures in Thai children. WHO Bull 2003. [In press]

60. Warrell MJ, Warrell DJ, Suntharasamai P, et al. An economical regimen of human diploid cell strain anti-rabies vaccine for post-exposure prophylaxis. Lancet 1983;2:301–4.

61. Phanuphak P, Khawplod P, Srivichayakul S, et al. Humoral and cell mediated immune response to various economical regimens of purified Vero-cell rabies vaccine. Asia Pac J Allergy Immunol 1987;5:33–7.

62. Jaiaroensup W, Lang J, Thipkong P, et al. Safety and efficacy of purified Vero cell rabies vaccine given intramuscularly and intradermally. Results of a prospective randomized trial. Vaccine 1998;16:1559–62.

63. Dutta JK. Adverse reactions to purified chick embryo cell rabies vaccine. Vaccine 1994;12:1484.

64. Briggs DJ, Banzhoff A, Nicolay U, et al. Antibody response of patients after postexposure rabies vaccination with small intradermal doses of purified chick embryo cell vaccine or purified Vero cell vaccine. Bull World Health Organ 2000;78:693–8.

65. Chutivingse S, Wilde H, Benjavongkulchai M, et al. Postexposure rabies vaccination during pregnancy. Effect on 202 women and their infants. Clin Infect Dis 1995;4:818–20.

66. Tantawichien T, Benjavongkulchai M, Wilde H, et al. Value of skin testing for predicting reactions to equine rabies immune globulin. Clin Infect Dis 1995;3:660–2.

67. Wilde H, Sirikawin S, Subcharoen A, et al. Failure of post-exposure treatment of rabies in children. Clin Infect Dis 1996;22:228–32.

68. Hemachudha T, Mitrabhakdi E, Wilde H, et al. Additional reports of failure to respond to treatment after rabies exposure in Thailand. Clin Infect Dis 1999;28:143–4.

69. Wilde H, Hemachudha T. Rabies [video]. Lyon (France): CME Video, Fondation Merieux; 2001.

70. Jackson AC, Warrell MJ, Rupprecht CE, et al. Management of rabies in humans. Clin Infect Dis 2003;36:60–3.

71. World Health Organization. Recommendations on rabies postexposure treatment and the correct technique of intradermal immunization against rabies. EMC.ZOO 96.6. Geneva (Switz.): WHO; 1996.

72. Khawplod P, Wilde H, Tepsumethanon S, et al. Prospective immunogenicity study of multiple intradermal injections of rabies vaccine (an effort to obtain an early immune response without using immunoglobulin). Clin Infect Dis 2002;35:1562–5.

73. Sriaroon C, Daviratanasilpa S, Sansomranjai P, et al. Rabies in a Thai child treated with the 8-site postexposure regimen without immune globulin. Vaccine 2003. [In press]

74. Rupprecht CE, Hanlon CA, Hemachudha T. Rabies re-examined. Lancet Infect Dis 2002;2:337–53.

75. Khawplod P, Wilde H, Chomchey P, et al. What is an acceptable delay in rabies immune globulin administration when vaccine alone had been given previously? Vaccine 1996;14(5):389–91.

76. Modelska A, Dietzschold B, Sleysh N, et al. Immunization against rabies with plant-derived antigen. Proc Natl Acad Sci U S A 1998;95:2481–5.

77. Kammer AR, Ertl HC. Rabies vaccines from the past to the 21st century. Hybrid Hybridomics 2002;21:123–7.

78. Hanlon CA, De Mattos CA, De Mattos CC, et al. Experimental utility of rabies virus neutralizing human monoclonal antibody in post-exposure prophylaxis. Vaccine 2001;19:3834–42.

79. Selhorst T, Thulke HH, Muller T. Cost-efficient vaccination of foxes *(Vulpes vulpes)* against rabies and the need for a new baiting strategy. Prev Vet Med 2001;51:95–109.

80. Rosatte RC, Lawson KF. Acceptance of baits for delivery of oral rabies vaccine to raccoons. J Wildl Dis 2001;37:730–9.

81. Alibek K, Handelman S. Biohazard. New York: Random House/Dell; 1999.

82. Sage G, Khawplod P, Wilde H, et al. Immune response to rabies vaccine in Alaskan dogs. Failure to achieve a consistently protective antibody response. Trans R Soc Trop Med Hyg 1993;5:593–5.

83. Siwasontiwat D, Lumlertdacha B, Polsuwan C, et al. Rabies. Is provocation of the biting dog relevant for risk assessment? Trans R Soc Trop Med Hyg 1992;4:443.

84. Kamoltham T, Khawplod P, Wilde H, et al. Rabies postexposure vaccination using reconstituted and stored vaccine. Vaccine 2002;20:3272–6.

85. Khawplod P, Wilde H, Tantawichien T, et al. Potency, sterility and immunogenicity of rabies tissue culture vaccine after reconstitution and refrigerated storage for 1 week. Vaccine 2002;20:3272–6.

86. Kamoltham T, Singseh J, Promsaraull U, et al. Elimination of rabies in a canine endemic province of Thailand; five-year program. Bull WHO 2003;81:375–81.

Chapter 10

Japanese Encephalitis Vaccine

Tom Solomon

For most people, the first time they have ever heard of Japanese encephalitis (JE) is when visiting a travel clinic in preparation for a trip to Asia. They are then faced with the seemingly impossible decision of whether to spend money on a vaccine that has a rather bad reputation or to risk developing the disease, which would be much worse.[1] Many of the physicians that have to advise them feel ill equipped to do so. From a Western perspective, JE is considered a rare and exotic disease, but for those living and working in southern and eastern Asia, JE is a daily reality. Although confined to this region, the arthropod-borne JE virus (JEV) is numerically one of the most important causes of viral encephalitis worldwide, with an estimated 50,000 cases and 15,000 deaths annually.[2,3] In addition to the large number of deaths, approximately half the survivors of JE have severe neuropsychiatric sequelae, imposing a large socioeconomic burden on the community. Yet, ironically, this is a disease for which several safe and effective vaccines exist, and newer ones are in development. A safe and effective formalin-inactivated vaccine has been available for nearly 40 years, but production difficulties and its cost have restricted its usage in Asia to wealthier countries, whereas its use by Western travelers is limited by concerns over side effects. In the absence of robust epidemiologic data, vaccination practices have at times fluctuated according to highly publicized cases of JE in travelers or of adverse events related to vaccination. A newer live attenuated vaccine, developed by the Chinese, is cheaper to produce, but its uptake outside China has been limited by regulatory issues and concerns over its production. In recent years, the application of molecular biologic approaches have helped elucidate the structure of flaviviruses, giving insights into viral pathogenesis and have allowed development of newer recombinant vaccines.

Sadly, some remarkable achievements in vaccinology have not always been matched by equal vigor in public health policy and implementation, and the disease continues to grow in importance globally. This chapter reviews the epidemiology, clinical features, and pathogenesis of JE and then focuses on the formalin-inactivated mouse brain–derived (BIKEN) vaccine, which is available to travelers, before briefly considering some of the other vaccines used in Asia as well as newer vaccines in development.

HISTORIC PERSPECTIVE

Epidemics of encephalitis were described in Japan from the 1870s onward, with major epidemics approximately every 10 years. In September 1923, Japan suffered a large earthquake, and in the following summer, which was particularly dry, one of the largest encephalitis outbreaks occurred, with 6,551 cases in 6 months and a 55% case fatality rate.[4–7] The term type B encephalitis was originally used to distinguish these summer epidemics from von Economo's encephalitis lethargica ("sleeping sickness," known as type A), but the B has since been dropped. In 1933, a filterable agent was transmitted from the brain of a fatal case and caused encephalitis in monkeys. The prototype Nakayama strain of JEV was isolated from the brain of a fatal case in 1935, and the disease has been recognized across Asia since then (Figure 10-1).[8] The virus was later shown to be a member of the genus *Flavivirus* (family Flaviviridae), named after the prototype yellow fever virus (L *flavus* yellow). Although of no taxonomic significance, the ecologic term arbovirus ("arthropod-borne virus") is used to describe the fact that JEV is one of more than 500 viruses transmitted between vertebrate hosts by arthropods (insects, ticks, sand flies, and biting midges).[9]

INFECTIOUS AGENT

Flaviviruses

The *Flavivirus* genus is one of three genera in the family Flaviviridae. The other two are the genus *Hepacivirus*, which includes hepatitis C virus, and the genus *Pestivirus*, which includes bovine viral diarrhea viruses. The *Flavivirus* genus contains approximately 70 members and includes many important

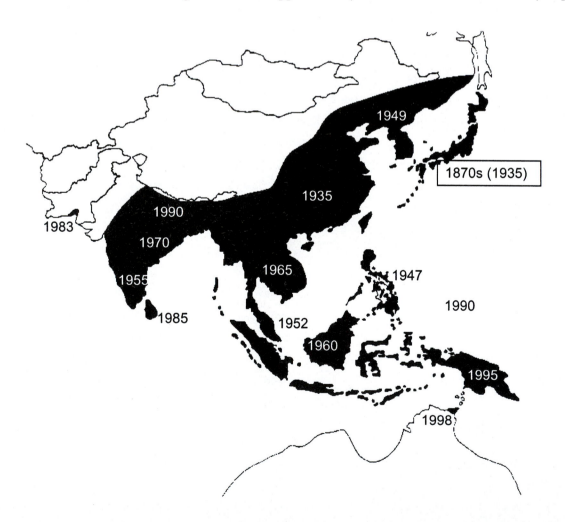

Figure 10-1. Current distribution of Japanese encephalitis. The approximate dates of the first major outbreaks or first virus isolations since epidemics of encephalitis were first described in Japan in the 1870s are shown. Adapted from Solomon T.[8]

Table 10-1. **Medically Important Flaviviruses**

Virus	Main Clinical Syndromes*	Main Vectors	Natural Hosts	Main Geographic Area
Mosquito-borne viruses				
Japanese encephalitis	CNS	*Culex tritaeniorhyncus* and others	Waterfowl (egrets, herons), chickens, pigs	Asian subcontinent, Southeast Asia, Pacific Rim
West Nile	FAR, CNS	*Culex pipiens* and others	Passeriform birds (jays, blackbirds, sparrows, crows)	Africa, Middle East, southern Europe, North America
St. Louis encephalitis	CNS	*Culex pipiens, C. tarsalis, C. nigripalpus*	Passeriform birds (pigeons, sparrows)	North and South America
Murray Valley encephalitis	CNS	*Culex annulirostris*	Waterfowl, rabbits, marsupials	New Guinea, Australia
Dengue (serotypes 1–4)	FAR, HF	*Aedes aegypti, A. albopictus*	Humans, (macaque monkeys in Africa)	Most countries in the tropics
Yellow fever	Hepatitis, HF	*Aedes* and other species	Primates (monkeys, chimpanzees, baboons), humans	South America, Africa
Tick-borne viruses				
Tick-borne encephalitis	CNS	*Ixodes* spp[†]	Forest rodents (mice, hedgehogs)	Commonwealth of Soviet States
Omsk hemorrhagic fever	HF	*Dermacentor* spp	Rodents (muskrats, voles)	Siberia
Kyasanur forest disease virus	HF	*Haemaphysalis* spp	Rodents, birds, bats, monkeys	Karnataka State, India

Adapted from Solomon T and Mallewa MJ.[11]

*CNS = central nervous system infection; FAR = fever arthralgia rash syndrome; HF = hemorrhagic fever.

[†]Tick-borne encephalitis virus is also transmitted via infected milk.

causes of human disease (Table 10-1).[10,11] Flaviviruses are thought to have evolved from a common ancestor as recently as 10,000 years ago and are rapidly evolving to fill new ecologic niches.[12,13] Within the genus, the JE serogroup contains JEV, West Nile virus, St. Louis encephalitis virus, and Murray Valley encephalitis virus.[14,15] Other flaviviruses that cause hemorrhagic fever include yellow fever virus (see Chapter 5, "Yellow Fever Vaccine") and dengue viruses (see Chapter 13, "Dengue Fever Vaccine"). Dengue viruses are endemic in much of Asia and are serologically cross-reactive with JEV, which has implications for diagnosis and pathogenesis. Additional flaviviruses circulating in Asia include Tembusu in Thailand and Langat in Malaysia, but these do not appear to be important causes of disease.

Structure and Replication Strategy

Flaviviruses consist of a single strand of positive-sense ribonucleic acid (RNA) wrapped in a nucleocapsid and surrounded by a glycoprotein-containing envelope. The RNA comprises a short 5' untranslated region (UTR), a longer 3' UTR, and between them a single open reading frame.[16] This codes for a single polyprotein, which is co- and post-translationally cleaved by viral and host proteases into three structural proteins (core or C; premembrane or PrM; and envelope or E) and seven nonstructural (NS) proteins (NS1, NS2A, NS2B, NS3, NS4A, NS4B, NS5). The C protein is highly basic and combines with the RNA to form the nucleocapsid. The PrM is closely associated with the E protein, forming a heterodimer, and is thought to act as a "chaperone" to it, impairing its function until after virion release. Immediately prior to virion release, the PrM protein is cleaved by a furin-like protease to its mature M protein form. This allows the formation of E protein homodimers, which are thus activated.[17] The E protein is the largest structural protein, consisting of nearly 500 amino acids with up two potential gylcosylation sites. It is the major target for the humoral immune response and is thought to be important in viral entry into host cells. The flavivirus receptor has yet to be identified, but a highly sulphated heparan sulphate molecule might contribute to receptor binding.[18,19] Studies with monoclonal antibodies and, more recently, x-ray crystallography have determined the composition of the E protein's three domains.[20,21] Domain III is the putative receptor-binding domain (by which virions attach to the yet-to-be-identified host cell receptor), domain II is the dimerization domain, and domain I has a central beta barrel and is the hinge domain that links the other two. Following viral attachment to the cell surface, flaviviruses enter cells by endocytosis. Subsequent fusion of the virus's lipid membrane with the endosome membrane allows viral RNA to penetrate into the cytoplasm of the infected cell.[16] Recent cryoelectron microscopy studies have shown an arrangement of 90 E protein dimers lying flat on the surface of the virion that rearrange to form E homodimers as the pH drops, exposing an internal fusion peptide and a patch of viral membrane for fusion. Interestingly, recent studies have shown that the E1 protein of alphaviruses has a striking similarity to the flavivirus E protein in terms of structure and function.[22] Together, they have been labeled class II fusion peptides.[23]

Prototypes and Genotypes of Japanese Encephalitis Virus

Soon after the identification of the prototype Nakayama JEV strain, other strains were isolated that have proved to be important in the history of vaccine development. Beijing-1 was isolated in the People's Republic of China (referred to hereafter as China) in 1949 and P3 soon after in 1950. (At this time, the capital of China was known as Peking—hence the letter P.) In 1982, the Chinese isolated strain SA14, from which the live attenuated vaccine strain (SA14-14-2) would ultimately be derived. JaOARS982 was isolated by the Japanese in 1982 and became important as the first fully sequenced strain.

Comparisons of virus strains by serologic cross-reactivity, and later by the use of monoclonal antibodies, suggested that viruses could be grouped according to antigenic differences.[24,25] Based on limited nucleotide sequencing of the *PrM* and *E* genes, four genotypes of virus were identified (differentiated by at least 12% divergence), which roughly correlated with the antigenic groupings, though a single isolate might represent a putative fifth genotype.[25–28] The different genotypes are not evenly distributed across Asia. Because genotypes I and III were found mainly in northern areas where JE occurs in large summer epidemics and II and IV were found in southern endemic areas, it was postulated that the different genotypes were responsible for the different epidemiologic patterns.[26,27,29] However, recent, more detailed studies have shown that all genotypes of JEV are found in the Indonesia-Malaysia region, but in other parts of Asia only the less divergent, more recently evolved genotypes (I, II, and III) are found.[30] These findings suggest that the virus arose from its flavivirus ancestor in the Indonesia-Malaysia region and evolved here into the different genotypes, only the more recent of which have spread to new geographic areas.[8,31] It has been suggested that differences between the genotypes could have implications for vaccine development, but there are few data to support this (see below).

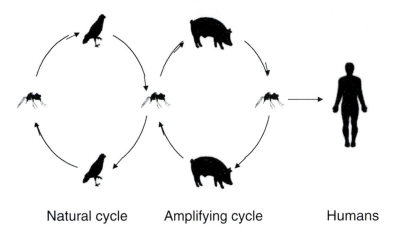

Natural cycle   Amplifying cycle   Humans

Figure 10-2. The transmission cycle of Japanese encephalitis virus. The virus is transmitted naturally between aquatic birds by *Culex* mosquitoes; during the rainy season, when there is an increase in the number of mosquitoes, the virus "overflows" into pigs and other domestic animals and then into humans, who do not transmit the virus further (dead-end hosts).

EPIDEMIOLOGY

Enzootic Cycle

JEV is transmitted naturally in an enzootic cycle between birds, pigs, and other vertebrate hosts by mosquitoes, especially *Culex tritaeniorhyncus, Culex vishnui, Culex pseudovishnui, Culex gelidus,* and other species that breed in pools of stagnant water (such as rice paddies) (Figure 10-2). Although many animals can be infected with JEV, only those with high viremias are important for the natural cycle. Birds are thought to be important in maintaining and amplifying JEV in the environment, and migrating birds, particularly the black-crowned night heron (*Nycticorax nycticorax*) and the Asiatic cattle egret (*Bubulcus ibis coromandus*), are thought to be important in the virus's dispersal to new geographic areas.[32,33] In addition, windblown mosquitoes might have a role.[34] The means by which JEV overwinters (ie, survives the winter months when there is little mosquito activity) is not certain. The virus can be transmitted vertically from an infected female into her eggs, and overwintering in the eggs of *Aedes* mosquitoes might be one mechanism.[35] In many parts of Asia, pigs are kept close to the home, and they thus serve as important bridging hosts, bringing the virus close to humans. In Indonesia, the lower prevalence of the antibody to JEV in Borneo than in neighboring Bali has been attributed to the near-absence of swine in the predominantly Muslim culture.[36] Whereas the virus does not normally cause encephalitis in birds or pigs, it can cause pregnant sows to abort, and it also causes encephalitis in horses.

Geographic Distribution

In the past 50 years, the geographic area affected by JEV has expanded (see Figure 10-1; Table 10-2).[37,38] Differences in diagnostic capabilities and in reporting of encephalitis make it impossible to plot this expansion precisely. However, the timing of the first reported cases or new epidemics in each area gives an impression of the relentless spread of JE. In China, outbreaks of summer encephalitis occurred from 1935, and the virus was first isolated there in 1940; there are currently 10,000 to 20,000 cases per year, though in the early 1970s there were more than 80,000 cases annually.[39] In the far eastern states of the former Soviet Union, JE first occurred in 1938. In 1949, large epidemics of JE were reported from

Table 10–2. Risk of Japanese Encephalitis by Country

Country	Affected Areas	Transmission Season	Comments
Australia	Islands of Torres Strait	Probably year-round transmission risk	Localized outbreak in Torres Strait in 1995 and sporadic cases in 1998 in Torres Strait and on mainland Australia at Cape York Peninsula
Bangladesh	Little data but probably widespread	Possibly July to December as in northern India	Outbreak reported from Tangail District, Dhaka Division; sporadic cases in Rajshahi Division
Bhutan	No data	No data	No comments
Brunei	Presumed to be sporadic-endemic as in Malaysia	Presumed year-round transmission	No comments
Burma (Myanmar)	Presumed to be endemic-hyperendemic countrywide	Presumed to be May to October	Repeated outbreaks in Shan State in Chiang Mai valley
Cambodia	Presumed to be endemic-hyperendemic countrywide	Presumed to be May to October	Cases reported from refugee camps on Thai border and from Phnom Penh
India	Reported cases from all states and union territories except Arunachal Pradesh, Dadra, Daman, Diu, Gujarat, Himachal, Jammu, Kashmir, Lakshadweep, Meghalaya, Nagar Haveli, Orissa, Punjab, Rajasthan, and Sikkim	South India, May to October in Goa, October to January in Tamil Nadu, and August to December in Karnataka, second peak April to June in Mandhya Pradesh District; Andhra Pradesh, September to December; northern India, July to December	Outbreaks in Andhra Pradesh, Assam, western Bengal, Bihar, Goa, Karnataka, Manipur, Tamil Nadu, and Uttar Pradesh; urban cases reported (eg, in Luchnow)
Indonesia	Bali, Irian Jaya (Papua), Kalimantan, Lombok, Moluccas, Nusa Tenggara, and Sulawesi	Probably year-round risk; varies by island; peak risks associated with rainfall, rice cultivation, and presence of pigs; peak periods of risk November to March, also June and July in some years	Human cases recognized on Bali, Java, and possibly in Lombok
Japan	Rare-sporadic cases on all islands except Hokkaido	June to September, except April to December on Ryukyu Islands (Okinawa)	Vaccine not routinely recommended for travel to Tokyo and other major cities; enzootic transmission without human cases observed on Hokkaido
Korea	North Korea, no data; South Korea, sporadic-endemic with occasional outbreaks	July to October	Last major outbreaks in 1982 and 1983; sporadic cases reported in 1994 and 1998
Laos	Presumed to be endemic-hyperendemic countrywide	Presumed to be May to October	No comments
Malaysia	Sporadic-endemic in all states of Peninsula, Sarawak, and probably Sabah	Year-round transmission; October to February in Sarawak	Most cases from Johor, Penang, Perak, Sarawak, and Selangor

Continued on next page

Table 10-2. **Risk of Japanese Encephalitis by Country** (*Continued*)

Country	Affected Areas	Transmission Season	Comments
Nepal	Hyperendemic in southern lowlands (Terai)	July to December	Vaccine not recommended for travelers visiting only high-altitude areas
Pakistan	Might be transmitted in central deltas	Presumed to be June to January	Cases reported near Karachi; endemic areas overlap those for West Nile virus; lower Indus Valley might be an endemic area
Papua New Guinea	Normanby Islands and Western Province	Probably year-round risk	Localized sporadic cases
People's Republic of China	Cases in all provinces except Xizang (Tibet), Xinjiang, Qinghai; endemic–periodically epidemic in temperate areas; Hong Kong, rare cases in new territories; Taiwan, endemic, sporadic cases islandwide; hyperendemic in southern China	Northern China, May to September; southern China, April to October (southern Fujian, Guangdong, Guangxi, Guizhou, Hunan, Jiangxi, Sichuan, and Yunnan provinces); Hong Kong, April to October; Taiwan, April to October with a June peak	Vaccine not routinely recommended for travelers to urban areas only; Taiwan, cases reported in and around Taipei and the Kaohsiung-Pingtung river basins
Philippines	Presumed to be endemic on all islands	Uncertain; speculations based on locations and agroecosystems; West Luzon, Mindoro, Negros, and Palawan, April to November; elsewhere year-round, with greatest risk April to January	Outbreaks described in Luzon, Manila, and Nueva Ecija
Russia	Far-eastern maritime areas south of Khabarousk	Peak period July to September	First human cases in 30 years recently reported
Singapore	Rare cases	Year-round transmission, with April peak	Vaccine not routinely recommended
Sri Lanka	Endemic in all but mountainous areas; periodically epidemic in northern and central provinces	October to January; secondary peak of enzootic transmission May to June	Recent outbreaks in central (Anuradhapura) and northwestern provinces
Thailand	Hyperendemic in north; sporadic-endemic in south	May to October	Annual outbreaks in Chiang Mai Valley; sporadic cases in Bangkok suburbs
Vietnam	Endemic-hyperendemic in all provinces	May to October in the North, year-round in the South	Highest rates in and near Hanoi
Western Pacific	Two epidemics reported in Guam and Saipan since 1947	Uncertain; possibly September to January	Enzootic cycle might not be sustainable; epidemics might follow introductions of virus

Adapted from the Centers for Disease Control and Prevention[37,38] and updated following the Global Alliance for Vaccines and Immunizations, Southeast Asia and Western Pacific Regional Working Group's Japanese Encephalitis Meeting: Setting the Global Agenda on Public Health Solutions and National Needs, Bangkok, Thailand, 2002.

South Korea for the first time. Epidemics in northern Vietnam followed in 1965 (currently 1,000 to 3,000 cases nationally per year) and in Chiang Mai, northern Thailand, in 1969 (currently 1,500 to 2,500 cases nationally each year). JE was recognized in southern India from 1955 but was confined to the south until the 1970s. Since then, large outbreaks (2,000 to 7,000 cases per year) have been reported from eastern and northeastern states. The fact that adults and children were equally affected in these Indian states supports the idea that the virus was introduced here for the first time. The late 1970s also saw the first cases in Burma (Myanmar) and Bangladesh and large epidemics (up to 500 cases per year) in Nepal. In 1985, Sri Lanka experienced its first epidemic, with 410 cases and 75 deaths. JEV continues to spread west, with cases occurring in Pakistan and new epidemics in the Kathmandu valley of Nepal.[40–42]

Charting the progression of JE southeast across Asia and the Pacific Rim is difficult because sporadic cases in endemic areas do not command the same attention as the massive epidemics associated with temperate climates. JE has appeared sporadically on the Western Pacific islands, with outbreaks in Guam in 1947 and Saipan (Northern Mariana Islands) in 1990.[43,44] In Malaysia, the disease is endemic, with the virus first isolated in the 1950s and approximately 100 cases annually.[45] Further east, JE occurs sporadically in the Philippines and New Guinea. The first cases occurred in the Australian Torres Strait islands in 1995, and JE was reported for the first time on the Australian mainland, north of Cairns, in 1998.[34,46]

The reasons for the spread of JE are incompletely understood but probably include changing agricultural practices, such as increasing irrigation (which allows mosquito breeding) and animal husbandry (which provides host animals). A single rice paddy can produce more than 30,000 adult mosquitoes in a day.[47] The risk of acquiring JE after a single mosquito bite is low. Even where transmission is intense, the infection rate of mosquitoes rarely exceeds 3%.[48] However, by one estimate, the minimum probability of an infectious mosquito bite in Tamil Nadu, India, was 0.47 to 0.77 per year.[49,50]

In developed countries, such as Japan, Taiwan, and South Korea, the number of cases of JE has fallen, probably because of a combination of mass vaccination of children, spraying of pesticides, changing pig-rearing practices, separation of housing from farming, better housing with air conditioning, and less availability of mosquito breeding pools.[51] The impact of factors other than vaccination is best demonstrated in Singapore. This country was previously endemic for JE but now has no disease, even though there is no vaccination program.[48] In some developed Asian countries, although JE is now rare in children, it is still seen in adults, particularly the elderly.[39]

Epidemic versus Endemic Disease

Broadly speaking, two epidemiologic patterns of JE are recognized.[39] In northern areas (northern Vietnam, northern Thailand, Korea, Japan, Taiwan, China, Nepal, and northern India), large epidemics occur during the summer months, whereas in southern areas (southern Vietnam, southern Thailand, Indonesia, Malaysia, Philippines, Sri Lanka), JE tends to be endemic; cases occur sporadically throughout the year, with a peak after the start of the rainy season.[39]

A variety of explanations for this different pattern have been offered. The observation that JEV genotypes I and III circulate in northern "epidemic" regions and II and IV in southern "endemic" regions led to the proposal that different genotypes might explain the differing clinical epidemiology.[26,27] However, the recent arrival of a "northern genotype I" isolate in Australia, the observation that genotype III is associated with epidemic disease in northern Vietnam and endemic disease in southern Vietnam, and the identification of a putative fifth genotype suggested that this paradigm was not right.[28,52,53] The distribution of genotypes is now thought to relate to the virus's origin in the Indonesia-Malaysia region and that the spread of the more recently evolved genotypes is from there also.[8,31]

An alternative hypothesis is that the clinical epidemiology relates to climate. Comparisons of climatic data from northern and southern Vietnam suggested that temperature might be a key determinant of disease pattern.[53] Whereas rainfall patterns are almost identical in northern and southern Vietnam, the temperature is very different, and the number of encephalitis cases appears to follow temperature closely. In the south, the temperature remains high throughout the year, and the number of cases each month is unchanged. In the north, a rise in JE cases during the summer months corresponds with a rise in temperature. The prolonged mosquito larval development time and longer extrinsic incubation period of JEV at cooler temperatures, which thus reduce the rate of virus transmission, could be one explanation for these observations.

Epidemiology of Human Disease

Humans become infected with JEV coincidentally when living or traveling in close proximity to the virus's enzootic cycle. Although most cases occur in rural areas, JEV is also found on the edge of some Asian cities, including Ho Chi Minh City in Vietnam and Bangkok in Thailand, and outbreaks have been reported from Lucknow, India.[48,54] Epidemiologic studies have shown that following the monsoon rains, mosquitoes breed prolifically, and as their numbers grow, so does their carriage of JEV and the infection rate of pigs.[55,56] Human infection soon follows. In sentinel studies, previously unexposed pigs placed in endemic areas were infected with the virus within weeks.[57]

Although the virus has occasionally been isolated from human peripheral blood, viremias are usually brief and titers low; thus, man is considered a dead-end host from which transmission does not normally occur (see Figure 10-2).[58] Cross-sectional serologic surveys have shown that in rural Asia, the majority of the population is infected with JEV during childhood or early adulthood.[59] Approximately 10% of the susceptible population is infected each year.[38] However, most infections of humans are asymptomatic or result in a nonspecific, flu-like illness; estimates of the ratio of symptomatic to asymptomatic infection vary between 1 in 25 and 1 in 1,000.[60,61]

When epidemics first occur in new locations, for example, in Sri Lanka, India, and Nepal, adults as well as children are affected.[62] The susceptibility of immunologically naive adults was also demonstrated by the incidence of JE among American troops during conflicts in Japan, Korea, and Vietnam.[63–67] The risk of developing symptoms seems to be higher in these troops than in the local population (possibly because for the local population, previous exposure to other flaviviruses reduces the severity of infection with JEV).

Incidence

Although JE is a disease that is reportable to the World Health Organization (WHO), official figures vastly underestimate the true incidence. For example, in the Philippines and Indonesia, few cases are officially reported, yet hospital-based studies show up to 50% of encephalitis patients have JE. One reason for underreporting has been the difficulty in establishing the diagnosis, but with the availability of new diagnostic tests based on immunoglobulin M (IgM) capture enzyme-linked immunosorbant assays (ELISAs), this should become easier.[68–71] JE is primarily a disease of children and young adults. In most affected areas, the incidence is 1 to 10 per 10,000. In northern Thailand, the incidence has been estimated to be up to 40 per 100,000 for ages 5 to 25 years, declining to almost zero for those over 35 years.[59,72] The incidence is lower in infants and young children (< 3 years old) than in older children, possibly reflecting behavioral factors, for example, playing outside, particularly after dusk.[39]

Although a figure of 35,000 to 50,000 reported cases is often quoted, estimates of the disease burden based on incidence rates suggest that the number of cases is much higher. Data from Taiwan and Thailand looking at the incidence among nonvaccinated children during placebo-control JE vaccine trials suggest an incidence of 1.8 to 2.5 per 10,000, whereas unvaccinated children in trials in China had an incidence of 5.7 to 64 per 10,000.[48,59,73] Using 1994 population estimates that 700 million Asian children (< 15 years) live in rural areas at risk of JEV and assuming a representative incidence rate of 2.5 per 10,000 (and no vaccination), the annual incidence of JE was estimated to be 175,000 cases, with 43,750 deaths and 78,750 survivors having severe disabilities.[73] Allowing for vaccine coverage, the expected number of cases was more than 125,000.[73]

Epidemiology among Travelers and Expatriates

Until the 1980s, vaccination against JE was rarely considered for travelers and expatriates. Then, in 1982, an American student who was spending a year at Peking University developed JE and died. His father, a Washington lawyer, was outraged that the vaccine was not even an option in the United States and used his good connections with government officials to ensure that the vaccine soon became available through the United States Centers for Disease Control and Prevention (CDC) as an investigational new drug.[74] The vaccine subsequently received full licensure after efficacy trials conducted by the United States Army in Thailand (see "Efficacy").

No systematically collected data exist on the incidence of JE among travelers or expatriates (including military personnel and other foreign residents), though cases are reported in the literature and have been surveyed informally.[48] A review of 24 cases reported to the CDC between 1978 and 1992 showed that 11 had occurred in expatriates, 8 of whom were military personnel or their dependents and 1 or 2 of whom were thought to be tourists.[38] Outcome information was available for 15, of whom 6 died: 5 were disabled, and 4 recovered. Taking Department of Transport figures indicating that 2 to 3 million US citizens travel by air to Asia each year, and allowing for the fact that most travelers have brief itineraries that do not include staying in areas with an exposure risk and that some will have been immunized, an annual incidence was estimated at roughly one per million. Based on these data, immunization against JE was recommended by the United States Advisory Committee on Immunization Practices (ACIP) for those staying in Asia for a month or more, or a shorter time if likely to be at a greater risk of exposure (see following discussion).[38] However, with so many unknown variables, it is difficult to know how reliable this estimate of risk really is. An alternative approach is to extrapolate from the incidence rates in the local population. Assuming an annual incidence of 10 per 10,000 and recognizing that most cases occur in a 5-month period, the risk of developing JE during a 1-month visit in the transmission season was estimated at 1 per 5,000 or 1 per 20,000 per week.[38] These rates are similar to the attack rates for nonimmunized Western military personnel exposed during field operations in Asia between 1945 and 1991 (0.05 to 2.1 per 10,000 per week).[60,75]

The cases of JE that have occurred in tourists have shown limitations in our understanding of the risk factors. Three foreigners staying in hotels in Bali, Indonesia, for 2 weeks or less developed JE. In the 1980s, an Australian child developed the disease after a 2-week holiday but recovered.[76] A female Swedish tourist developed JE in March 1994, and a fatal case occurred in January 1995 in a Danish man.[77,78] Two of these cases occurred after the ACIP recommendations had been published and in line with those recommendations, the tourists had not been vaccinated because they were on short trips and were not visiting a known epidemic area. It has been suggested that Bali might reflect a unique situation because of the close proximity of tourist hotels and beaches to areas with intense enzootic viral transmission. Although it might be argued that there will inevitably be some unlucky individuals who will develop disease despite following the recommendations for vaccination, it could alternatively be argued that these cases in Bali indicate the failings of the vaccination policy. The recently published guidelines are less specific about the duration of a trip. Further cases among travelers were reported in 1996, but none appear to have been reported since then, possibly because the publicity caused by these cases resulted in more travelers being vaccinated.[48]

Vaccination policies in countries other than the United States have tended to follow this reactive rather than proactive approach. For example, the Israeli public health authorities now recommend JE vaccine for all Israeli travelers going to Thailand following a single case that occurred in a nonvaccinated traveler.[1] In the Kathmandu valley of Nepal, JE cases have been seen among Nepalis since 1995, and serosurveys of pigs have shown widespread virus activity.[41,79] Long-term expatriates are now being vaccinated, but, unfortunately, it seems that vaccination for travelers will not be recommended until the first case in a traveler is seen.[1]

CLINICAL FEATURES

Patients with JE typically present after a few days of nonspecific febrile illness, which can include coryza, diarrhea, and rigors. This is followed by headache, vomiting, and a reduced level of consciousness, often heralded by a convulsion. In some patients, particularly older children and adults, abnormal behavior might be the only presenting feature, resulting in an initial diagnosis of mental illness: during the Korean conflict, American servicemen with JE were initially diagnosed as having "war neurosis."[65] A proportion of patients make a rapid, spontaneous recovery (so-called abortive encephalitis). Others present with aseptic meningitis and have no encephalopathic features.[80]

Seizures

Seizures occur frequently in JE and have been reported in up to 85% of children and 10% of adults.[64,81,82] In some children, a single seizure is followed by a rapid recovery of consciousness, resulting in a clinical diagnosis of febrile seizure. Generalized tonic-clonic seizures occur more often than focal motor seizures. Multiple or prolonged seizures and status epilepticus are associated with hypoxic brain metabolism, raised intracranial pressure, clinical signs consistent with brainstem herniation, and a poor prognosis.[80] In a proportion of children, subtle motor seizures occur, causing twitching of a digit, an eye, or the mouth; eye deviation; nystagmus; excess salivation; or irregular respiration. Without electroencephalographic monitoring, these subtle motor seizures might be difficult to document.[80]

Parkinsonism and Other Movement Disorders

The classic description of JE includes a Parkinson's disease–like dull, flat, "mask-like" facies with wide, unblinking eyes, tremor, generalized hypertonia, and cogwheel rigidity. These features were reported in 70 to 80% of American service personnel and 20 to 40% of Asian children.[81,83] Opisthotonos (Figure 10-3) and rigidity spasms, particularly on stimulation, occur in about 15% of patients and are associated with a

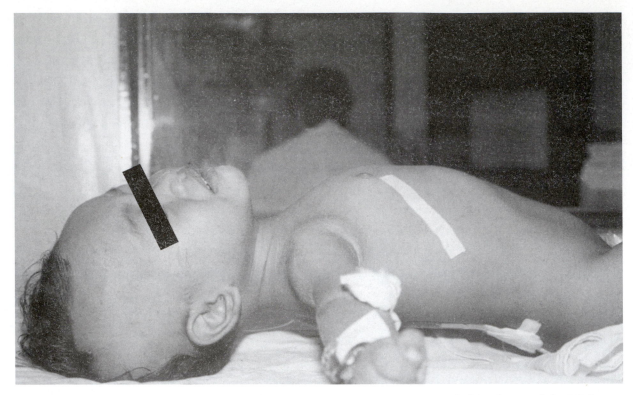

Figure 10-3. Opisthotonos and other movement disorders are common in Japanese encephalitis. Photograph by T. Solomon reproduced with permission from Solomon T.[84]

poor prognosis.[81,83,84] Other extrapyramidal features include head nodding and pill-rolling movements, opsoclonus-myoclonus, choreoathetosis, bizarre facial grimacing, and lip smacking.[81,83,85] Radiologic studies support earlier pathologic studies implicating the basal ganglia and thalamus in the parkinsonian syndromes seen in JE.[85–87] Upper motor neuron facial nerve palsies occur in approximately 10% of children and can be subtle or intermittent.

Acute Flaccid Paralysis

A subgroup of patients infected with JEV present with a poliomyelitis-like acute flaccid paralysis.[88] Following a short febrile illness, there is a rapid onset of flaccid paralysis in one or more limbs, despite a normal level of consciousness. Weakness occurs more frequently in the legs than in the arms and is usually asymmetric. Of these patients, 30% subsequently developed encephalitis, with a reduced level of consciousness and upper motor neuron signs, but, in the majority, acute flaccid paralysis is the only feature. At follow-up (1 to 2 years later), there is persistent weakness and marked wasting in the affected limbs (Figure 10-4).[88] Nerve conduction studies demonstrated markedly reduced compound muscle action potentials, and electromyography showed a chronic partial denervation pattern, suggesting anterior horn cell damage.[88] Flaccid paralysis also occurs in comatose patients with JE, being reported in 5 to 20%.[64,89] Electrophysiologic studies have confirmed anterior horn cell damage, and magnetic resonance imaging (MRI) of the spinal cord has shown abnormal signal intensity on T2-weighted images, which is probably the radiologic correlate of the inflammation in the anterior horn of the spinal cord that is seen at autopsy.[7,86]

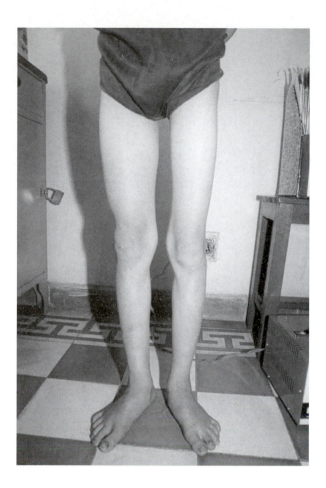

Figure 10-4. Poliomyelitis-like acute flaccid paralysis. This child has marked weakness and wasting a year after the initial presentation. Photograph by T. Solomon reproduced with permission from Solomon T et al.[88]

Investigations

A peripheral neutrophil leukocytosis is seen in most patients, and hyponatremia can occur as a consequence of the syndrome of inappropriate antidiuretic hormone secretion (SIADH). The cerebrospinal fluid (CSF) opening pressure is elevated in approximately 50% of patients. Typically, there is a moderate CSF pleocytosis of 10 to 100 cells per mm^3, with predominant lymphocytes, mildly elevated protein (50 to 200 mg %), and a normal glucose ratio. However, polymorphonuclear cells may predominate early in the disease or there might be no CSF pleocytosis.[81]

In approximately 50% of patients with JE, computed tomography (CT) scans show bilateral, nonenhancing, low-density areas in one or more of the thalamus, basal ganglia, midbrain, pons, and medulla.[90,91] MRI is more sensitive, typically demonstrating more extensive lesions, including damage in the cerebral hemispheres, cerebellum, and anterior spinal cord of patients with flaccid paralysis.[86,92] Thalamic lesions of mixed intensity on T1 and T2 are often seen and are suggestive of hemorrhage.[85,86] They may be useful in distinguishing JE from herpes simplex encephalitis, where the changes are characteristically frontoparietal.[93] Single photon emission CT (SPECT) studies carried out acutely can show hyperperfusion in the thalamus and putamen.[94] Follow-up studies have shown hypoperfusion in the same areas as well as in the frontal lobes.[85]

A variety of electroencephalographic abnormalities have been reported in JE, including theta and delta coma, burst suppression, periodic lateralized epileptiform discharges and other epileptiform activity and, occasionally, alpha coma.[80,91,93,95]

Diagnosis

The differential diagnosis of JE is broad and includes other viral encephalitides (arboviruses, herpesviruses, enteroviruses, postinfectious and postvaccination encephalomyelitis), other central nervous system (CNS) infections (bacterial and fungal meninigitis, tuberculosis, cerebral malaria, leptospirosis, tetanus, abscesses), other infectious diseases with CNS manifestations (typhoid encephalopathy, febrile convulsions), and noninfectious diseases (tumors, cerebrovascular accidents, Reye's syndrome, toxic and alcoholic encephalopathies, epilepsy).[3] Distinguishing encephalitis from partially pretreated bacterial meningitis and cerebral malaria might be particularly difficult.

Attempts at isolating JEV from clinical specimens are usually unsuccessful, probably because of low viral titers and the rapid production of neutralizing antibodies. Isolates can sometimes be obtained from brain tissue (either at autopsy or from a postmortem needle biopsy) or from CSF, in which case it is associated with a failure of antibody production and a high mortality rate.[96] Immunohistochemical staining of CSF cells or autopsy tissue with anti-JEV polyclonal antibodies can be positive.[97,98] However, in most cases, JE is diagnosed serologically. The hemagglutination inhibition test was used for many years, but it had various practical limitations and, because it required paired sera, could not give an early diagnosis.[99] In the 1980s, IgM and IgG capture ELISAs were developed and have become the accepted standard for diagnosis of JE.[69,100] The presence of anti-JEV IgM in the CSF has a sensitivity and specificity of greater than 95% for CNS infection with JEV.[101] ELISAs are now commercially available and have also been modified to a kit form that requires no specialist equipment, which might be useful for diagnosing JE in small rural hospitals.[70,71] JEV ribonucleic acid (RNA) has been detected in human CSF samples using reverse transcriptase polymerase chain reaction.[40,102] However, its reliability as a routine diagnostic test has not been shown.

MANAGEMENT AND ANTIVIRAL TREATMENT

Treatment for JE is supportive and involves controlling convulsions and raised intracranial pressure when they occur. For many years, corticosteroids were given, but a double-blind randomized placebo-controlled trial of dexamethasone failed to show any benefit.[103] Aspiration pneumonia is a common occurrence in patients with a reduced gag reflex. Careful nursing care and physiotherapy are needed to reduce the risk of bedsores, malnutrition, and contractures. There is no established antiviral treatment for JE or any other flavivirus infection. A variety of compounds have shown antiviral activity in vitro and/or in animal models of infection.[104] In animal studies, passive immunization with polyclonal or mixed monoclonal antibodies given peripherally and intrathecally was effective.[105] This has also been attempted in a small number of patients, but experience from similar treatment of tick-borne encephalitis suggests it is unlikely to be useful unless given before encephalitis has developed and might even worsen outcome.[106,107]

Recently, salicylates and nonsteroidal anti-inflammatory drugs were shown to suppress the in vitro replication of JEV and prevent apoptosis of infected cells.[108,109] This did not appear to be via suppression of nuclear factor κB activation but might be via mitogen-activated kinase.[109] Interferon-α, a glycoprotein cytokine that is produced naturally in response to viral infections, including JE, had been the most promising antiviral candidate.[110] In tissue culture, recombinant interferon is effective against JEV and other arboviruses, including West Nile virus.[111,112] In the 1980s, it was given in open trials to a small number of Thai JE patients with encouraging results[113] However, a recently completed double-

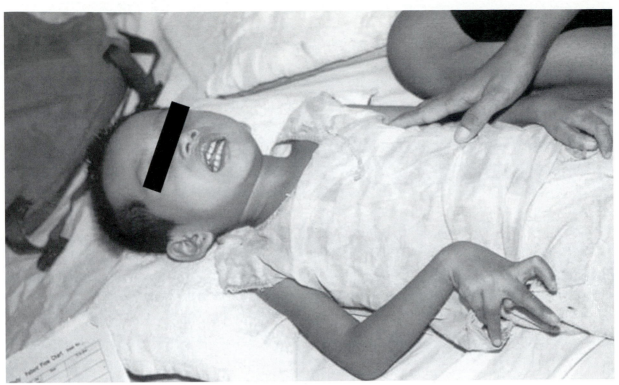

Figure 10-5. Sequelae of Japanese encephalitis: flexion deformities are apparent in this child 2 months after the initial illness. Photograph by T. Solomon reproduced with permission from Solomon T.[84]

blind placebo-controlled trial in Vietnamese children with JE (the first randomized controlled antiviral trial for any flavivirus) showed that it made no impact on the overall outcome.[114]

Outcome

Approximately 30% of hospitalized patients with JE die, and around half of the survivors have severe neurologic sequelae. However, in areas with better hospital facilities, there is a reduction in mortality but a concomitant increase in the number of patients with severe sequelae. Poor prognostic indicators include a depressed level of consciousness, abnormal breathing and decerebrate posturing, multiple seizures, raised intracranial pressure, isolation of virus from the CSF, low levels of JE virus–specific IgM and IgG in CSF and serum, and immune complexes in the CSF.[80,81,115,116] Other indicators that have been found in some, but not all, populations studied include higher admission temperature, absent abdominal reflexes, hyponatremia, low serum iron, and elevated CSF white cell counts and protein.[80,81,117–119] Approximately 30% of survivors have frank motor deficits. These result in a mixture of upper and lower motor neuron weakness and cerebellar and extrapyramidal deficits.[66,120] Hyperextension of the legs, with "equine feet," and fixed-flexion deformities of the arms are common (Figure 10-5). Twenty percent of patients have severe cognitive and language impairment (most with motor impairment too), and 20% have convulsions.[121,122] A higher rate of sequelae is reported for children than for adults.[123] In addition, the more detailed studies have shown that approximately half of those who were classed in the "good recovery" group have subtle sequelae, such as learning difficulties, behavioral problems, and subtle neurologic signs.[121]

Pathogenesis

Only about 1 in 25 to 1 in 1,000 humans infected with JEV develop clinical features of infection.[60,61] These can range from a mild, flulike illness to a fatal meningoencephalomyelitis. The factors determining which of all the humans infected with JEV will develop disease are unknown but could include viral factors, such as route of entry, titer of the inoculum, strain virulence, and host factors such as age, genetic make-up, general health, and preexisting immunity.

Humans become infected from the bite of an infected mosquito. Following inoculation, the virus is thought to replicate in the skin before being transported to local lymph nodes. Langerhans' dendritic cells migrating from the skin to the lymph nodes have recently been implicated in this transport in experimental intradermal infection of BALB/c mice with West Nile virus and in volunteers receiving candidate live attenuated dengue virus vaccines.[124,125]

The means by which JEV crosses the blood-brain barrier is unknown. In experimental studies with a hamster model of the related flavivirus, St. Louis encephalitis virus, the olfactory route was shown to be important.[126] Intranasal spraying is also an effective means of experimentally inoculating monkeys.[127] However, immunohistochemical staining of human JE autopsy material has shown diffuse infection throughout the brain, indicating a hematogenous route of entry.[98] Although experimental evidence suggests that replication within endothelial cells might be an important means of crossing the blood-brain barrier in some flaviviruses, for JEV, passive transfer across the endothelial cells appears a more likely mechanism.[128,129] Other factors that compromise the integrity of the blood-brain barrier have also been implicated as risk factors for neuroinvasion. In several studies, a disproportionate number of fatal cases had neurocysticercosis at autopsy, and it has been suggested that head trauma (eg, due to a road traffic accident) during the incubation period could facilitate viral entry into the central nervous system.[130–132]

Virulence Determinants

In animal models, JEV strains differ in both their neuroinvasiveness (following peripheral inoculation) and neurovirulence (following intracranial inoculation). This might be a consequence of the high viremia achieved by some strains. In mice, JEV strains with higher neurovirulence produce higher viremias than those with lower neurovirulence.[133,134] An analysis of the nucleotide and amino acid sequence showed that changes in the structural, nonstructural, and noncoding regions were associated with neurovirulent strains. The E protein has been shown to have a major role in determination of the virulence phenotype, and single amino acid substitutions are sufficient to cause loss of neurovirulence or neuroinvasiveness.[135,136] Two mechanisms mediated by the E protein might be involved: attachment of the virus to the receptor and fusion of viral and host cell membranes. The putative receptor-binding site of flaviviruses lies in an exposed hydrophilic region of domain III of the envelope protein, which in some mosquito-borne flaviviruses includes the integrin-binding motif arginine-glysine-aspartate (RGD). Substitutions around position E-306 on the exposed lateral surface of domain III, at or close to this RGD motif, are associated with loss of neuroinvasiveness.[133,137,138] Another group of flavivirus variants with altered virulence has amino acid changes in the putative hinge region. For example, in several studies of JEV and Murray Valley encephalitis virus, neutralization escape variants with low neuroinvasiveness for mice have shown changes around positions 52 and 270 to 277 of the E protein, both of which lie in this hinge region.[139–141] A substation at E279 in a chimeric yellow fever–Japanese encephalitis virus (see below) was recently shown to affect neurovirulence for mice and monkeys.[142]

Histopathology

At autopsy, CNS findings in JE reflect the inflammatory response to widespread neuronal infection with the virus.[7,143,144] The leptomeninges are normal or hazy. The brain parenchyma is congested with focal petechiae or hemorrhage in the gray matter. When survival is prolonged beyond 7 days, blotchy, necrolytic zones are seen. The white matter usually appears normal. In some patients, the gray matter of the spinal cord is confluently discolored, resembling that of poliomyelitis.[145] The thalamus, basal ganglia, and midbrain are heavily affected, providing anatomic correlates for the tremor and dystonias that characterize JE. At the histologic level, invasion of neurons by JEV is followed by perivascular cuffing, infiltration of inflammatory cells (T cells and macrophages) into the parenchyma, and phagocytosis of infected cells.[7,143] T cells in the brains of fatal cases stained with monoclonal antibodies are CD8+ and CD8− (presumed to be CD4+) and are localized at the perivascular cuff. Both cell types are found in the CSF in acute infection, though the predominant cell type is CD4+.[143] In patients that die rapidly, there might be no histologic signs of inflammation, but immunohistochemical studies reveal viral antigen in morphologically normal neurons.[143,146] This might explain the normal CSF findings in a proportion of patients with Japanese encephalitis.

Immune Response

Interferon and interferon inducers are active against JEV in mice and monkeys, and endogenous interferon-α has been detected in the plasma and CSF of humans with JE.[101,147,148] In addition, both humoral and cellular immune responses occur following infection with JEV. The humoral immune response in JE has been well characterized. In primary infection (ie, when JEV is the first flavivirus with which an individual has been infected), a rapid and potent IgM response occurs in serum and CSF within days of infection. By day 7, most patients have elevated titers.[101] Attempts to isolate virus are usually negative in such patients. However, the failure to mount an IgM response is associated with positive virus isolation and a fatal outcome.[96] Antibodies to JEV may protect the host by restricting viral replication during the viremic phase, before the virus crosses the blood-brain barrier.[149] Evidence from other flaviviruses suggests it may also limit damage during established encephalitis by neutralizing extracellular virus and facilitating lysis of infected cells by antibody-dependent cellular cytotoxicity.[150]

In surviving patients, class switching occurs, and within 30 days, most have IgG in the serum and CSF. Asymptomatic infection with JEV is also associated with elevated IgM in the serum but not in the CSF. In patients with secondary infection (ie, those who have previously been infected with a different flavivirus such as dengue infection or yellow fever vaccination), there is an anamnestic response to flavivirus group common antigens.[100] This secondary pattern of antibody activation is characterized by an early rise in IgG with a subsequent slow rise in IgM.

In animal models of JE, the cellular immune response appears to contribute to the prevention of disease during acute infection by restricting virus replication before the nervous system is invaded. Athymic nude mice have increased susceptibility to experimental infection with JEV and transfer of spleen cells from mice immunized with live attenuated virus conveys immunity to infection.[151,152] Spider monkeys, which are normally unaffected by intracerebrally inoculated JEV, develop rapidly progressive encephalitis when T-cell function has been impaired by cyclophosphamide.[153]

In humans infected with St. Louis encephalitis virus, impairment of T-cell function by human immunodeficiency virus (HIV) appears to increase the risk of developing encephalitis.[154] By analogy with other human viral infections, including influenza, HIV, Epstein-Barr virus, and dengue, cytotoxic T lymphocytes might be important in the control and, possibly, the clearance of JEV.[155,156] Preliminary experimental evidence is in agreement with this: T-lymphocyte responses were characterized in 7 convalescent JE patients and 10 vaccine recipients of the formalin-inactivated vaccine, JEV-specific T-cell proliferation (including CD4+ and CD8+ T-lymphocyte responses) was demonstrated in both groups.[157] JEV-specific and flavivirus–cross-reactive CD4+ T lymphocytes that recognize E protein in an HLA-restricted manner were recently demonstrated in two vaccine recipients.[158]

Effect of Heterologous Antiflavivirus Antibodies

Many JE-endemic areas are also endemic for dengue and other flaviviruses, such as Tembusu and Langat viruses. In dengue infection, the presence of heterologous antibodies to other dengue virus serotypes appears to be associated with more severe disease (due to a postulated Fc-γ receptor–mediated antibody-dependent enhancement of virus entry into macrophages) (see Chapter 13, "Dengue Fever Vaccine").[159–161] However, in JE the evidence suggests that rather than making the disease more severe, the presence of prior dengue antibodies might afford some protection against severe disease.[72,118,162,163] Thus, patients with a secondary flavivirus infection are less likely to die or have severe sequelae than are those with primary infection.[118] Younger children with JE tend to have a worse outcome, which might be a reflection of their having had less exposure to other flaviviruses.[123] Preexisting dengue virus antibodies have also been postulated as one reason why the apparent-to-inapparent infection ratio is much lower in indigenous populations (1 in 300) than it was in nonindigenous American service personnel (1 in 25).[39,60] In a similar way, during the 1962 Florida epidemic of St. Louis encephalitis virus, the age-adjusted clinical attack rates were much lower in those with prior dengue immunity than in those without.[164]

NONVACCINE PREVENTIVE MEASURES

Broadly speaking, measures to control JE include those that interfere with the virus's enzootic cycle and those that prevent disease in humans. Measures to control breeding of *Culex* mosquitoes, such as the application of larvicides to rice fields and insecticide spraying, have largely proved ineffectual. Alternative, more ecologically friendly methods that might be useful include the application of the natural insecticide neem (which is also a fertilizer for the rice) to rice fields, placing larvivorous fish in rice paddies, and using intermittent irrigation of rice paddies, which disrupts the mosquitoes' breeding but does not impair rice yields (indeed, it might provide better yields for the water consumed).[165,166] *Culex* mosquitoes breed preferentially on cattle, yet cattle are dead-end hosts for JEV. Thus, using cattle to divert mosquitoes away from swine and humans (zooprophylaxis) might have a role.[167,168]

Inactivated and live attenuated vaccines (described below) have been used to protect swine against JEV; however, widespread vaccination is not feasible in most settings. Residents and travelers to endemic areas should take personal protection to reduce the number of *Culex* bites. These include minimizing outdoor exposure at dusk and dawn, wearing clothing that leaves a minimum of exposed skin, using insect repellents containing at least 30% DEET (N,N-diethyl-3-methlybenzamide), and sleeping under bed nets. Although these measures might be possible for the short-term visitor, they are not practical for many residents of endemic areas.

Table 10-3. **Summary of Vaccines against Japanese Encephalitis**

Description	Virus Strain	Common Name	Manufacture/Developer	Notes
INACTIVATED VACCINES				
Mouse brain	Nakayama	BIKEN	BIKEN, Japan	Manufactured for international distribution
	Nakayama	Green Cross	Green Cross, S. Korea	Some available internationally
	Beijing-1	—	Japan	Manufactured for the domestic market
Primary hamster kidney	P3	—	China	Previously China's principal vaccine
Vero cell	P3	—	China	Recently licensed in China
	Beijing-1	—	Japan	In development
	SA14-14-2	—	US Army	In development
	P3	—	Aventis Pasteur	Abandoned after it caused febrile reactions in clinical trials
LIVE ATTENUATED VACCINES				
Primary hamster kidney	SA14-14-2	—	China	Widely used in China, also in trials in Nepal and South Korea
	SA14-5-3	—	China	Abandoned after clinical trials because poorly immmunogenic
RECOMBINANT VACCINES				
Canarypox vectored	—	NYVAC-JE	—	Abandoned because poorly immunogenic
Vaccinia vectored	—	ALVAC-JE	—	Abandoned because poorly immunogenic in vaccinia-immune individuals
17D yellow fever vectored	SA14-14-2	ChimeriVax-JE	Acambis	In development
DNA vaccine	Various	—	Japan	In development

VACCINES FOR JAPANESE ENCEPHALITIS

The only JE vaccine currently available for travelers is a formalin-inactivated mouse brain–derived vaccine. This comes from the Research Foundation for Microbial Disease of Osaka University (BIKEN), Japan and is distributed by Aventis Pasteur (Table 10-3).[169] A vaccine is also sometimes internationally available from Green Cross in Korea. In addition, formalin-inactivated mouse brain–derived vaccines are produced for local use in Taiwan, Thailand, and Vietnam. Two other vaccines are used widely in China: an inactivated vaccine grown in primary hamster kidney (PHK) cells and a live attenuated vaccine, known as SA14-14-2, which is having a great impact on JE control in China. In addition, a formalin-inactivated Vero cell–derived vaccine has recently been licensed in China, and other tissue culture–derived vaccines and genetically engineered recombinant vaccines are in development.

Inactivated Mouse Brain–Derived JE Vaccine

Work on inactivated mouse brain–derived vaccines began soon after JEV was first isolated in the 1930s in Japan. An immunogenic, efficacious, and relatively safe inactivated vaccine has been available for at least 30 years and has been used widely in wealthier Asian countries. In poorer Asian countries, its use has been limited by cost, difficulty of production, and issues over availability, whereas its use in travelers has been dominated by issues related to vaccine safety.

Vaccine Production

Following the isolation of JEV in the 1930s, the Japanese and Russians produced crude vaccines by growing the virus in mouse brain and then inactivating it in formalin.[170,171] During World War II, a similar vaccine was developed for the US Army by Albert Sabin (later of poliomyelitis fame) and colleagues. It was shown to be immunogenic and was given to 60,000 American soldiers during an encephalitis outbreak in Okinawa in 1945.[63] For several years postwar, the US armed forces used a chick embryo–derived inactivated vaccine but later abandoned it because the available data suggested it was not immunogenic or efficacious. Since the 1950s, the mouse brain vaccine has been refined by research institutes in Japan, and by 1966 it had been introduced for routine use in children. The current vaccine undergoes centrifugation, ultrafiltration, protamine sulphate precipitation, and then formalin inactivation, followed by further clarification, ultrafiltration and concentration, ammonium sulphate precipitation, ultracentrifugation on a sucrose density gradient, and then dialysis and concentration.[48] National standards in Japan specify minimal immunogenicity and potency in mice (compared with a vaccine standard), maximal protein content, and undetectable myelin basic protein (assay limit of detection 2 ng/mL). The vaccine is stabilized with gelatin and sodium glutamate and preserved with thimerosal. In Japan, the vaccine is distributed in liquid form, but for international distribution it is lyophilized (freeze dried). The production procedures of formalin-inactivated mouse brain vaccine in other Asian countries are similar to that in Japan.

Stability and Storage

The liquid and freeze-dried inactivated vaccines should be stored at 2°C to 8°C but should not be frozen. Lyophilized vaccine is stable at 4°C for at least a year. It retains more than 90% of its potency after 28 weeks at 22°C and 95% of its potency after 4 weeks at 37°C. Once it has been reconstituted, inactivated vaccine is stable for at least 2 weeks at 22°C, but at 37°C, the potency declines to 85%.[172]

Virus Strains Used

Most formalin-inactivated vaccines (including the BIKEN and Green Cross vaccines) are based on the original Nakayama strain of JEV isolated in 1935 and maintained by continuous mouse brain passage since then. However, since 1989 the vaccine produced for the domestic market in Japan has been prepared using the Beijing-1 strain, isolated in China in 1948 (see Table 10-3). The Beijing-1 strain has a higher potency, and in challenge experiments in mice, it elicited broader cross-reacting antibodies against various wild-type strains of JEV.[173] However, during a phase III clinical trial comparing monovalent Nakayama vaccine to bivalent Nakayama/Beijing-1 vaccine, the efficacy of the two vaccines was the same (see "Efficacy").[59] Recently, the question of whether these vaccines (which are based on genotype III strains of virus) are efficacious against other genotypes of JEV has been raised. A WHO-supported study is addressing this question, but no clinical or epidemiologic data suggest that it is a problem.

Dosage and Route

A variety of dosage regimens are used depending on the setting. The differing immunization schedules have been derived from immunogenicity studies, though, as explained later in this chapter, these have not always been conducted to a single standard. The volume of Nakayama-based vaccine administered per dose is 1 mL subcutaneously (0.5 mL for children age 1 to 2 years; 1.0 mL for children 3 years and older). Because the Beijing-1 vaccine is more potent, it is given at half this volume.

Immunogenicity Studies

Assays of Humoral Immunity. To determine the neutralizing antibody titer that is protective against JEV, mice were passively immunized with anti-JEV antibody and then challenged with live virus. The dose of challenge virus used in these experiments was 105 median lethal dose (MLD) of JEV (ie, 105 times the lethal dose50—the dose that kills 50% of the unimmunized mice), which is thought to be a typical dose transmitted by an infectious mosquito bite. In such challenge experiments, mice that had neutralizing antibody titers greater than 1 in 10 were found to be protected, whereas mice with lower titers were not.[174,175] Neutralizing antibody titers greater than 1 in 10 are also therefore taken to indicate postvaccination seroconversion and protection in humans, though no direct data support this.[48]

To measure neutralizing antibody titers, the plaque reduction neutralization test is most often used. The essence of the test is that when JEV is grown on a monolayer of Vero cells, or other appropriate cell substrate, it causes plaques to form. The number of plaques formed is reduced if the virus has been mixed with serum containing neutralizing antibody, and this reduction in plaques gives a measure of the antibody titer. No international standard for the exact procedure or choice of end points has been established. Thus, the challenge virus strains, cell systems, addition of exogenous complement (which facilitates binding of antibody to virus), and end points (ranging from 50% to 90% reduction in plaques) vary between laboratories. A comparison of results from three laboratories showed good correlation, and the issue is currently being examined further with the support of the WHO initiative for vaccine research.[176]

Immune Responses to Inactivated Vaccine. Studies of the immune response in vaccine recipients revealed important differences between residents of endemic areas and travelers, which have led to different vaccination schedules being recommended. When Asian children were vaccinated with a primary regimen of two doses of Nakayama or Beijing-1 strain–derived vaccines, 94 to 100% had neutralizing antibody to the homologous strain, though seroconversion rates against heterologous antigenic groups were lower.[177] Nearly 100% seroconversion was achieved following a 1-year booster dose. In contrast, seroconversion rates in travelers and military personnel from the United Kingdom and United States following a two-dose primary vaccination regimen were lower (33 to 80%).[178–181] By 6 to 12 months after vaccination, only 10% of vaccinees still had antibody titers greater than 1 in 8. A three-dose primary schedule was more effective, giving seroconversion in more than 90% of recipients and higher geometric mean titers.[180,181] The difference in vaccine immunogenicity between the two populations is presumed to be due to a degree of natural immunity among the Asian children because of exposure to JEV and other flaviviruses, particularly dengue; however, the differences in the age of the populations studied (most of the travelers and military personnel are adults) might also be important.

Cellular Immunity

Although immunogenicity studies of vaccine efficacy have focused on humoral immunity, cellular immune responses produced by inactivated vaccines might also be important. CD4+ and CD8+ T-cell memory has been demonstrated by lymphoproliferative responses to JE antigens in virus-like particles containing only structural proteins.[157] In addition, as described above, inactivated JE vaccine induces both JE-specific and flavivirus cross-reactive human leukocyte antigen (HLA)-restricted CD4+ cytotoxic T cells directed against the E protein of the virus. Thus, T-cell memory could be protective even in vaccinees who appear to be seronegative.[157,158]

Primary Vaccination Schedules

In endemic parts of Asia, a two-dose primary immunization schedule is used. Children typically receive their first dose at any age between 12 and 36 months; the second dose is given 7 to 30 days later (Table 10-4).[169] A booster dose is given at 1 year and then additional boosters are given every 1 to 3 years. In Japan and South Korea, where the incidence of JE has declined, the first dose is given at 18 months to 3 years. In Thailand, vaccination is initiated at 18 months, whereas in Sarawak, Malaysia, it is started at 9 months.

For travelers (and military personnel), a three-dose primary schedule is recommended because, as explained previously, a two-dose regimen fails to produce neutralizing antibody in approximately 20% of subjects (Table 10-5). ACIP recommends three doses on days 0, 7, and 30. If there is insufficient time available before departure, an accelerated regimen (days 0, 7, and 14) is recommended.[38] Both regimens produce nearly 100% seroconversion, but the accelerated regimen produces lower antibody titers when measured subsequently. Although not ideal, even two doses given 7 days apart produce antibody in 80% of recipients and so might be better than nothing. An interval of at least 10 days is recommended between the last dose of vaccine and the commencement of a trip because of the low risk of adverse events requiring medical attention (see "Adverse Events").[38,169]

Booster Doses

Precise recommendations are not possible because only limited data are available. Studies of US Army vaccine recipients showed that antibody titers were maintained for up to 3 years in nearly 95% of recipients, but field studies suggested greater variability.[180] Boosters at 2 to 3 years are currently recommended. In different parts of Asia, the practice has varied over time: annual boosters during childhood were given in Korea until the 1980s; in Japan boosters are given approximately every 5 years; in poorer countries that are able to afford only primary vaccination in a limited number of children, no boosters are given at all. Natural boosting by exposure to JEV, dengue, or other flaviviruses might be important in parts of Asia.

Immunosuppressed Recipients, Pregnancy, and Lactation

Because it is not a live vaccine, the BIKEN and other inactivated JE vaccines are safe in immunosuppressed individuals. In one comparison of infants with vertically acquired HIV and HIV-negative infants of HIV-infected women, there was a trend toward lower JEV seroconversion rates after vaccination in the HIV-positive children.[182] No specific information is available on vaccination in pregnancy or in lactation.

Table 10-4. **Vaccination Policy in Countries at Risk of Japanese Encephalitis**

Country	Policy	Vaccine Used	Schedule	Manufacture and Distribution
Australia	High-risk areas (Torres Strait islands)	Inactivated Nakayama mouse brain	3 doses given to adults and children in affected areas	5,000 doses, imported from Japan
China	All children	Inactivated P3 in PHK cells	2 doses, 1 wk apart at age 0–6 mos; boosters at 2, 3, and 7 yrs	100 million doses manufactured in total, being phased out
		Vero cell–derived inactivated P3	Used as booster for those that received PHK-derived P3 for primary immunization	200,000 doses in 2001
		Live attenuated SA14-14-2	0–2 yrs, boosters at age 2 and age 7 yrs	50 million doses annually
India	In response to epidemics	Inactivated Nakayama mouse brain	Children, 2 doses	Imported from Japan and Vietnam
Japan	All children	Inactivated Beijing-1 mouse brain	2 doses up to 4 wks apart at age 3 yrs; boosters at 1 yr, 9–12 yrs, and 14–15 yrs	11 million doses, manufactured locally
Malaysia	Implemented in stages, beginning with Sarawak	Inactivated Nakayama mouse brain	2 doses 1 mo apart at age 9 mos; booster at 18 mos	Imported from Japan
Nepal	Children in high-risk areas	Inactivated Nakayama mouse brain; live attenuated SA14-14-2 also used in trials	2 doses of inactivated; live attenuated used as a single dose	Inactivated imported from Japan; live attenuated imported from China
North Korea	All children	Inactivated Nakayama mouse brain	—	3.5 million doses manufactured locally
South Korea	All children	Inactivated Nakayama mouse brain; live attenuated SA14-14-2 has also been used in trials	2 doses, 1 to 4 wks apart at age 3 yrs; boosters at 1 yr and every 2 yrs up to age 14	6 million doses of inactivated manufactured locally; live attenuated imported from China
Taiwan	All children	Inactivated Nakayama mouse brain	2 doses 2 wks apart at age 15–27 mos; boosters at 1 yr and age 6 yrs	1.5 million doses manufactured locally
Thailand	Targeted to children in high-risk areas; incorporated into EPI* in northern provinces	Inactivated Nakayama mouse brain	2 doses up to 4 wks apart at age 18–24 mos; booster at 1 yr and age 7 yrs	1–2 million doses manufactured in country
Vietnam	Targeted to children in high-risk areas; being incorporated into EPI	Inactivated Nakayama mouse brain	2 doses 1 wk apart in children aged 1–5 yrs; booster 1 yr later	7 million doses manufactured in Hanoi in 2002 (previously 2 million annually)

Adapted from Monath[169] and updated following the Global Alliance for Vaccines and Immunizations, Southeast Asia and Western Pacific Regional Working Group's Japanese Encephalitis Meeting: Setting the Global Agenda on Public Health Solutions and National Needs, Bangkok, Thailand 2002.

The following countries have no vaccination policy: Bangladesh, Brunei, Cambodia, Indonesia, Laos, Myanmar (Burma), and Philippines .

EPI = Expanded Program on Immunization; PHK = primary hamster kidneys.

Table 10-5. **Summary of Information for Travelers**

General measures

In the evenings, travelers should wear clothing with long sleeves and trousers and use insect repellent containing DEET to minimize the risk of mosquito bites. They should stay in air-conditioned or screened rooms, or use bed nets, aerosol insecticides, and mosquito coils.

Indications for vaccination

BIKEN formalin-inactivated vaccine is recommended for travelers spending prolonged periods in rural areas where JE is endemic or epidemic (see Table 10-2), or those on shorter trips if likely to include extensive outdoor evening and night-time exposure to biting mosquitoes in rural areas. Previously, "prolonged" was specified as a month or more, but because in some parts of Asia the epidemiology is not well described and JE has occurred in short-term travelers, recent guidelines have been less specific, and some authors have recommended more liberal use of vaccine.*

Primary dosage schedules

- Preferred regimen: three 1.0 mL doses of BIKEN formalin-inactivated vaccine given subcutaneously on days 0, 7, and 30

- Accelerated 2 week regimen if traveling soon: three 1.0 mL doses of formalin-inactivated vaccine given on days 0, 7, and 14 (this regimen gives near 100% protection but lower antibody titers)

- One-week regimen: two 1.0 mL doses of formalin-inactivated vaccine given on days 0 and 7 (gives seroconversion in 80% of recipients, so is probably better than nothing)

For any regimen, the last dose should be given at least 10 days before travel to allow time for the immune response to develop and access to medical care in the event of a delayed adverse reaction. For infants and children < 3 years, a 0.5 mL dose should be given using the same routes and the same schedules. The vaccine is not recommended in pregnancy unless the risk of acquiring JE outweighs the theoretic risks of the vaccine

Boosters

Recommended at 2 years, then every 2 to 3 years if continuing risk of exposure to JEV (though conclusive data are lacking)

Adverse events

Approximately 20% of vaccinees have local cutaneous or mild systemic reactions (fever, headache, myalgias). Approximately 0.6% of vaccinees have had more serious allergic reactions (urticaria, angioedema, respiratory distress, anaphylaxis) that respond to adrenaline, antihistamines, or steroids. Vaccinees should be observed for 30 minutes after vaccination. Those with a history of urticaria or allergic reactions are at greater risk of adverse events. Severe neurologic adverse events are very rare (approximately 1 per million doses).

Adapted from Shlim DR and Solomon T[1] and the US Centers for Disease Control.[37,38]
DEET = N,N-diethyl-3-methylbenzamide; JEV = Japanese encephalitis vaccine.

Because of the theoretic risk to the fetus, vaccine is not normally recommended in pregnant women unless there is thought to be a strong risk of infection.

Efficacy

Two randomized double-blind placebo-controlled trials have assessed the efficacy of formalin-inactivated JE vaccines. In 1965, nearly 134,000 individuals in Taiwan were given either a single dose (22,000) or a double dose (112,000) of the Nakayama vaccine (a less purified form than today's vaccine), and nearly 132,000 children were given tetanus toxoid as placebo. The JE attack rates per 100,000 recipients were 18.2 in the placebo group, 9.0 in the single-dose group, and 3.6 in the double-dose group. Thus, a single dose of vaccine yielded 50% (95% CI: 26% to 88%) efficacy, and two doses gave 80% (95% CI: 71% to 93%) efficacy. The BIKEN JE vaccine was assessed in northern Thailand in the 1980s.[59] Children aged 1 year or older, in three groups of approximately 22,000, received two doses (1 week apart) of the BIKEN Nakayama vaccine, two doses of bivalent Nakayama/Beijing-1 vaccine, or tetanus toxoid as placebo. After a 2-year observation period, the JE attack rate in the placebo group was 51 per 100,000, whereas in both vaccine groups it was 5 per 100,000, giving a protective efficacy of 91% (95% CI: 70% to 90%).[59] These results were accepted by the United States Food and Drug Administration as evidence for efficacy, leading to licensure of the BIKEN vaccine.[38] Interestingly, during the follow-up period, the risks of dengue and dengue hemorrhagic fever were slightly lower in the vaccinated groups, which does not support the theoretic possibility that vaccination against JE might increase the risk of severe dengue disease (as discussed in "Effects of Heterologous Antiflavivirus Antibodies").

Adverse Events

Local and Nonspecific Adverse Events. In studies in the United States, Thailand, and the United Kingdom, approximately 20% of individuals reported localized tenderness, redness, or swelling, and 5 to 10% reported mild systemic side effects (headache, low-grade fever, myalgias, malaise, and gastrointestinal symptoms).[59,176,178,181,183,184] The incidence of these adverse events decreased with each dose in the three-dose primary vaccine series.

Neurologic Adverse Events. Because of the vaccine's neural-tissue substrate (mouse brain) there has always been a concern that an immune response raised against mouse neural tissue could attack the human nervous system causing autoimmune-type conditions such as acute disseminated encephalomyelitis (ADEM), Guillain-Barré syndrome, or related neuritis, polyneuritis, and demyelinating diseases. As discussed previously, the current purification procedures ensure that the amount of myelin basic protein in the vaccine is below the limit of detection (< 2 ng/mL), though there are no reported data on measurements of other neural proteins known to be associated with ADEM, such as proteolipid protein and myelin-oligodendrocyte glycoprotein. Experimental infection of guinea pigs and cynomolgus monkeys with 50 times the normal dose of vaccine did not result in clinical or histopathologic evidence of encephalomyelitis. Furthermore, as outlined later in this chapter, data from clinical studies suggest that the risk of serious neurologic adverse events is about one in a million, which is comparable to that for other vaccines, such as measles.

Most attempts at early monitoring of adverse events were simply documented cases, with no attempt at examining a control group. Eight neurologic reactions (mostly neuritis) were reported among 53,000 American soldiers vaccinated in 1945 with a crude, inactivated vaccine on Okinawa island, Japan, but similar cases occurred among nonvaccinees.[63] In Japan, a countrywide survey between 1957 and 1966 found 26 temporally-related events (meningitis, convulsions, demyelinating disease, polyneuritis), but the rates of vaccination and comparison with controls were not available.[171] Surveillance data from the manufacturers in Japan from 1965 through to 1989 suggested neurologic adverse events rates in children of 1 to 2.2 per million doses.[171,185,186] In the 1990s, following two ADEM cases temporally related to vaccination, a retrospective survey of 162 Japanese medical institutions identified 7 further cases over 22 years and estimated the incidence to be less than one per million vaccinees, though the denominator of vaccine recipients was poorly defined.[186,187] Similarly, ADEM following JE vaccination in a Danish traveler prompted a review of the national database for further cases.[185] This identified 2 additional cases in adults and gave an estimated risk of 1 in 50,000 to 1 in 75,000 vaccinees, far greater than in any other report.[188] In total, 16 ADEM cases were reported between 1992 and 1996 from Japan, South Korea, and Denmark (identified by passive reporting and retrospective case finding). Guillain-Barré, optic neuritis, and Bell's palsy have also on occasion been reported following JE vaccination, but the causal relationship is uncertain.

Hypersensitivity Reactions. As the formalin-inactivated JE vaccine became available to travelers from Europe, North America, and Australia, hypersensitivity reactions not previously reported were described.

These consisted of urticaria, angioedema, and bronchospasm. The incidence is reported to be 2 to 6 per 1,000 vaccinees in travelers and military personnel, whereas a study in Korean children gave a risk factor of 0.3 per 1,000 for similar reactions.[183,189–192] A review of vaccine administration data from Okinawa in 1945 suggests that allergic side effects were also seen there.[63] In a prospective study of nearly 15,000 US marines, the median time interval between immunization and onset of symptoms was 16 to 24 hours after the first dose and 96 hours after the second dose, though it could occur up to 14 days later.[189,190] Reactions could occur after the second or third dose even if the first dose had been given uneventfully. Most cases respond to outpatient treatment with antihistamines or corticosteroids, but hospitalization and intravenous steroids have been required. Three deaths due to anaphylaxis, or possibly a cardiovascular collapse syndrome with a different pathogenesis, have been attributed to the vaccine.[169,193,194] Other allergic phenomena reported include transient generalized pruritus and, rarely, erythema multiforme, erythema nodosum, and serum sickness–like disease with joint manifestations. Because of the risk of adverse reactions, vaccinees should be observed for 30 minutes after vaccination, and immunization should be completed at least 10 days before departure.[38]

The cause of these allergic reactions is not known. Numerous lots from different manufacturers have been implicated. Case-control studies have indicated an increased risk in those with a history of allergic disorders, such as urticaria and rhinitis, or of asthma; female sex; and young (adult) age.[189,191] Alcohol consumption in the prior 48 hours might also be implicated.[195] IgE antibodies to gelatin (used as a vaccine stabilizer) were demonstrated in three Japanese children with systemic allergic reactions, whereas IgG against gelatin appeared to be more important in those with later cutaneous reactions.[196,197]

The risk of adverse events was assessed by examining the postmarketing surveillance data from Japan and the United States. The rate of total adverse events per 100,000 doses was 2.8 in Japan and 15.0 in the United States. In Japan, 17 neurologic disorders were reported from April 1996 to October 1998, for a rate of 0.2 per 100,000 doses. In the United States, no serious neurologic adverse events temporally associated with JE vaccine were reported from January 1993 to June 1999. Rates for systemic hypersensitivity reactions were 0.8 and 6.3 per 100,000 doses in Japan and the United States, respectively. Data passively collected by the United States' Vaccine Adverse Events Reporting System (VAERS) indicate that characteristic hypersensitivity reactions with a delayed onset continue to occur among JE vaccine recipients.[198]

Inactivated Cell Culture–Derived Vaccines

Because of the limitations of the formalin-inactivated vaccines grown in mouse brain (cost, complexity of production, and concerns over adverse reactions) and the desire to improve immunogenicity, attention has focused on inactivated vaccines grown in cell culture. A variety of JEV strains have been used in a range of different tissues.

Studies in China showed primary hamster kidney cells (PHK cells, primary cell cultures derived from the kidneys of Syrian golden hamsters) gave the highest yield of JEV.

A formalin-inactivated vaccine produced from growing the P3 strain of JEV in PHK cells has been used in China since the 1960s and for many years was the country's principal JE vaccine.[48] The vaccine, which is not purified, is stabilized with 0.1% human serum albumin and presented as a liquid formulation. The primary course consists of two 0.5 mL subcutaneous doses given 1 week apart to children age 6 to 12 months, then boosters at 1 year, school entry, and age 10 years. After primary immunization, 60 to 70% of children have seroconverted, and booster doses elicit good recall immunity.[169] In five randomized field trials in

China involving a total of 480,000 children, the vaccine's efficacy ranged from 76 to 95%.[48] However, the need for repeated booster doses and its relatively low efficacy have meant that the vaccine is gradually being replaced with the live attenuated vaccine (see below).

Vaccines grown in Vero cells have also been developed. Vero is a continuous cell line derived from African green monkeys and is a conventional substrate for vaccine production with the advantage of quality, absence of animal proteins and allergens, and lower cost. One such vaccine, a formalin-inactivated P3 virus grown in Vero cells, has recently been licensed in China, and 200,000 doses were produced in 2001.[199] A similar vaccine developed by Aventis Pasteur reached clinical trials but was discontinued because of nonspecific febrile reactions, the cause of which was not known.[169] An inactivated Vero cell Beijing-1 strain vaccine is being developed by two Japanese companies, and a Vero cell–derived inactivated vaccine based on the live attenuated SA14-14-2 strain (see below) is being developed by the Walter Reed Army Institute of Research (WRAIR) in the United States.[200] Because this uses an attenuated rather than a virulent virus, production is easier, requiring only biosafety level 2 rather than level 3 facilities. In clinical trials, immune responses were disappointing after primary immunization (40 to 70%) but better after a booster dose.[169]

Live Attenuated SA14-14-2 Vaccine

The accomplishment by Dr. Yu Yong Xin and colleagues in developing a live attenuated vaccine against JEV has been likened to Max Theiler's Nobel prize–winning derivation of the 17D yellow fever vaccine strain.[73,201] Live attenuated SA14-14-2 vaccine was licensed in China in 1988, and more than 200 million doses have been delivered since then with an excellent record of safety and efficacy.

Vaccine Development

To produce a live attenuated JEV strain, wild-type strains were passaged empirically in a range of cell culture systems, including PHK, chick embryo (CE), and mouse embryo skin cells. A lack of virulence in mice, hamsters, or pigs suggested the possibility of safe use in humans. JEV strain SA14 was isolated from *Culex pipiens* larvae collected in Xian, China, in 1954.[201] It was passaged 11 times in weanling mice, then 100 times in PHK cells, at which stage it was no longer neurovirulent in monkeys but was not stable. To produce a stable, avirulent virus, it was then inoculated intraperitoneally into mice, harvested from the spleen, plaque-purified further in CE cells, and passaged subcutaneously in mice and orally in hamsters before further purification in PHK cells.[48] The resultant strain, SA14-5-3, did not revert to virulence after intracerebral passage in suckling mice and was still immunogenic. It was safe in humans but in large field trials in southern China had poor immunogenicity in flavivirus-naive subjects. To increase immunogenicity, the virus was therefore passaged subcutaneously in suckling mice five times and twice plaque-purified on PHK cells to produce strain 14-14-2, which was equally attenuated. SA14-14-2 is more immunogenic for mice than inactivated PHK vaccines and was protective against challenge experiments with JEV strains from Thailand, Indonesia, and Vietnam, which represented diverse genotypes.[202] The vaccine is produced from seed virus by infecting PHK cells and is manufactured as a freeze-dried product stabilized with gelatin and sorbitol. After reconstitution with normal saline, the vaccine must be used within 4 hours.

Biologic Characteristics. The virus neurovirulence in animals has been studied extensively. Compared with the parental SA14 strain, SA14-14-2 is attenuated in immunocompetent mice, hamsters, and nude and cytoxan-treated mice and in monkeys inoculated by the intrathalamic and intraspinal routes.[48] The virus replicates in C6/36 mosquito cells and also in *Culex tritaeniorhyncus* and other mosquitoes.[203] As for any live virus, one safety concern is the possibility of continuous circulation and reversion to a virulent form. There is a theoretic possibility that by feeding on a viremic, recently vaccinated human, a mosquito could become infected with SA14-14-2, and replicating in the mosquito, the strain could revert to virulence. However, the evidence suggests that this is unlikely to occur. Human viremias following vaccination are likely to be below the oral infection threshold of mosquitoes, and a related vaccine strain (SA-14-2-8) did not infect *Culex tritaeniorhyncus* orally.[169,204]

Genetic Basis of Attenuation. Although there are many silent mutations and amino acid changes between SA14-14-2 and the parental strain SA14, comparison with two other attenuated strains from earlier in the vaccine's development (SA14-2-8 and SA14-5-3) suggests that eight common amino acid changes from SA14 are important in attenuation; these include six changes in the virus's E protein (E107, E138, E176, E279, E315, E439) and single changes in nonstructural proteins NS2B, NS3, and NS4. Plotting the E-protein mutations onto the three-dimensional model of the flavivirus envelope protein showed they occurred in domains I, II, and III.[21,169] To examine which combination of E-protein changes might be important in attenuation, the mutations were reverted to wild-type sequence singly or in combinations using an infectious chimeric clone that incorporates the structural genes of SA14-14-2 into the yellow fever 17D backbone (see "Chimeric Yellow Fever–JE Vaccine").[205] Virulence was assessed by intra-cerebral inoculation of mice. These studies showed that attenuation depended on at least three or four mutations, making it extremely unlikely that the virus would revert to a virulent form.[169]

Immunogenicity, Efficacy, and Adverse Events

SA14-14-2 vaccine has undergone many clinical trials in China and, more recently, South Korea and Nepal. After a single dose of SA14-14-2, 85 to 100% of children had seroconverted, but two doses given 1 to 3 months apart gave 99 to 100% seroconversion with higher geometric mean titers.[48,201,206,207] This regimen allows full protection of infants born before or during the summer transmission season and is compatible with incorporation into the Expanded Program on Immunization (EPI) schedule at 9 and 12 months of age. Currently, a third dose at school entry is administered in China, but it is not certain that this is necessary.

The vaccine's efficacy was demonstrated in five open-label field studies in China between 1988 and 1993 that involved nearly 600,000 children.[48] Comparisons of the incidence of JE in vaccinated and unvaccinated children showed a protective efficacy of approximately 98%. These findings were confirmed in a more rigorous, relatively simple and inexpensive postlicensure case-control study in which the prevalence of immunization was compared between 56 JE cases and 1,299 age- and village-matched controls.[208] The effectiveness of one dose was 80% (95% CI: 44% to 93%) and of two doses 1 year apart, 97.5% (CI: 86% to 99.6%). The efficacy of single-dose vaccine given just before the JE season was assessed in a similar case-control study in Nepal in 1999, when approximately 160,000 children were vaccinated.[209] None of 20 JE cases had received vaccine, compared with 326 of 557 age- and sex-matched village controls, giving a protective efficacy of 99.3% (CI: 94.9% to 100%). Interestingly, the data suggested protection occurred a median 2 weeks after vaccination. The mechanism of this early protection is unknown, and whether this single-dose vaccination with SA14-14-2 gives longer term protection is under investigation.

In the field studies involving more than 600,000 children, the vaccine had a very low incidence of side effects, which included fever, rash, nausea, and dizziness. Fever occurred in less than 5 per 10,000 recipients.[48]

Vaccine safety was also assessed in a postlicensure, randomized, placebo-controlled trial in 26,000 children.[210] One month after vaccination, the two groups had similar rates of hospitalization and illness. There were no cases of postvaccine anaphylaxis or neurologic disease.

The Vaccine's Future

SA14-14-2 vaccine has not had regulatory approval outside of China because of concerns about the PHK substrate, which is not an accepted cell line for vaccine production; uncertainty about the quality control tests for adventitious agents; and other issues related to good manufacturing practice (GMP). However, the WHO has recently developed guidelines to facilitate the international acceptance of the vaccine.[73] The key issues identified are testing of the hamster colonies (which should preferably be closed, "specified pathogen–free" colonies) and testing of the vaccine seeds to prove freedom from adventitious agents. In addition, evidence of continued attenuation for batches in animal tests and evidence of phenotypic stability will be important. Concerns have also been expressed about documentation of the raw materials, including bovine serum and hamster cells, used in the production of the original seed virus. These might be harder to address retrospectively, but given the vaccine's efficacy and apparent safety and the more experience with the vaccine grows, the less important these are likely to be.

COST-EFFECTIVENESS OF JE VACCINATION IN ASIA

Cost effectiveness analyses of JE vaccination have been conducted in Thailand and China.[211,212] In Thailand, it was estimated that incorporating the inactivated vaccine into routine immunization at 18 months (at a cost of $2.28 (US) per person) would prevent 124 cases (per 100,000 people), with a cost-effectiveness of $15,715, and would save $72,922 (in treatment costs, disability care, and loss of future earnings) for each prevented JE case. JE vaccination was thought to be worth implementing unless the incidence was below 3 per 100,000 population.[211] In Shanghai, China, a cost-effectiveness analysis estimated that immunization with inactivated P3 vaccine would prevent 420 JE cases and 105 deaths, saving 6,456 disability-adjusted life years (DALYs) per 100,000 people. The live attenuated SA14-14-2 vaccine would prevent a similar number of cases and deaths. Both vaccines resulted in costs savings compared with no vaccination, but the live vaccine would result in a greater cost saving ($512,456 per 100,000 people versus $348,246) because it is cheaper to produce.[212]

VACCINES IN DEVELOPMENT

Newer JE vaccines in development include genetically engineered recombinant vaccines, in which the JEV structural genes are delivered by established vaccine strains and DNA vaccines.

Vaccinia-Vectored Vaccines

Replication-deficient canarypox (ALVAC) and highly attenuated vaccinia viruses (NYVAC) have been used as vectors for delivering *PrM-E* or *PrM-E-NS1* genes.[213,214] The recombinant vaccines induced protective immunity in mice and monkeys in challenge experiments and proceeded to clinical studies. Because of the possibility that prior vaccination against smallpox would limit the response to these pox-vectored vaccines, the recombinant vaccines were tested in vaccinia-immune and vaccinia-naive individuals.[215]

ALVAC-JE was poorly immunogenic in all subjects. In contrast, NYVAC-JE elicited neutralizing antibody and T-cell responses in vaccinia-naive recipients but not in those that had previously been vaccinated against smallpox. Because the main commercial interest was for immunization of adult travelers, approximately half of whom were likely to be vaccinia immune, development of the vaccine has not continued.[169]

Chimeric Yellow Fever–JE Vaccine

In an alternative approach, the *PrM-E* genes of attenuated JEV strain SA14-14-2 were inserted into an infectious clone of the 17D yellow fever vaccine strain.[216] The chimeric virus (ChimeriVax-JE; Acambis, Cambridge, UK) replicated efficiently in vitro and was shown to be immunogenic, efficacious, and safe in mice and nonhuman primates, being even more attenuated than the original 17D yellow fever strain.[217,218] Attenuation of the chimeric virus was shown to depend on clusters of at least three of the six amino acid changes in the E protein.[205] The chimeric virus was incapable of infecting mosquitoes by oral feeding and had reduced replication after indirect intrathoracic inoculation, allaying fears of secondary transmission after vaccination and suggesting that it is unlikely to be transmitted by mosquitoes' biting recently vaccinated individuals.[203] The vaccine has been given to 12 human volunteers in a phase I trial and was shown to be safe and immunogenic.[219] Interestingly, in both humans and monkeys, prior yellow fever immunity did not reduce the response to the chimeric vaccine.[217] A similar approach using the same 17D yellow fever virus backbone is being used to develop chimeric vaccines against West Nile virus and dengue (see Chapter 13, "Dengue Fever Vaccine").[220]

DNA Vaccine

Plasmid DNA vaccines containing JEV *PrM-E* genes under the control of a cytomegalovirus promoter have produced promising results in mice and swine. In mice, intramuscular or intradermal inoculation with two doses of plasmid DNA produced neutralizing antibodies, T-cell memory, and CD8+ cytotoxic T-cell responses against the E protein, and protected against lethal JE challenge.[221] In swine, two intramuscular doses produced high antibody titers and high anamnestic responses to challenge with live attenuated virus.[222] Another vaccine in development includes the secretory signal sequence derived from tissue plasminogen activator fused to either the full-length or partial JEV envelope protein gene. Cells transfected with the latter construct secreted E protein and produced better protection against intracerebral challenge in mice.[223]

CONCLUDING COMMENTS

Since outbreaks of encephalitis were first recognized in Japan in the 1870s, the story of JE has been one of remarkable achievements in virology and vaccine development against a disease that continues to spread and for which there is no antiviral treatment. In some parts of Asia, these achievements have translated into public health policy and have had a large impact on disease control, whereas in developing countries, JE is still a major cause of morbidity and death. For travelers, uncertainties still remain about the risk-benefit ratio of the inactivated JE vaccine. The development of newer, safe vaccines might make these decisions easier for travelers, but there is a need to ensure that such vaccines reach those most in need of them.

ACKNOWLEDGMENTS

I thank David Vaughn, Scott Halstead, Julie Jacobson, and Jane Cardosa for helpful discussions and all the participants of the Global Alliance for Vaccines and Immunizations, Southeast Asia and Western Pacific Regional Working Group's Japanese Encephalitis Meeting: Setting the Global Agenda on Public Health Solutions and National Needs, Bangkok, Thailand 2002, for regional updates on Japanese encephalitis disease burden and vaccination policy. Some of the work described was funded by the Wellcome Trust of Great Britain.

REFERENCES

1. Shlim DR, Solomon T. Japanese encephalitis vaccine for travelers. Exploring the limits of risk. Clin Infect Dis 2002;35:183–8.
2. Tsai TF. Factors in the changing epidemiology of Japanese encephalitis and West Nile fever. In: Saluzzo JF, Dodet B, editors. Factors in the emergence of arbovirus diseases. Paris: Elsevier; 1997. p. 179–89.
3. Solomon T. Viral encephalitis in Southeast Asia. Neurol Infect Epidemiol 1997;2:191–9.
4. Barker F, Bird GA. The Japanese earthquake, notes from Koby on the medical history. BMJ 1924:469.
5. Anonymous. Infectious diseases abroad: outbreak in Japan of a disease resembling encephalitis lethargica. Lancet 1924:1251–2.
6. Kaneko R, Aoki Y. Uber die Encephalitis epidemica in Japan. Engebrisse der Inneren Medizin Kinderheilkunde 1928;34:342–456.
7. Miyake M. The pathology of Japanese encephalitis. Bull World Health Organ 1964;30:153–60.
8. Solomon T. Recent advances in Japanese encephalitis. J Neurovirol 2003;9:274–83.
9. Solomon T, Whitley RJ. Arthropod-borne viral encephalitides. In: Scheld M, Whitley RJ, Marra C, editors. Infections of the central nervous system. Philadelphia, PA: Lippincott Williams and Wilkins; 2004. p.
10. Solomon T. Viral haemorrhagic fevers. In: Cook G, Zumlar A, editors. Manson's tropical diseases. London: WB Saunders; 2002. p. 773–93.
11. Solomon T, Mallewa MJ. Dengue and other emerging flaviviruses. J Infect 2001;42:104–15.
12. Zanotto PM, Gould EA, Gao GF, et al. Population dynamics of flaviviruses revealed by molecular phylogenies. Proc Natl Acad Sci U S A 1996;93:548–53.
13. Gould EA, Zanotto PM, Holmes EC. The genetic evolution of flaviviruses. In: Saluzzo JF, Dodet B, editors. Factors in the emergence of arbovirus diseases. Paris: Elsevier; 1997. p. 51–63.
14. Tsai TF, Popovici F, Cernescu C, et al. West Nile encephalitis epidemic in southeastern Romania. Lancet 1998;352:767–71.
15. Petersen LR, Marfin AA. West Nile virus. A primer for the clinician. Ann Intern Med 2002;137:173–9.
16. Chambers TJ, Hahn CS, Galler R, Rice CM. Flavivirus genome organisation, expression and replication. Annu Rev Microbiol 1990;44:649–88.
17. Stadler K, Allison SL, Schalich J, Heinz FX. Proteolytic activation of tick-borne encephalitis virus by furin. J Virol 1997;71:8475–81.
18. Chen Y, Maguire T, Hileman RE, et al. Dengue virus infectivity depends on envelope protein binding to target cell heparan sulphate. Nat Med 1997;3:866–71.
19. Su CM, Liao CL, Lee YL, Lin YL. Highly sulfated forms of heparin sulfate are involved in Japanese encephalitis virus infection. Virology 2001;286:206–15.
20. Roehrig JT, Hunt AR, Johnson AJ, Hawkes RA. Synthetic peptides derived from the deduced amino acid sequence of the E-glycoprotein of Murray Valley encephalitis virus elicit antiviral antibody. Virology 1989;171:49–60.
21. Rey FA, Heinz FX, Mandl C, et al. The envelope glycoprotein from tick-borne encephalitis virus at 2Å resolution. Nature 1995;375:291–8.
22. Lescar J, Roussel A, Wien MW, et al. The fusion glycoprotein shell of Semliki Forest virus. An icosahedral assembly primed for fusogenic activation at endosomal pH. Cell 2001;105:137–48.
23. Heinz FX, Allison SL. The machinery for flavivirus fusion with host cell membranes. Curr Opin Microbiol 2001;4:450–5.
24. Kobayashi Y, Hasegawa H, Oyama T, et al. Antigenic analysis of Japanese encephalitis virus by using monoclonal antibodies. Infect Immun 1984;44:117–23.
25. Hasegawa H, Yoshida M, Fujita S, Kobayashi Y. Comparison of structural proteins among antigenically different Japanese encephalitis virus strains. Vaccine 1994;12:841–4.

26. Chen WR, Tesh RB, Rico-Hesse R. Genetic variation of Japanese encephalitis virus in nature. J Gen Virol 1990;71:2915–22.

27. Chen WR, Rico-Hesse R, Tesh RB. A new genotype of Japanese virus from Indonesia. Am J Trop Med Hyg 1992;47:61–9.

28. Uchil PD, Satchidanandam V. Phylogenetic analysis of Japanese encephalitis virus. Envelope gene based analysis reveals a fifth genotype, geographic clustering, and multiple introductions of the virus into the Indian subcontinent. Am J Trop Med Hyg 2001;65:242–51.

29. Williams DT, Wang LF, Daniels PW, Mackenzie JS. Molecular characterization of the first Australian isolate of Japanese encephalitis virus, the FU strain. J Gen Virol 2000;81:2471–80.

30. Solomon T, Ni H, Beasley DW, et al. Origin and evolution of Japanese encephalitis virus in Southeast Asia. J Virol 2003;77:3091–8.

31. Solomon T, Ni H, Beasley DW, et al. The origin and evolution of Japanese encephalitis virus. New evidence from the fourth genotype, ICID 2002. 2002.

32. Johnsen DO, Edelman R, Grossman RA, et al. Study of Japanese encephalitis virus in Chiangmai Valley, Thailand. V. Animal infections. Am J Epidemiol 1974;100:57–68.

33. Rodrigues FM, Guttikar SN, Pinto BD. Prevalence of antibodies to Japanese encephalitis and West Nile viruses among wild birds in the Krishna-Godavari Delta, Andhra Pradesh, India. Trans R Soc Trop Med Hyg 1981;75:258–62.

34. Hanna J, Ritchie S, Phillips DA, et al. An outbreak of Japanese encephalitis in the Torres Strait, Australia, 1995. Med J Aust 1996;165:256–60.

35. Rosen L. The natural history of Japanese encephalitis virus. Annu Rev Microbiol 1980;40:395–414.

36. Wuryadi S, Suroso T. Japanese encephalitis in Indonesia. Southeast Asian J Trop Med Public Health 1989;20:575–80.

37. Centers for Disease Control and Prevention. Encephalitis, Japanese. In: CDC, editor. Health information for international travel 2003-2004. Atlanta (GA): CDC; 2003.

38. Centers for Disease Control and Prevention. Inactivated Japanese encephalitis virus vaccine. Recommendations of the Advisory Committee on Immunization Practices (ACIP). MMWR Morb Mortal Wkly Rep 1993;42:1–14.

39. Vaughn DW, Hoke CH. The epidemiology of Japanese encephalitis. Prospects for prevention. Epidemiol Rev 1992;14:197–221.

40. Igarashi A, Tanaka M, Morita K, et al. Detection of West Nile and Japanese encephalitis viral genome sequences in cerebrospinal fluid from acute encephalitis cases in Karachi, Pakistan. Microbiol Immunol 1994;38:827–30.

41. Zimmerman MD, Scott RM, Vaughn DW, et al. Short report. An outbreak of Japanese encephalitis in Kathmandu, Nepal. Am J Trop Med Hyg 1997;57:283–4.

42. Akiba T, Osaka K, Tang S, et al. Analysis of Japanese encephalitis epidemic in western Nepal in 1997. Epidemiol Infect 2001;126:81–8.

43. Hammon WM, Tiggert WD, Sather GE. Epidemiologic studies of concurrent "virgin" epidemics of Japanese B encephalitis and mumps on Guam, 1947–1948, with subsequent observations including dengue through 1957. Am J Trop Med Hyg 1958;67:441–67.

44. Paul WS, Moore PS, Karabatsos N, et al. Outbreak of Japanese encephalitis on the island of Saipan, 1990. J Infect Dis 1993;167:1053–8.

45. Paterson PY, Ley HL Jr, Wisseman CL Jr, et al. Japanese encephalitis in Malaya. Am J Hyg 1952;56:320–33.

46. Anonymous. Japanese encephalitis on the Australian mainland. Commun Dis Intell 1998;22:80.

47. Olson JG, Atmosoedjono S, Lee VH, Ksiazek TG. Correlation between population indices of *Culex tritaeniorhynchus* and *Cx. gelidus* (*Diptera: Culicidae*) and rainfall in Kapuk, Indonesia. J Med Entomol 1983;20:108–9.

48. Tsai TF, Chang J, Yu XX. Japanese encephalitis vaccines. In: Plotkin SA, Orenstein WA, editors. Vaccines. Philadelphia: WB Saunders; 1999. p. 672–710.

49. Gajanana A, Rajendran R, Samuel PP, et al. Japanese encephalitis in south Arcot district, Tamil Nadu, India. A three-year longitudinal study of vector abundance and infection frequency. J Med Entomol 1997;34:651–9.

50. Gajanana A, Thenmozhi V, Samuel PP, Reuben R. A community-based study of subclinical flavivirus infections in children in an area of Tamil Nadu, India, where Japanese encephalitis is endemic. Bull World Health Organ 1995;73:237–44.

51. Innis BL. Japanese encephalitis. In: Porterfield JS, editor. Exotic viral infections. London: Chapman and Hall; 1995. p. 147–74.

52. Pyke AT, Williams DT, Nisbet DJ, et al. The appearance of a second genotype of Japanese encephalitis virus in the Australasian region. Am J Trop Med Hyg 2001;65:747–53.

53. Solomon T, Dung NM, Kneen R, et al. Japanese encephalitis. J Neurol Neurosurg Psychiatry 2000;68:405–15.

54. Gingrich J, Nisalak A, Latendresse JR, et al. Japanese encephalitis virus in Bangkok. Factors influencing vector infections in three suburban communities. J Med Entomol 1992;29:426–44.

55. Buescher EL, Schere WF. Ecological studies of Japanese encephaltis in Japan. IX. Epidemiological correlations and conclusions. Am J Trop Med Hyg 1959;8:719–22.

56. Peiris JSM, Amerasinghe FP, Amerasinghe PH, et al. Japanese encephalitis in Sri Lanka—the study of an epidemic. Vector incrimination, porcine infection, and human disease. Trans R Soc Trop Med Hyg 1992;86:307–13.

57. Burke DS, Ussery M, Elwell MR, et al. Isolation of Japanese encephalitis virus strains from sentinel pigs in northern Thailand, 1982. Trans R Soc Trop Med Hyg 1985;79:420–1.

58. Chan YC, Loh TF. Isolation of Japanese encephalitis virus from the blood of a child in Singapore. Am J Trop Med Hyg 1966;15:567–72.

59. Hoke CH, Nisalak A, Sangawhipa N, et al. Protection against Japanese encephalitis by inactivated vaccines. N Engl J Med 1988;319:608–14.

60. Halstead SB, Grosz CR. Subclinical Japanese encephalitis. I. Infection of Americans with limited residence in Korea. Am J Hyg 1962;75:190–201.

61. Huang CH. Studies of Japanese encephalitis in China. Adv Virus Res 1982;27:71–101.

62. Umenai T, Krzysko R, Bektimorov TA, Assaad FA. Japanese encephalitis. Current worldwide status. Bull World Health Organ 1985;63:625–31.

63. Sabin AB. Epidemic encephalitis in military personnel. Isolation of Japanese B virus on Okiowa in 1945, serologic diagnosis, clinical manifestations, epidemiological aspects, and use of mouse brain vaccine. JAMA 1947;13:281–93.

64. Dickerson RB, Newton JR, Hansen JE. Diagnosis and immediate prognosis of Japanese B encephalitis. Am J Med 1952;12:277–88.

65. Lincoln AF, Silvertson SE. Acute phase of Japanese B encephalitis. Two hundred and one cases in American soldiers, Korea 1950. JAMA 1952;150:268–73.

66. Richter RW, Shimojyo S. Neurologic sequelae of Japanese B encephalitis. Neurology 1961;11:553–9.

67. Ketel WB, Ognibene AJ. Japanese B encephalitis in Vietnam. Am J Med Sci 1971;261:271–9.

68. Burke DS, Nisalak A. Detection of Japanese encephalitis virus immunoglobulin M antibodies in serum by antibody capture radioimmunoassay. J Clin Microbiol 1982;15:353–61.

69. Bundo K, Igarashi A. Antibody-capture ELISA for detection of immunoglobulin M antibodies in sera from Japanese encephalitis and dengue hemorrhagic fever patients. J Virol Methods 1985;11:15–22.

70. Solomon T, Thao LTT, Dung NM, et al. Rapid diagnosis of Japanese encephalitis by using an IgM dot enzyme immunoassay. J Clin Microbiol 1998;36:2030–4.

71. Cuzzubbo AJ, Endy TP, Vaughn DW, et al. Evaluation of a new commercially available immunoglobulin M capture enzyme-linked immunosorbant assay for diagnosis of Japanese encephalitis infections. J Clin Microbiol 1999;37:3738–41.

72. Grossman RA, Edelman R, Chiewanich P, et al. Study of Japanese encephalitis virus in Chiangmai valley, Thailand. II. Human clinical infections. Am J Epidemiol 1973;98:121–32.

73. Tsai TF. New initiatives for the control of Japanese encephalitis by vaccination. Minutes of a WHO/CVI meeting, Bangkok, Thailand, 13–15 October 1998. Vaccine 2000;18 Suppl 2:1–25.

74. Trillin C. American chronicles. The New Yorker 1985:61-94.

75. Benenson MW, Top FH, Gresso W, et al. The virulence to man of Japanese encephalitis virus in Thailand. Am J Trop Med Hyg 1975;24:974–80.

76. MacDonald WBG, Tink AR, Ouvrier RA, et al. Japanese encephalitis after a two-week holiday in Bali. Med J Aust 1989;150:558–66.

77. Wittesjö B, Eitrem R, Niklasson B, et al. Japanese encephalitis after a 10-day holiday in Bali. Lancet 1995;345:856.

78. Buhl MR, Black FT, Andersen PL, Laursen A. Fatal Japanese encephalitis in a Danish tourist visiting Bali for 12 days. Scand J Infect Dis 1996;28:189.

79. Basnyat B, Zimmerman MD, Shrestha Y, et al. Persistent Japanese encephalitis in Kathmandu. The need for immunization. J Travel Med 2001;8:270–1.

80. Solomon T, Dung NM, Kneen R, et al. Seizures and raised intracranial pressure in Vietnamese patients with Japanese encephalitis. Brain 2002;125:1084–93.

81. Kumar R, Mathur A, Kumar A, et al. Clinical features and prognostic indicators of Japanese encephalitis in children in Lucknow (India). Indian J Med Res 1990;91:321–7.

82. Poneprasert B. Japanese encephalitis in children in northern Thailand. Southeast Asian J Trop Med Public Health 1989;20:599–603.

83. Solomon T, Thao LTT, Dung NM, et al. Clinical features of Japanese encephalitis. Prognostic and pathophysiological significance in 50 patients. Paper presented at the Seventh International Congress for Infectious Diseases, Hong Kong, 1996.

84. Solomon T. Japanese encephalitis. In: Gilman S, Goldstein GW, Waxman SG, editors. Neurobase. Vol. 4. San Diego: Medlink Publishing; 2000.

85. Misra UK, Kalita J. Movement disorders in Japanese encephalitis. J Neurol 1997;244:299–303.

86. Kumar S, Misra UK, Kalita J, et al. MRI in Japanese encephalitis. Am J Med Sci 1997;39:180–4.

87. Murgod UA, Muthane UB, Ravi V, et al. Persistent movement disorders following Japanese encephalitis. Neurology 2001;57:2313–5.

88. Solomon T, Kneen R, Dung NM, et al. Poliomyelitis-like illness due to Japanese encephalitis virus. Lancet 1998;351:1094–7.

89. Kumar R, Agarwal SP, Waklu I, Misra PK. Japanese encephalitis—an encephalomyelitis. Indian Pediatr 1991;23:1525–33.

90. Shoji H, Murakamo T, Murai I, et al. A follow-up study by CT and MRI in 3 cases of Japanese encephalitis. Neuroradiology 1990;32:215–9.

91. Misra UK, Kalita J, Jain SK, Mathur A. Radiological and neurophysiological changes in Japanese encephalitis. J Neurol Neurosurg Psychiatry 1994;57:1484–7.

92. Huang CR, Chang WN, Lui CC, et al. Neuroimages of Japanese encephalitis. Report of 3 patients. Chin Med J (Engl) 1997;60:105–8.

93. Misra UK, Kalita J. A comparative study of Japanese and herpes simplex encephalitis. Electromyogr Clin Neurophysiol 1998;38:41–6.

94. Kimura K, Dosaka A, Hashimoto Y, et al. Single-photon emission CT findings in acute Japanese encephalitis. Am J Neuroradiol 1997;18:465–9.

95. Gourie-Devi M, Deshpande DH. Japanese encephalitis. In: Prasad LS, Kulczycki LL, editors. Paediatric problems. New Delhi: S Chand; 1982. p. 340–56.

96. Leake CJ, Burke DS, Nisalak A, Hoke CH. Isolation of Japanese encephalitis virus from clinical specimens using a continuous mosquito cell line. Am J Trop Med Hyg 1986;35:1045–50.

97. Mathur A, Kumar R, Sharma S, et al. Rapid diagnosis of Japanese encephalitis by immunofluorescent examination of cerebrospinal fluid. Indian J Med Res 1990;91:1–4.

98. Desai A, Shankar SK, Ravi V, Chandramuki A. Japanese encephalitis virus antigen in the brain and its topographical distribution. Acta Neuropathol (Berl) 1995;89:368–73.

99. Clark CH, Casals J. Techniques for hemagglutination inhibition with arthropod viruses. Am J Trop Med Hyg 1958;7:561–73.

100. Innis BL, Nisalak A, Nimmannitya S, et al. An enzyme-linked immunosorbent assay to characterize dengue infections where dengue and Japanese encephalitis co-circulate. Am J Trop Med Hyg 1989;40:418–27.

101. Burke DS, Nisalak A, Ussery MA, et al. Kinetics of IgM and IgG responses to Japanese encephalitis virus in human serum and cerebrospinal fluid. J Infect Dis 1985;151:1093–9.

102. Meiyu F, Huosheng C, Cuihua C, et al. Detection of flavivirus by reverse transcriptase-polymerase chain reaction with the universal primer set. Microbiol Immunol 1997;41:209–13.

103. Hoke CH, Vaughn DW, Nisalak A, et al. Effect of high dose dexamethasone on the outcome of acute encephalitis due to Japanese encephalitis virus. J Infect Dis 1992;165:631–7.

104. Leyssen P, De Clercq E, Neyts J. Perspectives for the treatment of infections with Flaviviridae. Clin Microbiol Rev 2000;13:67–82.

105. Zhang M, Wang M, Jiang S, Ma W. Passive protection of mice, goats, and monkeys against Japanese encephalitis with monoclonal antibodies. J Med Virol 1989;29:133–8.

106. Ma WY, Jiang SZ, Zhang MJ, et al. Preliminary observations on treatment of patients with Japanese B encephalitis with monoclonal antibody. J Med Coll PLA 1992;7:299–302.

107. Waldvogel K, Bossart W, Huisman T, et al. Severe tick-borne encephalitis following passive immunization. Eur J Pediatr 1996;155:775–9.

108. Chen CJ, Raung SL, Kuo MD, Wang YM. Suppression of Japanese encephalitis virus infection by non-steroidal anti-inflammatory drugs. J Gen Virol 2002;83:1897–905.

109. Liao CL, Lin YL, Wu BC, et al. Salicylates inhibit flavivirus replication independently of blocking nuclear factor kappa B activation. J Virol 2001;75:7828–39.

110. Burke DS, Morill JC. Levels of interferon in the plasma and cerebrospinal fluid of patients with acute Japanese encephalitis. J Infect Dis 1987;155:797–9.

111. Harinasuta C, Wasi C, Vithanomsat S. The effect of interferon on Japanese encephalitis virus *in vitro*. 1984;15:564–8.

112. Anderson JF, Rahal JJ. Efficacy of interferon alpha-2b and ribavirin against West Nile virus *in vitro*. Emerg Infect Dis 2002;8:107–8.

113. Harinasuta C, Nimmanitya S, Titsyakorn U. The effect of interferon alpha on two cases of Japanese encephalitis in Thailand. Southeast Asian J Trop Med Public Health 1985;16:332–6.

114. Solomon T, Dung NM, Wills B, et al. Interferon alfa-2a in Japanese encephalitis. A randomised double-blind placebo-controlled trial. Lancet 2003;361:821–6.

115. Burke DS, Lorsomrudee W, Leake CJ, et al. Fatal outcome in Japanese encephalitis. Am J Trop Med Hyg 1985;34:1203–10.

116. Desai A, Ravi V, Guru SC, et al. Detection of autoantibodies to neural antigens in the CSF of Japanese encephalitis patients and correlation of findings with the outcome. J Neurol Sci 1994;122:109–16.

117. Dapeng L, Jindou S, Huijun Y, Renguo Y, Ze W. Prognostic factors of early sequelae and fatal outcome of Japanese encephalitis. Southeast Asian J Trop Med Public Health 1995;26:694–8.

118. Libraty DH, Nisalak A, Endy TP, et al. Clinical and immunological risk factors for severe disease in Japanese encephalitis. Trans R Soc Trop Med Hyg 2002;96:173–8.

119. Misra UK, Kalita J, Srivastava M. Prognosis of Japanese encephalitis. A multivariate analysis. J Neurol Sci 1998;161:143–7.

120. Simpson TW, Meiklehohn G. Sequelae of Japanese B encephalitis. Am J Trop Med Hyg 1947;27:727–31.

121. Kumar R, Mathur A, Singh KB, et al. Clinical sequelae of Japanese encephalitis in children. Indian J Med Res 1993;97:9–13.

122. Huy BV, Tu HC, Luan TV, Lindqvist R. Early mental and neurological sequelae after Japanese B encephalitis. Southeast Asian J Trop Med Public Health 1994;25:549–53.

123. Schneider RJ, Firestone MH, Edelman R, et al. Clinical sequelae after Japanese encephalitis. A one year follow up study in Thailand. Southeast Asian J Trop Med Public Health 1974;5:560–8.

124. Johnston LJ, Halliday GM, King NJ. Langerhans cells migrate to local lymph nodes following cutaneous infection with an arbovirus. J Invest Dermatol 2000;114:560–8.

125. Wu SJ, Grouard-Vogel G, Sun W, et al. Human skin Langerhans cells are targets of dengue virus infection. Nat Med 2000;6:816–20.

126. Monath TP, Cropp CP, Harrison AK. Mode of entry of a neurotropic virus into the central nervous system. Reinvestigation of an old controversy. Lab Invest 1983;48:399–410.

127. Myint KSA, Raengsakulrach B, Young GD, et al. Immunocytochemical detection of Japanese encephalitis (JE) virus antigen in the CNS of rhesus macaques inoculated intranasally with JE virus. Am J Trop Med Hyg 1994;51 Suppl:274.

128. Dropulie B, Masters CL. Entry of neurotropic arboviruses into the central nervous system. An in vitro study using mouse brain endothelium. J Infect Dis 1990;161:685–91.

129. Liou ML, Hsu CY. Japanese encephalitis virus is transported across the cerebral blood vessels by endocytosis in mouse brain. Cell Tissue Res 1998;293:389–94.

130. Liu YF, Teng CL, Liu K. Cerebral cysticercosis as a factor aggravating Japanese B encephalitis. Chin Med J (Engl) 1957;75:1010.

131. Shankar SK, Rao TV, Mruthyunjayana BP, et al. Autopsy study of brains during an epidemic of Japanese encephalitis in Karnataka. Indian J Med Res 1983;78:431–41.

132. Shiraki H. Encephalitis due to arboviruses. Japanese encephalitis. In: Celers RDaJH, editor. Clinical virology. The evaluation and management of human viral infections. Philadelphia: WB Saunders; 1970. p. 155–75.

133. Ni H, Barrett ADT. Molecular differences between wild-type Japanese encephalitis virus strains of high and low mouse neuroinvasiveness. J Gen Virol 1996;77:1449–55.

134. Huang CH, Wong C. Relation of the peripheral multiplication of Japanese B encephalitis virus to the pathogenesis of the infection in mice. Acta Virol 1963;7:322–30.

135. Ni H, Burns NJ, Chang GJ, et al. Comparison of nucleotide and deduced amino acid sequence of the 5′ non-coding region and structural protein genes of the wild-type Japanese encephalitis virus strain SA14 and its attenuated vaccine derivatives. J Gen Virol 1994;75:1505–10.

136. Ni H, Chang GJ, Xie H, et al. Molecular basis of attenuation of neurovirulence of wild-type Japanese encephalitis virus strain SA14. J Gen Virol 1995;76:409–13.

137. Holzmann H, Heinz FX, Mandl C, et al. A single amino acid substitution in envelope protein of tick borne encephalitis virus leads to attenuation in the mouse model. J Gen Virol 1990;64:5156–9.

138. Lee E, Lobigs M. Substitutions at the putative receptor-binding site of an encephalitic flavivirus alter virulence and host cell tropism and reveal a role for glycosaminoglycans in entry. J Virol 2000;74:8867–75.

139. Hasegawa H, Yoshida M, Shiosaka T, et al. Mutations in the envelope protein of Japanese encephalitis virus affect entry into cultured cells and virulence in mice. Virology 1992;191:158–65.

140. Cecilia D, Gould EA. Nucleotide changes responsible for loss of neuroinvasiveness in Japanese encephalitis virus neutralisation-resistant mice. Virology 1991;181:70–7.

141. McMinn PC, Dalgarno L, Weir RC. A comparison of the spread of Murray Valley encephalitis viruses of high or low neuroinvasiveness in the tissues of Swiss mice after peripheral inoculation. Virology 1996;220:414–23.

142. Monath TP, Arroyo J, Levenbook I, et al. Single mutation in the flavivirus envelope protein hinge region increases neurovirulence for mice and monkeys but decreases viscerotropism for monkeys. Relevance to development and safety testing of live, attenuated vaccines. J Virol 2002;76:1932–43.

143. Johnson RT, Burke DS, Elwell M, et al. Japanese encephalitis. Immunocytochemical studies of viral antigen and inflammatory cells in fatal cases. Ann Neurol 1985;18:567–73.

144. Zimmerman HM. The pathology of Japanese B encephalitis. Am J Pathol 1946;22:965–91.

145. Haymaker W, Sabin AB. Topographic distribution of lesions in central nervous system in Japanese B encephalitis. Nature of the lesions with report of a case on Okinawa. Arch Neurol Psychiatry 1947;57:673–92.

146. Li ZS, Hong SF, Gong NL. Immunohistochemical study of Japanese B encephalitis. Chin Med J (Engl) 1988;101:768–71.

147. Liu JL. Protective effect of interferon alpha on mice experimentally infected with Japanese encephalitis virus. Chin J Microbiol 1972;5:1–9.

148. Ghosh SN, Goverdhan MK, Sathe PS, et al. Protective effect of 6-MFA, a fungal interferon inducer against Japanese encephalitis virus in bonnet macaques. Indian J Med Res 1990;91:408–13.

149. Hammon WM, Sather GE. Passive immunity for arbovirus infection. I. Artificially induced prophylaxis in man and mouse for Japanese (B) encephalitis. Am J Trop Med Hyg 1973;22:524–34.

150. Carmenaga DL, Nathonson N, Cole GA. Cyclophosphamide-potentiated West Nile encephalitis. Relative influence of cellular and humoral factors. J Infect Dis 1974;130:634–41.

151. Yu WX, Wang JF, Zheng GM, Li HM. Response of normal and athymic mice to infection by virulent and attenuated Japanese encephalitis virus. Chin J Virol 1985;1:203–9.

152. Jia LL, Zheng A, Yu YX. Study on the immune mechanism of JE attenuated live vaccine (SA_{14}-14-2 strain) in immune inhibited mice. Chin J Immunol Microbiol 1992;12:364.

153. Nathanson N, Cole GA. Fatal Japanese encephalitis virus infection in immunosuppressed spider monkeys. Clin Exp Immunol 1970;6:161–6.

154. Okhuysen PC, Crane JK, Pappas J. St. Louis encephalitis in patients with human immunodeficiency virus infection. Clin Infect Dis 1993;17:140–1.

155. Bukowski JF, Kurane I, Lai CJ, et al. Dengue virus-specific cross-reactive CD8+ human cytotoxic T lymphocytes. J Virol 1989;63:5086–91.

156. McMichael AJ. Cytotoxic T lymphocyte specific for influenza virus. Curr Top Microbiol Immunol 1994;189:75–91.

157. Konishi E, Mason PW, Innis BI, Ennis FA. Japanese encephalitis virus-specific proliferative responses of human peripheral blood T lymphocytes. Am J Trop Med Hyg 1995;53:278–83.

158. Aihara H, Takasaki T, Matsutani T, et al. Establishment and characterization of Japanese encephalitis virus-specific, human CD4+ T-cell clones. Flavivirus cross-reactivity, protein recognition, and cytotoxic activity. J Virol 1998;72:8032–6.

159. Halstead SB. Pathogenesis of dengue. Challenges to molecular biology. Science 1988;239:476–81.

160. Halstead SB, O'Rourke EJ. Antibody-enhanced dengue virus infection in primate leukocytes. Nature 1977;265:739–41.

161. Gollins SW, Porterfield JS. Flavivirus infection enhancement in macrophages. An electron microscopic study of viral cellular entry. J Gen Virol 1985;66:1969–82.

162. Edelman R, Schneider R, Chieowanich P, et al. The effect of dengue virus infection on the clinical sequelae of Japanese encephalitis. A one year follow-up study in Thailand. Southeast Asian J Trop Med Public Health 1975;6:308–15.

163. Grossman RA, Edelman R, Willhight M, et al. Study of Japanese encephalitis virus in Chiangmai Valley, Thailand. 3. Human seroepidemiology and inapparent infections. Am J Epidemiol 1973;98:133–49.

164. Bond JO. St. Louis encephalitis and dengue fever in the Caribbean area. Evidence of possible cross protection. Bull World Health Organ 1969;:160–3.

165. Rao DR, Reuben R, Nagasampagi BA. Development of combined use of neem (*Azadirachta indica*) and water management for the control of culicine mosquitoes in rice fields. Med Vet Entomol 1995;9:25–33.

166. Rao DR, Reuben R, Venugopal MS, et al. Evaluation of neem, *Azadirachta indica*, with and without water management, for the control of culicine mosquito larvae in rice-fields. Med Vet Entomol 1992;6:318–24.

167. Lacey LA, Lacey CM. The medical importance of riceland mosquitoes and their control using alternatives to chemical insecticides. J Am Mosq Control Assoc Suppl 1990;2:1–93.

168. Reuben R, Thenmozhi V, Samuel PP, et al. Mosquito blood feeding patterns as a factor in the epidemiology of Japanese encephalitis in southern India. Am J Trop Med Hyg 1992;46:654–63.

169. Monath TP. Japanese encephalitis vaccines. Current vaccines and future prospects. Curr Top Microbiol Immunol 2002;267:105–38.

170. Smorodintsev AA, Shubladse AK, Neustroer VD. Etiology of autumn encephalitis in the far east of the USSR. Arch Ges Virus Forsch 1940;1:549–59.

171. Tsai TF, Yu YX. Japanese encephalitis vaccines. In: Plotkin SA, Mortimer EAJ, editors. Vaccines. Philadelphia: WB Saunders; 1994. p. 671–713.

172. Gowal D, Singh G, Bhau LN, Saxena SN. Thermostability of Japanese encephalitis vaccine produced in India. Biologicals 1991;19:37–40.

173. Kitano T, Yabe S, Kobayashi M, et al. Immunogenicity of JE Nakayama and Beijing-1 vaccines. JE and HFRS Bull 1986;1:37–41.

174. Lubiniecki AS, Cypess RH, Hammon WM. Passive immunity for arbovirus infection. II. Quantitative aspects of naturally and artificially acquired protection in mice for Japanese (B) encephalitis virus. Am J Trop Med Hyg 1973;22:535–42.

175. Oya A. Japanese encephalitis vaccine. Acta Paediatr Jpn 1988;30:175–84.

176. Defraites RF, Gambel JM, Hoke CH Jr, et al. Japanese encephalitis vaccine (inactivated, BIKEN) in US soldiers. Immunogenicity and safety of vaccine administered in two dosing regimens. Am J Trop Med Hyg 1999;61:288–93.

177. Nimmannitya S, Hutamai S, Kalayanarooj S, Rojanasuphot S. A field study on Nakayama and Beijing strains of Japanese encephalitis vaccines. Southeast Asian J Trop Med Public Health 1995;26:689–93.

178. Poland JD, Cropp CB, Craven RB, Monath TP. Evaluation of the potency and safety of inactivated Japanese encephalitis vaccine in US inhabitants. J Infect Dis 1990;161:878–82.

179. Henderson A. Immunisation against Japanese encephalitis in Nepal. Experience of 1152 subjects. J R Army Med Corps 1984;130:188–91.

180. Gambel JM, DeFraites R, Hoke C Jr, et al. Japanese encephalitis vaccine. Persistence of antibody up to 3 years after a three-dose primary series. J Infect Dis 1995;171:1074.

181. Sanchez JL, Hoke CH, McCowan J, et al. Further experience with Japanese encephalitis vaccine. Lancet 1990;335:972–3.

182. Rojanasuphot S, Shaffer N, Chotpitayasunondh T, et al. Response to JE vaccine among HIV-infected children, Bangkok, Thailand. Southeast Asian J Trop Med Public Health 1998;29:443–50.

183. Ruff TA, Eisen D, Fuller A, Kass R. Adverse reactions to Japanese encephalitis vaccine. Lancet 1991;338:881–2.

184. Andersen MM, Ronne T. Side-effects with Japanese encephalitis vaccine. Lancet 1991;337:1044.

185. Plesner AM, Arlien-Soborg P, Herning M. Neurological complications and Japanese encephalitis vaccination. Lancet 1996;348:202–3.

186. Ohtaki E, Matsuishi T, Hirano Y, Maekawa K. Acute disseminated encephalomyelitis after treatment with Japanese B encephalitis vaccine (Nakayama-Yoken and Beijing strains). J Neurol Neurosurg Psychiatry 1995;59:316–7.

187. Ohtaki E, Murakami Y, Komori H, et al. Acute disseminated encephalomyelitis after Japanese B encephalitis vaccination. Pediatr Neurol 1992;8:137–9.

188. Plesner AM, Arlien-Soborg P, Herning M. Neurological complications to vaccination against Japanese encephalitis. Eur J Neurol 1998;5:479–85.

189. Berg SW, Mitchell BS, Hanson RK, et al. Systemic reactions in US Marine Corps personnel who received Japanese encephalitis vaccine. Clin Infect Dis 1997;24:265–6.

190. Plesner AM, Ronne T. Allergic mucocutaneous reactions to Japanese encephalitis vaccine. Vaccine 1997;15:1239–43.

191. Plesner A, Ronne T, Wachmann H. Case-control study of allergic reactions to Japanese encephalitis vaccine. Vaccine 2000;18:1830–6.

192. Sohn YM. Japanese encephalitis immunization in South Korea. Past, present, and future. Emerg Infect Dis 2000;6:17–24.

193. Sakaguchi M, Nakashima K, Takahashi H, et al. Anaphylaxis to Japanese encephalitis vaccine. Allergy 2001;56:804–5.

194. Sakaguchi M, Inouye S. Two patterns of systemic immediate-type reactions to Japanese encephalitis vaccines. Vaccine 1998;16:68–9.

195. Robinson P, Ruff T, Kass R. Australian case-control study of adverse reactions to Japanese encephalitis vaccine. J Travel Med 1995;2:159–64.

196. Sakaguchi M, Yoshida M, Kuroda W, et al. Systemic immediate-type reactions to gelatin included in Japanese encephalitis vaccines. Vaccine 1997;15:121–2.

197. Sakaguchi M, Miyazawa H, Inouye S. Specific IgE and IgG to gelatin in children with systemic cutaneous reactions to Japanese encephalitis vaccines. Allergy 2001;56:536–9.

198. Takahashi H, Pool V, Tsai TF, Chen RT. Adverse events after Japanese encephalitis vaccination. Review of post-marketing surveillance data from Japan and the United States. The VAERS Working Group. Vaccine 2000;18:2963–9.

199. Ding Z, Shi H, Pang C. [Production of purified Japanese encephalitis vaccine from Vero cells with roller bottles]. Zhonghua Yi Xue Za Zhi 1998;78:261–2.

200. Sugawara K, Nishiyama K, Ishikawa Y, et al. Development of Vero cell-derived inactivated Japanese encephalitis vaccine. Biologicals 2002;30:303–14.

201. Xin YY, Ming ZG, Peng GY, et al. Safety of a live-attenuated Japanese encephalitis virus vaccine (SA14-14-2) for children. Am J Trop Med Hyg 1988;39:214–7.

202. Xin YY, Zhang GM, Zheng Z. Studies of the immunogenicity of live and killed Japanese encephalitis (JE) vaccines to challenge with different Japanese encephalitis virus strains. Chin J Virol 1989;5:106–10.

203. Bhatt TR, Crabtree MB, Guirakhoo F, et al. Growth characteristics of the chimeric Japanese encephalitis virus vaccine candidate, ChimeriVax-JE (YF/JE SA14-14-2), in *Culex tritaeniorhynchus*, *Aedes albopictus*, and *Aedes aegypti* mosquitoes. Am J Trop Med Hyg 2000;62:480–4.

204. Chen BQ, Beaty BJ. Japanese encephalitis vaccine (2-8 strain) and parent (SA 14 strain) viruses in *Culex tritaeniorhynchus* mosquitoes. Am J Trop Med Hyg 1982;31:403–7.

205. Arroyo J, Guirakhoo F, Fenner S, et al. Molecular basis for attenuation of neurovirulence of a yellow fever virus/Japanese encephalitis virus chimera vaccine (ChimeriVax-JE). J Virol 2001;75:934–42.

206. Tsai TF, Yong-Xin Y, Putvatan R, et al. Immunogenicity of live attenuated SA14-14-2 Japanese encephalitis vaccine— a comparison of 1- and 3-month immunization schedules. J Infect Dis 1998;177:221–3.

207. Sohn YM, Park MS, Rho HO, et al. Primary and booster immune responses to SA14-14-2 Japanese encephalitis vaccine in Korean infants. Vaccine 1999;17:2259–64.

208. Hennessy S, Zhengle L, Tsai TF, et al. Effectiveness of live-attenuated Japanese encephalitis vaccine (SA14-14-2). A case control study. Lancet 1996;347:1583–6.

209. Bista MB, Banerjee MK, Shin SH, et al. Efficacy of single-dose SA 14-14-2 vaccine against Japanese encephalitis. A case control study. Lancet 2001;358:791–5.

210. Liu ZL, Hennessy S, Strom BL, et al. Short-term safety of live attenuated Japanese encephalitis vaccine (SA14-14-2). Results of a randomized trial with 26,239 subjects. J Infect Dis 1997;176:1366–9.

211. Siraprapasiri T, Sawaddiwudhipong W, Rojanasuphot S. Cost benefit analysis of Japanese encephalitis vaccination program in Thailand. Southeast Asian J Trop Med Public Health 1997;28:143–8.

212. Ding D, Kilgore PE, Clemens JD, et al. Cost-effectiveness of routine immunization to control Japanese encephalitis in Shanghai, China. Bull World Health Organ 2003;81:334–42.

213. Konishi E, Pincus S, Paoletti E, et al. A highly attenuated host range-restricted vaccinia virus strain, NYVAC, encoding the *prM*, *E* and *NS1* genes of Japanese encephalitis virus prevents JEV viremia in swine. Virology 1992;190:454–8.

214. Mason PW, Pincus S, Fournier MJ, et al. Japanese encephalitis virus-vaccinia recombinants produce particulate forms of the structural proteins and induce high levels of protection against lethal JEV infection. Virology 1991;180:294–305.

215. Kanesa-thasan N, Smucny JJ, Hoke CH, et al. Safety and immunogenicity of NYVAC-JEV and ALVAC-JEV attenuated recombinant Japanese encephalitis virus—poxvirus vaccines in vaccinia-nonimmune and vaccinia-immune humans. Vaccine 2000;19:483–91.

216. Chambers TJ, Nestorowicz A, Mason PW, Rice CM. Yellow fever/Japanese encephalitis chimeric viruses. Construction and biological properties. J Virol 1999;73:3095–101.

217. Guirakhoo F, Zhang ZX, Chambers TJ, et al. Immunogenicity, genetic stability, and protective efficacy of a recombinant, chimeric yellow fever-Japanese encephalitis virus (ChimeriVax-JE) as a live, attenuated vaccine candidate against Japanese encephalitis. Virology 1999;257:363–72.

218. Monath TP, Levenbook I, Soike K, et al. Chimeric yellow fever virus 17D-Japanese encephalitis virus vaccine. Dose-response effectiveness and extended safety testing in rhesus monkeys. J Virol 2000;74:1742–51.

219. Monath TP, McCarthy K, Bedford P, et al. Clinical proof of principle for ChimeriVax. Recombinant live, attenuated vaccines against flavivirus infections. Vaccine 2002;20:1004–18.

220. Guirakhoo F, Pugachev K, Arroyo J, et al. Viremia and immunogenicity in nonhuman primates of a tetravalent yellow fever-dengue chimeric vaccine. Genetic reconstructions, dose adjustment, and antibody responses against wild-type dengue virus isolates. Virology 2002;298:146–59.

221. Konishi E, Yamaoka M, Khin Sane W, et al. Induction of protective immunity against Japanese encephalitis in mice by immunization with a plasmid encoding Japanese encephalitis virus premembrane and envelope genes. J Virol 1998;72:4925–30.

222. Konishi E, Yamaoka M, Kurane I, Mason PW. Japanese encephalitis DNA vaccine candidates expressing premembrane and envelope genes induce virus-specific memory B cells and long-lasting antibodies in swine. Virology 2000;268:49–55.

223. Ashok MS, Rangarajan PN. Protective efficacy of a plasmid DNA encoding Japanese encephalitis virus envelope protein fused to tissue plasminogen activator signal sequences. Studies in a murine intracerebral virus challenge model. Vaccine 2002;20:1563–70.

Chapter 11

BCG Vaccine and Tuberculosis Vaccines

Clydette Powell

The first reported cases of tuberculosis (TB) date back to 3000 BC; the disease has been discovered in Egyptian mummies. Reported to have claimed 100 million lives over the past 100 years, TB persists to the present time. Furthermore, with numbers of case reports increasing, it has reemerged since the onset of human immunodeficiency virus/acquired immunodeficiency syndrome (HIV/AIDS) in the 1980s. The resurgence of tuberculosis has been fueled in part by that epidemic, but its incidence is also increasing in places where the public health infrastructure either has deteriorated or has never been effective in the first place. According to World Health Organization (WHO) estimates, TB's cumulative prevalence in the world numbers about 88 million. One-third of the world (two billion people) is infected with TB (the latent form), with some 8,000,000 new cases (active disease) occurring each year. This growing problem led WHO to declare in 1993 that TB is a global health emergency.

Although TB has predilections for certain populations, overall it is no respecter of persons. It is capable of affecting any age, either gender, any socioeconomic class, and any nationality. In effect, all who breathe are at risk. However, the poor, the marginalized, the homeless, the prisoner, the injecting drug user, the immunocompromised, the refugee, and the immigrant are especially targeted. In spite of the fact that 98% of TB occurs in the developing world, the international traveler now finds him- or herself exposed through airborne transmission; cases acquired during international flights have been documented.[1] Although a misnomer, some have referred to TB as "Ebola with wings," to give emphasis to the rapidity of its spread and the fear it can evoke.

Caused by *Mycobacterium tuberculosis (M.tb)*, TB is a chronic infection that primarily affects the lungs, its usual portal of entry. From the lungs, through hematogenous spread, it can reside in any organ of the body, lying dormant until reactivation many years later due to either natural or acquired immunocompromise. In addition, it can smolder over many years, causing debilitation and disability or it may develop into a fulminant disease that claims the life of its victim in spite of medical intervention. *M. tuberculosis* is part of a complex of bacilli that includes *Mycobacterium bovis*, *Mycobacterium africanum*, and *Mycobacterium microti*. Most cases of TB are caused by *M. tb*, although in some regions infections occur with *M. bovis*.

With the renewed recognition of tuberculosis as both a communicable disease and an important public health problem, attention has been refocused on methods to prevent and control TB. Four main interventions are used in public health and clinical settings to reach these goals: (1) treatment of persons with infectious disease, (2) drug prophylaxis to prevent infection (eg, in HIV-positive patients), (3) treatment of subclinical (latent) infection to reduce the progression to clinical disease, and (4) infant vaccination before exposure occurs. This chapter focuses on this last intervention: vaccination.

VACCINE HISTORY

The vaccine against tuberculosis that is used today had an interesting start 100 years ago. In 1902, Edmond Isidore Etienne Nocard isolated a virulent strain of *M. bovis* (part of the *M. tb* complex) from a cow with tuberculous mastitis. Over the next 13 years, Albert Calmette and Camille Guérin of the Institut Pasteur, Paris, inoculated a medium with this strain and subcultured it multiple times. That strain was named bacille Calmette-Guérin, or BCG, and it was originally intended for vaccination of goats and cattle.[2] The first use of BCG vaccine in humans occurred in 1921. The vaccine was given orally in three portions every 48 hours until 30 mg were administered.[3] Hundreds of thousands of children coming from households with TB exposure were vaccinated in such a way.

Advances in molecular biology have led to observations on the genetic basis of BCG's attenuation from virulent *M.bovis*. Three distinct genomic regions have been found to be deleted from BCG, designated RD1, RD2, and RD3. The RD3 DNA segment was absent in BCG strains but found in virulent laboratory strains of *M.bovis* and *M. tuberculosis* and 84% of virulent clinical isolates. RD2 was deleted only from substrains derived from the original BCG Pasteur strain after 1925. RD1 was deleted in all BCG substrains tested, and further studies suggested that RD1 has a role in regulation of multiple genetic loci that may be related to virulence.[4] Since the isolation of the original BCG strain at the Institut Pasteur in 1921, at least 13 substrains have been generated. There are seven major BCG vaccine strains in present use. Four of the vaccine strains contain the RD2 deletion: they are manufactured by Aventis Pasteur (Paris), the Statens Serum Institut (Copenhagen), Evans Medeva (formerly Glaxo), and the BCG laboratory in Japan. The three remaining strains, the Moreau (Brazilian) strain, another Japanese strain, and a Russian strain retain the RD2 segment. The historic implications of the RD2 segment differences among BCG vaccines are unclear. Among the seven major strains, Copenhagen 1331 has the greatest use around the world. For the rare instances in which BCG is used in the United States as a preventive strategy for persons meeting specific criteria, the Tice strain (1934) is the only one licensed and administered in the United States.

BCG Impact

Whether BCG has had an impact in the past and whether it will have such an impact on the incidence of childhood TB complications in the future may be hard to determine. This is in part because the first use of BCG occurred when TB rates were already declining and when health care providers were improving their case detection and treatment approaches. Second, the advent of HIV/AIDS in the late twentieth century has slowed the decline in TB rates that might have been attributable to BCG vaccination. Moreover, BCG's target population is children, who represent a small percentage of the world's TB burden. To demonstrate impact in this cohort, many observational years are needed; questions about duration of protection afforded by BCG make that outcome even less clear. In addition, as infected children do not constitute the major transmitters of *M. tb*, BCG would have little impact on transmission rates in the adult population. On the other hand, the experience in the United Kingdom and Scandinavia was that TB rates decreased with BCG vaccination; when those countries discontinued BCG, surveillance findings reported increases in TB meningitis and glandular disease. Though outside the scope of this chapter, some alternative benefits of variable significance derived from BCG vaccines have been documented in the literature for allergy and asthma, leprosy, Buruli ulcer (*Mycobacterium ulcerans*), lymphadenopathy secondary to *Mycobacterium avium*, and bladder cancer (as an adjunct to surgery). However, BCG's impact on these conditions has not been quantified and requires more scientific scrutiny.

VACCINE SAFETY AND ADVERSE EFFECTS

Although BCG is a live vaccine, large reviews show it to be a safe one. Early on in the 1930s, questions had arisen as to BCG's safety, especially when a cluster of deaths occurred in BCG-vaccinated German children; later studies revealed that a mixture containing virulent bacilli, and not BCG, was the reason for the fatalities.[5,6] Since its inception in the 1920s, millions of people have been vaccinated without ill effect. Where adverse events have occurred, dose, strain, and method of administration may be among the possible explanations. More serious events might be more frequent in those with symptomatic HIV infection.

Complications from BCG, though not common, can include regional suppurative lymphadenitis, hypersensitivity reactions (erythema multiforme), and disseminated mycobacteriosis (including pulmonary TB). In addition, cutaneous lesions (ulceration and fistula), musculoskeletal lesions, osteomyelitis, and osteoarticular mycobacteriosis may occur. Some of these complications can appear as late as 5 months following vaccination and may persist for months. Treatment options vary from no treatment at all to single drugs, combinations of drugs, or surgical interventions.

The most serious complication is disseminated BCG infection. BCG osteitis, especially of the long bones, can occur anywhere from 4 months to 2 years following BCG vaccination. Studies indicate that the incidence of this complication varies with the strain of BCG used and the method of production. Osteitis can be treated either with anti-TB drugs or surgically. Fatal disseminated BCG disease is rare and has been seen primarily in the immunocompromised; treatment is with anti-TB drugs except for pyrazinamide, to which all BCG strains are resistant.

Concerns have been voiced about the use of BCG in HIV-infected persons. Zambian studies have shown that mycobacteremia due to BCG in HIV-symptomatic infants is rare.[7] WHO recommends that BCG be given to HIV-infected but not to HIV-symptomatic children.[8] Other African studies of BCG given to infants of HIV-positive and -negative mothers demonstrated no increased adverse reactions in babies of either group.[9] In the United States, studies have not been done regarding the safety (and efficacy) of BCG in such populations; for this reason, among others, the use of BCG is not recommended for HIV-infected persons in the United States.[10]

In some instances, BCG has been shown to be tolerated poorly in adults. In a small study of BCG vaccination in 20 persons who were both purified protein derivative (PPD) and HIV negative, all had erythema, induration, and tenderness at the site of the injection. In addition, 14 experienced local ulceration.[11] When adverse reactions do appear, they should be reported to the vaccine manufacturer as well as to the Vaccine Adverse Event Reporting System (VAERS).

BCG VACCINE EFFICACY AND EFFECTIVENESS

Controversy has swirled around the efficacy (in an ideal setting, the theoretic ability to produce an effect) and effectiveness of BCG vaccine. Early twentieth-century successes indicated that BCG appeared to reduce case fatality rates in children and to protect health workers with heavy exposure. Following these human experiments, BCG was put to trials to evaluate its impact. Over the years, single studies with varying methodologies and validity have produced efficacy rates ranging from 0 to 80%, leading to reluctance on the part of researchers to state overall protective efficacy by BCG.

Questions about study design reduced the acceptance of positive results of BCG vaccination, even where case fatality rate had been reduced dramatically. Such an example is the 1935 classic study by Aronson and Dannenburg, who compared case fatality rates from TB among newborns and demonstrated an 85% reduction in deaths.[12] However, suspicion or conflicting conclusions about many other studies persisted and influenced decisions, particularly in Britain and the United States, about BCG vaccine policies for decades, up to the present time.[13,14] Studies in the United States using the BCG Tice strain in persons of varying ages who were PPD negative showed little or no vaccine protection.[15] The United States and the Netherlands decided not to use BCG but, rather, to pursue policies concerning contact tracing and tuberculin skin testing (TST) to identify persons for whom preventive therapy is indicated. In contrast, in the United Kingdom, where the Copenhagen strain was used in PPD-negative 13-year-olds, protection was demonstrated. These British studies in schoolchildren demonstrated protection lasting 10 years and then dropping off rapidly.[16]

Other international studies have come to various conclusions. A large community-based controlled trial (1968–1971) of BCG in India showed no protective effect 5 years later and only 17% 15 years later in vaccinated children.[17] This small effect was not observed in those vaccinated as adolescents or adults. In some instances, there were more TB cases among those vaccinated as adolescents or adults 5 years after vaccination. Researchers who claim that BCG protects not against pulmonary TB but only against severe and disseminated infections quote a Finnish autopsy study to support their view.[18]

Meta-analyses of the BCG Vaccine

In an attempt to put to rest the concerns over BCG vaccine efficacy and effectiveness, researchers have conducted meta-analyses. Fundamental to any discussion of such analyses is the distinction between vaccine efficacy and effectiveness. Reflecting ideal conditions, efficacy rates are best investigated through prospective studies, such as randomized controlled trials (RCT). On the other hand, effectiveness is best ascertained from field experience, for example, in retrospective or case-control, studies (CC) where real conditions, confounders, and effect modifiers are at work. In RCTs, researchers begin their study with an exposure (BCG vaccination) and then follow the study participants for development of TB. In CCs, researchers start with outcomes (TB cases) and then look back in time for a history of BCG exposure. In general, CCs are cheaper and easier to conduct and avoid the ethical concerns in RCTs, where giving either placebo or vaccine may result in marked disadvantages to recipients. Incomparability of controls and selection bias, however, limit the usefulness and conclusions that can be drawn from CCs. The reader of literature on meta-analyses should be aware of these distinctions in study design and outcome measures.

Two notable meta-analyses were done in the early 1990s. The first examined 18 studies dating back to 1950: 10 RCTs and 8 CCs. The review of the RCTs showed an 86% (confidence interval [CI]: 65–95%) protective efficacy against meningeal and miliary TB in children. The CC showed 75% effectiveness (CI: 61–84%). However, for pulmonary TB efficacy rates, the meta-analysts noted significant enough differences in the rates to preclude an estimation of protection.[19] The second meta-analysis was done by the Harvard School of Public Health at the request of the US Centers for Disease Control and Prevention (CDC). They reviewed 1,264 titles or abstracts from work done between 1933 and 1991 and scrutinized 70 of those; 26 met the investigators' inclusion criteria for study design and validity (such as surveillance completeness, equality between vaccinees and controls, and diagnostic confirmation).[20] Of these 26

Table 11-1. **Efficacy and Effectiveness of BCG Vaccine: A Summary of Findings from Randomized Controlled Trials and Case Control Studies**

Study Focus	Prospective Studies	Percent Efficacy	Retrospective Studies	Percent Effectiveness
Protection against disseminated, meningeal, and death	4 1	> 80 0	8 3	> 80 50–80
Newborns and infants	5	50–80	9 3 1	> 50 30–50 0 (HIV+), 60 (HIV−)
Children > 1 year of age	2 1	0–30 −10	3	16–74
Adolescents and adults	4 2	35–80 −30 to −50	2	10–60
Varying ages	2 4	80 0–15	1	—

Adapted from International Union Against Tuberculosis and Lung Disease.[69]
HIV = human immunodeficiency virus.

studies, 14 were RCTs and 12 were CCs. The investigators determined vaccine efficacy for each study design, for different outcome variables, and by age group and diagnostic criteria. The meta-analysis concluded that efficacy was 78% for disseminated TB, 71% for TB deaths, and 64% for TB meningitis. Studies that confirmed diagnosis using culture and/or histology had higher efficacy scores of 83%. In the RCTs, estimates revealed an overall efficacy of 51% (CI: 30–66%) and an overall effectiveness of 50% (CI: 36–61%) in the CCs. This meta-analysis concluded that vaccine efficacy was greater in children than in adults and that the strain of BCG vaccine was not a factor.[21] However, a key flaw in this estimate of efficacy was that the researchers used weighted averages, which is misleading.[22]

More recently, the International Union Against Tuberculosis and Lung Disease (IUATLD) has reviewed and discussed the findings from 25 RCTs and 30 CCs, as shown in Table 11-1.[23] From this, one can conclude that BCG is protective against death from TB as well as against disseminated and meningeal TB and that at least 50% protection is conferred by BCG vaccination of newborns and infants. In general, vaccination of older children does not confer the same degree of protection as it does at an earlier age; in fact, vaccination of adolescents or adults is not indicated and is rarely effective. Specific studies examine in greater depth the details within Table 11-1. Of note are the Zambian studies, which showed that the 60% protection in HIV-negative children was not seen at all in HIV-positive children.[24]

Widely divergent results from vaccine efficacy and effectiveness studies have led researchers to formulate hypotheses for such variations. Characteristics of the study population (age, genetic make-up, HIV status), environmental factors (exposure to nontuberculous mycobacteria), presence of other organisms (helminths), and geographic factors (latitude) are some explanations proffered. Vaccine (strains, phenotype, genotype, virulence) and methods of vaccine administration (route, dosage) are all proposed to have influenced results and have led to varying conclusions. Moreover, sample size, susceptibility status, case definitions, bacteriologic confirmation, lack of comparability to controls, incomplete follow-up, and questions about ongoing exposure have plagued analyses. The fact that most studies have enrolled infants or children rather than adults makes it harder to draw statistically significant conclusions about some population subsets.

Smith and Fine have examined these hypotheses closely.[25] Diverse reasons are assessed for such variation in results: methodologic stringency, vaccine virulence, risk attributable to exogenous re-infection, prevalence of infection with environmental mycobacteria, nutritional status and genetic make-up of vaccinees, and helminthic infestation. However, some investigators state that methodologic flaws do not explain all the differences.[26] Studies that are higher in quality from a methodologic point of view have also shown higher efficacy.[27] Nevertheless, questions remain when other studies show that different BCG vaccines have the same efficacy in the same populations and that the same vaccines have different efficacies in different populations. Genetic differences in the host population have been discounted as reasons for differences in results, and researchers have suggested that genetic markers in individuals with and without TB or between populations where BCG appears to work to different degrees should be studied.[22,28]

Some researchers have investigated whether vaccine strains produced by different manufacturers can have different microbiologic properties or produce variable immunogenicity, thereby explaining differences in vaccine efficacy and effectiveness.[29,30] They concluded that vaccine strain is not a key explanation. However, opposing conclusions have been drawn by meta-analyses in the United States and Hong Kong.[15]

A number of factors may modify the efficacy of BCG. Environmental mycobacterial infection can mask the protection of BCG, and helminthic infestation can alter human thymus-dependent lymphocyte (T cell) responses.[31] Protection attributable to exogenous re-infection, differences in genetic make-up, or nutritional status of vaccinees do not explain the differences in study results. Arguments that poor nutritional status blunts the effectiveness of BCG vaccine are countered by vaccine results in leprosy populations, where the vaccine provided better protection against leprosy than against TB. The failure against TB, therefore, is not related to nutritional impairment alone. Studies conducted at sites farther from the equator have been associated with higher efficacy, with geographic latitude accounting for up to 40% of the differences.[32] This may be explained in part by the fact that environmental (nontuberculous) mycobacteria (NTM) thrive in warmer climates (lower latitudes) and that BCG cannot improve on the "natural immunity" afforded by NTM in the environment. Temperature, humidity, ultraviolet (UV) radiation, and skin pigmentation have also been said to explain such differences.

The role of environmental bacteria has been successfully invoked as an explanation for variation in the efficacy of BCG vaccination.[33] NTM are ubiquitous, diverse, and vary geographically. Animal studies have led researchers to believe that NTM provide some protection against TB; conversely, BCG vaccine may protect against infection with some NTM, such as *M. avium-intracellulare*.[34,35] In some studies, however, the protection afforded by BCG appears to be relatively low; this might be due to population characteristics, such as high previous NTM exposure and infection. Moreover, this circumstance would make BCG efficacy in newborns appear higher simply because they had not "benefited" from exposure to NTM.

The Chingleput study of India often enters into analyses of BCG efficacy and effectiveness with regard to study validity as an explanation for efficacy and effectiveness results. The study was initiated in 1968 by the Indian Council of Medical Research, WHO, and the US Public Health Service, with data publicized in 1980.[36] This highly scientific study, scrutinized by WHO's Scientific Group, showed no protection against TB.[37] In addition, hypotheses about the use of different vaccine strains artificially influencing outcomes are neutralized by this study; two highly efficacious vaccine strains (Pasteur and Danish strains) at two different doses showed no efficacy in Chingleput.[38] Observations about vaccine doses and routes are also contradicted by the Chingleput study and other controlled trials.[39]

Target Populations for Vaccination

Children

For children living outside the United States, WHO has strongly recommended that BCG vaccine be given to newborns or as early in life as possible. As part of the Expanded Program on Immunization (EPI) and the Global Program on Vaccinations of WHO, BCG is given intradermally as a single dose.[40] In fact, each year approximately 100 million children are vaccinated with BCG.[41] In some countries (eg, Bulgaria, Azerbaijan, and other former Soviet block nations), the policy is to vaccinate and revaccinate children of various ages and settings (at birth, at school entry, at school departure), but these practices lack proven utility. The United States and the Netherlands do not use BCG in the standard vaccination schedule for children. Those decisions are based on historic data as described previously.

Children usually acquire TB from adults with infectious pulmonary disease who are either undiagnosed, early in their treatment course and still coughing, or noncompliant with their treatment regimen. According to CDC guidelines, within the United States, if a child is continuously exposed to such an infected person and cannot either be removed from such a setting or given preventive treatment, then BCG should be considered.[42] This approach is especially critical if the infected adult has multiple-drug–resistant TB (MDR-TB). Assurance that the child is TST negative is the first step before vaccination. If the child is TST positive, then a diagnostic work-up and full course of treatment with anti-TB drugs is indicated for the child.

Adolescents and Adults in the General Population

BCG should not be regarded as a primary strategy, largely because studies have not proven BCG to be either efficacious or effective in this population age group.

Health Care Workers

Prevention of infection is the first step in both low- and high-risk settings. Comprehensive infection control measures and prompt identification, isolation, and treatment of persons with active TB are the critical steps. These measures will reduce the likelihood of exposure and transmission to health care workers (HCW), other persons at a facility, and visitors to the facility. BCG should not be regarded as the primary strategy. However, case-by-case considerations can be made for BCG for those working in high-exposure settings.[43] Where the prevalence of MDR-TB is high, where transmission of MDR-TB to HCWs is likely, and where implementation of infection control precautions has failed, BCG vaccination can be entertained. HCWs should be counseled about the variability of protection by the vaccine, the implications for future TST, and the possibility of complications for immunosuppressed persons. HCWs with HIV infection should be counseled to seek employment in places where TB transmission is the lowest possible.

HIV-Infected Persons

Inconsistent study results on the safety of BCG vaccine in HIV-infected populations have led to some debate as to whether HIV-infected persons should receive BCG. The CDC does not recommend BCG for persons with HIV infection. On the other hand, WHO recommends that BCG be given to asymptomatic

HIV-infected children who have acquired HIV through maternal transmission. Studies have shown, however, that HIV infection lowers BCG's protective effect against extrapulmonary TB.[44]

Pregnant Women

BCG's use in pregnancy is not recommended, although no evidence exists for harmful effects to the developing fetus.

Contraindications

The CDC does not support the administration of BCG to HIV-infected persons who are symptomatic, as risks and benefits have not been clearly defined. In addition, BCG should not be administered to persons with congenital immunodeficiency, leukemia, lymphoma, generalized malignancy, or on long-term regimens of immunosuppression (eg, steroids, radiation, alkylating agents, or antimetabolites). Of note is that WHO's only contraindication is for persons with symptomatic HIV/AIDS; for children who are HIV infected but asymptomatic, WHO does recommend BCG.[45]

VACCINE ADMINISTRATION

Given the CDC guidelines for limited BCG vaccine use, practitioners considering its use should first reflect on several factors: (1) the variable protection levels afforded by BCG vaccine, especially in adults; (2) potential difficulties interpreting TST results after vaccination; (3) possible risks of exposure to immunocompromised persons; and (4) the lowered likelihood of implementation of other effective public health measures. Before administering BCG vaccine, providers and practitioners are advised to consult first with local TB control program personnel and the CDC Division of TB Elimination in Atlanta, Georgia.

BCG vaccine comes freeze dried and should remain refrigerated until reconstitution, just prior to use. It should be used within 8 hours of reconstitution. As it is very light sensitive, it should be protected from such exposure. A dose of 0.3 mL of reconstituted vaccine is placed on the lower deltoid area and then delivered percutaneously through a multipuncture disk. Babies less than 1 month old should receive a half-dose by increasing the diluent added to the lyophilized vaccine. If these children remain at risk and their TST reaction (using 5 tuberculin units [TU] of PPD tuberculin) remains at less than 5 mm of induration, they should receive the full dose at 1 year.

Alternatively, an intradermal injection of 0.05 mL for children less than 1 year of age (0.1 mL for children 1 year and older) into the deltoid using a 25-gauge needle is the standard method and amount of delivery recommended by manufacturers who provide vaccine for UNICEF.[46]

Normally, within 2 or 3 weeks following the multipuncture administration of BCG, a blue-red pustule forms. This pustule ulcerates approximately 6 weeks after the administration and forms a lesion roughly 5 mm in diameter. The scab forms and then heals in 3 months, resulting in a permanent scar. This process may be accelerated if a vaccinee has a prior history of infection with *M. tb*. About one-third of vaccinees will develop hypertrophic scars, and a smaller percentage (2–4%) have keloid reactions. It should be noted that a scar is not a correlate of protection and that less permanent scars occur in infants compared with children and adolescents; this may be due to the half dose used in infants. The presence or absence of a scar is used in vaccine uptake surveys and prevalence studies but may not give entirely accurate community BCG rates.

Similarly, following the intradermal administration of BCG, a red induration of 5 to 15 mm occurs, with a soft-centered crust around the induration persisting for up to a month. Between 6 and 10 weeks later, the crust falls off, leaving a flat, permanent scar of 3 to 7 mm. Regional (axillary and cervical) lymphadenopathy is part of a normal reaction, even in the absence of erythema or vesicles. Subcutaneous administration of BCG may be more likely to provoke local soreness, erythema, and drainage.

Revaccination

Because the protective effect of BCG wanes over 15 to 20 years, some countries advocate revaccination at age 5 to 14 years. However, no evidence exists to support BCG's protection against TB in this age group, and WHO discourages revaccination.[40] Moreover, persons of these ages are among those at the lowest risk for TB, and studies for these ages have demonstrated neither the efficacy nor the effectiveness of vaccination. In addition, revaccination campaigns at school entry tend to be inefficient, whereas capture of susceptible newborns and infants is relatively cost-efficient. Of note, however, is that revaccination with BCG has been shown to confer some protection against leprosy.[47]

Low-Prevalence Settings

Where TB prevalence is quite low and, therefore, the cost-benefit ratio may be unfavorable, some countries have opted to forego BCG vaccination. The IUATLD has put forth recommendations for the discontinuation of mass BCG campaigns.[48] These recommendations are informed by three key issues: (1) the local level of efficacy of BCG vaccine, (2) the risk-benefit of serious forms of TB versus frequency of adverse reactions, and (3) the value placed on the usefulness of TST conversions where preventive chemotherapy would be indicated.

Tuberculin Skin Testing

The question arises as to the need for or the significance of TST following BCG vaccination.[42] What is known is that the reaction can be nonexistent or as large as 19 mm at the TST site.[49,50] The presence and size do not correlate with protection and do not indicate if the reaction is due to the vaccination or to infection itself. Moreover, the reactivity will wane over time and usually is not present 10 years after BCG vaccination, assuming that the vaccinee has not had any other *M. tb* exposure and infection.

If TST is done following BCG vaccination, it is recommended that it be performed 3 months after BCG administration; however, reactivity can develop as early as 6 weeks. Results, expressed as mm of induration, should be documented in the person's medical record. An indication of unsuccessful immunization is an induration of less than 5 mm. However, vaccinees who have a positive TST reaction of 5 mm or greater should not enroll in ongoing periodic testing (eg, as is done for health care workers). Rather, they should be retested only if they have been exposed to an individual with an infectious case of tuberculosis. An increase in diameter of induration of 10 mm or more in individuals below 35 years of age and 15 mm or more in those 35 years or older may indicate a recent infection with *M. tb*.

Although some have argued that the utility of TST is markedly diminished, or even eliminated, in those who have received BCG, this is not the case. TST can still be used to support or exclude the diagnosis of *M. tb* infection. If such a BCG-vaccinated person has a TST reaction (induration) of 10 mm or greater, the diagnosis of latent TB infection should be entertained and curative therapy should be considered, especially in any of the following circumstances: (1) the BCG-vaccinated person has a history of contact with an infected person (particularly if that infectious contact is known to have transmitted *M. tb* to others); (2) he or she was either born or has lived in a country where TB prevalence is high; or (3) he or she works as an employee or volunteer in a setting where contact with infected people is both close and continuous, for example, homeless shelters, TB treatment facilities, or drug treatment centers.[51] A difference of at least 15 mm in induration diameter between a previous test and a more recent one following a possible exposure is thought to be indicative of newly acquired *M. tb* infection.[52] The TST, however, is far from an ideal test, and newer diagnostics are critically needed.

Decreased or absent TST reactivity can be seen in HIV-infected persons. Among HIV-infected persons who have also been BCG vaccinated, a TST reaction of more than 5 mm's induration, or even nonreactivity, is an indicator for TB preventive therapy in patients at risk of *M. tb* infection. Moreover, symptoms of TB infection, regardless of TST reaction or HIV status, should lead health care providers to consider a diagnosis of active TB among BCG vaccinees, especially if they have had recent exposure to a person with an infectious case.

FUTURE VACCINE DEVELOPMENTS

Why a New Vaccine?

Many reasons exist for the need for a new vaccine against TB. Although the present vaccine is 80 years old, its questionable effectiveness is the strongest argument for a new vaccine. In addition, current drug treatment strategies using a "short-course" chemotherapy are fraught with provider and patient compliance failures; the appearance of multiple-drug resistance (MDR-TB) is attributable to the latter. New vaccines could circumvent these problems to some extent. In spite of global progress made in coverage by directly observed treatment, short-course strategies (DOTS), the burden of TB worldwide is increasing rapidly, predominantly in the poorest of developing countries. Furthermore, some of these poor nations are simultaneously battling HIV/AIDS but have neither the human nor the fiscal resources to do so effectively.

Although BCG vaccine has been used in humans since 1921, no other vaccine has been fully developed; until recently, no new TB candidate vaccine clinical trials had been conducted. This is surprising, given that more than three billion individuals worldwide have received this vaccine and that much controversy has centered on the vaccine's efficacy and effectiveness. The fact remains that some individuals who received BCG have still contracted TB. BCG does not decrease the risk of infection; however, it does decrease the risk of progression from latent to active disease.[53]

Cost-Effectiveness

There is a strong economic argument to be made for more effective vaccines in the fight against TB. From this viewpoint, the productivity of a nation is reflected by the health of its people and the resultant quality of their lives. Illness and disability mean lost productivity, lost goods and services to the public, and loss of wages to the employee; loss of wages means entry into a cycle of poverty and higher risk of TB and HIV/AIDS. Death means loss of a workforce, and, in homes, death means loss of parents, leaving orphans. Not to be overlooked is that rising TB rates in some countries could adversely affect tourism, which may be a large revenue-generating activity for a nation.

It has been said that a vaccine with only 50% efficacy would save millions of lives each year and possibly be more effective in reducing the global TB burden than DOTS delivered with 100% efficiency.[54] Moreover, economic modeling has shown that a 75% effective vaccine that lasted 10 years would save a billion people at least $25 (US) each in their medical costs.[55] Of course, a vaccine would not mean that medical systems could forego screening, diagnostic testing, or prevention measures, but it could equate to lowered treatment costs. Because children represent about 10% of the TB burden, the impact of the present BCG vaccine has been relatively small on the overall burden of TB. Although reporting deficiencies may underestimate that figure, children stand as sentinel cases for TB in the community. New vaccines would have to address entire populations, not just children, to demonstrate cost-effectiveness.

Vaccine Development

Many aspects characterize the ideal vaccine: a high safety profile and no adverse effects, a demonstrated protection in animal models, protection against infection versus disease, single dosage in a noninjectable form, heat stability with a long shelf life, ease of transportation and storage, lack of interference or cross-reactivity with other vaccines, and a clear indication of conversion in the vaccinee. Unfortunately, the costs of moving many novel vaccine candidates from academia to clinical settings may be prohibitive when there is minimal commercial interest. The challenges with any vaccine are the degree of protection, the economic return, and lengthy and costly clinical trials.

The good news, however, is that vaccine research has benefited from advances in comparative proteomics, transcription analysis, and genomics. Characterizing the TB genome, with its 4,000,000 base pairs and nearly 4,000 protein-coding genes, has represented a major breakthrough in scientists' understanding of the *Mycobacterium* and in their ability to devise ways to stop its infection and disease-producing functions.[56]

Knowing the basics of the *Mycobacterium*'s functions informs new vaccine development strategies. Mycobacteria take up residence in the macrophages of the host during the primary infection. Most individuals are able to mount a sufficient immune response such that the infection does not progress to disease. Within the macrophage, *M. Tb* locates itself in a separate compartment called a phagosome, protected from lysosomes but with access to major histocompatibility complex (MHC) antigens (class I molecules) and a processing pathway. This presentation of the mycobacterial antigens by the MHC molecule to the MHC pathway stimulates cytokines and activates both CD4 T cells and CD8 T cells. In turn, these T cells produce interferon-γ (IFN-γ), which plays a key role in the macrophage's microbicidal functions; IFN-γ aids in recognition of the mycobacterial glycolipids and subsequent killing of the intracellular *M. Tb*.

Scientists believe that cell-mediated immunity (CMI), rather than antibody formation, plays a large role in protection against TB infection following exposure. When CD4 cell function is disrupted and the ability to produce IFN is diminished, then TB bacilli are more likely to take up residence in the host. Cytotoxic T lymphocytes, cytokines, lymphokines, and macrophages play critical roles as well. In addition, CD8 cells are thought to work synergistically with CD4 cells to contain a latent infection and prevent its development to an active case.

Vaccine Types

Potentially, three vaccine types are needed: (1) one to prevent infection, a preexposure vaccine; (2) one to prevent progression to disease, a postexposure or preventive therapeutic vaccine; and (3) one to treat

Table 11-2. New Antituberculosis Vaccines in Preclinical Development

	Recombinant	*Peptide*	*DNA*
Product	Recombinant BCG overexpressing Ag 85A	MHC-promiscuous peptides admixed with polyarginine	*Mycobacterium leprae* heat shock protein–65 in plasmid
Indication	Replacement for BCG in neonates	Booster for neonatal BCG, in adolescents	Use with drug therapy to reduce relapse
Clinical material	Ongoing production (Korea)	Ongoing production (Intercell, AG)	Ongoing production (Cobra Pharmaceuticals)
Preclinical studies	Planned	Planned	Planned
Clinical trial site	NIH/TBRU; San Francisco	Selection under way	Selection under way
Clinical trials	2002	2002 and 2003	2003

Adapted from Sequella Global TB Foundation 2002.[57]
BCG = bacille Calmette-Guérin; DNA = deoxyribonucleic acid; MHC = major histocompatibility complex; NIH National Institutes of Health; TBRU = Tuberculosis Research Unit.

those with active disease, a therapeutic vaccine. The first category could be used for those who are immunologically naive to *M. tb*; this is the key function of the standard BCG vaccine. The second category would be useful for those with latent infection, which includes one-third of the world's population (an estimated two billion people). In addition, preventive therapeutic vaccines are of interest for persons with latent infection because of the 10% whose disease might be reactivated during their lifetime and, in particular, for those with HIV infection in whom the reactivation risk is 10% each year. The third vaccine would interrupt or reverse the disease pathology in individuals who have clinical cases of TB, either diagnosed or suspected. Some interest has been generated in postexposure vaccines, and a fast-tracked approval process is in place because of the perceived threat of bioterrorism.

Other functions of a new vaccine could also be envisioned. One alternative would be to enhance the BCG protection already afforded by the primary vaccination. For example, the vaccine could provide better BCG protection against TB meningitis or induce antipulmonary and extrapulmonary TB effects in both children and adults. Therapeutic vaccines could be designed to enhance drug effectiveness in MDR-TB cases, shorten the treatment duration with first-line TB drugs, or enhance the preventive drug treatment used in those at risk of TB to avoid the transition from latent to active disease.

At the time of this writing, a handful of new anti-TB vaccines are in preclinical development (Table 11-2).[57]

Candidate Vaccines

The more than 200 candidate vaccines, all of whose strategies are to stimulate an immune response, can be classified into four basic categories: (1) subunit vaccines, (2) naked deoxyribonucleic acid (DNA) vaccines, (3) recombinant BCG or live attenuated mycobacteria, and (4) vaccines using live attenuated nonmycobacterial vectors. The elaboration of the *M. tb* genome and of BCG and nonpathogenic mycobacteria enlarges the pool of possible vaccine candidates. By the time of this writing, 213 vaccines had been tested at the National Institutes of Health. About half, or 103, are subunit vaccines, 37 are DNA vaccines, 23 are recombinant vaccines, and 7 are adjuvant vaccines.

Subunits

Subunits can be proteins, lipids, or carbohydrates. Mycobacteria secrete antigens, such as ESAT-6 and Ag 85A, which are recognized by T cells and provoke an immune response. Some components of disease-producing organisms can induce either protective immune responses or pathologic changes; therefore, vaccine research selects the optimum packaging of one or more subunits into potential vaccine candidates. Moreover, antigens fused with other antigens may have additive, or synergistic, effects. The ESAT-6 subunit vaccine in genetic fusion with Ag 85B shows such potential. Fusion proteins could create new T-cell epitopes, not yet seen as detrimental.

Because the immune memory for BCG can wane over time, subunit vaccines can also be used as booster doses in place of simple revaccination with BCG alone. Priming with naked (purified) DNA and later boosting with a protein may increase protection, all the while maintaining the role of the original BCG vaccine in lieu of replacing it altogether. A notable limitation is that such boosting cannot be done in people who are PPD positive because of concerns of hyperreactivity.

DNA Vaccines

DNA vaccines that encode mycobacterial antigens, such as heat shock protein (HSP) 65 and, especially, Ag 85A, induce protection by eliciting cellular and humoral responses. Nevertheless, because they may create adverse immunogenicity of proteins and lipoproteins, they are more likely to be used to screen and identify vaccine candidates, in a process that some have called vaccinomics.[58]

Recombinants

Recombinant vaccines use existing microorganisms that are genetically altered to produce additional antigens. Recombinant vaccines, including recombinant BCG (rBCG), use live attenuated mycobacteria that express immunodominant antigens and cytokines. MVA-Ag85A is such an example. With support from Wellcome Trust, a large British charity, a booster made of vaccinia virus that produces antigen 85 (a protein produced by *M. tb*), MVA-Ag85A, is the first to reach human testing. A new TB vaccine used in tandem with BCG has been manufactured in Germany and is undergoing phase I safety and immunogenicity trials with three arms: (1) BCG alone, mapping immune response; (2) MVA-Ag85A alone, mapping immune response and monitoring safety; and (3) BCG as a prime, followed by a boost with MVA-Ag85A. This will be started with parallel trials in endemic countries. A recombinant poxvirus, FP9, also expressing Ag85A, is another candidate in this prime-boost strategy.

Other Candidates

Comparing genomes of virulent and nonvirulent mycobacteria, as well as comparing various strains of BCG, will further elucidate why some strains produce disease and others do not. Moreover, the RD1 deletion of *M. bovis*, which led to the creation of BCG, has been incorporated into *M. tb*.[59] Researchers will test this attenuated form to see if it can persist enough to generate a protective immune response. A heat-inactivated form of an environmental mycobacterium (*M. vaccae*) is being tested in HIV-positive persons.[60]

Improving BCG

Some workers suggest that improvements on the effectiveness of the BCG vaccine might be the most realistic goal. This improvement could be achieved by modifying mycobacteria whose more virulent genes have been deleted, thereby creating a mutant for a live but attenuated vaccine. Such mutants may not be able to produce a cell wall or may be deficient in an enzyme, for example. This would mean that they could not exist in the host for long periods of time, thereby making them safer than the currently available vaccines, especially in immunocompromised persons.

Testing such a BCG mutant at lower doses or in prime-boost combination is a strategy proposed by some researchers.[61] Prime doses are followed a few weeks later by booster doses that are thought to add to the efficacy of the single dose. These booster doses can be the same as the prime or may use alternative routes (eg, oral vs intradermal). Prime-boost strategies may also combine BCG with another novel candidate vaccine to improve the performance of the BCG vaccine.

Complementary Developmental Needs

Not to be overlooked is the fact that surrogate markers, adjuvants, and new animal-model methodology complement the progress made in vaccines against TB. In fact, progress could not be made without advances in these areas.

Surrogate Markers

Clear surrogate markers are critical in the testing of vaccine candidates. GlaxoSmithKline's Action TB Initiative, the TB Research Unit of the National Institute for Allergy and Infectious Diseases, and groups in London and South Africa are studying markers that correlate with immunologic protection as part of vaccine trials. In the past, TST was used as an indicator of the "take" of the BCG vaccine. However, such reactivity is variable and depends on many factors, such as the type of vaccine, doses, time since the BCG vaccination, age at BCG vaccination, host genetics, exposure to nonmycobacterial antigens, and past exposure to tuberculin.[53,62] In fact, research has shown that TST does not predict immunity to TB.[63] This means that delayed-type hypersensitivity (DTH) cannot be used reliably as a marker for vaccine efficacy. The cell types, cytokines, and the resultant pathology produced by cell-mediated immunity (CMI) and DTH, though both mediated by T cells, use different pathways. For example, CMI activates macrophages, whereas DTH is associated with tissue damage and caseation.[64]

Adjuvants

Adjuvants may reduce the amount, number, or frequency of administration or enhance vaccine efficacy, especially in patients who are immunocompromised or have poor immune responses. Antigens may be more versatile when used with either synthetic or host cell adjuvants. Synthetic adjuvants, such as monophosphoryl lipid A (MPL) and dimethyl dioctadecyclammonium (DDA), have been used with ESAT-6 or Ag 85A to enhance specific antibody and cellular proliferative response. The optimum delivery of the vaccine has led to exploration of other mechanisms, such as dendritic cells, pox viruses, DNA, recombinant BCG, and microspheres with protein or with DNA. Adjuvants are needed to stimulate long-lasting immunity in T cells. In addition, their safety profile makes them attractive.

Animal Models for Vaccines

A key step in vaccine research progress is the standardization of experimental models and vaccine candidate protocols, including route, dose, and time of evaluation. Initial screening is done using mice, mostly for reasons of cost, and, then if protection is demonstrated, follow-up studies with guinea pigs are conducted. Guinea pigs are good models because they are susceptible to skin testing and the progression of disease is like that in humans. Final testing is done in nonhuman primates. Although animal studies can be costly, they lessen the likelihood of failure in phase III clinical trials, which can be a more expensive and untimely finding. Animal models that better simulate the conditions and circumstances of human experience, including exposures, pathology, and duration of protection in humans, will better inform researchers about up-and-coming vaccine candidates.

Partnerships for Recent Vaccine Developments

WHO organized the Global Forum on TB Vaccine Research and Development, which is dedicated to making progress in new TB vaccines to explore the issues confronting the TB community. A TB vaccine advisory committee—the Tuberculosis Vaccine Initiative Advisory Committee (TBVIAC)—is now working in conjunction with the WHO/UNAIDS (Joint United Nations Program on HIV/AIDS) Initiative for Vaccine Research (IVR) as well as the Stop TB Global Partnership.[65] They have made many recommendations focused on clinical investigations, such as the need to establish multicenter clinical trials networks, coordination with current international AIDS and malaria vaccine testing programs, and ethical and clinical guidelines to address complex issues. In addition, the Global Forum is well aware of the hurdles of meeting standards set by regulatory authorities.[66]

The TBVIAC and the Global Forum recognize the critical role played by public/private partnerships with national and multinational companies for large-scale production. Smaller entities, ranging from universities to private biotechnology laboratories and bioinformatics offices, have joined hands with corporate partners, such as pharmaceutical companies and business groups, to pursue TB vaccine research through the nonprofit organization Sequella Global TB Foundation. Early in 2002, Sequella formed a TB Vaccine Collaboration program funded with $25,000,000 (US) from the Bill and Melinda Gates Foundation to make TB vaccines a global reality by moving discoveries in basic science from the laboratory into the clinic and then out to health care workers. Three groups are engaged in improving BCG, developing a preinfection vaccine, or developing a postexposure vaccine. The European Commission and some smaller laboratories have formed and funded a European consortium to screen vaccine candidates.[67] Finally, the United States National Institutes of Health, the largest public funder of TB research, had a budget of $80,000,000 (US) in the year 2000 to expand its research in TB.[69]

Constraints to TB Vaccine Progress

Prospective studies, also known as efficacy studies or RCTs, are long, complex, and costly. Vaccine trials in uninfected individuals would require follow-up for as many as 15 to 20 years. Such studies would provide the most unambiguous data and possibly resolve questions raised by efficacy trials. The ethics of withholding BCG during RCTs and testing for vaccine safety in immunodeficient individuals add layers of complexity as well. Clearer surrogate markers of immune status and animal models that better mimic the human condition are additional challenges. A significant hurdle is the major financial outlay by pharmaceutical research and development companies to produce a vaccine that is both safe and effective for use in humans. Regulatory standards for new vaccine products pose another challenge and vary from country to country. Finally, market potential is largely among the poorest countries, where 98% of persons with TB reside and where the risk is high owing to malnutrition, immunocompromise by HIV, and the factors associated with poverty. These countries can ill afford to support such vaccine development costs or to consider buying the products of technology.

CONCLUSION

TB vaccine development is at a crossroads. Current and upcoming vaccine research and development will address the long gap in appropriate TB vaccines for both the developing world and developed nations. These vaccines will require reproducible markers of protective immunity, consensus on outcome measures, better diagnostic tests than presently available in sputum smear microscopy, and an advanced appreciation of the modifying influences on vaccine efficacy and effectiveness. Ethical concerns in trials all the way to marketing interests, among many factors, will shape the direction and focus of investigation. Not to be overlooked are regulatory standards that will have to be addressed. Strategies to implement vaccine policies for adults as well as children will require approaches akin to the EPI. Strong research and development partnerships, fully funded and committed to fast-track progress, will be needed to complement such endeavors if researchers and public health specialists alike are to prevent and control TB for coming generations around the world.

REFERENCES

1. Kenyon TA, Valmay SE, Inle WW, et al. Transmission of multiple-drug resistance *Mycobacterium tuberculosis* during a long airplane flight. N Engl J Med 1996;334:933–8.

2. Guérin C. The history of BCG. In: Rosenthal SR, editor. BCG vaccination against tuberculosis. Boston: Little, Brown; 1957. p. 48–53.

3. Calmette A. Preventive vaccination against tuberculosis with BCG. Proc R Soc Med 1931;24:85–94.

4. Mahairas GG, Sobo PJ, Hickey MJ, et al. Molecular analysis of genetic diferences between *Mycobacterium bovis* BCG and virulent *M. bovis*. J Bacteriol 1996;178:1274–82.

5. Lange B. Untersuchungen zur klarung der ursachen der im anschluss an die Calmette-Impfung aufgetretenen sauglingserkrankungen in Lubeck. Z Tuberkulose 1930;59:1–18.

6. Moegling A. Die epidemiologie der Lubecker sauglingstuberkulose. Arb Reichsges Amt 1935;69:1–24.

7. Waddell RD, Lishimpi K, Fordahm von Reyn C, et al. Bacteremia due to *Mycobacterium tuberculosis* or *M. bovis*, Bacille Calmette-Guérin (BCG) among HIV-positive children and adults in Zambia. AIDS 2001;15:55–60.

8. World Health Organization. Special Programme on AIDS and Expanded Programme on Immunization Joint Statement. Consultation on human immunodeficiency virus (HIV) and routine childhood immunization. Wkly Epidemiol Rec 1987;62:297–9.

9. O'Brien KL, Ruff AJ, Louis MA, et al. Bacille Calmette-Guérin complications in children born to HIV-1 infected women with a review of the literature. Pediatrics 1995;95:414–8.

10. Centers for Disease Control and Prevention. The role of BCG vaccine in the prevention and control of tuberculosis in the United States. A joint statement by the Advisory Council for the Elimination of Tuberculosis and the Advisory Committee on Immunization Practices. MMWR Morb Mortal Wkly Rep 1996;45:12–3.

11. Brewer MA, Edwards KM, Palmer PS, Hinson HP. BCG immunization in normal healthy adults. J Infect Dis 1994; 170:476–9.

12. Aronson JD, Dannenberg AM. Effect of vaccination with BCG on tuberculosis in infancy and in childhood. Correlation of reactions to tuberculin tests, roentgenologic diagnosis, and mortality. Am J Dis Child 1935;50:1117–30.

13. Dormandy T. The white death. 1st ed. London: Hambledon Press; 1999.

14. Feldberg GD. Disease and class. Tuberculosis and the shaping of modern North American society. 1st ed. New Brunswick (NJ): Rutgers University Press; 1995.

15. Comstock GW, Palmer CE. Long-term results of BCG vaccination in the southern US. Am Rev Respir Dis 1996;93(2):171–83.

16. Hart PDA, Sutherland I. BCG and vole bacillus vaccines in the prevention of tuberculosis in adolescence and early adult life. Final report to the Medical Research Council. BMJ 1977;2:293–5.

17. Tripathy SP. Fifteen year follow-up of the Indian BCG prevention trial. In: International Journal of Tuberculosis and Lung Disease, editor. Proceedings of the XXVIth IUAT World Conference on Tuberculosis and Respiratory Diseases. Singapore: Professional Postgraduate Services International; 1987. p. 69–72.

18. Sutherland I, Lindgren I. The protective effect of BCG vaccination as indicated by autopsy studies. Tubercle 1979;60:225–31.

19. Rodrigues LC, Diwan VK, Wheeler JG. Protective effect of BCG against tuberculous meningitis and military tuberculosis. A meta-analysis. Int J Epidemiol 1993;22:1154–8.

20. Technology Assessment Group. Report to the Centers for Disease Control and Prevention. Boston: Harvard School of Public Health; 1993.

21. Colditz GA, Brewer TF, Berkey CS, et al. The efficacy of BCG in the prevention of tuberculosis. Meta-analysis of the published literature. JAMA 1994;271:698–702.

22. Fine PEM. BCG vaccines and vaccination. In: Reichman LB, Hershfield ES, editors. Tuberculosis. A comprehensive international approach. 2nd ed. New York: Marcel Dekker; 2000. p. 490–521.

23. Rieder H. Interventions for tuberculosis control and elimination. IJTLD 2002;107–15.

24. Bhat GJ, Diwan VK, Chintu C, et al. HIV, BCG, and TB in children. A case control study in Lusaka, Zambia. J Trop Pediatr 1993;39:219–23.

25. Smith PG, Fine PEM. BCG vaccination. In: Davies PDO, editor. Clinical tuberculosis. London: Chapman and Hall Medical; 1998. p. 417–31.

26. Clemens JD, Jackie JH, Chuong JH, Feinstein AR. The BCG controversy. A methodological and statistical reappraisal. JAMA 1983;249:23623–9.

27. Colditz GA, Berkey CS, Mosteller F, et al. The efficacy of bacillus Calmette-Guérin vaccination of newborns and infants in the prevention of tuberculosis. Meta-analysis of the published literature. Pediatrics 1995;96:29–35.

28. Milstein JB, Gibson JJ. Quality control of BCG vaccines by WHO. A review of factors that may influence vaccine effectiveness and safety. Bull World Health Organ 1990;68:93–108.

29. Hart PDA. Efficacy and applicability of mass BCG vaccination in TB control. BMJ 1967;1:1587–92.

30. Fine PEM, Vynnycky E. The effect of heterologous immunity upon the apparent efficacy of (eg, BCG) vaccines. Vaccine 1998;16:1923–8.

31. Elias D, Wolday D, Akuffo H, et al. Effect of deworming on human T Cell responses to mycobacterial antigens in helminth exposed individuals before and after bacilli Calmette-Guérin (BCG) vaccination. Clin Exp Immunol 2001;123:219–25.

32. Wilson ME, Fineberg HV, Colditz GA. Geographic latitude and the efficacy of bacillus Calmette-Guérin vaccine. Clin Infect Dis 1995;20:982–91.

33. Palmer CE, Long MW. Effects of infection with atypical mycobacteria on BCG vaccination and tuberculosis. Am Rev Respir Dis 1966;94;553–68.

34. Katila ML, Brander E, Backman A. Neonatal BCG vaccination and mycobacterial cervical adenitis in childhood. Tubercle 1987;68:291–6.

35. Wickman K. Clinical significance of nontuberculous mycobacteria. A bacteriological survey of Swedish strains isolated between 1973 and 1981. Scand J Infect Dis 1986;18:337–45.

36. Tuberculosis Prevention Trials in Madras. Trial of BCG vaccines in South India for TB prevention. Indian J Med Res 1980;72 Suppl:1–74.

37. Indian Council on Medical Research, WHO Scientific Group. Vaccination against TB. World Health Organ Tech Rep Ser 1980;651.

38. Tuberculosis Prevention Trial. Trial of BCG vaccines in south India for tuberculosis prevention. First report. Bull World Health Organ 1979;57:819–27.

39. Tuberculosis Research Centre (ICMR) Chennai. Fifteen year follow up of trial of BCG vaccines in south India for tuberculosis prevention. Indian J Med Res 1999;110:56–69.

40. World Health Organization. Global Tuberculosis Program and Global Programme on Vaccines. Statement on BCG revaccination for the prevention of tuberculosis. Wkly Epidemiol Rec 1995;70:229–31.

41. World Health Organization. BCG in immunization programmes. Wkly Epidemiol Rec 2001;76:33–9.

42. Centers for Disease Control and Prevention. The role of BCG vaccine in the prevention and control of tuberculosis in the United States. A joint statement by the Advisory Council for the Elimination of Tuberculosis and the Advisory Committee on Immunization Practices. MMWR Morb Mortal Wkly Rep 1996;45:8–9.

43. Centers for Disease Control and Prevention. Guidelines for preventing the transmission of *M. tb* in health care settings. MMWR Morb Mortal Wkly Rep 1994;43:1–132.

44. Arbelaez MP, Nelson KE, Munoz A. BCG vaccine effectiveness on preventing tuberculosis and its interaction with human immunodeficiency virus infection. Int J Epidemiol 2000;29:1085–91.

45. World Health Organization. Immunization Policy. Global Programme for Vaccines and Immunization. Geneva: WHO; 1996.

46. Fine PEM, Carneiro IAM, Milstein JB, Clements CJ. Issues relating to the use of BCG in immunization programmes. A discussion document. WHO/V&B/-99.23. Geneva: WHO; 1999.

47. Karonga Prevention Trial Group. Randomised controlled trial of single BCG, repeated BCG, or combined BCG and killed *Mycobacterium leprae* vaccine for prevention of leprosy and tuberculosis in Malawi. Lancet 1996;348:17–24.

48. International Union Against Tuberculosis and Lung Disease. Criteria for discontinuation of vaccination programmes using bacille Calmette-Guérin (BCG) in countries with a low prevalence of tuberculosis. A statement of the International Union Against Tuberculosis and Lung Disease. Tuberc Lung Dis 1994;75:179–80.

49. Comstock GW, Edwards LB, Nabangxang H. Tuberculin sensitivity after eight to fifteen years after BCG vaccination. Am Rev Respir Dis 1971;103:572–5.

50. Horwitz O, Bunch-Christensen K. Correlation between tuberculin sensitivity after 2 months and 5 years among BCG vaccinated subjects. Bull World Health Organ 1968;39:829–36.

51. Horowitz HW, Luciano BB, Kadel J, Wormser JP. Tuberculin skin test conversion in hospital employees vaccinated with bacille Calmette-Guérin. Recent *M. tb* infection or booster effect. Am J Infect Control 1995;23:181–7.

52. Baily GVJ, Narain R, Mayurnath S, et al. Trial of BCG vaccine in South India for tuberculosis prevention. Tuberculosis prevention trial, Madras. Indian J Med Res 1980;72 Suppl:1–74.

53. ten Daam HG. Research on BCG vaccination. Adv Tuberc Res 1984;21:79–106.

54. Lietman T, Blower SM. Potential impact of tuberculosis vaccines as epidemic control agents. Clin Infect Dis 2000;Suppl 3:S316–22.

55. Bishai DM, Mercer D. Modeling the economic benefits of better TB vaccines. Int J Tuberc Lung Dis 2001;5:984–93.

56. Cole ST, Brosch R, Parkhill J, et al. Deciphering the biology of *Mycobacterium tuberculosis* from the complete genome sequence. Nature 1998;393:537–44.

57. Sequella Global Tuberculosis Foundation. World TB Day presentation, Washington, DC. 2002.

58. Collins HL, Kauffman SHE. Prospects for better tuberculosis vaccines. Lancet Infect Dis 2001;1:21–8.

59. Behr MA, Wilson MA, Gill WP, et al. Comparative genomics of BCG vaccines by whole-genome DNA microarray. Science 1999;284:1520–3.

60. Waddell RD, Chintu C, Lein AD, et al. Safety and immunogenicity of a five-dose series for inactivated *Mycobacterium vaccae* vaccination for the prevention of HIV-associated tuberculosis. Clin Infect Dis 2000;30 Suppl 3:S309–15.

61. Brooks JV, Frank AA, Keen MA, et al. Boosting vaccine for tuberculosis. Infect Immun 2001;69:2714–7.

62. Menzies R, Viscandjee B. Effect of bacille Calmette-Guérin vaccination on tuberculin reactivity. Am Rev Respir Dis 1992;145:621–5.

63. Hart PD, Sutherland T, Thomas J. The immunity conferred by effective BCG and vole bacillus vaccines, in relation to individual variations in tuberculin sensitivity and to technical variations in the vaccines. Tubercle 1967;48:201–10.

64. Wilson ME. Applying experiences from trials of bacille Calmette-Guérin vaccine. Clin Infect Dis 2000;30 Suppl 3: S262–5.

65. Brennan MJ, Fruth U. Global forum on TB vaccine research and development, World Health Organization, June 7–8, 2002, Geneva. Tuberculosis (Edinb) 2001;81(5/6);365–8.

66. Brennan MJ, Collins FM, Morris SM. Propelling novel vaccines directed against tuberculosis through the regulatory process. Tuberc Lung Dis 1999;79:145–51.

67. European Commission TB Vaccine Cluster. Paris: Institut Pasteur; 2000. Available at: http://www.pasteur.fr/rechereche/EC_Tbvaccine/html/Game.html (accessed June 26, 2002).

68. Ginsberg A. What's new in tuberculosis vaccines? Bull World Health Organ 2002;80:483–8.

69. International Union Against Tuberculosis and Lung Disease. Interventions for tuberculosis control and elimination. Paris: IUATLD; 2002.

Chapter 12

ETEC AND ENTERIC VACCINES

David R. Tribble, Thomas Larry Hale, and David N. Taylor

Diarrheal disease is the most common illness reported by travelers to less developed countries.[1,2] Traveler's diarrhea (TD) is typically self-limited, with duration of illness of less than a week.[3,4] However, during that time, the traveler can be uncomfortable, inconvenienced, and often must be attentive to rehydration and bed rest, with potential itinerary changes. Short-term medical management, adjunctive nonantimicrobial therapies (ie, antimotility agents), and antibiotics speed recovery but add further logistic challenges for the traveler (ie, acquiring medications, frequent self-diagnosis and treatment, and, occasionally, ambulatory or inpatient care during travel). Acute infectious diarrhea in travelers is caused primarily by bacterial pathogens. Common causes of traveler's diarrhea are enterotoxin-producing *Escherichia coli* (ETEC), *Shigella* species, and *Campylobacter jejuni*. Other bacterial species such as nontyphoidal forms of *Salmonella* and other pathogenic *E. coli* are also important causes. The bacterial agents primarily responsible for TD—ETEC, *Shigella*, *Campylobacter*, and *Salmonella*—have become increasingly resistant to antimicrobial treatment, serving as a major stimulus for vaccine development.[5,6] TD vaccine development targeting common agents of TD, such as ETEC, *Shigella* species, and *C. jejuni*, is a daunting task given the multiplicity of agents responsible for the syndrome, the existence of numerous serotypes, and the current state of knowledge of certain agents' pathogenesis and mucosal immunity in general. Efforts in developing these vaccines have potential promise, beyond application in travelers, to alleviate a significant component of childhood diarrheal disease morbidity and mortality in developing countries. In this chapter, we will summarize the epidemiology, the common immunologic considerations, and the foundations for pathogenesis and immunity leading to current efforts for vaccine candidates in clinical testing targeting ETEC, *Shigella* species, and *C. jejuni*, concluding with an overall assessment of current prospects and future needs.

TRAVELER'S DIARRHEA CLINICAL SYNDROME AND EPIDEMIOLOGY

"Typical" traveler's diarrhea represents a spectrum of illness from a fleeting, mild diarrhea without associated symptoms or activity limitation to a serious dehydrating and/or febrile dysentery requiring hospitalization. Most commonly, the diarrheal illness is self-limited, lasting 3 to 5 days.[3,4] The number of loose or liquid bowel movements occurring daily during illness can be 1 to 2 (~20%), 3 to 5 (~25%), and ≥ 6 (~55%).[7] Associated symptoms are not uncommon, including abdominal cramps (70%), nausea (50%), fever (20–25%), blood in stools (10–20%), and vomiting (10–15%). Overall, approximately one-fifth of affected persons have evidence (fever and/or bloody stools) of inflammatory disease. This does not take into account further laboratory evidence of fecal leukocytes, which frequently increases the proportion of patients with evidence of inflammatory disease up to approximately 50%. The mean duration of symptoms without treatment is about 4 days (median 2 days). Acute bacterial diarrhea is frequently categorized clinically as watery diarrhea or dysentery (bloody diarrhea). Considerable syndrome overlap occurs for various bacterial enteropathogens. Pathogens such as ETEC, known to cause predominantly a watery, noninflammatory diarrhea, demonstrate little overlap with inflammatory diarrhea. On the other hand, *Campylobacter*, *Shigella*, and nontyphoidal *Salmonella* can present anywhere along the spectrum of illness.

The naive or semi-immune traveler leaving his or her relatively low-risk environment for an area hyperendemic for bacterial enteropathogens has an approximately 40% diarrhea risk.[8,9] In most traveler's diarrhea series in tourists and military personnel, ETEC predominates as the most commonly identified agent, representing between 5 and 40% of cases.[10,11] *Campylobacter jejuni* (3–45%), *Shigella* spp. (2–10%), and nontyphoidal *Salmonella* spp. (2–10%) are other commonly identified etiologic agents. Significant regional and seasonal variability affects the relative distribution of etiologic agents (ie, ETEC more common in summer vs *Campylobacter* more common in winter in semitropical regions; ETEC and *Shigella* predominant in Southwest Asia vs *Campylobacter* and *Salmonella* more common in Thailand).[10–13] In addition to these commonly identified agents, there remains a substantial proportion, often up to 50%, of diarrhea cases with unidentified etiologies.[10] Other bacterial enteropathogens, as well as viral (*Rotavirus* and Norwalk virus, 5–10%) and parasitic agents (*Giardia*, *Cryptosporidium*, *Cyclospora*, and *Entamoeba histolytica*, < 5%) account for additional cases. *Aeromonas*, *Vibrio cholerae*, noncholera vibrios, and *Plesiomonas* typically represent no more than 5% of identified etiologies in most series. The continuously evolving spectrum of *E. coli*–related diarrheal diseases, such as enteroinvasive *E. coli* (EIEC), causing febrile dysentery, and enteroadherent *E. coli*, causing watery diarrhea, are increasingly being shown to account for 5 to 10% of the previously undiagnosed cases.[14] Another type of *E. coli*, known as aggregative *E. coli*, is currently being evaluated as another possible cause of TD.[15] Enterohemorrhagic *E. coli* (most commonly *E. coli* 0157:H7), although now recognized as a major food-borne threat in industrialized countries and as the most common cause of bloody diarrhea and the associated complication of hemolytic uremic syndrome, has not been identified as a traveler's diarrhea threat.[16]

The rationale supporting TD vaccine development is based on the high disease incidence, limited ability for effective behavioral modification, disadvantages of chemoprophylaxis and limited efficacy of nonpharmacologic prevention strategies, and increasing antimicrobial resistance challenging the efficacy of empiric antibiotic-based regimens.[3–6,17] Prophylactic measures that can be employed against traveler's diarrhea pathogens include inhibition with colonizing nonpathogenic microbes, chemical inhibition through nonantibiotic and antimicrobial means, passive immune inhibition with pathogen-specific immunoglobulin (Ig), and active immunization. The studies with probiotic colonizing flora have shown low protective efficacy (PE), up to approximately 40% compared with intermediate (~ 65%) and high (~ 90%) for bismuth subsalicylate and antibiotics, respectively.[18–21] The potential for adverse effects and the complexity in managing a prophylaxis failure are much greater for the antibiotic options. Passive immunization with pathogen-specific Ig shows promise as a well-tolerated approach with high PE; however, it might be limited by a narrow pathogen spectrum of protection.[22] The prophylactic measures discussed above require varying degrees of individual commitment (once to four times daily dosing) during a time period when an individual is typically feeling well, actively involved in new activities, and not following a routine amenable to regimen compliance. The majority of bacterial enteropathogen vaccine development efforts in the past decade have focused on mucosal vaccination strategies.

IMMUNOLOGIC CONSIDERATIONS

In general for bacterial enteropathogens, there is a body of evidence to support the concept of acquired immunity and the potential for vaccine development. Residents of endemic regions experience reduced age-related pathogen-specific disease rates within the first few years of life.[23–27] In addition, epidemiologic studies have further demonstrated reduced duration of pathogen excretion, apparent colonization resistance, and, in the case of certain pathogens, elevated pathogen-specific Ig levels (maternally derived in breast milk and/or serology).[24,28,29] Experimental infection studies involving volunteers from industrialized countries have further supported the acquisition of protective immunity.[30–32] Although there is evidence for acquired immunity, it is short lived because travelers who return to endemic areas after living several months in a sanitary environment are fully susceptible.[33]

Vaccines targeting mucosal enteric pathogens must successfully stimulate the gut-associated lymphoid system to be efficacious.[34–36] Because of redistribution of locally stimulated immune cells, immunization at one mucosal surface can elicit secretory antibodies at sites distant from the immunizing site, a phenomenon known as the common mucosal immune system.[34,37] Parenteral vaccines generally fail to elicit mucosal secretory IgA responses. Parenterally delivered bacterial enteropathogen vaccines do to not provide protection against mucosal pathogens that lack a systemic pathogenesis phase, although there is concern that these earlier vaccines failed to induce systemic IgG responses that might be sufficient, as seen in the documented efficacy of a parenteral *Shigella* conjugate vaccine in providing protection for certain enteropathogens.[38] Immunization strategies have included attenuated mutant strains (as vaccine or vector of pathogen antigens), nonliving microparticles (such as liposomes, microspheres, or the killed bacteria itself), adhesive antigens (or conjugates), and addition of bacterial products (or modified, less toxic molecules) with adjuvant properties (such as cholera toxin or heat-labile toxin of ETEC).

There is a range of outcomes that could be considered reasonable goals in the development of a TD vaccine. These range from sterile immunity with protection against intestinal colonization, protection from disease but not infection, or protection from severe illness only. The optimal protective efficacy outcome of sterile vaccine–induced immunity is likely not realistic or necessary. The median infective dose (ID_{50}), as determined through mathematic modeling from outbreak investigations and volunteer experimental infection studies, is frequently very low ($\sim 10^2$ organisms) for many enteropathogens.[39] The potential for an infectious inoculum that would overwhelm vaccine-induced immunity seems reasonably high and might lead to breakthroughs in protection. Epidemiologic studies in developing-world children document increasing rates of asymptomatic infection and less ability to isolate the bacteria in resident adult populations despite the hyperendemic setting and probable frequent exposure. Repeated exposure, with or without associated clinical disease, of live, presumably fully virulent bacteria, appears to lead to acquired immunity, particularly with regard to protection against disease manifestations. However, the level of antigenic exposure needed to achieve protective immunity is not clear. These observations emphasize the challenges faced in acquiring vaccine-induced immunity and determining the appropriateness of targeting disease attenuation as the primary efficacy outcome and the probable requirement for booster vaccinations. Cholera vaccine development provides illustrative examples of mucosal immunization strategies using oral delivery through divergent approaches, inactivated whole cells and attenuated bacteria, with both demonstrating evidence of mucosal immune system induction and protective efficacy.[40–43]

CHOLERA VACCINE DEVELOPMENT MODEL

Inactivated Whole Cell Approach

Inactivated microorganisms offer some advantages as potential vaccines for mucosal immunization. Physically, they are naturally occurring microparticles that should enhance interactions between their surface and mucosal lymphoid tissues. As vaccines, they are inexpensive to produce and contain multiple antigens that might be important for protection. Formulations could potentially be modified to offer protection against prevalent serotypes over time or in different geographic regions, as is done for influenza. Presentation of multiple antigens might be particularly important for pathogens like *Campylobacter*, for which protective antigens are not known. Although not suitable for parenteral administration, whole cell preparations are safe for mucosal immunization.

The inactivated cholera vaccine contains heat and formalin–killed *Vibrio cholerae* whole cells (WC) of several biotypes and serotypes plus the nontoxic B subunit (BS) of cholera toxin.[44] A randomized, double-blind placebo-controlled field trial involving 63,000 individuals in rural Bangladesh established the safety, immunogenicity, and efficacy of the WC-BS vaccine against cholera.[41,44] Two or three doses of the WC-BS vaccine conferred 85% protection against cholera for the first 6 months in all age groups tested and 51% overall protection after 3 years. More recently, a new formulation of the WC-BS cholera vaccine containing a recombinant cholera toxin B subunit (rBS-WC) was also found to be safe and gave high levels of protection against symptomatic cholera in Peruvian military recruits, but larger-scale studies of civilian populations in Peru showed efficacy only after a 1-year booster dose.[42,45] Although not as immunogenic as live attenuated *V. cholerae* strains, these vaccines have provided evidence that an orally administered whole cell vaccine can be safe and provide reasonable protection against an enteric pathogen.

Live Attenuated Approach

Live attenuated oral vaccines also have the potential to deliver the full complement of protective antigens, even if they have not been identified, and to be effective after only a single dose. However, the virulence determinants do need to be identified so that these genes can be deleted to reduce vaccine reactogenicity. Several live attenuated oral vaccines have been shown to stimulate mucosal immunity effectively and provide excellent protection in field or volunteer challenge studies. These include vaccines attenuated by serial passage (oral polio), chemical mutagenesis (the Ty2lA vaccine strain of *Salmonella enterica* serovar Typhi), or targeted deletion of genes encoding for important virulence factors, such as cholera toxin A subunit deleted from the cholera vaccine CVD 103-HgR.[46–48] CVD 103-HgR has been demonstrated to be safe and highly immunogenic and to provide protection in experimental cholera challenge studies (100% efficacy against severe disease and 76% for any diarrhea), but it did not demonstrate efficacy in a field trial in Indonesia.[43,49]

Peru-15 is another live attenuated oral vaccine derived from a *Vibrio cholerae* O1 El Tor Inaba strain by a series of deletions and modifications, including deletion of the entire cholera toxin (CT) genetic element.[50] Peru-15 is a stable, motility-defective strain and is unable to recombine with homologous deoxyribonucleic acid (DNA). A single oral dose of Peru-15 was evaluated for preliminary protective efficacy against moderate and severe diarrhea in a randomized, double-blind, placebo-controlled human volunteer cholera challenge model. A total of 59 volunteers were randomly allocated to groups to receive either 2×10^8 colony-forming units (CFUs) of reconstituted, lyophilized Peru-15 vaccine diluted in CeraVacx (CeraProduct, Jessup, MD) buffer or placebo (CeraVacx buffer alone). Approximately 3 months after vaccination, 36 of these volunteers were challenged with approximately 10^5 CFU of virulent *V. cholerae* O1 El Tor Inaba strain N16961 prepared from a standardized frozen inoculum. Among vaccinees, 98% showed at least a fourfold increase in vibriocidal antibody titers. After challenge, 5 (42%) of the 12 placebo recipients and none (0%) of the 24 vaccinees had moderate or severe diarrhea ($\geq 3,000$ g of diarrheal stool) ($p = .002$; protective efficacy, 100%; lower one-sided 95% confidence limit, 75%). A total of 7 (58%) of the 12 placebo recipients and 1 (4%) of the 24 vaccinees had any diarrhea ($p < .001$; protective efficacy, 93%; lower one-sided 95% confidence limit, 62%). Peru-15 is a well-tolerated and immunogenic oral single-dose cholera vaccine that affords protective efficacy against life-threatening cholera diarrhea in a human volunteer challenge model. These vaccines provide strong support for an attenuated enteric vaccine approach that might be amenable to the common bacterial agents causing traveler's diarrhea.

ENTEROTOXIGENIC *ESCHERICIA COLI*

Pathogenesis and Immunity

Enterotoxigenic *E. coli* (ETEC) is the cause of an estimated 650 million diarrheal episodes resulting in more than 800,000 deaths annually, most of them in children below 5 years of age in developing countries.[51] ETEC is also the single most common cause of TD in regions with poorer sanitary conditions, being isolated in 30 to 50% of these episodes.[10] DuPont and colleagues tested isolates from ill American soldiers in Vietnam in the classic study on the pathogenesis of ETEC diarrhea.[52] Toxigenic diarrhea is a similar term describing watery, noninflammatory diarrhea best represented by cholera and ETEC. ETEC causes intestinal secretion of fluids and electrolytes by production of one or more enterotoxins that overwhelm the intestine's absorptive capacity, leading to watery diarrhea.[53,54]

ETEC are defined as *E. coli* that produce heat-labile enterotoxins (LT), heat-stable enterotoxins (ST), or both. In surveys, ETEC are nearly equally divided into those that produce LT, ST, or both toxins.[14] To produce illness, ETEC must first adhere to mucosal epithelial cells through binding proteins called colonization factors (CF), then cause secretory diarrhea by expressing toxins. CF interact with receptors on the host epithelial cells allowing for adherence of the ETEC to the mucosa.[14] The majority of ETEC strains express one of three main CF antigen (CFA) groups: CFA/I, CFA/II, or CFA/IV. CFA/II is composed of coli surface antigen 3 (CS3) alone or in combination with CS1 or CS2. Similarly, CFA/IV is composed of coli surface antigen CS6, alone or in combination with CS4 or CS5. This antigenic variability in ETEC strains has made vaccine development difficult. The serotypes (O:H antigens) of *E. coli* are well-characterized surface structures. The O serogroup is based on the polysaccharide chain of lipopolysaccharide (LPS), and the H serogroup is based on the proteinaceous flagella. Some serotypes are common in ETEC, but 110 combinations have been reported, and the most common account for only 15% of the ETEC. Given their great variety, it would be impractical to design a vaccine based on O or H antigens. However, there is less variability between the CF, with three of the antigens (CFA/I, CS3, and CS6) collectively expressed by a majority of ETEC isolates. Any viable subunit ETEC vaccine strategy must, at a minimum, include some form of CFA/I and the common antigenic components of CFA/II (ie, CS3) and CFA/IV (ie, CS6). Additional CF might also be required to broaden vaccine coverage. Vaccine development against ETEC is focused on generating mucosal antibody responses that (a) prevent the initial colonization of the bacteria in the gut and (b) neutralize toxins produced by the bacteria.

Vaccine Approaches

Killed Whole Cells

Studies with an oral killed whole cell plus recombinant B–subunit cholera vaccine (rBS-WC) have demonstrated partial short-term protection against ETEC-induced diarrhea.[55,56] ETEC cross-protection was not observed with the whole cell cholera vaccine without the B subunit of cholera toxin. This finding was theorized as being due to antibody responses to the B subunit of the LT of *E. coli*, which shares extensive antigenic relatedness to those against cholera toxin B subunit.[57,58] Based on this observation and their experience with the oral killed whole cell cholera vaccine, Svennerholm and Holmgren, in collaboration with SBL Vaccin AB (Stockholm), designed a killed whole cell ETEC vaccine.[59,60] This oral ETEC vaccine consists of formalin-killed *E. coli* expressing CFA/I and coli surface antigen components of CFA/II and CFA/IV. The enterotoxin component is provided by cholera toxin B (CTB) from the cholera vaccine. The vaccine strains were common ETEC O-groups, which express the different fimbriae in high concentrations. Formalin inactivation killed the bacteria without causing significant loss in the antigenicity of the CFA. The Swedish Bacteriological Laboratory (SBL, Stockholm) has manufactured several lots of the ETEC vaccine, some of which were tested in Swedish, Bangladeshi, American, and Israeli adults and children.[51,61–66] This formulation exhibited minimal reactogenicity and stimulated relevant mucosal immune responses.[51,61–63,65,67–69]

The vaccine is currently completing phase III field efficacy testing in Egyptian children and American travelers to Central America. Sequential phase II studies in adults, schoolchildren, toddlers, and infants have undertaken prior to the initiation of the phase III trial in Egypt.[62,63,66] The vaccine was found to be safe and to induce vaccine antigen–specific serologic and antibody-secreting cell responses with reasonable correlation between these responses.[62,63,67] A two-dose regimen was tested in all age groups except the infants, in whom a three-dose regimen (14-day intervals) was assessed. In the infant cohort (age < 2 years), IgA seroconversion after any dose was observed in vaccinees more commonly than placebo recipients for the following vaccine antigens: recombinant cholera toxin B subunit (97% vs 46%), CFA/I (61% vs 18%), and CS4 (39% vs 4%). A similar finding was observed for IgG seroconversion rates in the vaccine and control groups, with 97% and 21% to recombinant CTB, 64% and 29% for CFA/I, 53% and 21% for CS2, and 58% and 4% for CS4, respectively. The third vaccine dose was followed by augmented IgG antitoxin titers, leading to the decision to use the three-dose regimen in the phase III trial. The preliminary results of the phase III trial in US travelers to Central America was recently presented in abstract form.[70] This double-blind, randomized placebo-controlled trial evaluated approximately 1,350 volunteers. The vaccine schedule used was a two-dose regimen (14-day interval), with the last dose 1 week prior to travel and 28-day monitoring for primary outcome events (ETEC-associated diarrhea with vaccine-homologous antigens) during their stay. The total number of diarrheal cases was not different between vaccine and control groups; however, there were fewer frequent severe ETEC-associated cases among vaccinees. Complete reviews of these efficacy trial results in concert with vaccine formulation will be necessary to determine the future direction for killed whole cell ETEC vaccine approaches.

Live Attenuated Vaccines

An attenuated ETEC vaccine approach was previously investigated at the University of Maryland in the 1980s using a nontoxigenic *E. coli*–expressing CFA/II (designated E1392-75-2A).[71,72] In an earlier trial in 1986 at the Center for Vaccine Development (CVD), 12 volunteers were given a single dose of 5×10^{10} CFU of E1392-75-2A as a vaccine and then challenged with 5×10^8 CFU of E23477A, a pathogenic ETEC strain with a different O:H serotype but the same CFA/II antigen components (coli surface antigens 1 and 3) as the vaccine strain.[71,72] Protective efficacy was demonstrated with 3 of 12 vaccinees, and 6 of 6 controls developed diarrhea ($p < .005$). However, 2 of 19 volunteers developed mild diarrhea after ingesting the vaccine strain, suggesting that further attenuation was needed. Further attenuation of the E1392-75-2A strain has been achieved by deletion of specific gene combinations.[73] Two attenuated vaccine candidates have been constructed, PTL-002 by deletion of the *AROC* and *OMPR* genes and PTL-003 by deletion of the *AROC*, *OMPC*, and *OMPF* genes. Both constructs retained their ability to express CFA/II, thought to be the protective antigen. These vaccine candidates have entered clinical testing.

Subunit Vaccines

Microsphere Oral Delivery. Colonization factors are logical targets for inhibiting the interaction between pathogen and host. Antibody to colonization factors should block initial adherence to the host cell. Vaccine efforts focused on anti-CF immunity have been successful in farm animals.[74,75] All CF are large macromolecular surface structures composed of protein subunits, which are immunogenic. Because of the wide variety of ETEC serotypes, CF are thought to be one of the most important antigenic targets. A polyvalent vaccine specific for organisms with CFA/I, CS3, and CS6 as well as LT could potentially be protective in up to 85% of ETEC.[76] Passive immunization using a milk anti-CF immunoglobulin preparation, produced by immunizing cows with purified CFAs, prevented ETEC diarrhea in the human challenge model but required multiple doses given with antacid.[22] These studies provide support for a subunit ETEC vaccine approach based on purified CFAs; however, delivery has been problematic. One approach is to deliver the antigens in poly(lactide-co-glycolide) (PLGA) polymer microspheres. Biodegradable PLGA polymers have been used safely as resorbable sutures. PLGA microspheres are biodegradable and permit slow and continued release of antigen. In animals, antigens delivered in these microspheres are taken up and processed by Peyer's patches, and they stimulate local and systemic immune responses.[72,77] Several CFAs have been purified and microencapsulated with material that allows uptake in the M cells and slow release

A microencapsulated CFA/II antigen was tested as a vaccine at the University of Maryland.[78] In this study, volunteers were given 1 mg of microencapsulated CFA/II vaccine four times. After the last dose, 5 of the 10 vaccinated volunteers developed IgA antibody-secreting cells (ASC) to the vaccine. Fifty-seven days after vaccination, the 10 vaccinees and 10 controls were challenged with ETEC-expressing CFA/II. All of the unvaccinated controls and 7 of 10 vaccinees developed diarrhea. Two of the protected volunteers had the highest number of IgA anti-CFA/II ASC (700–800 spots at 7 days) and the highest fecal IgA anti-CFA/II titers (respective titers of > 256 and 64), providing limited evidence for anti-CFA immune correlate of protection.

A vaccine made up of microspheres with incorporated CS6 colonization factor was produced at the Walter Reed Army Institute of Research (WRAIR) bioproduction facility. The CS6 used in the test material was produced from genes cloned from ETEC strain E8775.[79] A phase I study found that the CS6 vaccine was safe and well tolerated when delivered as a three-dose oral vaccination, 1 or 5 mg doses at 2-week intervals.[80] The immune response seen in this study was similar in magnitude to experimental infection using a pathogenic strain of ETEC-expressing CS6 (T. Coster, unpublished data). Most peak responses were seen after the third dose of the vaccine, which supports the use of three doses in subsequent studies. The study was a small nonplacebo-controlled trial that evaluated several variables (microencapsulation, CS6 dose, and use of buffered solution). No clearly superior regimen was evident; however, the 1 mg dose of microencapsulated CS6 in buffer demonstrated the best, albeit moderate, immune response. Future studies will evaluate the effect a mucosal adjuvant will have on the immune response, leading to assessment of preliminary efficacy in experimental infection studies.

Transcutaneous Immunization. Transcutaneous immunization (TCI) is an innovative approach to vaccine delivery accomplished by topical application of an aqueous protein solution (containing antigen and adjuvant) to intact skin using a simple occlusive patch (to hydrate the skin).[81] The topical application of vaccine formulations on the skin provides access to the skin immune system dominated by densely distributed and potent professional antigen-presenting cells, Langerhans' cells, that can be manipulated to yield specific, robust immune responses. TCI has the potential to be a safe and painless method of administering vaccine antigens. In animals, LT and the closely related CT were found to be potent immunogens and adjuvants when given transcutaneously.[82–84] In a phase I study, LT application onto human skin did not cause local skin findings or systemic toxicity and induced systemic and mucosal IgA and IgG anti-LT antibodies.[81]

A follow-up open label study evaluated the safety and immunogenicity of a transcutaneously administered vaccine containing graded doses of CS6 (250 µg to 2 mg) with or without LT (500 µg).[85] Nineteen volunteers received the LT/CS6 combination, and 10 received CS6 only. Three immunizations were given over a period of 3 months. The combination of LT and CS6 was safe and immunogenic. The only vaccine-related adverse event was mild delayed-type hypersensitivity (DTH), suggesting T-cell responses, seen in 14 of 19 volunteers receiving LT and CS6; no DTH was seen in subjects receiving CS6 alone. The DTH appeared within 24 hours in the area of patch application after the second or third dose. There were no immune responses to CS6 in the absence of LT, combined to further differentiate it from the group that received CS6 alone. LT responses were observed in all volunteers receiving LT/CS6 (100% anti-LT IgG, 90% anti-LT IgA, 79% anti-LT IgG ASC, and 37% anti-LT IgA ASC). This study demonstrated that a subunit ETEC CS6 vaccine candidate, in the presence of LT adjuvant, induced immune responses comparable to challenge with B7A, a wild-type ETEC-expressing CS6, and the microencapsulated oral CS6 candidate vaccine.

SHIGELLA

Pathogenesis and Immunity

The Institute of Medicine estimates that bacteria of the genus *Shigella* cause 250 million cases of diarrhea and 654,000 deaths annually.[86] Although *Shigella sonnei* is the principal species causing diarrhea in industrialized countries and in travelers to less developed countries, *Shigella flexneri* is a major problem in less developed countries. Shigellae are ingested by the host, usually following fecal-oral transmission, and pass to the terminal ileum and colon where they invade and proliferate within enterocytes, produce cell death, incite an inflammatory reaction, and induce intestinal fluid secretion. This multistep process involves many highly regulated virulence properties encoded by both chromosomal and plasmid genes.[87,88]

The term dysentery is used to describe a more severe clinical form of an inflammatory diarrhea specifically manifesting with gross blood. The inflammatory process is marked by clinical symptoms and signs, such as fever, chills, tenesmus, and gross blood in stools, and stool laboratory analysis, such as fecal leukocytes, stool lactoferrin, and occult blood. The colon is the anatomic location most often associated with dysentery; however, the small intestine (particularly the ileum) also can be involved. A range of bacterial enteropathogens is associated with this syndrome, with *Shigella* being the prototype for bacillary dysentery. Shigellosis is classically described as a triphasic illness with the first phase presenting as systemic symptoms ("flulike"), with moderate to high fever, followed by a phase of large-volume watery stools with upper abdominal cramping and, finally, by small-volume, bloody stools with lower abdominal cramps and tenesmus.[89] The presence of each phase and the specific order is frequently not observed. *Shigella* causes disease via invasion of colonic epithelial cells followed by cell-to-cell spreading, eventually forming superficial ulceration. *S. sonnei* and *S. flexneri* are the most important causes of endemic shigellosis. *Shigella dysenteriae* type 1 causes epidemic shigellosis.

Serotype-specific immunity arises after natural infection.[90] Natural infection induces a serum immune response to the LPS.[26,91] As shown by epidemiologic and challenge data in humans, as well as challenge data in primates, type-specific serum antibody recognizing the O-specific polysaccharide portion of the LPS somatic antigen of shigellae is associated with protection against shigellosis.[26,91–93] However, parenteral immunization with killed whole shigellae has been found to be ineffective both in a challenge study in monkeys and in a well-controlled field trial despite induction of significant serum antibody responses.[93,94] These observations are consistent with the principle that local intestinal immunity is a prime protective mechanism against enteric *Shigella* infection. Serum antibodies can be viewed as surrogate markers that reflect the protective mechanisms mediated by local antibodies operating at intestinal mucosal sites. More recently, clinical trial evidence of protective efficacy of parenteral *Shigella* vaccines (see *Shigella* "Subunit Vaccines: Parenteral Conjugates,") led to questions concerning the sufficiency of this vaccine approach and the possibility that protective immunity can be induced by various means.[38]

Vaccine Approaches

Live Attenuated Vaccines

Live attenuated vaccines with targeted genetic mutations have been made possible by recent strides in understanding the genetics of *Shigella* pathogenesis.[95] These vaccine candidates, following successful attenuation, can be fermented and lyophilized at a low cost. The packaging may be more expensive than the actual vaccine. WRAIR investigators, in collaboration with Sansonnetti's group at Institut Pasteur, have constructed attenuated vaccine candidates of *S. flexneri* type 2a, *S. sonnei*, and *S. dysenteriae* type 1.[95,96] These vaccines have all been attenuated in the same manner, by removing the *ICSA/VIRG* gene, which enables the bacteria to spread from cell to cell, in this way limiting the infection.[95]

A prototype vaccine strain (SC5700) was constructed in *S. flexneri* 5 by site-directed mutation of both the *ICSA/VIRG* gene and the *IUCA-IUT* chromosomal locus (encoding the aerobactin iron-binding siderophore).[96] Intragastric challenge of rhesus monkeys with SC5700 demonstrated both attenuation and protective immunity against intragastric challenge with the parent *S. flexneri* 5 strain (M90T). After the initial studies with *S. flexneri* 5, an *ICSA-IUC* double deletion mutant was constructed from the more common *S. flexneri* 2a using strain 454 (Centre national de référence des shigelles, Institut Pasteur).[96] Preclinical studies showed that the SC602 vaccine was both safe and efficacious in the guinea pig Sereny test and in the intragastric rhesus monkey model. Inpatient dose ranging studies (10^2 to 10^8 CFU range) established 10^4 CFU of SC602 as a safe dose, with no vaccinees experiencing severe constitutional or intestinal symptoms. Vaccinated subjects ($n = 7$) receiving this dose returned for a challenge with wild-type *Shigella flexneri* 2a 8 weeks after vaccination.[97] Seven *Shigella*-naive volunteers were recruited as controls. After ingesting 10^3 CFU of virulent shigellae, the vaccinees experienced no fever or severe shigellosis, whereas 6 (86%) controls experienced one or both of these symptoms. Three of the challenged vaccinees (43%) experienced mild diarrhea, indicating that disease symptom attenuation is a primary vaccine outcome.

In further studies involving 58 North American volunteers receiving the 10^4 CFU dose of SC602, approximately 20% of subjects experienced quantifiable diarrhea or febrile reactions of brief duration, and approximately 10% of vaccinees experienced headaches or cramps of sufficient severity to modify normal activities (T. Coster, unpublished data). Approximately 70% of vaccinees had a highly significant (≥ 10) IgA or IgG ASC per 10^6 peripheral blood lymphocytes (PBL) response recognizing *S. flexneri* 2a LPS. About 60% of the ASC responders also had greater than or equal to threefold increase in serum IgA—recognizing 2a LPS (40% of all vaccinees). SC602 vaccinees who had relatively high levels of anti-LPS IgA were protected against all symptoms of shigellosis. On the other hand, vaccinees who had < 10 IgA ASC and no serum IgA response were likely to have mild diarrhea rather than the severe shigellosis seen in control volunteers who ingested virulent *S. flexneri* 2a.[97] This modest level of protection has been difficult to achieve in the human challenge model without inducing clinical shigellosis.[98] Nonetheless, the residual reactogenicity of SC602 for up to 20% of vaccinees ingesting a four-log dose might discourage the development of this candidate as a commercial product. In addition, regulatory agencies are concerned about the spread of excreted SC602 to nonvaccinated contacts. Additional community-based trials of the four-log dose of SC602 are planned to determine consumer acceptance of the symptoms associated with vaccination. In addition, adventitious spread of SC602 to household contacts will be monitored carefully in these trials.

The live oral *S. sonnei* vaccine candidate designated WRSS1 is attenuated by a deletion in the *VIRG* gene similar to SC602 *S. flexneri* 2a vaccine.[99] Inpatient studies have evaluated the safety and immunogenicity of this candidate vaccine in randomized double-blind, placebo-controlled trials conducted in the Research Isolation Ward of the University of Maryland CVD.[100] Four WRSS1 doses ranging from 10^3 CFU to 10^6 CFU were tested. Six of 27 volunteers met the definition of illness (diarrhea and/or fever) that was possibly vaccine related, but only 2 subjects reported a symptom (headache) that interfered with normal activity. WRSS1 elicited vigorous IgA ASC anti-LPS responses at all doses tested, with counts exceeding 100 per 10^6 PBL in most subjects. Geometric mean peak postvaccination anti-LPS serum IgG and fecal IgA titers were also robust, with most subjects exhibiting a fourfold rise in serum and/or fecal anti-LPS antibody. WRAIR is currently sponsoring phase II studies with WRSS1 in Israel to define more fully the safety profile, immunogenicity, and potential for secondary spread to household contacts.

The CVD has constructed and evaluated a series of *S. flexneri* 2a vaccines (CVD 1204, CVD 1207, and CVD 1208) that are attenuated by a deletion in the *GUABA* operon.[101,102] This locus regulates two enzymes in the distal de novo purine biosynthesis pathway. This mutation results in low infectivity (< 1% HeLa cell invasive capacity of the 2457T parent), and it limits the ability of vaccine to multiply in the cytoplasm of mammalian cells. In addition to *GUABA*, CVD 1207 has genetically engineered deletions in the *ICSA/VIRG* intercellular spread gene and deletions of two putative enterotoxin genes (*SET* and *SEN*). CVD 1207 has been tested by CVD in outpatient trials at doses of up to 10^{10} CFU. The highest dosage caused watery diarrhea in 20% of volunteers, and there was a strong IgA ASC response against *S. flexneri* 2a LPS in all subjects. CVD 1207 was less reactogenic at 10^9 CFU or 10^8 CFU, but the percentage of IgA responders decreased to 50% at these doses. Recently, the CVD has conducted phase I trials on two additional *GUABA* candidate vaccines: CVD 1204 (attenuated by *GUABA* alone) and CVD 1208 (attenuated by *GUABA, SEN,* and *SET*). Neither of these candidates has the *ICSA/VIRG* intercellular spread mutation. CVD 1204 caused diarrhea and fever at a 10^7 CFU dose, but CVD 1208 caused only short-term fever with no diarrhea at doses up to 10^9 CFU. Both candidate vaccines were much more immunogenic than CVD 1207. CVD 1208 (*guaBA, sen, set*) has been chosen for further evaluation in clinical trials at the University of Maryland (K. Kotloff, personal communication, June 2003).

S. flexneri and *S. sonnei* vaccines attenuated by *ICSA/VIRG* or *GUABA* are highly immunogenic and, for the most part, safe, although some side effects, such as low-grade fever or diarrhea, have been observed in volunteers receiving these vaccines. These studies demonstrate the feasibility of the live attenuated approach for *Shigella* vaccine development, but the residual reactogenicity is a problem for commercial development. Perhaps even more daunting is the concern of regulatory agencies that these live, excreted vaccines will colonize contacts who have not consented to vaccination. This risk is now being assessed in phase II trials with the WRSS1 and SC602 vaccines.

Subunit Vaccines

Parenteral Conjugates. The successes with polysaccharide conjugate vaccines for *Haemophilus influenzae* type B (Hib) led scientists at the US National Institutes for Health (NIH) to experiment with an O-specific polysaccharide–protein conjugate vaccine for shigellosis. Previous evidence suggests that the O-specific polysaccharide (O-SP) domain of the LPS cell wall is both an essential virulence factor and a protective antigen of *Shigella* strains, as previously discussed. *Shigella* LPS is purified, and then the lipid portion of the LPS is removed to decrease pyrogenicity, leaving the O-SP to induce an immune response.[103,104] An injection of O-SP does not elicit an effective immune response because polysaccharides are T-independent antigens. To make the polysaccharide vaccine T dependent and produce an anamnestic response, it is covalently conjugated to a carrier protein, commonly tetanus toxoids (TT), *Pseudomonas aeruginosa* exoprotein A (rEPA), or *Corynebacterium diphtheriae* CRM9.

Initial preclinical studies with *S. dysenteriae* type 1–TT conjugates were found to be stable, elicited IgG O–SP antibodies, and exhibited a booster effect when additional injections were given.[105] Conjugate vaccines were made for the more commonly occurring *S. flexneri* type 2a and *S. sonnei* using rEPA as the carrier protein. These vaccines were tested for safety and immunogenicity first in mice and then in a small group of volunteers.[106] In 116 human volunteers, increased IgG, IgM, and IgA antibody levels were elicited by the O-SP–protein conjugates ($p < .001$). However, no booster response was observed, and adsorption onto alum did not appear to increase immunogenicity of the vaccine. The few adverse reactions observed were mild. The anti–OS-P antibody levels were comparable to those observed in previous studies of immune response to natural *Shigella* infection.

Given the observed safety and immunogenicity, Cohen and colleagues designed a randomized clinical trial to elucidate further the potential of *Shigella* conjugate vaccines.[104] They randomized 192 Israeli soldiers to receive *S. flexneri* or *S. sonnei* bound to rEPA or hepatitis B vaccine. Fourfold or greater increases in IgG and IgA levels were observed in 90% of *S. sonnei*–rEPA recipients and in 73 to 77% of the *S. flexneri*–rEPA recipients 2 weeks after vaccination ($p < .01$). These antibody levels decreased over time yet were still observed to be higher than the prevaccination levels when measured 2 years later. No booster response was observed with an additional dose.

Field efficacy was evaluated in male Israeli military recruits in a double-blind vaccine-controlled trial ($n = 1,446$).[38] The soldiers were randomized to receive *S. sonnei*–rEPA, *E. coli/S. flexneri* 2a (EcSf2a-2, an oral, live attenuated hybrid vaccine), or meningococcal tetravalent control vaccine. Cases of *S. sonnei* shigellosis occurred in four of the seven surveillance sites. The protective efficacy of the conjugate vaccine against *S. sonnei* shigellosis in three of the groups was found to be 74% ($p = .006$, 95% CI 28–100%). Shigellosis cases occurred 70 to 155 days after vaccination in these three groups. In the fourth group, an outbreak occurred 1 to 17 days after vaccination. In the case of the early outbreak, the efficacy of the vaccine was reduced to 43% ($p = .039$, 95% CI 4–82%). This suggests the possible utility of the vaccine in an outbreak situation, but additional studies are needed. In all four groups, among those soldiers who received the vaccine, those who developed shigellosis tended to have lower IgG and IgA levels than those who did not develop disease, and these differences were significant after 17 days (IgG) and 129 days (IgA). A mechanism proposed for this immune response is the activity of serum antibodies in the jejunum, acting to overwhelm the invading pathogens before they can colonize. The authors concluded that one injection of *S. sonnei*–rEPA is adequate to elicit an immune response in young adults. A more cautious conclusion would be that there appears to be an adequate immune response; however, because of the epidemiology of *Shigella* and the wide confidence intervals of the efficacy, additional studies with more power are needed.

Ashkenazi and colleagues tested the safety and immunogenicity of two conjugate vaccines, *S. sonnei*–rEPA and *S. flexneri* 2a–rEPA in children 4 to 7 years of age.[107] The study was randomized, controlled, and unblinded. Sixty children received *S. sonnei*–rEPA, 60 received *S. flexneri* 2a–rEPA, and the control group of 27 children received hepatitis B vaccine. Adverse events associated with the vaccines were minimal and consisted mainly of mild local reactions. Significant serum antibody (IgG, IgA, and IgM) anti–O-SP response was observed in both of the conjugate vaccine groups and remained significantly elevated 6 months following vaccination. A second dose of *S. flexneri* 2a–rEPA administered 6 weeks later elicited a booster response.

To determine the best vaccine formulation, Passwell and colleagues randomly assigned 152 volunteers to receive one of five experimental vaccines: O-SP conjugates of *S. sonnei* and *S. flexneri* 2a bound to succinylated rEPA or native or succinylated *C. diphtheriae* toxin CRM9.[108] Succinylation was expected to improve the immunogenicity of the conjugates. All three of the *S. sonnei* conjugates elicited high levels of anti–O-SP antibodies within a week of vaccination ($p < .001$), and these levels remained higher than prevaccination levels 26 weeks later ($p < .0001$). *S. flexneri* 2a–rEPA$_{succ}$ elicited consistently significantly higher levels of antibodies than *S. flexneri* 2a–rCRM9$_{succ}$ and, therefore, was chosen by the authors to evaluate in children.

Polysaccharide-protein conjugate *Shigella* vaccines have been shown to be safe and immunogenic in randomized double-blind clinical trials; however, they are expensive to manufacture and have not yet been adopted by pharmaceutical companies. In the future, less expensive methods (synthetic saccharides, for instance) of producing conjugate vaccines might be developed so that they can be used worldwide.

Proteosome Intranasal Vaccine Delivery. Subunit mucosal vaccine delivery systems have been developed in an attempt to elicit both systemic and mucosal type-specific protective immune responses and to avoid the safety issues sometimes present with live attenuated vaccines. Proteosomes have been applied to the development of mucosal vaccines for *Shigella*.[109–111] A *Shigella* proteosome vaccine has been evaluated in humans, the proteosome–*S. flexneri* 2a LPS vaccine.[110,112] The term proteosome refers to purified preparations of meningococcal outer membrane proteins that form multimolecular vesicular structures with antigens noncovalently complexed to them via hydrophobic interactions.[113] Proteosomes have been shown in animal models to enhance the immune responses to peptides, proteins, gangliosides, and LPS following both parenteral and mucosal immunization.[113] Proteosome-LPS vaccines are designed for mucosal application. They have been given orally, but most experience has been with intranasal dosing.

The subunit proteosome *Shigella* vaccine consists of *S. flexneri* 2a LPS complexed to proteosomes prepared from *Neisseria meningitidis*.[110] Dosage is based on protein content; the protein:LPS ratio is approximately 1.0. Prior studies in 35 human subjects have evaluated this product at doses up to 1.5 mg intranasally.[110] There have been no deaths or serious adverse events. The majority (60–70%) of vaccine recipients at doses ≤ 1.0 mg experience transient rhinorrhea and nasal congestion, but these are generally mild and interfere with normal daily activities only infrequently. Nasal discharge, where present, is scanty and clear. No purulent nasal discharge has been noted, and no evidence of erosion of the nasal mucosae, sinusitis, or fever has been reported. At the higher doses, 90% of subjects who received the vaccine had an IgA-ASC response, and all had an ASC response in one or more isotype. The ASC responses to intranasal proteosome–*Plesiomonas shigelloides* LPS vaccine were similar, with IgA-ASC in 75% and 100% with significant ASC responses in one or more antibody isotype. Both proteosome-LPS vaccines induced three- to fourfold increases in serum antibodies (rises similar to clinical shigellosis). The proteosome–*S. flexneri* 2a LPS vaccine was further evaluated in a volunteer challenge model.[112] In this placebo-controlled, double-blind study, 27 volunteers previously vaccinated with a two-dose intranasal regimen, as used in the previous phase I study, were admitted and challenged 4 to 9 weeks postvaccination. Protective efficacy for primary outcomes of dysentery, diarrhea, and fever ranged from 24 to 32%. Volunteers challenged earlier (4 to 6 weeks after completing vaccine series) or with higher levels of anti–*S. flexneri* 2a LPS IgA serology demonstrated protection from severe disease/fever (protective efficacy 56–78%) or reduced rates of diarrhea/any disease ($p ≤ .02$), respectively. These findings provided the first demonstration of an intranasal vaccine eliciting protection (albeit moderate) against enteric disease.

CAMPYLOBACTER JEJUNI

Pathogenesis and Immunity

Campylobacter jejuni is the most common cause of bacterial diarrhea in the United States and ranks as one of the most common bacterial etiologies of TD.[13,114–118] *C. jejuni*–associated illness presents along a spectrum of watery diarrhea to dysenteric illness similar to shigellosis.[114,119] Compared to ETEC and other noninvasive causes of diarrhea, *Campylobacter*-associated diarrhea is generally more severe, with a longer duration of symptoms and frequent occurrence of severe cramps, bloody stools, and fever. Isolation rates of *Campylobacter* in children with diarrheal disease (typically ≤ 2 years old) in developing countries range between 5 and 18%.[120,121] However, different from the traveler's diarrhea syndrome, asymptomatic infections are commonly observed with values as high as 15%.[122] Given the prevalence of this infection in healthy children, it is challenging to discriminate the impact of *Campylobacter* on child health in developing countries, although a recent birth cohort study in Egypt documented pathogenicity, evidenced by associated diarrheal disease, dehydration, and bloody diarrhea.[123]

A complete understanding of the determinants of *C. jejuni* pathogenesis is lacking.[124] *Campylobacter* spp. are known for characteristic motility linked to the presence of polar flagella and spiral morphology.[124] This aspect of campylobacters is the best characterized virulence determinant, likely providing the bacteria with the ability to penetrate intestinal mucous prior to adhesion, with resultant invasion and/or indirect damage through secreted toxins.[124–129] Flagellin is the immunodominant antigen recognized during infection and has been suggested to be a protective antigen.[130] Other putative virulence factors include the PEB proteins functioning as surface adhesins and cytolethal distending toxin-inducing cell cycle arrest and cytoplasm distention, with eventual cell death.[131–135] Given the clinical spectrum, *Campylobacter* pathogenesis is likely to be complex and multifactorial.

Campylobacter-associated diarrheal illness is particularly notable for the postinfectious complication of Guillain-Barré syndrome (GBS), a paralyzing neurologic illness.[136–138] Based on epidemiologic studies, approximately 30 to 40% of patients with GBS have had a *C. jejuni* infection in the preceding 10 to 21 days.[139] The pathogenesis of *Campylobacter*-associated GBS is unclear but might involve "molecular mimicry," whereby peripheral nerves share epitopes with some *C. jejuni* antigens, such as lipo-oligosaccharides (LOS), with resultant immune response postinfection directed against host nerve tissues.[140–142] The incomplete understanding of the mechanisms by which *Campylobacter* is able to induce Guillain-Barré syndrome precludes the use of a live attenuated strain at this time.

The nature of acquired immunity, correlates of protection, and the mechanism(s) of protection against this infection have not been elucidated. Evidence for acquired immunity to *C. jejuni* derives from epidemiologic studies of residents of developing countries and experimental infection studies in US volunteers. Children living in hyperendemic areas have frequent symptomatic infections in the first 1 to 3 years of life, but, with increasing age, infections are more commonly asymptomatic, with lower quantitative levels and duration of excretion of *C. jejuni* in stool specimens.[24,130,143,144] Volunteer experimental infection studies have documented homologous protection with repeat exposure approximately 1 month following initial challenge (D. Tribble, unpublished data).[32] Volunteers with the highest prechallenge levels of anti-*Campylobacter* serum IgA were the least likely to develop disease.[32] The level of mucosal antibody is likely to be more important than serum levels. Antiflagellar IgA identified in human breast milk has been shown to protect children from *C. jejuni* diarrhea.[28,29,145–147] A vaccine challenge study conducted at Naval Medical Research Center (NMRC)also suggests a protective role of *Campylobacter*-specific fecal IgA (D. Tribble, unpublished data). Cellular responses are likely to be important in the protective response to *Campylobacter* infection given the invasive nature of the disease. A vigorous and sustained antigen-specific, IFN-γ–dependent lymphocyte proliferative response was seen in a naturally acquired *C. jejuni* infection.[148] Our existing unpublished data also support a crucial role of Th 1–type IFN-γ–dependent cell-mediated immune response in protecting volunteers from a homologous rechallenge with *C. jejuni.*

Vaccine Approaches

Whole Cell Vaccines

Given the recognized disease threat to deployed military personnel, the US Department of Defense (DOD), led by the NMRC, has sponsored a *Campylobacter* research program. A monovalent, formalin-inactivated, whole cell vaccine (CWC) made from *C. jejuni* 81-176 (Penner serotype 23/36; Lior serogroup 5) has been evaluated in clinical trials (D. Tribble, unpublished data).[149] This strain is invasive in cell culture and was originally isolated from the feces of a 9-year-old girl with diarrhea who became ill during a milk-borne outbreak in Minnesota.[129,150,151] In 1984, the strain was used in a human volunteer study at the CVD, University of Maryland.[32] The vaccine is grown under conditions that maximize motility/flagella expression and ability to invade eukaryotic cells in vitro.

NMRC has studied the hypothesis that a killed whole cell vaccine against *Campylobacter* could be safe, immunogenic, and protective against disease. Given the invasive nature of campylobacters and anticipated lower immunogenicity with inactivated vaccines delivered orally, studies were initiated to combine the vaccine with a mucosal adjuvant such as *E. coli* LT or one of its less toxic derivatives.[152,153] Preclinical studies in small animals (mice and ferrets) demonstrated the adjuvant potential of LT, as well as mutant LT, LT(R192G), when combined with the *Campylobacter* whole cell vaccine.[154–156] Small animal studies also provided preclinical efficacy evidence with the adjuvanted vaccine.[156,157]

Volunteer studies have shown the vaccine to be safe and moderately immunogenic. However, when given in a two-dose regimen like that used for the whole cell cholera vaccine, the vaccine did not protect in a volunteer challenge study, although there was a trend toward less severe disease in volunteers receiving the vaccine. Recent studies have shown that the immune response to the vaccine can be improved using a four-dose, short-interval vaccination regimen like that used for the oral typhoid vaccine Ty21a (D. Tribble, unpublished data). Specifically, although a two-dose, 14-day regimen induced no fecal IgA response, the four-dose regimen produced a mean 13-fold rise in fecal IgA. It is not yet known if the enhanced immune responses will be adequate to provide protection against disease.

Recombinant Protein Vaccine

Another approach is a recombinant protein vaccine based on a conserved, surfaced-exposed antigen that has been shown to induce an immune response after infection. Purified proteins could be delivered to the mucosa by oral or intranasal administration or given parenterally. *Campylobacter* flagellum–mediated motility contributes significantly to pathogenesis, as previously discussed. A single uni- or bipolar flagellum, composed of a major flagellin subunit, FlaA, and a minor FlaB subunit, imparts motility.[124,125,128] NMRC researchers have developed a recombinant subunit vaccine composed of truncated FlaA flagellin of *C. coli* VC167 fused to maltose-binding protein (MBP) of *Escherichia coli.*[158] The region of the *FLAA* gene encoding amino acids 5 to 337 was chosen because of its high conservation among different strains of *Campylobacter* and because this region has been demonstrated to be immunogenic. The recombinant truncated flagellin protein (rFla-MBP) has demonstrated cross-species protection in murine models of *C. jejuni* pathogenesis using intranasal rFla-MBP vaccination.[158] Clinical trial development is currently ongoing.

Table 12-1. Vaccines Currently in Clinical Development to Prevent Diarrhea (Excluding Cholera) and Dysentery

Pathogen	Approach	Components	Route	Number of Doses	Vaccine Interval	Phase of Clinical Development	Reference(s)
ETEC	Killed whole cell	Formalin-inactivated ETEC strains (*n* = 5; expressing CFA/I, CFA/II, and CFA/IV) + 1 mg cholera toxin rBS	PO	2–3	14 d	3	61–65
	Live attenuated	*ARO* (aromatic metabolism) *OMP* (outer membrane protein) mutant toxin-negative ETEC (CFA/II) strain (PTL-ETEC-003)	PO	1–2	10 d	2	73
	Subunit	Microencapsulated (PLGA polymer) CS6	PO	3	14 d	1	80
		CS6 + ETEC heat-labile toxin	TCI	3	0, 1, and 3 mo	1	85
Shigella	Live attenuated	*IUC* (aerobactin) *ICSA* (intercellular spread) mutant *S. flexneri* 2a (SC602)	PO	1	N/A	2	97
		IUC (aerobactin) *ICSA* (intercellular spread) mutant *S. sonnei* (WRSS1)	PO	1	N/A	1	100
		GUABA (purine biosynthesis) *SEN SET* (enterotoxin) mutant *S. flexneri* 2a (CVD 1208)	PO	1	N/A	1	102
	Subunit	*S. sonnei* bound to *Pseudomonas aeruginosa* rEPA	SC	1	N/A	2–3	38
		S. flexneri 2a bound to rEPA	SC	1	N/A	1-2	104, 107
		Proteosome (meningococcal OMP)–*S. flexneri* 2a LPS	IN	2	14 d	2	110, 112
Campylobacter jejuni	Killed whole cell	Monovalent formalin-inactivated *C. jejuni* strain 81-176 (Lior 5, Penner 23/36)	PO	4	2 d	2	(D. Tribble, unpublished data).

CFA = colonization factor antigen; CS = coli surface antigen; ETEC = enterotoxin-producing *Escherichia coli*; IN = intranasal; LPS = lipopolysaccharide; OMP = outer membrane protein; PLGA = poly(lactide-co-glycolide); PO = oral; SC = subcutaneous injection; TCI = transcutaneous; rBS = recombinant B subunit; rEPA = recombinant exoprotein A.

FUTURE RESEARCH NEEDS AND PROSPECTS

The number of vaccination approaches continues to grow with candidates, including live attenuated vectors, such as *Shigella flexneri* and *Salmonella* Typhi, expressing a heterologous virulence determinant from another enteropathogen, such as ETEC or *Campylobacter*; coadministration of mucosal adjuvants; DNA vaccines; and plant-based edible vaccines.[159–167] Research is under way to elucidate more fully the mechanisms involved in mucosal immune induction and how it differs based on the pathogen of interest, route of antigen delivery, vaccination regimen, and methods used to measure response. In addition, detailed immunologic analyses are evaluating issues such as the relative role of Th 1/Th 2 responses as it relates to specific pathogens (ie, invasive with intracellular phase) or mucosal adjuvant effect and homing of effector cells within the intestinal mucosa following antigenic exposure. Increased understanding of mucosal immunity will directly support enteric vaccine development.

The ever-growing list of enteropathogens, coupled with the inability to attribute as much as 25 to 50% of traveler's diarrhea episodes to an identified etiologic agent, challenges TD vaccine development efforts. However, there remain, with some regional variability, predominant agents as discussed in this chapter that would be the primary targets. From a regulatory perspective, there is a trend toward vaccine candidates with well-defined molecular factors rather than whole cell products.[168] Encouraging developments that increase the likelihood of discovering well-characterized vaccine candidates have been efforts to obtain complete genomic sequences for important enteropathogens.[169] This information has the potential to yield additional data on pathogenesis with subsequent identification of new vaccine candidates, especially when combined with microbial population data to assess for conserved epitopes and host immunology to assure that protective immune response is elicited. Several challenges and technical barriers remain; however, the diverse approaches to vaccine candidates and delivery methods (Table 12-1) provide optimism for future TD vaccine development.

The views expressed in this chapter are those of the authors and not necessarily those of the U.S. Navy or Army.

REFERENCES

1. Steffen R, van der Linde F, Gyr K, Schar M. Epidemiology of diarrhea in travelers. JAMA 1983;249:1176–80.
2. Steffen R, Rickenbach M, Wilhelm U, et al. Health problems after travel to developing countries. J Infect Dis 1987;156:84–91.
3. Ericsson CD, DuPont HL. Travelers' diarrhea. Approaches to prevention and treatment. Clin Infect Dis 1993;16:616–24.
4. DuPont HL, Ericsson CD. Prevention and treatment of traveler's diarrhea. N Engl J Med 1993;328:1821–7.
5. Sack RB, Rahman M, Yunus M, Khan EH. Antimicrobial resistance in organisms causing diarrheal disease. Clin Infect Dis 1997;24 Suppl 1:S102–5.
6. Hoge CW, Gambel JM, Srijan A, et al. Trends in antibiotic resistance among diarrheal pathogens isolated in Thailand over 15 years. Clin Infect Dis 1998;26:341–5.
7. Katelaris PH, Farthing MJ. Traveler's diarrhea. Clinical presentation and prognosis. Chemotherapy 1995;41 Suppl 1:40–7.
8. Steffen R. Epidemiologic studies of travelers' diarrhea, severe gastrointestinal infections, and cholera. Rev Infect Dis 1986;8 Suppl 2:S122–30.
9. Castelli F, Carosi G. Epidemiology of traveler's diarrhea. Chemotherapy 1995;41 Suppl 1:20–32.
10. Black RE. Epidemiology of travelers' diarrhea and relative importance of various pathogens. Rev Infect Dis 1990;12 Suppl 1:S73–9.
11. Hyams KC, Bourgeois AL, Merrell BR, et al. Diarrheal disease during Operation Desert Shield. N Engl J Med 1991;325:1423–8.
12. Mattila L, Siitonen A, Kyronseppa H, et al. Seasonal variation in etiology of travelers' diarrhea. Finnish-Moroccan Study Group. J Infect Dis 1992;165:385–8.
13. Echeverria P, Jackson LR, Hoge CW, et al. Diarrhea in U.S. troops deployed to Thailand. J Clin Microbiol 1993;31:3351–2.
14. Nataro JP, Kaper JB. Diarrheagenic *Escherichia coli*. Clin Microbiol Rev 1998;11:142–201.
15. Adachi JA, Jiang ZD, Mathewson JJ, et al. Enteroaggregative *Escherichia coli* as a major etiologic agent in traveler's diarrhea in 3 regions of the world. Clin Infect Dis 2001;32:1706–9.
16. Slutsker L, Altekruse SF, Swerdlow DL. Foodborne diseases. Emerging pathogens and trends. Infect Dis Clin North Am 1998;12:199–216.
17. Ansdell VE, Ericsson CD. Prevention and empiric treatment of traveler's diarrhea. Med Clin North Am 1999;83:945–73, vi.
18. Oksanen PJ, Salminen S, Saxelin M, et al. Prevention of travellers' diarrhoea by *Lactobacillus* GG. Ann Med 1990;22:53–6.

19. Scott DA, Haberberger RL, Thornton SA, Hyams KC. Norfloxacin for the prophylaxis of travelers' diarrhea in U.S. military personnel. Am J Trop Med Hyg 1990;42:160–4.

20. DuPont HL, Galindo E, Evans DG, et al. Prevention of travelers' diarrhea with trimethoprim-sulfamethoxazole and trimethoprim alone. Gastroenterology 1983;84:75–80.

21. Steffen R. Worldwide efficacy of bismuth subsalicylate in the treatment of travelers' diarrhea. Rev Infect Dis 1990;12 Suppl 1:S80–6.

22. Freedman DJ, Tacket CO, Delehanty A, et al. Milk immunoglobulin with specific activity against purified colonization factor antigens can protect against oral challenge with enterotoxigenic *Escherichia coli*. J Infect Dis 1998;177:662–7.

23. Black RE, Merson MH, Rowe B, et al. Enterotoxigenic *Escherichia coli* diarrhoea. Acquired immunity and transmission in an endemic area. Bull World Health Organ 1981;59:263–8.

24. Taylor DN, Perlman DM, Echeverria PD, et al. *Campylobacter* immunity and quantitative excretion rates in Thai children. J Infect Dis 1993;168:754–8.

25. Calva JJ, Ruiz-Palacios GM, Lopez-Vidal AB, et al. Cohort study of intestinal infection with *Campylobacter* in Mexican children. Lancet 1988;1:503–6.

26. Cohen D, Green MS, Block C, et al. Serum antibodies to lipopolysaccharide and natural immunity to shigellosis in an Israeli military population. J Infect Dis 1988;157:1068–71.

27. Cohen D, Sela T, Slepon R, et al. Prospective cohort studies of shigellosis during military field training. Eur J Clin Microbiol Infect Dis 2001;20:123–6.

28. Georges-Courbot MC, Beraud-Cassel AM, Gouandjika I, Georges AJ. Prospective study of enteric *Campylobacter* infections in children from birth to 6 months in the Central African Republic. J Clin Microbiol 1987;25:836–9.

29. Ruiz-Palacios GM, Calva JJ, Pickering LK, et al. Protection of breast-fed infants against *Campylobacter* diarrhea by antibodies in human milk. J Pediatr 1990;116:707–13.

30. Levine MM, Nalin DR, Hoover DL, et al. Immunity to enterotoxigenic *Escherichia coli*. Infect Immun 1979;23:729–36.

31. DuPont HL, Hornick RB, Snyder MJ, et al. Immunity in shigellosis. I. Response of man to attenuated strains of *Shigella*. J Infect Dis 1972;125:5–11.

32. Black RE, Levine MM, Clements ML, et al. Experimental *Campylobacter jejuni* infection in humans. J Infect Dis 1988;157:472–9.

33. Merson MH, Morris GK, Sack DA, et al. Travelers' diarrhea in Mexico. A prospective study of physicians and family members attending a congress. N Engl J Med 1976;294:1299–305.

34. Mestecky J. The common mucosal immune system and current strategies for induction of immune responses in external secretions. J Clin Immunol 1987;7:265–76.

35. Holmgren J, Czerkinsky C, Lycke N, Svennerholm AM. Mucosal immunity. Implications for vaccine development. Immunobiology 1992;184:157–79.

36. Czerkinsky C, Svennerholm AM, Holmgren J. Induction and assessment of immunity at enteromucosal surfaces in humans. Implications for vaccine development. Clin Infect Dis 1993;16 Suppl 2:S106–16.

37. Holmgren J. Mucosal immunity and vaccination. FEMS Microbiol Immunol 1991;4:1–9.

38. Cohen D, Ashkenazi S, Green MS, et al. Double-blind vaccine-controlled randomised efficacy trial of an investigational *Shigella sonnei* conjugate vaccine in young adults. Lancet 1997;349:155–9.

39. Teunis PF, Nagelkerke NJ, Haas CN. Dose response models for infectious gastroenteritis. Risk Anal 1999;19:1251–60.

40. Black RE, Levine MM, Clements ML, et al. Protective efficacy in humans of killed whole-vibrio oral cholera vaccine with and without the B subunit of cholera toxin. Infect Immun 1987;55:1116–20.

41. Clemens JD, Sack DA, Harris JR, et al. Field trial of oral cholera vaccines in Bangladesh. Results from three-year follow-up. Lancet 1990;335:270–3.

42. Sanchez JL, Vasquez B, Begue RE, et al. Protective efficacy of oral whole-cell/recombinant-B-subunit cholera vaccine in Peruvian military recruits. Lancet 1994;344:1273–6.

43. Levine MM, Kaper JB, Herrington D, et al. Safety, immunogenicity, and efficacy of recombinant live oral cholera vaccines, CVD 103 and CVD 103-HgR. Lancet 1988;2:467–70.

44. Clemens JD, Harris JR, Sack DA, et al. Field trial of oral cholera vaccines in Bangladesh. Results of one year of follow-up. J Infect Dis 1988;158:60–9.

45. Taylor DN, Ciqm V, Sanchez JL, et al. Two-year study of the protective efficacy of the oral whole cell plus recombinant B subunit cholera vaccine in Peru. J Infect Dis 2000;181:1667–73.

46. Kaper JB, Lockman H, Baldini MM, Levine MM. Recombinant nontoxinogenic *Vibrio cholerae* strains as attenuated cholera vaccine candidates. Nature 1984;308:655–8.

47. Black RE, Levine MM, Ferreccio C, et al. Efficacy of one or two doses of Ty21a *Salmonella typhi* vaccine in enteric-coated capsules in a controlled field trial. Chilean Typhoid Committee. Vaccine 1990;8:81–4.

48. Sabin AB. Oral poliovirus vaccine. History of its development and prospects for eradication of poliomyelitis. JAMA 1965;194:872–6.

49. Richie EE, Punjabi NH, Sidharta YY, et al. Efficacy trial of single-dose live oral cholera vaccine CVD 103-HgR in North Jakarta, Indonesia, a cholera-endemic area. Vaccine 2000;18:2399–410.

50. Cohen MB, Giannella RA, Bean J, et al. Randomized, controlled human challenge study of the safety, immunogenicity, and protective efficacy of a single dose of Peru-15, a live attenuated oral cholera vaccine. Infect Immun 2002;70:1965–70.

51. New frontiers in the development of vaccines against enterotoxinogenic (ETEC) and enterohaemorrhagic (EHEC) E. coli infections. Part I. Wkly Epidemiol Rec 1999;74:98–101.

52. DuPont HL, Formal SB, Hornick RB, et al. Pathogenesis of Escherichia coli diarrhea. N Engl J Med 1971;285:1–9.

53. Crane JK, Guerrant, RL. Acute watery diarrhea. In: Blaser MJ, Smith PD, Ravdin JI, Greenberg HB, editors. Infections of the gastrointestinal tract. New York: Raven Press; 1995. p. 273–82.

54. Cohen MB, Giannella RA. Enterotoxigenic Escherichia coli. In: Blaser MJ, Smith PD, Ravdin JI, Greenberg HB, editors. Infections of the gastrointestinal tract. New York: Raven Press; 1995. p. 691–707.

55. Clemens JD, Sack DA, Harris JR, et al. Cross-protection by B subunit-whole cell cholera vaccine against diarrhea associated with heat-labile toxin-producing enterotoxigenic Escherichia coli. Results of a large-scale field trial. J Infect Dis 1988;158:372–7.

56. Peltola H, Siitonen A, Kyronseppa H, et al. Prevention of travellers' diarrhoea by oral B-subunit/whole-cell cholera vaccine. Lancet 1991;338:1285–9.

57. Svennerholm AM, Holmgren J, Black R, et al. Serologic differentiation between antitoxin responses to infection with Vibrio cholerae and enterotoxin-producing Escherichia coli. J Infect Dis 1983;147:514–22.

58. Clements JD, Finkelstein RA. Demonstration of shared and unique immunological determinants in enterotoxins from Vibrio cholerae and Escherichia coli. Infect Immun 1978;22:709–13.

59. Holmgren J, Svennerholm AM. Bacterial enteric infections and vaccine development. Gastroenterol Clin North Am 1992;21:283–302.

60. Svennerholm AM, Holmgren J, Sack DA. Development of oral vaccines against enterotoxinogenic Escherichia coli diarrhoea. Vaccine 1989;7:196–8.

61. Jertborn M, Ahren C, Holmgren J, Svennerholm AM. Safety and immunogenicity of an oral inactivated enterotoxigenic Escherichia coli vaccine. Vaccine 1998;16:255–60.

62. Savarino SJ, Brown FM, Hall E, et al. Safety and immunogenicity of an oral, killed enterotoxigenic Escherichia coli–cholera toxin B subunit vaccine in Egyptian adults. J Infect Dis 1998;177:796–9.

63. Savarino SJ, Hall ER, Bassily S, et al. Oral, inactivated, whole cell enterotoxigenic Escherichia coli plus cholera toxin B subunit vaccine. Results of the initial evaluation in children. PRIDE Study Group. J Infect Dis 1999;179:107–14.

64. Cohen D, Orr N, Haim M, et al. Safety and immunogenicity of two different lots of the oral, killed enterotoxigenic Escherichia coli-cholera toxin B subunit vaccine in Israeli young adults. Infect Immun 2000;68:4492–7.

65. Qadri F, Wenneras C, Ahmed F, et al. Safety and immunogenicity of an oral, inactivated enterotoxigenic Escherichia coli plus cholera toxin B subunit vaccine in Bangladeshi adults and children. Vaccine 2000;18:2704–12.

66. Savarino SJ, Hall ER, Bassily S, et al. Introductory evaluation of an oral, killed whole cell enterotoxigenic Escherichia coli plus cholera toxin B subunit vaccine in Egyptian infants. Pediatr Infect Dis J 2002;21:322–30.

67. Hall ER, Wierzba TF, Ahren C, et al. Induction of systemic antifimbria and antitoxin antibody responses in Egyptian children and adults by an oral, killed enterotoxigenic Escherichia coli plus cholera toxin B subunit vaccine. Infect Immun 2001;69:2853–7.

68. Wenneras C, Qadri F, Bardhan PK, et al. Intestinal immune responses in patients infected with enterotoxigenic Escherichia coli and in vaccinees. Infect Immun 1999;67:6234–41.

69. Ahren C, Jertborn M, Svennerholm AM. Intestinal immune responses to an inactivated oral enterotoxigenic Escherichia coli vaccine and associated immunoglobulin A responses in blood. Infect Immun 1998;66:3311–6.

70. Sack DA, Shimko J, Torres O, et al. Safety and efficacy of a killed oral vaccine for enterotoxigenic E. coli diarrhea in adult travelers to Guatemala and Mexico. Abstracts from the 42nd ICAAC, American Society for Microbiology; 2002 September 27–30; San Diego, CA.

71. Levine MM. Escherichia coli that cause diarrhea. Enterotoxigenic, enteropathogenic, enteroinvasive, enterohemorrhagic, and enteroadherent. J Infect Dis 1987;155:377–89.

72. Levine MM. Development of bacterial vaccines. In: Blaser M, Smith PD, Ravdin JI, et al, editors. Infections of the gastrointestinal tract. New York: Raven Press; 1995. p. 1441–70.

73. Turner AK, Terry TD, Sack DA, et al. Construction and characterization of genetically defined aro omp mutants of enterotoxigenic Escherichia coli and preliminary studies of safety and immunogenicity in humans. Infect Immun 2001;69:4969–79.

74. Marquardt RR, Jin LZ, Kim JW, et al. Passive protective effect of egg-yolk antibodies against enterotoxigenic *Escherichia coli* K88+ infection in neonatal and early-weaned piglets. FEMS Immunol Med Microbiol 1999;23:283–8.

75. Moon HW, Bunn TO. Vaccines for preventing enterotoxigenic *Escherichia coli* infections in farm animals. Vaccine 1993;11:213–200.

76. Wolf MK. Occurrence, distribution, and associations of O and H serogroups, colonization factor antigens, and toxins of enterotoxigenic *Escherichia coli*. Clin Microbiol Rev 1997;10:569–84.

77. Reid RH, Boedeker EC, McQueen CE, et al. Preclinical evaluation of microencapsulated CFA/II oral vaccine against enterotoxigenic *E. coli*. Vaccine 1993;11:159–67.

78. Tacket CO, Reid RH, Boedeker EC, et al. Enteral immunization and challenge of volunteers given enterotoxigenic *E. coli* CFA/II encapsulated in biodegradable microspheres. Vaccine 1994;12:1270–4.

79. Wolf MK, de Haan LA, Cassels FJ, et al. The CS6 colonization factor of human enterotoxigenic *Escherichia coli* contains two heterologous major subunits. FEMS Microbiol Lett 1997;148:35–42.

80. Katz DE, DeLormier AJ, Wolf MK, et al. Oral immunization of adult volunteers with microencapsulated enterotoxigenic *Escherichia coli* (ETEC) CS6 antigen. Vaccine 2003;21:341–6.

81. Glenn GM, Taylor DN, Li X, et al. Transcutaneous immunization. A human vaccine delivery strategy using a patch. Nat Med 2000;6:1403–6.

82. Yu J, Cassels F, Scharton-Kersten T, et al. Transcutaneous immunization using colonization factor and heat-labile enterotoxin induces correlates of protective immunity for enterotoxigenic *Escherichia coli*. Infect Immun 2002;70:1056–68.

83. Glenn GM, Scharton-Kersten T, Vassell R, et al. Transcutaneous immunization with bacterial ADP-ribosylating exotoxins as antigens and adjuvants. Infect Immun 1999;67:1100–6.

84. Glenn GM, Scharton-Kersten T, Vassell R, et al. Transcutaneous immunization with cholera toxin protects mice against lethal mucosal toxin challenge. J Immunol 1998;161:3211–4.

85. Guerena-Burgueno F, Hall ER, Taylor DN, et al. Safety and immunogenicity of a prototype enterotoxigenic *Escherichia coli* vaccine administered transcutaneously. Infect Immun 2002;70:1874–80.

86. Vaccine research and development. New strategies for accelerating *Shigella* vaccine development. Wkly Epidemiol Rec 1997;72:73–9.

87. Formal SB, Hale TL, Kapfer C. *Shigella* vaccines. Rev Infect Dis 1989;11 Suppl 3:S547–51.

88. Philpott DJ, Edgeworth JD, Sansonetti PJ. The pathogenesis of *Shigella flexneri* infection. Lessons from in vitro and in vivo studies. Philos Trans R Soc Lond B Biol Sci 2000;355:575–86.

89. Shears P. *Shigella* infections. Ann Trop Med Parasitol 1996;90:105–14.

90. Ferreccio C, Prado V, Ojeda A, et al. Epidemiologic patterns of acute diarrhea and endemic *Shigella* infections in children in a poor periurban setting in Santiago, Chile. Am J Epidemiol 1991;134:614–27.

91. Cohen D, Green MS, Block C, et al. Prospective study of the association between serum antibodies to lipopolysaccharide O antigen and the attack rate of shigellosis. J Clin Microbiol 1991;29:386–9.

92. Tacket CO, Binion SB, Bostwick E, et al. Efficacy of bovine milk immunoglobulin concentrate in preventing illness after *Shigella flexneri* challenge. Am J Trop Med Hyg 1992;47:276–83.

93. Formal SB, Maenza RM, Austin S, LaBrec EH. Failure of parenteral vaccines to protect monkeys against experimental shigellosis. Proc Soc Exp Biol Med 1967;125:347–9.

94. Higgins AR, Floyd TM, Kader MA. Studies in Shigellosis. III. A controlled evaluation of a monovalent *Shigella* vaccine in a highly endemic environment. Am J Trop Med Hyg 1955;4:281–8.

95. Sansonetti P, Phalipon A. Shigellosis. From molecular pathogenesis of infection to protective immunity and vaccine development. Res Immunol 1996;147:595–602.

96. Sansonetti PJ, Arondel J. Construction and evaluation of a double mutant of *Shigella flexneri* as a candidate for oral vaccination against shigellosis. Vaccine 1989;7:443–50.

97. Coster TS, Hoge CW, VanDeVerg LL, et al. Vaccination against shigellosis with attenuated *Shigella flexneri* 2a strain SC602. Infect Immun 1999;67:3437–43.

98. Kotloff KL, Nataro JP, Losonsky GA, et al. A modified *Shigella* volunteer challenge model in which the inoculum is administered with bicarbonate buffer. Clinical experience and implications for *Shigella* infectivity. Vaccine 1995;13:1488–94.

99. Hartman AB, Venkatesan MM. Construction of a stable attenuated *Shigella sonnei* DeltavirG vaccine strain, WRSS1, and protective efficacy and immunogenicity in the guinea pig keratoconjunctivitis model. Infect Immun 1998;66:4572–6.

100. Kotloff KL, Taylor DN, Sztein MB, et al. Phase I evaluation of delta virG *Shigella sonnei* live, attenuated, oral vaccine strain WRSS1 in healthy adults. Infect Immun 2002;70:2016–21.

101. Kotloff KL, Noriega F, Losonsky GA, et al. Safety, immunogenicity, and transmissibility in humans of CVD 1203, a live oral *Shigella flexneri* 2a vaccine candidate attenuated by deletions in aroA and virG. Infect Immun 1996;64:4542–8.

102. Kotloff KL, Noriega FR, Samandari T, et al. *Shigella flexneri* 2a strain CVD 1207, with specific deletions in virG, sen, set, and guaBA, is highly attenuated in humans. Infect Immun 2000;68:1034–9.

103. Robbins JB, Chu C, Watson DC, et al. O-specific side-chain toxin-protein conjugates as parenteral vaccines for the prevention of shigellosis and related diseases. Rev Infect Dis 1991;13 Suppl 4:S362–5.

104. Cohen D, Ashkenazi S, Green M, et al. Safety and immunogenicity of investigational *Shigella* conjugate vaccines in Israeli volunteers. Infect Immun 1996;64:4074–7.

105. Chu CY, Liu BK, Watson D, et al. Preparation, characterization, and immunogenicity of conjugates composed of the O-specific polysaccharide of *Shigella dysenteriae* type 1 (Shiga's bacillus) bound to tetanus toxoid. Infect Immun 1991;59:4450–8.

106. Taylor DN, Trofa AC, Sadoff J, et al. Synthesis, characterization, and clinical evaluation of conjugate vaccines composed of the O-specific polysaccharides of *Shigella dysenteriae* type 1, *Shigella flexneri* type 2a, and *Shigella sonnei* (*Plesiomonas shigelloides*) bound to bacterial toxoids. Infect Immun 1993;61:3678–87.

107. Ashkenazi S, Passwell JH, Harlev E, et al. Safety and immunogenicity of *Shigella sonnei* and *Shigella flexneri* 2a O-specific polysaccharide conjugates in children. J Infect Dis 1999;179:1565–8.

108. Passwell JH, Harlev E, Ashkenazi S, et al. Safety and immunogenicity of improved *Shigella* O-specific polysaccharide-protein conjugate vaccines in adults in Israel. Infect Immun 2001;69:1351–7.

109. Orr N, Robin G, Cohen D, et al. Immunogenicity and efficacy of oral or intranasal *Shigella flexneri* 2a and *Shigella sonnei* proteosome-lipopolysaccharide vaccines in animal models. Infect Immun 1993;61:2390–5.

110. Fries LF, Montemarano AD, Mallett CP, et al. Safety and immunogenicity of a proteosome–*Shigella flexneri* 2a lipopolysaccharide vaccine administered intranasally to healthy adults. Infect Immun 2001;69:4545–53.

111. Mallett CP, Hale TL, Kaminski RW, et al. Intranasal or intragastric immunization with proteosome–*Shigella* lipopolysaccharide vaccines protects against lethal pneumonia in a murine model of *Shigella* infection. Infect Immun 1995;63:2382–6.

112. Durbin AP, Bourgeois AL, McKenzie R. et al. Intranasal immunization with proteosome-*Shigella flexneri* 2a LPS vaccine. Factors associated with protection in a volunteer challenge model [abstract]. Thirty-ninth Meeting of the Infectious Diseases Society of America; 2001 October 25–28; San Francisco.

113. Lowell GH. Proteosomes for improved nasal, oral or injectable vaccines. In: Levine MM, Woodrow GC, Kaper JB, Cobon GS, editors. New generation vaccines. New York: Marcel Dekker; 1997. p. 193–206.

114. Blaser MJ. Epidemiologic and clinical features of *Campylobacter jejuni* infections. J Infect Dis 1997;176 Suppl 2:S103–5.

115. Preliminary FoodNet data on the incidence of foodborne illnesses—selected sites, United States, 2001. MMWR Morb Mortal Wkly Rep 2002;51:325–9.

116. Mattila L. Clinical features and duration of traveler's diarrhea in relation to its etiology. Clin Infect Dis 1994;19:728–34.

117. Taylor DN, Echeverria P. Etiology and epidemiology of travelers' diarrhea in Asia. Rev Infect Dis 1986;8 Suppl 2:S136–41.

118. Bourgeois AL, Gardiner CH, Thornton SA, et al. Etiology of acute diarrhea among United States military personnel deployed to South America and West Africa. Am J Trop Med Hyg 1993;48:243–8.

119. Blaser MJ, Berkowitz ID, LaForce FM, et al. *Campylobacter* enteritis. Clinical and epidemiologic features. Ann Intern Med 1979;91:179–85.

120. Glass RI, Stoll BJ, Huq MI, et al. Epidemiologic and clinical features of endemic *Campylobacter jejuni* infection in Bangladesh. J Infect Dis 1983;148:292–6.

121. Taylor D. *Campylobacter* infections in developing countries. Washington (DC): American Society for Microbiology; 1992.

122. Coker AO, Isokpehi RD, Thomas BN, et al. Human campylobacteriosis in developing countries. Emerg Infect Dis 2002;8:237–44.

123. Rao MR, Naficy AB, Savarino SJ, et al. Pathogenicity and convalescent excretion of *Campylobacter* in rural Egyptian children. Am J Epidemiol 2001;154:166–73.

124. Ketley JM. Pathogenesis of enteric infection by *Campylobacter*. Microbiology 1997;143 Pt 1:5–21.

125. Wassenaar TM, Bleumink-Pluym NM, van der Zeijst BA. Inactivation of *Campylobacter jejuni* flagellin genes by homologous recombination demonstrates that flaA but not flaB is required for invasion. EMBO J 1991;10:2055–61.

126. Wassenaar TM, Blaser MJ. Pathophysiology of *Campylobacter* jejuni infections of humans. Microbes Infect 1999;1:1023–33.

127. Guerry P, Alm RA, Power ME, et al. Role of two flagellin genes in *Campylobacter* motility. J Bacteriol 1991;173:4757–64.

128. Pavlovskis OR, Rollins DM, Haberberger RL Jr, et al. Significance of flagella in colonization resistance of rabbits immunized with *Campylobacter* spp. Infect Immun 1991;59:2259–64.

129. Yao R, Burr DH, Doig P, et al. Isolation of motile and non-motile insertional mutants of *Campylobacter jejuni*. The role of motility in adherence and invasion of eukaryotic cells. Mol Microbiol 1994;14:883–93.

130. Martin PM, Mathiot J, Ipero J, et al. Immune response to *Campylobacter jejuni* and *Campylobacter coli* in a cohort of children from birth to 2 years of age. Infect Immun 1989;57:2542–6.

131. Johnson WM, Lior H. Cytotoxic and cytotonic factors produced by *Campylobacter jejuni*, *Campylobacter coli*, and *Campylobacter laridis*. J Clin Microbiol 1986;24:275–81.

132. Whitehouse CA, Balbo PB, Pesci EC, et al. *Campylobacter jejuni* cytolethal distending toxin causes a G2-phase cell cycle block. Infect Immun 1998;66:1934–40.

133. Pickett CL, Pesci EC, Cottle DL, et al. Prevalence of cytolethal distending toxin production in *Campylobacter jejuni* and relatedness of *Campylobacter* sp. cdtB gene. Infect Immun 1996;64:2070–8.

134. Pei ZH, Ellison RTd, Blaser MJ. Identification, purification, and characterization of major antigenic proteins of *Campylobacter jejuni*. J Biol Chem 1991;266:16363–9.

135. Pei Z, Burucoa C, Grignon B, et al. Mutation in the peb1A locus of *Campylobacter jejuni* reduces interactions with epithelial cells and intestinal colonization of mice. Infect Immun 1998;66:938–43.

136. Kuroki S, Haruta T, Yoshioka M, et al. Guillain-Barré syndrome associated with *Campylobacter* infection. Pediatr Infect Dis J 1991;10:149–51.

137. Rees JH, Gregson NA, Griffiths PL, Hughes RA. *Campylobacter jejuni* and Guillain-Barré syndrome. QJM 1993;86:623–34.

138. Mishu B, Blaser MJ. Role of infection due to *Campylobacter jejuni* in the initiation of Guillain-Barré syndrome. Clin Infect Dis 1993;17:104–8.

139. Nachamkin I, Allos BM, Ho T. *Campylobacter* species and Guillain-Barré syndrome. Clin Microbiol Rev 1998;11:555–67.

140. Yuki N. Pathogenesis of axonal Guillain-Barré syndrome. Hypothesis. Muscle Nerve 1994;17:680–2.

141. Aspinall GO, Fujimoto S, McDonald AG, et al. Lipopolysaccharides from *Campylobacter jejuni* associated with Guillain-Barré syndrome patients mimic human gangliosides in structure. Infect Immun 1994;62:2122–5.

142. Prendergast MM, Moran AP. Lipopolysaccharides in the development of the Guillain-Barré syndrome and Miller Fisher syndrome forms of acute inflammatory peripheral neuropathies. J Endotoxin Res 2000;6:341–59.

143. Blaser MJ, Taylor DN, Feldman RA. Epidemiology of *Campylobacter jejuni* infections. Epidemiol Rev 1983;5:157–76.

144. Blaser MJ, Taylor DN, Echeverria P. Immune response to *Campylobacter jejuni* in a rural community in Thailand. J Infect Dis 1986;153:249–54.

145. Megraud F, Boudraa G, Bessaoud K, et al. Incidence of *Campylobacter* infection in infants in western Algeria and the possible protective role of breast feeding. Epidemiol Infect 1990;105:73–8.

146. Torres O, Cruz JR. Protection against *Campylobacter* diarrhea. Role of milk IgA antibodies against bacterial surface antigens. Acta Paediatr 1993;82:835-8.

147. Nachamkin I, Fischer SH, Yang XH, et al. Immunoglobulin A antibodies directed against *Campylobacter jejuni* flagellin present in breast-milk. Epidemiol Infect 1994;112:359–65.

148. Baqar S, Rice B, Lee L, et al. *Campylobacter jejuni* enteritis. Clin Infect Dis 2001;33:901–5.

149. Scott DA. Vaccines against *Campylobacter jejuni*. J Infect Dis 1997;176 Suppl 2:S183–8.

150. Oelschlaeger TA, Guerry P, Kopecko DJ. Unusual microtubule-dependent endocytosis mechanisms triggered by *Campylobacter jejuni* and *Citrobacter freundii*. Proc Natl Acad Sci U S A 1993;90:6884–8.

151. Korlath JA, Osterholm MT, Judy LA, et al. A point-source outbreak of campylobacteriosis associated with consumption of raw milk. J Infect Dis 1985;152:592–6.

152. Dickinson BL, Clements JD. Dissociation of *Escherichia coli* heat-labile enterotoxin adjuvanticity from ADP-ribosyltransferase activity. Infect Immun 1995;63:1617–23.

153. Cheng E, Cardenas-Freytag L, Clements JD. The role of cAMP in mucosal adjuvanticity of *Escherichia coli* heat-labile enterotoxin (LT). Vaccine 1999;18:38–49.

154. Rollwagen FM, Pacheco ND, Clements JD, et al. Killed *Campylobacter* elicits immune response and protection when administered with an oral adjuvant. Vaccine 1993;11:1316–20.

155. Pace JL, Rossi HA, Esposito VM, et al. Inactivated whole-cell bacterial vaccines. Current status and novel strategies. Vaccine 1998;16:1563–74.

156. Baqar S, Applebee LA, Bourgeois AL. Immunogenicity and protective efficacy of a prototype *Campylobacter* killed whole-cell vaccine in mice. Infect Immun 1995;63:3731–5.

157. Baqar S, Bourgeois AL, Applebee LA, et al. Murine intranasal challenge model for the study of *Campylobacter* pathogenesis and immunity. Infect Immun 1996;64:4933–9.

158. Lee LH, Burg E III, Baqar S, et al. Evaluation of a truncated recombinant flagellin subunit vaccine against *Campylobacter jejuni*. Infect Immun 1999;67:5799–805.

159. Koprowski H II, Levine MM, Anderson RJ, et al. Attenuated *Shigella flexneri* 2a vaccine strain CVD 1204 expressing colonization factor antigen I and mutant heat-labile enterotoxin of enterotoxigenic *Escherichia coli*. Infect Immun 2000;68:4884–92.

160. Medina E, Guzman CA. Use of live bacterial vaccine vectors for antigen delivery. Potential and limitations. Vaccine 2001;19:1573–80.

161. Altboum Z, Barry EM, Losonsky G, et al. Attenuated *Shigella flexneri* 2a Delta guaBA strain CVD 1204 expressing entero-toxigenic *Escherichia coli* (ETEC) CS2 and CS3 fimbriae as a live mucosal vaccine against *Shigella* and ETEC infection. Infect Immun 2001;69:3150–8.

162. Freytag LC, Clements JD. Bacterial toxins as mucosal adjuvants. Curr Top Microbiol Immunol 1999;236:215–36.

163. Boyaka PN, Marinaro M, Vancott JL, et al. Strategies for mucosal vaccine development. Am J Trop Med Hyg 1999;60:35–45.

164. Fujihashi K, Koga T, van Ginkel FW, et al. A dilemma for mucosal vaccination. Efficacy versus toxicity using enterotoxin-based adjuvants. Vaccine 2002;20:2431–8.

165. Alves AM, Lasaro MO, Almeida DF, Ferreira LC. DNA immunisation against the CFA/I fimbriae of enterotoxigenic *Escherichia coli* (ETEC). Vaccine 2000;19:788–95.

166. Artnzen CJ. Edible vaccines. Public Health Rep 1997;112:190–7.

167. Tacket CO, Mason HS. A review of oral vaccination with transgenic vegetables. Microbes Infect 1999;1:777–83.

168. Dougan G, Huett A, Clare S. Vaccines against human enteric bacterial pathogens. Br Med Bull 2002;62:113–23.

169. Moxon R, Rappuoli R. Bacterial pathogen genomics and vaccines. Br Med Bull 2002;62:45–58.

Chapter 13

Dengue Fever Vaccine

Scott B. Halstead and David W. Vaughn

Although there are no licensed vaccines to protect against dengue fever (DF), dengue hemorrhagic fever (DHF), or dengue shock syndrome (DSS) at the time of this writing, this chapter reviews some of the extensive literature on dengue vaccine development and highlights progress achieved for those vaccines farthest downstream. The current situation is somewhat ironic, given that the development of inactivated dengue vaccines began in 1929.[1,2] The first live attenuated vaccine was achieved by mouse-brain passage soon after the first isolations of dengue virus type 1 (DEN-1) in the 1940s.[3,4] Dengue virus type 2 (DEN-2), also recovered in the laboratory from infected soldiers during World War II, was similarly attenuated by serial mouse-brain passage.[5] Although DEN-1, passaged 33 times in mouse brain (MD-1), was satisfactorily attenuated and immunogenic, these early vaccines were abandoned because of the complications that might result from residual mouse brain myelin proteins in the vaccine preparations.[6] In the 1950s, with the recovery and characterization of dengue virus types 3 (DEN-3) and 4 (DEN-4), the challenge of developing a dengue vaccine became technically more demanding.[7]

From their original endemic focus in Southeast Asia, the four dengue virus serotypes have spread to nearly 100 tropical countries around the globe, where each year they cause tens of millions of cases of DF and 500,000 cases of DHF/DSS.[8] Because most tropical travel destinations are in dengue-endemic countries, dengue infections are a serious health threat to travelers. Among tourists, dengue occurs about as frequently as malaria and ranks just below respiratory disease and diarrhea (D. Gubler, US Centers for Disease Control [CDC], personal communication, May 2002). Travelers and their consulting physicians should be reminded that dengue viruses are transmitted by the bite of *Aedes aegypti*, a daytime-biting mosquito that breeds in water stored in or around human dwellings.

The development of a dengue vaccine has now become a public health imperative as national programs for the control of *Aedes aegypti* have conspicuously failed in the modern era.[9] A protective single-dose tetravalent vaccine would appear to be the essential requirement for a candidate dengue vaccine given the discovery that the life-threatening syndrome, DHF/DSS, is a high risk during a second dengue virus infection.[10,11] Furthermore, infants receiving passive transfer of dengue antibodies from their mothers at birth may also develop DHF/DSS during their initial dengue infection within the first year of life.[12,13] The at-risk status with regard to DHF/DSS appears to last for life following the first dengue infection.[14] Infection with a single dengue virus type results in a lifelong antibody response and solid protection to challenge with the same virus type.[1,15,16] However, after a short period of cross-protection, infection with a different dengue type occurs regularly, often resulting in an overt illness.[16]

VACCINES IN DEVELOPMENT

Live Attenuated Viruses (Cell Culture Passaged)

There are several licensed live attenuated viral vaccines, including the flavivirus vaccine for yellow fever. Live attenuated viral vaccines have been proven to raise both antibody and T-cell responses, most closely resembling those following natural infection. The challenge is to show that the agent does not cause disease or provoke other safety problems. Using the classic method of serial passage in non-human hosts, a live attenuated tetravalent dengue vaccine was developed and tested by investigators at Mahidol University in Bangkok, Thailand, and licensed to Aventis Pasteur (Lyon, France). Virus strains DEN-1 16007, DEN-2 16681, and DEN-4 1036 were passaged serially in primary dog kidney (PDK) cells at the University of Hawaii then transferred to Thailand for phase I testing.[17] Extensive studies in small groups of flavivirus-susceptible adult Thai volunteers who were given various PDK passage–level viruses resulted in the identification of strains with acceptable reactogenicity and immunogenicity for DEN-1, -2, and -4 viruses at passage levels PDK13, PDK53, and PDK48, respectively.[18–20] DEN-3 viruses consistently failed to replicate in PDK cells and, accordingly, were attenuated by serial passage in primary African green monkey kidney (GMK) cells. An acceptable vaccine candidate was found for DEN-3 16562 at the 48th GMK cell passage with 3 final passages in fetal rhesus lung (FRhL) cells.

A trial of vaccine candidate DEN-2 16681 PDK53 in 10 US Army soldiers raised neutralizing antibodies in all participants.[21] The four monovalent candidates elicited neutralizing antibody seroconversion in 3 of 5, 5 of 5, 5 of 5, and 5 of 5 American volunteers, respectively, after a single dose of approximately 10^3 to 10^4 plaque-forming units (PFU)[22] Bivalent and trivalent formulations using DEN-1, -2, and -4 vaccine candidates elicited uniform seroconversions in Thai subjects.[23] However, when all 4 serotypes were combined into a tetravalent vaccine, the predominant response was the development of DEN-3 viremia and neutralizing antibody only.[22] To overcome this apparent viral interference phenomenon, this vaccine was reformulated using lower doses of DEN-3 and is being administered using one or two booster doses. Indeed, a reformulated tetravalent vaccine resulted in seroconversions of 85%, 78%, 100%, and 71% for dengue virus serotypes 1 to 4, respectively, after two doses given at 0 and 6 months in a study in Thai adults (J. Lang, personal communication, June 2003). This vaccine is in long-term phase IIa evaluation in 73 children at this writing (J. Lang, personal communication, June 2003).

The Walter Reed Army Institute of Research (WRAIR) has also developed a tetravalent live attenuated dengue vaccine. Their effort involved serial passage of all four dengue viruses, including DEN-3, in PDK. Initial vaccine candidates (specific virus strains and PDK cell passage levels) were selected based on the results of a series of phase I safety and immunogenicity studies conducted at the WRAIR and the University of Maryland School of Medicine Center for Vaccine Development. Selected candidate vaccines were produced with terminal passage in FRhL cells: DEN-1 45AZ5 PDK20/FRhL3, DEN-2 16803 PDK50/FRhL3, DEN-3 CH53489 PDK20/FRhL3, and DEN-4 341750 PDK20/ FRhL4. Among the selected passage levels, the seroconversion rates were 100%, 92%, 46%, and 58% for a single dose of DEN-1 to -4, respectively. The WRAIR DEN-2, -3, and -4 vaccine viruses were well tolerated by volunteers. The DEN-1 PDK20/FRhL3 monovalent candidate was associated with increased reactogenicity, with 40% developing fever and generalized rash. Vaccine-related reactions consisted of modified symptoms of dengue fever including headache, myalgia, and rash.[24–26]

Sixteen formulations of the WRAIR tetravalent vaccine were tested in 64 adult volunteers.[26,27] The formulations were derived by using undiluted vaccine (5 to 6 logs of virus) or a 1:30 dilution for each virus serotype. Seroconversion rates after a single dose of tetravalent vaccine were 83%, 65%, 57%, and 25% to DEN-1 to -4, respectively, similar to those seen with monovalent vaccines. Few additional seroconversions were seen following a booster dose 1 month after the first dose. Though the sample size was small, a trend toward increased reactogenicity was observed when a full dose of the DEN-1 component was combined with lower doses of DEN-2 and/or DEN-4. With these viral strains, at the doses evaluated, viral interference did not affect antibody response but may have modified reactogenicity. In an attempt to reduce reactogenicity due to the DEN-1 component and to increase the immunogenicity of the DEN-4 component, a seventeenth formulation using DEN-1 45AZ5 PDK27 and DEN-4 341750 PDK6 was evaluated. Expanded testing of vaccine formulations along with booster doses at an interval of 6 months yielded higher seroconversion rates and acceptable reactogenicity in adults (W. Sun, personal communication, December 2002).

Because DHF/DSS is seen regularly in infants 2 years of age and older, it will be important to administer tetravalent vaccines early in life. Hospital-based studies in Thailand have shown that most primary dengue virus infections in young children are clinically silent.[28,29] It has been reasoned that a vaccine that is somewhat reactogenic in susceptible adult volunteers might demonstrate decreased reactogenicity in young children. Accordingly, phase I and II vaccine trials in 12- to 15-month-old flavivirus-naive Thai infants are planned (M.P. Mammen, personal communication, June 2003).

There are two safety issues with live dengue vaccines: enhanced disease accompanying breakthrough wild-type dengue virus infections in the event of incomplete protection or enhancement of vaccine reactogenicity in persons with existing dengue immunity. The principal concern is the theoretic risk of enhanced disease following incomplete dengue virus vaccination. A tetravalent vaccine approach is designed to induce primary-type immune responses to all four dengue viruses simultaneously, a phenomenon readily demonstrated in susceptible rhesus monkeys (*Macaca mulatta*).[30] The simultaneous production of neutralizing antibodies to all four dengue viruses is predicted to yield solid immunity, thereby minimizing the risk of disease enhancement following natural infection. Most adults in Southeast Asia have circulating neutralizing antibodies to all four dengue virus types and have demonstrable solid immunity. However, primary vaccine failures to one or more components in a tetravalent vaccine or the raising of nonprotective antibodies could result in partially immunized individuals who are at risk of antibody-enhanced disease during a subsequent infection with a wild-type dengue virus. Further vaccine development and testing will be needed to assure that tetravalent seroconversion to relevant viral epitopes occurs following immunization, resulting in cellular memory responses adequate for producing circulating antibodies that abort enhanced infections, even many years following vaccination.

Enhanced vaccine reactogenicity is also a possibility if a live attenuated dengue virus is administered to persons with preexisting antiflavivirus antibodies. To date, enhanced disease has not been observed in dengue-vaccinated yellow fever immunes, in volunteers receiving closely spaced sequential dengue viruses, or in dengue or Japanese encephalitis (JE)–immune volunteers given serially passaged dengue virus vaccines (S. Yoksan, personal communication, June 2003).[15,31,32] In this last group, volunteers were screened using the plaque reduction neutralization test (PRNT) for dengue viruses, although some of the preexisting flavivirus antibodies may have been nondengue. There have been recent suggestions that wild-type DEN-4 and DEN-2 viruses may cause less overt disease, that is, they are naturally attenuated in many flavivirus naive hosts.[33,34] The implication from this observation is that seemingly attenuated laboratory-passaged dengue strains inoculated in susceptible volunteers may actually be "virulent" in partially dengue-immune subjects and capable of producing antibody-enhanced infection and disease.

Because in nature, more than 95% of secondary dengue virus infections are inapparent, safety tests on live attenuated vaccines must be done on large numbers of partially dengue-immune volunteers to adequately assess this risk.[35] As yet, increased reactogenicity has not been observed in clinical trials, conducted in Thailand and in the United States, in which two doses of tetravalent vaccines were given 6 months apart (R. Edelman and J.F. Saluzzo, personal communications, November 2002). Perhaps the interval between doses controls the risk of disease enhancement. A better understanding of the immune mechanisms of vaccine protection and enhanced disease is needed to asses more accurately the risks associated with phase III field trials.

Other safety concerns with live attenuated dengue viral vaccines include the presence of cell culture–derived adventitious agents in the final vaccine product, community spread of vaccine virus present in viremic immunized humans by local vector mosquitoes, vaccine virus neurovirulence, and the effects of vaccine administration in immunocompromised hosts.

Chimeric Vaccines

The flavivirus genome is a single-stranded, positive-sense ribonucleic acid (RNA) molecule of nearly 11 kilobases containing a single open reading frame. The RNA is translated into a polyprotein that is processed into at least 10 gene products: the three structural proteins nucleocapsid, or core (C); pre-membrane (prM); envelope (E); and seven nonstructural (NS) proteins, NS1, NS2A, NS2B, NS3, NS4A, NS4B, and NS5. The untranslated regions of the genome at the 5′ and 3′ ends are crucial for protein translation and minus-strand transcription.[36]

Yellow Fever Virus as Molecular Backbone

Chimeric dengue vaccine viruses have been derived by replacing genes encoding dengue virus structural proteins for the equivalent genes from an attenuated yellow fever vaccine virus. The hypothesis is that the attenuation characteristics of the vaccine virus will assure the absence of dengue-like behavior by the chimera. Insertion of dengue genes into the cDNA backbone of yellow fever 17D was pioneered at the Washington University and the St. Louis University medical schools and is being developed commercially by Acambis (Cambridge, Massachusetts USA).[37–40] Vero cells serve as the substrate for vaccine virus production.

Dengue/yellow fever virus chimeras have been developed for each of the four dengue virus serotypes using the *PrM-E* genes from DEN-1 PUO-359, DEN-2 PUO-218, DEN-3 PaH881, and DEN-4 1228 viruses.[40] Neurovirulence in mice was reduced compared with the yellow fever 17D vaccine virus. Viremia in rhesus macaques is similar to that of yellow fever 17D virus and greatly reduced compared to wild-type dengue viruses. Seroconversion in rhesus monkeys was 100% using a tetravalent formulation composed of three logs of the DEN-2 chimera and five logs of DEN-1, -3, and -4 chimeras.[40] Lower DEN-3 and DEN-4 neutralizing antibody titers were seen with five logs of the DEN-2 component, suggesting interference, but rhesus monkeys were protected from viremia when challenged with all four wild-type dengue viruses.[40] Encouraging phase I data for the yellow fever 17D–Japanese encephalitis virus chimera (ChimeriVax-JE) suggest that this approach will also be effective for dengue.[41] Phase I evaluation of a monovalent DEN–2 vaccine started in 2002 (T. Monath, personal communication, October 2002).

If virus replication depends on nonstructural genes and/or noncoding regions of the genome, those chimeras using a common genetic backbone for all component viruses should not result in growth interference. However, with the yellow fever 17D–dengue virus chimera (ChimeriVax-DEN), different formulations of the four component viruses resulted in significantly different neutralizing antibody responses.[40] This suggests that interference can occur with chimeric vaccines. Recombination events might occur following administration of tetravalent chimeric vaccines, but such events are unlikely to result in reversion to a more virulent phenotype.

Dengue 2 Virus as Molecular Backbone

The CDC is developing a tetravalent chimeric dengue vaccine by introducing DEN-1, -3, and -4, *prM*, and *E* genes into cyclic deoxyribonucleic acid (cDNA) derived from the successfully attenuated DEN-2 component of the Mahidol University/Aventis Pasteur LAV vaccine (DEN-2 16681 PDK53).[21,42,43] Previously, this group had reported that the attenuation markers for DEN-2 vaccine reside outside the structural gene region, providing a justification for using this virus backbone to receive *C-PrM-E* genes from the other dengue virus types.[44] Chimeras for DEN-1 have been produced using structural genes from both the Mahidol DEN-1 PDK13 vaccine virus and the near–wild-type DEN-1 16007 virus. The structural genes of the DEN-1 16007 virus appear to be more immunogenic in mice than those of the PDK13 vaccine virus.[45] Chimeras for DEN-3 and DEN-4 have been constructed using the wild-type virus structural genes and are currently being characterized in monkeys (D. Gubler, personal communication, June 2003).

Molecularly Attenuated Viruses

Dengue 4

The cloning of a DEN-4 (WRAIR 814669, Dominica, 1981) by Lai and colleagues at the National Institutes of Health permitted the introduction of selected genes in a dengue genome and opened a new era of dengue vaccine research.[46]

A DEN-4 mutant (DEN-4 2AΔ30), transcribed from recombinant cDNA, with a 30-nucleotide deletion in the 3′ untranslated region (10478–10507) produced lower viremia and slightly decreased neutralizing antibody responses compared with wild type in rhesus macaques.[47] After being grown in Vero cells, this virus was recently evaluated in 20 volunteers.[48] Following inoculation of 10^5 PFU in 0.5 mL subcutaneously, there was no injection site soreness or swelling and only minimal systemic symptoms. Ten volunteers (50%) experienced a mild rash (unnoticed by the volunteers themselves). Seven volunteers reported mild headaches lasting less than 2 hours. One volunteer reported a fever of 38.6°C without other symptoms. A mild increase in serum transaminase levels was seen in five volunteers (25%), with a transient increase to five times the upper limit of normal (238 IU/L) for one volunteer. Seventy percent of volunteers had low-level viremia, and all developed neutralizing antibody (28 days following a single dose of candidate vaccine).

The DEN-4 cDNA described above may serve as a model for the other dengue virus serotypes. The DEN-4 vaccine virus was used to construct chimeric viruses with DEN-1 or DEN-2 antigenicity by substitution of the heterotypic genes coding for the respective viral structural proteins.[49,50] DEN-1 and DEN-2 *PrM-E* genes placed in the DEN-4 backbone resulted in chimeric viruses with reduced viremia compared with the wild-type DEN-4 virus. These chimeric viruses produced robust antibody responses and protection from challenge with wild-type viruses when used as either monovalent or bivalent vaccines in rhesus monkeys.[51] Work with the DEN-3/DEN-4 chimera is in progress.[52]

Because attenuation of this virus is the result of a large deletion mutation, it is likely to remain genetically stable in vaccinees. Because of evidence suggesting that wild-type DEN-4 infection in flavivirus naive adults seldom results in overt disease, a full evaluation of the safety of the mutagenized DEN-4 candidate vaccine will require vaccination of partial dengue-immune volunteers.[33]

Dengue 1

Investigators at the Center for Biologics Evaluation and Research at the US Food and Drug Administration (FDA) created a chimeric virus combining a DEN-2 with the terminal 3′ stem and loop structure of West Nile virus. This virus grew normally in (LLC-MK2) cells but was severely restricted for growth in C6/36 insect cells and was designated "mutant F," or "mutF."[53] A DEN-1 mutF virus was created starting with an infectious clone of the DEN-1 West Pacific; this virus shared the phenotype of restricted growth in insect cells and was evaluated in rhesus macaques.[54] Viremia in rhesus monkeys was greatly reduced compared with the DEN-1 West Pacific parent, suggesting that the chimera will be less reactogenic in humans.[24] Immune responses were similar to the wild-type virus: all animals seroconverted, with mean reciprocal neutralizing antibody titers of 320 and 240 for wild-type and DEN-1 mutF virus recipients, respectively. Monkeys challenged 12 or 17 months following a single dose of vaccine were protected from viremia. Phase I testing is planned.

The two approaches described may generate tetravalent dengue vaccines either by separately introducing 3′ terminus changes into each of the four dengue viruses or by making structural gene chimeras so as to include all four sets of dengue antigens. Such a vaccine may have advantages over empiric attenuation in cell culture because there is a known molecular basis to attenuation, and there will be a reduced risk of adventitious agents, resulting in lower product quality assurance costs. It remains to be determined if genetically altered viruses have lost dengue-like virulence and whether interference phenomena can occur when these viruses are given as a tetravalent formulation.

Inactivated or Subunit Vaccines

Infected Mosquitoes

In 1929, Simmons and colleagues attempted to develop an inactivated dengue vaccine prior to the laboratory characterization of dengue virus.[1] This vaccine consisted of 2010 *A. aegypti* mosquitoes that had fed on DEN-1–infected volunteers. The mosquitoes were ground in a sterile porcelain mortar and suspended in a salt solution with phenol and formalin added. The suspension was held for 10 days; clarified by centrifugation and tested for aerobic and anaerobic bacteria and for bacterial toxins; and safety tested in rabbits, guinea pigs, and white mice. All safety tests were normal. The authors and two additional volunteers were given two doses of vaccine 4 days apart and subsequently challenged by exposure to bites of DEN-1–infected mosquitoes a week after the second dose. At such a short interval between vaccination and challenge, it is not surprising that dengue fever was observed in all vaccinated volunteers. This vaccine was not evaluated further.

Tissue Culture–Based Vaccines

Purified, inactivated DEN-2 vaccines (D2-PIV) were prepared in Vero and FRhL cells under good manufacturing practices by the Department of Biologics Research, WRAIR.[55,56] For preparation of D2-PIV, D2 strain S16803, Vero cell passage 3 was propagated in certified Vero cells, which were maintained in serum-free Eagles minimum essential medium. Virus from the culture supernatant fluid was concentrated by ultrafiltration and purified on 15 to 60% sucrose gradients. The high-titer purified virus (approximately 9 $\log_{10}$ PFU/mL) was inactivated with 0.05% formalin at 22°C for 10 days. Following inactivation, residual formalin was neutralized with sodium bisulfite, and the D2-PIV was stored at 4°C prior to formulating with adjuvant. Two doses of D2-PIV with alum induced high PRNT antibody levels and 100% protection against viremia in a primate model.[55]

Recently, the immunogenicity and efficacy of D2-PIV formulated with four different adjuvants (alum and adjuvants SBAS4, SBAS5, and SBAS8 provided by GlaxoSmithKline Biologicals, Rixensart, Belgium) were evaluated in rhesus monkeys in groups of three animals each.[57] The WRAIR DEN2 S16803 PDK50 LAV vaccine and saline served as positive and negative controls, respectively. Two doses of D2-PIV, D2 LAV, or saline were given 3 months apart. The animals were challenged with wild-type D2 S16803 parent virus 3 months after the second dose, and their subsequent viremia and antibody responses were measured. All but one vaccinated animal seroconverted after the first dose of vaccine. Moreover, all vaccinated animals had anamnestic antibody rises following the second dose of vaccine, with mean reciprocal PRNT antibody titers 30 days after the second dose of vaccine of 4600 (D2-PIV/SBAS5), 3800 (D2-PIV/SBAS8), 680 (D2-PIV/SBAS4), 630 (D2 LAV vaccine), and 200 (D2-PIV/alum group). After virus challenge, viremia was detected by cell culture in the saline group (3 to 5 days of viremia for all animals, mean 4 days), the D2-PIV/alum group (2 animals without viremia, 1 animal with 2 days of low-titer viremia), and the D2-PIV/SBAS4 (2 animals without viremia, 1 animal with 2 days of low-titer viremia). No viremia was detected in the animals that received D2-PIV/SBAS5, D2-PIV/SBAS8, or D2 LAV. A subset of monkeys was rechallenged with wild-type virus 1 year later, when PRNT antibody titers had sharply decreased. The animals were protected against viremia.[57] A phase I evaluation of the DEN-2-PIV vaccine is planned.

Recombinant Subunit Vaccines

T- and B-cell epitopes have been mapped on dengue virus structural and nonstructural proteins.[58,59] The right combination of epitopes expressed in protein subunit vaccines could be the basis for an effective and safe vaccine at moderate cost.[60] Structural and nonstructural dengue virus proteins have been produced in adequate amounts in many expression systems, including *Escherichia coli*, baculovirus in *Spodoptera frugiperda* insect cells, yeast, vaccinia virus, and *Drosophila* cells.[57,61–71] The last approach, 80% *E* gene expression in *Drosophila* cells was explored by Hawaii Biotechnology (Alca, Hawaii). One microgram of DEN-2 E protein with the SBAS5 adjuvant partially protected rhesus monkeys from viremia following challenge with wild-type virus. A tetravalent formulation is undergoing evaluation in rhesus monkeys (R. Putnak, personal communication, May 2003).

Synthetic Peptides

Synthetic peptides containing B- and T-cell epitopes are immunogenic in mice, and combinations of peptides could be effective as subunit vaccines.[72,73] Antibodies directed to synthetic peptides have been detected in sera from patients convalescent from dengue infections.[74,75] Peptides are particularly problematic as vaccines to protect against dengue infection because they provide fewer epitopes than do other candidate vaccines and lack conformational epitopes.

Inactivated whole virus or subunit vaccines are the simplest approach to vaccine development. Such vaccines have two potential advantages compared with live attenuated vaccines: they cannot revert to a more pathogenic phenotype and when combined are unlikely to produce interference. Cell-mediated as well as humoral immune responses have been demonstrated with an inactivated flavivirus vaccine.[76] On the other hand, killed or subunit vaccines raise antibodies to only a portion of the structural proteins and normal virion-based structural conformation. Three-dimensional structural antigens crucial to protection may not be presented to B cells. Other disadvantages include the requirement for multiple doses to fully immunize plus the need to prepare sufficient quantities of antigens, which could result in increased cost per dose. Safety concerns in dengue may differ from those in viral encephalitis. Two inactivated vaccines have been licensed and are widely used, safe, and effective in preventing Japanese encephalitis and tick-borne encephalitis.[77,78] Because of antibody-dependent enhancement, inactivated or subunit dengue vaccines are unlikely to be used alone, although they may be useful in a prime-boost strategy with live or DNA vaccines.

DNA Vaccines

DNA vaccines consist of a plasmid or plasmids containing dengue genes reproduced to high copy number in bacteria such as *E. coli*.[79] The plasmid contains a eukaryotic promoter and termination sequence to drive transcription in the vaccine recipient. The transcribed RNA is translated to produce proteins to be processed and presented to the immune system in the context of major histocompatibility complex (MHC) molecules. Additional genes, such as intracellular trafficking and immunostimulatory sequences, can be added to the plasmid or provided in separate plasmids. The target organism's immune system recognizes the expressed antigen and generates antibodies and/or cell-mediated immune responses. DNA-based vaccine constructs can be modified without the need for subsequent viability, as is required when working with infectious clones. DNA vaccines afford numerous advantages over conventional vaccines, including ease of production, stability, and transport at room temperature, and they provide the possibility of immunizing against multiple pathogens with a single vaccine. Dengue DNA vaccines offer the possibility of achieving protective immunity with reduced concern about reactogenicity or the interference seen with multivalent live virus vaccines. The immunology of DNA vaccines has been reviewed recently.[80]

Workers at the Naval Medical Research Institute evaluated two eukaryotic plasmid expression vectors (pkCMVint-Polyli and pVR1012, Vical, San Diego, CA) expressing the prM protein and 92% of the E protein for DEN-2 virus (New Guinea C strain). Both constructs induced neutralizing antibody in all mice, with a subsequent improvement seen with the addition of immunostimulatory CpG motifs (pUC 19, Gibco BRL, Gaithersburg, MD).[81,82] Konishi and colleagues successfully immunized mice with a similar DEN-2 vaccine construct using *C-PrM-E* genes in the pcDNA3 vector (Invitrogen, San Diego, CA).[83]

In subsequent experiments using genes from the West Pacific 74 strain of DEN-1 virus and the pVR1012 plasmid, it was determined that the full-length *E* gene plus *PrM* was translated into a better immunogen and was shown to reduced the frequency and duration of viremia in rhesus macaques following challenge with wild-type virus.[84,85] At present, the DNA approach has produced modest neutralizing antibody levels in nonhuman primates with only a portion of animals fully protected from viremia for varying lengths of time (K. Porter and R. Putnak, personal communication, May 2003). With the recognition that skin dendritic cells are highly permissive for dengue virus replication, ongoing efforts may focus on vaccine delivery systems that target these cells.[86] Additional dengue gene sequences, immunostimulatory gene sequences, trafficking sequences, and codelivery of plasmids encoding cytokine genes are being evaluated to increase vaccine potency (G. Murphy, personal communication, January 2002).

DNA Shuffling

Tetravalent dengue vaccines have been created by shuffling the envelope genes from the four dengue viruses. Selected shuffled DNA was transfected into human cells, subjected to flow cytometry, and reacted with type-specific dengue antibodies. Antibody markers permitted rapid screening of libraries and identification of novel expressed chimeric antigens for all four dengue types. When mixtures of these DNA molecules were inoculated in mice, they raised cross-reactive and cross-neutralizing antibodies. Immunized mice survived challenge with lethal intracerebral doses of all four dengue viruses. Primate immunization and challenge studies are in progress (K. Porter, personal communication, May 2003).

DNA vaccines used in combination with other approaches, such as inactivated virus vaccines, discussed above, may increase the complexity and effectiveness of the immune response.[87,88] Preliminary studies in mice at the Naval Medical Research Institute suggest that this approach may be effective for dengue.[89] In the mice, DNA vaccination alone elicited primarily an immunoglobulin G2a (IgG2a) antibody response, whereas the recombinant protein elicited an exclusive IgG1 antibody response. Vaccination with different products either in sequence or simultaneously elicited a more balanced distribution of both antibody subclasses. However, for a vaccine targeted for one billion children in the tropics, an eight-component vaccine will present obstacles due to cost and complexity.

Although the DNA approach offers unique advantages, it also carries unique risks.[90] These include the theoretic risk of nucleic acid integration into the host's chromosomal DNA, which could inactivate tumor suppressor genes or activate oncogenes. This risk appears to be well below the spontaneous mutation frequency for mammalian cells.[91,92] However, if a mutation due to DNA integration is a part of a multiple-hit phenomenon leading to carcinogenesis, it could take many years before this problem became evident. Another concern is that foreign DNA might induce anti-DNA antibodies, leading to autoimmune diseases such as systemic lupus erythematosus. However, to date, studies in lupus-prone mice, normal mice, rabbits, and people have not validated this concern, and, in fact, DNA vaccines are being proposed as an approach to the management of autoimmune diseases.[93–96]

CONCLUSION

The development of safe and effective dengue vaccines faces many challenges. Four vaccines must be developed without the benefit of a full understanding of the pathogenesis of severe dengue disease or of an adequate or affordable animal disease model. Mice and monkeys can be used to demonstrate immunogenicity and protection from death following intracerebral virus challenge in mice and viremia in monkeys. Although mice have been reported to develop fatal hemorrhage following intraperitoneal inoculation with dengue virus, full advantage of this model has been pursued in only a single laboratory.[97,98] Monkeys do not show dengue-like signs and, like humans, rarely show evidence of increased vascular permeability when given wild-type dengue viruses.[99] Monkeys have, however, developed enhanced viremias during secondary infections with DEN-2 and also when DEN-2 was inoculated into animals receiving passively transferred dengue antibodies.[100,101]

Monkeys can be used to detect attenuation characteristics of live vaccine candidates. For example, reduced viremia in rhesus macaques has been associated with reduced reactogenicity in humans.[24] Without more data from inoculation of candidate dengue vaccines in humans, it cannot be known how accurately monkey responses predict protection or enhancement of dengue infections in humans. A major step in this direction has been accomplished by workers from WRAIR, who have produced mild dengue-like illness with near–wild-type DEN-1 and DEN-3 and reactogenic infections with DEN-4. Dengue strains producing symptomatic disease can be used in a human challenge model to provide a method of evaluating the protective efficacy of dengue vaccines without recourse to phase III efficacy trials involving many thousands of volunteers. Although a licensed dengue vaccine is not yet available, the scope and intensity of dengue vaccine development has increased dramatically in recent years.

REFERENCES

1. Simmons JS, St. John JH, Reynolds FHK. Experimental studies of dengue. Philippine J Sci 1931;44:1–252.

2. Blanc G, Caminopetros J. Recherches experimentales sur la dengue. Ann Inst Pasteur (Paris) 1930;44:367–436.

3. Sabin AB, Schlesinger RW. Production of immunity to dengue with virus modified by propagation in mice. Science 1945;101:640–2.

4. Hotta S. Experimental studies in dengue. I. Isolation, identification and modification of the virus. J Infect Dis 1952;90:1–9.

5. Schlesinger RW, Gordon I, Frankel JW, et al. Clinical and serologic response of man to immunization with attenuated dengue and yellow fever viruses. J Immunol 1956;77:352–64.

6. Wisseman CL Jr, Sweet BH, Rosenzweig EC, Eylar OR. Attenuated living type 1 dengue vaccines. Am J Trop Med Hyg 1963;12:620–3.

7. Hammon WM, Rudnick A, Sather GE. Viruses associated with epidemic hemorrhagic fevers of the Philippines and Thailand. Science 1960;131:1102–3.

8. Gubler DJ. Epidemic dengue/dengue hemorrhagic fever as a public health, social and economic problem in the 21st century. Trends Microbiol 2002;10:100–3.

9. Gubler DJ. Dengue and dengue hemorrhagic fever. Clin Microbiol Rev 1998;11:480–96.

10. Halstead SB, Nimmannitya S, Yamarat C, Russell PK. Hemorrhagic fever in Thailand. Recent knowledge regarding etiology. Jpn J Med Sci Biol 1967;20:96–103.

11. Halstead SB. Pathogenesis of dengue. Challenges to molecular biology. Science 1988;239:476–81.

12. Halstead SB, Nimmannitya S, Cohen SN. Observations related to pathogenesis of dengue hemorrhagic fever. IV. Relation of disease severity to antibody response and virus recovered. Yale J Biol Med 1970;42:311–28.

13. Kliks SC, Nimmannitya S, Nisalak A, Burke DS. Evidence that maternal dengue antibodies are important in the development of dengue hemorrhagic fever in infants. Am J Trop Med Hyg 1988;38:411–9.

14. Guzman MG, Kouri G, Valdes L, et al. Epidemiologic studies on dengue in Santiago de Cuba, 1997. Am J Epidemiol 2000;152:793–9.

15. Halstead SB. Etiologies of the experimental dengues of Siler and Simmons. Am J Trop Med Hyg 1974;23:974–82.

16. Sabin AB. Research on dengue during World War II. Am J Trop Med Hyg 1952;1:30–50.

17. Halstead SB, Marchette N. Biological properties of dengue viruses following serial passage in primary dog kidney cells. Am J Trop Med Hyg Suppl 2003. [In press]

18. Bhamarapravati N, Sutee Y. Live attenuated tetravalent dengue vaccine. Vaccine 2000;18 Suppl 2:44–7.

19. Bhamarapravati N, Yoksan S, Chayaniyayothin T, et al. Immunization with a live attenuated dengue-2-virus candidate vaccine (16681-PDK 53). Clinical, immunological and biological responses in adult volunteers. Bull World Health Organ 1987;65:189–95.

20. Bhamarapravati N, Yoksan S. Live attenuated tetravalent dengue vaccine. In: Gubler DJ, editor. Dengue and dengue hemorrhagic fever. New York: CAB International 1997. p. 367–77.

21. Vaughn DW, Hoke CH Jr, Yoksan S, et al. Testing of a dengue 2 live-attenuated vaccine (strain 16681 PDK 53) in ten American volunteers. Vaccine 1996;14:329–36.

22. Kanesa-Thasan N, Sun W, Kim-Ahn G, et al. Safety and immunogenicity of attenuated dengue virus vaccines (Aventis Pasteur) in human volunteers. Vaccine 2001;19:3179–88.

23. Bhamarapravati N, Yoksan S. Study of bivalent dengue vaccine in volunteers. Lancet 1989;1:1077.

24. Edelman R, Tacket CO, Wasserman SS, et al. A live attenuated dengue-1 vaccine candidate (45AZ5) passaged in primary dog kidney cell culture is attenuated and immunogenic for humans. J Infect Dis 1994;170:1448–55.

25. Mackowiak PA, Wasserman SS, Tacket CO, et al. Quantitative relationship between oral temperature and severity of illness following inoculation with candidate attenuated dengue virus vaccines. Clin Infect Dis 1994;19:948–50.

26. Sun W, Edelman R, Kanesa-Thasan N, et al. Vaccination of human volunteers with monovalent and tetravalent live-attenuated dengue vaccine candidates. Am J Trop Med Hyg Suppl 2002. [In press]

27. Edelman R, Wasserman SS, Bodison SA, et al. Phase 1 trial of 16 formulations of a tetravalent live-attenuated dengue vaccine. Am J Trop Med Hyg Suppl 2003. [In press]

28. Vaughn DW, Green S, Kalayanarooj S, et al. Dengue viremia titer, antibody response pattern, and virus serotype correlate with disease severity. J Infect Dis 2000;181:2–9.

29. Green S, Vaughn DW, Kalayanarooj S, et al. Early immune activation in acute dengue illness is related to development of plasma leakage and disease severity. J Infect Dis 1999;179:755–62.

30. Halstead SB, Palumbo NE. Studies on the immunization of monkeys against dengue. II. Protection following inoculation of combinations of viruses. Am J Trop Med Hyg 1973;22:375–81.

31. Bancroft WH, Scott RM, Eckels KH, et al. Dengue virus type 2 vaccine. Reactogenicity and immunogenicity in soldiers. J Infect Dis 1984;149:1005–10.

32. Kanesa-Thasan N. [Submitted]

33. Vaughn DW. Invited commentary. Dengue lessons from Cuba. Am J Epidemiol 2000;152:800–3.

34. Guzman MG, Kouri GP, Bravo J, et al. Dengue hemorrhagic fever in Cuba, 1981. A retrospective seroepidemiologic study. Am J Trop Med Hyg 1990;42:179–84.

35. Halstead SB. Immunological parameters of Togavirus disease syndromes. In: Schlesinger RW, editor. The togaviruses. Biology, structure, replication. New York: Academic Press; 1980. p.107–73.

36. Henchal EA, Putnak JR. The dengue viruses. Clin Microbiol Rev 1990;3(4):376–96.

37. Rice CM, Grakoui A, Galler R, Chambers TJ. Transcription of infectious yellow fever RNA from full-length cDNA templates produced by in vitro ligation. New Biologist 1989;1:285–96.

38. Guirakhoo F, Weltzin R, Chambers TJ, et al. Recombinant chimeric yellow fever–dengue type 2 virus is immunogenic and protective in nonhuman primates. J Virol 2000;74:5477–85.

39. Chambers TJ, Nestorowicz A, Mason PW, Rice CM. Yellow fever/Japanese encephalitis chimeric viruses. Construction and biological properties. J Virol 1999;73:3095–101.

40. Guirakhoo F, Arroyo J, Pugachev KV, et al. Construction, safety, and immunogenicity in nonhuman primates of a chimeric yellow fever–dengue virus tetravalent vaccine. J Virol 2001;75:7290–304.

41. Monath TP, McCarthy K, Bedford P, et al. Clinical proof of principle for ChimeriVax. Recombinant live, attenuated vaccines against flavivirus infections. Vaccine 2002;20:1004–18.

42. Kinney RM, Butrapet S, Chang GJ, et al. Construction of infectious cDNA clones for dengue 2 virus. Strain 16681 and its attenuated vaccine derivative, strain PDK-53. Virology 1997;230:300–8.

43. Kinney RM, Huang CY. Development of new vaccines against dengue fever and Japanese encephalitis. Intervirology 2001;44:176–97.

44. Butrapet S, Huang CY, Pierro DJ, et al. Attenuation markers of a candidate dengue type 2 vaccine virus, strain 16681 (PDK-53), are defined by mutations in the 5′ noncoding region and nonstructural proteins 1 and 3. J Virol 2000;74:3011–9.

45. Huang CY, Butrapet S, Pierro DJ, et al. Chimeric dengue type 2 (vaccine strain PDK-53)/dengue type 1 virus as a potential candidate dengue type 1 virus vaccine. J Virol 2000;74:3020–8.

46. Lai CJ, Zhao BT, Hori H, Bray M. Infectious RNA transcribed from stably cloned full-length cDNA of dengue type 4 virus. Proc Natl Acad Sci U S A 1991;88:5139–43.

47. Men R, Bray M, Clark D, et al. Dengue type 4 virus mutants containing deletions in the 3′ noncoding region of the RNA genome. Analysis of growth restriction in cell culture and altered viremia pattern and immunogenicity in rhesus monkeys. J Virol 1996;70:3930–7.

48. Durbin AP, Karron RA, Sun W, et al. Attenuation and immunogenicity in humans of a live dengue virus type-4 vaccine candidate with a 30 nucleotide deletion in its 3′-untranslated region. Am J Trop Med Hyg 2001;65:405–13.

49. Bray M, Lai CJ. Construction of intertypic chimeric dengue viruses by substitution of structural protein genes. Proc Natl Acad Sci U S A 1991;88:10342–6.

50. Lai CJ, Bray M, Men R, et al. Evaluation of molecular strategies to develop a live dengue vaccine [in process citation]. Clin Diagn Virol 1998;10:173–9.

51. Bray M, Men R, Lai CJ. Monkeys immunized with intertypic chimeric dengue viruses are protected against wild-type virus challenge. J Virol 1996;70:4162–6.

52. Chen W, Kawano H, Men R, et al. Construction of intertypic chimeric dengue viruses exhibiting type 3 antigenicity and neurovirulence for mice. J Virol 1995;69:5186–90.

53. Zeng L, Falgout B, Markoff L. Identification of specific nucleotide sequences within the conserved 3′-SL in the dengue type 2 virus genome required for replication. J Virol 1998;72:7510–22.

54. Markoff L, Pang X, Houng HS, et al. Derivation and characterization of a dengue type 1 host range-restricted mutant virus that is attenuated and highly immunogenic in monkeys. J Virol 2002;76:3318–28.

55. Putnak R, Barvir DA, Burrous JM, et al. Development of a purified, inactivated, dengue-2 virus vaccine prototype in Vero cells. Immunogenicity and protection in mice and rhesus monkeys. J Infect Dis 1996;174:1176–84.

56. Putnak R, Cassidy K, Conforti N, et al. Immunogenic and protective response in mice immunized with a purified, inactivated, Dengue-2 virus vaccine prototype made in fetal rhesus lung cells. Am J Trop Med Hyg 1996;55:504–10.

57. Putnak RI, Coller B-A, Voss G, et al. Recombinant subunit protein and inactivated virus vaccines for dengue type–2 formulated with new adjuvants induced high titered virus–neutralizing antibodies and confer porotection against virus challenge in rhesus monkeys. Vaccine [Submitted]

58. Brinton MA, Kurane I, Mathew A, et al. Immune mediated and inherited defences against flaviviruses. Clin Diagn Virol 1998;10:129–39.

59. Rey FA, Heinz FX, Mandl C, et al. The envelope glycoprotein from tick-borne encephalitis virus at 2 angstrom resolution. Nature 1995;375:291–8.

60. Trent DW, Kinney RM, Huang CY. Recombinant dengue virus vaccines. In: Gubler DJ, Kuno G, editors. Dengue and dengue hemorrhagic fever. New York: CAB International; 1997. p. 379–404.

61. Fonseca BA, Khoshnood K, Shope RE, Mason PW. Flavivirus type-specific antigens produced from fusions of a portion of the E protein gene with the *Escherichia coli* trpE gene. Am J Trop Med Hyg 1991;44:500–8.

62. Srivastava AK, Putnak JR, Warren RL, Hoke CH Jr. Mice immunized with a dengue type 2 virus E and NS1 fusion protein made in *Escherichia coli* are protected against lethal dengue virus infection. Vaccine 1995;13:1251–8.

63. Simmons M, Porter KR, Escamilla J, et al. Evaluation of recombinant viral envelope B domain protein antigens for the detection of dengue type specific antibodies. Am J Trop Med Hyg 1998;58:144–51.

64. Delenda C, Frenkiel MP, Deubel V. Protective efficacy in mice of a secreted form of recombinant dengue-2 virus envelope protein produced in baculovirus infected insect cells. Arch Virol 1994;139:197–207.

65. Delenda C, Staropoli I, Frenkiel MP, et al. Analysis of C-terminally truncated dengue 2 and dengue 3 virus envelope glycoproteins. Processing in insect cells and immunogenic properties in mice. J Gen Virol 1994;75:1569–78.

66. Velzing J, Groen J, Drouet MT, et al. Induction of protective immunity against dengue virus type 2. Comparison of candidate live attenuated and recombinant vaccines. Vaccine 1999;17:1312–20.

67. Bielefeldt Ohmann H, Beasley DW, Fitzpatrick DR, Aaskov JG. Analysis of a recombinant dengue-2 virus–dengue-3 virus hybrid envelope protein expressed in a secretory baculovirus system. J Gen Virol 1997;78:2723–33.

68. Sugrue RJ, Fu J, Howe J, Chan YC. Expression of the dengue virus structural proteins in *Pichia pastoris* leads to the generation of virus-like particles. J Gen Virol 1997;78:1861–6.

69. Zhao BT, Prince G, Horswood R, et al. Expression of dengue virus structural proteins and nonstructural protein NS1 by a recombinant vaccinia virus. J Virol 1987;61:4019–22.

70. Deubel V, Kinney RM, Esposito JJ, et al. Dengue 2 virus envelope protein expressed by a recombinant vaccinia virus fails to protect monkeys against dengue. J Gen Virol 1988;69:1921–9.

71. Men R, Wyatt L, Tokimatsu I, et al. Immunization of rhesus monkeys with a recombinant of modified vaccinia virus Ankara expressing a truncated envelope glycoprotein of dengue type 2 virus induced resistance to dengue type 2 virus challenge. Vaccine 2000;18:3113–22.

72. Roehrig JT, Johnson AJ, Hunt AR, et al. Enhancement of the antibody response to flavivirus B-cell epitopes by using homologous or heterologous T-cell epitopes. J Virol 1992;66:3385–90.

73. Becker Y. Dengue fever virus and Japanese encephalitis virus synthetic peptides, with motifs to fit HLA class I haplotypes prevalent in human populations in endemic regions, can be used for application to skin Langerhans cells to prime antiviral CD8(+) cytotoxic T cells (CTLs). A novel approach to the protection of humans. Virus Genes 1994;9:33–45.

74. Huang JH, Wey JJ, Sun YC, et al. Antibody responses to an immunodominant nonstructural 1 synthetic peptide in patients with dengue fever and dengue hemorrhagic fever. J Med Virol 1999;57:1–8.

75. Garcia G, Vaughn DW, Del Angel RM. Recognition of synthetic oligopeptides from nonstructural proteins NS1 and NS3 of dengue-4 virus by sera from dengue virus-infected children. Am J Trop Med Hyg 1997;56:466–70.

76. Aihara H, Takasaki T, Toyosaki–Maeda T, et al. T-cell activation and induction of antibodies and memory T cells by immunization with inactivated Japanese encephalitis vaccine. Viral Immunol 2000;13:179–86.

77. Hoke CH Jr, Nisalak A, Sangawhipa N, et al. Protection against Japanese encephalitis by inactivated vaccines. N Engl J Med 1988;319:608–14.

78. Craig SC, Pittman PR, Lewis TE, et al. An accelerated schedule for tick-borne encephalitis vaccine. The American military experience in Bosnia. Am J Trop Med Hyg 1999;61:874–8.

79. Whalen RG. DNA vaccines for emerging infectious diseases. What if ? Emerg Infect Dis 1996;2:168–75.

80. Gurunathan S, Klinman DM, Seder RA. DNA vaccines. Immunology, application, and optimization. Annu Rev Immunol 2000;18:927–74.

81. Kochel T, Wu SJ, Raviprakash K, et al. Inoculation of plasmids expressing the dengue-2 envelope gene elicit neutralizing antibodies in mice. Vaccine 1997;15:547–52.

82. Porter KR, Kochel TJ, Wu SJ, et al. Protective efficacy of a dengue 2 DNA vaccine in mice and the effect of CpG immunostimulatory motifs on antibody responses. Arch Virol 1998;143:997–1003.

83. Konishi E, Yamaoka M, Kurane I, Mason PW. A DNA vaccine expressing dengue type 2 virus premembrane and envelope genes induces neutralizing antibody and memory B cells in mice. Vaccine 2000;18:1133–9.

84. Raviprakash K, Kochel TJ, Ewing D, et al. Immunogenicity of dengue virus type 1 DNA vaccines expressing truncated and full length envelope protein. Vaccine 2000;18:2426–34.

85. Raviprakash K, Porter KR, Kochel TJ, et al. Dengue virus type 1 DNA vaccine induces protective immune responses in rhesus macaques. J Gen Virol 2000;81 Pt 7:1659–67.

86. Wu SJ, Grouard–Vogel G, Sun W, et al. Human skin Langerhans cells are targets of dengue virus infection [see comments]. Nat Med 2000;6:816–20.

87. Eo SK, Gierynska M, Kamar AA, Rouse BT. Prime-boost immunization with DNA vaccine. Mucosal route of administration changes the rules. J Immunol 2001;166:5473–9.

88. Tellier MC, Pu R, Pollock D, et al. Efficacy evaluation of prime-boost protocol. Canarypoxvirus-based feline immunodeficiency virus (FIV) vaccine and inactivated FIV-infected cell vaccine against heterologous FIV challenge in cats. AIDS 1998;12:11–8.

89. Simmons M, Murphy GS, Kochel T, et al. Characterization of antibody responses to combinations of a dengue-2 DNA and dengue recombinant subunit vaccine. Am J Trop Med Hyg 2001;65:420–6.

90. Klinman DM, Takeno M, Ichino M, et al. DNA vaccines. Safety and efficacy issues. Springer Semin Immunopathol 1997;19:245–56.

91. Nichols WW, Ledwith BJ, Manam SV, Troilo PJ. Potential DNA vaccine integration into host cell genome. Ann N Y Acad Sci 1995;772:30–9.

92. Martin T, Parker SE, Hedstrom R, et al. Plasmid DNA malaria vaccine. The potential for genomic integration after intramuscular injection. Hum Gene Ther 1999;10:759–68.

93. Parker SE, Borellini F, Wenk ML, et al. Plasmid DNA malaria vaccine. Tissue distribution and safety studies in mice and rabbits. Hum Gene Ther 1999;10:741–58.

94. Mor G, Singla M, Steinberg AD, et al. Do DNA vaccines induce autoimmune disease? Hum Gene Ther 1997;8:293–300.

95. Prud'homme GJ, Lawson BR, Chang Y, Theophilopoulos AN. Immunotherapeutic gene transfer into muscle. Trends Immunol 2001;22:149–55.

96. Karin N. Gene therapy for T cell mediated autoimmunity. Teaching the immune system how to restrain its own harmful activities by targeted DNA vaccines. Isr Med Assoc J 2000;2 Suppl:63–8.

97. Chaturvedi UC, Tandon P, Mathur A, Kumar A. Host defence mechanisms against dengue virus infection of mice. J Gen Virol 1978;39:293–302.

98. Chaturvedi UC, Nath P, Gulati L, et al. Subcellular changes in spleen cells of mice treated with the dengue virus-induced cytotoxic factor. Indian J Med Res 1987;86:284–9.

99. Halstead SB, Shotwell H, Casals J. Studies on the pathogenesis of dengue infection in monkeys. I. Clinical laboratory responses to primary infection. J Infect Dis 1973;128:7–14.

100. Halstead SB, Shotwell H, Casals J. Studies on the pathogenesis of dengue infection in monkeys. II. Clinical laboratory responses to heterologous infection. J Infect Dis 1973;128:15–22.

101. Halstead SB. In vivo enhancement of dengue virus infection in rhesus monkeys by passively transferred antibody. J Infect Dis 1979;140:527–33.

Chapter 14

MALARIA VACCINE

Thomas L. Richie and Stephen L. Hoffman

Of the nearly 700 million international tourist arrivals recorded in the year 2000, approximately 9 million were to West, Central, or East Africa, 37 million were to Southeast Asia, 6 million to South Asia, and 10 million to Oceania.[1] Although it is not possible to ascertain what proportion of these travelers visited malaria-endemic areas, an estimate of 20% would yield 12 million international travelers to these areas potentially exposed to malaria transmission. This estimate can be supplemented by arrivals to malarious areas of the Middle East, Caribbean, and South America, and by nontourist travel, such as the deployment of military personnel. Serologic studies of various traveling populations suggest that from 2 to 21% (but as high as 80%) of travelers are inoculated with malaria parasite sporozoites during their stay in the tropics.[2] Furthermore, in addition to international travelers, a growing number of people leave their homes in malaria-free regions of malaria-endemic countries for local travel to areas where malaria is transmitted.[3] Whether the purpose is tourism, family visits, business, government assignment, military deployment, religious or other service, emigration, or escape from civil strife or persecution, malaria is one of the most significant health risks faced by travelers today.

Those seeking medical advice prior to international travel from developed countries are counseled to use personal protective measures (PPM), such as insect repellents, and are prescribed drugs for prophylaxis (chemoprophylaxis). However, the inconvenience of PPM and the costs, side effects, and inconvenience of taking drugs reduce compliance and thus the effectiveness of these measures. For example, randomized, blinded clinical trials indicate that the recommended drugs such as mefloquine or doxycycline provide protection with efficacies on the order of 85 to 100% relative to placebo. These trials are conducted under carefully controlled conditions, with supervised drug administration. However, airport-based surveys of departing travelers heading for malarious areas indicate variable, but often very low, levels of preparedness, with as few as one-third intending to use chemoprophylaxis.[4–10] Thus, even prior to travel, a gap is created between potential pharmacologic efficacy and actual effectiveness (Table 14-1).

Within-country travelers may or may not have the same access to PPM and to recommended drugs as international travelers have or they might be unable to afford them, and migrants or refugees often have no access at all to medical care, as travel can be forced or unexpected or occur during periods when normal medical services are disrupted. There are also cases in which prophylaxis is relatively contraindicated, such as the use of doxycycline in children less than 9 years of age or in pregnant or lactating women or mefloquine in persons with a history of seizures or psychiatric disorder. Thus, a significant proportion of travelers are without protection against malaria as their travel begins.

Table 14-1. Issues Affecting Effectiveness of Chemoprophylaxis versus Vaccination

	Chemoprophylaxis				*Vaccination*
Pretravel					
Visit health professional*	2 weeks to 2 days before departure[†]				6 months to 2 days prior to departure, or no visit needed[‡]
Contraindication	Might be present				Unlikely
Purchase costs for trips lasting 7, 14, and 28 days[§]		7 days	14 days	28 days	Any duration up to 6 months $200 (estimate)
	Mefloquine				
	Lariam[‖]	$ 123.57	138.45	165.16	
	Generic	107.05	119.86	142.65	
	Doxycycline				
	Vibramycin[‖]	221.50	258.96	323.99	
	Generic	25.72	29.33	33.99	
	Atovaquone/proguanil				
	Malarone[‖]	114.40	159.57	248.54	
Side effects	*Mefloquine:* sleep disturbance, irritability, seizures, psychotic reactions *Doxycycline:* stomach pain, esophagitis, photosensitivity, yeast infection *Atovaquone/proguanil:* mild gastrointestinal upset				Pain and tenderness at injection site. *Systemic side effects:* for DNA vaccine, unlikely; for protein-based vaccine, occasional
During travel					
Compliance	Variable[#]				100%
Side effects	As above				None
Post-travel					
Compliance	Often poor				100%
Side effects	As above				None
Long-term issues					
Repeat trips within 6 months	Repeat all the above				Nothing required
Loss of efficacy due to evolution of resistance	Possible				Possible

Note: This comparison assumes that chemoprophylaxis and vaccination have equal efficacy for all four species of human malaria. Mefloquine and doxycycline do not eliminate hypnozoite stages, creating the possibility of late relapse post-travel. The table is highly speculative, given that there are no marketed malaria vaccines to use as a basis for comparison and that current vaccines under development are for *Plasmodium falciparum* only.

*Visiting a health professional is a key stumbling block for both modalities. The traveler must have access to adequate health care and must be willing to make the time and financial commitment to seek it. Adequate health care might be unavailable to many travelers, such as refugees. Vaccination would have the advantage of offering some level of protection even if the visit to the health professional was remote relative to the time of travel, depending on the duration of the immune response to the vaccine.

[†]This assumes that the traveler will begin mefloquine dosing 2 weeks, doxycycline 2 days, or atovaquone/proguanil 2 days prior to departure. Mefloquine can also be started 2 days before departure if given as a loading dose.

[‡]The initial vaccination series might require 6 months; a single booster 2 days prior to departure is needed for subsequent trips if the interval is greater than 6 months; no visit is required if the interval is less than 6 months.

[§]Costs were obtained from a US retail pharmacy chain in November 2002 and assume continuing mefloquine and doxycycline for 4 weeks and atovaquone/proguanil for 1 week following return.

[‖]Lariam, Roche Labs, Nutley, NJ, USA; Vibramycin, Pfizer, New York City, NY, USA; Malarone, GlaxoSmithKline, London, UK.

[#]Poor compliance can be purposeful (stopping drugs because of side effects), inadvertent (forgetting, losing drug), or forced (lost or damaged baggage, theft, unexpected prolongation of travel). Compliance might be better or worse as affected by weekly (eg, mefloquine) versus daily (eg, doxycycline) administration, depending on the individual's preferences.

Those who prepare prior to their journey must take their medicines according to schedule and tolerate any side effects. The difficulty of integrating these tasks with the constrained schedules and altered diets of travel introduces the potential for noncompliance. This is magnified after the return home, when reestablishing daily routines in a malaria-free environment reduces the motivation to continue the drug for the prescribed period, which ranges from 1 to 4 weeks. With these considerations, it is not surprising that the presence of malaria in returning travelers correlates strongly with lack of compliance with recommended chemoprophylaxis.[11] The large number of reported travel-related malaria cases, which likely underestimate the actual numbers by two- to threefold (approximate yearly figures: 1,000 for the United states, 1,900 for the United Kingdom, and 1,000 for France; data from industrialized nations[12]), and the problems associated with malaria diagnosis and treatment in returning travelers indicate the need to improve on the effectiveness of current preventive measures.[13]

These factors—availability, costs, contraindications, side effects, inconvenience, and noncompliance, coupled with the many cases of malaria in returning travelers and the threat of increasing drug resistance—form the rationale for a traveler's vaccine for the prevention of malaria (see Table 14-1). If a vaccine were available, medical practitioners would still face the challenge of ensuring that travelers received the vaccine before departure, but once it was administered, travelers would no longer risk acquiring malaria because of hurried departure or intentional or unintentional noncompliance, or experience drug-associated toxicity while traveling. We can anticipate that a vaccine would decrease side effects and also increase compliance, thereby reducing the number of cases of malaria among travelers. A vaccine would especially benefit individuals who are unable to take drugs; visiting areas with drug-resistant malaria; living or working in refugee camps, where large gatherings of displaced persons create conditions suitable for epidemic malaria transmission and where access to medical services may be limited; or residing for long periods in malarious areas and for whom taking medications for months or years is difficult.

The need to protect travelers must be considered in relation to the overwhelming need to protect residents of endemic areas against severe disease and death. There are between 1 and 3 million deaths worldwide due to malaria each year (more than 90% of these occurring in infants and young children living in sub-Saharan Africa), derived from 300 to 900 million clinical cases.[14] It is impractical for residents of endemic areas to undertake lifelong chemoprophylaxis; therefore, the need for an effective vaccine is acute. As will be explained below, it is a characteristic of malaria epidemiology and of the rationale for vaccine design that a vaccine intended for travelers could also protect residents of endemic areas and vice versa.

As there is no currently marketed malaria vaccine, this chapter will describe vaccine development efforts, focusing on the challenges of designing a vaccine able to induce an effective immune response against the complex malaria parasite, the exciting technologies that are being developed to meet this challenge, and the current status of clinical trials of prototype vaccines.

MALARIA LIFE CYCLE: STRATEGIES FOR VACCINE DESIGN

Transmission of the parasite *Plasmodium* (the protozoan parasite causing malaria) occurs via the bite of infected female *Anopheles* mosquitoes, which are active from dusk to dawn. Other routes of transmission, such as transfusions, rarely apply to travelers. Sporozoites (the infectious stage of the parasite—Figure 14-1) migrate via the bloodstream from the bite site to the liver where they multiply within hepatocytes, producing, in the case of *P. falciparum*, 10,000 to 40,000 progeny per infected cell. This new generation

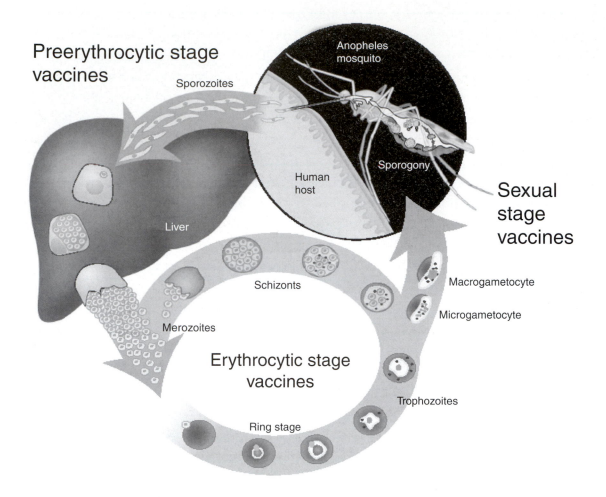

Figure 14-1. Approaches to designing malaria vaccines can be divided according to the target of the immune responses. **Preerythrocytic-stage vaccines** target sporozoites and infected hepatocytes. Killing the parasite at these stages would completely prevent any manifestations of disease as sporozoites and liver-stage parasites cause no measurable harm to the host, making this an ideal approach for a traveler's vaccine. The immune responses induced by preerythrocytic vaccines would not protect against subsequent stages, however, because antigen expression is generally stage specific. **Erythrocytic-stage vaccines** target merozoites, infected erythrocytes, or malaria toxins released from infected cells and are designed to limit the severity of disease by curtailing parasitemia and its toxic effects. These vaccines would serve as a second line of defense for travelers experiencing breakthrough blood-stage infections. Unless a preerythrocytic stage vaccine had an efficacy of more than 85 to 90%, travelers would best be served by a two-tiered vaccine incorporating antigens from both sporozoite/liver and blood-stage parasites. **Sexual-stage vaccines** target gametocytes, the form of the parasite transmitted to mosquitoes. These vaccines would not generally provide any direct benefit to the host, but they would aid in preventing the spread of escape mutants resistant to the immune responses generated by a preerythrocytic- or erythrocytic-stage vaccine. Reproduced with permission from Long CA and Hoffman SL.[117]

of parasites reenters the bloodstream as merozoites, expressing a set of antigens that is different from those expressed during the hepatic stages, and invades erythrocytes (red blood cells) where additional multiplication increases parasite numbers by approximately 10- to 15-fold every 48 hours. Unlike the 5- to 10-day period of development in the liver, which does not induce pathology or clinical illness, untreated blood stage infection causes hemolysis, shaking chills, high fevers, and prostration. In the case of *P. falciparum*, the most dangerous of the four species of *Plasmodium* that infect humans, the disease is complicated by disruption of microcirculatory flow and metabolic changes in vital organs, such as the brain, kidney, and lung, frequently leading to death in nonimmune patients if not treated quickly.

The strategy for designing a malaria vaccine is derived from the life cycle of the infecting protozoan. During their approximately 30-minute circulation in the blood, sporozoites are susceptible to neutralization by preexisting antibodies recognizing the sporozoite surface, such as the antigens responsible for mediating hepatocyte invasion. A minimum 5-day window follows, during which the parasite is sequestered within the protective membrane of the host cell but nevertheless can be targeted by T cells recognizing parasite-derived peptides bound to class I human leukocyte antigen (HLA) molecules on the surface of the hepatocyte. If the infection were cured by these immune mechanisms before any liver-derived merozoites emerged into the blood, it would be clinically silent and the human host protected against disease and death. On the other hand, the initiation of blood-stage replication by even a few parasites would again place the host at risk. For this reason, a separate set of immune responses directed against developing blood stage parasites, which express different antigens from liver stage parasites, would be a critical component of protection for an incompletely protective preerythrocytic-stage vaccine. These could comprise antibody responses against merozoites in the plasma, in particular targeting the antigens responsible for erythrocytic invasion, antibodies against parasite antigens expressed on the surface of erythrocytes, proteins that are responsible for adherence of infected erythrocytes to endothelial cells in the microcirculation, or cell-mediated responses (with or without antibody dependency) directed against infected erythrocytes, possibly mediated through the spleen.

The ideal traveler's vaccine, then, combines preerythrocytic-stage antigens as the primary component attempting to prevent all manifestations of disease, supplemented with erythrocytic-stage antigens to induce a "back-up" response in case of breakthrough blood-stage infection. However, it is possible that alternative strategies would suffice, for example, a highly effective liver-stage vaccine that consistently eliminated 100% of parasites, or a blood-stage vaccine that completely suppressed blood-stage development.

A combined preerythrocytic- and asexual erythrocytic-stage vaccine would likely benefit residents of endemic areas. Evidence that attacking the preerythrocytic stages of the parasite reduces morbidity and fatality rates comes from studies of insecticide-treated bed nets. The effect of bed nets might herald that of a preerythrocyte-stage vaccine because both reduce the number of parasites reaching the blood. Several studies have shown that the use of bed nets in endemic areas can reduce childhood morbidity and mortality rates.[15] The second component of the vaccine, which targets blood stage parasites, would also clearly benefit residents of endemic areas. As will be described below, antibody responses targeting blood stage antigens appear to provide very effective protection against clinical illness.

The sexual stage of the parasite—the gametocyte stage transmitted to the mosquito—could also be considered for incorporation into a traveler's vaccine.[16] A transmission-blocking component, however, would not benefit the recipient directly, as gametocytes are not pathogenic. It could also be argued that travelers would be unlikely to serve as gametocyte sources for transmission, so there would be little public health incentive to incorporate gametocyte antigens into a traveler's vaccine. On the other hand, if a traveler's vaccine, especially one that targeted only the asexual erythrocytic stages, was widely used by residents of endemic areas, the appearance of escape mutants resistant to the immune responses induced by the vaccine would be a concern, but the transmission of these resistant strains could be prevented by including transmission-blocking antigens.[17] It thus might be appropriate to include transmission-blocking components into a traveler's vaccine, on the assumption that its use would not be limited to travelers, and, therefore, resistance to the vaccine could develop. In addition, certain travelers, such as residents of refugee camps, might benefit directly from transmission-blocking vaccines if these vaccines prevented local epidemic transmission. Our assessment is that transmission-blocking antigens would be an appropriate addition to any vaccine as long as they did not interfere with its efficacy at preventing clinical malaria.

Many *P. falciparum* genes exhibit allelic heterogeneity, indicating that a malaria vaccine might require more than one allelic form of these proteins to protect against all *P. falciparum* strains. This might stem from heterogeneity at a single locus (eg, there are two major antigenic families of the leading blood-stage antigen, *P. falciparum* merozoite surface protein 1, *Pf*MSP1) or from the presence of multiple copies of a single gene. The best-known example of the latter is provided by the *VAR* (variable) gene family, which encodes the *P. falciparum* erythrocyte membrane protein 1 (*Pf*EMP1), an immunodominant molecule expressed on the surface of infected erythrocytes that mediates their adhesion to endothelial cells.[18] About 50 to 60 (59 in the 3D7 isolate) members of this family are present in the *P. falciparum* genome, each encoding an antigenically variant molecule.[19] Variant forms are expressed sequentially on the surface of infected erythrocytes, with each newly expressed variant allowing escape from the immune response generated against the previously expressed variant, resulting in a recurring waves of parasitemia. Although *Pf*EMP1 is a natural target for immune responses, a vaccine would have to include all members of the family or else employ conserved domains of the molecule.

MODELS OF IMMUNITY

We know that both preerythrocytic-stage and erythrocytic-stage vaccines are feasible, because there are functional human models for each. In humans, preerythrocytic-stage immunity can be induced by exposure to irradiated sporozoites,[20] and a clinically important degree of erythrocytic-stage immunity can be induced by exposure to repeated blood-stage infection.[21,22] In addition, all three types of protection obtained from vaccines—preerythrocytic, erythrocytic, and sexual stage (transmission blocking)—have been demonstrated in animal models.

The attenuated sporozoite vaccine is administered by preparing multiple batches of irradiated, infected mosquitoes and exposing vaccinees to at least 1,000 to 2,000 bites over the course of several months (Figure 14-2). These attenuated parasites undergo partial development in the liver but do not progress to the blood stage. They stimulate an immune response that is sporozoite and liver stage specific and, with a sufficient number of immunizations, able to sterilize subsequent challenge with intact sporozoites for up to 42 weeks.[20] However, this cumbersome procedure presents a technical barrier to large-scale immunization that has not been overcome, although there is considerable interest in doing so. Nevertheless, the induction of sterile immunity by attenuated sporozoites provides proof of the principle regarding the feasibility of a sporozoite–liver-stage malaria vaccine that prevents blood stage infection and clinical illness. This model also suggests a logical approach for making a preerythrocytic-stage vaccine: identify the antigenic targets of irradiated sporozoite-induced immunity and package these antigens in a vaccine formulation that is immunogenic and suitable for manufacture and administration. It is likely, although not proven, that the protection afforded by the irradiated sporozoite vaccine represents the summed immune responses against multiple antigens derived from the attenuated malaria parasite (Figure 14-3). Therefore, a multiantigen vaccine will probably be required to reproduce irradiated sporozoite–induced

A

Attenuated sporozoite immunization

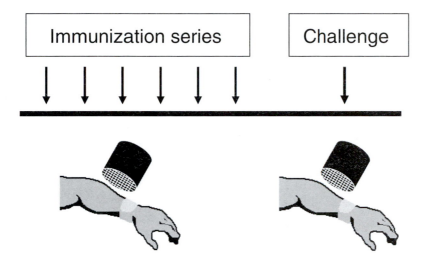

B

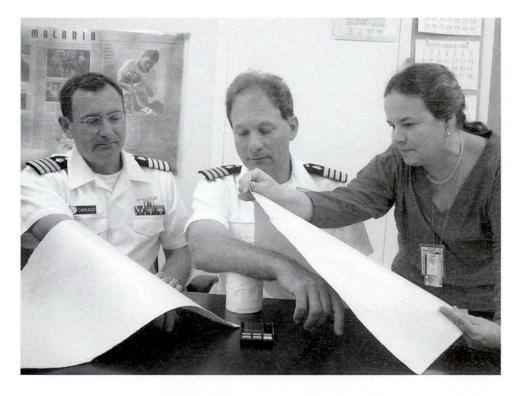

Figure 14-2. *A,* The most effective human malaria vaccine in existence, the attenuated sporozoite vaccine, is administered via the bites of irradiated, infected *Anopheles* mosquitoes. Batches of several hundred are permitted to feed on the arm of malaria-naive volunteers for two 5-minute periods. These immunizations are repeated every few weeks until 1,000 to 2,000 infectious bites have been delivered. Approximately 90 to 95% of such volunteers are protected for at least 42 weeks against challenge via the bites of five nonirradiated, infectious mosquitoes, even if the strain of *Plasmodium falciparum* used for challenge is different from the strain used for immunization.[20] Leukapheresis and serum sampling are often performed pre- and postimmunization to study the mechanisms of protection. *B,* Volunteers undergoing immunization. (Photograph by Yvonne Strausbaugh.)

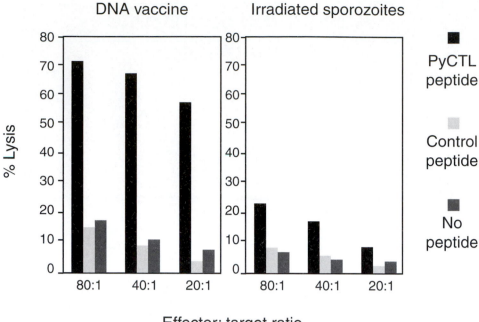

Figure 14-3. The high level of protection induced by the attenuated sporozoite vaccine might represent the combined effects of multiple immune responses directed against a wide variety of antigens contained in this whole organism vaccine. This figure portrays CD8+ T-lymphocyte responses against a peptide derived from the circumsporozoite protein (CSP), the principal surface protein of sporozoites and, presumably, an important component of the protective responses generated by the attenuated sporozoite vaccine. CD8+ T-cell responses against the CSP induced in mice by a CSP deoxyribonucleic acid (DNA) vaccine are stronger than those induced by attenuated sporozoites, even though the DNA vaccine provides considerably less protection against sporozoite challenge. Data such as these (and similar results obtained from antibody measurements) suggest that a multicomponent vaccine might be needed to successfully mimic attenuated sporozoites and induce similarly high levels of protection. Alternative interpretations of these data include that (1) CD8+ T-cell responses or antibodies are not the immune responses responsible for protection and (2) CSP and the other antigens tested to date that yield results such as these are not the antigens generating the protective responses. Understanding the mechanism of protection in the irradiated sporozoite model is an important research goal for malaria vaccine developers. Reproduced with permission from Sedegah M et al.[52]

immunity. This vaccine should be designed to induce the cell-mediated immune responses that are the primary effector mechanisms of liver-stage immunity.[23]

The second model of immunity to malaria in humans is termed naturally acquired immunity (NAI).[22] Residents of endemic areas, after repeated infections with *P. falciparum*, exhibit only mild clinical illness, if any, in association with parasitemia and also have lower parasitemias than those who are malaria naive. This antidisease/antiparasite immunity appears to be mediated, in part, by antibody responses to blood-stage antigens, based on the results of passive-transfer experiments in clinically ill children. Immunoglobulin transfusions derived from adults with NAI rapidly reduced parasitemia and led to resolution of symptoms in parasitemic recipients.[24–27] Some progress has been made identifying which blood-stage antigens are likely targets of NAI. An intriguing possibility is that there is a component of pathogenicity relating to the release of malaria toxins and that neutralization of these toxins via antibodies contributes to NAI and in theory could explain the beneficial effects of transfusions.[28] Whatever the mechanism of protection, the existence of NAI provides a strong rationale for including blood-stage antigens designed to induce antibody responses as the second tier of a two-tiered vaccine: preerythrocytic components to destroy the majority of developing parasites during the 5-day window of liver-stage development and erythrocytic components to protect against severe disease and death in individuals who experience breakthrough blood-stage infections.

Vaccine development has been prioritized for *P. falciparum* because this species causes nearly all cases of severe disease and death due to malaria and because multidrug resistance to *P. falciparum* is widespread. A successful *P. falciparum* vaccine should jump-start vaccine development for *Plasmodium vivax*, *Plasmodium malariae*, and *Plasmodium ovale*, the other three human malaria parasites, by directing the choice of antigens for these species.[29,30] For example, antigenic targets that are structural or functional orthologues to the *P. falciparum* antigens used in a successful *P. falciparum* vaccine would be leading candidates for inclusion in vaccines against the other species.

CANDIDATE VACCINES

Until recently, there has been only one approach to developing a malaria vaccine. The idea has been to identify parasite-derived proteins that are the targets of protective immune responses, and develop "subunit" (less than the whole parasite) vaccines that elicit protective immune responses. However, based on the exceptional protection demonstrated by immunizing volunteers by exposure to irradiated, infected mosquitoes, the practicality of developing an attenuated sporozoite vaccine has been reevaluated.[20] It is anticipated that such a vaccine will be assessed in the coming years. The rest of the vaccines reviewed in this chapter, however, consist of subunit vaccines.

In a 1998 review, Engers and Godal listed 17 *P. falciparum* subunit vaccines that had reached clinical testing.[31] These and additional vaccines tested since then reflect a variety of approaches, including recombinant malarial proteins, fusions of malarial with other proteins such as hepatitis B surface antigen (to enhance immunogenicity), long and short synthetic peptides (including multiantigen peptides, or MAPs), conjugates of synthetic peptides with proteins such as tetanus toxoid (also to enhance immunogenicity), virus-like particles with embedded antigens, recombinant plasmids encoding malarial genes or epitope strings, and recombinant bacteria (eg, *Salmonella*) and viruses (eg, New York Vaccine [NYVAC]) encoding malarial genes. These *P. falciparum* vaccines have typically shown good immunogenicity when assessed in animal models, and when a challenge model has been available, such as with the murine or simian malarias, significant levels of protection have been achieved using orthologues to the *P. falciparum* antigens. However, it has been much more difficult to demonstrate strong immunogenicity or protective efficacy in humans, with the notable exception of the protection afforded by the attenuated sporozoite vaccine. In a recent review of malaria vaccine trials, Greenwood and Alonso cited 12 trials employing experimental sporozoite challenge to assess the efficacy of candidate vaccines and 15 trials conducted in endemic areas.[32] None of these studies demonstrated efficacy on a par with that achieved with murine or simian malarias.

Protein-Based Vaccines

The difficulty of translating success in animals into success in humans is evident when tracing the history of the best-studied malarial protein, called the circumsporozoite protein (CSP), as a vaccine candidate.

CSP is found on the surface of sporozoites, and its attack by antibody responses can neutralize the infectivity of sporozoites. *P. falciparum* CSP (*Pf*CSP), formulated as a purified recombinant protein in the adjuvant aluminum hydroxide or a synthetic peptide conjugated to tetanus toxoid in aluminum hydroxide, was first tested in the human challenge model in 1987 and was shown to induce some protection.[33,34] It was not until 10 years later, however, after intensive efforts by a number of laboratories, that the combination of *Pf*CSP with a powerful adjuvant system achieved levels of protection against homologous sporozoite challenge approaching 50%.[35]

Development of this vaccine, called RTS,S/AS02A, was started in the late 1980s by GlaxoSmithKline Biologicals (GSKBio, Rixensart, Belgium) in collaboration with the Walter Reed Army Institute of Research. It is now the leading recombinant protein–based candidate malaria vaccine. In several phase IIa studies, RTS,S/AS02A has consistently protected 40 to 50% of immunized volunteers from homologous sporozoite challenge with the NF54 (clone 3D7) strain of *P. falciparum,* administered within 2 to 3 weeks following immunization and to prolong the prepatent period in nonprotected volunteers.[35,36] RTS,S contains 19 units of the *r*epeat region of the *Pf*CSP (R), included to induce antibody responses against sporozoites, and a portion of the C-terminal flanking region of *Pf*CSP containing a number of CD4 and CD8 *T*-cell epitopes (T), included to induce responses against infected hepatocytes expressing the *Pf*CSP on their surfaces. This RT section of the *Pf*CSP and the *s*urface antigen of hepatitis B (S) are coexpressed in yeast from a single open reading frame. The malaria-hepatitis fusion protein (RTS) spontaneously assembles into multimer particles when coexpressed with additional hepatitis B (S). RTS,S antigenic particles formulated with aluminum hydroxide were more immunogenic than previous formulations of the *Pf*CSP but did not induce protective immune responses in a significant proportion of humans until combined with GSKBio's proprietary AS02A oil-in-water adjuvant formulation, which contains 3-deacylated monophosphoryl lipid A and the saponin-derivative QS21, although even then, protection remains relatively short lived.[36–38] Immune responses include antibodies, lymphoproliferative responses, and CD4 T cell–mediated interferon-γ (IFN-γ) production, measured by ELISpot assay, but no consistent, reproducible CD8 T cell CTL or IFN-γ responses.[39]

RTS,S is prepared in lyophilized form and injected intramuscularly (IM) in the deltoid muscle after reconstitution with liquid AS02A. One to three injections spaced over 1 to 9 months have been assessed in various studies. In a study conducted by The Medical Research Council in The Gambia, in collaboration between GSKBio, the University of Oxford, and the London School of Hygiene & Tropical Medicine, adult Gambian men experienced a significant delay in re-infection rates following immunization with RTS,S/AS02A.[40] The GSKBio candidate vaccine will be assessed next in children in Mozambique, in a collaboration involving the Ministry of Health, the Centro de Investigaçao em Saude de Manhiça (CISM), and the Malaria Vaccine Initiative (MVI). Depending on the outcome of these and other trials, RTS,S/AS02A may be marketed toward the end of the decade as a vaccine for reducing morbidity and mortality rates in infants and children living in endemic areas. The potential benefits for travelers remain uncertain at this time, as the level of protection is not high enough for the vaccine to supplant chemoprophylaxis.

The derivation of RTS,S/AS02A from a single malaria antigen increases technical feasibility but might also limit the efficacy that can be achieved, especially for travelers who require a highly effective vaccine. This univalent vaccine also faces the possibility that widespread use could select for vaccine-resistant genotypes, although as yet there is no direct evidence that this will occur. Efforts have been initiated to combine this antigen with a second recombinant protein, first with a second liver-stage antigen (thrombospondin-related adherent protein, *Pf*TRAP, also called the sporozoite surface protein 2, *Pf*SSP2), which did not improve protection (K.E. Kester, unpublished data), and, most recently, with the blood-stage antigen *Pf*MSP1, a trial still under analysis. Further development is aimed at evaluating potential additional combinations, such as with other blood stage antigens, improved formulations, or alternative immunization approaches, such as prime-boost (see "Heterologous [Prime-Boost] Vaccines").

Additional protein vaccines based on the *Pf*CSP are under development. Researchers at the University of Lausanne, Switzerland, have tested the synthetic peptide vaccine *Pf*CSP 282-383 (also composed of a portion of the C-terminus of the molecule) formulated in Montanide ISA-720 (Seppic, Paris, France) and alum, demonstrating antibody, lymphoproliferative, and, most important, CD8-positive (CD8+) T cell–mediated IFN-γ responses to a series of three immunizations.[41] The biotechnology company Apovia (San Diego, CA), in collaboration with the US National Institutes of Health (NIH), New York University, MVI, and other institutions, is testing virus-like particles derived from hepatitis B core antigen and specific T- and B-cell epitopes from the *Pf*CSP.[42]

Single-valent synthetic (eg, long synthetic peptides) or recombinant protein–based vaccines derived from blood-stage antigens are also being assessed, including formulations of *Pf*MSP1 (Pasteur Institute, Paris; University of Oxford, England; US Army in collaboration with the US Agency for International Development [US AID]; and GSKBio), *P. falciparum* merozoite surface protein 3 (*Pf*MSP3) (University of Lausanne, Pasteur Institute, European Malaria Vaccine Initiative), *P. falciparum* glutamine-rich protein (*Pf*GLURP) (University of Nijmegen, European Malaria Vaccine Initiative), *P. falciparum* apical membrane antigen 1 (*Pf*AMA1) (US Army in collaboration with US AID; University of Nijmegen, European Malaria Vaccine Initiative), and several other antigens. In addition, the NIH is developing single-valent transmission-blocking protein vaccines for both *P. falciparum* and *P. vivax*.[43–47]

As far back as 1991, various laboratories initiated studies with multiantigen cocktails.[48] The first such vaccine to receive widespread testing, SPf66, was developed at the University of Colombia, Bogota, and consisted of three peptides, one of which was derived from *Pf*MSP1 and the other two of which have not been identified, linked by repeat sequences from the *Pf*CSP and adsorbed on aluminum hydroxide.[49] Despite evidence of some degree of protection afforded by this vaccine in South America, trials in Africa and Asia and some in South America have shown no consistent benefit, and it is unlikely that the vaccine will be licensed for widespread use.[50] Another vaccine, called Combo B, combined portions of three asexual blood-stage antigens (MSP1; merozoite surface protein 2, or MSP2; and ring-infected erythrocyte surface antigen, or RESA). This vaccine was assessed in children aged 5 to 9 years in Papua New Guinea and resulted in diminished parasite density and decreased frequency of clinical episodes associated with parasitemias greater than 1,000/μL.[51] Perhaps a portent of the future, this trial by itself apparently exerted a selection pressure on the local parasite population, which exhibited a major switch in MSP2 genotype frequencies following the trial.

Nucleic Acid–Based Vaccines

The discovery that recombinant DNA plasmids encoding the CSP of the murine malaria *Plasmodium yoelii* can induce protective immune responses in BALB/c mice has launched an intensive effort to develop this new technology for use in humans.[52,53] The ease of manufacturing DNA and its stability, ready combination into multiantigen cocktails, and ability to induce in humans the CD8 T cell–mediated immune responses believed to be critical to preerythrocytic-stage immunity make it an attractive approach.[52–57] The immunogenicity of "naked" DNA plasmids relies on their uptake by host cells, the transcription and translation of the malarial genes by host cell organelles, and the acquisition of the resulting malarial antigens by antigen-presenting cells (APCs). Protection has been achieved in murine models, and new approaches for delivering DNA may improve both its immunogenicity and protective efficacy.[52,58–62] For example, DNA can be delivered directly into host cells by particle-mediate gene transfer (PMGT) or targeted to dendritic cells by adsorption onto microparticles or by fusion with the constant (Fc) region of immunoglobulins.[63–69] The level of expression can be improved by the use of synthetic genes designed with codon usage patterns more efficiently translated by host cell ribosomes than the native constructs.[70] In addition, responses can be improved by the inclusion of costimulatory molecules, such as human cytokines or CpG motifs, or by fusion of the malaria gene with DNA-encoding hepatitis B surface antigen.[71–75] Other approaches have included using recombinant viral, bacterial, or protozoal vectors to express malarial DNA and the use of expression libraries for immunization.[76–84]

Two groups have made significant progress with human testing of DNA-based vaccines for the prevention of malaria.[85–87] The US Navy and Vical (San Diego, CA), in collaboration initially with Aventis Pasteur and, more recently, with US AID, have tested a single plasmid encoding full-length PfCSP in healthy malaria-naive adults and have demonstrated the induction of genetically restricted, antigen-specific CTL responses and of CD4+ and CD8+ T cell–dependent IFN-γ production, as measured by ELISpot assay.[56,57] Although the vaccine has appeared safe, no antibody responses have been induced.[88,89] More recently, this vaccine has been combined with four additional plasmids, each encoding a different preerythrocytic stage protein, and the cocktail administered either alone or in conjunction with a sixth plasmid encoding human granulocyte-macrophage colony–stimulating factor (hGM-CSF) to serve as an immunostimulant.[71] IFN-γ production was demonstrated against each of the five antigens, but the frequency and magnitude of these responses were not optimal; hGM-CSF did not appear to enhance responses (although the level of expression was not ascertained), and no antibodies were induced. However, immunization with this vaccine primed for boosting of antibody and T-cell responses by exposure to the parasite (T.L. Richie, unpublished data). Studies in mice of these same antigens indicate that poor immunogenicity may have reflected competition among plasmids in the mixture (M. Sedegah, unpublished data). However, this has not been confirmed in rhesus monkeys or in humans.[54] The Navy, partnering with Epimmune (San Diego, CA), is also developing multiepitope strings of T- and B-cell epitopes derived from malaria antigens, in which interepitope linking sequences have been adjusted to optimize expression and immunogenicity of the epitopes.[90,91]

At the University of Oxford, a single plasmid encoding a string of CTL epitopes derived from six P. falciparum preerythrocytic antigens fused to the full-sequence TRAP/SSP2 has now been extensively assessed in a series of phase I/IIa studies in the United Kingdom and in The Gambia, mostly in conjunction with heterologous prime-boost regimens with modified vaccinia virus Ankara (MVA) or fowlpox expressing the same fusion gene as the DNA plasmid.[87] As with the DNA vaccines tested by the Navy, these formulations appear to be safe and well tolerated and induce genetically restricted T-cell responses, including IFN-γ production as measured by ex vivo ELISpot assays, but no or negligible antibody responses. Promising results are now being obtained in human trials, in particular with a regimen in which the fowlpox construct is used for priming and the MVA construct for boosting (A.V.S. Hill, personal communication, September 2003).

Carbohydrate Vaccines

Fatalities from *P. falciparum* malaria are thought to result in part from pathologic reactions to the malarial toxin glycosylphosphatidylinositol (GPI). A recent exciting development has been the demonstration that mice can be immunized with a synthetic version of the glycan portion of *P. falciparum* GPI. This nontoxic carbohydrate coupled to a carrier protein substantially protected mice against malarial acidosis, pulmonary edema, cerebral syndrome, and fatality when challenged intraperitoneally with *Plasmodium berghei* ANKA blood-stage parasites.[28] If this success can be carried forward into human trials, malaria toxin, rendered nonpathogenic by deacylation, could become an important component of a malaria vaccine, inducing an immune response that offers protection against severe disease and death.

Heterologous (Prime-Boost) Vaccines

Currently, the most powerful approach, particularly for inducing CD8+ T-cell responses, which are likely critical to preerythrocyte-stage immunity, may be heterologous vaccination, in which two distinct formulations of the same antigen or antigens are injected sequentially.[92] For example, priming with a DNA plasmid encoding the CSP of *P. yoelii* and boosting with a poxvirus encoding the same antigen yielded improved immunogenicity, protection, and generation of memory against sporozoite challenge compared with either vaccine administered alone.[72,93,94] Prime-boost strategies can afford 100% protection against sporozoite challenge in some murine models.[95] In the rhesus monkey/*Plasmodium knowlesi* sporozoite challenge model, a DNA prime–poxvirus boost regimen protected 80% of monkeys against lethal sporozoite challenge.[96] A large variety of heterologous approaches are currently being assessed, including priming with DNA, poxviruses, or adenoviruses and boosting with protein, poxviruses, adenoviruses, or other constructs.[64,78,97–105]

As described above, the US Navy has now consistently protected 80% of rhesus monkeys against a normally lethal challenge with the simian malaria parasite *P. knowlesi*, using a four-antigen cocktail. Four separate plasmids, each encoding a liver-stage or a blood-stage antigen, were mixed together and injected in three (0, 4, and 8 weeks) or four doses (0, 4, 8, and 40 weeks), followed by boosting with a mixture of four recombinant COPAK (attenuated vaccinia) viruses, each encoding one of the four antigens, at 24 to 44 weeks. Two weeks later, the monkeys were challenged with 100 sporozoites injected into the saphenous vein. In two separate experiments, approximately 20% of the monkeys showed no parasitemia and were completely protected, 60% became parasitemic but controlled their infections without significant clinical illness, and only 20% experienced rapidly rising parasitemias similar to those exhibited by the control monkeys, all of which required treatment (Weiss, unpublished data).[96]

The prime-boost approach has already undergone clinical testing by the group at Oxford, as described above, and by the US Navy. A clinical trial has now been conducted in which volunteers initially immunized with the *Pf*CSP DNA vaccine were boosted 12 to 14 months later with RTS,S/ASO2A. As with the Oxford studies, preliminary results from this clinical trial are encouraging (R. Wang and J.E. Epstein, unpublished data). Although heterologous vaccination strategies represent a challenge for marketing and for vaccine delivery, particularly in endemic areas, it is likely that in the short term, our most successful subunit vaccines will use a heterologous approach. A long-term goal will be to formulate vaccines that, when delivered in a homologous regimen, are as effective as heterologous vaccines.[106]

GENOMES TO VACCINES

With the completion of the genomic sequence of *P. falciparum* and the murine malaria species *P. yoelii*, we have entered a new era in terms of target antigen discovery for malaria vaccine development. The genomic-sequence data presented in the recently published papers reporting the sequences of *P. falciparum* and *P. yoelii* have, and will be useful in identifying potential surface proteins based on their DNA sequence.[19,107] Furthermore, the data will be critical for conducting the gene expression and proteomics studies that will establish which proteins are expressed at which stages of the parasite life cycle.[108,109] Such data on subcellular localization and stage-specific expression will be fundamental for selecting the proteins to be included in subunit vaccines designed to duplicate naturally acquired and radiation-attenuated sporozoite-induced immunity.

Surface Proteins

There are more than 1,000 *P. falciparum* proteins predicted, based on their gene sequence, to be on the surface of cells. These proteins can be divided into two principal classes: proteins with extracellular modules specific to parasites like those that cause malaria (apicomplexans) and proteins containing conserved domains that are widespread across a broad range of organisms. The most prominent among the former are the variant gene families that are involved in cytoadherence of infected red cells and that are prominently clustered in the subtelomeric regions of the *P. falciparum* genome (*Pf*EMP or var, rifins, stevors). These are proteins now known to be expressed on the surface of infected erythrocytes. Additional examples include the Duffy-binding ligand (DBL) domain–containing, erythrocyte-binding antigen (EBA-175) –like gene family, and the rhoptry- and reticulocyte-binding protein gene families involved in red cell invasion, encoding proteins also known to be on the surface of parasites.[19,110] The second class of surface proteins contains conserved eukaryotic adhesion modules; these proteins might be involved in parasite invasion of cells and therefore might serve as attractive targets for vaccine development. In all such cases of surface proteins, vaccines designed to induce antibodies that recognize these proteins could restrict parasite development and thereby attenuate the disease.

Stage-Specific Protein Expression

Genomic-sequence data have provided the foundation for studies to determine mRNA and protein expression at different stages of the parasite life cycle.[111,112] The results of preliminary analyses to identify proteins expressed at specific stages of the parasite life cycle have now been reported.[19,108,109] This is especially important for vaccine development wherein subsets of proteins can be prioritized for T-cell vaccines based on their stage-specific expression (especially liver stage) and for antibody vaccines based on stage-specific expression (especially blood stage) and computationally predicted surface localization. Hence, defining the stage specificity of proteins with predicted transmembrane segments (approximately 1,400 proteins) is of paramount importance.

Contributions from the Human Genome

Host genomic data might also contribute to developing malaria vaccines. Case-control and association studies have now been successfully used to dissect the genetics of host susceptibility to malaria, generating a lengthening list of genetic markers associated with susceptibility to severe disease.[113] In addition, the recent completion of the mouse genome and the comparative genomic map of the two species will both complement and benefit from ongoing efforts to dissect determinants of host susceptibility and immune response in murine models of malaria, such as *P. yoelii*.[114,115] Future efforts aimed at identifying genetic correlates in populations at risk with biologic correlates of parasite invasion, parasite development, cytoadherence efficiency, and clinical outcomes will allow specific targeting of vaccination to the individuals most likely to benefit. In addition, human genomic data should permit a systems biology/immunology approach to monitoring human immune responses, wherein molecular, kinetic portraits of individuals provide a more comprehensive indication of the response to infection and immunization than do currently available cross-sectional single–immune response measurements. This should facilitate developing vaccines that maximize the magnitude, quality, and longevity of protective immune responses.

A broad overview of malaria "vaccinomics" is provided in Figure 14-4, which describes the scientific capabilities that have been facilitated by the emerging genomic data bases, including parasite genomics (contributing primarily to the endeavors listed at the top of the figure) and human genomics (contributing primarily to the endeavors listed at the bottom of the figure).[116]

LOOKING TO THE FUTURE FOR TRAVELERS

Currently, the only approach to immunization that has shown in human volunteers a level of efficacy and longevity of protective immunity suitable for travelers has been immunization by exposure of volunteers to the bites of irradiated, infected mosquitoes.[20] Heretofore, it had been considered impractical to develop such an approach as a vaccine, and it has been used only as a model for developing a subunit malaria vaccine. However, a reevaluation of this approach suggests that it is feasible (S.L. Hoffman, unpublished data), and it is anticipated that within 2 to 3 years, it will be determined if it is possible to produce an attenuated sporozoite vaccine for travelers and residents of endemic areas.

In regard to subunit vaccines, the vaccine currently most advanced in its development, RTS,S/AS02A, might not be marketed prior to the end of the decade and might not be able to substitute for chemoprophylaxis because of its modest efficacy and duration of protection. Nonetheless, there is also optimism regarding the likelihood of success for subunit malaria vaccine development in the long-term.[117]

As malaria infections are chronic, we face the conundrum of attempting to use the human immune system as a weapon to evict a parasite that is naturally able to evade human immune responses. This will require identifying potentially protective antigens and pushing immune responses to levels that exceed those occurring in response to natural infection. However, we do have human models for both pre-erythrocytic-stage and erythrocytic-stage vaccines (attenuated sporozoites and NAI, respectively), and as we better elucidate the protective mechanisms operative in these models, optimize the many vaccine enhancement strategies currently available, and learn how to formulate and deliver highly immunogenic vaccines, we should be able to reproduce the protective effects of these models. In particular, the sequencing of the *P. falciparum* genome and progress in defining high-throughput techniques for identifying new candidate antigens using genomic data hold promise for the future. The technologies developed in this fight against malaria might yield important benefits for vaccine development for other chronic parasitic infections, making the world much safer for travelers and residents of endemic areas alike.

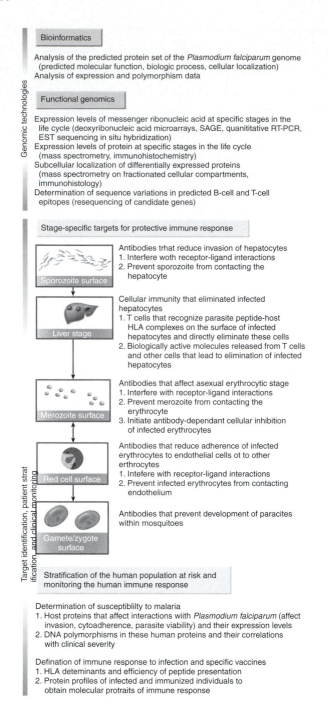

Figure 14-4. The emerging science of malaria "vaccinomics" uses parasite and host genomic-sequence data to enhance the development of effective malaria vaccines. New functionally or anatomically important candidate antigens will be identified from the parasite genome using a variety of techniques based on predicted protein sequences, stage-specific ribonucleic acid (RNA) isolation, microarrays, and mass spectrometry analysis of parasite proteomes (bioinformatics and functional genomics). On the host side, analysis of the human genome and its polymorphisms will allow targeting subpopulations for vaccine administration based on relevant genetic traits, such as those contributing to severe disease or those associated with the ability to respond immunologically to the vaccine (population stratification). Data from parasite and human genomics interface in the pairing of antigens and host genotype to induce the right combination of stage-specific immune responses required for protection (stage-specific targeting). Reproduced with permission from Hoffman SL et al.[116] EST = expressed sequence tag; HLA = human leukocyte antigen; RT-PCR = reverse transcriptase polymerase chain reaction; SAGE = serial analysis of gene expression.

ACKNOWLEDGMENTS

We thank Joe Cohen, Denise Doolan, Filip Dubovsky, Adrian Hill, Søren Jepsen, Kent Kester, Allan Saul, Robert Sauerwein, Nadia Tornieporth, and Walter Weiss for their comments on specific sections; Kevin Kain, Blaise Genton, and Patricia Schlagenhauf for providing references; and Alan Pariser of Giant Pharmacy (Clarksville, MD) for providing drug costs. Funding has been provided by the US Navy Bureau of Medicine, the US Army Military Infectious Disease Research Program, the Office of Naval Research, and the US Agency for International Development. The opinions and assertions herein are the private ones of the authors and are not to be construed as official or as reflecting the views of the US Navy or the US Government.

REFERENCES

1. World Tourism Organization. International tourist arrivals by (sub)region, June, 2002. Facts and figures. Available at: http://www.world-tourism.org/ (accessed September 2002).

2. Jelinek T. Evidence of malaria exposure in travelers. In: Schlagenhauf P, editor. Travelers' malaria. Hamilton (ON): BC Decker; 2001. p. 94–103.

3. Martens P, Hall L. Malaria on the move. Human population movement and malaria transmission. Emerg Infect Dis 2000;6:103–9.

4. Coole L, Wiselka MJ, Nicholson KG. Malaria prophylaxis in travellers from Britain. J Infect 1989;18:209–12.

5. Lobel HO, Phillips-Howard PA, Brandling-Bennett AD, et al. Malaria incidence and prevention among European and North American travellers to Kenya. Bull World Health Organ 1990;68:209–15.

6. Semaille C, Santin A, Prazuck T, et al. Malaria chemoprophylaxis of 3,446 French travelers departing from Paris to eight tropical countries. J Travel Med 1999;6:3–6.

7. dos Santos CC, Anvar A, Keystone JS, Kain KC. Survey of use of malaria prevention measures by Canadians visiting India. Can Med Assoc J 1999;160:195–200.

8. Molle I, Christensen KL, Hansen PS, et al. Use of medical chemoprophylaxis and antimosquito precautions in Danish malaria patients and their traveling companions. J Travel Med 2000;7:253–8.

9. Laver SM, Wetzels J, Behrens RH. Knowledge of malaria, risk perception, and compliance with prophylaxis and personal and environmental preventive measures in travelers exiting Zimbabwe from Harare and Victoria Falls International Airport. J Travel Med 2001;8:298–303.

10. Lobel HO, Baker MA, Gras FA, et al. Use of malaria prevention measures by North American and European travelers to East Africa. J Travel Med 2001;8:167–72.

11. D'Acremont V, Landry P, Mueller I, et al. Clinical and laboratory predictors of imported malaria in an outpatient setting. An aid to medical decision making in returning travelers with fever. Am J Trop Med Hyg 2002;66:481–6.

12. Muentener P, Schlagenhauf P, Steffen R. Imported malaria (1985–95). Trends and perspectives. Bull World Health Organ 1999;77:560–6.

13. Kain KC, Harrington MA, Tennyson S, Keystone JS. Imported malaria. Prospective analysis of problems in diagnosis and management. Clin Infect Dis 1998;27:142–9.

14. Breman JG. The ears of the hippopotamus. Manifestations, determinants, and estimates of the malaria burden. Am J Trop Med Hyg 2001;64 Suppl:1–11.

15. Lengeler C, Armstrong-Schellenberg J, D'Alessandro U, et al. Relative versus absolute risk of dying reduction after using insecticide-treated nets for malaria control in Africa. Trop Med Int Health 1998;3:286–90.

16. Carter R. Transmission blocking malaria vaccines. Vaccine 2001;19:2309–14.

17. Gandon S, Mackinnon MJ, Nee S, Read AF. Imperfect vaccines and the evolution of pathogen virulence. Nature 2001;414:751–6.

18. Duffy PE, Craig AG, Baruch DI. Variant proteins on the surface of malaria-infected erythrocytes—developing vaccines. Trends Parasitol 2001;17:354–6.

19. Gardner MJ, Hall N, Fung E, et al. Genome sequence of the human malaria parasite *Plasmodium falciparum*. Nature 2002;419:498–511.

20. Hoffman SL, Goh LM, Luke TC, et al. Protection of humans against malaria by immunization with radiation-attenuated *Plasmodium falciparum* sporozoites. J Infect Dis 2002;185:1155–64.

21. Jeffrey GM. Epidemiological significance of repeated infections with homologous and heterologous strains and species of *Plasmodium*. Bull World Health Organ 1996;35:873–82.

22. Baird JK. Host age as a determinant of naturally acquired immunity to *Plasmodium falciparum*. Parasitol Today 1995;11:105–11.

23. Doolan DL, Hoffman SL. The complexity of protective immunity against liver-stage malaria. J Immunol 2000;165:1453–62.

24. Cohen S, McGregor IA, Carrington S. Gamma globulin and acquired immunity to human malaria. Nature 1961;192:733–7.

25. Edozien, JC, Gilles HM, Udeozo IOK. Adult and cord-blood gamma globulin and immunity to malaria in Nigerians. Lancet 1962;ii:951–5.

26. McGregor IA, Carrington SP. Treatment of East African *P. falciparum* malaria with West African human γ-globulin. Trans R Soc Trop Med Hyg 1963;57:170–5.

27. Sabchareon A, Burnouf T, Ouattara D, et al. Parasitologic and clinical human response to immunoglobulin administration in falciparum malaria. Am J Trop Med Hyg 1991;45:297–308.

28. Schofield L, Hewitt MC, Evans K, et al. Synthetic GPI as a candidate anti-toxic vaccine in a model of malaria. Nature 2002;418:785–9.

29. Arevalo-Herrera M, Herrera S. *Plasmodium vivax* malaria vaccine development. Mol Immunol 2001;38:443–55.

30. Mendis K, Sina BJ, Marchesini P, Carter R. The neglected burden of *Plasmodium vivax* malaria. Am J Trop Med Hyg 2001;64(1 Suppl 2):97–106.

31. Engers HD, Godal T. Malaria vaccine development. Current status. Parasitol Today 1998;14:56–64.

32. Greenwood B, Alonso P. Malaria vaccine trials. Chem Immunol 2002;80:366–95.

33. Ballou WR, Hoffman SL, Sherwood JA, et al. Safety and efficacy of a recombinant DNA *Plasmodium falciparum* sporozoite vaccine. Lancet 1987;1(8545):1277–81.

34. Herrington DA, Clyde DF, Losonsky G, et al. Safety and immunogenicity in man of a synthetic peptide malaria vaccine against *Plasmodium falciparum* sporozoites. Nature 1987;328:257–9.

35. Stoute JA, Slaoui M, Heppner DG, et al. A preliminary evaluation of a recombinant circumsporozoite protein vaccine against *Plasmodium falciparum* malaria. RTS,S Malaria Vaccine Evaluation Group. N Engl J Med 1997;336:86–91.

36. Kester KE, McKinney DA, Tornieporth N, et al. Efficacy of recombinant circumsporozoite protein vaccine regimens against experimental *Plasmodium falciparum* malaria. J Infect Dis 2001;183:640–7.

37. Gordon DM, McGovern TW, Krzych U, et al. Safety, immunogenicity, and efficacy of a recombinantly produced *Plasmodium falciparum* circumsporozoite protein–hepatitis B surface antigen subunit vaccine. J Infect Dis 1995;171:1576–85.

38. Stoute JA, Kester KE, Krzych U, et al. Long-term efficacy and immune responses following immunization with the RTS,S malaria vaccine. J Infect Dis 1998;178:1139–44.

39. Lalvani A, Moris P, Voss G, et al. Potent induction of focused Th1-type cellular and humoral immune responses by RTS,S/SBAS2, a recombinant *Plasmodium falciparum* malaria vaccine. J Infect Dis 1999;180:1656–64.

40. Bojang KA, Milligan PJ, Pinder M, et al. Efficacy of RTS,S/AS02 malaria vaccine against *Plasmodium falciparum* infection in semi-immune adult men in The Gambia. A randomised trial. Lancet 2001;358:1927–34.

41. Lopez JA, Weilenman C, Audran R, et al. A synthetic malaria vaccine elicits a potent CD8(+) and CD4(+) T lymphocyte immune response in humans. Implications for vaccination strategies. Eur J Immunol 2001;31:1989–98.

42. Milich DR, Hughes J, Jones J, et al. Conversion of poorly immunogenic malaria repeat sequences into a highly immunogenic vaccine candidate. Vaccine 2001;20:771–88.

43. Lee EA, Palmer DR, Flanagan KL, et al. Induction of T helper type 1 and 2 responses to 19-kilodalton merozoite surface protein 1 in vaccinated healthy volunteers and adults naturally exposed to malaria. Infect Immun 2002;70:1417–21.

44. Theisen M, Dodoo D, Toure-Balde A, et al. Selection of glutamate-rich protein long synthetic peptides for vaccine development. Antigenicity and relationship with clinical protection and immunogenicity. Infect Immun 2001;69:5223–9.

45. Dutta S, Lalitha PV, Ware LA, et al. Purification, characterization, and immunogenicity of the refolded ectodomain of the *Plasmodium falciparum* apical membrane antigen 1 expressed in *Escherichia coli*. Infect Immun 2002;70:3101–10.

46. Kocken CH, Withers-Martinez C, Dubbeld MA, et al. High-level expression of the malaria blood-stage vaccine candidate *Plasmodium falciparum* apical membrane antigen 1 and induction of antibodies that inhibit erythrocyte invasion. Infect Immun 2002;70:4471–6.

47. Miles AP, Zhang Y, Saul A, Stowers AW. Large-scale purification and characterization of malaria vaccine candidate antigen Pvs25H for use in clinical trials. Protein Expr Purif 2002;25:87-96.

48. Caspers P, Etlinger H, Matile H, et al. A *Plasmodium falciparum* malaria vaccine candidate which contains epitopes from the circumsporozoite protein and a blood stage antigen, 5.1. Mol Biochem Parasitol 1991;47:143–50.

49. Amador R, Moreno A, Murillo LA, et al. Safety and immunogenicity of the synthetic malaria vaccine SPf66 in a large field trial. J Infect Dis 1992;166:139–44.

50. Graves P, Gelbrand H. Vaccines for preventing malaria. Cochrane Database Syst Rev 2001;3. Available at: http://www.cochrane.org/cochrane/revabstr/g070index.htm (accessed September 2002).

51. Genton B, Betuela I, Felger I, et al. A recombinant blood-stage malaria vaccine reduces *Plasmodium falciparum* density and exerts selective pressure on parasite populations in a phase 1-2b trial in Papua New Guinea. J Infect Dis 2002;185:820–7.

52. Sedegah M, Hedstrom R, Hobart P, Hoffman SL. Protection against malaria by immunization with plasmid DNA encoding circumsporozoite protein. Proc Natl Acad Sci U S A 1994;91:9866–70.

53. Doolan DL, Hoffman SL. Nucleic acid vaccines against malaria. Chem Immunol 2002;80:308–21.

54. Wang R, Doolan DL, Charoenvit Y, et al. Simultaneous induction of multiple antigen-specific cytotoxic T lymphocytes in nonhuman primates by immunization with a mixture of four *Plasmodium falciparum* DNA plasmids. Infect Immun 1998;66:4193–202.

55. Jones TR, Gramzinski RA, Aguiar JC, et al. Absence of antigenic competition in Aotus monkeys immunized with *Plasmodium falciparum* DNA vaccines delivered as a mixture. Vaccine 2002;20:1675–80.

56. Wang R, Doolan DL, Le TP, et al. Induction of antigen-specific cytotoxic T lymphocytes in humans by a malaria DNA vaccine. Science 1998;282:476–80.

57. Wang R, Epstein J, Baraceros FM, et al. Induction of CD4(+) T cell–dependent CD8(+) type 1 responses in humans by a malaria DNA vaccine. Proc Natl Acad Sci U S A 2001;98:10817–22.

58. Doolan DL, Sedegah M, Hedstrom RC, et al. Circumventing genetic restriction of protection against malaria with multigene DNA immunization. CD8+ cell–, interferon gamma–, and nitric oxide–dependent immunity. J Exp Med 1996;183:1739–46.

59. Becker SI, Wang R, Hedstrom RC, et al. Protection of mice against *Plasmodium yoelii* sporozoite challenge with *P. yoelii* merozoite surface protein 1 DNA vaccines. Infect Immun 1998;66:3457–61.

60. Sauzet JP, Perlaza BL, Brahimi K, et al. DNA immunization by *Plasmodium falciparum* liver-stage antigen 3 induces protection against *Plasmodium yoelii* sporozoite challenge. Infect Immun 2001;69:1202–6.

61. Dubensky TW Jr, Liu MA, Ulmer JB. Delivery systems for gene-based vaccines. Mol Med 2000;6:723–32.

62. Clark KR, Johnson PR. Gene delivery of vaccines for infectious disease. Curr Opin Mol Ther 2001;3:375–84.

63. Leitner WW, Seguin MC, Ballou WR, et al. Immune responses induced by intramuscular or gene gun injection of protective deoxyribonucleic acid vaccines that express the circumsporozoite protein from *Plasmodium berghei* malaria parasites. J Immunol 1997;159:6112–9.

64. Degano P, Schneider J, Hannan CM, et al. Gene gun intradermal DNA immunization followed by boosting with modified vaccinia virus Ankara. Enhanced CD8+ T cell immunogenicity and protective efficacy in the influenza and malaria models. Vaccine 1999;18:623–32.

65. Weiss R, Leitner WW, Scheiblhofer S, et al. Genetic vaccination against malaria infection by intradermal and epidermal injections of a plasmid containing the gene encoding the *Plasmodium berghei* circumsporozoite protein. Infect Immun 2000;68:5914–9.

66. Yoshida S, Kashiwamura SI, Hosoya Y, et al. Direct immunization of malaria DNA vaccine into the liver by gene gun protects against lethal challenge of *Plasmodium berghei* sporozoite. Biochem Biophys Res Commun 2000;271:107–15.

67. Singh M, Briones M, Ott G, O'Hagan D. Cationic microparticles. A potent delivery system for DNA vaccines. Proc Natl Acad Sci U S A 2000;97:811–6.

68. Rosas JE, Pedraz JL, Hernandez RM, et al. Remarkably high antibody levels and protection against *P. falciparum* malaria in Aotus monkeys after a single immunisation of SPf66 encapsulated in PLGA microspheres. Vaccine 2002;20:1707–10.

69. You Z, Huang X, Hester J, et al. Targeting dendritic cells to enhance DNA vaccine potency. Cancer Res 2001;61:3704–11.

70. Narum DL, Kumar S, Rogers WO, et al. Codon optimization of gene fragments encoding *Plasmodium falciparum* merozoite proteins enhances DNA vaccine protein expression and immunogenicity in mice. Infect Immun 2001;69(12):7250–3.

71. Weiss WR, Ishii KJ, Hedstrom RC, et al. A plasmid encoding murine granulocyte-macrophage colony-stimulating factor increases protection conferred by a malaria DNA vaccine. J Immunol 1998;161:2325–32.

72. Sedegah M, Weiss W, Sacci JB Jr, et al. Improving protective immunity induced by DNA-based immunization. Priming with antigen and GM-CSF–encoding plasmid DNA and boosting with antigen-expressing recombinant poxvirus. J Immunol 2000;164:5905–12.

73. Kumar S, Villinger F, Oakley M, et al. A DNA vaccine encoding the 42 kDa C-terminus of merozoite surface protein 1 of *Plasmodium falciparum* induces antibody, interferon-gamma and cytotoxic T cell responses in rhesus monkeys. Immuno-stimulatory effects of granulocyte macrophage-colony stimulating factor. Immunol Lett 2002;81:13–24.

74. Near KA, Stowers AW, Jankovic D, Kaslow DC. Improved immunogenicity and efficacy of the recombinant 19-kilodalton merozoite surface protein 1 by the addition of oligodeoxynucleotide and aluminum hydroxide gel in a murine malaria vaccine model. Infect Immun 2002;70:692–701.

75. Wunderlich G, Moura IC, del Portillo HA. Genetic immunization of BALB/c mice with a plasmid bearing the gene coding for a hybrid merozoite surface protein 1–hepatitis B virus surface protein fusion protects mice against lethal *Plasmodium chabaudi chabaudi* PC1 infection. Infect Immun 2000;68:5839–45.

76. Lanar DE, Tine JA, de Taisne C, et al. Attenuated vaccinia virus–circumsporozoite protein recombinants confer protection against rodent malaria. Infect Immun 1996;64:1666–71.

77. Ockenhouse CF, Sun PF, Lanar DE, et al. Phase I/IIa safety, immunogenicity, and efficacy trial of NYVAC-Pf7, a pox-vectored, multiantigen, multistage vaccine candidate for *Plasmodium falciparum* malaria. J Infect Dis 1998;177:1664–73.

78. Rodrigues EG, Zavala F, Nussenzweig RS, et al. Efficient induction of protective anti-malaria immunity by recombinant adenovirus. Vaccine 1998;16:1812–7.

79. Tsuji M, Bergmann CC, Takita-Sonoda Y, et al. Recombinant Sindbis viruses expressing a cytotoxic T-lymphocyte epitope of a malaria parasite or of influenza virus elicit protection against the corresponding pathogen in mice. J Virol 1998;72:6907–10.

80. Gonzalez C, Hone D, Noriega FR, et al. *Salmonella typhi* vaccine strain CVD 908 expressing the circumsporozoite protein of *Plasmodium falciparum*. Strain construction and safety and immunogenicity in humans. J Infect Dis 1994;169:927–31.

81. Matsumoto S, Yukitake H, Kanbara H, Yamada T. Long-lasting protective immunity against rodent malaria parasite infection at the blood stage by recombinant BCG secreting merozoite surface protein-1. Vaccine 1999;18:832–4.

82. Wu S, Beier M, Sztein MB, et al. Construction and immunogenicity in mice of attenuated *Salmonella typhi* expressing *Plasmodium falciparum* merozoite surface protein 1 (MSP-1) fused to tetanus toxin fragment C. J Biotechnol 2000;83:125–35.

83. Charest H, Sedegah M, Yap GS, et al. Recombinant attenuated *Toxoplasma gondii* expressing the *Plasmodium yoelii* circumsporozoite protein provides highly effective priming for CD8+ T cell–dependent protective immunity against malaria. J Immunol 2000;165:2084–92.

84. Smooker PM, Setiady YY, Rainczuk A, Spithill TW. Expression library immunization protects mice against a challenge with virulent rodent malaria. Vaccine 2000;18:2533–40.

85. Doolan DL, Hoffman SL. DNA-based vaccines against malaria. Status and promise of the multi-stage malaria DNA vaccine operation. Int J Parasitol 2001;31:753–62.

86. Kumar S, Epstein JE, Richie TL, et al. A multilateral effort to develop DNA vaccines against falciparum malaria. Trends Parasitol 2002;18:129–35.

87. Ferry G. First DNA malaria vaccine on trial in Africa. Curr Biol 2000;10:R810–1.

88. Le TP, Coonan KM, Hedstrom RC, et al. Safety, tolerability and humoral immune responses after intramuscular administration of a malaria DNA vaccine to healthy adult volunteers. Vaccine 2000;18:1893–901.

89. Epstein JE, Gorak EJ, Charoenvit Y, et al. Safety, tolerability, and lack of antibody responses after administration of a *Pf*CSP DNA malaria vaccine via needle or needle-free jet injection, and comparison of intramuscular and combination intramuscular/intradermal routes. Hum Gene Ther 2002;13:1551–60.

90. Doolan DL, Southwood S, Chesnut R, et al. HLA-DR–promiscuous T cell epitopes from *Plasmodium falciparum* pre-erythrocytic–stage antigens restricted by multiple HLA class II alleles. J Immunol 2000;165:1123–37.

91. Sette A, Keogh E, Ishioka G, et al. Epitope identification and vaccine design for cancer immunotherapy. Curr Opin Investig Drugs 2002;3:132–9.

92. Hill AV, Reece W, Gothard P, et al. DNA-based vaccines for malaria. A heterologous prime-boost immunisation strategy. Dev Biol Stand 2000;104:171–9.

93. Sedegah M, Jones TR, Kaur M, et al. Boosting with recombinant vaccinia increases immunogenicity and protective efficacy of malaria DNA vaccine. Proc Natl Acad Sci U S A 1998;95:7648–53.

94. Sedegah M, Brice GT, Rogers WO, et al. Persistence of protective immunity to malaria induced by DNA priming and poxvirus boosting. Characterization of effector and memory CD8(+)-T-cell populations. Infect Immun 2002;70:3493–9.

95. Schneider J, Gilbert SC, Blanchard TJ, et al. Enhanced immunogenicity for CD8+ T cell induction and complete protective efficacy of malaria DNA vaccination by boosting with modified vaccinia virus Ankara. Nat Med 1998;4:397–402.

96. Rogers WO, Weiss WR, Kumar A, et al. Protection of rhesus macaques against lethal *Plasmodium knowlesi* malaria by a heterologous DNA priming and poxvirus boosting immunization regimen. Infect Immun 2002;70:4329–35.

97. Li S, Rodrigues M, Rodriguez D, et al. Priming with recombinant influenza virus followed by administration of recombinant vaccinia virus induces CD8+ T-cell–mediated protective immunity against malaria. Proc Natl Acad Sci U S A 1993;90:5214–8.

98. Plebanski M, Gilbert SC, Schneider J, et al. Protection from *Plasmodium berghei* infection by priming and boosting T cells to a single class I–restricted epitope with recombinant carriers suitable for human use. Eur J Immunol 1998;28:4345–55.

99. Gilbert SC, Schneider J, Plebanski M, et al. Ty virus–like particles, DNA vaccines and modified vaccinia virus Ankara. Comparisons and combinations. Biol Chem 1999;380:299–303.

100. Haddad D, Liljeqvist S, Stahl S, et al. Characterization of antibody responses to a *Plasmodium falciparum* blood-stage antigen induced by a DNA prime/protein boost immunization protocol. Scand J Immunol 1999;49:506–14.

101. Oliveira-Ferreira J, Miyahira Y, Layton GT, et al. Immunogenicity of Ty-VLP bearing a CD8(+) T cell epitope of the CS protein of *P. yoelii*. Enhanced memory response by boosting with recombinant vaccinia virus. Vaccine 2000;18:1863–9.

102. Bruna-Romero O, Gonzalez-Aseguinolaza G, Hafalla JC, et al. Complete, long-lasting protection against malaria of mice primed and boosted with two distinct viral vectors expressing the same plasmodial antigen. Proc Natl Acad Sci U S A 2001;98:11491–6.

103. Jones TR, Narum DL, Gozalo AS, et al. Protection of Aotus monkeys by *Plasmodium falciparum* EBA-175 region II DNA prime-protein boost immunization regimen. J Infect Dis 2001;183:303–12.

104. Schneider J, Langermans JA, Gilbert SC, et al. A prime-boost immunisation regimen using DNA followed by recombinant modified vaccinia virus Ankara induces strong cellular immune responses against the *Plasmodium falciparum* TRAP antigen in chimpanzees. Vaccine 2001;19:4595–602.

105. Gilbert S, Schneider J, Hannan C, et al. Enhanced CD8 T cell immunogenicity and protective efficacy in a mouse malaria model using a recombinant adenoviral vaccine in heterologous prime-boost immunisation regimes. Vaccine 2002;20:1039–45.

106. Hoffman SL, Doolan DL. Can malaria DNA vaccines on their own be as immunogenic and protective as prime-boost approaches to immunization? Dev Biol Stand 2000;104:121–32.

107. Carlton JM, Angiuoli SV, Suh BB, et al. Genome sequence and comparative analysis of the model rodent malaria parasite *Plasmodium yoelii yoelii*. Nature 2002;419:512–9.

108. Florens L, Washburn MP, Raine JD, et al. A proteomic view of the *Plasmodium falciparum* life cycle. Nature 2002;419:520–6.

109. Lasonder E, Ishihama Y, Andersen JS, et al. Analysis of the *Plasmodium falciparum* proteome by high-accuracy mass spectrometry. Nature 2002;419:537–42.

110. Cowman AF, Crabb BS. The *Plasmodium falciparum* genome—a blueprint for erythrocyte invasion. Science 2002;298:126–8.

111. Gardner MJ, Tettelin H, Carucci DJ, et al. Chromosome 2 sequence of the human malaria parasite *Plasmodium falciparum*. Science 1998;282:1126–32.

112. Bowman S, Lawson D, Basham D, et al. The complete nucleotide sequence of chromosome 3 of *Plasmodium falciparum*. Nature 1999;400:532–8.

113. Miller LH, Baruch DI, Marsh K, Doumbo OK. The pathogenic basis of malaria. Nature 2002;415:673–9.

114. Marshall E. Genome sequencing. Celera assembles mouse genome. Public labs plan new strategy. Science 2001;292:822.

115. Fortin A, Cardon LR, Tam M, et al. Identification of a new malaria susceptibility locus (Char4) in recombinant congenic strains of mice. Proc Natl Acad Sci U S A 2001;98:10793–8.

116. Hoffman SL, Subramanian GM, Collins FH, Venter JC. Plasmodium, human and *Anopheles* genomics and malaria. Nature 2002;415:702–9.

117. Long CA, Hoffman SL. Malaria——from infants to genomics to vaccines. Science 2002;297:345–7.

Chapter 15

ROUTINE IMMUNIZATIONS FOR PEDIATRIC TRAVELERS: TRAVEL CONSIDERATION

Karl Neumann and Sheila M. Mackell

Preparing infants and children for overseas travel requires familiarity with the childhood disease patterns and vaccine practices in the countries to be visited.[1] Childhood diseases remain prevalent in many developing countries, and outbreaks continue to occur in countries where the diseases are rarely seen or are thought to have been eliminated. Some developed countries do not have universal vaccination programs against all vaccine-preventable childhood diseases or have poorly managed programs.[2,3] For example, in the year 2000, there was an outbreak of poliomyelitis in Haiti and the Dominican Republic (island of Hispaniola), where no polio had occurred in more than a decade.[4] This outbreak was due to a polio vaccine–derived virus. In the 1990s, there were outbreaks of measles and mumps in Ireland, pertussis in the Netherlands, and diphtheria in the countries of the former Soviet Union.[5–8] Although childhood immunizations are strongly recommended for international travelers, no such immunization is a prerequisite for entering any country.[9] Some countries that require an International Certificate of Vaccination waive the requirement for infants younger than 6 months or 1 year of age.

BASICS IN VACCINATING INFANTS AND CHILDREN FOR TRAVEL

Children in developed countries receive vaccines at the age at which their immune systems can generally respond with optimal, long-term protection from that disease.[10] However, this is not necessarily the age at which children first become susceptible. Optimal protection against childhood diseases is particularly important for children who will visit developing countries and, more so, if they will have close contact with local children. Children at particular risk are those of immigrants to developed countries returning to visit their developing country of origin. Parents of such children often do not seek travel health advice or, if they do, turn to the consular services of the countries that they are planning to visit, sources that might not have up-to-date or accurate recommendations.

Family travel plans might dictate that infants and young children receive vaccinations before the optimal ages, that the intervals between doses be shortened, and, because of time restraints before travel, that only one or two doses of a multipart vaccine series be given before the trip.[11] In most cases, starting vaccines at slightly younger ages than recommended and somewhat shortening intervals between doses results in acceptable, but not optimal, immunity. (See the schedule for routine dosing and for accelerating dosing, Table 15-1.) In such cases, doses might have to be repeated at a later age. Generally, supernumerary doses of vaccines do not cause any known serious side effects, though some vaccines might be associated with increased local reactions with additional doses (diphtheria- and tetanus-containing vaccines and rabies vaccines, for example).[12–14] With the exception of the oral typhoid vaccine, vaccines

Table 15-1. **Recommended and Minimum Ages and Intervals between Vaccine Doses**

Vaccine and Dose Number	Recommended Age for This Dose	Minimum Age for This Dose	Recommended Interval to Next Dose	Minimum Interval to Next Dose
Hepatitis B1*	Birth–2 mo	Birth	1–4 mo	4 wk
Hepatitis B2	1–4 mo	4 wk	2–17 mo	8 wk
Hepatitis B3†	6–18 mo	6 mo‡	—	—
Diphtheria and tetanus toxoids and acellular pertussis (DTaP)1	2 mo	6 wk	2 mo	4 wk
DTaP2	4 mo	10 wk	2 mo	4 wk
DTaP3	6 mo	14 wk	6–12 mo	6 mo‡§
DTaP4	15–18 mo	12 mo	3 yr	6 mo‡
DTaP5	4–6 yr	4 yr	—	—
Haemophilus influenzae type b (Hib)1*‖	2 mo	6 wk	2 mo	4 wk
Hib2	4 mo	10 wk	2 mo	4 wk
Hib3#	6 mo	14 wk	6–9 mo	8 wk
Hib4	12–15 mo**	12 mo	—	—
Inactivated poliovirus vaccine (IPV)1	2 mo	6 wk	2 mo	4 wk
IPV2	4 mo	10 wk	2–14 mo	4 wk
IPV3	6–18 mo	14 wk	3.5 yr	4 wk
IPV4	4–6 yr	18 wk	—	—
Pneumococcal conjugate vaccine (PCV)1‖	2 mo	6 wk	2 mo	4 wk
PCV2	4 mo	10 wk	2 mo	4 wk
PCV3	6 mo	14 wk	6 mo	8 wk
PCV4	12–15 mo	12 mo	—	—
Measles, mumps, and rubella (MMR)1	12–15 mo**	12 mo	3–5 yr	4 wk
MMR2	4–6 yr	13 mo	—	—
Varicella††	12–15 mo	12 mo	4 wk††	4 wk††
Hepatitis A1	2 yr	2 yr	6–18 mo‡	6 mo‡
Hepatitis A2	> 30 mo	30 mo	—	—
Influenza‡‡	—	6 mo‡	1 mo	4 wk
Pneumococcal polysaccharide vaccine (PPV)1	—	2 yr	5 yr§§	5 yr
PPV2	—	7 yr§§	—	—

Table continues next page.

Table 15-1. **Recommended and Minimum Ages and Intervals between Vaccine Doses** *(Continued)*

Combination vaccines are available. Using licensed combination vaccines is preferred over separate injections of their equivalent component vaccines.[60] When administering combination vaccines, the minimum age for administration is the oldest age for any of the individual components; the minimum interval between doses is equal to the greatest interval of any of the individual antigens.

*A combination hepatitis B–Hib vaccine is available (Comvax, manufactured by Merck Vaccine Division). This vaccine should not be administered to infants aged < 6 weeks because of the Hib component.

†Hepatitis B3 should be administered > 8 weeks after hepatitis B2 and 16 weeks after hepatitis B1, and it should not be administered before age 6 months.

‡This reference is to calendar months.

§The minimum interval between DTaP3 and DTaP4 is recommended to be > 6 months. However, DTaP4 does not need to be repeated if administered > 4 months after DTaP3.

‖For Hib and PCV, children receiving the first dose of vaccine at age > 7 months require fewer doses to complete the series.[33,42]

#For a regimen of only polyribosylribitol phosphate–meningococcal outer membrane protein (PRP-OMP, PedvaxHib, manufactured by Merck), a dose administered at age 6 months is not required.

**During a measles outbreak, if cases are occurring among infants aged < 12 months, measles vaccination of infants aged > 6 months can be undertaken as an outbreak control measure. However, doses administered at age < 12 months should not be counted as part of the series.[36]

††Children aged 12 months to 13 years require only one dose of varicella vaccine. Persons aged > 13 years should receive two doses separated by > 4 weeks.

‡‡Two doses of inactivated influenza vaccine, separated by 4 weeks, are recommended for children aged 6 months to 9 years who are receiving the vaccine for the first time. Children aged 6 months to 9 years who have previously received influenza vaccine and persons aged > 9 years require only one dose per influenza season.

§§Second doses of PPV are recommended for persons at highest risk of serious pneumococcal infection and those who are likely to have a rapid decline in pneumococcal antibody concentration. Revaccination 3 years after the previous dose can be considered for children at highest risk of severe pneumococcal infection who would be aged < 10 years at the time of revaccination.[61]

Adapted from the Centers for Disease Control and Prevention.[14]

given at longer-than-recommended intervals need not be repeated.[15] This is true even after prolonged lapses. However, children might not be optimally immunized until the series is completed.

Acute febrile and other minor illnesses in otherwise healthy children are not reasons to postpone immunizations.[15] Increasingly, parents ask for changes in recommended vaccination protocols; that polyvalent vaccines, such as MMR (measles-mumps-rubella), for example, be given in three separate monovalent doses or that vaccination be postponed until a child is older. There is no evidence that such changes reduce risk—if indeed, there is a risk—but delaying immunizations, obviously, delays protection.

Although all combinations of vaccines have not been evaluated thoroughly, it appears that numerous vaccines can be given at one time without affecting immunogenicity or increasing side reactions; seven vaccines have been administered at one time without untoward effects.[14] In developed countries, similar vaccines produced by different manufacturers appear to be compatible. Live-virus vaccines should be given either on the same day or more than 28 days apart. Live-virus vaccines—and certain acute infections—can create a temporary anergic state during which tuberculin skin tests can yield false-negative reactions. Therefore, tuberculin testing should be performed on the same day as the live vaccine is given or 28 or more days later.[15] Immunoglobulin (Ig) and Ig-containing products (blood, for example) can interfere with the replication of live-virus vaccines, diminishing the antibody response to the vaccine(s).

In the absence of written immunization records or documents, essential vaccines should be repeated.[15] When a parent reports a previous serious reaction to a specific vaccine and that vaccine is indicated, the child should be referred to a pediatrician with expertise in immunization practices. If a recommended immunization is not indicated for medical reasons, parents should be given a signed, dated, and stamped letter stating the reasons for the exemption.

Children less than 1 year of age should be vaccinated in the anterolateral part of the thigh and older children, in the deltoid area of the upper arm.[15] Some immunizations are intended for subcutaneous tissue, others for the muscle. Injections of hepatitis B or rabies vaccines, for example, must be given into muscle tissue to achieve optimal immunogenicity. Often, children must be physically restrained so that vaccines reach the tissue for which they are intended. Needle size is important.[15] For subcutaneous injections, the injection should be given with a 23- to 25-gauge needle 16 to 19 mm (⅝ to ¾ inch) in length and injected into a pinched-up fold of skin. For intramuscular injections, the optimal size and length of needle to be used depends on the size of the child. Needles should be 22 to 25 gauge, with lengths as follows: 2 month old—16 mm (⅝ inch); 4 month old—22 to 25 mm (⅞ to 1 inch); older child—25 to 38 mm (1 to 1½ inch). When multiple vaccines are administered, injections should be spaced 3 cm or more (1 inch) apart. Unless approved, individual vaccines should not be mixed in the same syringe to reduce the number of injections. Vaccinations administered improperly should be repeated at a later date (see Chapter 4, "Vaccine Administration: Technical Aspects").

Parents should be cautioned to avoid immunizations and other injections overseas, especially in developing countries.[16] When possible, infants and children remaining overseas for long periods should have their booster doses during visits home. Although vaccines used in most of the world appear to be effective, the storage of vaccines and the sterility of syringes and needles are suspect in many countries. (Therapeutic injections are rarely, if ever, needed for acute illnesses. In many countries, health care personnel are prone to treating minor illnesses by injections. Such injections can lead to hepatitis B or C, human immunodeficiency virus [HIV], and other infections.)

IMMUNE RESPONSES TO VACCINES IN THE PEDIATRIC AGE GROUP

Age and the presence of passively transferred maternal antibodies influence the immune response to vaccines in infants and children.[17] The infant immune system especially is characterized by impaired T-cell function and minimal collaboration between B and T cells, restricting the immunoglobulin repertoire. Antibody response to antigenic stimulation is generally of low affinity.[18] Maternal antibodies to pertussis, mumps, and polio, for example, is present transiently during the first 4 to 6 months of life and appears not to be protective. Furthermore, children less than 2 years of age are unable to make IgG2 subclass antibodies, the main response elicited by purified polysaccharide vaccines: meningococcal A, C, Y, W-135 polysaccharide; typhoid Vi polysaccharide; and early versions of the *Haemophilus influenzae* type b (Hib) vaccines. Oligosaccharide protein conjugate vaccines—newer Hib vaccines, seven-valent pneumococcal vaccine, and meningococcal A-C conjugate vaccines—are capable of stimulating the infant immune system and elicit booster responses. Schedules for vaccinating premature infants are identical to those of full-term infants, with one exception: hepatitis B seroconversion in preterm infants is optimal when the first dose is given at 2 months rather than at birth.[15]

VACCINES FOR INFANTS AND CHILDREN

Diphtheria

Diphtheria remains a problem in many parts of the world even though an effective, inexpensive vaccine has been readily available for almost 50 years.[2] The reasons for this are: failure to immunize all children, use of the adult tetanus/diphtheria vaccine (Td) containing a lower dose of diphtheria toxin than the pediatric diphtheria-pertussis-tetanus (DPT) or diphtheria and tetanus toxoids with acellular pertussis (DTaP) vaccines for the primary series in children, and failure to give booster Td doses to older children and adults. In the early and mid-1900s, there was a major diphtheria epidemic in the countries of the former Soviet Union, with more than 100,000 known cases and many deaths, including several deaths in travelers.[8] The apparent reason for the epidemic was Soviet soldiers returning from Afghanistan infected with the disease, coupled with an inadequately immunized Soviet population. Massive immunization programs have brought the epidemic under control (Figures 15-1 and 15-2). The bacteria still circulate most everywhere, however, and travelers should ensure that they are immune. The United States had two cases in the year 2001. Transmission is generally by close contact with an infected individual or asymptomatic carrier. Bacteria are spread by droplets expelled during talking, coughing, and sneezing.

The pediatric dose of diphtheria vaccine is generally combined with vaccines against tetanus and pertussis (whooping cough) (DPT or DTaP). In some countries, DPT or DTaP is further combined with Hib and/or hepatitis B vaccines, producing a pentavalent vaccine. The adult diphtheria vaccine is commonly combined with tetanus vaccine (Td).

In the year 1999, 80% of children in the world received at least three doses of diphtheria vaccine, the number of doses necessary for basic immunity.[2] This is about twice the number of children as in 1980. Worldwide coverage is now as follows: developed world, near 100%; East Asia and Pacific, 90%; Latin America and Caribbean, 80%; South Asia, 70%; and sub-Saharan Africa, 50% (see Figure 15-2).[2] Not known is how many of these children receive booster doses, which are necessary to maintain immunity. However, especially in the developing world, less-than-optimally vaccinated children are not necessarily susceptible; some have had the disease either clinically or subclinically and are, therefore, immune.

Optimal diphtheria protection requires a primary (pediatric) series consisting of five doses: three doses in the first year of life, one in the second year, and one more in the fourth or fifth year.[19] Adult booster doses to maintain immunity should be given at 10 to 15 years of age and then every 10 years thereafter.

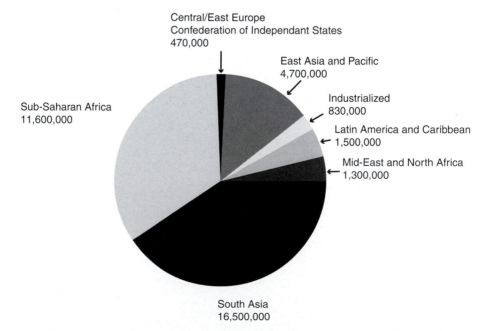

Figure 15-1. Diphtheria-tetanus-pertussis 3-dose vaccination: 34 million children not immunized in the year 1999. Shown here is the "best estimate" to reach 100% coverage. Adapted from the World Health Organization joint UNICEF/WHO review.

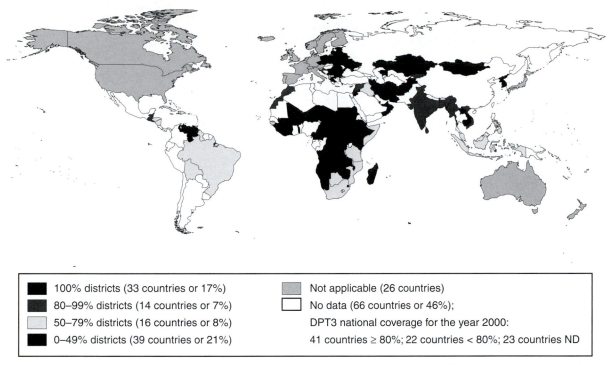

100% districts (33 countries or 17%)

80–99% districts (14 countries or 7%)

50–79% districts (16 countries or 8%)

0–49% districts (39 countries or 21%)

Not applicable (26 countries)

No data (66 countries or 46%);

DPT3 national coverage for the year 2000:

41 countries ≥ 80%; 22 countries < 80%; 23 countries ND

Figure 15-2. "Developing" countries with percentage of districts achieving at least 80% diphtheria-tetanus-pertussis (DTP3 coverage, in the year 2000. Indicated here are 188 developing countries and economies in transition per the United Nations' *World Economic and Social Survey* (2001) classification. Adapted from the World Health Organization/UNICEF joint reporting form, 2000.

Each dose of primary-series vaccine contains six or more lime floculate (Lf) units of antigen, the amount necessary to establish immunity.[20] Booster doses for older children and adults contain only 2 Lf units per dose. In the early years of diphtheria vaccination, it was found that giving older children and adults the larger pediatric dose often caused annoying adverse reactions (fever, aches and pains, several days lost from school and work) and that the smaller dose of antigen was sufficient to maintain immunity and also to establish immunity in nonimmune older children and adults. It is not known if adverse reactions would occur in older children and adults from present-day pediatric vaccines; present-day vaccines are more refined. Larger doses of antigen in booster doses could possibly increase the duration of vaccine protection.[21]

Diphtheria vaccine protects by producing circulating antibodies that neutralize the toxin produced by a natural infection; the vaccine does not prevent infection.[22] Antibody levels wane over time if not "boosted" by natural infection or vaccination. As the incidence of the disease decreases throughout the world, there is less boosting from natural disease.

Present recommendations for adults going to highly endemic areas are to give one booster dose of diphtheria toxoid regardless of the time that has elapsed since the last dose. This recommendation is based on the assumption that the primary pediatric series was given, and was given correctly, and that adult booster doses were given on a fairly regular basis, assumptions that are often incorrect. For example, most individuals born before 1940 did not receive the primary series in their childhood, and people born in developing countries and in eastern Europe may have received no vaccine or the wrong strength of vaccine. Diphtheria vaccination recommendations are currently under review, and practitioners are advised to continue present recommendations.

Tetanus

The tetanus bacillus inhabits soil worldwide, especially soil contaminated by animal excreta, and it survives particularly well in tropical climates. Wounds need not be deep or obvious to allow tetanus organisms in the wound to multiply and secrete toxin. The schedule for tetanus vaccine is identical to that for diphtheria, and the two vaccines are generally combined in one product. Pediatric primary tetanus vaccine doses and adult booster doses contain identical amount of tetanus toxoid. Adverse reactions (pain and fever) are rare and generally not severe but tend to increase with subsequent doses.

Cases of tetanus are very rare in developed countries and probably never occur in properly vaccinated children and adults. In the United States, there were 67 known cases in the year 2001, almost all in elderly individuals who had never had tetanus vaccine or had not had a booster dose in their adult life. Older children and adults tend to receive booster doses for tetanus more often than boosters against diphtheria; a booster dose of tetanus is generally given for injuries that involve bleeding. Although tetanus booster doses are recommended every 10 years, protection might last longer, apparently longer than for diphtheria.[22] One way to increase diphtheria protection in the population is to give tetanus/diphtheria injections whenever tetanus is called for.

Tetanus immunity is important for travelers. Many developing countries lack facilities for adequate wound cleansing and may not have human-derived tetanus immunoglobulin (TIG) available. TIG provides immediate passive immunity and should be given concomitantly with tetanus vaccine when immunity is in doubt. When TIG is not available, animal-derived tetanus antitoxin can be used instead but can cause serious side effects. Availability of sterile needles and syringes is also a concern in developing countries. Travelers should have their tetanus status documented in their certificates of vaccination. Without clear documentation, health care workers in developing countries tend to vaccinate injured patients against tetanus routinely when wounds occur because the people they are accustomed to treating often lack immunity.

Pertussis

An estimated 60 million people are infected with pertussis annually worldwide, causing 600,000 deaths, most among children in developing countries. However, many cases also occur in developed countries, and the number increases when vaccination programs lag. In the 1970s, unfounded media reports of vaccine-related brain damage in Britain lowered vaccination rates from 77% (already low) to 45%, leading to 47,000 reported cases of pertussis resulting in many deaths and some cases of permanent brain damage. In recent years, there have been pertussis outbreaks in the Netherlands and New Zealand.[6,7,23] Transmission occurs by close contact with respiratory-tract secretions from individuals colonized with the organism but not necessarily symptomatic.

In the United States, virtually all children are vaccinated against pertussis in childhood, with the last dose generally given about the time of entrance into school.[15] Older children are not vaccinated because the disease becomes milder with age and because the vaccines used in the past (whole cell derived) were often associated with more severe adverse reactions in older age groups.

Pertussis vaccines are not 100% protective, and vaccinated children can still become infected, albeit the disease in such individuals tends to be milder. Moreover, immunity from vaccination wanes about 10 years after the last primary vaccination dose, making older teenagers and adults susceptible. However, the disease in these older age groups is of a milder form than occurs in children; the cough is generally indistinguishable from other coughs but lasts longer and can be transmitted to others. Pertussis acquired abroad by non- or semi-immune teenagers and adults is one reason that the disease continues to circulate in areas with optimal immunization. Presently, studies are under way to vaccinate teenagers and adults at risk—health care workers and travelers, for example—with the new acellular pertussis vaccines, which are associated with far fewer side reactions than previous cellular ones.

Poliomyelitis

In the late 1990s, the World Health Organization (WHO) predicted the worldwide eradication of polio by the year 2000 and the end of polio vaccination somewhere between 2005 and 2010.[24] Although the date for eradication has not been met and the date to end vaccination is now nowhere in sight, tremendous progress has been made in eliminating this disease.[25]

Poliovirus spreads by the fecal-oral and oral-oral (respiratory) routes. In the year 2001, WHO estimated that fewer than 1,000 cases of wild poliovirus disease occurred worldwide. Most of these cases occurred in small, remote pockets in sub-Saharan Africa, Afghanistan, and the Indian subcontinent. However, scattered cases were reported in the Asian countries of the former Soviet Union and in several countries in the Middle East. A small outbreak occurred in Bulgaria in groups of people traveling from India to Western Europe (Figure 15-3).[22]

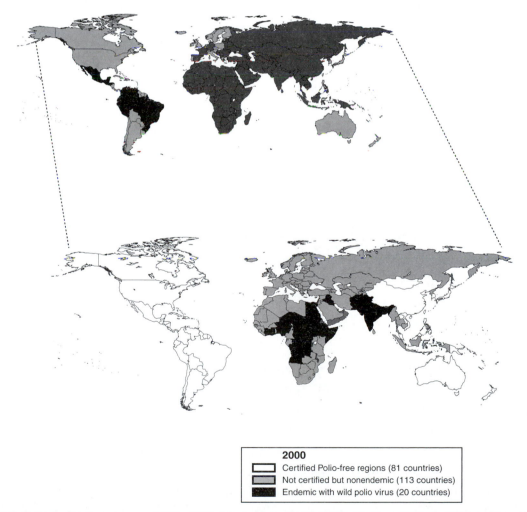

2000
- Certified Polio-free regions (81 countries)
- Not certified but nonendemic (113 countries)
- Endemic with wild polio virus (20 countries)

Figure 15-3. Polio eradication progress, 1988 to 2000. Adapted from the World Health Organization's AFP surveillance database, November 2001.

Although it appears that disease due to wild-type poliovirus will be eliminated in the next few years, cases of vaccine-derived poliovirus disease, such as the outbreak reported in Haiti and the Dominican Republic and the one in the Philippines in the year 2001, are major setbacks in the campaign to eliminate the disease.[21] The virus causing these outbreaks originated from the attenuated oral poliovirus vaccine (OPV) type l, one of the three polioviruses that constitute the vaccine. In areas of Haiti and the Dominican Republic where the outbreaks occurred, fewer than 20% of children were protected (ie, had a minimum of three doses), and some children had received no doses. Nucleotide sequence studies suggest that the virus either replicated in an immunodeficient individual or circulated for as long as 2 years in areas where vaccination coverage was very low, resulting in ongoing genetic changes. This caused the vaccine virus to reassume some of the characteristics of wild poliovirus type 1, in terms of both neurovirulence and transmissibility. The only other documented occurrence was in Egypt, about 15 years ago, involving type 2 OPV–derived virus, with 30 reported cases.

Although these outbreaks of polio vaccine–derived disease were quickly controlled by vaccination of susceptible children, the incidents raise concerns about the worldwide efforts to eradicate the disease.[4] Having large number of unvaccinated children in an area creates a prime breeding ground for vaccine-derived mutations.

OPV remains the vaccine of choice for eradicating polio in the developing world: the vaccine is relatively inexpensive and is oral and, therefore, can be administered by health care workers with minimal training; furthermore, because the attenuated live vaccine viruses are shed in the stool of recipients for up to 4 to 6 weeks after immunization, they spread to other people via sewage in areas of poor sanitation. This, in effect, "vaccinates" individuals who do not receive the vaccine directly. Discontinuing OPV vaccination programs will result in unvaccinated children being susceptible to poliovirus vaccine-derived mutant strains, if such a strain develops again, as well as to wild-type polioviruses. The longer that a given mutant strain circulates, the more virulent it could become. If at the same time the population of susceptible individuals increases, the risk of a flare-up of the disease from the mutant virus might also increase.

One solution is to vaccinate all children in the developing world with injectable (Salk) inactivated polio vaccine (IPV), as has been/is being done in most developed countries.[4] The IPV is as effective as OPV, but because it is inactivated, there is no chance for vaccine viruses to replicate and mutate in vaccine recipients. However, vaccinating all the children in the developing world with the Salk vaccine is an enormously complex and expensive undertaking that might require a decade or more to accomplish. More than a billion children would require vaccination with a relatively expensive vaccine that must be administered by injection, requiring a higher level of training for health care workers than does giving the oral vaccine.

Although both IPV and OPV prevent disease, immunization with IPV elicits serum immunity and does not necessarily prevent infection and transmission. Following exposure to wild poliovirus, the virus can replicate in the gastrointestinal (GI) tract of individuals who have received IPV and be excreted in the stool. However, in the developed world, should this happen, good hygiene and effective sanitation would prevent the virus from spreading to others. OPV stimulates mucosal immunity in the GI tract, discouraging poliovirus replication after exposure. However, in one in several million cases, OPV can cause vaccine-associated paralysis. Because this risk of vaccine-associated polio appears greater than the risk of exposure to wild poliovirus in most developed countries, OPV is no longer used or available in these countries.

Children fully immunized against polio—at least 3 doses of IPV, OPV, or any combination of the two—do not require additional doses of vaccine for travel; however, those not up-to-date might be at risk.[26] Children in most developed countries now receive 4 doses of IPV, given at 2 months, 4 months, 6 through 18 months, and 4 through 6 years. If accelerated protection is needed, the intervals between the first two doses can be reduced to 4 weeks, and the third can be given 2 months after the third. Though there are no good data on waning immunity, it is generally accepted that a single polio booster in adolescence is given for travel to endemic areas.

Hepatitis B

Hepatitis B is widespread in most developing countries, especially in Southeast Asia, sub-Saharan Africa, and the Amazon basin.[27] In some areas, more than 50% of individuals have or have had the disease. Common sources of transmission of the causative virus include body secretions (high virus content in blood, low in saliva), blood products, and blood-contaminated needles. However, many individuals, especially children, do not have an obvious source of infection. Many children in endemic areas appear to become infected when skin lesions such as insect bites or scratches become contaminated with minute amounts of blood from infected individuals. Skin lesions are especially common in tropical countries. Also, some travelers visit China specifically for acupuncture treatments. Needles are often reused and might be inadequately sterilized.[28] Equipment used for dental work, tattooing, ear piercing, and manicuring can also transmit the virus.[29] Hepatitis B causes few and generally mild immediate symptoms but often results in cirrhosis and cancer of the liver decades later.

The incidence of hepatitis B in most developed countries is low. In the United States, about 3 to 5% of the population has been infected, and about 1% is chronically infected. Many infected people belong to subgroups with far higher rates of hepatitis B than the general population: immigrants from endemic areas, individuals who have had many sexual partners, and intravenous drug users, for example.

In the United States, hepatitis B vaccination programs began in the mid-1980s when the early hepatitis B vaccines became available. Health care personnel and others exposed to blood and blood products in the workplace were vaccinated first. Routine immunization of children began in the 1990s. However, many countries, including some developed ones, still do not have universal hepatitis B immunization (Figure 15-4).[30] Presently, in developed countries, vaccines are made from baker's yeast that has been genetically modified to synthesize hepatitis B surface antigen. The original vaccines, prepared from the plasma of hepatitis B surface antigen carriers, might still be used in some parts of the world.

Hepatitis B vaccination is recommended for all travelers to endemic areas who anticipate close contact with local people, go to school, or intend to stay more than 6 months.[8] Parents-to-be going overseas to adopt children should be vaccinated. In the United States, there are nearly 20,000 foreign adoptions each year, the majority from Asia, eastern Europe, and Latin America, areas with high incidences of hepatitis B. Moreover, many of these children originate from backgrounds where the incidence of the disease is high.

Immunity requires three doses of hepatitis B vaccine at day 0, 1 month, and 6 months. If time is short, the third dose can be given at 3 months. Doses of some hepatitis B vaccines appear to be effective if given on days 0, 7, and 21.[31] With these accelerated schedules, a booster dose (fourth dose) should be given 12 months later. Two doses of certain hepatitis B vaccine formulations might be sufficient for teenagers. The vaccine must be injected into muscle (the anterolateral thigh in infants or the deltoid area of the arm

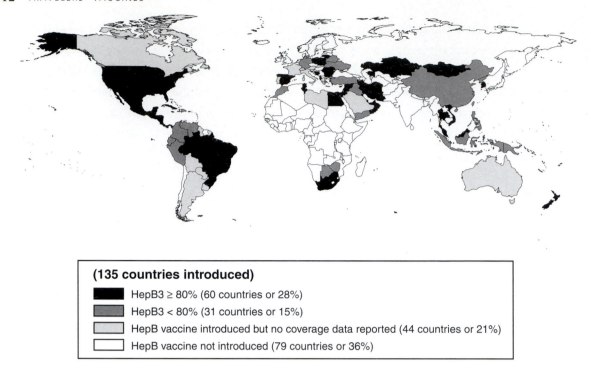

(135 countries introduced)

■ HepB3 ≥ 80% (60 countries or 28%)
■ HepB3 < 80% (31 countries or 15%)
□ HepB vaccine introduced but no coverage data reported (44 countries or 21%)
□ HepB vaccine not introduced (79 countries or 36%)

Figure 15-4. Countries that had introduced hepatitis B vaccine by the year 2001 and reported hepatitis B3 coverage by 2000. Adapted from the World Health Organization (WHO)/UNICEF joint reporting form, 2000; WHO country information, 2001.

in older children and adults). Injections into the gluteal area (buttock) might not reach muscle and therefore might be less effective. The duration of protection following hepatitis B immunization has not been determined but appears to be long; individuals vaccinated more than 15 years earlier have been shown to have protective antibodies (see Chapter 6, "Hepatitis A and Hepatitis B Vaccines").

Haemophilus influenzae Type b

Haemophilus influenzae type b vaccine has dramatically decreased the incidence of meningitis and other invasive diseases due to this organism. Vaccination is now universal in most developed countries and in an increasing number of developing countries.[32] Crowding appears to be a risk factor for acquiring the disease. Various forms of the vaccines, generally conjugated to a protein, are available in different countries. Some Hib vaccines are monovalent, requiring either three or four doses; others are combined with DPT or DTaP, polio (IPV), and/or hepatitis B, for example. Ideally, immunization should be started at 2 months and completed at about 15 to 18 months.[33] When vaccinations are delayed, fewer doses are indicated.[15] Healthy children over the age of 5 years need not be vaccinated (Figure 15-5).

Measles (Rubeola)

This disease might be eradicated worldwide by the year 2010.[34] All cases now occurring in the United States, for example, originate abroad imported by travelers, many of them foreign students attending US secondary schools and colleges. Measles continues to be a major health problem in many developing countries, especially in sub-Saharan Africa and on the Indian subcontinent; in some areas, fewer than half the children are optimally immunized with two doses (Figure 15-6). In poor areas of the world, the case fatality rate of measles is far higher than it is/was in the developed world, probably as a result of poor

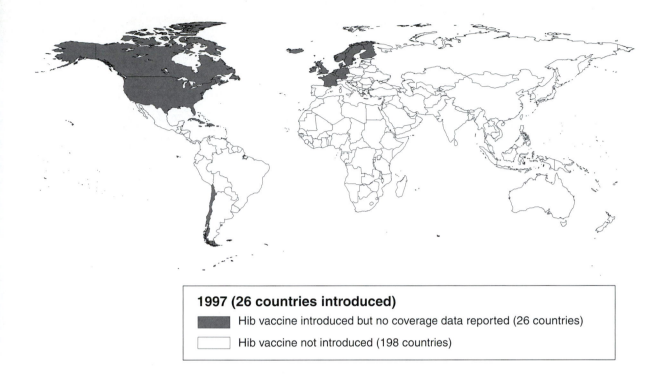

1997 (26 countries introduced)

Hib vaccine introduced but no coverage data reported (26 countries)

Hib vaccine not introduced (198 countries)

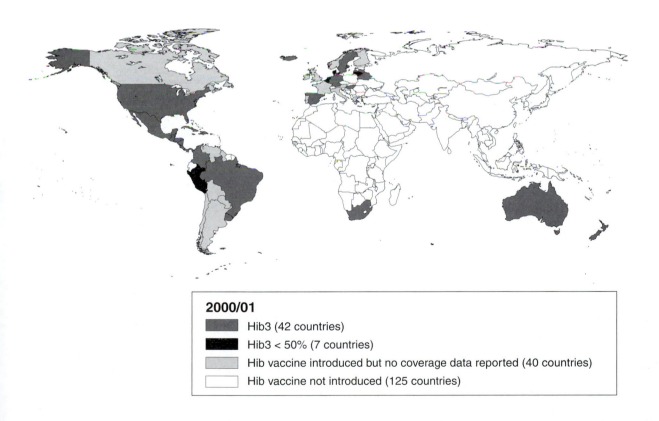

2000/01

Hib3 (42 countries)

Hib3 < 50% (7 countries)

Hib vaccine introduced but no coverage data reported (40 countries)

Hib vaccine not introduced (125 countries)

Figure 15-5. Countries that had introduced *Haemophilus influenzae* b (Hib) vaccine by the year 2001 and reported Hib3 coverage in 2000. Adapted from the World Health Organization (WHO)/UNICEF joint reporting form, 2000; WHO country information, 2001.

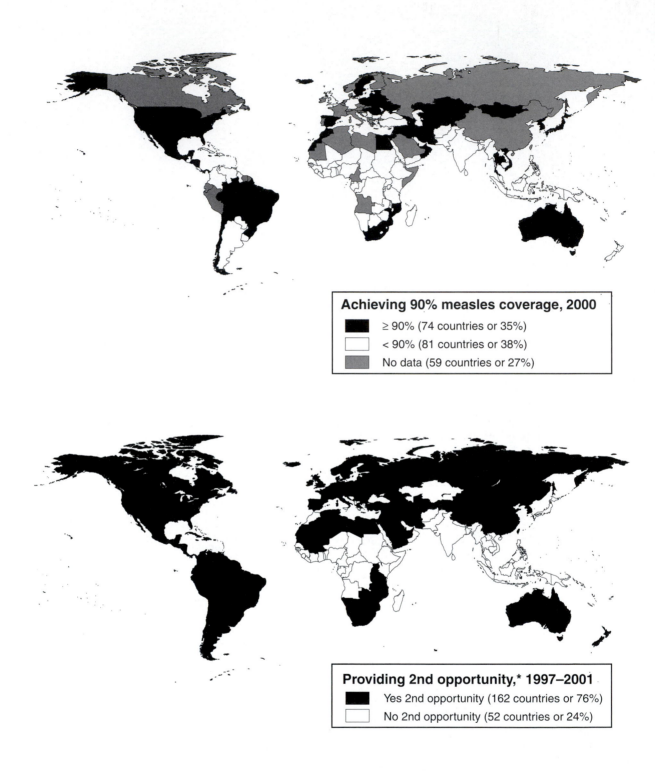

Figure 15-6. Countries that have implemented measles mortality reduction strategies. Adapted from the World Health Organization (WHO)/UNICEF joint reporting form, 2000; WHO country information, 2001. *2nd opportunity = country has implemented a two-dose routine measles schedule and/or within the last 4 years has conducted a national immunization campaign achieving ≥ 90% coverage of children < 5 years.

nutrition, not because of more virulent viruses. Vitamin A, for example, seems to reduce the severity of this disease. Measles spreads by direct contact with infectious droplets from infected individuals.

Travelers to developing countries should be immune to measles, either by having had the disease or by immunization. However, occasionally, there are reports of measles in developed countries: recent outbreaks have occurred in the Netherlands and Ireland.[5,35] The outbreak in the Netherlands occurred in a semi-isolated religious community whose members refuse immunizations. Such outbreaks present little risk to travelers. However, several thousand cases with several deaths were reported in the year 2000 in Ireland in the general population. Therefore, all travelers should be immune.

In most industrialized countries, children receive measles vaccine between age 12 and 15 months and again at 4 years.[36] The measles vaccine is generally combined with mumps and rubella (MMR) vaccines. Children traveling to areas where measles is still prevalent might need an extra dose at 6 months; protection from maternal measles antibodies wanes after 6 months, and measles can be a serious illness in infants. Parents should check their own immune status for MMR. Traveling with children may increase parents' frequency of exposure to local children.

Some adults in developed countries are not immune to measles.[37] Vaccination in the United States, for example, began in the late 1950s. People born in 1956 or before are assumed to have had the disease during childhood and, therefore, have lifelong immunity.[14] However, some individuals, by chance, did not acquire the disease until adulthood, and the number of such adult cases is higher than is generally appreciated. The same is true for mumps, rubella, and varicella (chickenpox). All of these diseases are far more severe when infection occurs in adulthood. Also, measles vaccines used in the late 1950s and early 1960s were poorly immunogenic.[15] In addition, immunoglobulin sometimes was given simultaneously to reduce side reactions but it also reduced immunogenicity. Between 1963 and 1967, killed virus vaccine was used, resulting in short-term immunity. In the mid-1960s, when the live-virus vaccine was introduced, many people received only one dose. Experience has shown that one dose immunizes only about 90% of recipients; the second dose immunizes 90% of the rest, thus the reason for the two doses.[38] Many developing countries still give only one dose because of cost and logistic problems. Susceptible adults should receive at least one dose, preferably two, given a month apart. There are no known harmful effects when immunizing people already immune.

Rubella and Mumps

Many countries, including some developed ones, do not have universal rubella and mumps vaccination programs, making these common diseases in those countries, with most cases occurring in childhood.[39] A few countries vaccinate only prepubertal females against rubella. If rubella is contracted during pregnancy, the fetus can be severely damaged. Rarely, mumps causes sterility in adult men. Spread of both diseases is by direct or droplet contact with nasopharyngeal secretions.

Most adults are immune to mumps and rubella by having contracted the disease or by immunization. In the United States, large-scale vaccination programs began in the early 1970s and included most children and teenagers. Rubella and mumps vaccines give excellent, probably lifelong immunity from one dose.[15] Vaccination against rubella may be indicated for women contemplating becoming pregnant and not certain of their immunity; however, a blood test can determine immunity. Nearly all children receive two doses of these vaccines, generally as MMR vaccine. Mumps and rubella need not be given before a year as these are generally benign diseases in this age group.

Varicella (Chickenpox)

Varicella is a more serious illness than is generally realized, especially for teenagers and adults; varicella during pregnancy can cause as serious damage to the fetus as rubella.[40] Transmission occurs primarily by direct, close contact with individuals who have the disease or, rarely, with someone who has herpes zoster (caused by the same virus).

Travelers without a definite history of having had varicella should be vaccinated. As with measles, some adults escaped infection in their childhood. Presently, only the United States and Japan have universal varicella vaccination programs, meaning that the disease is still prevalent in most of the world. In developing countries, varicella is commonly seen in young adults. In the tropics, the disease is more likely to result in secondary skin infections.

Vaccination was introduced in the United States in the mid-1990s, but only about 80 to 90% of children are presently being immunized. This results in fewer cases of natural disease in young children, raising the age at which people contract the disease. Experience has shown that vaccinating programs that reach fewer than 90% of children may worsen the morbidity and mortality from "childhood" diseases as compared to vaccinating no one. (In a study in Greece several years ago, only about one-half of all children were receiving rubella vaccine.[41] This raised the average age at which people were having the disease—often to the child-bearing age. The result: an increase in the number of cases of congenital rubella syndrome.)

Children receive one dose of vaccine, usually at age 12 to 15 months. Individuals more than 13 years of age receive two doses, given at least one month apart.[15] The seroconversion rate from one dose is about 80% for the older group compared with more than 95% for those less than 13 years of age. The period of protection is still unknown but appears to be at least 20 years and may be much longer.

Pneumococcal Vaccines

Two pneumococcal vaccines are available in the United States and in some other countries, causing some confusion. The 23-valent polysaccharide vaccine has been available for at least a decade and is generally recommended for adults with chronic illnesses and for the elderly. Individuals with influenza and other upper respiratory infections appear to be at increased risk of pneumococcal infections. In some parts of the world, many strains of pneumococcal bacteria are multidrug resistant. Transmission is from person to person, presumably by respiratory droplet contact.

A seven-valent pneumococcal polysaccharide conjugate vaccine was introduced in the United States in the year 2000. It is intended only for children under the age of 5 years and commonly is given only to children under the age of 2 years.[42] The pneumococcal serogroups that the vaccine protects against are the ones most likely to cause disease in this age group and most likely to be resistant to penicillin. The vast majority of United States children are now being immunized with this vaccine. Crowding increases the incidence of pneumococcal infections and skews the infection to the younger pediatric age groups. Infants traveling overseas may benefit from the vaccine. Optimal protection requires four doses at 2, 4, 6, and about 15 months.[15]

Meningococcal Meningitis

Sporadic cases occur in all countries at all times, but there is an increased incidence among pilgrims to Mecca, Saudi Arabia, for the annual hajj, for people living in the "meningitis belt" in the northern part of sub-Saharan Africa, and during outbreaks that crop up in different parts of the world.[43,44] The meningitis belt extends from Senegal and Guinea on the Atlantic Coast to Ethiopia on the Indian Ocean. In 1996, the largest outbreak ever recorded occurred in the "belt," with an estimated 250,000 cases and 25,000 deaths. In the 1990s, there were limited outbreaks in India, Nepal, Brazil, and southern Africa. Young children and the elderly might be more susceptible to the disease than other age groups. Vaccination is mandatory for entry into Saudi Arabia during the hajj period and is recommended for travelers to endemic areas in Africa, especially during the dry season. Transmission of the causative bacteria is from person to person via minute droplets of upper respiratory secretions. The majority of infected persons are asymptomatic and are carriers of the infection. Vaccination should be completed 10 days before possible exposure. The vaccines appear to be 85 to 90% effective in preventing disease.

Different meningococcal meningitis vaccines are licensed in various countries. The purified polysaccharide vaccine available in North America and other countries is effective against serogroups A, C, Y, and W-135 but not against group B, the cause of sporadic cases and some epidemics.[45] Protection elicited by this quadrivalent vaccine lasts 2 to 3 years, but this vaccine is poorly immunogenic for children less than 2 years of age. In the United States, immunization is recommended for first-year college students living in dormitories because of the risk of predominantly group C infections reported in this population. The incidence in these students, although still low, is almost four times that in the general population. Vaccination may also be indicated for children attending summer camps; several cases have been reported in recent years in such settings. Individuals with certain immune deficiency diseases are also at increased risk and should be vaccinated.

Protein conjugate vaccines for serogroups A and C are available in Great Britain and several other countries.[46] These vaccines produce an immune response in children less than 2 years of age. The recommended schedule for vaccination is ages 2, 4, and 6 months and an additional dose between ages 1 and 4 years (see Chapter 8, "Meningococcal Vaccine").

Tuberculosis

Although tuberculosis (TB) is not generally thought of as a travel-related disease, travel plays an important role in its epidemiology. In an area of California with a high immigrant population, the incidence of positive TB skin tests among children born in the United States and who had traveled to a country with a high incidence of TB was 4.7 times that of matched children who had not traveled (Figure 15-7).[47] In the same area of California, children who had a household visitor from such a country were 2.4 times more likely to have a positive test than those who did not. The risk of TB infection in long-term Dutch travelers to countries with a high incidence of TB is almost of the magnitude of that of the local population.[48] This was true regardless of whether the traveler was involved in health care. Transmission is via inhalation of contaminated droplets produced by the coughing and sneezing of infected individuals. On rare occasions, TB has been contracted in-flight from a passenger seated nearby.[49]

In many countries, both developed and developing, BCG (bacille Calmette-Guérin) vaccine is given to all children, usually at birth.[50] Some developed countries give BCG to travelers, especially children, who will have prolonged and close contact with local populations in countries with high incidences of TB (children of missionaries, for example). BCG might be more effective in preventing complications of TB (meningitis, for example) than in preventing the disease itself.[51] In the United States, BCG is very

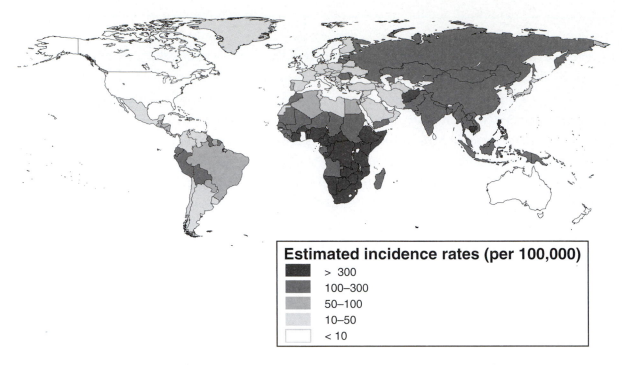

Figure 15-7. Tuberculosis in the year 2000. Adapted from the World Health Organization, 2001 WHO report, Geneva, Switzerland.

rarely used; recommendations are to skin test travelers at risk before and after trips and to treat individuals with positive skin tests with appropriate anti-TB drugs[52] (see Chapter 11, "BCG Vaccine and Tuberculosis Vaccines").

MIGRANTS, IMMIGRANTS, REFUGEES, AND ADOPTEES

Millions of migrant workers, immigrants, and refugees travel across international borders each year, generally from developing countries to developed ones, and many of them are accompanied by children. Most developed countries have regulations concerning health procedures for such groups, but specifics vary greatly from country to country.[53] In addition, large numbers of people, some with children, cross borders illegally and fall between the cracks of health care systems.[54]

Increasingly, migration includes children for adoption.[55] In the United States alone, in 2001, there were almost 20,000 international adoptions, with most of the children originating in Asia (China, Korea, India, Cambodia, the Philippines, and Vietnam), Central and South America (Guatemala and Colombia), and eastern Europe (Russia, Romania, and the Ukraine).[56]

The majority of the children in these categories of travelers come from deprived backgrounds and have had limited access to health care.[57] Many of the children have no written records of immunizations or have records that are incomplete, unacceptable (because of vaccine doses given at inappropriate ages or at improper intervals, for example), or fraudulent (doses dated before the child was born, for example). Children sometimes do not have demonstrable antibodies to diseases that their records show that they were immunized against. However, the validity of such studies might be limited by the methodology used—inability to detect protective antibodies to vaccines used in the country of the child's origin, for example. Most vaccines currently used worldwide are produced with adequate quality control standards and are considered immunogenic. Testing for antibody levels can help reduce the number of injections that need to be given.

Most experts believe that written documentation should be accepted as evidence of previous immunization if the vaccines, dates of administration, intervals between doses, and age of the child at the time of immunization are comparable with current WHO or local schedules. Detailed information on routine recommended schedules by country can be found on the World Health Organization Web site. Many countries also have their own Web sites. For the United States, information about vaccinations and other health issues regarding international adoptees is available at the State Department Web site.

IMMUNOSUPPRESSION AND TRAVEL

Virtually no data exist concerning travel for children who are immunosuppressed. Vaccinating such children is best done by people with expertise in pediatric vaccinology and immunosuppression, in consultation with experts in travel medicine and, if necessary, tropical medicine. Issues that need addressing include the importance of the trip, the age of the child, the cause and degree of suppression (the CD4+ lymphocyte count, for example), the risk of acquiring a particular disease during travel and the possible consequences of that disease, the effects of each vaccine on an immunosuppressed child, and the accessibility and quality of health services available during travel, to mention just a few. In some cases, from a medical standpoint, travel might be contraindicated, and parents must be apprised of such facts. Causes of immunosuppression in children include infection with HIV; congenital immunodeficiency states, malignant diseases, and associated medications and radiation therapy used to treat such diseases, and organ transplants. At times, immunosuppression is temporary, the result of radiation or chemotherapy, and travel can be postponed until several weeks or months after treatment is concluded.

Immunosuppressed children are especially susceptible to many infectious diseases. Furthermore, immunosuppression can alter the effects of vaccines, generally making them less immunogenic and resulting in susceptibility to the disease even after optimal vaccination, and shorten the period of protection. With live vaccines, immunosuppressed recipients may be unable to contain the replicating vaccine virus, causing vaccine-related disease, which can be as severe, or more so, than the wild disease. Generally, the greater the degree of immunosuppression, the poorer the immune response. In some cases, additional vaccine doses supplement for poorer response per dose. Often, antibody titers can determine immunity. In some situations, protection with disease-specific immunoglobulin can substitute for vaccination (varicella, for example). If travel is to a country that requires yellow fever vaccine as a condition of entry but the travel is to an area in that country with little or no disease, it might be prudent to advise maximum insect protection and give the family a letter explaining the situation. Such letters are generally honored.

Generally, inactivated, conjugated, and polysaccharide vaccines (DTaP, pneumococcal, *Haemophilus influenzae*, hepatitis A and B, and inactivated polio) are safe in immunocompromised individuals, albeit the immune response may be less than optimal. However, live-viruses vaccines (MMR, varicella, yellow fever, oral typhoid, and oral polio) should be given only by experts in this field and after weighing the risks and benefits. The severity and type of immunosuppression may determine whether these vaccines should be given (see Chapter 17, "Travel Immunizations for Special Risk Groups: Pregnant, Immune Compromised").

HYPERSENSITIVITY REACTIONS TO COMMONLY USED CHILDHOOD AND TRAVEL-RELATED VACCINES

Significant hypersensitivity reactions to routine pediatric vaccines are extremely rare. Nevertheless, health care professionals who administer vaccines, especially to infants and children, must be aware of the components of vaccines and potential reactions from vaccines and be prepared to deal with reactions, including anaphylaxis.[58] Vaccines contain numerous ingredients in addition to the immunizing antigen. These ingredients include suspending fluids (egg protein in the cases of some vaccines), preservatives, antibiotics, and adjuvants (substances such as aluminum to enhance immunogenicity, for example). Ingredients vary from one vaccine to the next and between similar vaccines produced by different manufacturers.

Parents should be asked about previous reactions to vaccines and about other allergies. Measles and mumps vaccines, for example, are derived from chick embryo fibroblasts tissue culture but do not contain significant amounts of egg protein. Children with egg allergies can be given these vaccines without skin testing. Yellow fever and influenza vaccines contain egg protein and, rarely, induce immediate allergic reactions, including anaphylaxis[59] Skin testing for yellow fever vaccine sensitivity should be performed before administration to persons reporting egg allergies, especially to those with a history of systemic anaphylactic symptoms (see Chapter 5, "Yellow Fever Vaccine"). For yellow fever vaccine, the risk-to-benefit ratio might favor not vaccinating. Severe reactions are sometimes seen to gelatin and neomycin, which are present in many vaccines. Techniques for testing for allergens are available in most pediatrics and allergy/immunology textbooks.

REFERENCES

1. Knirsch CA. Travel medicine and health issues for families traveling with children. Adv Pediatr Infect Dis 1999;14:163–89.

2. World Health Organization. Department of Vaccines and Biologicals. Vaccine preventable diseases, 2001 global summary. Geneva: WHO; 2001.

3. Reaney EA, Tohani VK, Devine MJ, et al. Mumps outbreak among young people in Northern Ireland. Commun Dis Public Health 2001;4:311–5.

4. Kew O, Morris-Glasgow V, Landavere M, et al. Outbreak of poliomyelitis in Hispaniola associated with circulating type 1 vaccine–derived poliovirus. Science 2002;296:356–9.

5. Coughlan S, Connell J, Cohen B, et al. Suboptimal measles-mumps-rubella vaccination coverage facilitates an imported measles outbreak in Ireland. Clin Infect Dis 2002;35:84–6.

6. de Melker HE, Conyn–van Spaedonck MA, et al. Pertussis in the Netherlands. An outbreak despite high levels of immunization with whole-cell vaccine. Emerg Infect Dis 1997;3(2):175–8.

7. Sheldon T. Dutch whooping cough epidemic puzzles scientists. BMJ 1998;316(7125):92.

8. Centers for Disease Control and Prevention. Diphtheria epidemic in the new independent states of the former Soviet Union, 1990–1994. MMWR Morb Mortal Wkly Rep 1995;44:177–81.

9. Centers for Disease Control and Prevention. Health information for international travel, 2001–2002. Atlanta (GA): Department of Health and Human Services, Public Health Services; 2001.

10. Centers for Disease Control and Prevention. Standards for pediatric immunization practices. Recommended by the National Vaccine Advisory Committee, approved by the U.S. Public Health Service. MMWR Morb Mortal Wkly Rep 1993;42(RR-5):1–13.

11. Barnett ED, Chen R. Children and international travel. Immunization. Pediatr Infect Dis J 1995;14:982–92.

12. King GE, Hadler SC. Simultaneous administration of childhood vaccines. An important public health policy that is safe and efficacious. Pediatr Infect Dis J 1994;13:394–407.

13. Dashefsky B, Wald E, Guerra N, et al. Safety, tolerability, and immunogenicity of concurrent administration of *Haemophilus influenzae* type B conjugate vaccine (meningococcal protein conjugate) with either measles-mumps-rubella vaccine or diphtheria. Pediatrics 1990;85(4 Pt 2):682–9.

14. Centers for Disease Control and Prevention. General recommendations on immunizations. Recommendations of the Advisory Committee on Immunization Practices and the American Academy of Family Practices. MMWR Morb Mortal Wkly Rep 2002;51(RR-2):1–27.

15. Pickering LK. Report of the Committee on Infectious Diseases. Elk Grove Village (IL): American Academy of Pediatrics; 2000.

16. Simonsen L, Kane A, Loyd J, et al. Unsafe injections in the developing world and transmission of bloodborne pathogens. A review. Bull World Health Organ 1999;77:789–800.

17. Siegrist CA, Cordova M, Brandt C, et al. Determinants of infant responses to vaccines in presence of maternal antibodies. Vaccine 1998;16:1409–14.

18. Siegrist CA. Vaccination in the neonatal period and early infancy. Int Rev Immunol 2000;19:195–219.

19. Centers for Disease Control and Prevention. Diphtheria, tetanus, and pertussis. Recommendations for vaccine use and other preventive measures. Recommendations of the Immunization Practices Advisory Committee. MMWR Morb Mortal Wkly Rep 1991;40(RR-10):1–28.

20. Mortimer EA Jr, Wharton M. Diphtheria toxoid. In: Plotkin SA, Orenstein WA, editors. Vaccines. 3rd ed. Philadelphia: WB Saunders 1999.

21. Centers for Disease Control and Prevention. Acute flaccid paralysis associated with circulating vaccine-derived poliovirus—Philippines, 2001. MMWR Morb Mortal Wkly Rep 2001;50:874–5.

22. Centers for Disease Control and Prevention. Imported wild poliovirus causing poliomyelitis—Bulgaria, 2001. MMWR Morb Mortal Wkly Rep 2001;50:1033–5.

23. Blakely TA, Mansoor O, Baker M, et al. The 1996 pertussis epidemic in New Zealand. Vaccine effectiveness. N Z Med J 1999;112:118–20.

24. World Health Organization. "Endgame" issues for the global polio eradication initiative. Technical Consultative Group on the Global Eradication of Poliomyelitis. Clin Infect Dis 2002;34:72–7.

25. Centers for Disease Control and Prevention. Laboratory surveillance for wild poliovirus and vaccine-derived poliovirus, 2000–2001. MMWR Morb Mortal Wkly Rep 2002;51:369–71.

26. Centers for Disease Control and Prevention. Poliomyelitis prevention in the United States. Updated recommendations of the Advisory Committee on Immunization Practices. MMWR Morb Mortal Wkly Rep 2000;49(RR-5):1–22.

27. World Health Organization. Department of Vaccines and Biologicals Vaccine Assessment and Monitoring Team. Countries using hepatitis B vaccine in their national immunization system (2000). Geneva: WHO; 2002.

28. World Health Organization. Safety of injections. Facts and figures. Fact Sheet No. 232. October 1999. Available at http://www.who.int/vaccines-surveillance/ISPP/CDRom/alldocs/allothers/fs232sftyofinjctnsfactseng.htm (accessed April 4 2003).

29. Kane A, Lloyd J, Zaffran M, et al. Transmission of hepatitis B, hepatitis C and human immunodeficiency viruses through unsafe injections in the developing world. Model-based regional estimates. Bull World Health Organ 1999;77:801–7.

30. Centers for Disease Control and Prevention. Hepatitis B virus. A comprehensive strategy for eliminating transmission in the United States through universal childhood vaccination. MMWR Morb Mortal Wkly Rep 1991;40(RR1-13).

31. Nothdurft HD, Dietrich M, Zuckerman JN, et al. A new accelerated vaccination schedule for rapid protection against hepatitis A and B. Vaccine 2002;20:1157–62.

32. Global Programme for Vaccines and Immunization (GPV). The WHO position paper on *Haemophilus influenza* type b conjugate vaccines. Wkly Epidemiol Rec 1998;73:64–8.

33. Centers for Disease Control and Prevention. *Haemophilus* b conjugate vaccines for prevention of *Haemophilus influenzae* type b disease among infants and children two months of age and older. Recommendations of the Immunization Practices Advisory Committee. MMWR Morb Mortal Wkly Rep 1991;40(RR-1):1–7.

34. Orenstein WA, Strebel PM, et al. Measles eradication. Is it in our future? Am J Public Health 2000;90:1521–5.

35. Conyn–van Spaendock MA, van den Hof S, Meffre CM, et al. Measles outbreak in a community with very low vaccine coverage, the Netherlands. Emerg Infect Dis 2001;7(3 Suppl):593–7.

36. Centers for Disease Control and Prevention. Measles, mumps, and rubella-vaccine use and strategies for elimination of measles, rubella, and congenital rubella syndrome and control of mumps. Recommendations of the Advisory Committee on Immunization Practices. MMWR Morb Mortal Wkly Rep 1998;47(RR-8):1–57.

37. Centers for Disease Control and Prevention. Measles—United States, 2000. MMWR Morb Mortal Wkly Rep 2002;51:120–3.

38. Centers for Disease Control and Prevention. Measles eradication. MMWR Morb Mortal Wkly Rep 1997;46(RR-11):1–19.

39. Plotkin SA. Rubella eradication. Vaccine 2001;19:3311–9.

40. Centers for Disease Control and Prevention. Prevention of varicella. Recommendations of the Advisory Committee on Immunization Practices. MMWR Morb Mortal Wkly Rep 1996;45(RR-11):8.

41. Panagiotopoulos T, Antoniadou I, Volassi-Adam E, et al. Increase in congenital rubella occurrence after immunisation in Greece. Retrospective survey and systematic review. BMJ 1999;319:1462–7.

42. Centers for Disease Control and Prevention. Preventing pneumococcal disease among infants and young children. Recommendations of the Advisory Committee on Immunization Practices. MMWR Morb Mortal Wkly Rep 2000;49(RR-9):1–35.

43. Pollard AJ, Shlim DR. Epidemic meningococcal disease and travel. J Travel Med 2002;9:29–33.

44. Memish ZA. Meningococcal disease and travel. Clin Infect Dis 2002;34:84–90.

45. Centers for Disease Control and Prevention. Control and prevention of meningococcal disease. MMWR Morb Mortal Wkly Rep 1997;46(RR-5):1–21.

46. Maiden MC, Spratt BG. Meningococcal conjugate vaccines. New opportunities and new challenges. Lancet 1999;354:615–6.

47. Lobato MN, Hopewell PC. Mycobacterium tuberculosis infection after travel to or contact with visitors from countries with a high prevalence of tuberculosis. Am J Respir Crit Care Med 1998;158:1871–5.

48. Cobelens FG, van Deutekom H, Draayer-Jansen IW, et al. Risk of infection with *Mycobacterium tuberculosis* in travellers to areas of high tuberculosis endemicity. Lancet 2000;356:461–5.

49. WHO guidelines address risk of tuberculosis transmission during air travel. Cent Eur J Public Health 1999;7:144,154.

50. Houston S. Tuberculosis risk and prevention in travelers. What about BCG? J Travel Med 1997;4:76–82.

51. Colditz GA, Berkey CS, Mosteller F, et al. The efficacy of bacillus Calmette-Guérin vaccination of newborns and infants in the prevention of tuberculosis. Meta-analyses of the published literature. Pediatrics 1995;96:29-35.

52. Centers for Disease Control and Prevention. The role of BCG vaccine in the prevention and control of tuberculosis in the United States. A joint statement by the Advisory Committee on Immunization Practices and Advisory Council for the Elimination of Tuberculosis. MMWR Morb Mortal Wkly Rep 1996;45(RR-4):1–1.

53. World Health Organization. Monitoring immunization coverage of migrants. Expanded programme for vaccines and immunizations. Geneva (Switz): WHO; 1998.

54. Loutan L, Ghaznawi H. The migrant as a traveler. In: DuPont HL, Steffen R, editors. Textbook of travel medicine and health. Hamilton (Canada): BC Decker; 2001;1–18.

55. Hostetter MK, Johnson DE. Immunization status of adoptees from China Russia, and Eastern Europe [abstract 851]. Paper presented at the 1998 Pediatric Academic Societies Annual Meeting, New Orleans, May 5, 1998.

56. Department of State. International adoptions. Washington (DC): Department of State; 2001.

57. Saiman L, Aronson J, Zhou J, et al. Prevalence of infectious diseases among internationally adopted children. Pediatrics 2001;108:608–12.

58. Grabenstein JD. Clinical management of hypersensitivities to vaccine components. Hosp Pharm 1997;32:77–87.

59. James JM, Zeiger RS, Lester MR, et al. Safe administration of influenza vaccine to patients with egg allergy. J Pediatr 1998;133:624–8.

60. Centers for Disease Control. Combination vaccines for childhood immunization. Recommendations of the Advisory Committee on Immunization Practices (ACIP), the American Academy of Pediatrics (AAP), and the American Academy of Family Physicians (AAFP). MMWR Morb Mortal Wkly 1999;48(RR-5):5.

61. Centers for Disease Control. Prevention of pneumococcal disease. Recommendations of the Advisory Committee on Immunization Practices (ACIP). MMWR Morb Mortal Wkly 1997;46(RR-8):1–24.

Chapter 16

AMERICAN COLLEGE HEALTH PERSPECTIVE: ROUTINE AND TRAVEL IMMUNIZATIONS IN COLLEGE-AGED AND OLDER ADULTS

Betty Anne Johnson

The enrollment of large numbers of foreign students in colleges and universities in the United States has resulted in the need for detailed information on immunization practices and student health requirements on US campuses, which vary from state to state. Such information can guide families and health care providers in the students' home countries who are responsible for preparing the students to meet entry requirements for student health. On the other hand, the growth in participation of American-born students in international programs and exchanges means that student health centers and other providers in the United States must be knowledgeable about immunization practices and communicable diseases in the destination countries abroad.

In the United States, one of the greatest public health achievements of the twentieth century has been the development and universal use of vaccines against many common infectious diseases. Since 1955, when federal funds were first used to promote polio vaccine use among all children, state and local governments and public and private health care providers have collaborated with the federal government in developing and maintaining the vaccine delivery system in the United States.[1] By 1990, vaccines for nine diseases (smallpox, diphtheria, pertussis, tetanus, polio, measles, mumps, rubella, and *Haemophilus influenzae* type b) had been used in routine childhood immunization programs, and morbidity for these diseases had either been eliminated (smallpox, wild-type polio) or had declined by nearly 100%.

Since 1990, new vaccines have come into routine use, namely, hepatitis A and B and varicella. The Advisory Committee on Immunization Practices (ACIP) at the Centers for Disease Control and Prevention (CDC) regularly issues guidelines that (1) incorporate new vaccines into the schedule for routine immunization of children and (2) make provision for "catch-up" immunization of older children and adolescents. Although there is no national immunization law, most states mandate that routine immunizations be received and documented prior to entry into day care or the school systems, whether public or private, and, therefore, vaccine coverage of 90 to 100% is the norm for children.[2]

For adults, however, there is no similar coercive mechanism to ensure high vaccine coverage rates across all populations. There is, in general, a lower rate of coverage with regard to the recommended vaccines covered by the *Recommended Adult Immunization Schedule—United States, 2002–2003*.[3]

In addition to being immunized against childhood diseases, adults need booster shots of tetanus and diphtheria, and they might also need to be immunized against hepatitis A and B, influenza, and pneumococcal infections. Prior to embarking on international travel, boosters or additional doses of vaccines against measles-mumps-rubella (MMR) and polio might be recommended, and immunity to varicella (chickenpox) should be verified.

VACCINES AND COLLEGE HEALTH

Individual institutions of higher education, in conjunction with the American College Health Association (ACHA), ACIP, and state governments, determine these prematriculation immunization requirements, and college health services enforce them, usually by denying access to ongoing registration for classes unless immunization requirements are fulfilled.

For institutions of higher education that have college health services on campus, oversight of prematriculation immunization requirements is a major role of the student health service. Computerized medical information systems with tracking mechanisms have assisted in this task, but lack of written, dated documentation of previous immunizations is one of the major obstacles faced by college health services managing these programs. Although all states and the District of Columbia have adopted official immunization cards, students and parents often cannot supply this information. With the exception of pneumococcal vaccination, the ACIP advises against accepting self-reporting of immunization doses.[4,5] Therefore, if records cannot be located, age-appropriate immunizations are begun, or, alternatively, students may have serum antibody tests to determine immunity against measles, mumps, rubella, varicella, hepatitis B, and, rarely, tetanus, diphtheria, and/or polio. The current ACHA recommendations for immunizations prior to college entry are shown in Table 16-1. However, there is freedom to interpret these requirements, as evidenced by a recent survey of ACHA-affiliated schools. Of the 716 respondents to a survey on immunization practices sent to 1,200 schools in the year 1999, only 71% indicated that their prematriculation immunization requirements were mandated by their state government.[6]

The 1999 college immunization survey indicated that although 93 to 99% of schools routinely view vaccine coverage for measles, mumps, and rubella as a requirement, vaccine coverage for diphtheria, tetanus, and, most particularly, polio are subject to less rigorous review (Figure 16-1), as these diseases are sometimes perceived as less of a public health threat on campus. In addition, until the ACIP changed its recommendations to an all-inactivated virus vaccine schedule for routine immunization against polio, college health practitioners, because of the fear of vaccine-associated paralytic poliomyelitis, were reluctant to use oral polio vaccine to complete deficiencies in vaccination histories.[7]

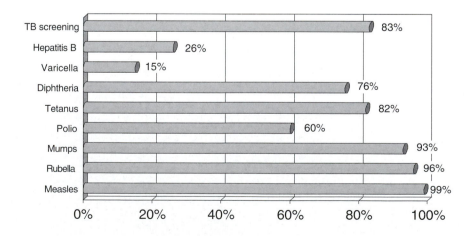

Figure 16-1. Prematriculation immunization requirements in postsecondary schools affiliated with the American College Health Association. Adapted from Capparella et al.[68] TB = tuberculosis.

Table 16-1. American College Health Association Recommendations for Institutional Prematriculation Immunizations

Vaccine[†]	Age Indicated	Major Indications	Major Precautions
Measles, mumps, rubella (MMR)	First dose at age 12–15 mo or later; second dose at age 4–6 yr or later	All entering college students born after 1956	Pregnancy; history of anaphylactic reaction to eggs or neomycin; immunosuppression; appropriate for HIV+ persons
Tetanus, diphtheria, pertussis	Primary series in childhood with DTaP or DTP, booster at age 11–12 yr with Td, then every 10 yr	All college students	History of neurologic hypersensitivity reaction following a previous dose
Polio vaccine	Primary series in childhood with IPV alone, OPV alone, or IPV/OPV sequentially; booster only if needed for travel after age 18 yr	IPV for certain international travelers	OPV should not be given to immunocompromised or HIV+ persons
Varicella	Childhood, adolescence, young adulthood	All entering college students without history of the disease or without age-appropriate immunization or with a negative antibody titer (2 doses ≥ 1 mo apart, if age > 13 yr)	Pregnancy
Hepatitis B	Series of 3 doses (given at 0, 1–2 mo, and 6–12 mo) prior to college entry	All college students	None
Meningococcal quadrivalent polysaccharide vaccine	> 2 yr, repeat every 3–5 yr	Certain high-risk groups, including persons with terminal complement deficiencies or those with asplenia; research/laboratory personnel who might be exposed to aerosolized meningococci*	None

DTaP = diphtheria and tetanus toxoids and acellular pertussis vaccine; DTP = diphtheria-tetanus-pertussis vaccine; HIV = human immunodeficiency virus; IPV = inactivated poliovirus vaccine; OPV = oral poliovirus vaccine.

*The Advisory Committee on Immunization Practices (ACIP) revised its recommendations for the use of the meningococcal quadrivalent polysaccharide vaccine in college students. It should continue to be used to control outbreaks of serogroups C, Y, W-135, and A. Furthermore, based on evidence that college freshmen living in dormitories or residence halls are at modestly increased risk of meningococcal disease relative to other persons their age, a final recommendation was published as follows. Practitioners who provide medical care to freshmen, particularly those who live in or plan to live in dormitories should

• inform students and their parents about meningococcal disease and the benefits of vaccination,
• provide vaccine or make it easily available to those freshmen who wish to reduce their risk of disease, and
• offer vaccine to other undergraduates < 25 yr who wish to reduce their risk.[49]

†Other recommendations:
• ACIP and American College Health Association (ACHA) encourage all college students (particularly those at high risk of complications from influenza or those living in dormitories) to receive influenza vaccine annually during autumn to minimize disruption of routine activities during campus-wide epidemics.
• Immunization requirements and recommendations for international travel may vary depending on personal medical history and travel destination. Anyone anticipating international travel should contact a health care provider for specific information.

Although the ACHA recommends immunization against hepatitis B for all college students who are not already immune, relatively few institutions (28/665; 4.2%) mandate this vaccine for entry except for those students entering health sciences programs.[6] Cost to the student was the primary concern cited by college health services for not mandating hepatitis B immunization.[6] Although the series of three vaccinations for adolescents is covered under most health insurance plans or under state childhood immunization programs for children and adolescents up to and including 18 years of age, it can cost approximately $100 to $150 (US) for the uninsured.

Varicella vaccine is another ACHA-recommended vaccine that is rarely mandated for college entry except for students entering health sciences programs. In the 1999 college immunization survey, among student health service users, 1,091 cases of varicella were reported on 335 campuses during the 1996 to 1997 school year. An additional 1,148 cases of varicella and 1,339 cases of herpes zoster were reported in 1997 to 1998 on 394 campuses.[6] However, formal surveillance of the incidence of varicella and herpes zoster on college campuses has not been conducted since varicella vaccine was added to the routine childhood immunization schedule in the United States in 1996.[8]

Some student health services contract outside vendors to deliver large-volume immunization clinics during the fall semester. These vendors take care of marketing, supplies, staffing, and billing, thus relieving the staff of the student health service of these tasks but incurring additional administrative costs. Often, influenza and meningococcal vaccinations are targeted during these clinics.

VACCINES AND INTERNATIONAL STUDENTS

Every year, more than 500,000 international students enter the United States to pursue postsecondary studies. As is true for American-born students, international students must comply with institutional prematriculation immunization requirements; however, interpreting immunization information supplied by international students can be difficult. As documented by the World Health Organization (WHO), routine immunization programs in other countries are very different from those in the United States.[9] Only written documentation should be accepted. These records are more likely to predict protection if the vaccines, dates of administration, intervals between doses, and age of the student at the time of immunization are similar to US standards.[5] If doubt exists, either revaccination or serum antibody tests are recommended to ensure immunity. Varicella and hepatitis B might not be routine immunizations in other countries. Quadrivalent A, C, Y, W-135 meningococcal polysaccharide vaccine that is given in the United States might not be available in many countries, but the A-C and C-conjugate vaccines given in many countries should provide protection against the serogroup C meningococcal disease outbreaks that have been reported as a particular risk for freshman living in dormitories on US campuses.

VACCINE ADVERSE REACTIONS IN COLLEGE STUDENTS

All vaccines have the potential to cause adverse reactions. Adverse reactions are classified into three general categories. (1) Local reactions include pain and swelling at the injection site. These reactions are the most frequent and the least severe. (2) Systemic reactions, including fever, occur less frequently than do local reactions. (3) Serious allergic reactions, such as anaphylaxis, are rare.

Health care providers who administer vaccines should be prepared to manage acute allergic reactions and should have emergency procedures in place. In adolescents and young adults, vasovagal or vasodepressor syncope occurs more frequently than in other age groups. Forty percent of syncopal episodes reported to the Vaccine Adverse Event Reporting System (VAERS) occurred among persons aged 10 to 18 years.[5] Approximately 12% of syncopal events result in hospitalization and serious injury, including skull fracture and cerebral bleeding. Observing the patient for 15 to 20 minutes after administration of vaccine can reduce the likelihood of serious injury.

DISEASE-SPECIFIC VACCINES

Measles, Mumps, and Rubella

Measles

Measles (rubeola) is a highly contagious respiratory viral disease characterized by fever, malaise, cough, coryza, and conjunctivitis with lacrimation. A characteristic rash is the hallmark of the disease. The rash is erythematous, nonpruritic, and maculopapular. It begins at the hairline and behind the ears and spreads down the trunk and limbs to involve the palms and soles. Koplik's spots (1–2 mm bluish-white spots on a red background) can appear on the buccal mucosa near the second molars before the rash and are diagnostic of the disease. The disease is more severe in adults than in children.

Complications from the disease can be respiratory (primary viral pneumonia or secondary bacterial pneumonias), neurologic (postinfectious encephalomyelitis; subacute sclerosing, panencephalitis; or transverse myelitis), or gastrointestinal (gastroenteritis, hepatitis, appendicitis, ileocolitis, or mesenteric adenitis).

Measles is transmitted by exposure to respiratory secretions. Humans are the only natural host, and the distribution of the disease is worldwide in countries where measles vaccine is not in routine use.

In the United States, both inactivated and attenuated live measles vaccines were used from 1963 to 1967. Because inactivated vaccine proved to be less effective than live attenuated vaccine, individuals vaccinated prior to 1968 should be revaccinated using the current protocol. Since 1968, only attenuated vaccine has been used. The number of measles cases increased in the United States in 1990 because of incomplete primary vaccination of infants and young children but also, in some cases, because of waning immunity. By 1993, after instituting a two-dose measles vaccine requirement (49 states have such a requirement for school-age children), transmission of indigenous measles in the United States was interrupted.[10] Of the 86 cases of measles reported in the United States in the year 2000, most were importation associated.[10] However, measles remains a serious problem. In 1999, an estimated 30 million cases of measles with 875,000 deaths occurred worldwide.[11]

Measles Vaccine Indication. Because most cases of measles in the United States are now imported, college health providers should scrutinize carefully the immunization records of entering international students for evidence of measles immunity. Adults who might be at increased risk of exposure or transmission of disease, including persons attending college or working in health care facilities, should receive special consideration for vaccination. Furthermore, as measles remains endemic in many developing nations worldwide, prior to traveling or living abroad, individuals should ensure that they have adequate immunity to measles as indicated by any one of the following conditions:

- They have documented administration of two doses of live measles virus vaccine given after 1967. The first dose should have been given on or after the first birthday. The second dose should be administered no earlier than 28 days after the first dose.
- They have laboratory evidence of immunity (immunoglobulin [Ig]G antibody).
- They were born before 1957 (likely to have been infected naturally and are not susceptible).
- They have documentation of physician-diagnosed measles.[12]

The trivalent MMR vaccine should be used whenever any of the individual components of the vaccine is indicated. There is no evidence that giving the trivalent MMR increases the risk of adverse reactions among persons who are already immune to measles, mumps, or rubella because of previous infection or vaccination.[5]

Measles Vaccine Composition. Measles vaccine can be given as a monovalent vaccine, a combined vaccine with rubella, or a combined vaccine with mumps and rubella (MMR). Each dose of either monovalent or combined vaccine contains approximately 0.3 mg of human albumin, 25 µg of neomycin, 14.5 mg of sorbitol, and 14.5 mg of hydrolyzed gelatin.[13] Live measles vaccine is produced in chick embryo cell culture (Table 16-2).

Pregnancy. Measles vaccination is contraindicated during pregnancy. Health providers should counsel reproductive-age women to avoid pregnancy for at least 28 days after administration of rubella-containing vaccines.[13]

Contraindications. Measles vaccine is a live vaccine and should not be given to persons in severe immunocompromised states, including individuals with congenital immunodeficiency disorders, leukemia, lymphoma, or generalized malignancy or to those whose immunologic response has been compromised by steroids, chemotherapeutic agents, or radiation. The degree to which a patient is immunocompromised should be determined by a physician. Guidelines exist for vaccination of persons with altered immunocompetence.[12,14] Measles vaccine should not be given to pregnant women or to individuals with hypersensitivity or a history of anaphylaxis to any of the components in the vaccine, particularly gelatin.[4] Routine vaccination should be deferred during acute illness.

Mumps

Mumps is a highly contagious respiratory viral infection characterized by swelling of one or both of the parotid glands. The virus replicates in the respiratory tract and then spreads via the bloodstream to other glandular tissue and/or the central nervous system. The disease is accompanied by fever, malaise, myalgia, and anorexia. Complications can include orchitis, oophoritis, and aseptic meningitis, encephalitis, and a variety of other nervous system disorders. Mumps is spread by droplet nuclei, saliva, and fomites.

Mumps is endemic in many countries of the world where childhood vaccination is not routine. Mumps vaccine was introduced in the United States in 1967, and the current live attenuated mumps vaccine (Jeryl Lynn strain) is highly effective.[12] Mumps incidence has been at record lows in all areas of the United States in the past few years, possibly reflecting the change to the two-dose MMR schedule, whereby the second dose of vaccine serves to immunize children who failed to respond to the initial dose. Mumps vaccine is usually administered as part of the trivalent MMR vaccine at age 12 to 15 months and again at 4 to 12 years. MMR is generally also used for adolescents and adults who need any one of the components of this vaccine.

Table 16-2. **Measles, Mumps, and Rubella Vaccines Available in the United States**

	Attenuvax	*Mumpsvax*	*Meruvax*	*M-R-Vax*	*Biavax II*	*M-M-R II*
Manufacturer	Merck	Merck	Merck	Merck	Merck	Merck
Viability	Live attenuated measles virus	Live attenuated mumps virus	Live attenuated rubella virus	Live attenuated measles and rubella viruses	Live attenuated mumps and rubella viruses	Live attenuated measles, mumps, and rubella viruses
How supplied	Single-dose and 10 mL vial	Single-dose vial	Single-dose vial	Single-dose and 10 mL vial	Single-dose syringe and 10 mL vial	Single-dose and 10-dose vial
Protection						
Onset	Within 2–3 weeks of the first dose for measles and mumps; within 2–6 weeks of the first dose for rubella					
Duration	Probably lifelong in most persons					
Efficacy	Measles: > 99% of individuals who receive two doses of vaccine after their first birthday will develop serologic evidence of immunity Mumps: > 97% of individuals vaccinated with mumps vaccine will develop measurable antibody; field studies indicate that the vaccine efficacy ranges from 75 to 95% in preventing disease Rubella: seroconversion in > 95% of recipients ≥ 12 mo; clinical studies indicate vaccine efficacy > 90%[12]					
Pregnancy	Contraindicated; reproductive-age women should avoid pregnancy for at least 28 days after administration of measles-containing vaccines.[13]					
Contraindications	Severe immunocompromise; hypersensitivity or history of anaphylaxis to any vaccine component, particularly gelatin; acute illness (defer routine immunization)*					
Dosage, route, and site	0.5 mL injection SC in the outer aspect of the upper arm with a 25-gauge (⅝ inch) needle					
Drug interactions	Can be administered at the same time as other live or inactivated vaccines;[3,12] live virus vaccines not administered on the same day should be administered ≥ 4 weeks apart whenever possible; blood and other antibody-containing products can inhibit the production of measles antibody for 3 months or greater; a tuberculin skin test should be placed at the same time as administration of measles vaccine to avoid false-negative reactions; measles vaccine does not interfere with the reading of the skin test in 48–72 h[12]					

Adapted from Centers for Disease Control and Prevention.[5,14]

SC = subcutaneous.

*See "Contraindications" subsection in the "Measles" section of this chapter.

Mumps Vaccine Indication. Mumps vaccine is indicated for any child or adult who lacks immunity to the disease. Adults who are at increased risk of exposure or transmission of disease, including persons attending college or working in health care facilities, should receive special consideration in vaccination. Because mumps remains endemic in many developing nations worldwide, prior to traveling or living abroad, individuals should ensure that they have adequate immunity to mumps by having

- documented administration of one dose of live mumps virus vaccine, given on or after the first birthday and after June 1967 (in general, the trivalent MMR vaccine should be used whenever any of the individual components of the vaccine is indicated), or
- laboratory evidence of immunity, or
- birth date before 1957, or
- documentation of physician-diagnosed mumps.[12]

Mumps Vaccine Composition. Mumps vaccine is available either in monovalent mumps or in combination. Each dose of either monovalent or combined vaccine contains approximately 0.3 mg of human albumin, 25 μg of neomycin, 14.5 mg of sorbitol, and 14.5 mg of hydrolyzed gelatin.[12] Live mumps vaccine is produced in chick embryo cell culture (see Table 16-2).

Rubella (German Measles)

Rubella is an acute respiratory viral infection of children and adults. Although a high percentage of infections are subclinical, symptoms that characterize the disease include rash, fever, and lymphadenopathy. Adults can develop arthritis, and rubella during the first trimester of pregnancy leads to a constellation of significant malformations known as congenital rubella syndrome (CRS).

Rubella is spread through respiratory secretions. Prior to the introduction of the vaccine in 1969, major epidemics occurred every 6 to 9 years, most often affecting schoolchildren. The last epidemic in the United States occurred in 1964 to 1965 and involved 12 million cases, including 20,000 cases of CRS. Since 1969, there have been no epidemics, and the number of cases of rubella and CRS has decreased dramatically. Further improvement occurred in 1977 when the ACIP modified its vaccine recommendations to include postpubertal girls and women. At the same time, the National Childhood Immunization Initiative sought to improve immunization rates to more than 90% of children by enforcing vaccination requirements prior to school entry.[13]

Analysis of US data from the 1990s reveals that whereas the incidence of rubella in children younger than 15 years has decreased (0.63 vs 0.06/100,000 in 1990 vs 1999), the incidence in adults aged 15 to 44 has increased (0.13 vs 0.24/100,000).[15] Lack of epidemiologic evidence of endemic transmission, together with molecular typing of viral strains, suggests that indigenous rubella is on the verge of elimination in the United States. At-risk populations in the United States, however, include the foreign born, particularly foreign-born Hispanic adults.

Worldwide, rubella remains endemic in countries where childhood immunizations are not routine, and prior to traveling or living in developing countries, travelers should ensure adequate immunity.

Rubella Vaccine Indications. Rubella vaccine is indicated for children or for adults who lack immunity. Adults who might be at increased risk of exposure or transmission of disease, including persons attending college or working in health care facilities, should receive special consideration for vaccination. Prior to traveling or living abroad, individuals should ensure that they have adequate immunity to rubella by having

- documented administration of one dose of rubella virus vaccine, given on or after the first birthday and after June 1969 (in general, the trivalent MMR vaccine should be used whenever any of the individual components of the vaccine is indicated), or
- laboratory evidence of immunity, or
- birth date before 1957 (except for women who could become pregnant).[12]

Rubella Vaccine Composition. Live rubella virus vaccine produced in the United States contains virus strain RA 27/3 and was licensed in 1969. It is prepared in human diploid cell culture (see Table 16-2).

Side Effects. Rubella vaccine can cause arthralgias or arthritis, especially in adult women. These complications are generally self-limited, with frank arthritis usually lasting only about a week.

Poliomyelitis

Poliomyelitis is caused by three serotypes of poliovirus: types 1, 2, and 3. In countries where wild-type virus still exists, paralytic disease is most commonly caused by serotype 1 or, less frequently, 3.[16] Global transmission of serotype 2 has apparently been interrupted, with the last case occurring in India in October 1999.[17] Direct fecal-oral contact is responsible for most person-to-person transmission of poliovirus, but it can be transmitted by indirect contact with infectious saliva or feces or by contaminated sewage and water.[16]

The introduction of inactivated poliovirus vaccine (IPV) in the 1950s followed by oral poliovirus vaccine (OPV) in the 1960s has resulted in eradication of indigenous wild-type poliomyelitis in numerous countries worldwide. The Americas region was declared free of indigenous poliovirus in 1994.[16] In the United States, the last case occurred in 1979, and the last case detected in the Americas occurred in Peru in 1991.[18,19] The WHO regions of the Western Pacific and Europe were certified free of polio in 2000 and 2002, respectively, although vulnerability to importation of wild-type virus was demonstrated in Bulgaria in 2001 with an outbreak of a strain of poliovirus type 1 closely related to a strain circulating in Uttar Pradesh, India.[20,21]

In addition to communities with suboptimal immunity, which exist in all European countries, wild-type poliovirus transmission is still occurring in Africa, Asia, and some countries of the eastern mediterranean. As of the year 2000 in Africa, wild poliovirus transmission was reported most frequently in central Africa and the horn of Africa, with Nigeria, the Democratic Republic of Congo (DRC), and Angola representing the countries with the largest poliovirus reservoirs.[22] The eastern Mediterranean region reported 261 cases of wild poliovirus in 2000. Pakistan is considered one of the global wild-type poliovirus reservoirs, and outbreaks continue to occur in Afghanistan, Sudan, Somalia, and Upper Egypt.[22,23] The Southeast Asia region reported 272 cases of wild poliovirus in 2000, most cases occurring in Uttar Pradesh and Bihar in northern India. Nepal reported cases from its border with Uttar Pradesh and Bangladesh, and Myanmar also reported cases along their shared border.[22]

Outbreaks of paralytic poliomyelitis also have continued to occur in countries where indigenous virus has been eradicated because OPV-derived strains have recovered the capacity to cause paralysis and because of person-to-person transmission. Recent outbreaks have been reported in the Philippines and on the Caribbean island of Hispaniola (Haiti and the Dominican Republic).[24,25] In the United States, where high levels of immunity predominate and concern exists concerning cases of vaccine-derived paralytic polio, the ACIP phased out the use of OPV for routine immunization as of January 1, 2000.

Polio Vaccine

In the United States, enhanced-potency inactivated poliovirus vaccine (e-IPV) is recommended for primary vaccination of infants, to vaccinate adults, and for vaccination of immunocompromised patients and their contacts. It is more potent and immunogenic than older IPV formulations. In contrast, OPV remains the vaccine of choice in developing countries because of the ease of administration, lower cost, and the induction of intestinal immunity, which reduces transmission of wild-type virus.

Polio Vaccine Indications

In the United States, routine poliovirus vaccination of adults 18 years and older is not necessary. Adults who might have greater risk of exposure to polioviruses than the general population should be vaccinated. These include

- travelers to areas of the world where polio is epidemic or endemic,
- members of communities or specific populations with disease caused by wild-type poliovirus,
- laboratory workers who handle specimens that might contain poliovirus,
- health care workers who might have close contact with patients excreting wild poliovirus, and
- unvaccinated adults whose children will be receiving oral polio vaccine.

Vaccine Series and Accelerated Schedule for Adults

Unvaccinated adults and those without documentation of vaccination status should receive a primary vaccination series with three doses of e-IPV. Two doses of IPV should be given at intervals of 4 to 8 weeks; a third dose should be administered 6 to 12 months after the second. If there is insufficient time to administer three doses prior to travel, the following alternatives are recommended:

- If more than 8 weeks are available prior to travel, three doses of e-IPV should be administered at least 4 weeks apart.
- If more than 4 but less than 8 weeks are available prior to travel, two doses of e-IPV should be administered at least 4 weeks apart.
- If less than 4 weeks are available prior to travel, one dose of e-IPV should be administered.[16]

Adults who have received a primary series of either OPV or IPV should receive another dose of e-IPV before travel to developing countries. There is no indication that more than one lifetime booster dose of IPV is necessary.

Polio Vaccine Composition

Two IPV products are licensed for use in the United States, although only one (IPOL, Aventis Pasteur, Swiftwater, PA) is both licensed and distributed in the United States. This product does not contain thimerosal. This vaccine consists of a suspension of three types of poliovirus grown in monkey kidney cells and inactivated with formaldehyde. Each dose contains 0.5% of 2-phenoxyethanol and up to 200 ppm of formaldehyde as preservatives and trace amounts of neomycin, streptomycin, and polymyxin B (Table 16-3).

Tetanus and Diphtheria

Tetanus

Tetanus is a neurologic disorder caused by *Clostridium tetani* an anaerobic gram-positive rod. The disease

Table 16-3. Polio Vaccines Available in the United States

	IPOL
Manufacturer	Aventis Pasteur; Swiftwater, PA
Viability	Inactivated
How supplied	Single-dose syringe with 25-gauge, ⅝-inch needle; package of 10 syringes
Onset	Within 1–2 weeks
Duration of protection	Many years*
Efficacy	99–100% seroconversion to each type after 3 doses[16]
Pregnancy	Category C†
Contraindications	History of hypersensitivity to any vaccine components
Dosage, route, and site	A primary series in adults consists of 0.5 mL SC in the deltoid ≤ 3 doses; booster dose several years after the primary series‡
Drug interactions	Concurrent use of corticosteroids or other immunosuppressants might result in inadequate immunity

SC = subcutaneous.
*In Sweden, more than 90% of vaccinated persons had serum antibodies to poliovirus 25 years after the fourth dose.[16]
†For a discussion of the Food and Drug Administration categories for pregnancy, see Chapter 17, Appendix 1.
‡Multiple doses in the primary series are used to ensure immunity to all three types of virus.

is characterized by increased muscle tone and spasm caused by a potent toxin produced by the organism. Tetanus can occur as generalized or localized disease. Generalized disease is more common and is characterized by spasms in large-muscle groups, including the masseter muscles (trismus, or lockjaw) as well as the back, abdominal, and proximal limb muscles. Some patients develop paroxysmal muscle spasm precipitated by the slightest stimulus. Life-threatening complications include apnea and laryngospasm. Autonomic dysfunction can complicate serious cases and includes symptoms such as hypertension, tachycardia, dysrhythmias, and hyperpyrexia. Neonatal disease is usually generalized and frequently develops after unsterile treatment of the umbilical stump. Local disease is uncommon and is characterized by muscle spasm near a contaminated wound, which is usually easily treated.

Clostridium tetani is found worldwide in the soil, in animal feces, and, occasionally, in human feces. Although the disease is uncommon in the United States, where most cases are a consequence of an acute injury, the disease burden remains heavy worldwide. Tetanus is common in rural areas where farming and soil cultivation occur, in warm climates, during the summer months, and among males. In 2002, 3 cases of tetanus, 2 of which were fatal, were reported by the Puerto Rico Department of Health.[27] Neonates and children suffer the highest burden of disease in countries without successful childhood immunization programs.

Diphtheria

Diphtheria is caused by *Corynebacterium diphtheriae,* an aerobic gram-positive rod. Disease can occur on the mucous membranes and in skin and is characterized by the formation of pseudomembranes. Respiratory diphtheria is usually caused by toxinogenic organisms. The toxin can cause myocarditis, polyneuritis, and other systemic toxic effects. Cutaneous diphtheria is frequently caused by nontoxinogenic strains.

Humans are the principal reservoir for *C. diphtheriae*, which is transmitted by close personal contact. In temperate climates, respiratory diphtheria predominates and prior to the immunization era caused devastating epidemics involving up to 10% of children, with death rates higher than 50% among those infected. Routine immunization of children has decreased the incidence of disease in the United States from more than 200,000 cases in the year 1921 to less than 5 cases a year since 1980. Worldwide, epidemics continue to occur in developing nations. In the states of the former Soviet Union, more than 157,000 cases with 5,000 deaths occurred in the 1990s. In the tropics, cutaneous diphtheria is more common than respiratory disease and often develops as a secondary infection, complicating other disorders that compromise skin integrity.

Tetanus Vaccine Indications

In the United States, the primary tetanus-diptheria toxoids (Td) series is usually administered in childhood and consists of three doses (in combination with pertussis, DTaP). In the rare event that an adult might have missed the primary childhood series, the first dose of Td should be given followed by a second dose after 1 month and a third dose 6 to 12 months later. A booster dose of Td is currently recommended at 10-year intervals throughout life or once at the age of 50 years.[27]

Tetanus spores are ubiquitous in soil. For travelers, maintaining active tetanus immunity obviates the need for treatment of contaminated wounds with equine tetanus antitoxin, a replacement for human tetanus immunoglobulin commonly used in other countries. Complications of treatment with equine tetanus antitoxin may include hypersensitivity reactions and serum sickness.

Travelers to certain countries remain at substantial risk of exposure to toxigenic strains of *C. diphtheriae*. Risk increases with prolonged stays, extensive contact with children, or exposure to poor hygiene. Areas of highest risk are the following:

- Africa: Algeria, Egypt, and sub-Saharan Africa
- Americas: Brazil, Dominican Republic, Ecuador, and Haiti
- Asia/Oceania: Afghanistan, Bangladesh, Cambodia, China, India, Indonesia, Iran, Iraq, Laos, Mongolia, Myanmar, Nepal, Pakistan, Philippines, Syria, Thailand, Turkey, Vietnam, and Yemen
- Europe: Albania and all countries of the former Soviet Union[28]

Td Vaccine Composition

Each 0.5 mL dose contains 5 limit of flocculation (Lf) units of tetanus toxoid and 2 Lf units of diphtheria toxoid. Both toxins are detoxified with formaldehyde. As much as 0.28 mg of aluminum may be present. Thimerosal is added as a preservative (Table 16-4).

Pregnancy

In the United States, it is generally not necessary to immunize pregnant women because nearly all women receive their primary series during childhood. However, the ACIP advises that Td can be considered a routine vaccine in pregnancy.[5] Worldwide, immunization of pregnant women with tetanus toxoid at least 6 weeks prior to delivery protects the neonate against tetanus neonatorum and protects the woman against puerperal tetanus. There is no evidence of adverse effects on mother or fetus.[29]

Table 16-4. **Diphtheria and Tetanus Vaccines**

	Tetanus and Diphtheria Toxoids Adsorbed, for Adult Use (Td)
Manufacturer	Aventis Pasteur; Swiftwater, PA
Viability	Inactivated
How supplied	Single-dose syringe and 10-dose vial
Protection	
Onset	Within days after the third dose
Duration	Lifelong reduction of severity of disease after completion of the primary series; one booster dose at age 50–65 years is probably adequate
Efficacy	Extremely high
Pregnancy	Generally not necessary to immunize in the US; ACIP considers Td routine during pregnancy; no evidence exists of adverse effects on mother or fetus[29]
Contraindications	Demonstrated hypersensitivity to any vaccine component; acute illness (defer routine vaccination)
Dosage, route, and site	0.5 mL IM or jet injection; should not be given ID or SC; IM injections should be given in the deltoid area of the arm or in the midlateral muscle of the thigh
Drug interactions	Concurrent use of corticosteroids or other immunosuppressants might result in inadequate immunity

Adapted from Centers for Disease Control and Prevention.[5]

ID = intradermal; IM = intramuscular; SC = subcutaneous.

Hepatitis A

Hepatitis A is a viral infection of the liver that is transmitted almost exclusively via the fecal-oral route. The prodromal symptoms are variable and can include low-grade fever, fatigue, malaise, anorexia, nausea, vomiting, myalgias, and arthralgias. Dark urine, clay-colored stools, and jaundice might then appear along with right-upper-quadrant pain from an enlarged and tender liver. During the posticteric phase, some liver enlargement and abnormal liver function tests might persist.

Hepatitis A is spread through poor personal hygiene and overcrowding. Outbreaks have been traced to contaminated uncooked food, water, ice, milk, and raw or partially cooked shellfish harvested from polluted waters. Hepatitis A outbreaks have also been identified in day care centers and neonatal intensive care units and among homosexual men with multiple partners and injection drug users. In the United States, the prevalence of hepatitis A has been decreasing since the 1970s, but the incidence remains higher than 20 per 100,000 in 11 Western states, prompting the ACIP to recommend hepatitis A vaccine as a routine childhood immunization in these states (Figure 16-2).

In developing countries, children are almost universally exposed and infected, and they develop lifelong immunity. Susceptible travelers, however, can become infected in endemic countries by eating food grown in contaminated soil or handled by infected workers. The risk of infection increases with length of stay and is highest for those travelers living in or traveling to rural areas, trekking in the backcountry, or eating and drinking in settings of poor sanitation.[30]

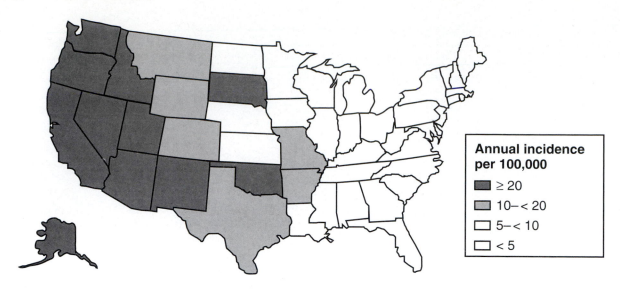

Figure 16-2. Geographic distribution of hepatitis A in the United States. Adapted from the Centers for Disease Control and Prevention.

Vaccine Indications

Immunity to hepatitis A is lifelong for those who have acquired the infection naturally. In some populations, it might be reasonable to test for anti–hepatitis A antibody prior to vaccination. The ACIP advises that in cases where the expected cost of screening is one-third the cost of the vaccination series, it is probably cost-effective to do prevaccination testing on (1) adults who were either born or lived for extensive periods of time in hepatitis A–endemic areas, (2) older adolescents or adults in some population groups (eg, American Indians, Alaskan Natives, and Hispanics), (3) injection drug users, and, possibly, (4) all adults over 40 years of age.[31]

Hepatitis A remains one of the most common vaccine-preventable diseases in the United States. An effective vaccine became available in 1995, and by 1999, the ACIP began advising routine immunization of children in states, counties, and communities where the incidence of hepatitis A is more than 20 per 100,000. Other high-risk groups include men who have sex with men, illegal-drug users (injecting and noninjecting), persons who work with hepatitis A virus in laboratories, persons administered clotting-factor concentrates, and travelers.[31]

Travelers to Africa, Asia (including Turkey but excepting Japan and Singapore), Latin America, parts of the Caribbean (mainly Hispaniola), and remote parts of eastern Europe should be vaccinated. Travelers to the major tourist countries of southern Europe (Italy, Spain, Portugal, and Greece) do not need to be vaccinated. In addition, European tourists visiting the western United States (with an incidence similar to Italy) do not need to be vaccinated.[30] Figure 16-3 shows the worldwide prevalence of hepatitis A infection.

The CDC no longer recommends coverage with immune globulin (0.2 mL/kg) if the traveler is leaving for a high-risk area less than 4 weeks after the initial dose of hepatitis A vaccine.[32] Hepatitis A vaccine has been shown to be effective in stopping community outbreaks, indicating rapid onset of protection. In Europe, vaccine alone is given even if departure is imminent, and cases of hepatitis A disease have not been reported where this strategy has been used (see Chapetr 6, "Hepatitis A vaccine and Hepatitis B vaccine").[30]

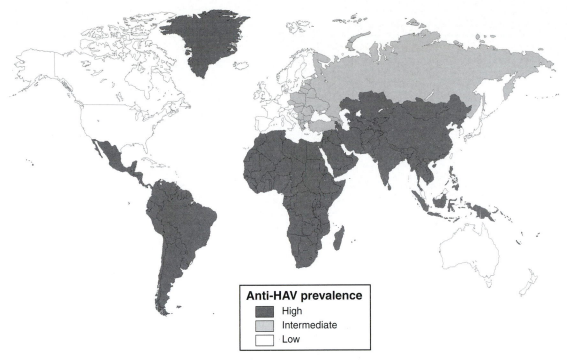

Figure 16-3. Geographic distribution of hepatitis A infection. HAV = hepatitis A virus.

Vaccine Composition

Two products are licensed for use in the United States. Both consist of inactivated virus adsorbed to aluminum hydroxide as an adjuvant. Havrix contains 2-phenoxyethanol as a preservative, whereas VAQTA is preservative free (Table 16-5). In addition, a combination product, Twinrix, provides immunization against hepatitis A and B. Twinrix will be discussed in detail in the section on hepatitis B.

Hepatitis B

Hepatitis B is a viral infection that predominantly affects the liver. It is caused by a hepadnavirus that replicates in the liver and causes acute hepatitis, manifested by malaise, fatigue, anorexia, nausea, and jaundice. Approximately 10% of adults and 35% of children become chronic carriers of the infection. Chronic carriers are at risk of developing cirrhosis of the liver and primary hepatocellular carcinoma.

In the United States, most hepatitis B infections occur in adolescents or adults. It is transmitted by parenteral contact with infected blood and/or blood products and is also transmitted sexually, especially among homosexual men and persons with multiple heterosexual partners. It is also transmitted by parenteral drug use through sharing of needles with an infected individual. Health care workers are at risk through needle sticks and other injuries associated with the care of infected patients. Other risk factors include household contact with a person who has acute hepatitis B or who is a chronic carrier, perinatal transmission, hemodialysis, and receipt of certain blood products. However, more than one-third of patients with acute hepatitis B infection have no identifiable risk factors.[33]

Routine childhood immunization for hepatitis B began in the United States in 1991.[33] Prior to that date, only high-risk groups had been targeted for hepatitis B vaccination, but this strategy failed to decrease the incidence of hepatitis B infections because it was not possible to vaccinate persons engaged in high-risk behaviors, lifestyles, or occupations before they became infected. The current childhood immunization

Table 16-5. Hepatitis A Vaccines, Recommended Doses, and Schedules of Immunization

	Havrix		*VAQTA*	
Manufacturer	GlaxoSmithKline		Merck	
Viability	Inactivated hepatitis A antigen		Inactivated hepatitis A antigen	
How supplied	Single-dose vial, prefilled syringe, prefilled syringe with detachable, locking needle (Tip-Lok), or multidose vial		Single dose vial or prefilled syringe	
Recommended dosage by age group	2–18 yr	> 18 yr	2–18 yr	≥ 19 yr
Dose	720 ELU	1,440 ELU	25 U	50 U
Volume (mL)	0.5	1.0	0.5	1.0
Number of doses	2	2	2	2
Schedule (mo)	0, 6–12	0, 6–12	0, 6–18	0, 6
Protection				
Onset	Within 2–4 weeks of initial vaccination			
Duration	≥ 20 years; possibly lifelong			
Efficacy	94–100% of those age ≥ 19 yr develop protective antibodies within 1 mo			
Accelerated vaccine schedule	See hepatitis B, Table 16-6, accelerated dosing of Twinrix			
Lapsed vaccination	Longer-than-recommended intervals between doses do not reduce final antibody concentrations; interruption in a vaccination schedule does not require restarting the entire series[5]			
Pregnancy	Category C*			
Contraindications	Known hypersensitivity to any vaccine component; package insert details the composition of each vaccine			
Dosage, route, and site	For adults, dose varies with product; the vaccine is administered IM in the deltoid			
Drug interactions	Concurrent use of corticosteroids or other immunosuppressants might result in inadequate immunity			

Adapted from Centers for Disease Control and Prevention (CDC).[67]
ELU=enzyme-linked immunosorbent assay (ELISA) units; IM = intramuscular.
*For a discussion of the Food and Drug Administration categories for pregnancy, see Chapter 17, Appendix 1.

schedule completes the series of three vaccinations by 18 months and provides for catch-up immunizations at 11 to 12 years. In the United States, 34 states now have middle school hepatitis B immunization laws.

Because hepatitis B is considered a sexually transmitted disease, routine immunization of adolescents and young adults has been prioritized, and, as a result, more students are entering college with immunization complete. Because of cost, assessment of antibody response to the immunization series is not recommended except for those individuals who are likely to experience occupational exposure to blood or body fluids. In this case, postexposure management for blood-borne pathogens is simplified if there is evidence that the exposed individual responded to hepatitis B immunization in the past.[34] However, at the time of routine immunization, children and adolescents obviously do not know whether they will

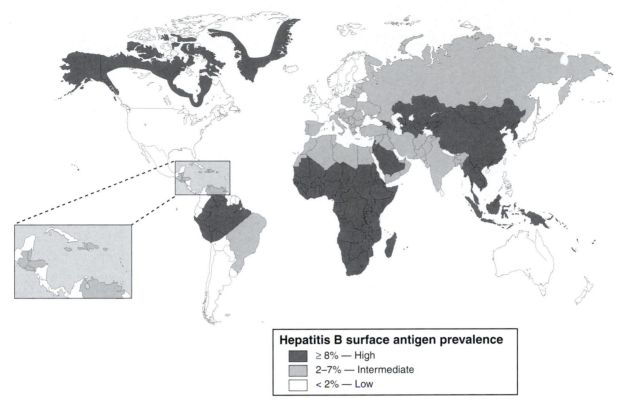

Hepatitis B surface antigen prevalence
- ≥ 8% — High
- 2–7% — Intermediate
- < 2% — Low

Figure 16-4. Geographic distribution of chronic hepatitis B infection.

enter the health care professions in the future. Therefore, in years to come, more health care workers will have received hepatitis B immunization during childhood without confirming immunity serologically, and the ACIP will need to propose a new strategy for postexposure management.

Worldwide, chronic hepatitis B remains endemic in many developing countries (Figure 16-4). Increasingly, immunization of children and adolescents is becoming routine in many of these countries, but the burden of disease remains large. WHO recommends hepatitis B immunization for travelers to Africa, Asia, South America (except Argentina, Chile, Bolivia, and Uruguay), parts of Central America (Guatemala, El Salvador), the island of Hispaniola, Alaska, northern Canada, and Greenland if the stay will exceed a month.[30] Travelers who stay in these areas for a shorter period in a single trip but whose cumulative exposure over several trips is likely to exceed a month are also encouraged to be immunized. For the CDC, a planned stay of 6 months or longer in close contact with local populations in hepatitis B endemic areas is used as a condition for hepatitis B immunization.[33]

Vaccine Indications

Prevaccination testing might be cost-effective in certain populations, as naturally acquired hepatitis B infection can confer lifelong immunity. Serologic evidence of current or previous hepatitis B infection is seen in 50 to 80% of individuals from countries with the highest prevalence rates.[35] Furthermore, first-generation immigrant populations have carrier rates similar to those of individuals in their country of origin. Therefore, for an adult born in or whose parents were born in any of the endemic areas mentioned in the previous sections, prevaccination testing should be considered. Other high-risk groups include injection drug users, homosexual men with multiple partners, and household contacts of hepatitis B carriers.

Hepatitis B vaccine is indicated for all adults at risk of hepatitis B infection. Three doses are given, with the second dose 1 month after the first and the third dose 6 months after the first but at least 2 months after the second.

In general, hepatitis B vaccination prior to travel is recommended because accidental injuries during international travel occur frequently, and contact with blood or blood products might be unavoidable. Travelers who are likely to have contact with blood or blood products (eg, health care workers or those who plan tattooing, body piercing, or acupuncture) or who will have sexual contact with residents in areas with high or intermediate rates of hepatitis B infection should also be vaccinated. Ideally, vaccination should begin 6 months prior to travel so that the series of three vaccinations can be completed.[33]

Vaccine Composition

In the United States, there are two licensed recombinant purified hepatitis B vaccines, one combination product of both hepatitis A and B antigens, and a third combination product, COMVAX (Merck, Whitehouse Station, NJ), which contains *Haemophilus* b conjugate, meningococcal protein conjugate, and hepatitis B recombinant. Because COMVAX is used only in children, it will not be discussed here. Worldwide, other hepatitis B products exist.[30]

All hepatitis B vaccines are produced in yeast and contain recombinant purified antigen of the hepatitis B surface coat proteins. The vaccines contain aluminum as an adjuvant and can contain thimerosal, 2-phenoxyethanol, neomycin, formalin, and yeast protein or plasmid deoxyribonucleic acid (DNA).[30] With the exception of the two-dose hepatitis B vaccination series for adolescents, all brands of hepatitis B vaccine are interchangeable (Table 16-6).[5]

Accelerated Vaccination Schedule

An accelerated vaccination schedule for 20 µg Engerix-B given at 0, 7, and 21 days, or at 0, 14, and 28 days, followed by a booster at 12 months is approved for use in some countries of western Europe.[36] Similarly, hepatitis A and B vaccine (Twinrix) can be given at 0, 7, and 21 days followed by a booster dose at 12 months. These schedules are pending Food and Drug Administration (FDA) approval at the time of writing. Alternately, there is a an FDA-approved accelerated schedule for Energix-B, consisting of 4 doses given on a 0, 1, 2, and 12 month schedule. When time is too short administer Twinrix on the accelerated schedule, monovalent adult doses of hepatitis A and B vaccines can be given initialy to elicit high-level protection against hepatitis A. The second and third doses of the series can then be completed using Twinrix at 1 and 6 months following the standard 0, 1, 6 month schedule .[30]

Influenza

Epidemic influenza is caused by two types of influenza virus, influenza A and B. Influenza A viruses are further subcategorized into types based on two surface antigens, hemagglutinin (H) and neuraminidase (N). Influenza B viruses are not subcategorized into types, but both A and B viruses are subgrouped based on antigenic characteristics. Frequent antigenic changes (ie, antigenic drift) result in new influenza virus variants. Influenza B viruses undergo antigenic drift less rapidly than do influenza A viruses.[37]

Influenza is transmitted from person to person through the spread of infected respiratory secretions by coughing and sneezing. Uncomplicated influenza infection results in the abrupt onset of both consti-

Table 16-6. Hepatitis B Vaccines, Recommended Dosages, and Schedules of Immunization

	Recombivax HB (adult, ≥ age 20, formulation)	*Engerix-B* (adult, > age 19, formulation)*	*Twinrix (adult, ≥ age 18, formulation)*
Manufacturer	Merck	GlaxoSmithKline	GlaxoSmithKline
Viability	Inactivated hepatitis B virus	Inactivated hepatitis B virus	Inactivated hepatitis A and hepatitis B virus
How supplied	Single-dose vial or glass syringe; 3 mL multidose vial	Single-dose vial, prefilled syringe, or prefilled syringe with detachable, locking needle (Tip-Lok)	Single-dose vial or prefilled syringe with detachable, locking needle (Tip-Lok)
Recommended dose			
Adult ≥ 18 yr			1 mL[†]
Birth through age 19[‡]	5 μg	10 μg	
Adults ≥ 20 yr	10 μg in 1 mL	20 μg in 1 mL	
Dialysis patients and other immunocompromised people	40 μg[§]	40 μg[‖]	
Protection			
Onset	70–80% after second dose; around 95% within 1–3 mo after third dose[32]		
Duration	Probably lifelong in most persons		
Efficacy	94–98% immunogenicity in adults 20–40 yr; 89% immunogenicity among adults > 40 yr		
Accelerated vaccination schedule	20 μg Engerix-B at 0, 7, and 21 days or at 0, 14, and 28 days; booster at 12 mo[#36] Twinrix at 0, 7, and 21 days followed by a booster dose at 12 months; if time too short for two doses of Twinrix, monovalent adult doses of hepatitis A and B vaccines can be given as the initial vaccines, and the second and third doses completed using Twinrix[30]		
Lapsed-vaccination schedule	Longer-than-recommended intervals between doses do not reduce final antibody concentrations; interruption in a vaccination schedule does not require restarting the entire series[5]		
Pregnancy	Recommended for at-risk pregnant women		
Contraindications	Hypersensitivity to any vaccine component (package inserts list vaccine contents of the vaccine); acute illness (defer immunization)		
Dosage, route, and site	Dose varies depending on product; administered IM in the deltoid		
Drug interactions	Concurrent use of corticosteroids or other immunosuppressants can result in inadequate immunity		

IM = intramuscular.

*Also licensed for a four-dose series.

[†]Each dose contains at least 720 enzyme-linked immunosorbent assay units of inactivated hepatitis A virus and 20 μg of recombinant hepatitis B surface antigen protein.

[‡]Recombivax-HB is also licensed for a two-dose schedule for 11- to 15-year-olds. Give the adult dose initially followed by a second adult dose at 4 to 6 months after the first dose.

[§]Special formulation.

[‖]Two 1.0 mL doses are given at the same time at two separate sites in a four-dose schedule at 0, 1, 2, and 6 months.

[#]Not Food and Drug Administration approved.

tutional and respiratory symptoms, such as fever, myalgias, headache, severe malaise, nonproductive cough, sore throat, and rhinitis. In most individuals, the acute illness resolves within several days, although the cough and malaise can linger for more than 2 weeks. In some persons, influenza can exacerbate underlying medical conditions and/or result in viral or secondary bacterial pneumonia. Other complications include encephalopathy, transverse myelitis, Reye's syndrome, myositis, myocarditis, and pericarditis. Persons with underlying health conditions such as pulmonary or cardiac disease or those 65 years of age or more are at higher risk of complications, hospitalizations, and death from influenza.[37]

Travelers experience variable risks of exposure to influenza depending on the time of year, destination, and type of travel. In the tropics, such as in the Caribbean, influenza viruses circulate throughout the year. In the temperate areas of the Southern Hemisphere, such as parts of Australia and South America, most influenza activity occurs from April through September. In countries in the Northern Hemisphere, such as the United States and Canada, influenza usually strikes between November and March. However, in the temperate regions of either the Northern or Southern Hemisphere, travelers can be exposed to influenza during their respective summer months, especially when traveling as part of large, organized tourist groups (cruises, land and sea tours), which can include travelers from areas of the world where influenza viruses are currently circulating.

Vaccine Indications

The CDC recommends annual influenza vaccination for any individuals older than 50 years with or without underlying medical problems and for individuals with high-risk medical conditions who are younger than 50 years.[38]

Travelers who should consider receiving influenza vaccine at least 2 weeks before travel if they were *not* vaccinated during the most recent fall or winter include
- individuals at high risk for complications of influenza and
- individuals who wish to decrease their chances of developing influenza *if*
  - traveling to the tropics at any time of year,
  - traveling to the Southern Hemisphere from April through September, or
  - traveling with a large organized tourist group at any time of year.

The previous season's vaccine might not be available to tourists during the summer months in North America. In this case, the traveler should discuss with his or her physician the possibility of carrying antiviral medications for either prophylaxis or treatment of influenza should it occur.

Any traveler at high risk for complications of influenza traveling in autumn or winter should receive the *current* season's vaccine.

Vaccine Composition

Influenza vaccine consists of three strains of virus (two type A and one type B), reflecting the virus strains most likely to circulate in the United States during a given season. The viruses are grown in embryonated hens' eggs and then inactivated or rendered noninfectious. In the United States, some vaccine manufacturers use thimerosal, a mercury-containing compound, as a preservative. Likewise, some manufacturers might use different inactivation agents or antibiotics to prevent bacterial contamination. The package insert will give the details of the content of the vaccine.

Table 16-7. **Influenza Vaccines***

Protection	
Onset	Within 2 weeks of vaccination
Duration	Can decline within a few months; annual revaccination is necessary even if the previous season's vaccine contained antigens anticipated to circulate in the current season's viral strains
Efficacy	Up to 70–90% in persons < 65 yr
Pregnancy	Recommended for women beyond first trimester of pregnancy during influenza season and for all pregnant women with chronic medical conditions that would increase their risk of influenza-related complications; no existing data indicate that thimerosal is harmful during pregnancy
Contraindications	Anaphylactic hypersensitivity to eggs or other components of the vaccine (manufacturer's package insert lists composition of the vaccine); acute febrile illness
Dosage, route, and site	IM, in the deltoid with a needle ≥1 inch (2.5 cm) in length to ensure penetration of muscle tissue in adults
Drug interactions	Can be administered simultaneously (albeit at separate anatomic sites) with pneumococcal vaccine if the traveler has not yet received this one-time vaccine

Adapted from Centers for Disease Control and Prevention.[5]
IM = intramuscular.
*New vaccines are produced for each influenza season. The vaccine consists of three strains of virus (two type A and one type B), reflecting the strains most likely to circulate in the United States during a given season. Proprietary name may vary.

Efficacy

When the vaccine and circulating viruses are antigenically similar and the vaccinee is healthy, the vaccine protects against influenza illness in 70 to 90% of persons less than 65 years of age. Elderly persons or those with chronic medical conditions can develop lower postvaccination antibody titers than healthy young adults do. However, even in these circumstances, the vaccine protects against secondary complications and might prevent hospitalizations and death (Table 16-7). A live attenuated influenza vaccine (LAIV) branded "FluMist" (Wyeth Philadelphia) was approved by the FDA in 2003. The LAIV is approved for immunization of healthy persons between the ages of 5 and 49 years old, and is administered by an intranasal spray.[39]

Meningococcal Disease

Neisseria meningitidis is a leading cause of bacterial meningitis and sepsis in children and young adults in the United States. Meningococcal disease is difficult to diagnose in the early stages, often resembling a viral illness, yet the organism can replicate at an astonishing rate, causing the infected person to deteriorate from good health to irreversible shock and death within hours. In addition to a case fatality rate of 10 to 15%, survivors can experience substantial morbidity, including permanent neurologic damage, hearing loss, limb amputation, or kidney failure. The organism is transmitted through contact with droplets of infected respiratory secretions and through oral contact with shared items such as cigarettes or drinking glasses.

Five serogroups of *N. meningitidis* account for the majority of disease. Four serogroups (A, C, Y, and W-135) are covered by the quadrivalent meningococcal vaccine. Serogroup B is currently not covered by the commercially available vaccine, but efficacy has been demonstrated with several experimental vaccines in older children and adults.[40] Although the quadrivalent meningococcal polysaccharide vaccine protects against meningococcal disease, it might not protect against asymptomatic nasopharyngeal carriage of the organism, which can then be transmitted to contacts.

Meningococcal disease has long been of special concern for college health professionals. It is one of the few infectious diseases of young healthy adults that regularly cause significant morbidity and death. In addition, because college campuses represent highly congenial environments, sporadic cases as well as outbreaks result in a public health emergency requiring swift action, usually at substantial cost. Furthermore, meningococcal disease outbreaks have increased in frequency on college campuses since 1990, prompting the ACHA to recommend in 1997 that college students consider vaccination with the quadrivalent meningococcal polysaccharide vaccine.

To better define the incidence of meningococcal disease on college campuses, an active surveillance study was conducted in 1999 by the CDC, ACHA, and the Council of State and Territorial Epidemiologists (CSTE).[41] In this study, 96 cases of meningococcal disease occurred during the surveillance year, resulting in an incidence rate of 0.7 in 100,000 among undergraduates versus 1.4 in 100,000 for 18- to 23-year-old nonstudents. To define risk factors for the disease more accurately, cases and controls were enrolled in a risk factor study that identified the highest incidence group to be freshmen living in dormitories (5.1/100,000). The study also indicated that 68% of the cases resulted from serotypes that would have been covered by the quadrivalent polysaccharide vaccine.

Data from this study and others were used by ACIP and the American Academy of Pediatrics (AAP) to formulate new recommendations:

- that college freshmen, particularly those planning to live in dormitories, and their parents receive information about the risk of meningococcal disease and the availability of a safe and effective vaccine; and
- that college freshmen have increased access to the vaccine.[42–44]

In response to these new recommendations, college health centers increased efforts to educate entering students and their parents about the disease and the vaccine, and many began offering the vaccine in their clinics.

Since this time, several states have either passed legislation or have legislation pending that mandates education about meningococcal disease and the vaccine (Table 16-8). Two states, Maryland and Connecticut, have gone beyond the ACIP recommendations and have mandated that students planning to live in campus housing receive the vaccine. Because of the low number of vaccine-preventable cases and the high cost of vaccination, a cost-benefit analysis (from the societal perspective) of routine immunization of incoming first-year students living in dormitories indicated that vaccination was not cost saving.[45] However, the authors indicate that from the perspective of students and parents, the cost of vaccination might be worth the real or perceived benefit of reducing the risk of disease.

Worldwide, meningococcal disease is epidemic or hyperendemic in numerous countries, most notably in sub-Saharan Africa, an area known as the meningitis belt, which extends from Senegal in the west to Ethiopia in the east. Widespread epidemics sweep across this area every 8 to 12 years during the dry season, from December to June.[40,46] Outbreaks of meningococcal disease have also been associated with the Hajj, the annual pilgrimage to holy places in Saudi Arabia, and the CDC continues to recommend meningococcal vaccination to the approximately 15,000 US pilgrims who travel to the hajj annually.[47]

Vaccine Indications

In the United States, vaccination with the quadrivalent meningococcal vaccine is currently recommended for first-time freshmen living in college or university dormitories.[41,48] University students studying abroad

Table 16-8. State Legislation* Relating to Meningococcal Disease and Vaccine

Legislation Passed

Arkansas
Colleges and universities must notify students and parents of the increased risk of disease for students living in close quarters and the availability of the vaccine.

California
Public, non-University of California institutions of higher education must provide information to entering students and document their decision about the vaccine.

Connecticut
All students planning on living in campus housing must receive the vaccine. Waivers are granted only for religious or medical reasons.

Delaware
All entering students at 4-year public or private institutions either receive the vaccine or sign a waiver after receiving information.

Florida
Postsecondary education students must receive information about the disease and vaccine, and students residing in on-campus housing must receive the vaccine or sign a waiver.

Illinois
Entering freshmen and transfer students must receive information about the disease and vaccine.

Indiana
Students enrolled at a residential campus at a public university must receive detailed information about the disease and vaccine from the university.

Maryland
All students planning on living in university-owned housing must receive the vaccine or sign a declination to live in such housing.

Michigan
The Michigan Department of Health must provide information about the disease and vaccine to colleges, universities, and secondary schools so that it may be distributed to students.

New Jersey
All entering students in 4-year public or private institutions must receive information about the disease and vaccine.

Pennsylvania
All students planning to live in campus housing must receive the vaccine or sign a waiver after receiving information about the disease and vaccine.

South Carolina
All students entering public universities must receive information about the risk of meningococcal disease and hepatitis B if living in on-campus housing. Vaccination against these diseases must be recommended by the institutions.

Texas
Entering students at private or public institutions of higher education must sign a confirmation of receipt of information about the disease and vaccine.

Virginia
All entering students at 4-year public institutions must receive the vaccine or alternatively receive information about the disease and sign a waiver declining the vaccine.

Legislation Pending

Georgia
Students in secondary and postsecondary schools should receive information about the disease.

Massachusetts
Students at public or private institutions who plan to reside in on-campus housing must receive the vaccine or sign a waiver after receiving information.

Missouri
Meningococcal vaccine and hepatitis B would be added to the standard immunization requirements for attending public, private, parochial, or parish schools.

New York
Students who reside in "student residences" for a period of not less than 7 days (this includes residence in private boarding schools, camps, public and private colleges, sororities and fraternities) must receive the vaccine or sign a waiver after receiving information.

Ohio
Students living in on-campus housing must be vaccinated against meningitis or sign a waiver after receiving information.

*Information is current as of August 2002.

in the United Kingdom and planning to live in "catered hall accommodations" (the equivalent of dormitories) might wish to be vaccinated as well because higher rates of meningococcal disease have been reported on campuses with more than 10% of their students in such housing compared to campuses providing such housing to less than 10% of their students (15.3/100,000 vs 5.9/100,000, respectively).[49] Other targeted groups include those with terminal complement deficiencies or functional or anatomic asplenia and laboratory workers who handle the organism.

Table 16-9. Meningococcal Disease Vaccine

	Menomune-A,C,Y,W-135
Manufacturer	Aventis Pasteur
Viability	Inactivated
How supplied	Single-dose and 10-dose vials
Onset	Within 7–10 days
Duration of protection	At least 3 years
Efficacy	≥ 85% for serogroups A and C*
Pregnancy	Category C; CDC does not alter meningococcal vaccine recommendations during pregnancy[32]
Contraindications	None
Dosage, route, and site	0.5 mL SC or jet injection; should not be injected ID, IM, or IV; booster can be given every 3 years as long as exposure risk continues
Drug Interactions	Concurrent use of corticosteroids or other immunosuppressants might result in inadequate immunity

CDC = Centers for Disease Control and Prevention; ID = intradermal; IM = intramuscular; IV = intravenous; SC = subcutaneous.
*See further discussion in the text.
For a discussion of the Food and Drug Administration categories for pregnancy see Chapter 17, Appendix 1.

Immunization is also recommended prior to travel to any area of the world where meningococcal outbreaks have been reported, including those mentioned above. Health sciences students, in particular, should be immunized prior to participating in rotations in health care facilities in developing countries.

Vaccine Composition
Each dose consists of 50 µg of the 4 bacterial capsular polysaccharides (Table 16-9).

Vaccine Efficacy
Efficacy against disease in adults caused by serogroups A and C has been demonstrated to be at least 85%. Although clinical efficacy against serogroups Y and W-135 has not been demonstrated, these polysaccharides are safe and immunogenic, producing bactericidal antibodies in adults. Repeated doses of the vaccine do not reduce clinical efficacy, but immunologic tolerance can develop after repeated doses of group C polysaccharide.[48] The clinical significance of this is unknown.

Pneumococcal Infections

Streptococcus pneumoniae (pneumococcus), a bacterial organism, is a leading cause of illness and death in children and the elderly. It colonizes the nasopharynx and can be found in 5 to 10% of healthy adults and in 20 to 40% of healthy children. The organism can be spread from person to person in settings with extensive close contact, such as day care centers, military barracks, prisons, or shelters for the homeless. Pneumococcal infections include disseminated invasive infections such as bacteremia and meningitis;

pneumonia and lower respiratory tract infections; and upper respiratory tract infections, including sinusitis and otitis media.

There are 90 known serotypes of pneumococcus, each possessing a unique polysaccharide capsule. The Danish system of serotype naming groups the serotypes by antigenic similarities.

Pneumococcal Polysaccharide Vaccine, 23-Valent

Both available US vaccines contain 23 purified capsular polysaccharide antigens of S. pneumoniae (serotypes 1, 2, 3, 4, 5, 6B, 7F, 8, 9N, 9V, 10A, 11A, 12F, 14, 15B, 17F, 18C, 19A, 19F, 20, 22F, 23F, and 33F). These vaccines were licensed in 1983 and replaced the earlier 14-valent vaccine, which was licensed in 1977. A single 0.5 mL dose of the 23-valent vaccine contains 25 µg of each polysaccharide antigen in an isotonic saline solution, with phenol (0.25%) or thimerosal (0.01%) added as a preservative. The 23-valent vaccine protects against 80 to 95% of the serotypes that cause invasive pneumococcal disease among both children and adults in the United States. The six serotypes (6B, 9V, 14, 19A, 19F, and 23F) that are most frequently associated with invasive drug-resistant pneumococcal infections in the United States are covered by the 23-valent vaccine.[50]

Indications for Pneumococcal Vaccine, 23-Valent

All individuals aged 65 years or older (the ACIP lowers this age to 50) should receive a dose of the 23-valent vaccine. In addition, individuals aged 2 to 64 years with chronic cardiopulmonary disease, diabetes, alcoholism, chronic liver disease, or cerbrospinal fluid (CSF) leaks should also be vaccinated. Other high-risk groups include those with functional or anatomic asplenia, residents in long-term care facilities, Alaskan Natives and certain American Indian populations, and immunocompromised individuals.[51] In general, in the United States, pneumococcal vaccination coverage has lagged behind influenza vaccine coverage, and racial/ethnic and socioeconomic disparities in vaccine coverage continue to exist.[52]

Resistant strains of S. pneumoniae occur worldwide. In the event of a pneumococcal infection while traveling, access to effective antibiotics might be limited. Therefore, even healthy adults who plan to travel, work, or live in developing countries should consider immunization prior to travel.[53]

Vaccine Composition

Vaccine composition is listed in the section "Pneumococcal Polysaccharide Vaccine, 23-Valent," above (Table 16-10).

Booster Doses

The ACIP advises consideration of a booster dose for those aged 65 years or over if 5 years or more have elapsed since the first dose and one of the following risk factors is present: immune compromise, chronic renal failure/nephrotic syndrome, organ (bone marrow) transplant, or first dose prior to age 65 years.[50] Clinicians should also consider giving a booster dose for those aged 2 to 64 years if the following conditions exist.

- If the patient is more than 10 years of age, the vaccination should be repeated if at least 5 years have elapsed since the previous immunization and the patient has splenic dysfunction or is immuno-compromised.

Table 16-10. Pneumococcal Disease Vaccine

Proprietary Name	Pnu-Imune 23	Pneumovax 23
Manufacturer	Wyeth Lederle	Merck
Viability	Inactivated	Inactivated
How supplied	Single-dose syringe and 5-dose vial	Single-dose vial or syringe and 5-dose vial
Efficacy	Reduces disease incidence by 60–80%	
Onset	Within 2 to 3 weeks	
Duration of protection	≥ 5 years	
Pregnancy	Category C*	
Contraindications	Hypersensitivity to any vaccine component; acute illness (defer routine vaccination)	
Dosage, route, and site	0.5 mL IM or SC in the deltoid (arm) or midlateral thigh; should not be given ID or IV as severe reactions can occur	
Drug interactions	Concurrent use of corticosteroids or other immunosuppressants may result in inadequate immunity	

ID = intradermal; IM = intramuscular; IV = intravenous; SC = subcutaneous.

*For a discussion of the Food and Drug Administration categories for pregnancy see Chapter 17, Appendix 1.

- If the patient is aged 10 years or under, the vaccination should be repeated if at least 3 years have elapsed and the patient has splenic dysfunction or is immunocompromised.

Tuberculosis

The WHO estimates that one-third of the world's population (1.86 billion people) is infected with *Mycobacterium tuberculosis*. The annual incidence of active tuberculosis (TB) increased by 0.4 million in 1999 to 8.4 million, largely owing to a 20% increase in incidence in the African countries most affected by the human immunodeficiency virus/acquired immunodeficiency virus (HIV/AIDS) epidemic.[54] Eighty percent of the new cases of active TB are found in 23 high-incidence countries, with more than 50% of the cases found in 5 Southeast Asian countries (India, Indonesia, Bangladesh, Thailand, and Myanmar). Other countries in the top 23 include 9 in the African region (Nigeria, Ethiopia, South Africa, Democratic Republic of Congo, Kenya, the United Republic of Tanzania, Mozambique, Uganda, and Zimbabwe), 4 in the western Pacific region (China, the Philippines, Vietnam, and Cambodia), 2 in the eastern Mediterranean region (Pakistan, Afghanistan), 2 in the American region (Brazil, Peru), and 1 in the European region (Russian Federation).[54] For comparison, TB case rates in the United States are below 10 per 100,000, whereas the highest incidence rates per capita in Africa are more than 400 per 100,000.

The global burden of multidrug-resistant (MDR) TB is increasing as well. In a survey of 58 geographic areas from the years 1996 to 1999, the median prevalence of MDR among new cases of TB was 1%, but the prevalence was much higher in Estonia (14.1%), Henan Province in China (10.8%), Latvia (9.0%), the Russian oblasts of Ivanovo (9%) and Tomsk (6.5%), Iran (5.0%), and Zhejiang Province in China (4.5%).[55]

Two studies suggest that travelers who spend time in areas with high TB rates are more likely to return with positive tuberculin skin tests, indicating latent TB infection. In California, children below 6 years of age who had traveled to TB-endemic areas or were in contact with individuals from TB-endemic areas were 4.7 times more likely to have positive skin tests.[56] Among 656 Dutch travelers to areas of high TB endemicity (length of stay 3–12 months), 1.8% returned with positive tuberculin skin tests, and two had active TB disease.[57]

Before prolonged travel to a TB-endemic area, in most circumstances, the traveler should be tuberculin skin-tested and retested 8 to 10 weeks after returning home. If the skin test converts to positive, active tuberculosis should be ruled out and the traveler treated for latent TB infection according to standard protocols. Travelers who have a positive skin test prior to travel are unlikely to be reinfected during travel but should be aware of how to recognize signs and symptoms of active TB.

In some circumstances, the risk of TB exposure can be anticipated to be high prior to travel. Wilson has suggested that in considering the risk of exposure to TB for a traveler, the following factors are likely to be relevant: incidence rates in the region (including rates of TB drug resistance in the region), duration of stay, accommodations, and activities. Also important for the risk of development of active tuberculosis after exposure are host factors such as age, underlying medical problems or treatment, and prior history of TB.[58] Health care workers or missionaries who plan to work in health care facilities where cases of active pulmonary tuberculosis are likely should take a supply of disposable (nondisposable models are also available) N-95–certified, nonpowered air-purifying respirator masks (duckbills).[59] Fit-testing for these masks is necessary to determine the appropriate size.

In rare circumstances, bacille Calmette-Guérin (BCG) vaccine can be considered as an option prior to travel. Epidemiologic factors that might favor the use of BCG vaccine include prolonged stay in an area with high rates of MDR TB where work or frequent leisure activities are anticipated to occur in crowded, confined spaces. Another possible circumstance where BCG vaccine might be warranted would be in infants or young children who are planning to reside with a person with potentially contagious MDR TB.

Bacille Calmette-Guérin Vaccine

BCG vaccines are live vaccines derived from a strain of *Mycobacterium bovis* that was attenuated by Calmette and Guérin at the Pasteur Institute in Lille, France. Many different BCG vaccines are available worldwide, all derived from the original *M. bovis* strain but differing in their ability to induce an immune response.[60] The TICE strain was developed in Chicago at the University of Illinois from the original Pasteur Institute strain and is currently the only BCG vaccine licensed by the FDA for use in the United States.[60]

Efficacy

Although clinical trials have demonstrated that BCG vaccine is efficacious in preventing TB meningitis and miliary TB in young children, the vaccine has not been proven to prevent pulmonary TB in adolescents and adults.[60] The CDC currently recommends BCG vaccination only in very restricted circumstances and advises health care providers considering BCG vaccination for their patients to consult either locally with TB control experts or nationally with the CDC's Division of Tuberculosis Elimination (404-639-8120).

Vaccine Indications

Administration of BCG vaccine to an international traveler may be considered under the following conditions:

Table 16-11. Bacille Calmette-Guérin (BCG) Vaccine Currently Licensed in the United States

	TICE Strain
Manufacturer	University of Chicago
Viability	Live vaccine
Protection	
Onset	6–12 weeks after vaccination
Duration of protection	Skin-test reactivity to PPD wanes over time and is unlikely to persist > 10 years in the absence of *Mycobacterium tuberculosis* exposure and infection
Efficacy	See text
Pregnancy	Not recommended
Contraindications	Immunocompromise, including related to HIV infection, congenital immunodeficiency disorders, leukemia, lymphoma, or generalized malignancy, or immunologic response compromised by steroids, chemotherapeutic agents, or radiation
Dosage, route, and site	Multiple-puncture disk; 0.3 mL of reconstituted vaccine placed on the skin of the lower deltoid area (ie, the upper arm)*
Drug interactions	Another live vaccine should be given either simultaneously at separate anatomic sites or ≥ 4 weeks apart

HIV = human immunodeficiency virus; PPD = purified protein derivative.

*Freeze-dried vaccine should be reconstituted, protected from light, refrigerated when not in use, and used within 8 hours after reconstitution. The pustule that forms following vaccination ulcerates after about 6 weeks, leaving a lesion approximately 5 mm in diameter. All draining lesions should be kept clean and bandaged. A scar that is hypertrophic in about one-third of patients usually forms at the puncture site. A small percentage of vaccinees (2–4%) develop a keloid at the site.[60]

- the traveler has a reaction of less than 5 mm after skin testing with 5 tuberculin units of purified protein derivative (PPD) and
  - the traveler will be in a high-risk setting and
  - the likelihood of exposure to active MDR tuberculosis is high,
  - comprehensive TB infection control precautions either cannot be implemented or have been implemented and have been found to be unsuccessful, and
  - to tuberculin skin-test surveillance is not possible (Table 16-11).[60]

Varicella

Varicella (or chickenpox) is a highly contagious disease caused by varicella-zoster virus (VZV). Secondary attack rates can reach 90% in susceptible household contacts. VZV enters the host through the respiratory tract and is transmitted from person to person through direct contact, droplet or aerosol from vesicular fluid of skin lesions, or secretions from the respiratory tract. Primary VZV infection in adults can be more severe than in children, and adults are about 25 times more likely than children to experience complications, including varicella pneumonia.[61] VZV remains dormant in the sensory nerve ganglia and can reactivate at a later date as a painful vesicular rash (herpes zoster, or shingles) appearing in the dermatomal distribution of one or two sensory nerve roots.[62]

Worldwide, varicella infections continue to occur in all populations. If widespread varicella vaccination programs are not in effect, varicella is a common disease of childhood in temperate, industrialized nations, and most adults are immune from prior childhood infection. In tropical or subtropical countries, however, varicella infection is often delayed until adulthood.[58]

Vaccine Indications

The CDC recommends that varicella vaccine be administered to all nonimmune adults.[62] Adult travelers, especially those who will have prolonged contact with local populations and who do not have a history of varicella disease or varicella vaccination, should first be tested for varicella antibodies. If negative, the vaccine series should be administered prior to travel.

Vaccine Composition

The vaccine licensed for use in the United States is composed of more than 1,350 plaque forming units (PFU) of the Oka strain of live attenuated VZV. The vaccine is lyophilized and must be used within 30 minutes of reconstitution. The vaccine also contains hydrolyzed gelatin, trace amounts of neomycin and fetal bovine serum, sucrose, and residual components of DNA and protein from cells used in passage of the virus. There are no preservatives (Table 16-12).[62]

Table 16-12. **Varicella Vaccine**

	Varivax
Manufacturer	Merck
Viability	Live attenuated varicella virus
How supplied	Single-dose vial
Protection	
Onset	Protection begins within 2–4 weeks of initial vaccination
Duration	Unknown but likely to be long; 70–90% of vaccinees protected against infection and 95% against severe disease for 7–10 years after vaccination[62]
Efficacy	78% of adults seroconverted after first dose, 99% after second dose
Pregnancy	Contraindicated; nonpregnant women should be counseled not to attempt pregnancy for 1 month following each vaccination
Contraindications	Hypersensitivity to any vaccine component; immunocompromise, (eg, due to HIV infection, congenital immunodeficiency disorders, leukemia, lymphoma, or generalized malignancy, or reduced immunologic response due to steroids, chemotherapeutic agents, or radiation)
Dosage, route, and site	For adults and adolescents, 0.5 mL SC in the outer aspect of the upper arm, followed by a second 0.5 mL 4–8 weeks after initial dose; if lapse between the first and second doses > 8 weeks, the second dose may be given without restarting the series
Drug interactions	Can be given with another live vaccine either simultaneously at separate anatomic sites or with ≥ 4 wk between immunizations[63]

HIV = human immunodeficiency virus; SC = subcutaneous.

Drug Interactions

If the patient needs two live vaccines, they can be given either simultaneously at separate anatomic sites or with at least a 4-week interval between immunizations.[63]

PREPARING HEALTH SCIENCES STUDENTS FOR ROTATIONS IN DEVELOPING COUNTRIES

Health care workers, including students, face an additional set of challenges to that of the ordinary traveler when preparing for travel and work in developing countries. Working in health care facilities increases the likelihood of exposure to vaccine-preventable diseases such as polio, tetanus, diphtheria, measles, mumps, rubella, varicella, hepatitis A and B, and meningococcal disease. Students should be immunized completely and be current with all vaccines prior to travel.

In addition, although protection against the occupational transmission of blood-borne pathogens is a high priority in the United States, this is not true in resource-poor developing countries, where the prevalence of hepatitis B virus (HBV), hepatitis C virus (HCV), and HIV might be many times higher than in the United States. For example, whereas the prevalence of HBV and HCV in the United States is less than 5% and 2%, respectively, in sub-Saharan Africa, the rate of hepatitis B carriers might approach 19% and that of hepatitis C, 24%.[64]

Sagoe-Moses and colleagues have documented other problems that contribute to an increased risk of occupational transmission of blood-borne pathogens in developing countries: excessive handling of contaminated needles, reuse of nonsterile needles, unregulated disposal of biohazardous waste, improper sterilization procedures, and lack of safer equipment such as automatically retracting finger-stick lancets, plastic or plastic-wrapped capillary tubes, and autodisable syringes. Personal protective equipment, such as gloves, gowns, masks, and goggles, are also lacking.[64]

Student health services at academic medical centers often must prepare health sciences students for rotations in these high-risk settings. In addition to the usual education about standard precautions and basic first aid to the wound site, students must be educated on how to assess the risk of any exposure in terms of its potential to transmit HBV, HCV, or HIV. Detailed guidelines for both risk assessment and postexposure prophylaxis have been published.[34] These guidelines help the health provider to assess the significance of the exposure based on the type of body substance involved, the route and severity of the exposure, and the infectiousness of the source patient.

Several student health centers have developed proactive programs to help protect medical students rotating through health care facilities in developing countries. The State University of New York Health Science Center at Brooklyn provides students with a 5-day supply of triple-therapy postexposure HIV prophylaxis medications, sealed in a tamper-proof bag. In the event of an exposure or possible exposure to HIV, the students are instructed to begin triple therapy immediately and make arrangements to return to the health center for follow-up and continued postexposure management. If no exposures occur during the rotation, the student is to return the unopened bag to the health center. Because of the cost of these medications, if the drugs have not expired, they are sent with the next rotating medical student.

The University of Rochester, New York, has a similar program, supplying a week of HIV medications, which, if unused, are then sent with the next rotating student.[65] In the event of an exposure, students are advised to contact the health center immediately for expert consultation and assessment of the exposure risk, begin triple therapy if indicated, and make plans to return to the United States for continued care. Postexposure prophylaxis is funded by a special health fee assessed to all medical students.

The University of Washington dispenses 5 to 10 days (length of time depends on how close the student will be to a large city with an airport) of Combivir and nelfinavir. The student pays for these medications. In addition, the student is sent with a needle pack for personal use should he or she need health care while on the rotation. The students are also provided with the phone number and e-mail address of the student health service at the University of Washington so that consultation with experts can be undertaken in a timely fashion.

In some international health care settings, drug-resistant HIV in the source patient might be a concern. Students should obtain as much information as possible about the source patient, including any past or current antiretroviral treatment. This information should be relayed to the student's United States health center postexposure prophylaxis (PEP) personnel to assist with consultation regarding appropriate PEP medications. An additional source of information is the National Clinicians' Post-Exposure Prophylaxis Hotline (PEPline) run by the University of California-San Francisco/San Francisco General Hospital staff (888-448-4911). Resistance testing of the source patient is not practical or realistic.

Students should be encouraged to take a supply of personal protective equipment (PPE) with them. Gloves, gowns, masks, and goggles might not be available in resource-poor countries. Students should also be aware that in tropical regions there is potential for transmission of other lethal blood-borne pathogens besides HBV, HCV, and HIV. These include Lassa virus, Ebola virus, and other hemorrhagic fever viruses.

Another potential hazard for rotating health sciences students is exposure to tuberculosis. Students should have a tuberculin skin test placed and read prior to travel to TB-endemic areas and should be retested within 10 to 12 weeks following their return to the United States. New converters should be treated preventively as detailed in the *Core Curriculum on Tuberculosis, 2000*.[66] If students will be working where cases of active pulmonary tuberculosis are likely, they should take a supply of N-95 disposable (nondisposable models are also available), nonpowered air-purifying respirator masks (duckbills).[59] Students should be fit-tested for these masks to determine which size to take with them. Under rare circumstances, use of BCG vaccine prior to travel might be considered. Epidemiologic factors that might favor the use of BCG vaccine include prolonged stay in an area with high rates of MDR TB where work or frequent leisure activities are anticipated to occur in crowded, confined spaces. Prior to administering BCG, consultation is advised either locally with TB control experts or nationally with the CDC's Division of Tuberculosis Elimination (404-639-8120).

Finally, if the student will be working in villages or even medium-sized towns, he or she should consider obtaining three doses of the preexposure rabies vaccine series before the trip. Postexposure prophylaxis is not readily available, even in major capital cities.

REFERENCES

1. Centers for Disease Control and Prevention. Ten great public health achievements—United States, 1900–1999. MMWR Morb Mortal Wkly Rep 1999;48:241–64.

2. Levin A. Vaccines today. Ann Intern Med 2000;133:661–4.

3. Centers for Disease Control and Prevention. Recommended adult immunization schedule—United States, 2002–2003. MMWR Morb Mortal Wkly Rep 2002;51:904–8.

4. Centers for Disease Control and Prevention. Prevention pneumococcal disease. Recommendations of the Advisory Committee on Immunization Practices. MMWR Morb Mortal Wkly Rep 1997;46(RR-8):1–24.

5. Centers for Disease Control and Prevention. General recommendations on immunization. Recommendations of the Advisory Committee on Immunization Practices (ACIP) and the American Academy of Family Physicians (AAFP). MMWR Morb Mortal Wkly Rep 2002;51(RR-2):1–35.

6. Capparella J, Collins M, Singleton J, et al. 1999 College immunization survey. Philadelphia: American College Health Association and the Centers for Disease Control and Prevention; 1999.

7. Centers for Disease Control and Prevention. Notice to readers. Recommendations of the Advisory Committee on Immunization Practices. Revised recommendations for routine poliomyelitis vaccination. MMWR Morb Mortal Wkly Rep 1999;48:590.

8. Centers for Disease Control and Prevention. Prevention of varicella. Recommendations of the Advisory Committee on Immunization Practices. MMWR Morb Mortal Wkly Rep 1996;45(RR11):1–25.

9. World Health Organization. Summary of routine immunization requirements by country. Institute of International Education.

10. Centers for Disease Control and Prevention. Measles—United States, 2000. MMWR Morb Mortal Wkly Rep 2000;51:120–3.

11. Centers for Disease Control and Prevention. Measles incidence before and after supplementary vaccination activities—Lusaka, Zambia, 1996–2000. MMWR Morb Mortal Wkly Rep 2001;50:513–6.

12. Centers for Disease Control and Prevention. Measles, mumps, and rubella—vaccine use and strategies for elimination of measles, rubella, and congenital rubella syndrome and control of mumps. Recommendations of the Advisory Committee on Immunization Practices (ACIP). MMWR Morb Mortal Wkly Rep1998;47(RR-8):1–57.

13. Centers for Disease Control and Prevention. Notice to readers. Revised ACIP recommendation for avoiding pregnancy after receiving a rubella-containing vaccine. MMWR Morb Mortal Wkly Rep 2001;50:1117.

14. Centers for Disease Control and Prevention. Recommendations of the Advisory Committee on Immunization Practices (ACIP). Use of vaccines and immune globulins in persons with altered immunocompetence. MMWR Morb Mortal Wkly Rep 1993;42(RR-4):1–18.

15. Reef S, Frey T, Theall K, et al. The changing epidemiology of rubella in the 1990's. On the verge of elimination and new challenges for control and prevention. JAMA 2002;287:464–72.

16. Centers for Disease Control and Prevention. Poliomyelitis prevention in the United States. Updated recommendations of the Advisory Committee on Immunization Practices. MMWR Morb Mortal Wkly Rep 2000;49(RR-5):1–22.

17. Centers for Disease Control and Prevention. Apparent global interruption of wild poliovirus Type 2 transmission. MMWR Morb Mortal Wkly Rep 2001;50:1–4.

18. Streubel P, Sutter R, Cochi S, et al. Epidemiology of poliomyelitis in the United States one decade after the last reported case of indigenous wild virus-associated disease. Clin Infect Dis 1992;14:568–79.

19. Centers for Disease Control and Prevention. Update. Eradication of paralytic poliomyelitis in the Americas. MMWR Morb Mortal Wkly Rep 1992;41:681–3.

20. Centers for Disease Control and Prevention. Public health dispatch. Certification of poliomyelitis eradication—European Region, June, 2002. MMWR Morb Mortal Wkly Rep 2002;51:572–4.

21. Centers for Disease Control and Prevention. Imported wild poliovirus causing poliomyelitis—Bulgaria, 2001. MMWR Morb Mortal Wkly Rep 2001;50(46):1033–5.

22. Centers for Disease Control and Prevention. Progress toward global poliomyelitis eradication, 2000. MMWR Morb Mortal Wkly Rep 2001;50:1–6.

23. Centers for Disease Control and Prevention. Progress toward poliomyelitis eradication—Eastern Mediterranean Region, January 2000–September 2001. MMWR Morb Mortal Wkly Rep 2001;50(49):1113–6.

24. Centers for Disease Control and Prevention. Public Health Dispatch. Acute flaccid paralysis associated with circulating vaccine-derived poliomyelitis—Philippines, 2001. MMWR Morb Mortal Wkly Rep 2001;50(40):874–5.

25. Centers for Disease Control and Prevention. Public Health Dispatch. Update. Outbreak of poliomyelitis—Dominican Republic and Haiti, 2000–2001. MMWR Morb Mortal Wkly Rep 2001;50(39):855–6.

26. Centers for Disease Control and Prevention. Tetanus—Puerto Rico, 2002. MMWR Morb Mortal Wkly Rep 2002;51:613–5.

27. Gardner P, Peter G. Recommended schedules for routine immunization of children and adults. Infect Dis Clin North Am 2001;15:1–18.

28. Centers for Disease Control and Prevention. Notice to readers. Deferral of routine booster doses of tetanus and diphtheria toxoids for adolescents and adults. MMWR Morb Mortal Wkly Rep 2001;50(20):418–9.

29. Munoz F, Englund J. Vaccines in pregnancy. Infect Dis Clin North Am 2001;15:253–71.

30. Steffan R. Immunization against hepatitis A and hepatitis B infections. J Travel Med 2001;8 Suppl 1:S9–16.

31. Centers for Disease Control and Prevention. Prevention of hepatitis A through active or passive immunization. MMWR Morb Mortal Wkly Rep 1999;48(RR-12):1–39.

32. Centers for Disease Control and Prevention. Health information for the international traveler 2003–2004. Atlanta (GA): US Department of Health and Human Services; 2003.

33. Centers for Disease Control and Prevention. Hepatitis B virus. A comprehensive strategy for eliminating transmission in the United States through universal childhood vaccination. Recommendations of the immunization Practices Advisory Committee (ACIP). MMWR Morb Mortal Wkly Rep 1991;40(RR-13):1–19.

34. Centers for Disease Control and Prevention. Updated U.S. Public Health Service guidelines for the management of occupational exposures to HBV, HCV, and HIV and recommendations for posexposure prophylaxis. MMWR Morb Mortal Wkly Rep 2001;(RR-11):1–42.

35. Walker P, Jaranson J. Refugee and immigrant health care. Med Clin North Am 1999;83:1103–20.

36. Bock HL, Loscher T, Scheiermann N, et al. Accelerated schedule for hepatitis B immunization. J Travel Med 1995;2:213–7.

37. Centers for Disease Control and Prevention. Prevention and control of influenza. Recommendations of the Advisory Committee on Immunization Practices (ACIP). MMWR Morb Mortal Wkly Rep 2001;RR04:1–46.

38. Centers for Disease Control and Prevention. Prevention and control of influenza. Recommendations of the Advisory Committee on Immunization Practices (ACIP). MMWR Morb Mortal Wkly Rep 2000;49:1–38.

39. Centers for Disease Control and Prevention. Who shoiuld get the influenza (flu) vaccine: interim recommendations, Dec, 2003. Available at http://www.cdc.gov/flu/protect/vaccine.htm (accessed December 16, 2003).

40. Centers for Disease Control and Prevention. Control and prevention of meningococcal disease and control and prevention of serogroup C meningococcal disease. Evaluation and management of suspected outbreaks. MMWR Recomm Rep 1997;46(RR-5):1–21.

41. Bruce MG, Rosenstein NE, Capparella JM, et al. Risk factors for meningococcal disease in college students. JAMA 2001;286:688–93.

42. Harrison LH, Dwyer DM, Maples CT, Billmann L. Risk of meningococcal infection in college students. JAMA 1999;281:1906–10.

43. Froeshle JE. Meningococcal disease in college students. Clin Infect Dis 1999;29:215–6.

44. Neal KR, Nguyen VTJ, Monk P, et al. Invasive meningococcal disease among university undergraduates. Epidemiol Infect 1999;122:351–7.

45. Scott R, Meltzer M, Erickson L, et al. Vaccination first-year college students living in dormitories for meningococcal disease. An economic analysis. Am J Prev Med 2002;(23):98–105.

46. Rosenstein N, Fischer M, Tappero J. Meningococcal vaccines. Infect Dis Clin North Am 2001;15:155–69.

47. Centers for Disease Control and Prevention. Public health dispatch. Update. Assessment of risk for meningococal disease associated with the Hajj 2001. MMWR Morb Mortal Wkly Rep 2001;50(12):221–2.

48. Centers for Disease Control and Prevention. Prevention and control of meningococcal disease and meningococcal disease and college students. MMWR Morb Mortal Wkly Rep 2000;49(RR-7):1–20.

49. Centers for Disease Control and Prevention. Meningococcal disease and college students. Recommendations of the Advisory Committee on Immunization Practices. MMWR Morb Mortal Wkly Rep 2000;49(RR-7):11–20.

50. Centers for Disease Control and Prevention. Prevention of pneumococcal disease. Recommendations of the Advisory Committee on Immunization Practices (ACIP). MMWR Recomm Rep 1997;46(RR-8):1–24.

51. Poland G. The prevention of pneumococcal disease by vaccines. Promises and challenges. Infect Dis Clin North Am 2001;15:97–121.

52. Centers for Disease Control and Prevention. Influenza and pneumococcal vaccination levels among persons aged greater than or equal to 65 years—United States, 1999. MMWR Morb Mortal Wkly Rep 2001;50(25):532–7.

53. Jong E. Travel immunizations. Med Clin North Am 1999;83:903–22.

54. World Health Organization. Global tuberculosis control. WHO Report 2001. Geneva (Switz): Communicable Diseases Section, World Health Organization; 2001. p. 1–34.

55. Espinal M, Lazlo A, Simonsen L, et al. Global trends in resistance to antituberculosis drugs. New Engl J Med 2001;344:1294–303.

56. Lobato M, Hopewell P. *Mycobacterium tuberculosis* infection after travel to or contact with vistors from countries with a high prevalence of tuberculosis. Am J Respir Crit Care Med 1998;158:1871–5.

57. Cobelens F, Deutekom HV, Draayer-Jansen I, et al. Risk of infection with *Mycobacterium tuberculosis* in travellers to areas of high tuberculosis endemicity. Lancet 2000;356:461–5.

58. Wilson M. Travel-related vaccines. Infect Dis Clin North Am 2001;15:231–51.

59. Centers for Disease Control and Prevention. Guidelines for preventing the transmission of *Mycobacterium tuberculosis* in health-care facilities. MMWR Morb Mortal Wkly Rep 1994;RR-13.

60. Centers for Disease Control and Prevention. The role of BCG vaccine in the prevention and control of tuberculosis in the United States. MMWR Recomm Rep 1996;45(RR-4):1–18.

61. Gershon A. Live-attenuated varicella vaccine. Infect Dis Clin North Am 2001;15:65–81.

62. Centers for Disease Control and Prevention. Prevention of varicella. Recommendations of the Advisory Committee on Immunization Practices (ACIP). MMWR Recomm Rep 1996;45(RR-11):1-25.

63. Centers for Disease Control and Prevention. Simultaneous administration of varicella vaccine and other recommended childhood vaccines—United States, 1995–2001. MMWR Morb Mortal Wkly Rep 2001;50(47):1058–61.

64. Sagoe-Moses C, Pearson RD, Perry J, Jagger J. Risks to health care workers in developing countries. New Engl J Med 2001;345:538–40.

65. Tanzman E, Manchester R. Risks to health care workers in developing countries [letter to the editor]. New Engl J Med 2001;345:1916.

66. Centers for Disease Control and Prevention. Core curriculum on tuberculosis. What the clinician should know. 4th ed. Atlanta (GA): National Center for HIV, STD, and TB Prevention; 2000.

67. Centers for Disease Control and Prevention. Health Information for the International Traveler 2001–2002. Atlanta (GA): US Department of Health and Human Services, Public Health Service; 2001.

68. Capparella et al. The 1999 college immunization survey. Paper presented at the American College Health Association Annual Meeting, Philadelphia, 1999.

Chapter 17

TRAVEL IMMUNIZATIONS FOR SPECIAL RISK GROUPS:
PREGNANT AND IMMUNE COMPROMISED

Tanya Schreibman and Frank J. Bia

As global travel continues to increase, vaccination practices for compromised individuals assume increasing importance. The decision to vaccinate an immunocompromised or pregnant patient involves the balancing of multiple risks and benefits for each individual. Generalized vaccine recommendations are based on a variety of considerations, including the burden of disease as well as the safety, cost, risks, and immunogenic characteristics of a given vaccine. Patients with an altered immune state must receive separate attention for multiple reasons. First, they are at increased risk of certain vaccine-preventable diseases that could have serious consequences for an immunocompromised patient. Second, vaccination itself may be associated with increased risks in the immunocompromised host. Finally, vaccination may be less efficacious within certain immunosuppressed populations. Each compromised patient must thus be considered on an individual basis in terms of perceived risk for disease, the potential risks of vaccination, and the possibility of decreased vaccine efficacy.

To best approach these issues, we begin with a discussion highlighting the relevant characteristics of each vaccine. Childhood vaccinations will also be included in this discussion since they are also important to update prior to travel whenever the effects of primary vaccinations may have waned. We will consider the following categories of patients and the particular vaccinations that apply to them.

1. Immunocompromised hosts
   - cancer chemotherapy recipients
   - bone marrow transplant recipients
   - solid organ transplant recipients
   - chronic corticosteroid users
   - multiple sclerosis patients
   - those with autoimmune diseases
2. Human immunodeficiency virus (HIV)–infected patients
3. Pregnant women
4. Hosts with conditions causing limited immune deficiencies that do not contraindicate any particular vaccinations but for which specific vaccinations are recommended
   - asplenia
   - chronic renal failure
   - diabetes mellitus
   - chronic liver disease
   - chronic cardiac or pulmonary conditions
   - clotting factor deficiencies

The term "severely immunocompromised" is used frequently in this chapter. This is a subjective term, meant to refer to patients with end-stage HIV disease but not to patients with asymptomatic HIV infection. It also refers to patients who are on multiple immunosuppressive medications following bone marrow transplant but not to patients with a prior history of Hodgkin's disease.

THE VACCINES

We have grouped vaccines in the following manner: (1) routine, (2) travel, (3) rarely recommended, or (4) bioterrorism related. Immediately following the name of each vaccine is a description of the vaccine's type (eg, live attenuated, inactivated, exotoxin). Much of the chapter will focus on live viral and bacterial vaccines (yellow fever, oral polio, measles-mumps-rubella [MMR], oral typhoid, varicella, bacille Calmette-Guérin [BCG], vaccinia), the administration of which can lead to continued microbial replication in certain hosts. Detailed discussion regarding vaccination in specific hosts follows this overview.

There are only a few absolute contraindications that should be highlighted prior to our discussion:

1. the administration of MMR vaccination during pregnancy or in severely immunocompromised hosts,
2. the administration of varicella vaccination during pregnancy or in severely immunocompromised hosts, and
3. the administration of oral polio, oral typhoid, BCG, or vaccinia vaccination during pregnancy or in any immunocompromised hosts (including all HIV-infected patients). The inactivated polio or parenteral typhoid vaccines can be used as alternatives.

The remainder of this chapter details all other recommendations, which vary depending on the host, the vaccine, and the clinical scenario.

Routine Vaccinations

Routine childhood vaccinations now include *Haemophilus influenzae* type b conjugate vaccine (Hib), hepatitis B vaccine, diphtheria and tetanus toxoids and acellular pertussis vaccine (DTaP), inactivated polio vaccine (IPV), MMR vaccine, conjugate seven-valent pneumococcal vaccine, and varicella vaccine. Routine adult vaccinations include updating any vaccinations from the above list, as well the adult tetanus-diphtheria toxoid booster, the 23-valent pneumococcal polysaccharide vaccine, and the influenza vaccine (the latter two only in high-risk patients). Routine vaccination data should always be reviewed and updated in patients planning travel, particularly for measles and polio, which may be more common in the developing world. In the following discussion, routine vaccinations that are particularly important to consider during travel are marked with an asterisk (*).

Haemophilus influenzae *type b (Inactivated Polysaccharide Conjugate Vaccine)*
Hib is a routine childhood immunization considered to be both safe and effective. Specific issues to consider with this vaccine are administration in patients with chronic conditions or diseases, such as asplenia, known to be at increased risk for *H. influenzae*, as well as possible decreased vaccine efficacy in HIV-infected patients.[1] There are no travel-specific recommendations with this vaccine.

Hepatitis B (Inactivated Recombinant Vaccine)*

Hepatitis B is now part of routine childhood immunization and is considered to be both safe and efficacious for most recipients. Because hepatitis B is prevalent in much of the developing world and is transmitted via blood or body secretions, vaccination is recommended for all long-term travelers who may have close contact with blood or sexual contact with potentially infected local residents. Expatriate medical workers may be at particular risk.

Although vaccine efficacy may be diminished somewhat, immunization is also specifically recommended for patients with end-stage liver disease (ESLD), HIV infection, or end-stage renal disease (ESRD), the latter because of an increased risk of hepatitis B acquisition via blood products and hemodialysis.

Diminished vaccine efficacy is of great concern for many other recipients in addition to patients with ESLD, ESRD, and HIV infection. Groups include those with malignancies as well as the elderly. In addition, concern has been raised regarding the potential for vaccines to induce the onset of autoimmune disease or trigger a relapse in patients with multiple sclerosis. These issues will be discussed in more detail later in the chapter.

Influenza (Inactivated Whole Virus)

The inactivated influenza vaccines are considered safe for use in all hosts, and they should be administered to appropriate individuals traveling to epidemic areas. The controversial issues of potentially increased viral replication in the HIV-infected host, as well as case reports of relapses in MS patients, are discussed below. The live attenuated influenza vaccine (LAIV) is considered safe for use in healthy persons between the ages of 5 and 49 years old. The LAIV should not be administered to persons with compromised immunity and should not be administered to recipients such as health care workers and household or family members likely to be in close contact with such at risk populations.

Pneumococcus (Inactivated or Conjugate Polysaccharide)

The conjugate seven-valent polysaccharide pneumococcal vaccine is now part of routine childhood immunization and can be used with infants younger than 2 years. In addition, the 23-valent polysaccharide vaccine is recommended in all high-risk patients, including immunocompromised and HIV-infected hosts, even though decreased vaccine efficacy has been noted in the latter group. Vaccination should also be updated for all susceptible individuals prior to travel. The safety of pneumococcal vaccination in pregnant women has not been studied, but there are no current reports of adverse events.

Tetanus (Inactivated Detoxified Exotoxin)*

Tetanus immunization is a part of routine childhood vaccinations, with booster doses recommended every 10 years. Although there are no specific patient groups for whom vaccination is contraindicated, decreased vaccine efficacy in HIV-infected patients has been reported. Since tetanus is more prevalent in developing areas, reviewing tetanus booster history is important in preparing all travelers, particularly trekers, climbers, and those engaged in extreme sports.

Diphtheria (Detoxified Exotoxin)*

Diphtheria vaccine is usually administered together with tetanus and pertussis as part of routine childhood vaccinations and should be updated in adults prior to travel. Of note are outbreaks of diphtheria in eastern Europe and Russia.[2]

Pertussis (Killed Whole Cell Vaccine or Detoxified Toxin)

Pertussis vaccination is routinely administered with diphtheria and tetanus childhood vaccinations. There are no specific travel recommendations pertaining to this component of the vaccine.

Poliomyelitis (Inactivated Virus or Live Attenuated Virus)*

There had been two forms of vaccine available against polioviruses, oral polio vaccine (OPV) and IPV. Only the enhanced IPV is currently used and is considered part of routine childhood immunization.

Non–vaccine-related poliomyelitis no longer occurs in the United States, although vaccination is recommended for unimmunized travelers to developing countries where the risk of polio still exists. This includes any area in which polio is endemic or where there is a current epidemic, including most countries other than the Americas, Australia, New Zealand, Japan, and the majority of European countries.[3]

OPV is made from live attenuated poliovirus and is no longer available for primary or booster immunization because of the reported, but rare, risk of vaccine-associated paralytic poliomyelitis. It can still be used for control of community outbreaks. Since it is a live viral vaccine, OPV has been contraindicated in immunocompromised patients and their household contacts, as well as during pregnancy.

Varicella (Live Attenuated Virus)

The varicella vaccine was licensed in 1995 and is now part of routine childhood immunization. Since varicella is endemic in most countries, vaccination should be considered for international travelers who do not have clinical or serologic evidence of prior disease or immunity. Although the illness is considered a "childhood disease" in industrialized temperate climates, it actually occurs quite commonly among adults in tropical developing areas.[4]

The live viral varicella vaccine is contraindicated during pregnancy and for 1 month prior to pregnancy. It should not be administered to severely immunosuppressed individuals, although it should be given to close contacts of patients known to be at high risk.

Measles (Live Attenuated Viral Vaccine)*

Measles vaccination is part of the routine MMR vaccination recommended for all children. All individuals born after the year 1957 should be vaccinated against measles if they have not had the disease. Most born before 1957 are immune through natural exposure and infection. However, persons born between 1958 and 1980 likely received only one dose of vaccine and thus should receive a booster dose if traveling abroad.

Although measles shows a declining prevalence in the United States, it is still present in many areas of the world, including Europe and most developing countries. Immigrants with imported disease now account for a large proportion of cases in the United States. Confirming prior vaccination is particularly important for immunocompromised hosts or pregnant women, who have an increased incidence of serious complications from measles. In the event of measles exposure in a high-risk host, immunoglobulin (Ig) should be administered regardless of prior vaccine status.

As with all live viral vaccines, MMR is contraindicated in severely immunocompromised hosts and pregnant women.

Mumps (Live Attenuated Virus)

Mumps immunization is part of routine childhood vaccination, along with measles and rubella. As stated above, contraindications are pregnancy and a severely immunocompromised state.

Rubella (Live Attenuated Virus)

Rubella is administered with measles and mumps as part of routine childhood vaccination. It should be confirmed that women of childbearing age are immune to rubella. As with mumps and measles, contraindications to vaccination include severe immunocompromise and pregnancy.

Specific Travel-Related Vaccinations

Meningococcal Virus (Inactivated Polysaccharide Vaccine)

The meningococcal vaccine contains inactivated bacterial polysaccharides obtained from *Neisseria meningitidis* serogroups A, C, Y, and W-135. There is no commercial vaccine product currently available against meningococcus serotype B.

Meningococcal disease is endemic throughout the world, occurring most frequently during the winter and early spring months. Vaccination might be considered for travelers to areas with recognized epidemics, such as sub-Saharan Africa, northern India, and Nepal, or for travelers who expect to have prolonged contact with the residents of hyperendemic regions.[5] It is a legal requirement for pilgrims wishing to enter Mecca, Saudi Arabia, and for all visa applicants to Saudi Arabia.[6]

Vaccination is considered safe in all patient groups, although the vaccine may be less efficacious in HIV-infected individuals. Vaccination is routinely recommended for asplenic patients and for those who are deficient in terminal complement components.

Japanese B Encephalitis (Inactivated Whole Virus Vaccine)

Japanese B encephalitis vaccine is available in the United States as an inactivated mouse brain–derived product with an estimated vaccine efficacy of 80 to 90%. Serious adverse reactions, such as urticaria, angioedema, itching, and respiratory distress, are reported in up to 6 in 1,000 recipients.[7] Adverse neurologic reactions, including acute disseminated encephalomyelitis, have been reported in vaccinees, but a definitive causal role for the vaccine has not been established.[8]

Japanese encephalitis may be encountered in both northern tropical and temperate regions of the Far East and Southeast Asia, including Bangladesh, Cambodia, China, India, Korea, Laos, Myanmar (Burma), Nepal, Thailand, Vietnam, and the eastern areas of the former Soviet Union. Endemic areas include the tropical regions of Indonesia, Malaysia, the Philippines, Singapore, Sri Lanka, Taiwan, southern India, and Thailand. It occurs rarely in Hong Kong and Japan. Risk becomes highest with prolonged stays in rural areas during the late summer and fall.

In general, vaccination should be limited to travelers who will spend at least 30 days during the late summer and fall in an endemic region, especially in a rural area where pig farming occurs.[9] Although there are no absolute contraindications to vaccination, there is concern about potentially decreased efficacy in immunocompromised hosts and HIV-infected patients. There is also limited experience with the vaccine in pregnant women.

Typhoid (Inactivated Polysaccharide and Live Attenuated Bacterial Vaccine)

Three types of vaccinations against *Salmonella typhi* (typhoid fever) are currently available: (1) oral live attenuated vaccine, (2) parenteral capsular polysaccharide vaccine, and (3) parenteral heat- and phenol-killed vaccine, which is now rarely used. The oral vaccine is 70% effective and well tolerated but not yet considered safe for immunocompromised hosts. The polysaccharide parenteral vaccine is the preferred vaccine since it also offers 70% protection while being safe for use in immunocompromised patients.

S. Typhi is prevalent throughout Asia, Africa, and Latin America. The risk is greatest for those traveling to the Indian subcontinent, where antibiotic resistance is also increasing. Vaccination is recommended for all travelers to areas endemic for typhoid or for travelers who will have prolonged exposures to potentially contaminated food and water in developing countries.

As previously noted, live attenuated typhoid vaccine should not be administered to immunocompromised hosts or pregnant women. In addition, experience with the inactivated typhoid vaccine in pregnant women has also been limited. Older vaccines caused fevers, which should be avoided, particularly during the first trimester.

Hepatitis A (Inactivated Virus)

There are two available inactivated hepatitis A virus (HAV) vaccines that provide long-term immunity following complete series administration. Immune serum globulin (ISG) may also be administered as immediate passive immunization, but ISG is more expensive, provides only short-term protection, and is usually recommended only in children younger than 2 years of age, and others who cannot be immunized with hepatitis A vaccines.

Hepatitis A is prevalent in many developing countries and is the most common preventable infection in travelers (0.3% incidence per month of stay in unprotected travelers and 2% incidence per month for those with poor hygiene).[10] Vaccination is recommended for all gay men, patients with clotting factor deficiencies, intravenous drug users, and patients with ESLD. In addition, vaccination is recommended in all individuals traveling to countries where HAV is endemic. In general, the hepatitis A vaccines are safe and efficacious in all hosts, although there are limited data available on its use in pregnant women.[11] Always determine whether vaccination against hepatitis A and B would best be accomplished simultaneously using one of the available combined vaccines.

Yellow Fever (Live Attenuated Viral Vaccine)

Yellow fever 17D vaccine is a live viral vaccine prepared as an extract from embryonated hens' eggs. Resultant immunity is probably lifelong, although booster doses are recommended every 10 years. This is the only vaccine that must be administered at a designated yellow fever vaccination center. It is also the only vaccination required for entry into certain countries or following exit from such countries and before entering a nonendemic region. Vaccination requirements are updated yearly, and they are listed in the United States Centers for Disease Control and Prevention (CDC) publication.

Official reports of yellow fever are published by the CDC and the World Health Organization (WHO); however, many cases go undiagnosed and therefore unreported. Yellow fever is endemic in some urban and rural areas of Africa and equatorial South America. Infection rates are high when epidemics occur, appearing in more than 30% of the affected population, and the overall case fatality rate is about 20%.[9] Two fatal cases of yellow fever in unvaccinated US residents have been reported in the past, one in 1996 and one in 1999.[12]

General recommendations for vaccination include persons older than 9 months visiting any country where yellow fever is known to potentially exist or travelers coming from such endemic countries. Although vaccination is considered both safe and efficacious, serious adverse reactions have included hypersensitivity reactions, neuroencephalitis, and systemic infections similar to those caused by wild-type yellow fever virus (10 reported cases of the latter).[13–15] As with all live vaccines, yellow fever immunization is generally not recommended for patients with severe immunosuppression, including advanced HIV infections, or for pregnant women. As discussed below, the benefits of vaccination may outweigh such risks if travel to an endemic area is absolutely necessary for a nonimmune traveler.

Rabies (Inactivated Virus)

Three types of rabies vaccination are currently available: human diploid cell rabies vaccine (HDCV), fetal rhesus lung diploid cell culture, and purified chick embryo cell cultures (PCEC) vaccines. Rabies vaccine is used either prophylactically, in those who will be at increased risk, or after exposure to an animal thought to be rabid. Vaccination does *not* eliminate the need for postexposure treatment but does abbreviate the postexposure treatment course and obviate the need for rabies ISG, which is expensive and often in short supply.

Rabies can be found in almost any region, including Asia, Africa, Central and South America, Mexico, India, Nepal, the Philippines, Sri Lanka, Thailand, and Vietnam. Vaccination should be considered for travelers who anticipate contact with wild animals or who are living for more than a month in an area endemic for rabies. It should also be considered for young children, joggers, veterinarians, animal handlers, field workers, and persons working in remote areas.[16]

There are no known contraindications to rabies vaccination. Vaccination is of particular importance in immunocompromised hosts, who theoretically are at increased risk of disease if infected. However, the vaccine appears to be less immunogenic in immunocompromised patients, emphasizing the need for postexposure rabies ISG in these patients regardless of preexposure vaccination.

Rarely Recommended Vaccinations

Cholera (Inactivated Whole Organism Suspension)

Cholera vaccine is prepared from killed bacteria and is minimally effective (50%) against cholera group 01, which is common in Latin America, and likely not effective against cholera group 0139, common in Asia.[17] Routine immunization is no longer recommended for travelers.[18] Prior to 1988, WHO required vaccination for entry into some Latin American countries. Though local authorities may still require proof of vaccination prior to entry, this is no longer a WHO requirement.

There are no specific contraindications to the cholera vaccination.

Bacille Calmette-Guérin Vaccine (Live Attenuated)

Use of BCG vaccine in the United States is limited, although it is used widely throughout the world. Estimated overall efficacy of the vaccine against tuberculosis (TB) is 51%.[19] General vaccination recommendations remain controversial for those traveling to areas where tuberculosis is endemic. Some authorities do recommend vaccination for young children who have had prolonged close contact with a family member with active, and particularly drug-resistant, TB in order to prevent dissemination. Others do not recommend vaccination given its potential side effects and limited efficacy and the loss of skin test utility.

Immunocompromised hosts, including all adult patients with HIV infection, and pregnant women should not be given BCG vaccine because of the increased risk of disseminated BCG infection.

Tick-Borne Encephalitis (Inactivated Viral Vaccine)

Two effective inactivated vaccines are available in Europe. Vaccination can be considered for long term-travelers to forested endemic areas in parts of Russia and central and eastern Europe.[5,20] There are no specific contraindications to vaccination.

Vaccines against Bioterrorism

Smallpox (Vaccinia) (Live Attenuated)

The last reported case of smallpox was recorded in 1977. WHO has since removed smallpox from the list of required vaccinations, and Wyeth Laboratories, Madison, New Jersey, discontinued vaccine production in 1983. Fifteen million available doses remained by 2002, with expected increased production because of rising concerns over its use as an agent of bioterrorism. Until recently, it has been indicated only for those working with vaccinia or other orthopoxviruses.[21]

Vaccination is contraindicated for severely immunocompromised patients, as well as for their household contacts and all HIV-infected hosts, in addition to pregnant women.

Anthrax (Killed Virus)

Anthrax vaccine is prepared from microaerophilic cultures of an avirulent nonencapsulated strain of *Bacillus anthracis*. Although vaccine efficacy has been demonstrated for protection against cutaneous disease, and 90% or more of recipients produce antibodies, clinical efficacy is not guaranteed against inhaled anthrax.

Prior to recent bioterrorism events, vaccination was indicated only for those at high risk of exposure to anthrax, including military personnel and those coming into contact with material from anthrax-endemic areas.

There are no specific contraindications to anthrax immunization.

Plague (Killed Suspension)

Plague vaccination has undefined efficacy and is recommended only for use in plague-infected areas. The vaccine is not effective against pneumonic plague. It is indicated for those with a high probability of exposure in rural upland areas of South America, Africa, and Asia, and in New Mexico and Arizona.[22]

IMMUNOCOMPROMISED HOSTS

This section considers non–HIV-infected immunocompromised travelers, including patients with congenital immunodeficiencies, leukemia, lymphoma, or generalized malignancy, as well as patients receiving alkylating agents, antimetabolites, radiation, or high-dose corticosteroid therapy. We begin with some general principles regarding travel vaccinations for these individuals and then discuss specific patient groups. It should be noted that most data on vaccination in immunocompromised hosts are derived from small-group studies or from studies that have been extrapolated from those done in healthy individuals.

- Live vaccinations (oral polio, yellow fever, MMR, varicella, oral typhoid, BCG) should generally be avoided in immunocompromised hosts due to the potential risk of enhanced viral replication.[23] For example, prolonged viremia as a result of yellow fever vaccination may place these patients at risk of encephalitis, hepatitis, or invasion of the central nervous system. However, there are no official reports of adverse events occurring in immunocompromised persons.[24]

- Vaccination should be considered if travel to an endemic region is absolutely necessary. However, if an immuncompromised patient is entering a country that requires vaccination simply to meet entry requirements but the country is not endemic for yellow fever, then a letter of vaccine waiver may be issued.

- In the event that travel-related immunizations are absolutely necessary, any vaccination should always be considered in light of the risk of contracting a given disease if the immunization was not given. According to the CDC Advisory Committee on Immunization Practices (ACIP) guidelines, varicella, MMR, oral polio, and oral typhoid are considered absolutely contraindicated for severely immunocompromised patients. In addition, OPV must be avoided for household contacts of immunocompromised patients, although MMR is considered safe.[25] Parenteral typhoid and parenteral polio vaccinations should be used as alternatives to these oral vaccinations.

- When possible, immunization should precede immunosuppression, such as chemotherapy or high-dose corticosteroid therapy, by at least 2 weeks or follow it by more than 3 months. Patients may have weaker and less durable antibody responses if vaccinated later in the course of an immunosuppressive disease or its therapy. For patients vaccinated while on corticosteroid therapy or within 2 weeks of starting such therapy, revaccination should occur at least 3 months after discontinuation of therapy.

- Killed/inactivated vaccines may be administered as recommended for healthy persons, although the response may be suboptimal.

- Immune responses may be limited in certain hosts, thereby dictating higher vaccine dosages or more frequent booster doses.

Commentaries regarding specific groups of immunocompromised patients are listed below.

Cancer Chemotherapy Patients

Although all malignancies are associated with some degree of immunosuppression, patients with hematologic malignancies such as lymphoma and leukemia are most severely immuncompromised, particularly patients with myeloma or chronic lymphocytic leukemia.[26] Inadequate responses to vaccination are also observed in these patients; thus, higher vaccine doses or more frequent boosters should be considered. As outlined above, it is best to give all vaccinations as early in the disease course as possible and to avoid live viral vaccinations 2 weeks prior to and at least 3 months following chemotherapy.[5]

Bone Marrow Transplant Recipients

Patients who have undergone bone marrow transplant routinely lose immunity conferred by previous vaccinations (including MMR, tetanus, diphtheria, polio, Hib, pneumococcus) and require reimmunization beginning 12 to 24 months after transplantation. In general, live viral vaccinations should be avoided.[5]

Solid Organ Transplant

Solid organ transplant recipients commonly receive immunosuppressive agents such as cyclosporine and tacrolimus, which have an impact on T-cell function, or azathioprine and corticosteroids, which have an impact on neutrophil function. Given the resultant immunosuppression, an ideal time for vaccination is at least 1 month prior to transplantation, when antibody responses are greatest and risks of vaccine-associated complications are lowest. As with other immunocompromised hosts, these transplant recipients should not receive live viral vaccines. Administered vaccines typically produce weaker and less durable antibody responses. There is, however, no increased risk of organ rejection after vaccination.[5]

Of particular note is hepatitis A vaccine, which has been shown to be safe and immunogenic in both liver and renal transplant recipients.[27] Vaccination is indicated for all patients with chronic liver disease who are awaiting transplant.

Corticosteroid Usage

High-dose corticosteroid therapy (> 2 mg/kg/day or > 20 mg of prednisone per day for 14 days or more) for connective tissue diseases or other immune-mediated disorders results in defective cell-mediated immunity and blunted responses to immunizations.[28] Live viral vaccinations should be avoided during therapy and for at least 3 months following therapy. Of note, this does not apply to patients receiving short courses of prednisone (< 2 weeks), maintenance physiologic doses, alternate-day treatment with short-acting preparations, topical (skin or eyes) treatments, aerosol steroids, or intra-articular, bursal, or tendon injections.[29]

Multiple Sclerosis

The onset or worsening of multiple sclerosis (MS) following vaccination, particularly influenza and hepatitis B, has been a subject of longstanding controversy.[30] In addition, vaccination against rabies, smallpox, yellow fever, typhoid fever, and polio have all been reported to be of potential harm in patients with MS.[31] It has been postulated that activation of the immune system following vaccination may trigger the onset or worsening of MS. Vaccination should thus be avoided unless absolutely necessary during times of active disease, in particular while on immunomodulating therapy. In addition, live vaccinations should be avoided whenever possible in this patient population.

Hepatitis B

Recurrent central nervous system (CNS) demyelination following hepatitis B vaccination has been reported as well as the development of new neurologic symptoms following vaccination.[32,33] Immunization should be avoided other than in situations in which the risk of contracting the disease greatly outweighs the potential risks to the MS patient associated with vaccination itself.

Influenza

Case reports have suggested that influenza vaccinations may be temporally related to MS relapses; however, the majority of controlled trials have not shown this to be the case.[34–36] A prospective double-blind study of 104 MS patients found no significant difference in reported relapses between patients who had received vaccine (3 relapses) and those who received placebo (2 relapses). The overall benefits of influenza vaccination appear to outweigh the risks in this patient group, particularly given the high risk of relapse, possibly as high as 33%, in MS patients who actually contract influenza.[37]

Autoimmune Disease

Concerns regarding the safety of vaccination in patients with autoimmune or connective tissue disease are based on the possibility that vaccination may trigger autoantibody production via molecular mimicry or increased cell-mediated immunity. Although the onset of systemic lupus erythematosus (SLE) or rheumatoid arthritis (RA) following vaccination against tetanus, hepatitis B, and other diseases has been described in case reports, routine vaccinations are generally considered safe.[38,39] Furthermore, a recent study of the 23-valent polysaccharide pneumococcal vaccine found it to be both safe and immunogenic for patients with either RA or SLE, although a significant number of patients (33% of RA patients and 21% of SLE patients) responded to either none or only one of the polysaccharides.[40] For patients with autoimmune disease, travel vaccines should be considered and administered according to standard guidelines.

HIV-INFECTED PATIENTS

Limited literature and data exist regarding immunizations for travel in HIV-infected patients, yet this population is increasingly important as these patients live longer and travel more. In addition, much of the existing data are from the pre-HAART (highly active antiretroviral therapy) era, making it less relevant or applicable for the current population of HIV-infected hosts.

In addition to updating routine vaccinations, the specific travel vaccinations one might consider and administer according to routine guidelines are hepatitis A, inactivated typhoid, inactivated polio, meningococcus, Japanese encephalitis, and rabies vaccinations. Administration of the live viral vaccinations might pose additional risks to HIV-infected individuals and are discussed separately below.

Three other issues to consider when vaccinating any HIV-infected patient include

- increased inherent risk of disease associated with immunosuppression;
- risks associated with vaccination, including risks of live vaccines and potential for retroviral upregulation (increases in HIV viral load); and
- decreased vaccine efficacy.

Increased Inherent Risk of Disease

HIV-infected patients have defects in both cell-mediated and humoral immunity, making immunizations critically important because of the already increased risk of specific opportunistic and other diseases in this population. It is important for HIV-infected travelers to update all routine childhood immunizations prior to travel. The exceptions are administration of either MMR or live polio vaccine, which will be discussed further below. In addition, all HIV-infected patients should be immunized against pneumococcal disease (every 5 years), influenza (every year), hepatitis B, and hepatitis A (particularly patients already co-infected with hepatitis B or C). In general, asymptomatic individuals do not need to be screened for HIV infection prior to receiving live viral vaccines.

Risks Associated with Vaccination: Live Vaccines

Although inactivated vaccines are considered safe for the HIV-infected patient, live viral or bacterial vaccines (oral polio, oral typhoid, varicella, BCG, yellow fever, MMR) may carry risks of adverse reactions. Current CDC/ACIP recommendations are to avoid MMR and yellow fever vaccinations until the CD4 count is above 200 and to avoid oral polio, oral typhoid, BCG, and vaccinia vaccinations altogether in HIV-infected individuals.

MMR

Prevention of measles is critical given the severity of disease in immunocompromised patients. Mortality rates and incidence of giant cell pneumonitis are significantly higher in HIV-infected patients, particularly in patients with low CD4 counts.[41] However, the risk of measles exposure increases with travel to developing countries, and immunization needs to be carefully evaluated for HIV-infected patients.

Concern regarding measles vaccination of HIV-infected patients was initially raised after a 1992 case report of fatal pneumonitis in a 21-year-old college student following his second dose of measles vaccine. Genomic sequencing of bronchoscopy specimens confirmed a measles vaccine–like virus.[42]

Vaccination is currently recommended in all HIV-infected patients with CD4 counts greater than 200 who were not previously immunized against measles.[42,43] In addition, if an HIV-infected patient is exposed to measles, immunoglobulin should be administered regardless of vaccination status.
Minimal data are available concerning the risk or efficacy of mumps and rubella immunization in HIV-infected hosts. General recommendations are to proceed with vaccination in unimmunized HIV-infected patients with CD4 counts greater than 200.[44]

Yellow Fever

Yellow fever vaccination should be avoided, if possible, for any HIV-infected patient but particularly for patients with CD4 counts less than 200. However, a study of HIV-infected children with low CD4 counts did not reveal any adverse events following yellow fever vaccination.[45] Given the severity of most illnesses in HIV-infected hosts, when travel to yellow fever–endemic areas cannot be avoided, the vaccine should be administered.[46] One must recognize, however, that yellow fever vaccine may be less immunogenic in the HIV-infected patient. If an HIV-infected traveler is entering a country that requires vaccination to meet its entry requirements but the country is not endemic for yellow fever, then a letter to waive the vaccine may be provided.

Varicella

As this is a relatively new vaccine, limited data are available, and the vaccine should be avoided if possible in the HIV-infected host. Vaccination is an absolute contraindication in adult or pediatric patients with advanced HIV infection.[44]

Poliomyelitis

Oral polio vaccination is no longer available. It was associated with the development of fatal clinical polio, progressive neurologic impairment, and prolonged excretion of poliovirus in HIV-infected patients.[47–51] Unimmunized patients with HIV disease who will be at risk of exposure to polio should receive the inactivated polio vaccination, which appears to be safe though potentially less immunogenic for this population.[52,53] Special consideration should also be given to immunizing household members or close contacts of HIV-infected persons with IPV.[54]

Typhoid (Live Oral Vaccine)

Typhoid immunization in HIV-infected persons should be attempted using only an inactivated parenteral vaccine. For the general population, current recommendations are to administer typhoid vaccine to travelers to an endemic area for a stay longer than 3 weeks. However, vaccination should be considered in short-term HIV-infected travelers. The live oral typhoid vaccine poses a theoretic risk for HIV-infected individuals, although no adverse events have been reported.

BCG

BCG vaccination should not be administered to the HIV-infected host given the risk of disseminated disease.[55]

Potential Risks Associated with Vaccination: Viral Upregulation

Viral upregulation as a result of vaccination has been a longstanding subject of controversy, with most of the literature focusing on the influenza and pneumococcal vaccines.[56] Although some reports suggest an increase in viral replication associated with vaccination, others examining vaccine administration to HIV-infected patients show no significant changes in CD4 counts or viral loads.[57–60] Retroviral replication may transiently increase, but vaccinations have never been shown to have serious negative long-term effects on CD4 counts or patient survival in this population.[61–63] In addition, viral upregulation is more likely to occur in patients not on HAART.[54]

Decreased Vaccine Efficacy: Potential for an Inadequate Vaccine Response

The poorest responses to vaccination, including lower seroconversion rates and lower protective antibody titers, are seen in patients with more advanced HIV disease, characterized by lower CD4 counts and higher viral loads. Diminished antibody responses have been documented with many vaccinations, including Japanese encephalitis, rabies, diphtheria and tetanus (DT), influenza, polio, Hib, meningococcus, MMR, pneumococcus, yellow fever, hepatitis A, and hepatitis B.[64–67]

Of particular clinical concern are diminished responses to vaccination against hepatitis B, Japanese encephalitis, and rabies. Vaccination against hepatitis B has been associated with a 24 to 43% response rate in this group compared with a 90% response rate in the general population. Two studies that examined responses to vaccination in HIV-infected children were based in Thailand. One showed diminished antibody responses to Japanese B encephalitis vaccine (36% vs 67% in controls) with the other showing significantly lower antibody titers to rabies vaccine compared with controls.[68,69] In addition, it is thought that there is an interaction between the HIV and rabies viruses. A report by Adle-Biassette and colleagues in 1996 described a 46-year-old man with AIDS who was bitten by a dog in Mali and died 12 days later secondary to florid rabies encephalitis.[70] Despite antirabies serotherapy and vaccination, neuropathology only showed mild neuronal inflammation and abundant rabies virus. It was hypothesized that the weak inflammatory reaction and abundant viral replication seen in this case were due to the inadequate T-cell response secondary to HIV infection. This reinforces the importance of immediate antirabies treatment (immunoglobulin and vaccine) in the event of rabies exposure in an HIV-infected individual regardless of prior vaccination status.

Postvaccination serologic evaluation is possible with some vaccinations, and reimmunization is recommended for patients when antibody levels decline, although this practice remains a subject of controversy.[63] Better humoral responses to vaccination have been documented in patients when CD4 counts are greater than 300.[52,71] Immunization should thus be undertaken as early in the disease course as possible for optimal responses.[61]

PREGNANT TRAVELERS

Immunization of pregnant women is critical for disease prevention in both mother and fetus during this time of relative maternal immunosuppression. Pregnant women are capable of mounting an effective immune response, and maternal antibodies can cross the placenta to the fetus. The half-life of maternal IgG is 3 to 4 weeks in the newborn, and antibody titers wane during the first 6 months of life.[72]

The ideal time for such vaccinations is prior to pregnancy. However, if immunizations are necessary during pregnancy, it is always preferable to vaccinate during the later stages of pregnancy, when the fetus is more fully developed. The risks and benefits of each vaccine must be considered individually for pregnant patients. Ideally, the following three criteria should be met when vaccinating a pregnant woman:

- High risk of maternal/fetal exposure to infection must be present
- Infection would be potentially hazardous for mother or fetus
- Vaccination is not likely to cause harm to mother or fetus

In general, pregnant women should not receive live vaccines during pregnancy and within 3 months before becoming pregnant. This recommendation is based on theoretic risks only as there are no reports of adverse events occurring with live vaccines. Exceptions to this rule are yellow fever and polio vaccines, which should be administered if the mother must travel to high-risk areas (see below for more details). Many routine vaccines, such as DT, pneumococcal, and hepatitis vaccines, have not been well studied during the first trimester of pregnancy. Although theoretically safe, they should be avoided, if possible, during the first trimester (see Appendix; Category C).

Vaccinations to Consider During Pregnancy

Influenza
Although not usually considered a travel vaccination, immunization is critical since there is a significant increase in morbidity associated with influenza infection in pregnant women and young infants.[73] The highest risk occurs in women during their third trimester and with certain underlying medical conditions. The vaccine is derived from inactivated virus and has not been associated with adverse pregnancy outcomes.

Hepatitis B
Hepatitis B (HBV) vaccination is indicated for unimmunized pregnant women who will be traveling or residing in an endemic HBV area where they will either work in health care or have the unlikely risk of sexual encounters with local residents. Vaccination is important because infants and young children who

acquire HBV are at higher risk of liver disease and death than adults.[74] Inactivated vaccine has not been associated with harmful effects on the fetus, although there are limited data available regarding vaccination during the first trimester.

Hepatitis A

Vaccination against HAV is indicated in nonimmunized pregnant women who are traveling to developing countries where the risk of HAV infection is high. Vaccination is particularly important because fulminant HAV during the third trimester of pregnancy has been associated with premature labor and fetal death.[29] There are limited data regarding the safety of vaccination for pregnant women. However, these are inactivated vaccines produced in a similar manner to inactivated polio vaccines and thus are theoretically safe for use in pregnant women.

Typhoid Fever

Pregnant women should avoid travel to areas where typhoid fever is endemic, but they can be vaccinated with the inactivated typhoid vaccine if travel is unavoidable. There are limited data regarding the safety of vaccination during pregnancy.

Japanese Encephalitis

Travel to areas endemic for Japanese encephalitis should be avoided by pregnant women. Vaccination can be administered in the event that travel is mandatory, though limited data exist to support vaccine safety in pregnant women.

Meningococcus

The safety of meningococcal vaccination has not been evaluated in pregnant women, and thus it should be administered only if travel to a high-risk area is planned.

Plague

The inactivated plague vaccine may be administered to pregnant women at high risk of disease.

Rabies

Vaccination against rabies is considered safe during pregnancy, and vaccine should be administered when indicated for either pre- or postexposure prophylaxis.

Vaccinations to Avoid during Pregnancy Unless Absolutely Necessary

Yellow Fever

Pregnant women should avoid travel to those areas that are endemic or epidemic for yellow fever. In cases where travel must be pursued, vaccination is recommended because of the high fatality rates associated with yellow fever in pregnant women and in infants. Opinions vary regarding the safety of vaccination during pregnancy. Some studies have shown no adverse events when yellow fever vaccination was administered during pregnancy.[24,75,76] Others have shown subclinical congenital yellow fever and an increased risk of spontaneous abortions.[77] Vaccination is known to be less immunogenic in pregnant women.[80]

Revaccination should be undertaken after parturition. Travel to certain countries requires documentation of yellow fever vaccination. If yellow fever is not a current threat but a certification of vaccination is required for entry, a waiver can be provided for pregnant women.

Polio

Pregnant women should avoid travel to areas where polio is endemic given the high rates of maternal morbidity, in addition to fetal morbidity and mortality, when polio is contracted during pregnancy. If travel is not avoidable, pregnant women should be immunized with a booster dose of IPV prior to travel.[75] For those not previously immunized, the full course of inactivated polio vaccinations should be administered. There are no documented adverse effects of inactivated polio vaccination during pregnancy, although limited data are available.

Vaccinations Contraindicated During Pregnancy

Varicella

Live viral varicella vaccination is contraindicated both during pregnancy and for 1 month prior to pregnancy. A VARIVAX registry has been created to track pregnancy outcomes when vaccination occurred within 3 months of or during pregnancy. As of March 2000, no cases of congenital varicella syndrome had been identified among infants of mothers vaccinated during pregnancy.

Because natural varicella infection during the first half of pregnancy can cause significant congenital abnormalities, such as low birth weight, cutaneous scarring, limb hypoplasia, microcephaly, cortical atrophy, chorioretinitis, and cataracts, it is critical for unimmunized women to avoid exposure during pregnancy.[79]

MMR

MMR is a live attenuated viral vaccine and should be administered prior to pregnancy for those who are not immune. Women should not be vaccinated during pregnancy, and they should avoid conception for 30 days following vaccination. This recommendation has recently been diminished from a waiting period of 3 months following vaccination. Furthermore, vaccination is not considered a reason to terminate pregnancy in the event that vaccination is inadvertently administered during pregnancy.

Measles during pregnancy has been associated with premature labor and spontaneous abortions.[80] Unimmunized women should avoid travel to developing countries where there is an increased incidence of measles. In the event of documented exposure to measles in a nonimmune pregnant woman, IG should be administered immediately.

Infection with rubella during pregnancy can lead to congenital rubella syndrome, miscarriage, and death. Rubella vaccine can cross the placenta and infect fetal tissue, though congenital rubella had not been documented in a study of women who received rubella vaccine during pregnancy.[81]

BCG

BCG is contraindicated in pregnant women.

Vaccinia

Vaccinia is contraindicated in pregnant women.

MEDICAL CONDITIONS ASSOCIATED WITH SPECIFIC INDICATIONS FOR VACCINATION

The medical conditions listed in this section all predispose patients to specific diseases, thus indicating a need for certain vaccinations. The patients discussed in this section are not considered immunosuppressed and can receive all routine vaccinations, including the live vaccines, without the concerns as raised in the above section for immunocompromised hosts.

Asplenic Travelers

Splenic dysfunction may be functional or anatomic, both representing important groups given the critical role of the spleen in immune function. The spleen is the body's largest lymphoid organ and has a variety of immunologic functions, including immune regulatory activities, immune clearance, phago-cytosis, and immune surveillance. Although the spleen was once viewed as a nonessential organ, the relationship between asplenia and severe infection, referred to as overwhelming postsplenectomy infec-tion (OPSI) or postsplenectomy sepsis (PSS), is well known.[5,26]

Patients with functional asplenia include those with sickle cell (SC) anemia, hemoglobin SC disease, splenic atrophy, congenital asplenia, and, less commonly, patients with systemic amyloidosis, lupus ery-thematosus, and rheumatoid arthritis. Anatomic asplenia occurs in adults secondary to trauma or removal for hypersplenia and in children secondary to malignancy or hematologic disease. The situations that resulted in splenectomy are of importance in defining a patient's risks of infection. A landmark study in the year 1990 evaluated the risk of fatal PSS and found the lowest risks in patients who had suffered trauma; intermediate risks were seen in patients with spherocytosis, idiopathic thrombocytopenic pur-pura (ITP), or portal hypertension; and highest risks were seen in patients with thalassemia or Hodgkin's disease as their respective indications for splenectomy.[82]

OPSI has a short prodrome of fever, myalgia, and chills followed by an abrupt clinical deterioration, often marked by disseminated intravascular coagulation (DIC), seizures, coma, and cardiovascular collapse. Typical organisms include the encapsulated bacteria, such as pneumococci, meningococci, and *Haemophilus influenzae* type b. Death rates from sepsis in OPSI are up to 600 times greater than in the general population. The actual lifetime incidence of OPSI varies in different reports and is dependent on the indication for splenectomy, but it has been reported to be as high as 25% after childhood splenectomy for hematologic disorders.

Of critical importance for the splenectomized patient is vaccination against encapsulated bacteria (pneumococci, meningococci, *H. influenzae* type b). However, it should be noted that vaccination may be less immunogenic in the splenectomized host.[83,84] There are no contraindications to vaccination in splenectomized patients, and live vaccinations are all considered to be safe for use in this group.[85] Ideally, all patients should be vaccinated at least 2 weeks prior to elective splenectomy.

Renal Failure

Patients with ESRD, in particular patients with nephrotic syndrome, are at high risk of pneumococcal and hepatitis B infections. However, vaccination is often associated with poor antibody responses in patients with uremia.[86] The response to vaccines appears to correlate with the degree of renal failure, and immunization is most efficacious if given as early in the course of renal disease as possible—ideally, prior to initiation of dialysis. In addition to hepatitis B and pneumococcus, all patients with ESRD should receive an annual influenza vaccination.[87–89]

Diabetes Mellitus

Diabetic patients are at higher risk of cardiovascular, renal, and other diseases. Both pneumococcal and annual influenza vaccinations are recommended for these patients. Vaccination is safe and effective in this patient group and does not interfere with antidiabetic agents or glucose control. Tetanus boosters are important for this group of patients, which is predisposed to foot ulcers.

Alcoholic Cirrhosis and Chronic Liver Disease

Patients with ESLD are at increased risk of infections because of defective host defenses, including leukopenia, decreased complement activity, chemotactic defects, and impaired cell-mediated immunity. Pneumococcal and annual influenza vaccination is recommended for this group. Patients should also be vaccinated against hepatitis B and hepatitis A, recognizing that vaccination may be less immunogenic in this population.

Chronic Cardiac and Pulmonary Conditions

Routine pneumococcal and influenza vaccination are recommended.

Clotting Factor Deficiency

Hepatitis A and B vaccines are recommended in this patient group in order to preserve whatever residual capacity the liver has to produce clotting factors.

SUMMARY

Many issues arise when vaccinating any immunocompromised patient, given the increased risk of diseases that may have more severe consequences in these populations. In addition, decreased vaccine efficacy as well as possible increased risk of vaccine-induced disease must be taken into account, particularly when considering immunization with live viral vaccines. Finally, special concern must be given to specific patient populations in need of vaccinations, including pregnant women and splenectomized patients. Of utmost importance is the decision made by a health provider to take into account the specific vaccines and clinical scenarios unique to a given patient.

REFERENCES

1. Peters VB, Sood SK. Immunity to *Haemophilus influenzae* type b after reimmunization with oligosaccharide CRM197 conjugate vaccine in children with human immunodeficiency virus infection. Pediatr Infect Dis J 1997;16:711–3.
2. Centers for Disease Control and Prevention. Diphtheria acquired by U.S. citizens in the Russian Federation and Ukraine—1994. MMWR Morb Mortal Wkly Rep 1995;34:237–44.
3. Centers for Disease Control and Prevention. Progress toward poliomyelitis eradication—Eastern Mediterranean Region, January 2000–September 2001. MMWR Morb Mortal Wkly Rep 2001;50:1113–6.
4. Sinha DP. Chickenpox—a disease predominantly affecting adults in rural West Bengal, India. Int J Epidemiol 1976;5:367–74.
5. Mileno MD, Bia FJ. The compromised traveler. Infect Dis Clin North Am 1998;12:369–412.
6. Orenstein W, Wharton, M, Bart, KJ, et al. Immunization. In: Mandell G, Bennett J, Dolin R, editors. Principles and practice of infectious diseases. Philadelphia (PA): Churchill Livingstone; 2000. p. 3207–34.

7. Nothdurft HD, Jelinek T, Marschang A, et al. Adverse reactions to Japanese encephalitis vaccine in travellers. J Infect 1996;32:119–22.

8. Plesner AM, Arlien-Soborg P, Herning M. Neurological complications and Japanese encephalitis vaccination. Lancet 1996;348:202–3.

9. Wilson ME. Travel-related vaccines. Infect Dis Clin North Am 2001;15:231–51.

10. Steffen RK, MA, Shapiro CN, et al. Epidemiology and prevention of hepatitis A in travelers. JAMA 1994;272:885.

11. Duff B, Duff P. Hepatitis A vaccine. Ready for prime time. Obstet Gynecol 1998;91:468.

12. Centers for Disease Control and Prevention. Fatal yellow fever in a traveler returning from Venezuela, 1999. MMWR Morb Mortal Wkly Rep 2000;49:303–5.

13. Vasconcelos PF, Luna EJ, Galler R, et al. Serious adverse events associated with yellow fever 17DD vaccine in Brazil. A report of two cases. Lancet 2001;358:91–7.

14. Martin M, Tsai TF, Cropp B, et al. Fever and multisystem organ failure associated with 17D-204 yellow fever vaccination. A report of four cases. Lancet 2001;358:98–104.

15. Chan RC, Penney DJ, Little D, et al. Hepatitis and death following vaccination with 17D-204 yellow fever vaccine. Lancet 2001;358:121–2.

16. Centers for Disease Control and Prevention. Human rabies prevention—United States, 1999. Recommendations of the Advisory Committee on Immunization Practices (ACIP). MMWR Morb Mortal Wkly Rep 1998;48:1–21.

17. Centers for Disease Control and Prevention. Health information for international travel 1999–2000. 1999.

18. MacPherson DW, Tonkin M. Cholera vaccination. A decision analysis. Can Med Assoc J 1992;146:1947–52.

19. Colditz GA, Brewer TF, Berkey CS, et al. Efficacy of BCG vaccine in the prevention of tuberculosis. Meta-analysis of the published literature. JAMA 1994;271:698–702.

20. McNeil JG, Lednar WM, Stansfield SK, et al. Central European tick-borne encephalitis. Assessment of risk for persons in the armed services and vacationers. J Infect Dis 1985;152:650–1.

21. Centers for Disease Control and Prevention. Vaccinia (smallpox) vaccine. Recommendations of the Immunization Practices Advisory Committee (ACIP). MMWR Recomm Rep 1991;40:1–10.

22. Centers for Disease Control and Prevention. Imported bubonic plague–District of Columbia. MMWR Morb Mortal Wkly Rep 1990;39:895,901.

23. Hibberd PL, Rubin RH. Approach to immunization in the immunosuppressed host. Infect Dis Clin North Am 1990;4:123–42.

24. Monath T, Cetron MS. Prevention of yellow fever in persons traveling to the tropics. Clin Infect Dis 2002;34:1369–78.

25. Centers for Disease Control and Prevention. Recommendations of the Advisory Committee on Immunization Practices (ACIP). Use of vaccines and immune globulins in persons with altered immunocompetence. MMWR Morb Mortal Wkly Rep 1993;42:1–18.

26. Mileno MD SK, Keystone JS, Bia FJ. Special high-risk travel groups. Immunocompromised, older, disabled and chronically ill travelers. In: Zuckerman J, editor. Principles and practice of travel medicine. New York: John Wiley; 2001.

27. Stark K, Gunther M, Neuhaus R, et al. Immunogenicity and safety of hepatitis A vaccine in liver and renal transplant recipients. J Infect Dis 1999;180:2014–7.

28. McDonald E, Jarrett MP, Schiffman G, Grayzel AI. Persistence of pneumococcal antibodies after immunization in patients with systemic lupus erythematosus. J Rheumatol 1984;11:306–8.

29. Centers for Disease Control and Prevention. Vaccine recommendations for travelers with altered immunocompetence, including HIV. National Center for Infectious Diseases: Travelers' Health 2001–2002.

30. Jeffrey D. The use of vaccinations in patients with multiple sclerosis. Infect Med 2002;19:73–9.

31. Miller H, Cendrowski W, Shapira K. Multiple sclerosis and vaccination. BMJ 1967;2:210–3.

32. Tourbah A, Gout O, Liblau R, et al. Encephalitis after hepatitis B vaccination. Recurrent disseminated encephalitis or MS? Neurology 1999;53:396–401.

33. Herroelen L, de Keyser J, Ebinger G. Central-nervous-system demyelination after immunisation with recombinant hepatitis B vaccine. Lancet 1991;338:1174–5.

34. Panitch HS, Hirsch RL, Haley AS, Johnson KP. Exacerbations of multiple sclerosis in patients treated with gamma interferon. Lancet 1987;1:893–5.

35. Kepes JJ. Large focal tumor-like demyelinating lesions of the brain. Intermediate entity between multiple sclerosis and acute disseminated encephalomyelitis? A study of 31 patients. Ann Neurol 1993;33:18–27.

36. Miller AE, Morgante LA, Buchwald LY, et al. A multicenter, randomized, double-blind, placebo-controlled trial of influenza immunization in multiple sclerosis. Neurology 1997;48:312–4.

37. De Keyser J, Zwanikken C, Boon M. Effects of influenza vaccination and influenza illness on exacerbations in multiple sclerosis. J Neurol Sci 1998;159:51–3.

38. Older SA, Battafarano DF, Enzenauer RJ, Krieg AM. Can immunization precipitate connective tissue disease? Report of five cases of systemic lupus erythematosus and review of the literature. Semin Arthritis Rheum 1999;29:131–9.

39. Aron-Maor A, Shoenfeld Y. Vaccination and systemic lupus erythematosus. The bidirectional dilemmas. Lupus 2001;10:237–40.

40. Elkayam O, Paran D, Caspi D, et al. Immunogenicity and safety of pneumococcal vaccination in patients with rheumatoid arthritis or systemic lupus erythematosus. Clin Infect Dis 2002;34:147–53.

41. Karp CL, Neva FA. Tropical infectious diseases in human immunodeficiency virus-infected patients. Clin Infect Dis 1999;28:947–63.

42. Centers for Disease Control and Prevention. Measles pneumonitis following measles-mumps-rubella vaccination of a patient with HIV infection, 1993. MMWR Morb Mortal Wkly Rep 1996;45:603–6.

43. Wallace MR, Hooper DG, Graves SJ, Malone JL. Measles seroprevalence and vaccine response in HIV-infected adults. Vaccine 1994;12:1222–4.

44. Leder K. HIV-infected travelers. What precautions should they take? J Respir Dis 2002;23:259–69.

45. Sibailly TS, Wiktor SZ, Tsai TF, et al. Poor antibody response to yellow fever vaccination in children infected with human immunodeficiency virus type 1. Pediatr Infect Dis J 1997;19:1177.

46. Kemper CA, Linett A, Kane C, Deresinski SC. Travels with HIV. The compliance and health of HIV-infected adults who travel. Int J STD AIDS 1997;8:44–9.

47. Centers for Disease Control and Prevention. Prolonged poliovirus excretion in an immunodeficient person with vaccine-associated paralytic poliomyelitis. MMWR Morb Mortal Wkly Rep 1997;46:641–3.

48. Groom SN, Clewley J, Litton PA, Brown DW. Vaccine-associated poliomyelitis. Lancet 1994;343:609–10.

49. Ion-Nedelcu N, Dobrescu A, Strebel PM, Sutter RW. Vaccine-associated paralytic poliomyelitis and HIV infection. Lancet 1994;343:51–2.

50. Bellmunt A, May G, Zell R, et al. Evolution of poliovirus type I during 5.5 years of prolonged enteral replication in an immunodeficient patient. Virology 1999;265:178–84.

51. Davis LE, Bodian D, Price D, et al. Chronic progressive poliomyelitis secondary to vaccination of an immunodeficient child. N Engl J Med 1977;297:241–5.

52. Kroon FP, van Dissel JT, Labadie J, et al. Antibody response to diphtheria, tetanus, and poliomyelitis vaccines in relation to the number of CD4+ T lymphocytes in adults infected with human immunodeficiency virus. Clin Infect Dis 1995;21:1197–203.

53. Mathisen GE, Allen AD. Inactivated polio vaccine hyperimmunization in adults with HIV disease. A placebo-controlled study. AIDS 1992;6:737–8.

54. Leder K. HIV-infected travelers. What precautions should they take? J Respir Dis 2002;23(4):259–69.

55. Edwards KM, Kernodle DS. Possible hazards of routine bacillus Calmette–Guerin immunization in human immunodeficiency virus-infected children. Pediatr Infect Dis J 1996;15:836–8.

56. Stanley S, Ostrowski MA, Justement JS, et al. Effect of immunization with a common recall antigen on viral expression in patients infected with human immunodeficiency virus type 1. N Engl J Med 1996;334:1222–30.

57. Brichacek B, Swindells S, Janoff EN, et al. Increased plasma human immunodeficiency virus type 1 burden following antigenic challenge with pneumococcal vaccine. J Infect Dis 1996;174:1191–9.

58. Ramilo O, Hicks PJ, Borvak J, et al. T cell activation and human immunodeficiency virus replication after influenza immunization of infected children. Pediatr Infect Dis J 1996;15:197–203.

59. Jackson CR, Vavro CL, Valentine ME, et al. Effect of influenza immunization on immunologic and virologic characteristics of pediatric patients infected with human immunodeficiency virus. Pediatr Infect Dis J 1997;16:200–4.

60. Tasker SA, Wallace MR, Rubins JB, et al. Reimmunization with 23-valent pneumococcal vaccine for patients infected with human immunodeficiency virus type 1. Clinical, immunologic, and virologic responses. Clin Infect Dis 2002;34:813–21.

61. Glesby MJ, Hoover DR, Farzadegan H, et al. The effect of influenza vaccination on human immunodeficiency virus type 1 load. A randomized, double-blind, placebo-controlled study. J Infect Dis 1996;174:1332–6.

62. Staprans SI, Hamilton BL, Follansbee SE, et al. Activation of virus replication after vaccination of HIV-1-infected individuals. J Exp Med 1995;182:1727–37.

63. Tasker SA, Wallace MR. Vaccination in HIV-infected patients. Curr Infect Dis Rep 2000;2:245–56.

64. Nitta AT, Douglas JM, Arakere G, Ebens JB. Disseminated meningococcal infection in HIV-seropositive patients. AIDS 1993;7:87–90.

65. Arpadi SM, Markowitz LE, Baughman AL, et al. Measles antibody in vaccinated human immunodeficiency virus type 1-infected children. Pediatrics 1996;97:653–7.

66. Sibailly TS, Wiktor SZ, Tsai TF, et al. Poor antibody response to yellow fever vaccination in children infected with human immunodeficiency virus type 1. Pediatr Infect Dis J 1997;16:1177–9.

67. Neilsen GA, Bodsworth NJ, Watts N. Response to hepatitis A vaccination in human immunodeficiency virus-infected and -uninfected homosexual men. J Infect Dis 1997;176:1064–7.

68. Rojanasuphot S, Shaffer, N, Chotpitayasunondh, T, et al. Response to JE vaccine among HIV-infected children, Bangkok, Thailand. Southeast Asian J Trop Med Public Health 1998;29:443.

69. Thisyakorn U, Pancharoen C, Ruxrungtham K, et al. Safety and immunogenicity of preexposure rabies vaccination in children infected with human immunodeficiency virus type 1. Clin Infect Dis 2000;30:218.

70. Adle-Biassette H, Bourhy H, Gisselbrecht M, et al. Rabies encephalitis in a patient with AIDS. A clinicopathological study. Acta Neuropathol 1996;92:415–20.

71. Birx DL, Rhoads JL, Wright JC, et al. Immunologic parameters in early-stage HIV-seropositive subjects associated with vaccine responsiveness. J Acquir Immun Defic Syndr Hum Retrovirol 1991;4:188–96.

72. Sarvas H, Seppala I, Kurikka S, et al. Half-life of the maternal IgG1 allotype in infants. J Clin Immunol 1993;13:145–51.

73. Neuzil KM RG, Mitchell EF, et al. Impact of influenza on acute cardiopulmonary hospitalization in pregnant women. Am J Epidemiol 1998;148:1094.

74. American Academy of Pediatrics. Poliovirus infections. Red Book Report of the Committee on Infectious Diseases. ed 25. Elk Grove Village (IL): American Academy of Pediatrics; 2000. p. 465–70.

75. Munoz FM, Englund JA. Vaccines in pregnancy. Infect Dis Clin North Am 2001;15:253–71.

76. Nishioka S, Nunes-Aravjo FR, Pires WP, et al. Yellow fever vaccination during pregnancy and spontaneous abortion. A case control study. Trop Med Int Health 1998;3:29.

77. Tsai TF, Paul R, Lynberg MC, Letson GW. Congenital yellow fever virus infection after immunization in pregnancy. J Infect Dis 1993;168:1520–3.

78. Nasidi A, Monath TP, Vandenberg J, et al. Yellow fever vaccination and pregnancy. A four-year prospective study. Trans R Soc Trop Med Hyg 1993;87:337–9.

79. Pastuszak AL. Outcome after maternal varicella infection in the first 20 weeks of pregnancy. N Engl J Med 1994;330:901.

80. Siegal M, Fuerst, HT. Low birth weight and maternal virus diseases. A prospective study of rubella, measles, mumps, chickenpox and hepatitis. JAMA 1966;197:88.

81. Mandell G, Bennet J, Dolin R. Principles and practice of infectious diseases. 5th ed. Philadelphia (PA): Churchill Livingstone; 2000.

82. Styrt B. Infection associated with asplenia. Risks, mechanisms, and prevention. Am J Med 1990;88:33N–42N.

83. Centers for Disease Control and Prevention. Prevention of pneumococcal disease. Recommendations of the Advisory Committee on Immunization Practices (ACIP). MMWR Recomm Rep 1997;46:1–24.

84. Centers for Disease Control and Prevention. Guidelines for the prevention and treatment of infection in patients with an absent or dysfunctional spleen. Working Party of the British Committee for Standards in Haematology Clinical Haematology Task Force. BMJ 1996;312:430–4.

85. Conlon CP. Travel and the immunocompromised host. Hosp Med 2000;61:167–70.

86. Schwebke J, Mujais S. Vaccination in hemodialysis patients. Int J Artif Organs 1989;12:481–4.

87. Buti M, Viladomiu L, Jardi R, et al. Long-term immunogenicity and efficacy of hepatitis B vaccine in hemodialysis patients. Am J Nephrol 1992;12:144–7.

88. Lefebure AF, Verpooten GA, Couttenye MM, De Broe ME. Immunogenicity of a recombinant DNA hepatitis B vaccine in renal transplant patients. Vaccine 1993;11:397–9.

89. Rangel MC, Coronado VG, Euler GL, Strikas RA. Vaccine recommendations for patients on chronic dialysis. The Advisory Committee on Immunization Practices and the American Academy of Pediatrics. Semin Dial 2000;13:101–7.

APPENDIX 1

US Food and Drug Administration (FDA) Pregnancy Categories

Documented problems in humans with the use of a drug during pregnancy are included in vaccine package inserts. Where appropriate, information is provided on fertility, pregnancy, labor, delivery, and postpartum effects. In addition, reference is made to problems documented in animal studies, even though the significance of such findings to humans might not be known. Pregnancy categories assigned by the US Food and Drug Administration (FDA) are included whenever available. These categories are as follows.

A. Adequate and well-controlled studies have failed to demonstrate a risk to the fetus in the first trimester of pregnancy (and there is no evidence of risk in later trimesters).

B. Animal reproduction studies have failed to demonstrate a risk to the fetus, and there are no adequate and well-controlled studies in pregnant woman.

C. Animal reproduction studies have shown an adverse effect on the fetus, and there are no adequate and well-controlled studies in humans, but potential benefits might warrant use of the drug in pregnant women despite potential risks.

D. Positive evidence exists of human fetal risk based on adverse-reaction data from investigational or marketing experience or studies in humans. However, potential benefits might warrant use of the drug in pregnant women despite potential risks if the drug is needed in a life-threatening situation or for a serious disease for which safer drugs cannot be used or are ineffective.

E. Studies in animals or humans have demonstrated fetal abnormalities, and/or there is positive evidence of human fetal risk based on adverse-reaction data from pregnant women who have used the drug. The risks clearly outweigh potential benefits.

Chapter 18

Vaccine Safety: Surveillance of Adverse Reactions, Public Policy, Risk Management

Elizabeth D. Barnett

Vaccine safety has received increased worldwide attention in the past decade. Eradication of wild-type polio in the United States focused attention on paralytic polio due to live oral polio vaccine, resulting in a change to an all-inactivated poliovirus vaccine schedule. Concern about adverse events associated with mercury-containing vaccines is leading to a change to nonmercury-containing products in many countries. Description of a new constellation of adverse events following yellow fever vaccine led to a reappraisal of the safety of this vaccine. Finally, adverse events associated with vaccination against smallpox have received unprecedented attention from scientists and the media.

Immunization is one of the most successful public health initiatives, with the reduction in incidence of some diseases exceeding 99%.[1] As disease incidence becomes very low, the imperative to assure vaccine safety becomes even more important. For diseases of low incidence, there is a continual challenge to balance the risk of disease with adverse events due to vaccines. Assessing risk of adverse events to travel vaccines presents special challenges. First, the epidemiology of diseases to which travelers are exposed might not be well described in the destination country, limiting accuracy of risk estimates. Second, disease risk can vary by geography, climate, presence of an outbreak, and travel circumstances, even within a given country. Third, risk estimates derived for the indigenous population might not be generalizable to travelers because of different exposure patterns or immunization programs in the area. Fourth, adverse events to vaccines given to travelers might not be well described in the population of travelers, though they may have been studied in trials in endemic areas. Finally, interpretation of risks can differ by provider or patient: some may favor protection against very rare but untreatable and potentially fatal diseases, whereas others might not wish to risk vaccine adverse events when the risk of disease is extremely low.

Travel medicine practitioners face the task of deciphering information about the risk of diseases throughout the world, vaccine efficacy, and the risk of vaccine adverse events, translating these risks for patients and aiding patients in making thoughtful, rational choices about vaccines for international travel.

Information about the risk of disease and use of medical history and particulars of travel style is presented in chapters 4, 15, 16, and 17. This chapter will focus on information about vaccine safety and approaches to balancing this information with the risk of disease to make choices about vaccine administration.

SAFETY MONITORING OF VACCINES

Prelicensure assessment of safety is carried out during vaccine trials. However, several limitations are present in these studies. First, sample sizes for trials are based on assessment of efficacy, and trials might not include enough subjects for assessment of rare adverse events. Second, the period of monitoring of subjects might be short (14–30 days) and might not allow for identification of late-appearing adverse events. Third, vaccines used in travelers might have been studied in populations that differ from travelers in demographic characteristics and/or in types of likely exposures. For example, efficacy studies of hepatitis A vaccines were conducted in areas where disease prevalence was high, in individuals residing in these locations who might have had exposures that differ from those experienced by typical travelers.[2–4] On the other hand, trials that assess vaccine safety usually do not permit administration of concurrent vaccines or medications, and subjects are followed and assessed in a systematic manner making it easier to determine a causal relationship between a vaccine and a specific adverse event.

Postlicensure, or postmarketing, surveillance for vaccine adverse events poses significant challenges. Passive surveillance, on which postmarketing surveillance usually relies, might be limited by the recall bias inherent in voluntary reporting of adverse events. There can be many confounding factors present, including concurrently administered vaccines or medications. Observational studies of vaccine adverse events also can be subject to recall bias. In contrast to the rigor and elegance of prelicensure studies, the monitoring of adverse events following licensure poses significant methodologic challenges.

Surveillance Systems for Vaccine Adverse Events

National and regional reporting systems for vaccine adverse events have been developed in many countries, including Australia, Canada, Denmark, France, Italy, Mexico, the Netherlands, New Zealand, Sao Paolo State in Brazil, Sweden, the United Kingdom, and the United States.[1] Most systems involve passive surveillance, relying on voluntary reporting of adverse events either through a system designed specifically for vaccine adverse events or through channels developed for the reporting of adverse drug reactions. The United States implemented the Vaccine Adverse Event Reporting System (VAERS) in 1990 to systematically collect information about adverse events after immunization.[5] Canada's Vaccine Associated Adverse Event (VAAE) reporting system was initiated in 1987 and began to be supplemented in 1990 by the Immunization Monitoring Program, Active (IMPACT), a hospital-based system assessing all admissions for possible relationships to immunizations.[6] Other countries and regions also have developed methods of monitoring vaccine safety.

Assessment of Causality

Demonstrating an association between an event (immunization) and a specific adverse event is a complex process. Occurrence of a unique laboratory finding or clinical syndrome following a specific vaccine implies a causal relationship between the vaccine and adverse event. Examples include paralytic polio following oral poliovirus vaccine, yellow fever vaccine–associated viscerotropic disease, and meningitis following Urabe mumps vaccine.[7–9] A causal relationship also can be demonstrated by the reoccurrence of an adverse event in the same individual on rechallenge with the same vaccine, such as when alopecia occurs following rechallenge with hepatitis B vaccine.[10] When an event occurs following immunization that is similar to signs or symptoms caused by wild-type disease, such as arthralgia or arthritis following rubella vaccine, causation is plausible.[11]

Most associations between vaccines and subsequent events are less clear than those just described, and demonstration of causality must be made based on a combination of factors, including temporal association of the vaccine and adverse event, lack of alternative causes for the event, and the presence of other similar cases. In 1986, the United States Institute of Medicine (IOM) established a committee to address vaccine safety issues. They identified limitations to establishing causality of many of the implicated adverse events to vaccines. These limitations included lack of understanding of biologic mechanisms of vaccine adverse events; insufficient or inconsistent information from case reports of vaccinees; insufficient size and inadequate length of follow-up of many population-based studies addressing vaccine adverse events; limitations of vaccine safety surveillance systems; and lack of experimental studies addressing causality of vaccine adverse events.[1,12] Many of these limitations are being addressed by the improvement of passive surveillance systems, the implementation of active surveillance for specific adverse events, and the establishment of programs designed to address investigation of rare vaccine adverse events.

COMMUNICATION OF RISK ABOUT TRAVEL VACCINE SAFETY

Travelers accept many risks associated with international travel by the very nature of choosing to travel. Individuals who travel, however, may have a diverse tolerance for risk and might interpret differently the risk associated with vaccines. Can the travel medicine professional practice in a consistent manner yet give different vaccines to patients with similar travel plans?

Principles of risk perception gleaned from other disciplines have been applied to immunizations.[13] First, when risks of action (receiving a vaccine) and inaction (exposure to a disease) are equivalent, individuals often prefer risks of inaction.[14] Second, voluntary risks (eg, traveling to areas where exposure to mosquitoes is likely) are usually perceived to be more acceptable than involuntary risks (mandated immunizations). Third, perception of risks varies widely from individual to individual, based on personality, previous life experiences, education, and perception of control over individual destiny. Fourth, patients rely on the advice of health professionals when there is uncertainty about risk. Understanding these principles helps to place the issues of vaccine safety in context and allows professionals to feel comfortable when different choices are made by patients to whom seemingly identical risks have been communicated.

Safety of Travel Vaccines

Scientific information about risks associated with routine pediatric vaccines was evaluated in the United States by the IOM in the early 1990s.[15,16] Evidence linking vaccines with specific adverse events was evaluated systematically and assigned to one of five categories representing a spectrum between no causal relationship and established causal relationship. To date, such a rigorous analysis has not been done for travel vaccines. Travel medicine practitioners have had to rely on data available from case reports, efficacy studies that might have sample sizes too small to identify rare adverse events, and passive surveillance systems that do not provide data appropriate for accurate calculation of rates. Recently, a more rigorous approach to the safety of travel vaccines and balancing this with the risk of contracting disease has been advocated. Work done by Shlim and Solomon in addressing the appropriate use of Japanese encephalitis vaccine and by scientists at the US Centers for Disease Control and Prevention (CDC) and other sites on yellow fever vaccine have advanced the field of travel vaccine safety.[8,17]

Travel Medicine Practice: Balancing Risk of Disease and Vaccine Adverse Events

The process of administering any vaccine involves discussion about adverse events. Health professionals, who are aware of the manifestations of the diseases prevented by routine immunizations and who might have seen severe or fatal complications of vaccine-preventable diseases, have a different perspective from those of their patients. Patients sometimes regard many vaccine-preventable diseases as having been eradicated and therefore place the risk associated with the vaccine as more immediate than the risk associated with the disease. The societal imperative for maintenance of a minimal level of vaccine coverage to preserve low disease incidence might not be persuasive to some individuals. The situation for travel vaccines might be complicated by several additional factors: travel medicine professionals might be less knowledgeable about diseases prevented by travel vaccines; there are few official requirements for travel vaccines, which might lead to the impression that vaccines are not needed for travel; and there are few mechanisms for compensation of individuals who suffer severe adverse events following travel vaccines. In some situations, practitioners might feel they are balancing the risks of giving a vaccine, including a low but present risk of an adverse event, with the risk of omitting the vaccine and thus placing a patient at risk of contracting a severe vaccine-preventable disease.

Table 18-1 summarizes data about the risk of disease, vaccine efficacy, risk of vaccines adverse events, the risk benefit of routine administration of vaccine, and factors that could alter this risk-benefit ratio. Unsurprisingly, the vaccines with the most favorable benefit-to-risk ratios are those that are given most frequently to travelers.

Hepatitis A

Hepatitis A vaccine is an example of a vaccine used for travelers to prevent a disease that is widely present and occurs frequently in unimmunized travelers. The vaccine is highly effective with generally mild adverse events.[18] The balance falls heavily in favor of offering this vaccine widely.

Typhoid

Typhoid is caused by *Salmonella enterica* serovar Typhi bacteria that are present in food and water contaminated with enteric bacteria. The disease is moderate to severe and can be fatal, but it is treatable with antibacterial agents. Available vaccines have incomplete efficacy; side effects are generally mild.[19] Because of the widespread nature of typhoid, the balance falls in favor of immunizing against the disease despite the less-than-optimal vaccine efficacy and treatable nature of the disease. Vaccine protection can be augmented by careful attention to the selection of food and water.

Meningococcal Disease

Disease caused by *Neisseria meningitidis* is serious and can be fatal. Adverse events to vaccine are generally mild. Vaccine efficacy of currently available polysaccharide vaccines is good in older children and adults but fair to poor in infants and young children; furthermore, the vaccine does not protect against all serogroups. Conjugate vaccines against meningococcus have better efficacy in infants and young children. Risk of meningococcal disease in the typical traveler is low but can increase in some circumstances, such as participating in the annual hajj in Saudi Arabia.[20] Of note, most data on the use of meningococcal vaccine in travelers address the risk of the disease caused by serogroup A meningococcus in the "meningitis belt" in Africa. Increased risk of disease caused by serogroup C meningococcus, which could be experienced by travelers from North America to the British Isles or to Australia, has not been addressed in a rigorous way.

Risk to the typical traveler of contracting meningococcal disease is very low. The disease is present worldwide. For travel to sub-Saharan Africa, the balance falls slightly in favor of offering this vaccine. In circumstances of increased risk, such as attending the hajj, vaccine use is even more beneficial.

Table 18-1. Disease Risk, Vaccine Efficacy, and Vaccine Safety for Six Vaccine-Preventable Diseases Associated with Travel

Disease/Vaccine	Disease Risk for the Typical Traveler	Disease Severity/ Treatment	Vaccine Efficacy	Vaccine Adverse Events	Benefit:Risk Ratio of Giving Vaccine	Factors Increasing Vaccine Benefit	Factors Increasing Vaccine Risk
Hepatitis A	Moderate to high	Mild to severe, no specific treatment	High	Generally mild	Benefit >>> risk	Increased risk of disease, patient at risk of severe disease	—
Typhoid	Low to moderate	Moderate to severe, rarely fatal; treatable with antibacterial agents	Moderate	Generally mild	Benefit >> risk	High disease prevalence	—
Meningococcal meningitis/sepsis	Very low	Moderate to severe, sometimes fatal or with severe sequelae; treatable with antibacterial agents	Moderate to high; fair in children < 2 years	Generally mild	Benefit > risk	Travel to the hajj; epidemic situation; contact with local population at risk	—
Yellow fever	Low but highly variable; increased in epidemic situations	Severe, sometimes fatal	High	Generally mild; rare serious, sometimes fatal adverse events	Benefit > risk	High disease prevalence (endemic area or outbreak)	Immunocompromise; extremes of age (< 4 mo, elderly); ? pregnancy
Japanese encephalitis	Very low to low; variable by season and location	Mild to severe, sometimes fatal or with neurologic sequelae	High	Generally mild; rare serious adverse events	Benefit ≅ risk	Long-term travel in endemic/epidemic areas; travel to high-risk rural areas (farming, rice growing)	History of severe allergic reactions; allergy to gelatin
Cholera	Extremely low	Mild to severe; easily treatable	Moderate	Generally mild	Benefit ≅ risk	Travel to area where an outbreak is occurring and hygienic conditions are poor	—

Yellow Fever

Yellow fever occurs only in Africa and South America; the disease is severe and can be fatal, and no specific treatment is available. Risk of illness and death in unvaccinated travelers has been estimated to be 1:2,000 and 1:10,000, respectively, for a 2-week journey in an endemic area in Africa and as high as 1:267 and 1:1,333 during an epidemic. Risk is thought to be as much as 10 times lower in South America, with risks being highly variable by location and season.[21] Yellow fever vaccine is highly effective and had been considered one of the safest vaccines.

Serious adverse events to yellow fever vaccine include yellow fever vaccine–associated neurotropic disease (YEL-AND, formerly postvaccinal encephalitis) and the recently described yellow fever vaccine–associated viscerotropic disease. Encephalitis has been reported in 23 patients among more than 200 million doses of vaccine distributed since 1945; 16 cases occurred in those less than 9 months of age.[8] A new syndrome of fever, jaundice, and multiple organ system failure following yellow fever vaccine has been reported in 10 patients worldwide since 1996 (4 in the United States, 2 in Brazil, and 1 each in Australia, Switzerland, Germany, and the United Kingdom, ranging in age from 5 to 79 years).[22–28] This syndrome, initially called febrile multiple organ system failure, ranges in severity from moderate disease with focal organ dysfunction to severe multisystem failure and death and may include neurotropic disease. Recently, two new suspected cases of viscerotropic disease and four suspected cases of neurotropic disease were reported in US recipients of yellow fever vaccine.[29] A study of reports submitted to the VAERS in the United States identified advanced age as a risk factor for adverse events associated with yellow fever immunization, though cases have occurred in younger individuals.[30]

YEL-AND has been estimated to occur in 0.5 to 4 per 1,000 very young infants and in fewer than 1 in 8 million vaccinees over 9 months of age in the United States.[31] Estimates of the incidence of YEL-AND have been made based on the number of doses distributed to the civilian population, safety monitoring data for doses distributed between 1990 and 1998 in the United States, and the number of cases identified using enhanced surveillance of yellow fever vaccine adverse events through the VAERS database. These data yield an estimated reported incidence of 2.5 adverse events per 1 million doses distributed.[8] Limitations of this estimate include possible underreporting of cases and lack of exact information about the number of doses administered.

The benefit of vaccine outweighs risk when a traveler is going to an area where yellow fever is known to be present, especially when epidemic activity is occurring. The existence of rare but serious adverse events compels the clinician to discuss factors in the patient's medical history that might change the balance of risk and to review the patient's itinerary carefully to be sure the trip actually involves travel to a yellow fever area.

Japanese Encephalitis

Japanese encephalitis (JE) is a mosquito-borne illness present throughout Asia. It is a potentially serious, and sometimes fatal, disease for which there is no specific treatment. The risk to travelers of contracting Japanese encephalitis has been estimated to be about 1 per million but might be higher in rural endemic areas in transmission season. Cases have occurred in travelers.[32]

Japanese encephalitis vaccine is very effective, with a moderate amount of local and mild systemic side effects. Severe adverse reactions to JE vaccine are rare. Neurologic events, including acute disseminated encephalomyelitis, have been reported, both in Japanese children receiving routine immunization and in adults receiving travel immunizations.[33,34] Severe neurologic events occurred at a rate of 1 to 2.3 per million vaccinees during an 8-year period of surveillance in Japan (1965–1973).[35] A new pattern of adverse events occurring primarily in travelers has been reported since 1989. These events included generalized urticaria and angioedema, but not anaphylaxis, occurring from within minutes to as long as 2 weeks after immunization. Some of these events might have occurred in individuals sensitized to gelatin, as has been shown in Japanese children.[36] Surveillance of Danish vaccinees between 1983 and 1995 identified a rate of 1 to 17 cases per 10,000 vaccine recipients.[37] In the United States, the rate of urticaria or angioedema was 6.3 cases per 100,000 doses distributed.[38]

For the traveler with a typical tourist itinerary, the risk of Japanese encephalitis will be similar to that of serious adverse events to vaccine. For this reason, detailed information should be obtained to assess whether the itinerary will place the traveler in circumstances of greater risk.[17] The traveler's preference about risk acceptance (risk of rare disease vs risk of rare vaccine adverse event) should be taken into consideration in making decisions about this vaccine.

Cholera

Cholera is an example of an easily treatable disease for which vaccines provide incomplete protection. Most travelers on typical itineraries will have little to no risk of contracting cholera. Cholera vaccine, though available in Europe and other areas, is no longer licensed or available in the United States.[39] Adverse events to the available vaccines generally are minor. Most travelers, even those who believe they need immunization against cholera, are able to balance information provided by travel professionals about the low risk of disease, the incomplete efficacy of vaccine, the treatable nature of the disease, and the availability of other methods to prevent disease and arrive at the conclusion that the vaccine is not needed for most itineraries.[40] Factors that would sway the balance toward immunizing would be entering a situation with greatly increased risk of contracting cholera, such as might be borne by relief workers in an area of an active outbreak of the disease. For new vaccines under development targeted toward travelers, a minor increase in vaccine-associated adverse events would be unacceptable for cholera vaccines given the low incidence of the disease and its treatable nature.

CONCLUSION

Logical steps can be taken to address vaccine safety issues with travelers. The travel medicine professional will need to feel comfortable with the possibility of reaching different conclusions about which vaccines to give for patients with similar itineraries. Many patients will want to be active participants in planning their care, but others will rely more heavily on provider expertise. Written materials can augment information given verbally.

Steps that travel medicine professionals can take include

1. providing information about the risk of disease that is as accurate as possible based on the travelers' itinerary, style of travel, and epidemiology of disease, including status of current outbreaks;
2. discussing tolerance for risk frankly with the patient in the context of passive exposure to disease and active immunization against disease;
3. providing information about vaccine efficacy;

4. presenting information about other possible methods for preventing disease that could be used instead of, or in addition to, immunization, including insect avoidance strategies, dietary restrictions, or placing some restrictions on the itinerary;

5. presenting the most accurate information possible about adverse events to vaccine, placing them in the context of the patient's medical history, age, or underlying medical problems, which might make the individual more or less susceptible to certain adverse events; and

6. reaching a consensus with the patient about which vaccines will be used and why and documenting the discussion and conclusions in the medical record.

Future directions for research on travel vaccine safety include enhanced surveillance, especially for rare and serious adverse events; identification of host risk factors for serious adverse events; and improving laboratory and other techniques for demonstrating causality. When combined with improved information about disease epidemiology and advances in development of safer vaccines, the decisions about travel vaccines faced by travelers and their travel medicine specialists can be made in a more educated and informed manner.

REFERENCES

1. Chen RT. Safety of vaccines. In: Plotkin SA, Orenstein WA, editors. Vaccines. 3rd ed. Philadelphia: WB Saunders; 1999. p. 1144–63.

2. Innis BL, Snitbhan R, Kunasol P, et al. Protection against hepatitis A by an inactivated vaccine. JAMA 1994;271:1328–34.

3. Werzberger A, Mensch B, Kuter B, et al. A controlled trial of a formalin-inactivated hepatitis A vaccine in healthy children. N Engl J Med 1992;327:453–7.

4. Riedermann S, Reinhardt G, Forsner GG, et al. Placebo-controlled efficacy study of hepatitis A vaccine in Valdivia, Chile. Vaccine 1992;10 Suppl 1:S152–5.

5. Chen RT, Rastogi SC, Mullen JR, et al. The Vaccine Adverse Event Reporting System (VAERS). Vaccine 1994;12:542–50.

6. Morris R, Halperin S, Dery P, et al. IMPACT monitoring network. A better mousetrap. Can J Infect Dis 1993;4:194–5.

7. Henderson DA, Witte JJ, Morris L, et al. Paralytic disease associated with oral polio vaccines. JAMA 1964;190:153–60.

8. Centers for Disease Control and Prevention. Yellow fever vaccine. Recommendations of the Advisory Committee on Immunization Practices (ACIP). MMWR Morb Mortal Wkly Rep 2002;51(RR-17):4–6.

9. Forsey T, Mawn JA, Yates PJ, et al. Differentiation of vaccine and wild mumps viruses using the polymerase chain reaction and dideoxinucleotide. J Gen Virol 1990;71:987–90.

10. Wise R, Kiminyo K, Salive M. Hair loss after routine immunization. JAMA 1997;278:1176–8.

11. Centers for Disease Control. Rubella prevention: recommendations of the Immunization Practices Advisory Committee (ACIP). MMWR Morb Mortal Wkly Rep 1990;39(RR-15):1–18.

12. Stratton KR, Howe CJ, Johnston RB, editors. Adverse events associated with childhood vaccines. Evidence bearing on causality. Washington DC: National Academy Press; 1994.

13. Bostrom A. Vaccine risk communication. Lessons from risk perception, decision making and environmental risk communication research. Risk Health Saf Environ 1997;8:173–200.

14. Asch D, Baron J, Hershey JC, et al. Omission bias and pertussis vaccine. Med Decis Making 1994;14:118–23.

15. Howson CP, Howe CJ, Fineberg HV, editors. Adverse effects of pertussis and rubella vaccines. Washington DC: National Academy Press; 1991.

16. Stratton KR, Howe CJ, Johnston RB. Adverse events associated with childhood vaccines other than pertussis and rubella. Summary of a report from the Institute of Medicine. JAMA 1994;271:1602–5.

17. Shlim DR, Solomon T. Japanese encephalitis vaccine for travelers. Exploring the limits of risk. Clin Infect Dis 2002;35:183–8.

18. Centers for Disease Control and Prevention. Prevention of hepatitis A through active or passive immunization. Recommendations of the Advisory Committee on Immunization Practices (ACIP). MMWR Morb Mortal Wkly Rep 1999;48(RR-12):1–37.

19. Centers for Disease Control and Prevention. Health information for international travel 2003–2004. Atlanta (GA): US Department of Health and Human Services, Public Health Service; 2003. p. 148–50.

20. Memish ZA. Meningococcal disease and travel. Clin Infect Dis 2002;34:84–90.

21. Monath TP, Cetron MS. Prevention of yellow fever in persons traveling to the tropics. Clin Infect Dis 2002;34:1369–78.

22. Vasconcelos PFC, Luna EJ, Galler R, et al. Serious adverse events associated with yellow fever 17DD vaccine in Brazil. A report of two cases. Lancet 2001;358:91–7.

23. Chan RC, Penney DJ, Little D, et al. Hepatitis and death following vaccination with 17D-204 yellow fever vaccine. Lancet 2001:358:121–2.

24. Martin M, Tsai RF, Cropp B, et al. Fever and multisystem organ failure associated with 17D-204 yellow fever vaccination. A report of four cases. Lancet 2001;358:98–104.

25. Adhiyaman V, Oke A, Cefai C. Effects of yellow fever vaccination [letter]. Lancet 2001;358:1907–8.

26. Troillet N, Laurencet F. Effects of yellow fever vaccination [letter]. Lancet 2001;358:1908–9.

27. Werfel U, Popp W. Effects of yellow fever vaccination [letter]. Lancet 2001;358:1909.

28. Centers for Disease Control and Prevention. Fever, jaundice, and multiple organ system failure associated with 17D-derived yellow fever vaccination, 1996–2001. MMWR Morb Mortal Wkly Rep 2001;50:643–5.

29. Centers for Disease Control and Prevention. Adverse events associated with 17D-derived yellow fever vaccination— United States, 2001–2002. MMWR Morb Mortal Wkly Rep 2002;51:989–93.

30. Martin M, Weld LH, Tsai RF, et al. Advanced age a risk factor for illness temporally associated with yellow fever vaccination. Emerg Infect Dis 2001;7:945–51.

31. Monath TP. Yellow fever. In: Plotkin SA, Orentstein WA, editors. Vaccines. 3rd ed. Philadelphia: WB Saunders; 1999. p. 815–79.

32. Centers for Disease Control and Prevention. Inactivated Japanese encephalitis virus vaccine. Recommendations of the Advisory Committee on Immunization Practices (ACIP). MMWR Morb Mortal Wkly Rep 1993;42(RR-1):6.

33. Ohtaki B, Matsuishi T, Hirano Y, Maekawa K. Acute disseminated encephalomyelitis after treatment with Japanese B encephalitis vaccine (Nakayama-Yoken and Beijing strains). J Neurol Neurosurg Psychiatry 1995;59:316–7.

34. Plesner A, Arlien-Soborg P, Herning M. Neurological complications and Japanese encephalitis vaccination. Lancet 1996;348:202–3.

35. Kitaoka M. Follow-up on use of vaccine in children in Japan. In: McHammond W, Kitaoka M, Downs WG, editors. Immunization for Japanese encephalitis. Amsterdam, the Netherlands: Excerpta Medica; 1972. p. 275–7.

36. Sakaguchi M, Miyazawa H, Inouye S. Specific IgE and IgG to gelatin in children with systemic cutaneous reactions to Japanese encephalitis vaccines. Allergy 2001;56:536–9.

37. Plesner A, Ronne T. Allergic mucocutaneous reactions to Japanese encephalitis vaccine. Vaccine 1997;15:1239–43.

38. Takahashi H, Pool V, Tsai TF, et al. Adverse events after Japanese encephalitis vaccination. Review of post-marketing surveillance data from Japan and the United States. Vaccine 2000;18:2963–9.

39. Sanchez JL, Taylor DN. Cholera. Lancet 1997;349:1825–30.

40. Steffen R. New cholera vaccines. For whom? Lancet 1994;344:1241–2.

Chapter 19

VACCINE HEALTH ECONOMICS: APPROACH TO COST-BENEFIT ANALYSIS

Jennifer A. Roberts and Punam Mangtani

Opposite the deepwater port of Mahon in the Mediterranean lies a quarantine island. Those on any ship that had a person on board with an infectious disease were given sanctuary in this idyllic prison. How many died there or how many were left alive after the 40 days' quarantine we do not know, but many lost their lives trying to escape by swimming ashore. Fortunately, travelers today do not suffer the same indiscriminate treatment, and for an increasing number of infections, there exists the option of vaccination to protect them and those whom they might infect. This is indeed fortunate, as the number of travelers increases yearly: it has been estimated that 2 billion people cross borders per day. This includes a million travelers per week between developed and developing countries. The speed of travel is such that some develop illnesses only once they have returned home, but many have visits for business, leisure, or family ties blighted by an infection and find themselves facing large medical bills in a distant country. Visitors with symptoms of an infection, such as rash, fever, cough, and/or diarrhea can find entry into a country affected and if admitted may find health care expensive and access to services complicated. For those attempting to control travel-related infections, the multiplicity of destinations further complicates the picture by the addition of new, exotic diseases to the old scourges that continue to plague us. Outsiders have always been blamed for the spread of infectious diseases, and travelers have sometimes been seen as a threat to the civic state.

Apart from the basic human instinct to blame the "foreigner," there were fundamental economic reasons why precautions were taken to avoid the importation of infection. Infection affected trade—closed ports, depleted the supply of sailors to man the fleets—and caused infection among the local inhabitants. The civic costs were quickly recognized, and quarantine was seen as a worthwhile investment to protect the state: it was seen to be the cost-beneficial option.

Regulations were put in place to deal with those with infection entering ports, especially travelers from places known to have certain infections—although if it was in the interests of the state to keep the knowledge of infection secret, that too was, and is still, done. Part of the burden of infection was borne by the merchants and the civic authorities, and they had a role in formulating regulations to deal with it. The burden to individuals was great, and the remedies available to them were small: they could walk around with charms and plants around their necks, but many just had to accept their fate. Quarantine, to prevent those infected from transmitting the infection, might have been a worthwhile investment for the state, but it imposed a significant cost on the incarcerated as it increased their risk of infection and prevented them from carrying on normal activities.

Today, the burden is still shared among various organizations and individuals. Industry stands to lose business because of infection. Municipal agencies and insurers can find themselves footing the bill for looking after those who are ill and those whom the ill infect, but preventive interventions such as vaccinations are now an option in many cases. The question that needs to be addressed is, "Are these interventions worthwhile?" It is in response to questions such as these that economic evaluations find a role. They can be used to inform decisions that need to be made by individuals and organizations about the likely benefits of participation in a preventive vaccination program.

In this conceptual chapter, we begin with a discussion of some of the infectious diseases associated with travel that might be modified or avoided by vaccination. We go on to discuss the economic characteristics of infectious disease that set it apart from other illnesses and the implications these characteristics have for the economic analysis used and for those whose task it is to control infection. Methods of economic evaluation such as cost-benefit and cost-effectiveness techniques will be introduced, and the information required to carry out economic evaluations of vaccination will be specified. Examples of work that has been carried out will be discussed and suggestions made about further work that would improve the information on the costs, effects, and benefits of vaccination for travelers.

TRAVEL-RELATED INFECTIONS

Let us consider briefly a selection of infections to which today's travelers are exposed and for which vaccinations are possible. These infections and the vaccines related to them are discussed in detail in Section III: Travelers' Vaccines: State-of-the-art.

Infectious intestinal disease is commonly associated with travel. Travel was associated with an increased risk of intestinal infectious disease (IID) in the report of a large survey of IID in England.[1] This report found that significantly increased risks of *Campylobacter jejuni* and enteroaggregative *Escherichia coli* infections were linked to travel, but the numbers of other organisms were too small to reach statistical significance. There was a distinct gradient in the risks associated with travel: traveling in northern Europe posed no additional risk to UK travelers, but the risk was elevated for travel in southern Europe and the Mediterranean and was substantially increased for travel elsewhere. Other studies have indicated that 20% of infections with nontyphoid *Salmonella* and *Campylobacter* and most cases of *Salmonella* Typhi, *Salmonella paratyphi*, and *Salmonella dysenteriae* were acquired abroad.[1]

It has been suggested that vaccination for *S.* Typhi would reduce the burden of one of the more severe infections. At present, the low incidence of infection, the side effects of the vaccines, and the relatively poor protective effects suggest that vaccines are not recommended.[2] This situation might change as better vaccines become available. Until then, it remains a strategy for high-risk patients to high-risk areas. However, the number of IIDs that might pose a problem is great, and it is unlikely that all of these can be protected against by vaccination. Unless this point is appreciated, vaccination for any particular gastrointestinal organism might offer a false sense of security to travelers, who must observe the preventive strategies recommended to reduce their risk of infections.

Travel is associated with an increased risk of viral hepatitis, with 60% of cases of hepatitis in travelers associated with hepatitis A, 15% with hepatitis B, and 25% with hepatitis C.[3] A study based on serologic testing suggests that for hepatitis A, the mean attack rate for visitors to countries in the developing world was 80 per 100,000 compared with 1.5 per 100,000 for travelers in southern Europe.[4] A study of reported hepatitis A in the United States indicated that 9% of cases were associated with travel to Central and South America in the previous 2 to 6 weeks, and some had spent a very short time abroad.[4] The incidence of travel-related disease is particularly high when travelers from countries where there is a low level of prevalence of hepatitis A visit countries of high prevalence where sanitation and safe disposal of feces are not developed. (In rural areas, nearly all children have been infected by the age of 5 years.) It is therefore not just the travel but the type of travel embarked on that affects the rates: those visiting and staying in high-quality hotels have a much lower infection rate than do those who backpack. Vaccines are recommended for travelers over 4 years of age to countries where they might be at risk.[5] This is made necessary because of the rapid falls in seroimmunity levels that have been found in community serosurveys as a result of the population's never having been exposed to the infection rather than to waning immunity following immunization. Seroprevalence was less than 10% in the Netherlands for those under 35 years of age in 1995 to 1997 and only 5% in the US Navy and Marine forces.[6] Because of the differential immunity by country and age group, it has been suggested that testing for immunity to hepatitis A should precede any vaccination procedure. This is not generally recommended in the United Kingdom except for those born before the year 1945, of whom a high proportion are likely to have immunity. [5]

Hepatitis B is endemic in almost all African countries and in countries of eastern Europe, Latin America, and Asia other than Japan. The risk for travelers to these countries is due to clinical treatment (surgery, injected medication with reused needles and/or syringes, dental treatment) with inadequate infection control, unprotected sexual exposure to a hepatitis B–infected person or carrier, or injecting drugs with reused drug-giving paraphernalia. It has been estimated that 13% of cases in England and Wales were linked to overseas travel, and a quarter of these individuals had become infected by unsafe medical procedures.[7]

Malaria, a potentially life-threatening disease, is increasingly observed in travelers returning from areas where malaria is endemic. Transmission rates are high in areas in South America, Southeast Asia, and sub-Saharan Africa. Travelers returning from rural areas, often migrants returning from visits to their families, are particularly prone to the disease.[8] Depending on the malaria strain, symptoms and signs might not be recognized by the physician, and those with partial immunity because of previous infection or exposure have mild illness. Malaria symptoms differ depending on the type of malaria acquired. It might be missed if it is vivax, but if it is falciparum or ovale, the patient is likely to be very ill and investigated because of persistent fever of unknown origin. Prophylaxis is available and effective, although resistance is increasing.

Risks of infection increase when a large number of people are grouped together in a confined area for any length of time, such as is the case of pilgrims to Mecca for the hajj. When an epidemic strain of meningococcus W-135 was recognized in 1999 and cases in developed countries, including southern England, were linked to the hajj, the Saudi authorities quickly took advice from the World Health Organization (WHO) and made immunization with the quadrivalent meningococcal vaccine (A, C, Y, W=135) an entry visa requirement for pilgrims. This has controlled the risk in Saudi Arabia. However, a similar, though larger, epidemic occurred in Burkina Faso in 2002, only partially managed by immunizing only those at risk because of financial constraints.[9]

Infectious diseases pose problems for any economist attempting to analyze the market for primary prevention, including vaccination, whether by vaccination or other means.

ECONOMIC ASPECTS OF INFECTIOUS DISEASE

Normally, market forces determine the value of a commodity. Those who wish to buy and those who wish to sell come together to trade for mutual advantage. It is difficult to ensure that all those who stand to benefit or lose from a transaction concerning infection control are able to come together to trade: many are excluded from the decision-making process. For example, if nursing and medical personnel have been vaccinated against HBV, a patient might benefit, but it would be difficult for the patient to contribute to the cost of the vaccinations nor would it be easy for the patient to persuade individuals at risk to be vaccinated, although the patient would benefit if they were. These "spillover" effects, or externalities, should be taken into account in decision-making processes if the number vaccinated is to be optimal. Sometimes, if the parties are known, it is possible to internalize these externalities by bringing the parties together to bargain, but when it is not possible, then some intervention might be required of the state or local authorities if an efficient level of provision is to be attained.

Externalities are not the only problems that have to be contended with in choosing the appropriate provision of infection control. Infectious disease control, including vaccination, has public as well as individual consequences: it is a "public good." It often affects everybody, and no one can be excluded. It might be inexhaustible, insofar as one person's consumption does not diminish the amount available to anyone else. If no one can be excluded, who will be willing to pay? Would people not just "free-ride"? If one extra person can benefit from a good without depleting the benefit to anyone else, what charge should be made? A charge might prevent benefits accruing: it would be inefficient. Some other means of financing the venture has to be found. Thus, public health activities are often funded directly from tax-based state funds. An example might be activities to clean up pollution. Everyone benefits from the clean air, and no one can be excluded, but it might be difficult to ensure that everyone contributes to the provision: they will be tempted to free-ride unless the state or municipality imposes a charge in the form of taxation. Many infection control activities have some features of a public good.

Another feature that one faces in using the marketplace for infection control is lack of information on which to base choices. Few have information about the risks of contracting an illness or the effect it might have if they did become infected, nor is information about efficacy of the drug likely to be known, although, increasingly, this information is available on the Internet.

Infectious disease often cannot be predicted; there is a great deal of uncertainty about when and where a particular organism might strike, although the rates of occurrence can be stable from year to year. Viral infections are particularly difficult to predict, for example, influenza (flu) or small round structured virus (SRSV), though good surveillance helps researchers to understand disease patterns. Uncertainty, unlike risk, for which a probability can be estimated, is an unknown quantity. One does not know. Uncertainty makes it difficult for the market to arrive at an efficient solution.

In many societies, equity of access to services is thought to be desirable; thus, some attempt will be made to help those less able to acquire a good or service. The help can take many forms, from income support to direct provision of services. Not only might it be considered appropriate to ensure equity of access to infection control for egalitarian reasons, it might also be imperative, as those too poor to protect themselves might be a reservoir infecting others. As a general rule, infection is no respecter of persons, although some might be more vulnerable than others. For all of these reasons—externalities, public good, uncertainty, and equity—the market might not produce the most appropriate level of infectious disease control; some form of state intervention might be required.[10] If this is the case, then economic evaluation can be used to assist decision making.

An economic evaluation would attempt to assess whether it is worthwhile to intervene and to determine the level of intervention required. If intervention is deemed worthwhile, it can take the form of advice, regulations, subsidization, or direct provision. Vaccination is an important vehicle of infectious disease control, and it is important to know whether it is a cost-beneficial policy. The technique used by economists to assess whether a project is "worthwhile" is cost-benefit analysis.

ECONOMIC EVALUATION

Cost-benefit is the traditional method employed by economists to evaluate projects that cannot easily be evaluated by market processes. Cost-benefit analysis has been employed quite extensively in areas of education, health, and transport.[11] It is an attempt to identify and evaluate costs and benefits wherever and whenever they occur. It is "information" hungry as a technique but if adequately conducted does enable one to answer questions such as "Does it represent a rate of return that is equal to that which could be earned elsewhere?" For example, does vaccination yield as much benefit as a screening program or a new road scheme? Furthermore, there are occasions when a project is deemed worthwhile but there are alternative ways of producing it. In such circumstances, a cost-effectiveness study might be the most useful approach to adopt when choosing among these options. This compares products having the same impact to determine which uses resources most efficiently: produce at least cost or produce most from a given budget. One might consider, for example, that malaria prophylaxis was worthwhile but wish to esti- mate which among the alternative products available would be the most cost-effective. Often different alternatives have different effects that need comparing one with another. A scale has been developed by health economists that enables different aspects of health, for example, pain, mobility, and sleep, to be assessed and aggregated to generate a quality-adjusted life year, or QALY. Some economists place great weight on such scales, whereas others feel that these health-based scales are too narrow to encompass all the features of health that are of value.[12] These researchers might wish to include these additional features, adopting what has come to be known as a cost-consequences approach. Neither of these approaches, QALY nor cost-consequences, enables trade-offs to be compared between health and other goods in soci- ety, and so they have limited value in determining the optimum amount that society should produce. In addition to these techniques of economic evaluation, it is often useful to policy makers to have some information about how much a disease costs. Although the mere cost does not enable one to compare projects, it does provide some initial guidance as to the magnitude of the resources used.

Some time ago, Behrens and Roberts set about trying to measure the burden of disease to the various parties of various infections, most of which were associated with travel, to estimate the cost-benefits of the interventions and to indicate the options that were most cost-effective.[13] The basic economic notion adopted was that those who stood to bear the burden arising from the infection would be likely to want to intervene in some way to prevent its occurrence or limit its spread. The health sector, in this context, was the publicly funded UK National Health Service (NHS). It was postulated that the NHS would find the information useful as it faced the bills for caring for the primary cases and any secondary spread and was responsible for picking up the bill for treatment of any sequelae that follow the initial infection. Therefore, there was a prima facie case for the NHS to intervene to prevent infection if the intervention was cost-beneficial. The simple assumption was that if the costs of the illness—costs of health care, costs to patients and their families, and the value of lost production—were greater than the cost of the vaccine (having taken into account the side effects of the vaccine), then it was cost beneficial, and it would be cost saving to vaccinate.

To estimate the impact of the infection and the intervention, there was a need for some good epidemiologic data and some reliable estimates about the use of health service resources that could be costed. Use had to be made of available data. Ideally, some data about the value individuals placed on avoiding illness would have been incorporated into the evaluation. It was necessary to rely on estimates for some parameters as good data were not readily available. Much work on the economics of travel-related illness is required, but it is hampered by lack of data. Let us review the information needed to carry out any economic evaluation of a vaccination program for travelers

INFORMATION REQUIRED TO EVALUATE A VACCINE PROGRAM

Clinical Path of Disease

We need to know the clinical path of the disease to assess its impact on the individual at the time of the acute phase and over the subsequent months and, in some cases, years, for example, hepatitis B and C. The clinical pathway is well documented in the literature for illnesses of short acute duration, but rarely is it well defined for diseases with prolonged morbidity or those with long-term sequelae. From the clinical path, we can calculate the resources required to treat the disease at each stage of the illness.[14]

Epidemiology

We need reliable information about the epidemiology of the disease. It is important to know something about the incidence and, if possible, seroprevalence of the disease in the population in the country of origin and in the countries that the travelers will visit or from which visitors will come, together with any risk factors associated with the infection that might be relevant to the vaccination program. This will include data about travel destinations and duration and frequency of travel. These epidemiologic building blocks are fundamental to any economic evaluation.

Efficacy of Vaccine

The first task that an economist has when setting up an evaluative study is to determine the product to be evaluated. It is then necessary to determine whether it is effective. It makes no sense to cost and evaluate a product that is shown to have no efficacy, but it is possible to assess the costs and benefits of various levels of efficacy. The efficacy might not be a simple rate for the whole population but might differ significantly, for example, by age. It might give protection for only a limited time, its efficacy declining in a linear or nonlinear fashion over time. For some infections, vaccination might have to be repeated, sometimes annually, to keep pace with the changing nature of the circulating virus, as in the case of flu, or, more frequently, immunoglobulin (Ig), which provides protection against hepatitis A for only 6 months. However, IgG is not recommended in developed countries that have the hepatitis A virus (HAV) vaccine, as it bears the theoretic risk of transmitting new variant Creutzfeldt-Jakob disease (nvCJD), thereby posing difficulties for those attempting a full economic evaluation. Active immunization with HAV and pneumococcal vaccines gives protection for 10 years that can be boosted every 10 years for continuing protection. Other vaccinations that offer protection of 10 years or longer are a full course of polio and tetanus immunizations, which probably give lifetime protection; bacille Calmette-Guérin

(BCG in infancy), lasting 10 to 20 years; meningitis C, which might give lifetime protection; *Haemophilus influenzae* group b (Hib), which gives prolonged protection, although some breakthrough cases have been observed; and smallpox vaccines.

There might be contraindications to vaccination for those suffering from compromised immune systems (eg, human immunodeficiency virus [HIV]) or liable to allergic reactions.

Options Other than Vaccination

As well as the need to know what vaccines are available, we need to know what alternatives are available to limit the infection that might be adopted instead of vaccination. Often travel arrangements are such that travelers spend many hours in close proximity to each other, breathing in any bacteria or viruses that might be circulating in the airplane. An option, other than ensuring that all passengers have flu and BCG vaccinations, would be to ensure that air filters are changed regularly. If we are not clear about the options available in the various settings, then the evaluation is likely to be biased, as costs and effects of these alternatives will not have been considered. Economists are often entrapped by the lack of full disclosure of options by their clients.

Having obtained the information about the disease, the population at risk and the nature of their exposure to infection, and the effectiveness of alternative strategies, one can proceed to explore the economic implications.

Costing Infection and Prevention

The costs of an infection are the opportunities lost in dealing with the infection rather than other things. These include the costs of the illness: treatment for the acute phase might be inexpensive for a case of gastroenteritis or very expensive for a case of botulism. Value of lost activity, whether it is leisure or work, should be estimated. This should include the value of the time of those who look after the sick person or who take on the responsibilities of the sick, such as looking after their children. The resources used at each stage of the illness need to be quantified and costed. These costs should include costs to the health care sector, both hospitals and primary care, and costs to patients that arise as a direct result of the infection as well as those that arise indirectly because the person cannot work or participate in normal activities.

A number of price or cost vectors are required. These include

- the costs of the vaccine, which should include the costs of the drug and the costs of storage and delivering the vaccine;
- the costs of treatment of the disease, which might include over-the-counter medicines, special foods, visits to primary care providers, visits to emergency rooms in hospitals, hospital in-patient stays, out-patient or ambulatory care visits to hospital, prescribed medicines, and laboratory tests;
- out-of-pocket expenses for travel to and from hospital or community services for the case and persons who might be accompanying them;
- costs of time, including time off work as a result of the infection by persons infected and those who take care of them, and time off work by those who might be infectious or incubating the disease and who work in situations that facilitate transmission (eg, catering); and
- costs of secondary cases caused by transmission by the infected case.

Once costs are estimated, one can proceed to estimate benefits.

Benefits of Prevention

Benefits are sometimes calculated as costs avoided. This assumes that the benefits of prevention can be approximated to the cost savings following vaccination. However, as we pointed out above, the simple costs-avoided approach to benefits does not necessarily reflect the value that individuals might place on avoiding an illness. It is this subjective evaluation of risk avoidance that is the true measure of the value of the intervention and that enables us to see how the rate of return to the investment in the vaccination compares with the rate of return to other activities.

Willingness to Pay

Because costs avoided might not capture the value to individuals of the avoidance of the infection, we might wish to construct a willingness-to-pay study to determine how much a given population might be willing to pay for the vaccination or to accept their not being given a vaccination. Willingness-to-pay studies have much to offer the economist seeking the most efficient investment to make in a program, but they are difficult to construct.[15]

One factor affecting the willingness to pay is the knowledge or beliefs about the disease, and another is the likely burden of the disease. Thus, when constructing studies of willingness to pay, it is important to provide data for the individual about the disease and its consequences and the impact vaccination might have on the probability of their acquiring infection. Given the same information and the same impact, some individuals are likely to be more risk averse than others. What seems worth risking to one person might be a risk too far for others and cause them to seek the protection of vaccination. This will affect their willingness to pay for a vaccination.

The perception of risk can be affected by many things including the likelihood of being infected; the perceived effect of the illness, including the possibility of fatal consequences; and the availability of a remedy. The status of the person affected in terms of responsibilities either to family or work commitments and their concerns about transmitting the infection might also influence the decision.

Time

The time dimension is very important in estimating the impact of a disease, as the benefits and costs might be experienced over a long time period. For example, hepatitis B vaccination can provide benefits some 30 years later in the form of liver cancers and liver transplants avoided. It is thus important that the time path of the illness as well as the duration of the immunity be taken into account and suitably discounted to ensure comparability with other vaccination programs.

REVIEW OF SOME ECONOMIC EVALUATIONS OF VACCINATIONS AND PROPHYLAXIS

The study by Behrens and Roberts considered hepatitis A, malaria, and typhoid.[13] A reexamination of this and subsequent work that considered some of these interventions might be a good way of illustrating the issues that need to be taken into account in conducting an economic evaluation as outlined above. This will indicate the type of assumptions that had to be made and the way in which new factors would need to be taken on board to refine the studies.

Behrens and Roberts concluded that malaria prophylaxis was a worthwhile investment, whereas vaccination for hepatitis A and typhoid were not.[15] The cost of prophylaxis represented only 0.3 or 0.5 of the cost of malaria, but the cost of the vaccine was 5.8 times larger than the costs of a case of typhoid and 3.8 times greater for a case of hepatitis A. This was largely because of the shorter duration of these illnesses and the low costs they imposed on the health care sector.

Hepatitis A

The estimate of the incidence of hepatitis A was .05 per 100,000, taken from the surveillance data adjusted for underreporting, using material reported by Zuckerman, which was considerably lower than that estimated in Swiss studies.[14,16] However, the latter were based on only a small number of cases. More exploration of the reliability of rates would be undertaken if the evaluation were to be re-estimated.

The assumptions made about the immunity in the general population would also need to be adjusted, as the prevelance of 54% used by Zuckerman is now much lower. Seropositive rates have been falling rapidly, and now prevelance for the over 40 year olds in the United Kingdom is 25%. Testing is of dubious value in most cases, but some studies have estimated that screening for antibodies is likely to be cost-effective if the immunity levels exceed 35%.[17] Age is a crucial variable affecting the prevelance of seropositive cases; this should be taken into account in further work. The information about hospitalization rates now available also shows variability by age, with older people being hospitalized more frequently and for longer than younger persons.[5] No estimate was made of the likely impact on transmission from cases to the community. Estimates of the impact of transmission should be included in subsequent work. The estimation of benefits in our study was that of costs avoided; subsequent work could include an assessment of the willingness to pay for vaccination.

To summarize, a revised evaluation of the prevention of hepatitis A would include

- stratified data to take account of seroimmunity by age,
- seroprevalence of the country visited,
- hospitalization rates by age, and
- an estimation of the willingness to pay for vaccination.

Typhoid

The incidence estimated for typhoid of .07 by Behrens and Roberts is lower than that in other studies, which have estimated rates ranging from 1.5 to 80 per 100,000 for southern Europe and developing countries, respectively. The incidence data on which the study was based has been criticized by Thompson and Booth, who felt that the low frequency assumed was biased because of the poor quality of surveillance data.[2] Technologic changes affect economic evaluations, and since the study was undertaken, new vaccines have become available, some giving combined protection from hepatitis A and typhoid. The implications of this new approach would need to be incorporated into a new analysis.

Subsequent work would

- adjust rates if required,
- examine the effectiveness of the new vaccines,
- contain an analysis stratified by age and country of destination,
- estimate the impact of costs and coverage of using the combined vaccine, and
- estimate both the willingness-to-pay and the cost-avoided benefits.

Malaria

Malaria prophylaxis was the one intervention that was found to have a positive benefit in the cost-benefit analysis. Adjustments for underreporting were made using work by Davidson and colleagues.[18] Further refinements might include estimates for the semi-immune cases and stratification according to the areas within countries as well as countries visited.[8] This estimate would now need to be modified to take into account the resistance to antimalaria drugs that is appearing. This would imply a structured study by country.

The adjustments would include

- improved estimates of cases;
- type of malaria including its implications for treatment, as duration and prophylaxis vary;
- country of destination;
- visits to rural areas where malaria is endemic;
- attention to partial-immune cases;
- inclusion of resistance data; and
- willingness-to-pay analysis.

Thus, any new economic evaluation would be stratified much more than the first study.

Other Diseases

The other big change that is clearly necessary is the incorporation of more vaccine-preventable diseases into the analysis. Of particular relevance would be a study of hepatitis B.

Studies of the cost-effectiveness of hepatitis B vaccination in travelers are badly needed. They could be stratified by country according to prevalence rates there. These could include the risky behavior in which the traveler might be involved. They could also include a model of the benefits of opportunistic vaccination for hepatitis A and B often recommended in the literature.

Some recent experiments in control would make interesting case studies for economic evaluation. Meningitis, in particular infection associated with large groups of people congregating in close quarters such as that experienced during the hajj, is a contender for further exploration. The benefits would be felt both in Saudi Arabia and in the countries to which the pilgrims return.

MODELING THE IMPACT OF VACCINATION ON TRAVEL-ASSOCIATED INFECTIONS

The number of economic evaluations of vaccination programs is small, yet the information that they can bring to bear on decision making is considerable. As it is unlikely that a whole raft of empiric evaluations will be forthcoming in the near future on the range of travel-related vaccines, it might be useful to construct hypothetic models of costs and benefits of the various vaccines.[19] Some work along these lines was conducted some while ago for the UK Health Protection Agency (formerly Public Health Laboratory Service [PHLS]) to estimate the costs of certain common infectious diseases. The work proved to be quite reliable and comparable to empiric studies carried out subsequently on an outbreak of *Escherichia coli* O157.[20,21]

Models of travel-related vaccines using assumptions relating to the many issues described above could be conducted for populations of a given county or region for a selection of infectious diseases. The frequency and duration of travel would be included in the model. This would provide a matrix of payoffs in terms of costs avoided for the various vaccines. The benefits could also be estimated using synthetic willingness-to-pay studies by surveying groups of individuals about their travel behavior and the amount they would be willing to pay for various levels of protection. The model would provide a structure into which new material could be incorporated as it became available. Without some tool of this type, we are faced with a number of ad hoc studies from which it is difficult to generalize as they relate to specific places at different times and often lack both accurate efficacy and comprehensive costing data.

POLICY IMPLICATIONS

The results of the Behrens and Roberts study led to the recommendation that the NHS continue to provide malaria prophylaxis but not the vaccine for hepatitis A and typhoid.[13] A few months later, malaria prophylaxis ceased to be provided under prescription by the NHS. This is a salutary reminder that economic evaluation can only suggest policies: governments choose whether to adopt them.

A component of the model showed the distribution between the parties. We would in general consider that when the burden of care for unvaccinated cases falls on health care systems or insurance companies, they would provide incentives or impose penalties to encourage uptake of the vaccines. The health sectors, particularly centrally funded ones, might be inclined to subsidize vaccination for those diseases that imposed substantial burden on the service and, ideally, on the society as a whole, although insurers might be tempted to add clauses exempting them from liability for infections acquired abroad if the necessary vaccination regimens had not been followed. Business firms might want to ensure the staff are fit enough to do the job they are sent out to do and to return without risk to themselves or others, and they have the duty of care, imposed on them by the UK Health and Safety at Work Act of 1992, which holds them responsible for harm to an employee whether in the workplace in England and Wales or abroad unless risks are assessed and minimized as far as possible. They might adopt a vaccination policy as recommended by government authorities and make it effective by making immunization mandatory in terms of employment or travel insurance. They are likely to pay for or subsidize workers' vaccinations. Taking aside different levels of risk aversion, we would expect the traveler to be more inclined toward vaccination for the more life-threatening events and the ones that had most impact on their lives. Many of the costs fall on individuals, who, in most health care systems, including that in the United Kingdom, have to pay for vaccination. Such charges are not inconsiderable and can represent a substantial proportion of the costs of a holiday. Many travelers are tourists taking holidays in popular holiday resorts who might find such costs prohibitive. Furthermore, more tourists are taking adventure holiday treks to remote places and hazardous places that expose them to unfamiliar and sometimes rare organisms, and they might find they have no option but to receive vaccinations to get a visa to travel. Others travelers might take trips on cruise liners and be exposed to water, food, and airborne organisms while onboard. Whole ships can be laid up and voyages cancelled if an infection is encountered.[22] The cost to the shipping line can be enormous as deep cleaning might need to be employed and voyages cancelled. Cancelled voyages also represent lost opportunities for the travelers.

States might be keen to ensure that visitors to their countries do not contract infections that would cause the state expense or deter visitors or business investment. They may choose to do this by linking certain immunization requirements to visa entry, such as the requirement for yellow fever immunizations for many countries in Africa and South America. Alternatively, some areas require quarantine for 6 days, the incubation period of the disease. This deflects cost onto the traveler seeking entry but protects the state from responsibilities for treating sick individuals and losing face. States might also wish to ensure that their citizens visiting countries with endemic infections are fully protected. This they can do by mandatory regulations or by recommendations and provision of services. Most countries have a list of vaccines that are recommended for visitors to certain destinations. This is the state stepping in to fill the information gap in the market and empowering individuals to make an informed choice (see Chapter 3, "Travel Vaccine Requirements and Recommendations," and <www.doh.gov.uk/traveladvice/imsum.htm>), one that they hope will also have the spillover effect of saving the state funds. Economic data could supplement such advice for the benefit of all the decision makers.[22]

ACKNOWLEDGMENTS

The authors are grateful to Elizabeth Haworth for her advice and comments.

REFERENCES

1. Food Standards Agency. A report of the study of infectious intestinal disease in England. London: Queen's Printer; 2000.

2. Thomson MA, Booth IW. Treatment of traveller's diarrhoea. Economic aspects. Pharmacoeconomics 1996;5:382–9.

3. Apotheloz M, Grob PJ, Steffen R, Schar M. Auslandreisenden ist ein Impfschutz gegen Hepatitis zu empfehlen? Soz Praventivmed 1982;27:264–5. In Steffen R, Kane MA, Craig, et al. Review. JAMA 1994;272:885–9.

4. Steffen R, Kane, MA, Shapiro CN, et al. Epidemiology and prevention of hepatitis A in travellers. JAMA 1994;272:885–9.

5. Crowcroft NS, Walsh B, Davison KL, Gungabissoon U. Guidelines for the control of hepatitis A virus infection. Commun Dis Public Health 2001;4:213–27.

6. Hawkins RE, Malone JD, Cloninger LA, et al. Risk of viral hepatitis among military personnel assigned to US navy ships. J Infect Dis 1992;18. In Stefan R, Kane MA, Shapiro CN. AJAM 1994;272:885–9.

7. Mangtani P, Heptonstall J, Hall AJ. Enhanced surveillance of acute symptomatic hepatitis B in England and Wales. Commun Dis Public Health 1998;1:114–20.

8. Sanjiv Shah Tanowwitz et al. The ethnic traveler. Travel Med 1998;12:523–41.

9. Hanne SJ, Gray SJ, Agulera, JF, et al. W135 meningococcal disease in England and Wales associated with Hajj 2000 and 2001. Lancet 2002;359:582–3. In Department of Health. Getting ahead of the curve. London: Queen's Printer; 2002.

10. Stiglitz JE. Economics of the public sector. London: Norton; 1988.

11. Drummond MF, O'Brien B, Stoddart GL, et al. Methods for the economic evaluation of health care program. New York: Oxford University Press; 1997.

12. Williams A. Economics of coronary artery bypass grafting. BMJ 1985;291:326–9.

13. Behrens RH, Roberts JA. Is travel prophylaxis worth while? Economic appraisal of prophylactic measures against malarial, hepatitis A and typhoid in travellers. BMJ 1994;309:918–22.

14. Zuckerman AJ. Notification of viral hepatitis. BMJ 1991;303:909.

15. Pauly MV. Valuing health care. Benefits in money terms. In: Sloan FA, editor. Valuing health care. Cambridge, UK: Cambridge University Press; 1995. p. 99–124.

16. Steffen R, Rickenbach M, Ura W, et al. Health problems after travel to developing countries. J Infect Dis 1987;156:84–91.

17. van Doorslaer E, Tormans G, van Damme P. Cost-effectiveness analysis of indications for prevention of hepatitis A in travellers. J Med Virol 1994;44:463–9.

18. Davidson, RN, Scott JA, Behrens RH, Warhurst D. Under reporting of malaria a notifiable disease. J Infect 1993;303:991.

19. Dusheiko M, Roberts JA. Treatment of chronic type B and C hepatitis with interferon alfa. An economic appraisal [special article]. Hepatology 1995;22:1863–72.

20. Roberts JA. Economics of surveillance report for PHLS. London; Public Health Laboratory Service; 1994.

21. Roberts JA, Upton PA. E. coli O157. An economic assessment of an outbreak, and an executive summary. Edinburgh (Scotland): Lothian Health and London School of Hygiene; 2000.

22. Koo D, Maloney K, Taux R. Epidemiology of diarrhoeal disease outbreaks on cruise ships, 1986 through 1993. JAMA 1996;275.

INDEX